PL
CRICKET ANNUAL 2017

70th edition

EDITED BY IAN MARSHALL

All statistics by the Editor unless otherwise stated

FOREWORD

The domestic 2016 season was a superb one. New County Championship sponsors Specsavers were granted a campaign in which each game in the last round of fixtures in the First Division had a bearing on who would be champions and who would be relegated. As it was, the decisive action at the top came with only minutes of the season to go. Toby Roland-Jones took a hat-trick, dismissing Azeem Rafiq, Andy Hodd and Ryan Sidebottom to secure a nail-biting win for Middlesex over Yorkshire, ensuring that Somerset missed out on their first title. For the Lord's outfit, this was a deserved reward. In the NatWest t20 Blast, unfavoured Northamptonshire managed to triumph against all the odds, despite the county's small squad and financial difficulties.

You might have thought that would satisfy the ECB. But a winter of change, debate and a great deal of dissatisfaction followed. Despite such a dramatic climax, it had been decided to revamp the Championship. So the First Division was cut to eight teams and the Second Division expanded to ten, but in 2017 all counties will play 14 Championship games. While trying to do something to improve the quality of what is on offer is to be welcomed, it is fair to say that the reduction in the amount of cricket that members will get to see has not been greeted with unbridled joy from that community.

Then, heavily indebted Durham were bailed out by the ECB, but their punishment was relegation from Division One, and they will start the 2017 season with a 48-point deduction, almost guaranteeing they will remain in Division Two for two years. Furthermore, the Emirates Riverside was stripped of its Test match status. Not least because Durham have done great work in producing their own talent (none more so than Ben Stokes, now the most valuable overseas IPL recruit of all time, and last year's cover star), many believed that this was too harsh, especially when the ECB is itself sitting on a large pile of cash, some of which comes from revenue generated from the grounds that host Test matches.

But perhaps the biggest debate centred on the idea that we should try to mimic the format of the IPL and the Big Bash, with a city-based T20 competition. Early plans for this tournament suggested it might run alongside the 50-over series, if and when it is finally launched in 2020. The idea is, once more, that the quality of the cricket will draw in a new audience – and one suspects new TV rights income and sponsorship. England players may struggle to appear if they have international commitments, but they can still be selected to 'promote' a team. When the Blast already attracts global stars of the calibre of Chris Gayle, Brendon McCullum and Kevin Pietersen, what really will improve? Just five players from the best side in the country in 2016 would have a chance to compete in it. Despite the support of some players and a few in the media, it was notable how little enthusiasm the whole idea gained from the cricket-watching public. And without that, it is hard to see how the ECB will generate the anticipated £1.3 million each county will earn per year from it.

For the national team, it was a mixed year. Alastair Cook stepped down as Test captain after a record-breaking 59 matches in charge. His replacement – Joe Root (2015's cover star) – was the obvious man for the job, and he will start his new role with series against South Africa and West Indies this summer, before going Down Under to try to retain the Ashes. One of the key players in the team, Jonny Bairstow, is the deserving cover star this year. In 2016, he scored 1470 Test runs (a record for a wicket-keeper in a calendar year) and he racked up a world record 70 dismissals in the year.

During the season I will do my best to keep people up to date on the latest records and personal landmarks via Twitter, so do follow me on @IanPlayfair. The website www.playfair.co.uk will provide weekly match reports, as well as updates to the players' register if anyone new arrives on the county scene. This year – I suspect for the first time – the season runs for more than six months, from 28 March to 29 September, so there is no excuse not to go to watch some cricket, especially with the Champions Trophy and the Women's World Cup to enjoy. Floodlit cricket in April may prove chilly, but from a personal perspective I am delighted to see that Eastbourne CC's Saffrons ground will be hosting a Royal London Cup game on 14 May – I can't wait.

Ian Marshall
Eastbourne, 9 March 2017

GUIDE TO USING PLAYFAIR

The basic layout of *Playfair* has remained the same for this edition. The Annual is divided into five sections, as follows: Test match cricket, county cricket, international limited-overs cricket (including Twenty20), other cricket (IPL and women's international cricket), and fixtures for the coming season. Each section, where applicable, begins with a preview of forthcoming events, followed by events during the previous year, then come the player records, and finally the records sections.

Within the players' register, there has been some debate with the county scorers over those who are defined as 'Released/Retired', as some players are drafted in for a game or two, and may re-appear in the current season, despite not having a contract as the book goes to press. What I try to do is to ensure that everyone who appeared in last season's games is included somewhere – this way, at least, if they do play in 2017 their details are available to readers. Players' Second XI Championship debuts and their England Under-19 Test appearances are given for those under the age of 25.

In the county limited-overs records in the Register, those records denoted by '50ov' cover any limited-overs game of 50 or more overs – in the early days, each team could have as many as 65 overs per innings. The '40ov' section refers to games of 40 or 45 overs per innings.

Records are provided for two formats of the women's game – limited-overs and T20 – and there is an England women's register. Fixtures for the women's Super League are provided, as well as for the Women's World Cup.

ACKNOWLEDGEMENTS AND THANKS

As always, this book could not have been compiled without the assistance of many people giving so generously of their time and expertise, so I must thank the following for all they have done to help ensure this edition of *Playfair Cricket Annual* could be written:

At the counties, I would like to thank the following for their help over the last year. Derbyshire – Chris Airey and John Brown; Durham – Matt Smith, Luke Bidwell and William Dobson; Essex – Alastair Cliffe and Tony Choat; Glamorgan – Andrew Hignell, Gloucestershire – Lizzie Allen and Adrian Bull; Hampshire – Tim Tremlett and Kevin Baker, Kent – Thomas Brown and Lorne Hart; Lancashire – Diana Lloyd and Chris Rimmer; Leicestershire – Jen Wilks and Paul Rogers; Middlesex – Steven Fletcher and Don Shelley; Northamptonshire – Tony Kingston; Nottinghamshire – Helen Palmer and Roger Marshall; Somerset – Spencer Bishop and Gerald Stickley; Surrey – Steve Howes and Keith Booth; Sussex – Colin Bowley and Mike Charman; Warwickshire – Keith Cook and Mel Smith; Worcestershire – Carrie Lloyd and Dawn Pugh; Yorkshire – Janet Bairstow and John Potter.

Thanks to Alan Fordham for the Principal and Second XI Fixtures, and Philip August for the Minor Counties. Philip Bailey once again provided the first-class and List A career records, and he continues to be a huge help in compiling the book. When a question arose over the correct order of a player's initials, he checked the register of births to ensure we – and the player's county – now have it right.

At Headline, my thanks as always go to Jonathan Taylor for his encouragement and help; Louise Rothwell reminded me of the vital importance of not missing my deadlines (!) and then ensured the book was printed in no time at all; Sam Habib administers the *Playfair* website with great enthusiasm, so the match reports and new arrivals are available as soon as possible. John Skermer did another great job checking the proofs, yet again turning things round at great speed. At Letterpart, the *Playfair* typesetter since 1994, Chris Leggett, Caroline Leggett and the whole team ensured the book was laid out superbly. Sadly, I had to miss out on my usual trip up to Caterham this year.

Finally, as ever, I have to thank my family for their help and patience. This time even my parents were roped in when I was chained to my desk finishing the book. Daughters Kiri and Sophia, despite losing me to the office as deadline day looms, have not been put off the sport – with Joe Root now a firm favourite of theirs. And finally, of course, there is no way I could manage to write the book at all, were it not for the support of my wife Sugra. Thank you all.

ENGLAND v SOUTH AFRICA

SERIES RECORDS

1928 to 2015-16
Key to grounds:
Durban – [1]Lord's, [2]Kingsmead; Johannesburg – [1]Old Wanderers, [2]Ellis Park, [3]Wanderers.

HIGHEST INNINGS TOTALS

England	in England	604-9d	The Oval	2003
	in South Africa	654-5	Durban[2]	1938-39
South Africa	in England	682-6d	Lord's	2003
	in South Africa	627-7d	Cape Town	2015-16

LOWEST INNINGS TOTALS

England	in England	76	Leeds	1907
	in South Africa	92	Cape Town	1898-99
South Africa	in England	30	Birmingham	1924
	in South Africa	30	Port Elizabeth	1895-96
HIGHEST MATCH AGGREGATE		1981 for 35 wickets	Durban[2]	1938-39
LOWEST MATCH AGGREGATE		378 for 30 wickets	The Oval	1912

HIGHEST INDIVIDUAL INNINGS

England	in England	219	M.E.Trescothick	The Oval	2003
	in South Africa	258	B.A.Stokes	Cape Town	2015-16
South Africa	in England	311*	H.M.Amla	The Oval	2012
	in South Africa	275	G.Kirsten	Durban[2]	1999-00

HIGHEST AGGREGATE OF RUNS IN A SERIES

England	in England	753	(av 94.12)	D.C.S.Compton	1947
	in South Africa	656	(av 72.88)	A.J.Strauss	2004-05
South Africa	in England	714	(av 79.33)	G.C.Smith	2003
	in South Africa	625	(av 69.44)	J.H.Kallis	2004-05

RECORD WICKET PARTNERSHIPS – ENGLAND

1st	359	L.Hutton (158)/C.Washbrook (195)	Johannesburg[2]	1948-49
2nd	280	P.A.Gibb (120)/W.J.Edrich (219)	Durban[2]	1938-39
3rd	370	W.J.Edrich (189)/D.C.S.Compton (208)	Lord's	1947
4th	286	K.P.Pietersen (152)/I.R.Bell (199)	Lord's	2008
5th	237	D.C.S.Compton (163)/N.W.D.Yardley (99)	Nottingham	1947
6th	399	B.A.Stokes (258)/J.M.Bairstow (150*)	Cape Town	2015-16
7th	152	I.R.Bell (199)/S.C.J.Broad (76)	Lord's	2008
8th	154	C.W.Wright (71)/H.R.Bromley-Davenport (84)	Johannesburg[1]	1895-96
9th	106	G.P.Swann (85)/J.M.Anderson (29)	Centurion	2009-10
10th	92	C.A.G.Russell (111)/A.E.R.Gilligan (39*)	Durban[2]	1922-23

RECORD WICKET PARTNERSHIPS – SOUTH AFRICA

1st	338	G.C.Smith (277)/H.H.Gibbs (179)	Birmingham	2003
2nd	259	G.C.Smith (131)/H.M.Amla (311*)	The Oval	2012
3rd	377*	H.M.Amla (311*)/J.H.Kallis (182*)	The Oval	2012
4th	214	H.W.Taylor (121)/H.G.Deane (93)	The Oval	1929
5th	212	A.G.Prince (149)/A.B.de Villiers (174)	Leeds	2008
6th	171	J.H.B.Waite (113)/P.L.Winslow (108)	Manchester	1955
7th	167	T.Bavuma (102*)/C.H.Morris (69)	Cape Town	2015-16
8th	150	G.Kirsten (130)/M.Zondeki (59)	Leeds	2003
9th	137	E.L.Dalton (117)/A.B.C.Langton (73*)	The Oval	1935
10th	103	H.G.Owen-Smith (129)/A.J.Bell (26*)	Leeds	1929

BEST INNINGS BOWLING ANALYSIS

England	in England	9- 57	D.E.Malcolm	The Oval	1994
	in South Africa	9- 28	G.A.Lohmann	Johannesburg[1]	1895-96
South Africa	in England	7- 65	S.J.Pegler	Lord's	1912
	in South Africa	9-113	H.J.Tayfield	Johannesburg[3]	1956-57

BEST MATCH BOWLING ANALYSIS

England	in England	15- 99	C.Blythe	Leeds	1907
	in South Africa	17-159	S.F.Barnes	Johannesburg[1]	1913-14
South Africa	in England	10- 87	P.M.Pollock	Nottingham	1965
	in South Africa	13-144	K.Rabada	Centurion	2015-16

HIGHEST AGGREGATE OF WICKETS IN A SERIES

England	in England	34	(av 8.29)	S.F.Barnes	1912
	in South Africa	49	(av 10.93)	S.F.Barnes	1913-14
South Africa	in England	33	(av 19.78)	A.A.Donald	1998
	in South Africa	37	(av 17.18)	H.J.Tayfield	1956-57

RESULTS SUMMARY

ENGLAND v SOUTH AFRICA – IN ENGLAND

		Series			Lord's			Leeds			The Oval			Birmingham			Manchester			Nottingham		
	Tests	*E*	*SA*	*D*	*E*	*SA*	*D*	*E*	*SA*	*D*	*E*	*SA*	*D*	*E*	*SA*	*D*	*E*	*SA*	*D*	*E*	*SA*	*D*
1907	3	1	–	2	–	–	1	1	–	–	–	–	1	–	–	–	–	–	–	–	–	–
1912	3	3	–	–	1	–	–	1	–	–	1	–	–	–	–	–	–	–	–	–	–	–
1924	5	3	–	2	1	–	–	1	–	–	–	–	1	1	–	–	–	–	1	–	–	–
1929	5	2	–	3	–	–	1	1	–	–	–	–	1	–	–	1	1	–	–	–	–	–
1935	5	–	1	4	–	1	–	–	–	1	–	–	1	–	–	–	–	–	1	–	–	1
1947	5	3	–	2	1	–	–	1	–	–	–	–	1	–	–	–	1	–	–	–	–	1
1951	5	3	1	1	1	–	–	–	–	1	1	–	–	–	–	–	1	–	–	–	1	–
1955	5	3	2	–	1	–		–	1	–	1	–	–	–	–	–	–	1	–	1	–	–
1960	5	3	–	2	1	–	–	–	–	–	–		1	1	–	–	–	–	1	1	–	–
1965	3		1	2	–	–	1	–	–	–		–	1	–	–	–	–	–	–	–	1	–
1994	3	1	1	1	–	1			–	1	1	–		–	–	–	–	–	–	–	–	–
1998	5	2	1	2	–	1	–	1	–	–	–	–	–	–	–	1	–	–	1	1		–
2003	5	2	2	1	–	1	–		1	–	1	–	–	–	–	1	–	–	–	1	–	–
2008	4	1	2	1	–	–	1	–	1	–	1	–	–	–	1	–	–	–	–	–	–	–
2012	3	–	2	1	–	1	–	–	–	1	–	1	–		–	–	–	–	–	–	–	–
	64	27	13	24	6	5	4	6	3	4	6	1	7	2	1	3	3	1	4	4	2	2

ENGLAND v SOUTH AFRICA – IN SOUTH AFRICA

		Series			Port Elizabeth			Cape Town			Johannesburg			Durban			Centurion		
	Tests	*E*	*SA*	*D*	*E*	*SA*	*D*	*E*	*SA*	*D*	*E*	*SA*	*D*	*E*	*SA*	*D*	*E*	*SA*	*D*
1888-89	2	2	–	–	1	–	–	1	–	–	–	–	–	–	–	–	–	–	–
1891-92	1	1	–	–	–	–	–	1	–	–	–	–	–	–	–	–	–	–	–
1895-96	3	3	–	–	1	–	–	1	–	–	1	–	–	–	–	–	–	–	–
1898-99	2	2	–	–	–	–	–	1	–	–	1	–	–	–	–	–	–	–	–
1905-06	5	1	4	–	–	–	–	1	1	–	–	3	–	–	–	–	–	–	–
1909-10	5	2	3	–	–	–	–	1	1	–	1	1	–	–	1	–	–	–	–
1913-14	5	4	–	1	1	–	–	–	–	–	2	–	–	1	–	1	–	–	–
1922-23	5	2	1	2	–	–	–	1	–	–	–	1	1	1	–	1	–	–	–
1927-28	5	2	2	1	–	–	–	1	–	–	1	1	–	–	1	1	–	–	–
1930-31	5	–	1	4	–	–	–	–	–	1	–	1	1	–	–	2	–	–	–
1938-39	5	1	–	4	–	–	–	–	–	1	–	–	2	1	–	1	–	–	–
1948-49	5	2	–	3	1	–	–	–	–	1	–	–	2	1	–	–	–	–	–
1956-57	5	2	2	1	–	1	–	1	–	–	1	1	–	–	–	1	–	–	–
1964-65	5	1	–	4	–	–	1	–	–	1	–	–	2	1	–	–	–	–	–
1995-96	5	–	1	4	–	–	1	–	1	–	–	–	1	–	–	1	–	–	1
1999-00	5	1	2	2	–	–	1	–	1	–	–	1	–	–	–	1	1	–	–
2004-05	5	2	1	2	1	–	–	–	1	–	1	–	–	–	–	1	–	–	1
2009-10	4	1	1	2	–	–	–	–	–	1	–	1	–	1	–	–	–	–	1
2015-16	4	2	1	1	–	–	–	–	–	1	1	–	–	1	–	–	–	1	–
	81	31	19	31	5	1	3	9	5	6	9	10	9	7	2	10	1	1	3
Totals	145	58	32	55															

ENGLAND v WEST INDIES

SERIES RECORDS

1928 to 2015

HIGHEST INNINGS TOTALS

England	in England	619-6d	Nottingham	1957
	in West Indies	849	Kingston	1929-30
West Indies	in England	692-8d	The Oval	1995
	in West Indies	751-5d	St John's	2003-04

LOWEST INNINGS TOTALS

England	in England	71	Manchester	1976
	in West Indies	46	Port-of-Spain	1993-94
West Indies	in England	54	Lord's	2000
	in West Indies	47	Kingston	2003-04

HIGHEST MATCH AGGREGATE 1815 for 34 wickets Kingston 1929-30
LOWEST MATCH AGGREGATE 309 for 29 wickets Bridgetown 1934-35

HIGHEST INDIVIDUAL INNINGS

England	in England	285*	P.B.H.May	Birmingham	1957
	in West Indies	325	A.Sandham	Kingston	1929-30
West Indies	in England	291	I.V.A.Richards	The Oval	1976
	in West Indies	400*	B.C.Lara	St John's	2003-04

HIGHEST AGGREGATE OF RUNS IN A SERIES

England	in England	506	(av 42.16)	G.P.Thorpe (*6 Tests*)	1995
	in West Indies	693	(av 115.50)	E.H.Hendren	1929-30
West Indies	in England	829	(av 118.42)	I.V.A.Richards	1976
	in West Indies	798	(av 99.75)	B.C.Lara	1993-94

RECORD WICKET PARTNERSHIPS – ENGLAND

1st	229	A.J.Strauss (142)/A.N.Cook (94)	Bridgetown	2008-09
2nd	291	A.J.Strauss (137)/R.W.T.Key (221)	Lord's	2004
3rd	303	M.A.Atherton (135)/R.A.Smith (175)	St John's	1993-94
4th	411	P.B.H.May (285*)/M.C.Cowdrey (154)	Birmingham	1957
5th	218	P.D.Collingwood (161)/M.J.Prior (131*)	Port-of-Spain	2008-09
6th	205	M.R.Ramprakash (154)/G.P.Thorpe (103)	Bridgetown	1997-98
7th	197	M.J.K.Smith (96)/J.M.Parks (101*)	Port-of-Spain	1959-60
8th	217	T.W.Graveney (165)/J.T.Murray (112)	The Oval	1966
9th	109	G.A.R.Lock (89)/P.I.Pocock (13)	Georgetown	1967-68
10th	128	K.Higgs (63)/J.A.Snow (59*)	The Oval	1966

RECORD WICKET PARTNERSHIPS – WEST INDIES

1st	298	C.G.Greenidge (149)/D.L.Haynes (167)	St John's	1989-90
2nd	287*	C.G.Greenidge (214*)/H.A.Gomes (92*)	Lord's	1984
3rd	338	E.de C.Weekes (206)/F.M.M.Worrell (167)	Port-of-Spain	1953-54
4th	399	G.St A.Sobers (226)/F.M.M.Worrell (197*)	Bridgetown	1959-60
5th	265	S.M.Nurse (137)/G.St A.Sobers (174)	Leeds	1966
6th	282*	B.C.Lara (400*)/R.D.Jacobs (107*)	St John's	2003-04
7th	204	M.N.Samuels (117)/D.J.G.Sammy (106)	Nottingham	2012
8th	99	C.A.McWatt (54)/J.K.Holt (48*)	Georgetown	1953-54
9th	150	E.A.E.Baptiste (87*)/M.A.Holding (69)	Birmingham	1984
10th	143	D.Ramdin (107*)/T.L.Best (95)	Birmingham	2012

BEST INNINGS BOWLING ANALYSIS

England	in England	8-103	I.T.Botham	Lord's	1984
	in West Indies	8- 53	A.R.C.Fraser	Port-of-Spain	1997-98
West Indies	in England	8- 92	M.A.Holding	The Oval	1976
	in West Indies	8- 45	C.E.L.Ambrose	Bridgetown	1989-90

BEST MATCH BOWLING ANALYSIS

England	in England	12-119	F.S.Trueman	Birmingham	1963
	in West Indies	13-156	A.W.Greig	Port-of-Spain	1973-74
West Indies	in England	14-149	M.A.Holding	The Oval	1976
	in West Indies	11- 84	C.E.L.Ambrose	Port-of-Spain	1993-94

HIGHEST AGGREGATE OF WICKETS IN A SERIES

England	in England	34	(av 17.47)	F.S.Trueman	1963
	in West Indies	27	(av 18.66)	J.A.Snow	1967-68
		27	(av 18.22)	A.R.C.Fraser	1997-98
West Indies	in England	35	(av 12.65)	M.D.Marshall	1988
	in West Indies	30	(av 14.26)	C.E.L.Ambrose	1997-98

RESULTS SUMMARY – ENGLAND v WEST INDIES – IN ENGLAND

		Series			Lord's			Manchester			The Oval			Nottingham			Birmingham			Leeds			Chester-le-St		
	Tests	*E*	*WI*	*D*	*E*	*WI*	*D*	*E*	*WI*	*D*	*E*	*WI*	*D*	*E*	*WI*	*D*	*E*	*WI*	*D*	*E*	*WI*	*D*	*E*	*WI*	*D*
1928	3	3	–	–	1	–	–	1	–	–	1	–	–	–	–	–	–	–	–	–	–	–	–	–	–
1933	3	2	–	1	1	–	–	–	–	1	1	–	–	–	–	–	–	–	–	–	–	–	–	–	–
1939	3	1	–	2	1	–	–	–	–	1	–	–	1	–	–	–	–	–	–	–	–	–	–	–	–
1950	4	1	3	–	–	1	–	1	–	–	–	1	–	–	1	–	–	–	–	–	–	–	–	–	–
1957	5	3	–	2	1	–	–	–	–	–	1	–	–	–	–	1	–	–	1	1	–	–	–	–	–
1963	5	1	3	1	–	–	1	–	1	–	–	1	–	–	–	–	1	–	–	–	1	–	–	–	–
1966	5	1	3	1	–	–	1	–	1	–	1	–	–	–	1	–	–	–	–	–	1	–	–	–	–
1969	3	2	–	1		–	1	1	–	–	–	–	–	–	–	–	–	–	–	1	–	–	–	–	–
1973	3	–	2	1	–	1	–	–	–	–	–	1	–	–	–	–	–	–	1	–	–	–	–	–	–
1976	5	–	3	2	–	–	1	–	1	–	–	1	–	–	–	1	–	–	–	–	1	–	–	–	–
1980	5	–	1	4	–	–	1	–	–	1	–	–	1	–	1	–	–	–	–	–	–	1	–	–	–
1984	5	–	5	–	–	1	–	–	1	–	–	1	–	–	–	–	–	1	–	–	1	–	–	–	–
1988	5	–	4	1	–	1	–	–	1	–	–	1	–	–	–	1	–	–	–	–	1	–	–	–	–
1991	5	2	2	1	–	–	1	–	–	–	1	–	–	–	1	–	–	1	–	1	–	–	–	–	–
1995	6	2	2	2	1	–	–	1	–	–	–	–	1	–	–	1	–	1	–	–	1	–	–	–	–
2000	5	3	1	1	1	–	–	–	–	1	1	–	–	–	–	–	–	1	–	1	–	–	–	–	–
2004	4	4	–	–	1	–	–	1	–	–	1	–	–	–	–	–	1	–	–	–	–	–	–	–	–
2007	4	3	–	1	–	–	1	1	–	–	–	–	–	–	–	–	–	–	–	1	–	–	1	–	–
2009	2	2	–	–	1	–	–	–	–	–	–	–	–	–	–	–	–	–	–	–	–	–	1	–	–
2012	3	2	–	1	1	–	–	–	–	–	–	–	–	1	–	–	–	–	1	–	–	–	–	–	–
	83	32	29	22	9	4	7	6	5	4	7	6	3	1	4	4	2	4	3	5	6	1	2	–	–

ENGLAND v WEST INDIES – IN WEST INDIES

		Series			Bridgetown			Port-of-Spain			Georgetown			Kingston			St John's			N Sound			St George's		
	Tests	*E*	*WI*	*D*	*E*	*WI*	*D*	*E*	*WI*	*D*	*E*	*WI*	*D*	*E*	*WI*	*D*	*E*	*WI*	*D*	*E*	*WI*	*D*	*E*	*WI*	*D*
1929-30	4	1	1	2	–	–	1	1	–	–	–	1	–	–		1	–	–	–	–	–	–	–	–	–
1934-35	4	1	2	1	1	–	–	–	1	–		–	1	–	1	–	–	–	–	–	–	–	–	–	–
1947-48	4	–	2	2	–	–	1	–	–	1	–	1	–	–	1	–	–	–	–	–	–	–	–	–	–
1953-54	5	2	2	1	–	1	–	–	–	1	1	–	–	1	1	–	–	–	–	–	–	–	–	–	–
1959-60	5	1	–	4	–	–	1	1	–	1	–	–	1	–	–	1	–	–	–	–	–	–	–	–	–
1967-68	5	1	–	4	–	–	1	1	–	1	–	–	1	–	–	1	–	–	–	–	–	–	–	–	–
1973-74	5	1	1	3	–	–	1	1	1	–	–	–	1	–	–	1	–	–	–	–	–	–	–	–	–
1980-81	4	–	2	2	–	1	–	–	1	–	–	–	–	–	–	1	–	–	1	–	–	–	–	–	–
1985-86	5	–	5	–	–	1	–	–	2	–	–	–	–	–	1	–	–	1	–	–	–	–	–	–	–
1989-90	4	1	2	1	–	1	–	–	–	1	–	–	–	1	–	–	–	1	–	–	–	–	–	–	–
1993-94	5	1	3	1	1	–	–	–	1	–	–	1	–	–	1	–	–	–	1	–	–	–	–	–	–
1997-98	6	1	3	2	–	–	1	1	1	–	–	1	–	–	–	1	–	1	–	–	–	–	–	–	–
2003-04	4	3	–	1	1	–	–	1	–	–	–	–	–	1	–	–	–	–	1	–	–	–	–	–	–
2008-09	5	–	1	4	–	–	1	–	–	1	–	–	–	–	1	–	–	–	1	–	–	1	–	–	–
2015	3	1	1	1	–	1	–	–	–	–	–	–	–	–	–	–	–	–	–	–	–	1	1	–	–
	68	14	25	29	3	5	7	6	7	6	1	4	4	3	6	6	–	3	4	–	–	2	1	–	–
Totals	151	46	54	51																					

TOURING TEAMS REGISTER 2017

Neither South Africa nor West Indies had selected their 2017 touring teams at the time of going to press. The following players, who had represented those teams in Test matches since 10 December 2015, were still available for selection:

SOUTH AFRICA

Full Names	*Birthdate*	*Birthplace*	*Team*	*Type*	*F-C Debut*
AMLA, Hashim Mahomed	31.03.83	Durban	Cape Cobras	RHB/RM	1999-00
BAVUMA, Temba	17.05.90	Cape Town	Lions	RHB/RM	2008-09
CCOK, Stephen Craig	29.11.82	Johannesburg	Lions	RHB/RM	2000-01
DE KOCK, Quinton	17.12.92	Johannesburg	Titans	LHB/WK	2009-10
DU PLESSIS, Francois 'Faf'	13.07.84	Pretoria	Titans	RHB/LB	2003-04
DUMINY, Jean-Paul	14.04.84	Cape Town	Cape Cobras	LHB/OB	2001-02
ELGAR, Dean	11.06.87	Welkom	Titans	LHB/SLA	2005-06
IMRAN TAHIR, Mohammad	27.03.79	Lahore, Pakistan	Dolphins	RHB/LBG	1996-97
MAHARAJ, Keshav Athmanand	07.02.90	Durban	Dolphins	RHB/SLA	2006-07
MORKEL, Morne	06.10.84	Vereeniging	Titans	LHB/RF	2003-04
MORRIS, Christopher Henry	30.04.87	Pretoria	Titans	RHB/RFM	2009-10
OLIVIER, Duanne	09.05.92	Groblersdal	Knights	RHB/RFM	2010-11
PARNELL, Wayne Dillon	30.07.89	Port Elizabeth	Cape Cobras	LHB/LFM	2006-07
PHILANDER, Vernon Darryl	24.06.85	Bellville	Cape Cobras	RHB/RMF	2003-04
PIEDT, Dane Lee-Roy	06.03.90	Cape Town	Cape Cobras	RHB/OB	2009-10
RABADA, Kagiso	25.05.95	Johannesburg	Lions	LHB/RF	2013-14
SHAMSI, Tabraiz	18.02.90	Johannesburg	Titans	RHB/SLC	2009-10
STEYN, Dale Willem	27.06.83	Phalaborwa	Cape Cobras	RHB/RF	2003-04

WEST INDIES

Full Names	*Birthdate*	*Birthplace*	*Team*	*Type*	*F-C Debut*
BISHOO, Devendra	06.11.85	New Amsterdam	Guyana	LHB/LB	2007-08
BLACKWOOD, Jermaine	20.11.91	St Elizabeth	Jamaica	RHB/OB	2011-12
BRATHWAITE, Carlos Ricardo	18.07.88	Christ Church	Barbados	RHB/RFM	2010-11
BRATHWAITE, Kraigg Clairmonte	01.12.92	St Michael	Barbados	RHB/OB	2008-09
BRAVO, Darren Michael	06.02.89	Santa Cruz	Trinidad	LHB/RM	2006-07
CHANDRIKA, Rajendra	08.08.89	Demarara	Guyana	RHB/OB	2009-10
CHASE, Roston Lamar	22.03.92	Christ Church	Barbados	RHB/OB	2010-11
CUMMINS, Miguel Lamar	05.09.90	St Michael	Barbados	LHB/RF	2011-12
DOWRICH, Shane Omari	30.10.91	St James	Barbados	RHB/WK	2009-10
GABRIEL, Shannon Terry	28.04.88	Trinidad	Trinidad	RHB/RFM	2009-10
HOLDER, Jason Omar	05.11.91	St George	Barbados	RHB/RMF	2008-09
HOPE, Shai Diego	10.11.93	Barbados	Barbados	RHB/WK	2012-13
JOHNSON, Leon Rayon	08.08.87	Georgetown	Guyana	LHB/LB	2003-04
JOSEPH, Alzarri Shaheim	20.11.96	Antigua	Leeward Is	RHB/RFM	2014-15
RAMDIN, Denesh	13.03.85	Couva	Trinidad	RHB/WK	2003-04
ROACH, Kemar Andre Jamal	30.06.88	St Lucy	Barbados	RHB/RF	2007-08
SAMUELS, Marlon Nathaniel	05.01.81	Kingston	Leeward Is	RHB/OB	1996-97
TAYLOR, Jerome Everton	22.06.84	St Elizabeth	Jamaica	RHB/RF	2002-03
WARRICAN, Jomel Andrel	20.05.92	Richmond Hill	Barbados	RHB/SLA	2011-12

STATISTICAL HIGHLIGHTS IN 2016 TESTS

Including Tests from No. 2195 (Australia v West Indies, 3rd Test) and No. 2197 (South Africa v England, 2nd Test) to No 2241 (Australia v Pakistan, 2nd Test) and No 2243 (South Africa v Sri Lanka, 1st Test).

† = National record

TEAM HIGHLIGHTS

HIGHEST INNINGS TOTALS

759-7d†	India v England	Chennai
631	India v England	Mumbai
629-6d	England v South Africa	Cape Town
627-7d	South Africa v England	Cape Town
624-8d	Australia v Pakistan	Melbourne

HIGHEST FOURTH INNINGS TOTAL

450†	Pakistan (set 490) v Australia	Brisbane

LOWEST INNINGS TOTALS

83	South Africa v England	Johannesburg
85	Australia v South Africa	Hobart
91	Sri Lanka v England	Leeds

HIGHEST MATCH AGGREGATE

1457-29	India (488 & 172-6) v England (537 & 260-3d)	Rajkot

BATSMEN'S MATCH (Qualification: 1200 runs, average 60 per wicket)

74.47 (1415-19)	South Africa (627-7d) v England (629-6d & 159-6)	Cape Town

LARGE MARGINS OF VICTORY

Inns & 117 runs	New Zealand (576-6d) beat Zimbabwe (164 & 295)	Bulawayo
330 runs	England (589-8d & 173-1d) beat Pakistan (198 & 234)	Manchester
321 runs	India (557-5d & 216-3d) beat New Zealand (299 & 153)	Indore

NARROW MARGINS OF VICTORY

22 runs	England (293 & 240) beat Bangladesh (248 & 263)	Chittagong

ALL ELEVEN SCORING DOUBLE FIGURES

South Africa (313) v England	Johannesburg

Uniquely in Tests, in the same innings no player made a fifty.

BATTING HIGHLIGHTS

TRIPLE HUNDREDS

Azhar Ali	302*	Pakistan v West Indies	Dubai (DSC)
K.K.Nair	303*	India v England	Chennai

DOUBLE HUNDREDS

H.M.Amla	201	South Africa v England	Cape Town
Azhar Ali	205*	Pakistan v Australia	Melbourne
V.Kohli (3)	200	India v West Indies	North Sound
	211	India v New Zealand	Indore
	235	India v England	Mumbai
J.E.Root	254	England v Pakistan	Manchester
B.A.Stokes	258	England v South Africa	Cape Town

The second fastest 200 in Test history (163 balls).

A.C.Voges	239	Australia v New Zealand	Wellington
Younus Khan	218	Pakistan v England	The Oval

HUNDREDS IN THREE CONSECUTIVE INNINGS

A.C.Voges	269*	Australia v West Indies	Hobart
	106*	Australia v West Indies	Melbourne
	239	Australia v New Zealand	Wellington

Voges scored a Test world record 614 runs between dismissals.

FASTEST HUNDRED

B.B.McCullum (145) 54 balls New Zealand v Australia Christchurch

The fastest Test century ever (79 balls, 21 fours, 6 sixes).

HUNDRED RUNS SCORED BEFORE LUNCH

B.A.Stokes (74-204*) England v South Africa Cape Town

On Day 2; most runs ever scored before lunch in Tests.

MOST SIXES IN AN INNINGS

11† B.A.Stokes (258) England v South Africa Cape Town

150 RUNS OR MORE IN BOUNDARIES IN AN INNINGS

Runs	*6s*	*4s*			
186	11	30	B.A.Stokes	England v South Africa	Cape Town
152	4	32	K.K.Nair	India v England	Chennai

HUNDRED ON TEST DEBUT

S.C.Cook (115) South Africa v England Centurion

The 100th batsman to score a century on Test debut.

K.K.Jennings (112) England v India Mumbai

CARRYING BAT THROUGH COMPLETED INNINGS

K.C.Brathwaite (142*) West Indies (337) v Pakistan Sharjah

LONG INNINGS (Qualification: 600 mins and/or 400 balls)

Mins	*Balls*			
707	477	H.M.Amla (201)	South Africa v England	Cape Town
658	469	Azhar Ali (302*)	Pakistan v West Indies	Dubai (DSC)
614	406	J.E.Root (254)	England v Pakistan	Manchester

LONG PARTNERSHIP WITHOUT SCORING

Balls			
154	P.M.Nevill/S.N.J.O'Keefe	Australia v Sri Lanka	Pallekele

This set a new world record.

FIRST-WICKET PARTNERSHIP OF 100 IN EACH INNINGS

104/116 S.C.Cook/D.Elgar South Africa v Sri Lanka Port Elizabeth

OTHER NOTABLE PARTNERSHIPS

Qualifications: 1st-4th wkts: 250 runs; 5th-6th: 225; 7th: 200; 8th: 175; 9th: 150; 10th: 100.

Third Wicket

289	J.A.Burns/S.P.D.Smith	Australia v New Zealand	Christchurch
250	D.Elgar/J.P.Duminy	South Africa v Australia	Perth

Fourth Wicket

365†	V.Kohli/A.M.Rahane	India v New Zealand	Indore

Sixth Wicket

399†	B.A.Stokes/J.M.Bairstow	England v South Africa	Cape Town

A world record Test partnership for the sixth wicket.

253	L.R.P.L.Taylor/B.J.Watling	New Zealand v Zimbabwe	Bulawayo

Eighth Wicket

241†	V.Kohli/J.Yadav	India v England	Mumbai

BOWLING HIGHLIGHTS

EIGHT WICKETS IN AN INNINGS

D.Bishoo	8-49	West Indies v Pakistan	Dubai (DSC)
H.M.R.K.B.Herath	8-63	Sri Lanka v Zimbabwe	Harare

TEN WICKETS IN A MATCH

J.M.Anderson	10- 45	England v Sri Lanka	Leeds
R.Ashwin (3)	10-225	India v New Zealand	Kanpur
	13-140	India v New Zealand	Indore
	12-167	India v England	Mumbai
D.Bishoo	10-174	West Indies v Pakistan	Dubai (DSC)
H.M.R.K.B.Herath (2)	13-145	Sri Lanka v Australia	Colombo (SSC)
	13-152	Sri Lanka v Zimbabwe	Harare
R.A.Jadeja	10-154	India v England	Chennai
Mehedi Hasan	12-159	Bangladesh v England	Dhaka
M.D.K.Perera	10- 99	Sri Lanka v Australia	Galle
K.Rabada	13-144	South Africa v England	Centurion
M.A.Starc	11- 94	Australia v Sri Lanka	Galle
C.R.Woakes	11-102	England v Pakistan	Lord's
Yasir Shah (2)	10-141	Pakistan v England	Lord's
	10-210	Pakistan v West Indies	Abu Dhabi

FIVE WICKETS IN AN INNINGS ON DEBUT

Mehedi Hasan	6-80	Bangladesh v England	Chittagong
C.de Grandhomme	6-41	New Zealand v Pakistan	Christchurch

HAT-TRICK

H.M.R.K.B.Herath		Sri Lanka v Australia	Galle

MOST OVERS IN AN INNINGS

A.U.Rashid	55.3-5-192-4	England v India	Mumbai

200 RUNS CONCEDED IN AN INNINGS

Yasir Shah	54-6-213-1	Pakistan v England	Manchester
Yasir Shah	41-2-207-3	Pakistan v Australia	Melbourne

ALL-ROUND HIGHLIGHTS

MATCH DOUBLE (HUNDRED AND FIVE DISMISSALS IN AN INNINGS)

J.M.Bairstow	(140 & 5ct)	England v Sri Lanka	Leeds

WICKET-KEEPING HIGHLIGHTS

SIX WICKET-KEEPING DISMISSALS IN AN INNINGS

J.M.Bairstow	6ct	England v South Africa	Johannesburg
W.P.Saha	5ct, 1st	India v West Indies	North Sound

NINE OR MORE WICKET-KEEPING DISMISSALS IN A MATCH

J.M.Bairstow	9ct	England v South Africa	Johannesburg
J.M.Bairstow	9ct	England v Sri Lanka	Leeds

NO BYES CONCEDED IN AN INNINGS OF 550

589-8d	Sarfraz Ahmed	Pakistan v England	Manchester

FIELDING HIGHLIGHTS

FOUR CATCHES IN AN INNINGS IN THE FIELD

J.E.Root	4ct	England v Pakistan	Manchester

SIX CATCHES IN A MATCH IN THE FIELD

S.P.D.Smith	6ct	Australia v Sri Lanka	Colombo (SSC)

LEADING TEST AGGREGATES IN 2016

1000 RUNS IN 2016

	M	*I*	*NO*	*HS*	*Runs*	*Avge*	*100*	*50*
J.E.Root (E)	17	32	2	254	**1477**	49.23	3	10
J.M.Bairstow (E)	17	29	4	167*	**1470**	58.80	3	8
A.N.Cook (E)	17	33	3	130	**1270**	42.33	2	7
V.Kohli (I)	12	18	2	235	**1215**	75.93	4	2
Azhar Ali (P)	11	22	3	302*	**1198**	63.05	3	4
S.P.D.Smith (A)	11	18	3	165*	**1079**	71.93	4	5
M.M.Ali (E)	17	29	6	155*	**1078**	46.86	4	5

RECORD CALENDAR YEAR RUNS AGGREGATE

	M	*I*	*NO*	*HS*	*Runs*	*Avge*	*100*	*50*
M.Yousuf (P) (2006)	11	19	1	202	**1788**	99.33	9	3

RECORD CALENDAR YEAR RUNS AVERAGE

	M	*I*	*NO*	*HS*	*Runs*	*Avge*	*100*	*50*
G.St A.Sobers (WI) (1958)	7	12	3	365*	**1193**	132.55	5	3

1000 RUNS IN DEBUT CALENDAR YEAR

	M	*I*	*NO*	*HS*	*Runs*	*Avge*	*100*	*50*
M.A.Taylor (A) (1989)	11	20	1	219	**1219**	64.15	4	5
A.C.Voges (A) (2015)	12	18	6	269*	**1028**	85.66	4	3
A.N.Cook (E) (2006)	13	24	2	127	**1013**	46.04	4	3

50 WICKETS IN 2016

	M	*O*	*R*	*W*	*Avge*	*Best*	*5wI*	*10wM*
R.Ashwin (I)	12	584.4	1721	72	**23.90**	7-59	8	3
H.M.R.K.B.Herath (SL)	9	412.2	1079	57	**18.92**	8-63	5	2
M.A.Starc (A)	8	325.4	1129	50	**22.58**	6-50	3	1

RECORD CALENDAR YEAR WICKETS AGGREGATE

	M	*O*	*R*	*W*	*Avge*	*Best*	*5wI*	*10wM*
M.Muralitharan (SL) (2006)	11	588.4	1521	90	**16.90**	8-70	9	5
S.K.Warne (A) (2005)	14	691.4	2043	90	**22.70**	6-46	6	2

50 WICKET-KEEPING DISMISSALS IN 2016

	M	*Dis*	*Ct*	*St*
J.M.Bairstow (E)	17	70	66	4

RECORD CALENDAR YEAR DISMISSALS AGGREGATE

	M	*Dis*	*Ct*	*St*
J.M.Bairstow (E) (2016)	17	70	66	4

20 CATCHES BY FIELDERS IN 2016

	M	*Ct*
S.P.D.Smith (A)	11	29
J.E.Root (E)	17	26

RECORD CALENDAR YEAR FIELDER'S AGGREGATE

	M	*Ct*
G.C.Smith (SA) (2008)	15	30

TEST MATCH SCORES
ENGLAND v SRI LANKA (1st Test)

At Headingley, Leeds, on 19, 20, 21 May 2016.
Toss: Sri Lanka. Result: **ENGLAND** won by an innings and 88 runs.
Debuts: England – J.M.Vince; Sri Lanka – M.D.Shanaka.

ENGLAND

*A.N.Cook	c Chandimal b Shanaka	16
A.D.Hales	c Chameera b Herath	86
N.R.D.Compton	c Thirimanne b Shanaka	0
J.E.Root	c Mendis b Shanaka	0
J.M.Vince	c Mendis b Eranga	9
B.A.Stokes	c Mathews b Fernando	12
†J.M.Bairstow	c Fernando b Chameera	140
M.M.Ali	c Mendis b Chameera	0
S.C.J.Broad	b Chameera	2
S.T.Finn	st Chandimal b Herath	17
J.M.Anderson	not out	1
Extras	(LB 8, W 4, NB 3)	15
Total	**(90.3 overs)**	**298**

SRI LANKA

F.D.M.Karunaratne	c Bairstow b Broad	0	c Bairstow b Anderson	7
J.K.Silva	c Bairstow b Anderson	11	c Bairstow b Anderson	14
B.K.G.Mendis	c Bairstow b Broad	0	b Anderson	53
†L.D.Chandimal	c Vince b Stokes	15	b Ali	8
*A.D.Mathews	lbw b Anderson	34	c Bairstow b Broad	5
H.D.R.L.Thirimanne	c Finn b Broad	22	c Root b Finn	16
M.D.Shanaka	c Bairstow b Anderson	0	c Bairstow b Anderson	4
H.M.R.K.B.Herath	c Stokes b Anderson	1	c Broad b Finn	4
P.V.D.Chameera	c Finn b Broad	2	c Compton b Finn	0
R.M.S.Eranga	c Bairstow b Anderson	1	not out	2
A.N.P.R.Fernando	not out	0	b Anderson	0
Extras	(NB 5)	5	(LB 5, NB 1)	6
Total	**(36.4 overs)**	**91**	**(35.3 overs)**	**119**

SRI LANKA	O	M	R	W		O	M	R	W
Eranga	19	4	68	1					
Fernando	19	7	56	1					
Mathews	11	2	31	0					
Chameera	17	0	64	3					
Shanaka	13	3	46	3					
Herath	11.3	1	25	2					
ENGLAND									
Anderson	11.4	6	16	5		13.3	5	29	5
Broad	10	1	21	4		13	0	57	1
Stokes	7	2	25	1					
Vince	1	0	10	0					
Finn	7	0	19	0	(3)	8	0	26	3
Ali					(4)	1	0	2	1

FALL OF WICKETS	E	SL	SL
Wkt	*1st*	*1st*	*2nd*
1st	49	10	10
2nd	49	12	35
3rd	51	12	79
4th	70	43	93
5th	83	77	93
6th	224	81	101
7th	231	83	111
8th	233	90	117
9th	289	91	118
10th	298	91	119

Umpires: Alim Dar (*Pakistan*) (102) and R.J.Tucker (*Australia*) (42).
Referee: A.J.Pycroft (*Zimbabwe*) (44). **Test No. 2202/29 (E970/SL246)**

ENGLAND v SRI LANKA (2nd Test)

At Riverside Ground, Chester-le-Street, on 27, 28, 29, 30 May 2016.
Toss: England. Result: **ENGLAND** won by nine wickets.
Debuts: None.

ENGLAND

*A.N.Cook	c Karunaratne b Lakmal	15	not out	47
A.D.Hales	c Mathews b Siriwardana	83	b Siriwardana	11
N.R.D.Compton	c Lakmal b Fernando	9	not out	22
J.E.Root	c Silva b Fernando	80		
J.M.Vince	c Thirimanne b Siriwardana	35		
†J.M.Bairstow	c Chandimal b Fernando	48		
M.M.Ali	not out	155		
C.R.Woakes	c Mendis b Lakmal	39		
S.C.J.Broad	c Mendis b Fernando	7		
S.T.Finn	c and b Herath	10		
J.M.Anderson	not out	8		
Extras	(B 1, LB 8)	9		–
Total	**(9 wkts dec; 132 overs)**	**498**	**(1 wkt; 23.2 overs)**	**80**

SRI LANKA

F.D.M.Karunaratne	b Anderson	9		c Root b Woakes	26
J.K.Silva	c Bairstow b Broad	13		c Bairstow b Finn	60
B.K.G.Mendis	c Anderson b Woakes	35		c Bairstow b Anderson	26
†L.D.Chandimal	c Cook b Anderson	4	(6)	b Broad	126
*A.D.Mathews	c Bairstow b Woakes	3		c Bairstow b Anderson	80
H.D.R.L.Thirimanne	c Compton b Anderson	19	(4)	b Ali	13
T.A.M.Siriwardana	c Bairstow b Woakes	0		c Hales b Anderson	35
H.M.R.K.B.Herath	c Anderson b Broad	12		lbw b Anderson	61
R.M.S.Eranga	c Root b Broad	2		b Anderson	1
R.A.S.Lakmal	c Bairstow b Broad	0		c Broad b Woakes	11
A.N.P.R.Fernando	not out	2		not out	13
Extras	(LB 1, NB 1)	2		(B 5, LB 11, W 1, NB 6)	23
Total	**(43.3 overs)**	**101**		**(128.2 overs)**	**475**

SRI LANKA	O	M	R	W		O	M	R	W
Eranga	27	3	100	0	(5)	1	0	4	0
Lakmal	29	4	115	2	(4)	3	0	9	0
Fernando	33	5	107	4	(2)	2	0	12	0
Herath	29	1	116	1	(1)	10	3	18	0
Mathews	6	2	16	0					
Siriwardana	8	0	35	2	(3)	7.2	0	37	1
ENGLAND									
Anderson	12.3	2	36	3		27	9	58	5
Broad	13	2	40	4		24	6	71	1
Woakes	7	4	9	3		27.2	8	103	2
Finn	7	3	15	0		19	0	78	1
Ali	4	4	0	0		28	5	136	1
Vince						1	1	0	0
Root						2	0	13	0

FALL OF WICKETS

	E	SL	SL	E
Wkt	*1st*	*1st*	*2nd*	*2nd*
1st	39	10	38	35
2nd	64	44	79	–
3rd	160	53	100	–
4th	219	58	182	–
5th	227	67	222	–
6th	297	67	314	–
7th	389	88	430	–
8th	400	90	442	–
9th	472	93	453	–
10th	–	101	475	–

Umpires: Alim Dar (*Pakistan*) (103) and S.Ravi (*India*) (11).
Referee: A.J.Pycroft (*Zimbabwe*) (45). **Test No. 2203/30 (E971/SL247)**

ENGLAND v SRI LANKA (3rd Test)

At Lord's, London, on 9, 10, 11, 12, 13 June 2016.
Toss: England. Result: **MATCH DRAWN**.
Debuts: None.

ENGLAND

*A.N.Cook	lbw b Fernando	85	(7)	not out	49
A.D.Hales	c Mathews b Herath	18		lbw b Mathews	94
N.R.D.Compton	c Chandimal b Lakmal	1	(1)	c Chandimal b Eranga	19
J.E.Root	lbw b Lakmal	3	(3)	b Fernando	4
J.M.Vince	b Fernando	10	(4)	b Fernando	0
†J.M.Bairstow	not out	167	(5)	b Fernando	32
M.M.Ali	c Mathews b Herath	25	(8)	c Herath b Eranga	9
C.R.Woakes	c and b Herath	66	(9)	not out	0
S.C.J.Broad	c Mendis b Lakmal	14			
S.T.Finn	c Lakmal b Herath	7	(6)	lbw b Eranga	7
J.M.Anderson	c Chandimal b Eranga	4			
Extras	(LB 16)	16		(B 6, LB 4, W 1, NB 8)	19
Total	**(128.4 overs)**	**416**		**(7 wkts dec; 71 overs)**	**233**

SRI LANKA

F.D.M.Karunaratne	c Bairstow b Finn	50	not out	37
J.K.Silva	c Bairstow b Broad	79	lbw b Anderson	16
B.K.G.Mendis	lbw b Woakes	25	not out	17
H.D.R.L.Thirimanne	c Root b Finn	17		
*A.D.Mathews	c Root b Woakes	3		
†L.D.Chandimal	lbw b Finn	19		
M.D.K.J.Perera	c Bairstow b Anderson	42		
H.M.R.K.B.Herath	b Broad	31		
R.M.S.Eranga	c Vince b Woakes	1		
R.A.S.Lakmal	c Root b Anderson	0		
A.N.P.R.Fernando	not out	0		
Extras	(B 4, LB 16, W 1)	21	(B 1, LB 6, NB 1)	8
Total	**(95.1 overs)**	**288**	**(1 wkt; 24.2 overs)**	**78**

SRI LANKA	O	M	R	W		O	M	R	W
Eranga	25.4	2	94	1	(2)	14	1	58	3
Lakmal	27	2	90	3	(1)	13	2	45	0
Fernando	27	4	104	2		15	5	37	3
Mathews	13	5	31	0	(5)	9	3	20	1
Herath	36	8	81	4	(4)	20	2	63	0
ENGLAND									
Anderson	23	6	61	2	(2)	9	2	27	1
Broad	23	7	79	2	(1)	11	4	27	0
Finn	18	1	59	3					
Woakes	17.1	5	31	3	(3)	2	1	7	0
Ali	14	2	38	0	(4)	2	1	4	0
Root					(5)	0.2	0	6	0

FALL OF WICKETS

	E	SL	E	SL
Wkt	*1st*	*1st*	*2nd*	*2nd*
1st	56	108	45	45
2nd	67	162	50	–
3rd	71	166	50	–
4th	84	169	101	–
5th	164	202	120	–
6th	227	205	202	–
7th	371	276	224	–
8th	396	288	–	–
9th	411	288	–	–
10th	416	288	–	–

Umpires: S.Ravi (*India*) (12) and R.J.Tucker (*Australia*) (43).
Referee: A.J.Pycroft (*Zimbabwe*) (46). **Test No. 2204/31 (E972/SL248)**

ENGLAND v PAKISTAN (1st Test)

At Lord's, London, on 14, 15, 16, 17 July 2016.
Toss: Pakistan. Result: **PAKISTAN** won by 75 runs.
Debut: England – J.T.Ball.

PAKISTAN

Mohammad Hafeez	c Bairstow b Woakes	40		c Root b Broad	0
Shan Masood	c Bairstow b Woakes	7		c Cook b Woakes	24
Azhar Ali	lbw b Ball	7		lbw b Woakes	23
Younus Khan	c Ali b Broad	33		b Ali	25
*Misbah-ul-Haq	b Broad	114		c Hales b Ali	0
Asad Shafiq	c Bairstow b Woakes	73		b Woakes	49
Rahat Ali	b Woakes	0	(11)	not out	0
†Sarfraz Ahmed	c Vince b Woakes	25	(7)	c Bairstow b Woakes	45
Wahab Riaz	b Woakes	0		c Bairstow b Woakes	0
Mohammad Amir	c Root b Broad	12		c Bairstow b Broad	1
Yasir Shah	not out	11	(8)	c Bairstow b Broad	30
Extras	(B 4, LB 10, W 2, NB 1)	17		(B 6, LB 11, NB 1)	18
Total	**(99.2 overs)**	**339**		**(79.1 overs)**	**215**

ENGLAND

*A.N.Cook	b Amir	81	c Ahmed b Rahat	8
A.D.Hales	c Azhar b Rahat	6	c Hafeez b Rahat	16
J.E.Root	c Hafeez b Shah	48	c Shah b Rahat	9
J.M.Vince	lbw b Shah	16	c Khan b Riaz	42
G.S.Ballance	lbw b Shah	6	b Shah	43
†J.M.Bairstow	b Shah	29	b Shah	48
M.M.Ali	lbw b Shah	23	b Shah	2
C.R.Woakes	not out	35	c Khan b Shah	23
S.C.J.Broad	b Riaz	17	b Amir	1
S.T.Finn	lbw b Shah	5	not out	4
J.T.Ball	run out	4	b Amir	3
Extras	(NB 2)	2	(B 1, LB 5, W 1, NB 1)	8
Total	**(79.1 overs)**	**272**	**(75.5 overs)**	**207**

ENGLAND	O	M	R	W		O	M	R	W
Broad	27.2	9	71	3		19.1	7	38	3
Ball	19	5	51	1		16	7	37	0
Woakes	24	7	70	6	(4)	18	6	32	5
Finn	21	2	86	0	(3)	13	4	42	0
Ali	7	0	46	0		13	3	49	2
Vince	1	0	1	0					
PAKISTAN									
Mohammad Amir	18	2	65	1		17.5	4	39	2
Rahat Ali	14	1	68	1		14	0	47	3
Wahab Riaz	18.1	0	67	1	(4)	13	1	46	1
Yasir Shah	29	6	72	6	(3)	31	9	69	4

FALL OF WICKETS

	P	E	P	E
Wkt	*1st*	*1st*	*2nd*	*2nd*
1st	38	8	2	19
2nd	51	118	44	32
3rd	77	139	59	47
4th	134	147	60	96
5th	282	173	129	135
6th	282	193	168	139
7th	310	232	208	195
8th	310	260	214	196
9th	316	267	214	204
10th	339	272	215	207

Umpires: H.D.P.K.Dharmasena (*Sri Lanka*) (37) and J.S.Wilson (*West Indies*) (2).
Referee: R.B.Richardson (*West Indies*) (1). **Test No. 2205/78 (E973/P395)**

ENGLAND v PAKISTAN (2nd Test)

At Old Trafford, Manchester, on 22, 23, 24, 25 July 2016.
Toss: England. Result: **ENGLAND** won by 330 runs.
Debuts: None.

ENGLAND

*A.N.Cook	b Amir	105		not out	76
A.D.Hales	b Amir	10		c Ahmed b Amir	24
J.E.Root	c Hafeez b Riaz	254		not out	71
J.M.Vince	c Ahmed b Rahat	18			
G.S.Ballance	b Rahat	23			
C.R.Woakes	c and b Shah	58			
B.A.Stokes	c Ahmed b Riaz	34			
†J.M.Bairstow	c Misbah b Riaz	58			
M.M.Ali	not out	2			
S.C.J.Broad					
J.M.Anderson					
Extras	(LB 9, W 8, NB 10)	27		(LB 2)	2
Total	**(8 wkts dec; 152.2 overs)**	**589**		**(1 wkt dec; 30 overs)**	**173**

PAKISTAN

Mohammad Hafeez	c Root b Woakes	18		c Ballance b Ali	42
Shan Masood	c Root b Anderson	39		c Cook b Anderson	1
Azhar Ali	c and b Woakes	1		lbw b Anderson	8
Younus Khan	c Bairstow b Stokes	1		c Hales b Ali	28
Rahat Ali	c Ballance b Stokes	4	(11)	not out	8
*Misbah-ul-Haq	c Cook b Ali	52	(5)	b Woakes	35
Asad Shafiq	c Hales b Broad	4	(6)	lbw b Anderson	39
†Sarfraz Ahmed	c Root b Stokes	26	(7)	c Bairstow b Woakes	7
Yasir Shah	c Root b Woakes	1	(8)	lbw b Ali	10
Wahab Riaz	c Hales b Ali	39	(9)	c Cook b Root	19
Mohammad Amir	not out	9	(10)	c Broad b Woakes	29
Extras	(LB 2, NB 2)	4		(B 2, LB 4, W 1, NB 1)	8
Total	**(63.4 overs)**	**198**		**(70.3 overs)**	**234**

PAKISTAN	O	M	R	W		O	M	R	W
Mohammad Amir	29	6	89	2		11	2	43	1
Rahat Ali	29	4	101	2		8	0	54	0
Wahab Riaz	26.2	1	106	3					
Yasir Shah	54	6	213	1	(3)	9	0	53	0
Azhar Ali	11	0	52	0	(4)	2	0	21	0
Shan Masood	3	0	19	0					
ENGLAND									
Anderson	13	5	27	1		16	2	41	3
Broad	12	5	20	1		14	3	37	0
Ali	7.4	0	43	2	(4)	18.4	1	88	3
Woakes	16	1	67	4	(5)	15.3	2	41	3
Stokes	15	1	39	2	(3)	5.2	0	21	0
Root						1	1	0	1

FALL OF WICKETS

	E	P	E	P
Wkt	*1st*	*1st*	*2nd*	*2nd*
1st	25	27	68	7
2nd	210	43	–	25
3rd	238	48	–	83
4th	311	53	–	102
5th	414	71	–	145
6th	471	76	–	163
7th	577	112	–	167
8th	589	119	–	190
9th	–	179	–	208
10th	–	198	–	234

Umpires: H.D.P.K.Dharmasena (*Sri Lanka*) (38) and R.J.Tucker (*Australia*) (44).
Referee: R.B.Richardson (*West Indies*) (2). **Test No. 2206/79 (E974/P396)**

ENGLAND v PAKISTAN (3rd Test)

At Edgbaston, Birmingham, on 3, 4, 5, 6, 7 August 2016.
Toss: Pakistan. Result: **ENGLAND** won by 141 runs.
Debuts: None.

ENGLAND

*A.N.Cook	lbw b Rahat	45	c Shah b Sohail	66
A.D.Hales	c Ahmed b Sohail	17	c Younus b Amir	54
J.E.Root	c Hafeez b Sohail	3	c Hafeez b Shah	62
J.M.Vince	c Younus b Sohail	39	c Younus b Amir	42
G.S.Ballance	c Ahmed b Shah	70	c Shafiq b Shah	28
†J.M.Bairstow	c Ahmed b Sohail	12	lbw b Sohail	83
M.M.Ali	c Ahmed b Amir	63	not out	86
C.R.Woakes	c Ahmed b Rahat	9	not out	3
S.C.J.Broad	c Azhar b Amir	13		
S.T.Finn	not out	15		
J.M.Anderson	lbw b Sohail	5		
Extras	(LB 1, W 1, NB 4)	6	(B 4, LB 7, W 2, NB 8)	21
Total	**(86 overs)**	**297**	**(6 wkts dec; 129 overs)**	**445**

PAKISTAN

Mohammad Hafeez	c Ballance b Anderson	0	c Woakes b Broad	2
Sami Aslam	run out	82	b Finn	70
Azhar Ali	c Cook b Woakes	139	c Cook b Ali	38
Younus Khan	c Bairstow b Woakes	31	c Bairstow b Anderson	4
*Misbah-ul-Haq	b Anderson	56	c Bairstow b Finn	10
Asad Shafiq	b Broad	0	lbw b Woakes	0
†Sarfraz Ahmed	not out	46	c Root b Woakes	0
Yasir Shah	run out	7	c Hales b Anderson	7
Mohammad Amir	lbw b Woakes	1	c Woakes b Broad	16
Sohail Khan	lbw b Broad	7	c and b Ali	36
Rahat Ali	c Root b Broad	4	not out	15
Extras	(B 5, LB 21, NB 1)	27	(LB 2, NB 1)	3
Total	**(136 overs)**	**400**	**(70.5 overs)**	**201**

PAKISTAN	O	M	R	W		O	M	R	W
Mohammad Amir	16	3	53	2		31	8	75	2
Sohail Khan	23	3	96	5		29	3	111	2
Rahat Ali	20	4	83	2		21	8	54	0
Yasir Shah	27	3	64	1		43	4	172	2
Azhar Ali						5	0	22	0
ENGLAND									
Anderson	29.1	7	54	2		13	3	31	2
Broad	30	4	83	3		15	7	24	2
Finn	27.5	7	76	0	(4)	13	5	38	2
Woakes	30	7	79	3	(3)	11	2	53	2
Ali	17	2	79	0		17.5	4	49	2
Vince	1	0	2	0					
Root	1	0	1	0	(6)	1	0	4	0

FALL OF WICKETS

	E	P	E	P
Wkt	*1st*	*1st*	*2nd*	*2nd*
1st	36	0	126	6
2nd	48	181	126	79
3rd	75	257	221	92
4th	144	274	257	124
5th	158	296	282	125
6th	224	358	434	125
7th	244	367	–	125
8th	276	368	–	149
9th	278	386	–	151
10th	297	400	–	201

Umpires: B.N.J.Oxenford (*Australia*) (32) and J.S.Wilson (*West Indies*) (3).
Referee: R.B.Richardson (*West Indies*) (3). **Test No. 2207/80 (E975/P397)**

ENGLAND v PAKISTAN (4th Test)

At The Oval, London, on 11, 12, 13, 14 August 2016.
Toss: England. Result: **PAKISTAN** won by ten wickets.
Debut: Pakistan – Iftikhar Ahmed.

ENGLAND

*A.N.Cook	b Sohail	35	c Iftikhar b Riaz	7
A.D.Hales	c Shah b Amir	6	lbw b Shah	12
J.E.Root	c Sarfraz b Riaz	26	lbw b Shah	39
J.M.Vince	c Sarfraz b Riaz	1	c Misbah b Shah	0
G.S.Ballance	c Azhar b Riaz	8	c Sarfraz b Sohail	17
†J.M.Bairstow	c Sarfraz b Amir	55	c Azhar b Riaz	81
M.M.Ali	c Shah b Sohail	108	c Sarfraz b Shah	32
C.R.Woakes	c Sarfraz b Sohail	45	run out	4
S.C.J.Broad	lbw b Sohail	0	c Younus b Shah	5
S.T.Finn	b Sohail	8	not out	16
J.M.Anderson	not out	6	lbw b Iftikhar	17
Extras	(B 8, LB 7, W 7, NB 8)	30	(B 8, LB 10, NB 5)	23
Total	**(76.4 overs)**	**328**	**(79.2 overs)**	**253**

PAKISTAN

Sami Aslam	lbw b Broad	3	not out	12
Azhar Ali	c Bairstow b Ali	49	not out	30
Yasir Shah	c Root b Finn	26		
Asad Shafiq	c Broad b Finn	109		
Younus Khan	lbw b Anderson	218		
*Misbah-ul-Haq	c Hales b Woakes	15		
Iftikhar Ahmed	c Ali b Woakes	4		
†Sarfraz Ahmed	c Bairstow b Woakes	44		
Wahab Riaz	st Bairstow b Ali	1		
Mohammad Amir	not out	39		
Sohail Khan	c Broad b Finn	2		
Extras	(B 18, LB 6, W 3, NB 2)	29		–
Total	**(146 overs)**	**542**	**(0 wkts; 13.1 overs)**	**42**

PAKISTAN	O	M	R	W		O	M	R	W
Mohammad Amir	18	1	80	2		21.4	7	65	0
Sohail Khan	20.4	1	68	5		15	2	50	1
Wahab Riaz	20	0	93	3		11.2	1	48	2
Yasir Shah	16	2	60	0		29	4	71	5
Iftikhar Ahmed	2	0	12	0		2.2	1	1	1
ENGLAND									
Anderson	29	10	78	1					
Broad	29	5	99	1					
Finn	30	1	110	3	(2)	0.2	0	0	0
Woakes	30	8	82	3	(1)	4	0	11	0
Ali	23	1	128	2	(3)	5.5	0	30	0
Root	5	0	21	0	(4)	3	2	1	0

FALL OF WICKETS

	E	P	E	P
Wkt	*1st*	*1st*	*2nd*	*2nd*
1st	23	3	14	–
2nd	69	52	49	–
3rd	73	127	55	–
4th	74	277	74	–
5th	110	316	128	–
6th	203	320	193	–
7th	282	397	209	–
8th	282	434	209	–
9th	296	531	221	–
10th	328	542	253	–

Umpires: M.Erasmus (*South Africa*) (36) and B.N.J.Oxenford (*Australia*) (33).
Referee: R.B.Richardson (*West Indies*) (4). **Test No. 2208/81 (E976/P398)**

WEST INDIES v INDIA (1st Test)

At Sir Vivian Richards Stadium, North Sound, Antigua, on 21, 22, 23, 24 July 2016.
Toss: India. Result: **INDIA** won by an innings and 92 runs.
Debut: West Indies – R.L.Chase.

INDIA

M.Vijay	c K.C.Brathwaite b Gabriel	7
S.Dhawan	lbw b Bishoo	84
C.A.Pujara	c K.C.Brathwaite b Bishoo	16
*V.Kohli	b Gabriel	200
A.M.Rahane	c Bravo b Bishoo	22
R.Ashwin	c Gabriel b K.C.Brathwaite	113
†W.P.Saha	st Dowrich b K.C.Brathwaite	40
A.Mishra	c Holder b K.C.Brathwaite	53
Mohammed Shami	not out	17
I.Sharma		
U.T.Yadav		
Extras	(B 6, LB 2, NB 6)	14
Total	**(8 wkts dec; 161.5 overs)**	**566**

WEST INDIES

K.C.Brathwaite	c Saha b Yadav	74		lbw b Sharma	2
R.Chandrika	c Saha b Shami	16		c Saha b Ashwin	31
D.Bishoo	st Saha b Mishra	12	(10)	c Pujara b Ashwin	45
D.M.Bravo	c Saha b Shami	11	(3)	c Rahane b Yadav	10
M.N.Samuels	c Saha b Shami	1	(4)	b Ashwin	50
J.Blackwood	c Rahane b Shami	0	(5)	c Kohli b Ashwin	0
R.L.Chase	c Kohli b Yadav	23	(6)	c sub (K.L.Rahul) b Ashwin	8
†S.O.Dowrich	not out	57	(7)	lbw b Mishra	9
*J.O.Holder	c Saha b Yadav	36	(8)	b Ashwin	16
C.R.Brathwaite	b Yadav	0	(9)	not out	51
S.T.Gabriel	b Mishra	2		b Ashwin	4
Extras	(B 4, LB 2, W 2, NB 3)	11		(NB 5)	5
Total	**(90.2 overs)**	**243**		**(78 overs)**	**231**

WEST INDIES	O	M	R	W		O	M	R	W
Gabriel	21	5	65	2					
Holder	24	4	83	0					
C.R.Brathwaite	25	5	80	0					
Chase	34	3	102	0					
Bishoo	43	1	163	3					
K.C.Brathwaite	14.5	1	65	3					
INDIA									
Sharma	20	7	44	0		11	2	27	1
Yadav	18	8	41	4	(3)	13	4	34	1
Mohammed Shami	20	4	66	4	(2)	10	3	26	0
Ashwin	17	5	43	0		25	8	83	7
Mishra	15.2	4	43	2		19	3	61	1

FALL OF WICKETS

	I	WI	WI
Wkt	*1st*	*1st*	*2nd*
1st	14	30	2
2nd	74	68	21
3rd	179	90	88
4th	236	92	92
5th	404	92	101
6th	475	139	106
7th	526	144	120
8th	566	213	132
9th	–	213	227
10th	–	243	231

Umpires: Alim Dar (*Pakistan*) (104) and I.J.Gould (*England*) (50).
Referee: R.S.Madugalle (*Sri Lanka*) (164). **Test No. 2209/91 (WI514/I496)**

WEST INDIES v INDIA (2nd Test)

At Sabina Park, Kingston, Jamaica, on 30, 31 July, 1, 2, 3 August 2016.
Toss: West Indies. Result: **MATCH DRAWN**.
Debut: West Indies – M.L.Cummins.

WEST INDIES

K.C.Brathwaite	c Pujara b Sharma	1	c Rahul b Mishra	23
R.Chandrika	c Rahul b Shami	5	b Sharma	1
D.M.Bravo	c Kohli b Sharma	0	c Rahul b Shami	20
M.N.Samuels	c Rahul b Ashwin	37	b Shami	0
J.Blackwood	lbw b Ashwin	62	c Pujara b Ashwin	63
R.L.Chase	c Dhawan b Shami	10	not out	137
†S.O.Dowrich	c Saha b Ashwin	5	lbw b Mishra	74
*J.O.Holder	c Rahul b Ashwin	13	not out	64
D.Bishoo	c Dhawan b Ashwin	12		
M.L.Cummins	not out	24		
S.T.Gabriel	c Kohli b Mishra	15		
Extras	(W 2, NB 10)	12	(LB 2, W 1, NB 3)	6
Total	**(52.3 overs)**	**196**	**(6 wkts; 104 overs)**	**388**

INDIA

K.L.Rahul	c Dowrich b Gabriel	158
S.Dhawan	c Bravo b Chase	27
C.A.Pujara	run out	46
*V.Kohli	c Chandrika b Chase	44
A.M.Rahane	not out	108
R.Ashwin	lbw b Bishoo	3
†W.P.Saha	lbw b Holder	47
A.Mishra	c Chandrika b Chase	21
Mohammed Shami	b Chase	0
U.T.Yadav	c Holder b Chase	19
I.Sharma		
Extras	(B 8, LB 3, W 6, NB 10)	27
Total	**(9 wkts dec; 171.1 overs)**	**500**

INDIA	O	M	R	W		O	M	R	W
Sharma	10	1	53	2		18	3	56	1
Mohammed Shami	10	3	23	2		19	3	82	2
Ashwin	16	2	52	5	(5)	30	4	114	1
Yadav	6	1	30	0		12	2	44	0
Mishra	10.3	3	38	1	(3)	25	6	90	2
WEST INDIES									
Gabriel	28	8	62	1					
Cummins	26.4	4	87	0					
Holder	34.2	12	72	1					
Chase	36.1	4	121	5					
Bishoo	35	5	107	1					
Brathwaite	11	0	40	0					

FALL OF WICKETS

	WI	I	WI
Wkt	*1st*	*1st*	*2nd*
1st	4	87	5
2nd	4	208	41
3rd	7	277	41
4th	88	310	48
5th	115	327	141
6th	127	425	285
7th	131	458	–
8th	151	458	–
9th	158	500	–
10th	196	–	–

Umpires: Alim Dar (*Pakistan*) (105) and I.J.Gould (*England*) (51).
Referee: R.S.Madugalle (*Sri Lanka*) (165). **Test No. 2210/92 (WI515/I497)**

WEST INDIES v INDIA (3rd Test)

At Darren Sammy National Cricket Stadium, Gros Islet, on 9, 10, 11‡, 12, 13 August 2016.
Toss: West Indies. Result: **INDIA** won by 237 runs.
Debut: West Indies – A.S.Joseph. ‡ (*no play*)

INDIA

K.L.Rahul	c Brathwaite b Chase	50		c Brathwaite b Cummins	28
S.Dhawan	c Dowrich b Gabriel	1		lbw b Chase	26
*V.Kohli	c Bravo b Joseph	3		lbw b Cummins	4
A.M.Rahane	b Chase	35		not out	78
R.G.Sharma	c Dowrich b Joseph	9		lbw b Cummins	41
R.Ashwin	c Blackwood b Cummins	118	(8)	c Brathwaite b Cummins	1
†W.P.Saha	c Dowrich b Joseph	104	(6)	c Dowrich b Cummins	14
R.A.Jadeja	c Dowrich b Cummins	6	(7)	c Samuels b Cummins	16
B.Kumar	c Johnson b Gabriel	0			
Mohammed Shami	not out	0			
I.Sharma	c Johnson b Cummins	0			
Extras	(B 7, LB 8, W 2, NB 10)	27		(B 1, LB 2, NB 6)	9
Total	**(129.4 overs)**	**353**		**(7 wkts dec; 48 overs)**	**217**

WEST INDIES

K.C.Brathwaite	c Saha b Ashwin	64		lbw b Kumar	4
L.R.Johnson	run out	23		c R.G.Sharma b Shami	0
D.M.Bravo	c Jadeja b I.Sharma	29		c R.G.Sharma b Shami	59
M.N.Samuels	b Kumar	48		b I.Sharma	12
J.Blackwood	c Kohli b Kumar	20	(6)	st Saha b Jadeja	1
R.L.Chase	c Rahane b Jadeja	2	(5)	b I.Sharma	10
†S.O.Dowrich	c Dhawan b Kumar	18		c Kohli b Shami	5
*J.O.Holder	lbw b Kumar	2		run out	1
A.S.Joseph	c Rahul b Kumar	0		c Shami b Ashwin	0
M.L.Cummins	c Saha b Ashwin	0		not out	2
S.T.Gabriel	not out	0		c Kumar b Jadeja	11
Extras	(B 13, LB 2, W 2, NB 2)	19		(LB 2, NB 1)	3
Total	**(103.4 overs)**	**225**		**(47.3 overs)**	**108**

WEST INDIES	O	M	R	W		O	M	R	W
Gabriel	23	4	84	2		3	0	19	0
Joseph	24	6	69	3		4	0	23	0
Cummins	21.4	8	54	3		11	1	48	6
Holder	19	7	34	0		9	1	50	0
Chase	33	9	70	2		11	1	41	1
Brathwaite	9	1	27	0		10	1	33	0
INDIA									
Kumar	23.4	10	33	5		12	6	13	1
Mohammed Shami	17	3	58	0		11	2	15	3
Ashwin	26	7	52	2	(4)	12	2	28	1
I.Sharma	13	2	40	1	(3)	7	0	30	2
Jadeja	24	9	27	1		5.3	1	20	2

FALL OF WICKETS

	I	WI	I	WI
Wkt	*1st*	*1st*	*2nd*	*2nd*
1st	9	59	49	4
2nd	19	129	58	4
3rd	77	135	72	35
4th	87	202	157	64
5th	126	203	181	68
6th	339	205	213	84
7th	351	212	217	88
8th	353	212	–	95
9th	353	221	–	95
10th	353	225	–	108

Umpires: N.J.Llong (*England*) (36) and R.J.Tucker (*Australia*) (45).
Referee: R.S.Madugalle (*Sri Lanka*) (166). **Test No. 2211/93 (WI516/I498)**

WEST INDIES v INDIA (4th Test)

At Queen's Park Oval, Port of Spain, Trinidad, on 18, 19‡, 20‡, 21‡, 22‡ August 2016.
Toss: West Indies. Result: **MATCH DRAWN**.
Debuts: None. ‡ (*no play*)

WEST INDIES

K.C.Brathwaite	not out	32
L.R.Johnson	c R.G.Sharma b I.Sharma	9
D.M.Bravo	b Ashwin	10
M.N.Samuels	not out	4
J.Blackwood		
R.L.Chase		
†S.O.Dowrich		
*J.O.Holder		
D.Bishoo		
M.L.Cummins		
S.T.Gabriel		
Extras	(LB 6, NB 1)	7
Total	**(2 wkts; 22 overs)**	**62**

INDIA

M.Vijay
K.L.Rahul
C.A.Pujara
*V.Kohli
A.M.Rahane
R.G.Sharma
R.Ashwin
†W.P.Saha
B.Kumar
Mohammed Shami
I.Sharma
Extras
Total

INDIA	O	M	R	W
Kumar	6	1	13	0
Mohammed Shami	6	2	14	0
I.Sharma	5	3	7	1
Ashwin	5	1	22	1

FALL OF WICKETS

	WI
Wkt	*1st*
1st	31
2nd	48
3rd	–
4th	–
5th	–
6th	–
7th	–
8th	–
9th	–
10th	–

Umpires: N.J.Llong (*England*) (37) and R.J.Tucker (*Australia*) (46).
Referee: R.S.Madugalle (*Sri Lanka*) (167). **Test No. 2212/94 (WI517/I499)**

SRI LANKA v AUSTRALIA (1st Test)

At Pallekele International Cricket Stadium, on 26, 27, 27, 29, 30 July 2016.
Toss: Sri Lanka. Result: **SRI LANKA** won by 106 runs.
Debuts: Sri Lanka – D.N.de Silva, P.A.D.L.R.Sandakan. ‡ (M.C.Henriques)

SRI LANKA

F.D.M.Karunaratne	lbw b Starc	5	(3)	lbw b Starc	0
J.K.Silva	c Voges b Hazlewood	4		lbw b O'Keefe	7
B.K.G.Mendis	lbw b Hazlewood	8	(4)	c Nevill b Starc	176
†L.D.Chandimal	c Nevill b Hazlewood	15	(6)	lbw b Marsh	42
*A.D.Mathews	c Smith b O'Keefe	15		c Burns b Lyon	9
D.M.de Silva	c Burns b Lyon	24	(7)	c Khawaja b Lyon	36
M.D.K.J.Perera	b Lyon	20	(1)	lbw b Starc	4
M.D.K.Perera	lbw b Lyon	0		lbw b Hazlewood	12
H.M.R.K.B.Herath	lbw b Starc	6		c sub‡ b Hazlewood	35
P.A.D.L.R.Sandakan	not out	19		b Starc	9
A.N.P.R.Fernando	c Smith b O'Keefe	0		not out	10
Extras	(LB 1)	1		(B 1, LB 12)	13
Total	**(34.2 overs)**	**117**		**(93.4 overs)**	**353**

AUSTRALIA

J.A.Burns	b Herath	3		b Sandakan	29
D.A.Warner	b Fernando	0		b Herath	1
U.T.Khawaja	lbw b Herath	26		lbw b M.D.K.Perera	18
*S.P.D.Smith	st Chandimal b Herath	30		lbw b Herath	55
A.C.Voges	c Mendis b Fernando	47		c and b Herath	12
M.R.Marsh	b Sandakan	31		lbw b Herath	25
†P.M.Nevill	c M.D.K.J.Perera b Herath	2		c Chandimal b de Silva	9
S.N.J.O'Keefe	c Mendis b Sandakan	23	(10)	b Herath	4
M.A.Starc	c M.D.K.J.Perera b Sandakan	11	(8)	c and b Sandakan	0
N.M.Lyon	lbw b Sandakan	17	(9)	lbw b Sandakan	8
J.R.Hazlewood	not out	2		not out	0
Extras	(B 4, LB 7)	11			–
Total	**(79.2 overs)**	**203**		**(88.3 overs)**	**161**

AUSTRALIA	O	M	R	W		O	M	R	W
Starc	11	1	51	2		19	4	84	4
Hazlewood	10	4	21	3		18.4	3	59	2
O'Keefe	10.2	3	32	2		16.2	3	42	1
Lyon	3	0	12	3		27	2	108	2
Warner						1	0	10	0
Voges						1.4	0	3	0
Marsh						9	1	33	1
Smith						1	0	1	0
SRI LANKA									
Fernando	16	6	36	2		6	3	16	0
Herath	25	8	49	4		33.3	16	54	5
M.D.K.Perera	14	1	43	0		13	3	30	1
Sandakan	21.2	3	58	4		25	8	49	3
Mathews	3	1	6	0					
De Silva					(5)	11	7	12	1

FALL OF WICKETS

	SL	A	SL	A
Wkt	*1st*	*1st*	*2nd*	*2nd*
1st	6	3	6	2
2nd	15	7	6	33
3rd	18	69	45	63
4th	43	70	86	96
5th	67	130	203	139
6th	87	137	274	140
7th	87	160	290	141
8th	94	179	314	157
9th	100	190	323	161
10th	117	203	353	161

Umpires: R.A.Kettleborough (*England*) (36) and S.Ravi (*India*) (13).
Referee: B.C.Broad (*England*) (78). **Test No. 2213/27 (SL249/A788)**

SRI LANKA v AUSTRALIA (2nd Test)

At Galle International Stadium, on 4, 5, 6 August 2016.
Toss: Sri Lanka. Result: **SRI LANKA** won by 229 runs.
Debuts: Sri Lanka – M.V.T.Fernando; Australia – J.M.Holland.

SRI LANKA

F.D.M.Karunaratne	c Burns b Starc	0	(2)	c Marsh b Starc	7
J.K.Silva	c Nevill b Starc	5	(1)	c Smith b Hazlewood	2
M.D.K.J.Perera	c Smith b Lyon	49		b Lyon	35
B.K.G.Mendis	c Nevill b Starc	86		c Nevill b Starc	7
*A.D.Mathews	c Nevill b Marsh	54		b Lyon	47
†L.D.Chandimal	c Khawaja b Hazlewood	5		c Nevill b Starc	13
D.M.de Silva	lbw b Holland	37		c Nevill b Starc	34
M.D.K.Perera	lbw b Lyon	16		b Starc	64
H.M.R.K.B.Herath	b Starc	14		b Holland	26
P.A.D.L.R.Sandakan	b Starc	1		not out	0
M.V.T.Fernando	not out	0		c Voges b Starc	0
Extras	(B 4, LB 10)	14		(LB 1, W 1)	2
Total	**(73.1 overs)**	**281**		**(59.3 overs)**	**237**

AUSTRALIA

J.A.Burns	c M.D.K.J.Perera b Fernando	0	(2)	c de Silva b Herath	2
D.A.Warner	c Mathews b M.D.K.Perera	42	(1)	lbw b M.D.K.Perera	41
U.T.Khawaja	b M.D.K.Perera	11	(4)	b M.D.K.Perera	0
*S.P.D.Smith	b Herath	5	(5)	c Silva b M.D.K.Perera	30
A.C.Voges	c Karunaratne b Herath	8	(6)	b M.D.K.Perera	28
M.R.Marsh	c Karunaratne b Sandakan	27	(7)	lbw b Sandakan	18
†P.M.Nevill	lbw b Herath	0	(8)	run out	24
M.A.Starc	lbw b Herath	0	(9)	b Herath	26
N.M.Lyon	c Mendis b M.D.K.Perera	4	(3)	c Silva b M.D.K.Perera	0
J.R.Hazlewood	c Mathews b M.D.K.Perera	3		c and b M.D.K.Perera	7
J.M.Holland	not out	0		not out	0
Extras	(B 5, LB 1)	6		(LB 7)	7
Total	**(33.2 overs)**	**106**		**(50.1 overs)**	**183**

AUSTRALIA	O	M	R	W		O	M	R	W
Starc	16.1	7	44	5		12.3	1	50	6
Hazlewood	15	3	51	1		9	3	13	1
Lyon	18	1	78	2		19	2	80	2
Marsh	9	0	30	1	(6)	4	1	7	0
Holland	15	0	64	1	(4)	10	1	69	1
Voges					(5)	1	0	4	0
Smith						4	0	13	0
SRI LANKA									
Fernando	2	0	16	1					
Herath	11	2	35	4	(1)	19.1	1	74	2
M.D.K.Perera	15	4	29	4	(2)	23	5	70	6
Mathews	3	1	13	0					
De Silva	2	1	7	0	(4)	2	0	2	0
Sandakan	0.2	0	0	1	(3)	6	1	30	1

FALL OF WICKETS

	SL	A	SL	A
Wkt	*1st*	*1st*	*2nd*	*2nd*
1st	0	0	5	3
2nd	9	54	9	10
3rd	117	59	31	10
4th	184	59	79	61
5th	199	80	98	80
6th	224	80	121	119
7th	259	80	172	123
8th	265	85	233	164
9th	274	89	237	181
10th	281	106	237	183

Umpires: C.B.Gaffaney (*New Zealand*) (8) and R.A.Kettleborough (*England*) (37).
Referee: B.C.Broad (*England*) (79). **Test No. 2214/28 (SL250/A789)**

SRI LANKA v AUSTRALIA (3rd Test)

At Sinhalese Sports Club, Colombo, on 13, 14, 15, 16, 17 August 2016.
Toss: Sri Lanka. Result: **SRI LANKA** won by 163 runs.
Debuts: None.

SRI LANKA

J.K.Silva	c Smith b Starc	0	(3)	c Smith b Holland	115
F.D.M.Karunaratne	b Starc	7		st Nevill b Lyon	22
M.D.K.J.Perera	c Smith b Lyon	16	(4)	c Nevill b Holland	24
B.K.G.Mendis	c Smith b Starc	1	(5)	lbw b Starc	18
*A.D.Mathews	c Starc b Lyon	1	(6)	c Smith b Lyon	26
†L.D.Chandimal	c Nevill b Starc	132	(7)	lbw b Lyon	43
D.M.de Silva	c S.E.Marsh b Lyon	129	(8)	not out	65
M.D.K.Perera	c Lyon b Holland	16	(1)	lbw b Starc	8
H.M.R.K.B.Herath	retired hurt	33		c Smith b Lyon	5
R.A.S.Lakmal	c M.R.Marsh b Starc	5		not out	4
P.A.D.L.R.Sandakan	not out	4			
Extras	(B 4, LB 7)	11		(B 8, LB 3, W 1, NB 5)	17
Total	**(141.1 overs)**	**355**		**(8 wkts dec; 99.3 overs)**	**347**

AUSTRALIA

D.A.Warner	c M.D.K.J.Perera b de Silva	11	(2)	b M.D.K.Perera	68
S.E.Marsh	b Lakmal	130	(1)	c Mendis b M.D.K.Perera	23
*S.P.D.Smith	st M.D.K.J.Perera b Herath	119		b Herath	8
A.C.Voges	lbw b Herath	22		lbw b Herath	1
M.C.Henriques	st M.D.K.J.Perera b Herath	4		run out	4
M.R.Marsh	c Mendis b Herath	53		c M.D.K.J.Perera b Herath	9
†P.M.Nevill	lbw b M.D.K.Perera	14		c Mathews b Herath	2
M.A.Starc	not out	9		c M.D.K.J.Perera b Herath	23
N.M.Lyon	c Mendis b M.D.K.Perera	3		lbw b Herath	12
J.R.Hazlewood	b Herath	0		st M.D.K.J.Perera b Herath	0
J.M.Holland	c Mathews b Herath	1		not out	0
Extras	(B 4, LB 9)	13		(B 4, LB 6)	10
Total	**(125.1 overs)**	**379**		**(44.1 overs)**	**160**

AUSTRALIA	O	M	R	W		O	M	R	W
Starc	25.1	11	63	5		19.3	4	72	2
Hazlewood	18	4	52	0	(4)	14	2	33	0
Lyon	50	11	110	3	(2)	37	7	123	4
Holland	37	8	69	1	(3)	20	4	72	2
Marsh	10	1	45	0	(6)	3	1	3	0
Smith	1	0	5	0	(5)	2	0	13	0
Henriques						2	0	9	0
Voges						2	0	11	0
SRI LANKA									
M.D.K.Perera	44	4	129	2	(2)	22	3	71	2
De Silva	7	0	27	1	(3)	4	0	15	0
Herath	38.1	11	81	6	(1)	18.1	3	64	7
Sandakan	19	0	70	0					
Lakmal	13	0	54	1					
Mathews	4	1	5	0					

FALL OF WICKETS

	SL	A	SL	A
Wkt	*1st*	*1st*	*2nd*	*2nd*
1st	2	21	8	77
2nd	21	267	44	100
3rd	23	275	69	102
4th	24	283	98	114
5th	26	316	156	115
6th	237	353	246	123
7th	267	367	276	140
8th	348	376	297	157
9th	355	377	–	159
10th	–	379	–	160

Umpires: C.B.Gaffaney (*New Zealand*) (9) and S.Ravi (*India*) (14).
Referee: B.C.Broad (*England*) (80). **Test No. 2215/29 (SL251/A790)**
H.M.R.K.B.Herath retired hurt at 340-7 in Sri Lanka's first innings.

ZIMBABWE v NEW ZEALAND (1st Test)

At Queens Sports Club, Bulawayo, on 28, 29, 30, 31 July 2016.
Toss: Zimbabwe. Result: **NEW ZEALAND** won by an innings and 117 runs.
Debuts: Zimbabwe – C.J.Chibhabha, M.T.Chinouya, P.S.Masvaure. ‡ (T.Muzarabani)

ZIMBABWE

B.B.Chari	c Guptill b Southee	4	(3)	b Boult	5
C.J.Chibhabha	c Latham b Wagner	15	(1)	c Taylor b Boult	7
H.Masakadza	c and b Santner	15	(2)	c Taylor b Southee	4
C.R.Ervine	st Watling b Santner	13		c Watling b Boult	50
S.C.Williams	c Sodhi b Wagner	1	(8)	c Williamson b Santner	119
Sikandar Raza	c Latham b Wagner	22		c Latham b Wagner	37
P.S.Masvaure	lbw b Southee	42	(5)	lbw b Boult	0
†R.W.Chakabva	c Watling b Wagner	0	(9)	b Southee	11
*A.G.Cremer	c Nicholls b Wagner	0	(7)	lbw b Sodhi	33
D.T.Tiripano	not out	49		c Watling b Wagner	14
M.T.Chinouya	b Wagner	1		not out	0
Extras	(LB 2)	2		(B 6, LB 9)	15
Total	**(77.5 overs)**	**164**		**(79 overs)**	**295**

NEW ZEALAND

M.J.Guptill	c Ervine b Chibhabha	40
T.W.M.Latham	c Chari b Masakadza	105
*K.S.Williamson	c Masakadza b Cremer	91
L.R.P.L.Taylor	not out	173
H.M.Nicholls	c Chari b Tiripano	18
I.S.Sodhi	c Chari b Chinouya	11
†B.J.Watling	c sub‡ b Sikandar Raza	107
M.J.Santner		
T.G.Southee		
N.Wagner		
T.A.Boult		
Extras	(B 15, W 4, NB 12)	31
Total	**(6 wkts dec; 166.5 overs)**	**576**

NEW ZEALAND	O	M	R	W		O	M	R	W
Southee	17	8	28	2		15	3	68	2
Boult	11	5	23	0		17	3	52	4
Santner	14	5	16	2	(4)	17	6	32	1
Wagner	20.5	8	41	6	(3)	17	1	62	2
Sodhi	15	3	54	0		12	1	66	1
Williamson						1	1	0	0
ZIMBABWE									
Chinouya	26	6	79	1					
Tiripano	28	4	82	1					
Masvaure	10	0	38	0					
Cremer	53	4	187	1					
Sikandar Raza	25.5	4	106	1					
Chibhabha	15	1	44	1					
Masakadza	9	1	25	1					

FALL OF WICKETS

	Z	NZ	Z
Wkt	*1st*	*1st*	*2nd*
1st	4	79	7
2nd	35	235	12
3rd	35	272	17
4th	36	299	17
5th	72	323	86
6th	72	576	124
7th	72	–	242
8th	72	–	277
9th	157	–	285
10th	164	–	295

Umpires: M.A.Gough (*England*) (1) and P.R.Reiffel (*Australia*) (23).
Referee: D.C.Boon (*Australia*) (31). **Test No. 2216/16 (Z98/NZ409)**

ZIMBABWE v NEW ZEALAND (2nd Test)

At Queens Sports Club, Bulawayo, on 6, 7, 8, 9, 10 August 2016.
Toss: New Zealand. Result: **NEW ZEALAND** won by 254 runs.
Debut: Zimbabwe – P.J.Moor.

NEW ZEALAND

M.J.Guptill	lbw b Tiripano	87	(2)	c Nyumbu b Chinouya	11
T.W.M.Latham	c and b Williams	136	(1)	c Moor b Tiripano	13
*K.S.Williamson	c Ervine b Chinouya	113		not out	68
L.R.P.L.Taylor	not out	124		not out	67
H.M.Nicholls	lbw b Cremer	15			
†B.J.Watling	not out	83			
M.J.Santner					
I.S.Sodhi					
T.G.Southee					
N.Wagner					
T.A.Boult					
Extras	(B 12, LB 3, W 1, NB 8)	24		(LB 4, W 3)	7
Total	**(4 wkts dec; 150 overs)**	**582**		**(2 wkts dec; 36 overs)**	**166**

ZIMBABWE

T.M.K.Mawoyo	b Southee	26		lbw b Boult	35
C.J.Chibhabha	c Williamson b Santner	60		c Guptill b Wagner	21
Sikandar Raza	c Williamson b Wagner	3		lbw b Southee	0
C.R.Ervine	c Wagner b Sodhi	146	(5)	c Watling b Guptill	27
P.S.Masvaure	b Santner	2	(6)	c Taylor b Sodhi	11
S.C.Williams	lbw b Sodhi	16	(7)	c Williamson b Guptill	11
†P.J.Moor	c Guptill b Sodhi	71	(8)	lbw b Sodhi	1
*A.G.Cremer	lbw b Boult	8	(9)	lbw b Guptill	1
D.T.Tiripano	lbw b Wagner	3	(4)	lbw b Santner	22
J.C.Nyumbu	c Santner b Sodhi	8		not out	0
M.T.Chinouya	not out	0		c Williamson b Sodhi	0
Extras	(B 12, LB 6, NB 1)	19		(B 1, LB 2)	3
Total	**(143.4 overs)**	**362**		**(68.4 overs)**	**132**

ZIMBABWE	O	M	R	W		O	M	R	W
Tiripano	25	4	102	1	(2)	6	1	14	1
Chinouya	22	6	64	1	(1)	9	2	45	1
Chibhabha	12	2	45	0		3	0	22	0
Cremer	36	2	147	1		11	0	59	0
Nyumbu	34	3	107	0		7	0	22	0
Williams	13	0	62	1					
Sikandar Raza	4	0	17	0					
Masvaure	4	0	23	0					
NEW ZEALAND									
Southee	28	14	73	1		14	7	35	1
Boult	27	13	45	1		12	4	26	1
Santner	35	8	105	2	(4)	12	4	15	1
Wagner	31	8	61	2	(3)	12	5	23	1
Sodhi	21.4	9	60	4		11.4	5	19	3
Guptill	1	1	0	0		7	4	11	3

FALL OF WICKETS

	NZ	Z	NZ	Z
Wkt	*1st*	*1st*	*2nd*	*2nd*
1st	169	65	24	45
2nd	329	83	26	58
3rd	369	107	–	58
4th	389	115	–	97
5th	–	147	–	112
6th	–	295	–	130
7th	–	319	–	131
8th	–	327	–	132
9th	–	352	–	132
10th	–	362	–	132

Umpires: M.A.Gough (*England*) (2) and P.R.Reiffel (*Australia*) (24).
Referee: D.C.Boon (*Australia*) (32). **Test No. 2217/17 (Z99/NZ410)**

SOUTH AFRICA v NEW ZEALAND (1st Test)

At Kingsmead, Durban, on 19, 20, 21 (*no play*), 22 (*no play*), 23 (*no play*) August 2016.
Toss: South Africa. Result: **MATCH DRAWN.**
Debuts: None.

SOUTH AFRICA

S.C.Cook	c Watling b Boult	20
D.Elgar	c Guptill b Bracewell	19
H.M.Amla	c Watling b Boult	53
J.P.Duminy	c Boult b Wagner	14
*F.du Plessis	c Williamson b Wagner	23
T.Bavuma	lbw b Santner	46
†Q.de Kock	c Bracewell b Santner	33
V.D.Philander	c Southee b Wagner	8
K.Rabada	not out	32
D.W.Steyn	b Southee	2
D.L.Piedt	c Watling b Boult	9
Extras	(LB 4)	4
Total	**(87.4 overs)**	**263**

NEW ZEALAND

M.J.Guptill	lbw b Steyn	7
T.W.M.Latham	c Amla b Steyn	4
*K.S.Williamson	not out	2
L.R.P.L.Taylor	not out	2
H.M.Nicholls		
†B.J.Watling		
M.J.Santner		
D.A.J.Bracewell		
T.G.Southee		
N.Wagner		
T.A.Boult		
Extras		
Total	**(2 wkts; 12 overs)**	**15**

NEW ZEALAND	O	M	R	W
Southee	23	3	80	1
Boult	21.4	5	52	3
Bracewell	16	6	53	1
Wagner	15	4	47	3
Santner	11	2	22	2
Guptill	1	0	5	0
SOUTH AFRICA				
Steyn	6	4	3	2
Philander	6	1	12	0

FALL OF WICKETS

	SA	NZ
Wkt	*1st*	*1st*
1st	33	7
2nd	41	12
3rd	102	–
4th	106	–
5th	160	–
6th	208	–
7th	208	–
8th	228	–
9th	236	–
10th	263	–

Umpires: I.J.Gould (*England*) (52) and R.K.Illingworth (*England*) (21).
Referee: A.J.Pycroft (*Zimbabwe*) (47). **Test No. 2218/41 (SA401/NZ411)**

SOUTH AFRICA v NEW ZEALAND (2nd Test)

At Centurion Park, on 27, 28, 29, 30 August 2016.
Toss: New Zealand. Result: **SOUTH AFRICA** won by 204 runs.
Debuts: None.

SOUTH AFRICA

S.C.Cook	c Williamson b Bracewell	56		lbw b Boult	4
†Q.de Kock	c Boult b Wagner	82		c Williamson b Bracewell	50
H.M.Amla	c Watling b Wagner	58		c Guptill b Southee	1
J.P.Duminy	c Watling b Southee	88		lbw b Southee	0
*F.du Plessis	not out	112		c Taylor b Boult	6
T.Bavuma	c Bracewell b Wagner	8		not out	40
S.van Zyl	c Taylor b Wagner	35		c Watling b Wagner	5
V.D.Philander	b Wagner	8		b Southee	14
K.Rabada	c Nicholls b Santner	7			
D.W.Steyn	not out	13			
D.L.Piedt			(9)	not out	0
Extras	(B 10, LB 4)	14		(B 4, LB 1, W 6, NB 1)	12
Total	**(8 wkts dec; 154 overs)**	**481**		**(7 wkts dec; 47 overs)**	**132**

NEW ZEALAND

M.J.Guptill	c van Zyl b Philander	8	(2)	c Amla b Steyn	0
T.W.M.Latham	c de Kock b Steyn	4	(1)	b Steyn	0
*K.S.Williamson	c de Kock b Rabada	77		c de Kock b Philander	5
L.R.P.L.Taylor	run out	1		lbw b Steyn	0
H.M.Nicholls	lbw b Rabada	36		c Rabada b Steyn	76
†B.J.Watling	c de Kock b Steyn	8		lbw b Piedt	32
M.J.Santner	b Philander	0		b Steyn	16
D.A.J.Bracewell	lbw b Rabada	18		lbw b Philander	30
T.G.Southee	c de Kock b Piedt	8		b Rabada	14
N.Wagner	c de Kock b Steyn	31		lbw b Rabada	3
T.A.Boult	not out	0		not out	0
Extras	(B 5, LB 2, W 15, NB 1)	23		(B 10, LB 7, W 2)	19
Total	**(58.3 overs)**	**214**		**(58.2 overs)**	**195**

NEW ZEALAND	O	M	R	W		O	M	R	W
Southee	35	5	114	1		16	6	46	3
Boult	35.4	7	107	0		14	3	44	2
Bracewell	30.2	9	98	1		7	2	19	1
Santner	14	1	62	1					
Wagner	39	8	86	5	(4)	10	1	18	1
SOUTH AFRICA									
Steyn	20	3	66	3		16.2	4	33	5
Philander	15	1	43	2		14	4	34	2
Rabada	16.3	4	62	3		13	2	54	2
Piedt	7	0	36	1	(5)	12	3	52	1
Van Zyl					(4)	3	1	5	0

FALL OF WICKETS

	SA	NZ	SA	NZ
Wkt	*1st*	*1st*	*2nd*	*2nd*
1st	133	13	31	0
2nd	151	13	32	3
3rd	246	26	32	5
4th	317	86	47	7
5th	342	106	82	75
6th	426	111	98	118
7th	442	144	129	164
8th	463	169	–	187
9th	–	214	–	195
10th	–	214	–	195

Umpires: I.J.Gould (*England*) (53) and P.R.Reiffel (*Australia*) (25).
Referee: A.J.Pycroft (*Zimbabwe*) (48). **Test No. 2219/42 (SA402/NZ412)**

INDIA v NEW ZEALAND (1st Test)

At Green Park, Kanpur, on 22, 23, 24, 25, 26 September 2016.
Toss: India. Result: **INDIA** won by 197 runs.
Debuts: None.

INDIA

K.L.Rahul	c Watling b Santner	32		c Taylor b Sodhi	38
M.Vijay	c Watling b Sodhi	65		lbw b Santner	76
C.A.Pujara	c and b Santner	62		c Taylor b Sodhi	78
*V.Kohli	c Sodhi b Wagner	9		c Sodhi b Craig	18
A.M.Rahane	c Latham b Craig	18		c Taylor b Santner	40
R.G.Sharma	c Sodhi b Santner	35		not out	68
R.Ashwin	c Taylor b Boult	40			
†W.P.Saha	b Boult	0			
R.A.Jadeja	not out	42	(7)	not out	50
Mohammed Shami	b Boult	0			
U.T.Yadav	c Watling b Wagner	9			
Extras	(B 5, LB 1)	6		(B 1, LB 8)	9
Total	**(97 overs)**	**318**		**(5 wkts dec; 107.2 overs)**	**377**

NEW ZEALAND

M.J.Guptill	lbw b Yadav	21	(2)	c Vijay b Ashwin	0
T.W.M.Latham	lbw b Ashwin	58	(1)	lbw b Ashwin	2
*K.S.Williamson	b Ashwin	75		lbw b Ashwin	25
L.R.P.L.Taylor	lbw b Jadeja	0		run out	17
L.Ronchi	lbw b Jadeja	38		c Ashwin b Jadeja	80
M.J.Santner	c Saha b Ashwin	32		c Sharma b Ashwin	71
†B.J.Watling	c and b Ashwin	21		lbw b Shami	18
M.D.Craig	lbw b Jadeja	2		b Shami	1
I.S.Sodhi	lbw b Jadeja	0		b Ashwin	17
T.A.Boult	c Sharma b Jadeja	0		not out	2
N.Wagner	not out	0		lbw b Ashwin	0
Extras	(B 8, LB 5, NB 2)	15		(LB 2, NB 1)	3
Total	**(95.5 overs)**	**262**		**(87.3 overs)**	**236**

NEW ZEALAND	O	M	R	W		O	M	R	W
Boult	20	3	67	3		9	0	34	0
Wagner	15	4	42	2	(4)	16	5	52	0
Santner	23	2	94	3	(2)	32.2	11	79	2
Craig	24	6	59	1	(3)	23	3	80	1
Sodhi	15	3	50	1		20	2	99	2
Guptill						4	0	17	0
Williamson						3	0	7	0
INDIA									
Mohammed Shami	11	1	35	0		8	2	18	2
Yadav	15	5	33	1	(4)	8	1	23	0
Jadeja	34	7	73	5		34	17	58	1
Ashwin	30.5	7	93	4	(2)	35.3	5	132	6
Vijay	4	0	10	0		2	0	3	0
Sharma	1	0	5	0					

FALL OF WICKETS

	I	NZ	I	NZ
Wkt	*1st*	*1st*	*2nd*	*2nd*
1st	42	35	52	2
2nd	154	159	185	3
3rd	167	160	214	43
4th	185	170	228	56
5th	209	219	277	158
6th	261	255	–	194
7th	262	258	–	196
8th	273	258	–	223
9th	277	258	–	236
10th	318	262	–	236

Umpires: R.A.Kettleborough (*England*) (38) and R.J.Tucker (*Australia*) (47).
Referee: D.C.Boon (*Australia*) (33). **Test No. 2220/55 (I500/NZ413)**

INDIA v NEW ZEALAND (2nd Test)

At Eden Gardens, Kolkata, on 30 September, 1, 2, 3, October 2016.
Toss: India. Result: **INDIA** won by 178 runs.
Debuts: None.

INDIA

S.Dhawan	b Henry	1	lbw b Boult	17
M.Vijay	c Watling b Henry	9	c Guptill b Henry	7
C.A.Pujara	c Guptill b Wagner	87	lbw b Henry	4
*V.Kohli	c Latham b Boult	9	lbw b Boult	45
A.M.Rahane	lbw b Patel	77	c Boult b Henry	1
R.G.Sharma	c Latham b Patel	2	c Ronchi b Santner	82
R.Ashwin	lbw b Henry	26	lbw b Santner	5
†W.P.Saha	not out	54	not out	58
R.A.Jadeja	c Henry b Wagner	14	c sub (J.D.S.Neesham) b Santner	6
B.Kumar	lbw b Santner	5	c Nicholls b Wagner	23
Mohammed Shami	c Henry b Boult	14	c Latham b Boult	1
Extras	(B 8, LB 10)	18	(B 10, LB 1, W 3)	14
Total	**(104.5 overs)**	**316**	**(76.5 overs)**	**263**

NEW ZEALAND

M.J.Guptill	b Kumar	13	(2)	lbw b Ashwin	24
T.W.M.Latham	lbw b Shami	1	(1)	c Saha b Ashwin	74
H.M.Nicholls	b Kumar	1		c Rahane b Jadeja	24
*L.R.P.L.Taylor	c Vijay b Kumar	36		lbw b Ashwin	4
L.Ronchi	lbw b Jadeja	35		b Jadeja	32
M.J.Santner	lbw b Kumar	11		lbw b Shami	9
†B.J.Watling	lbw b Shami	25		b Shami	1
M.J.Henry	b Kumar	0		c Kohli b Jadeja	18
J.S.Patel	c Shami b Ashwin	47		b Kumar	2
N.Wagner	lbw b Shami	10		not out	5
T.A.Boult	not out	6		c Vijay b Shami	4
Extras	(B 9, LB 4, W 5, NB 1)	19			–
Total	**(53 overs)**	**204**		**(81.1 overs)**	**197**

NEW ZEALAND	O	M	R	W		O	M	R	W
Boult	20.5	9	46	2		17.5	6	38	3
Henry	20	6	46	3		20	2	59	3
Wagner	20	5	57	2		15	3	45	1
Santner	23	5	83	1	(5)	16	2	60	3
Patel	21	3	66	2	(4)	8	0	50	0
INDIA									
Kumar	15	2	48	5		12	4	28	1
Mohammed Shami	18	1	70	3		18.1	5	46	3
Jadeja	12	4	40	1	(4)	20	3	41	3
Ashwin	8	3	33	1	(3)	31	6	82	3

FALL OF WICKETS

	I	NZ	I	NZ
Wkt	*1st*	*1st*	*2nd*	*2nd*
1st	1	10	12	55
2nd	28	18	24	104
3rd	46	23	34	115
4th	187	85	43	141
5th	193	104	91	154
6th	200	122	106	156
7th	231	122	209	175
8th	272	182	215	178
9th	281	187	251	190
10th	316	204	263	197

Umpires: R.A.Kettleborough (*England*) (39) and R.J.Tucker (*Australia*) (48).
Referee: D.C.Boon (*Australia*) (34). **Test No. 2221/56 (I501/NZ414)**

INDIA v NEW ZEALAND (3rd Test)

At Holkar Cricket Stadium, Indore, on 8, 9, 10, 11 October 2016.
Toss: India. Result: **INDIA** won by 321 runs.
Debuts: None.

INDIA

M.Vijay	c Latham b Patel	10	run out	19
G.Gambhir	lbw b Boult	29	c Guptill b Patel	50
C.A.Pujara	b Santner	41	not out	101
*V.Kohli	lbw b Patel	211	lbw b Patel	17
A.M.Rahane	c Watling b Boult	188	not out	23
R.G.Sharma	not out	51		
R.A.Jadeja	not out	17		
R.Ashwin				
†W.P.Saha				
Mohammed Shami				
U.T.Yadav				
Extras	(B 4, LB 3, W 1, NB 2)	10	(B 4, LB 1, W 1)	6
Total	**(5 wkts dec; 169 overs)**	**557**	**(3 wkts dec; 49 overs)**	**216**

NEW ZEALAND

M.J.Guptill	run out	72	(2)	lbw b Jadeja	29
T.W.M.Latham	c and b Ashwin	53	(1)	lbw b Yadav	6
*K.S.Williamson	b Ashwin	8		lbw b Ashwin	27
L.R.P.L.Taylor	c Rahane b Ashwin	0		b Ashwin	32
L.Ronchi	c Rahane b Ashwin	0		b Ashwin	15
J.D.S.Neesham	lbw b Ashwin	71		c Kohli b Jadeja	0
†B.J.Watling	c Rahane b Jadeja	23		not out	23
M.J.Santner	c Kohli b Jadeja	22		b Ashwin	14
J.S.Patel	run out	18		b Ashwin	0
M.J.Henry	not out	15		c Shami b Ashwin	0
T.A.Boult	c Pujara b Ashwin	0		c and b Ashwin	4
Extras	(B 6, LB 5, W 1, Pen 5)	17		(B 2, NB 1)	3
Total	**(90.2 overs)**	**299**		**(44.5 overs)**	**153**

NEW ZEALAND	O	M	R	W		O	M	R	W
Boult	32	2	113	2		7	0	35	0
Henry	35	3	127	0	(4)	7	1	22	0
Patel	40	5	120	2	(2)	14	0	56	2
Santner	44	4	137	1	(3)	17	1	71	0
Neesham	18	1	53	0		4	0	27	0
INDIA									
Mohammed Shami	13	1	40	0		7	0	34	0
Yadav	15	1	55	0		8	4	13	1
Ashwin	27.2	5	81	6		13.5	2	59	7
Jadeja	28	5	80	2		16	3	45	2
Vijay	7	0	27	0					

FALL OF WICKETS

	I	NZ	I	NZ
Wkt	*1st*	*1st*	*2nd*	*2nd*
1st	26	118	34	7
2nd	60	134	110	42
3rd	100	140	158	80
4th	465	148	–	102
5th	504	148	–	103
6th	–	201	–	112
7th	–	253	–	136
8th	–	276	–	138
9th	–	294	–	138
10th	–	299	–	153

Umpires: H.D.P.K.Dharmasena (*Sri Lanka*) (39) and B.N.J.Oxenford (*Australia*) (34).
Referee: D.C.Boon (*Australia*) (35). **Test No. 2222/57 (I502/NZ415)**
G.Gambhir retired hurt at 11-0 and resumed at 34-1.

PAKISTAN v WEST INDIES (1st Test)

At Dubai Sports City Stadium, on 13, 14, 15, 16, 17 October 2016 (day/night).
Toss: Pakistan. Result: **PAKISTAN** won by 56 runs.
Debuts: Pakistan – Babar Azam, Mohammad Nawaz[3].

PAKISTAN

Sami Aslam	b Chase	90	c Blackwood b Bishoo	44
Azhar Ali	not out	302	lbw b Gabriel	2
Asad Shafiq	c and b Bishoo	67	lbw b Bishoo	5
Babar Azam	c Holder b Bishoo	69	b Bishoo	21
*Misbah-ul-Haq	not out	29	b Bishoo	15
†Sarfraz Ahmed			st Dowrich b Bishoo	15
Mohammad Nawaz[3]			b Bishoo	0
Wahab Riaz			c Brathwaite b Bishoo	5
Yasir Shah			c and b Holder	2
Sohail Khan			not out	1
Mohammad Amir			b Bishoo	1
Extras	(B 1, LB 9, W 1, NB 11)	22	(B 10, NB 2)	12
Total	**(3 wkts dec; 155.3 overs)**	**579**	**(31.5 overs)**	**123**

WEST INDIES

K.C.Brathwaite	b Shah	32	b Amir	6
L.R.Johnson	lbw b Shah	15	lbw b Amir	47
D.M.Bravo	c Ali b Nawaz[3]	87	c and b Shah	116
M.N.Samuels	lbw b Khan	76	c Ahmed b Amir	4
J.Blackwood	c Ahmed b Riaz	37	lbw b Nawaz[3]	15
R.L.Chase	c Azam b Riaz	6	b Shah	35
†S.O.Dowrich	lbw b Shah	32	b Riaz	0
*J.O.Holder	b Shah	20	not out	40
D.Bishoo	b Nawaz[3]	17	lbw b Nawaz[3]	3
M.L.Cummins	b Shah	0	run out	1
S.T.Gabriel	not out	6	run out	1
Extras	(B 9, LB 8, W 1, NB 11)	29	(B 5, LB 7, W 5, NB 4)	21
Total	**(123.5 overs)**	**357**	**(109 overs)**	**289**

WEST INDIES	O	M	R	W		O	M	R	W
Gabriel	22	3	99	0		7	1	23	1
Cummins	25	2	99	0		7	0	29	0
Holder	25	4	73	0	(4)	4	0	12	1
Brathwaite	14	2	56	0					
Bishoo	35	4	125	2	(3)	13.5	1	49	8
Chase	33	2	109	1					
Blackwood	1.3	0	8	0					
PAKISTAN									
Mohammad Amir	22	6	54	0		23	5	63	3
Sohail Khan	16	2	56	1		10	1	22	0
Yasir Shah	43	15	121	5		41	6	113	2
Wahab Riaz	23.3	3	65	2	(5)	17	1	47	1
Mohammad Nawaz[3]	16.5	5	38	2	(4)	18	4	32	2
Azhar Ali	2.3	1	6	0					

FALL OF WICKETS

	P	WI	P	WI
Wkt	*1st*	*1st*	*2nd*	*2nd*
1st	215	42	13	27
2nd	352	69	20	87
3rd	517	182	77	95
4th	–	259	93	116
5th	–	266	112	193
6th	–	300	112	194
7th	–	325	118	263
8th	–	346	121	276
9th	–	351	121	277
10th	–	357	123	289

Umpires: R.K.Illingworth (*England*) (22) and P.R.Reiffel (*Australia*) (26).
Referee: J.J.Crowe (*New Zealand*) (77). **Test No. 2223/47 (P399/WI518)**

PAKISTAN v WEST INDIES (2nd Test)

At Sheikh Zayed Stadium, Abu Dhabi, on 21, 22, 23, 24, 25 October 2016.
Toss: Pakistan. Result: **PAKISTAN** won by 133 runs.
Debuts: None.

PAKISTAN

Sami Aslam	b Bishoo	6	c Hope b Gabriel	50
Azhar Ali	b Gabriel	0	c Holder b Cummins	79
Asad Shafiq	b Gabriel	68	not out	58
Younus Khan	c Chase b Brathwaite	127	not out	29
*Misbah-ul-Haq	lbw b Gabriel	96		
Yasir Shah	c Bishoo b Holder	23		
†Sarfraz Ahmed	b Gabriel	56		
Mohammad Nawaz[3]	b Holder	25		
Sohail Khan	c Johnson b Holder	26		
Zulfiqar Babar	c Hope b Gabriel	0		
Rahat Ali	not out	0		
Extras	(B 1, LB 15, NB 9)	25	(B 4, LB 3, W 1 NB 3)	11
Total	**(119.1 overs)**	**452**	**(2 wkts dec; 67 overs)**	**227**

WEST INDIES

L.R.Johnson	lbw b Rahat	12	(2)	b Shah	9
D.M.Bravo	lbw b Shah	43	(3)	c Nawaz[3] b Rahat	13
K.C.Brathwaite	run out	21	(1)	lbw b Nawaz[3]	67
M.N.Samuels	c Aslam b Rahat	30		c and b Shah	23
D.Bishoo	b Sohail	20	(9)	c Misbah b Babar	26
J.Blackwood	c Ahmed b Rahat	8	(5)	b Shah	95
R.L.Chase	c Shafiq b Shah	22	(6)	c Ahmed b Shah	20
†S.D.Hope	b Shah	11	(7)	c Younus b Babar	41
*J.O.Holder	not out	31	(8)	lbw b Shah	16
M.L.Cummins	b Sohail	3		b Shah	0
S.T.Gabriel	c Sohail b Shah	13		not out	7
Extras	(B 2, LB 7, NB 1)	10		(B 4, LB 1)	5
Total	**(94.4 overs)**	**224**		**(108 overs)**	**322**

WEST INDIES	O	M	R	W		O	M	R	W
Gabriel	23.1	1	96	5		12	2	36	1
Cummins	20	1	65	0		7	0	26	1
Holder	22	8	47	3	(5)	7	0	22	0
Bishoo	26	0	112	1		20	0	77	0
Chase	19	1	80	0	(6)	6	0	26	0
Brathwaite	9	0	36	1	(3)	15	2	33	0
PAKISTAN									
Rahat Ali	21	8	45	3	(2)	23	2	69	1
Sohail Khan	19	8	35	2	(1)	14	3	44	0
Zulfiqar Babar	21	6	39	0	(4)	22	5	51	2
Asad Shafiq	1	0	2	0					
Yasir Shah	28.4	6	86	4	(3)	39	5	124	6
Mohammad Nawaz[3]	4	1	8	0	(5)	10	0	29	1

FALL OF WICKETS

	P	WI	P	WI
Wkt	*1st*	*1st*	*2nd*	*2nd*
1st	6	27	93	28
2nd	42	65	164	63
3rd	129	106	–	112
4th	304	106	–	124
5th	332	121	–	187
6th	342	144	–	244
7th	412	169	–	266
8th	430	178	–	311
9th	452	197	–	312
10th	452	224	–	322

Umpires: M.A.Gough (*England*) (3) and R.K.Illingworth (*England*) (23).
Referee: J.J.Crowe (*New Zealand*) (78). **Test No. 2224/48 (P400/WI519)**

PAKISTAN v WEST INDIES (3rd Test)

At Sharjah Cricket Stadium, on 30, 31 October, 1, 2, 3 November 2016.
Toss: Pakistan. Result: **WEST INDIES** won by five wickets.
Debuts: None.

PAKISTAN

Sami Aslam	c Holder b Bishoo	74		c Joseph b Holder	17
Azhar Ali	c Brathwaite b Gabriel	0		c Bravo b Bishoo	91
Asad Shafiq	lbw b Gabriel	0		c Bravo b Holder	0
Younus Khan	c Johnson b Chase	51		c Dowrich b Holder	0
*Misbah-ul-Haq	c Dowrich b Bishoo	53		c Bishoo b Chase	4
†Sarfraz Ahmed	b Gabriel	51		c Bravo b Bishoo	42
Mohammad Nawaz[3]	st Dowrich b Bishoo	6		c Johnson b Bishoo	19
Wahab Riaz	lbw b Bishoo	4	(9)	c Johnson b Holder	1
Yasir Shah	b Joseph	12	(10)	lbw b Holder	0
Mohammad Amir	b Joseph	20	(8)	run out	8
Zulfiqar Babar	not out	1		not out	15
Extras	(LB 4, W 1, NB 4)	9		(B 2, LB 1, W 6 NB 2)	11
Total	**(90.5 overs)**	**281**		**(81.3 overs)**	**208**

WEST INDIES

K.C.Brathwaite	not out	142	not out	60
L.R.Johnson	lbw b Riaz	1	lbw b Shah	12
D.M.Bravo	c Amir b Babar	11	c Ahmed b Shah	3
M.N.Samuels	lbw b Shah	0	c Babar b Shah	10
J.Blackwood	c Shafiq b Amir	23	b Riaz	4
R.L.Chase	c Younus b Amir	50	c Nawaz[3] b Riaz	2
†S.O.Dowrich	b Riaz	47	not out	60
*J.O.Holder	b Amir	16		
D.Bishoo	c Ahmed b Riaz	27		
A.S.Joseph	c Shah b Riaz	6		
S.T.Gabriel	c Ahmed b Riaz	0		
Extras	(LB 6, NB 8)	14	(LB 2, NB 1)	3
Total	**(115.4 overs)**	**337**	**(5 wkts; 43.5 overs)**	**154**

WEST INDIES	O	M	R	W		O	M	R	W
Gabriel	21	1	67	3		15	1	36	0
Joseph	16.5	5	57	2		14	3	41	0
Holder	12	4	29	0		17.3	5	30	5
Chase	20	5	47	1	(5)	15	1	47	1
Bishoo	21	3	77	4	(6)	19	2	46	3
Brathwaite					(4)	1	0	5	0
PAKISTAN									
Mohammad Amir	25	5	71	3		9.5	0	43	0
Wahab Riaz	26.4	1	88	5		12	0	46	2
Yasir Shah	26	2	80	1		15	4	40	3
Zulfiqar Babar	21	3	56	1		3	1	3	0
Mohammad Nawaz[3]	11	2	20	0		4	0	20	0
Azhar Ali	6	0	16	0					

FALL OF WICKETS

	P	WI	P	WI
Wkt	*1st*	*1st*	*2nd*	*2nd*
1st	1	6	37	29
2nd	1	32	41	35
3rd	107	38	41	57
4th	150	68	48	63
5th	230	151	134	67
6th	242	234	175	–
7th	248	263	189	–
8th	248	323	192	–
9th	280	333	193	–
10th	281	337	208	–

Umpires: M.A.Gough (*England*) (4) and P.R.Reiffel (*Australia*) (27).
Referee: J.J.Crowe (*New Zealand*) (79). **Test No. 2225/49 (P401/WI520)**

BANGLADESH v ENGLAND (1st Test)

At Zohur Ahmed Chowdhury Stadium, Chittagong, on 20, 21, 22, 23, 24 October 2016.
Toss: England. Result: **ENGLAND** won by 22 runs.
Debuts: Bangladesh – Kamrul Islam, Mehedi Hasan, Sabbir Rahman; England – B.M.Duckett.

ENGLAND

*A.N.Cook	b Shakib	4		c Mahmudullah b Mehedi	12
B.M.Duckett	b Mehedi	14		c Mominul b Shakib	15
J.E.Root	c Sabbir b Mehedi	40		lbw b Shakib	1
G.S.Ballance	lbw b Mehedi	1		c Imrul b Taijul	9
M.M.Ali	c Mushfiqur b Mehedi	68		c Mushfiqur b Shakib	14
B.A.Stokes	b Shakib	18		lbw b Shakib	85
†J.M.Bairstow	b Mehedi	52		b Kamrul	47
C.R.Woakes	c Mominul b Taijul	36		not out	19
A.U.Rashid	c Sabbir b Taijul	26		lbw b Shakib	9
S.C.J.Broad	c Mushfiqur b Mehedi	13		run out	10
G.J.Batty	not out	1		lbw b Taijul	3
Extras	(B 14, LB 4, W 2)	20		(B 3, LB 8, Pen 5)	16
Total	**(105.5 overs)**	**293**		**(80.2 overs)**	**240**

BANGLADESH

Tamim Iqbal	c Bairstow b Batty	78		c Ballance b Ali	9
Imrul Kayes	b Ali	21		c Root b Rashid	43
Mominul Haque	c Stokes b Ali	0		lbw b Batty	27
Mahmudullah	c Root b Rashid	38		lbw b Batty	17
†*Mushfiqur Rahim	c Bairstow b Stokes	48	(6)	c Ballance b Batty	39
Shakib Al Hasan	st Bairstow b Ali	31	(5)	c Bairstow b Ali	24
Shafiul Islam	c Broad b Rashid	2	(11)	lbw b Stokes	0
Sabbir Rahman	c Cook b Stokes	19	(7)	not out	64
Mehedi Hasan	lbw b Stokes	1	(8)	lbw b Broad	1
Taijul Islam	not out	3		lbw b Stokes	16
Kamrul Islam	b Stokes	0	(9)	c Ballance b Broad	0
Extras	(B 2, LB 4, W 1)	7		(B 9, LB 13, W 1)	23
Total	**(86 overs)**	**248**		**(81.3 overs)**	**263**

BANGLADESH	O	M	R	W		O	M	R	W
Shafiul Islam	9	1	33	0	(6)	3	0	10	0
Mehedi Hasan	39.5	7	80	6	(1)	20	1	58	1
Kamrul Islam	8	0	41	0	(4)	8	0	24	1
Shakib Al Hasan	19	6	46	2	(2)	33	7	85	5
Taijul Islam	24	11	47	2	(3)	15.2	2	41	2
Sabbir Rahman	3	0	11	0					
Mahmudullah	2	0	17	0	(5)	1	0	6	0
Mominul Haque	1	1	0	0					
ENGLAND									
Broad	8	2	12	0	(5)	15	4	31	2
Batty	17	1	51	1	(1)	17	3	65	3
Woakes	7	2	15	0		7	3	10	0
Rashid	16	1	58	2		17	2	55	1
Ali	22	4	75	3	(2)	14	2	60	2
Stokes	14	5	26	4		11.3	2	20	2
Root	2	0	5	0					

FALL OF WICKETS

	E	B	E	B
Wkt	*1st*	*1st*	*2nd*	*2nd*
1st	18	29	26	35
2nd	18	29	27	81
3rd	21	119	28	103
4th	83	163	46	108
5th	106	221	62	140
6th	194	221	189	227
7th	237	238	197	234
8th	258	239	213	238
9th	289	248	233	263
10th	293	248	240	263

Umpires: H.D.P.K.Dharmasena (*Sri Lanka*) (40) and C.B.Gaffaney (*New Zealand*) (10).
Referee: R.S.Madugalle (*Sri Lanka*) (168). **Test No. 2226/9 (B94/E977)**

BANGLADESH v ENGLAND (2nd Test)

At Shere Bangla National Stadium, Mirpur, on 28, 29, 30 October 2016.
Toss: Bangladesh. Result: **BANGLADESH** won by 108 runs.
Debut: England – Z.S.Ansari.

BANGLADESH

Tamim Iqbal	lbw b Ali	104		c Cook b Ansari	40
Imrul Kayes	c Duckett b Woakes	1		lbw b Ali	78
Mominul Haque	b Ali	66		c Cook b Stokes	1
Mahmudullah	c Cook b Stokes	13		b Ansari	47
Shakib Al Hasan	c Bairstow b Woakes	10		b Rashid	41
†*Mushfiqur Rahim	c Cook b Ali	4		c Cook b Stokes	9
Sabbir Rahman	c Bairstow b Stokes	0		lbw b Rashid	15
Shuvagata Hom	c Bairstow b Woakes	6		not out	25
Mehedi Hasan	lbw b Ali	1	(10)	c Root b Rashid	2
Taijul Islam	not out	5	(9)	c Bairstow b Stokes	5
Kamrul Islam	c Root b Ali	0		c and b Rashid	7
Extras	(B 1, LB 9)	10		(B 17, LB 7, W 1, NB 1)	26
Total	**(63.5 overs)**	**220**		**(66.5 overs)**	**296**

ENGLAND

*A.N.Cook	lbw b Mehedi	14		c Mominul b Mehedi	59
B.M.Duckett	c Mushfiqur b Shakib	7		b Mehedi	56
J.E.Root	lbw b Taijul	56		lbw b Shakib	1
G.S.Ballance	c Mushfiqur b Mehedi	9		c Tamim b Mehedi	5
M.M.Ali	b Mehedi	10		lbw b Mehedi	0
B.A.Stokes	c Mominul b Taijul	0		b Shakib	25
†J.M.Bairstow	lbw b Mehedi	24		c Shuvagata b Mehedi	3
Z.S.Ansari	c Shuvagata b Mehedi	13	(10)	c Imrul b Shakib	0
C.R.Woakes	c Shuvagata b Mehedi	46	(8)	not out	9
A.U.Rashid	not out	44	(9)	lbw b Shakib	0
S.T.Finn	c Mushfiqur b Taijul	0		lbw b Mehedi	0
Extras	(B 13, LB 7, NB 1)	21		(B 4, LB 2)	6
Total	**(81.3 overs)**	**244**		**(45.3 overs)**	**164**

ENGLAND	O	M	R	W		O	M	R	W
Woakes	9	3	30	3	(6)	2	0	14	0
Finn	8	1	30	0	(1)	3	0	18	0
Ali	19.5	5	57	5	(2)	19	2	60	1
Ansari	6	0	36	0	(3)	19	0	76	2
Stokes	11	5	13	2	(4)	12	2	52	3
Rashid	10	0	44	0	(5)	11.5	1	52	4
BANGLADESH									
Mehedi Hasan	28	2	82	6		21.3	2	77	6
Shakib Al Hasan	16	5	41	1		13	1	49	4
Taijul Islam	25.3	3	65	3	(4)	5	2	7	0
Kamrul Islam	3	0	16	0					
Shuvagata Hom	4	0	8	0	(3)	6	0	25	0
Sabbir Rahman	5	0	12	0					

FALL OF WICKETS

	B	E	B	E
Wkt	*1st*	*1st*	*2nd*	*2nd*
1st	1	10	65	100
2nd	171	24	66	105
3rd	190	42	152	124
4th	196	64	200	124
5th	201	69	238	127
6th	202	114	238	139
7th	212	140	268	161
8th	213	144	273	161
9th	215	243	276	161
10th	220	244	296	164

Umpires: H.D.P.K.Dharmasena (*Sri Lanka*) (41) and S.Ravi (*India*) (15).
Referee: R.S.Madugalle (*Sri Lanka*) (169). **Test No. 2227/10 (B95/E978)**

ZIMBABWE v SRI LANKA (1st Test)

At Harare Sports Club, on 29, 30, 31 October, 1, 2 November 2016.
Toss: Sri Lanka. Result: **SRI LANKA** won by 225 runs.
Debuts: Zimbabwe – C.T.Mumba; Sri Lanka – D.A.S.Gunaratne, C.B.R.L.S.Kumara.

SRI LANKA

F.D.M.Karunaratne	c Mawoyo b Cremer	56	c and b Mpofu	110
J.K.Silva	c Williams b Waller	94	b Mumba	7
†M.D.K.J.Perera	c Waller b Cremer	110	c Masakadza b Waller	17
B.K.G.Mendis	c Moor b Cremer	34	c Cremer b Mumba	19
W.U.Tharanga	not out	110	c Moor b Mumba	1
D.M.de Silva	c Williams b Cremer	25	c Waller b Mumba	64
D.A.S.Gunaratne	c Cremer b Williams	54	not out	16
M.D.K.Perera	run out	23	not out	1
*H.M.R.K.B.Herath	c Waller b Mumba	7		
R.A.S.Lakmal	c Tiripano b Mpofu	7		
C.B.R.L.S.Kumara	c Moor b Mpofu	0		
Extras	(B 10, LB 7)	17	(B 6, LB 5, NB 1)	12
Total	**(155 overs)**	**537**	**(6 wkts dec; 61.5 overs)**	**247**

ZIMBABWE

T.M.K.Mawoyo	c Gunaratne b Lakmal	45	lbw b M.D.K.Perera	37
B.B.Chari	lbw b Herath	5	b Kumara	10
H.Masakadza	c Karunaratne b Lakmal	33	lbw b Lakmal	20
C.R.Ervine	lbw b M.D.K.Perera	12	lbw b M.D.K.Perera	0
S.C.Williams	c Gunaratne b Herath	10	c de Silva b Herath	40
M.N.Waller	lbw b M.D.K.Perera	22	lbw b Lakmal	0
†P.J.Moor	c M.D.K.Perera b Kumara	79	lbw b Kumara	7
*A.G.Cremer	not out	102	st M.D.K.J.Perera b Herath	43
D.T.Tiripano	lbw b Mendis	46	lbw b Herath	0
C.T.Mumba	b Herath	1	not out	10
C.B.Mpofu	b Lakmal	2	b M.D.K.Perera	0
Extras	(B 4, LB 4, W 7, NB 1)	16	(B 5, LB 13, W 1)	19
Total	**(107.5 overs)**	**373**	**(90.3 overs)**	**186**

ZIMBABWE	O	M	R	W		O	M	R	W
Mpofu	31	6	96	2		16	2	42	1
Mumba	24	2	101	1	(3)	11.5	2	50	4
Tiripano	26	7	71	0	(4)	8	0	33	0
Cremer	42	6	142	4	(2)	14	0	67	0
Masakadza	9	3	31	0	(7)	6	1	22	0
Williams	17	2	54	1		1	0	5	0
Waller	6	0	25	1	(5)	5	0	17	1
SRI LANKA									
Lakmal	21.5	3	69	3		24	6	43	2
Kumara	22	3	90	1	(3)	19	3	45	2
Herath	37	5	97	3	(2)	30	13	38	3
M.D.K.Perera	18	1	66	2		15.3	4	34	3
Gunaratne	3	0	23	0					
De Silva	2	0	10	0					
Mendis	4	0	10	1	(5)	2	1	8	0

FALL OF WICKETS

	SL	Z	SL	Z
Wkt	*1st*	*1st*	*2nd*	*2nd*
1st	123	21	17	31
2nd	198	92	72	68
3rd	282	92	111	74
4th	307	111	117	74
5th	351	134	211	74
6th	450	139	241	100
7th	498	271	–	139
8th	512	363	–	145
9th	536	366	–	183
10th	537	373	–	186

Umpires: S.D.Fry (*Australia*) (2) and I.J.Gould (*England*) (54).
Referee: B.C.Broad (*England*) (81). **Test No. 2228/16 (Z100/SL252)**

ZIMBABWE v SRI LANKA (2nd Test)

At Harare Sports Club, on 6, 7, 8, 9, 10 November 2016.
Toss: Zimbabwe. Result: **SRI LANKA** won by 257 runs.
Debuts: None.

SRI LANKA

F.D.M.Karunaratne	c Williams b Masakadza	26		lbw b Mpofu	88
J.K.Silva	lbw b Mpofu	37		c Waller b Mumba	6
†M.D.K.J.Perera	c Mumba b Masakadza	4	(7)	c Williams b Cremer	62
B.K.G.Mendis	c Moor b Tiripano	26	(3)	c Mpofu b Mumba	0
W.U.Tharanga	c Masakadza b Cremer	79	(4)	lbw b Cremer	17
D.M.de Silva	c and b Cremer	127	(5)	c Chari b Mumba	9
D.A.S.Gunaratne	st Moor b Williams	116	(6)	lbw b Tiripano	39
M.D.K.Perera	lbw b Cremer	34		c Masakadza b Cremer	2
*H.M.R.K.B.Herath	c Moor b Tiripano	27		b Cremer	4
R.A.S.Lakmal	b Tiripano	0		not out	21
C.B.R.L.S.Kumara	not out	7			
Extras	(B 9, LB 8, W 2, NB 2)	21		(B 6, LB 4)	10
Total	**(144.4 overs)**	**504**		**(9 wkts dec; 81.4 overs)**	**258**

ZIMBABWE

T.M.K.Mawoyo	lbw b Herath	3	c de Silva b Herath	15
B.B.Chari	b Herath	80	b Herath	8
H.Masakadza	c de Silva b Herath	0	lbw b Herath	10
C.R.Ervine	c Karunaratne b Lakmal	64	c de Silva b Herath	72
S.C.Williams	lbw b M.D.K.Perera	58	c Mendis b Kumara	45
M.N.Waller	c Silva b Herath	18	c M.D.K.J.Perera b de Silva	0
†P.J.Moor	lbw b M.D.K.Perera	33	c Mendis b Herath	20
*A.G.Cremer	c Karunaratne b M.D.K.Perera	3	b Herath	5
D.T.Tiripano	c Herath b Lakmal	3	not out	16
C.T.Mumba	lbw b Herath	2	lbw b Herath	1
C.B.Mpofu	not out	0	lbw b Herath	20
Extras	(B 2, LB 6)	8	(B 12, LB 6, W 3)	21
Total	**(82.1 overs)**	**272**	**(58 overs)**	**233**

ZIMBABWE	O	M	R	W		O	M	R	W
Mumba	23	4	80	0	(2)	19	4	67	3
Tiripano	32	4	91	3	(4)	11	4	14	1
Mpofu	23	4	92	1	(1)	21	8	51	1
Masakadza	13	4	34	2	(7)	2	1	1	0
Cremer	40	1	136	3	(3)	21.4	2	91	4
Williams	8.4	1	31	1	(5)	6	0	21	0
Waller	5	0	23	0					
Chari					(6)	1	0	3	0
SRI LANKA									
Lakmal	21.1	5	55	2		15	2	58	0
Herath	26	4	89	5		23	6	63	8
Kumara	14	0	60	0	(4)	9	0	42	1
M.D.K.Perera	18	2	51	3	(3)	8	1	42	0
Gunaratne	2	0	5	0					
De Silva	1	0	4	0	(5)	3	0	10	1

FALL OF WICKETS

	SL	Z	SL	Z
Wkt	*1st*	*1st*	*2nd*	*2nd*
1st	62	17	14	16
2nd	66	17	16	32
3rd	84	134	44	39
4th	112	173	84	113
5th	255	210	153	114
6th	342	253	198	166
7th	396	265	201	176
8th	471	268	211	195
9th	471	272	258	201
10th	504	272	–	233

Umpires: S.D.Fry (*Australia*) (3) and I.J.Gould (*England*) (55).
Referee: B.C.Broad (*England*) (82). **Test No. 2229/17 (Z101/SL253)**

AUSTRALIA v SOUTH AFRICA (1st Test)

At W.A.C.A. Ground, Perth, on 3, 4, 5, 6, 7 November 2016.
Toss: South Africa. Result: **SOUTH AFRICA** won by 177 runs.
Debut: South Africa – K.A.Maharaj.

SOUTH AFRICA

S.C.Cook	c M.R.Marsh b Starc	0	c S.E.Marsh b Siddle	12
D.Elgar	c Nevill b Hazlewood	12	c Starc b Hazlewood	127
H.M.Amla	c Smith b Hazlewood	0	b Hazlewood	1
J.P.Duminy	c Nevill b Siddle	11	c Nevill b Siddle	141
*F.du Plessis	c Voges b Starc	37	c Nevill b Starc	32
T.Bavuma	c S.E.Marsh b Lyon	51	c Khawaja b M.R.Marsh	8
†Q.de Kock	c S.E.Marsh b Hazlewood	84	c Voges b M.R.Marsh	64
V.D.Philander	b Starc	10	b Smith	73
K.A.Maharaj	c Warner b Lyon	16	not out	41
K.Rabada	not out	11		
D.W.Steyn	b Starc	4		
Extras	(B 4, W 2)	6	(B 10, LB 13, W 17, NB 1)	41
Total	**(63.4 overs)**	**242**	**(8 wkts dec; 160.1 overs)**	**540**

AUSTRALIA

D.A.Warner	c Amla b Steyn	97	(2) run out	35
S.E.Marsh	lbw b Philander	63	(1) c du Plessis b Rabada	15
U.T.Khawaja	b Rabada	4	lbw b Duminy	97
*S.P.D.Smith	lbw b Maharaj	0	c de Kock b Rabada	34
A.C.Voges	c and b Rabada	27	c de Kock b Rabada	1
M.R.Marsh	lbw b Philander	0	lbw b Rabada	26
†P.M.Nevill	c Amla b Maharaj	23	not out	60
M.A.Starc	c du Plessis b Maharaj	0	lbw b Rabada	13
P.M.Siddle	not out	18	lbw b Philander	13
J.R.Hazlewood	c Duminy b Philander	4	c Elgar b Bavuma	29
N.M.Lyon	c Elgar b Philander	0	lbw b Maharaj	8
Extras	(LB 3, NB 5)	8	(B 13, LB 11, W 4, NB 2)	30
Total	**(70.2 overs)**	**244**	**(119.1 overs)**	**361**

AUSTRALIA	O	M	R	W		O	M	R	W
Starc	18.4	2	71	4		31	8	114	1
Hazlewood	17	2	70	3		37	11	107	2
Siddle	12	3	36	1		26	9	62	2
M.R.Marsh	6	1	23	0		26	4	77	2
Lyon	10	1	38	2		34	3	146	0
Voges						5	1	8	0
Smith						1.1	0	3	1
SOUTH AFRICA									
Steyn	12.4	3	51	1					
Philander	19.2	2	56	4		22	7	55	1
Rabada	20	1	78	2	(1)	31	6	92	5
Maharaj	18.2	5	56	3		40.1	10	94	1
Duminy					(3)	17	1	51	1
Cook					(5)	2	0	16	0
Bavuma					(6)	7	1	29	1

FALL OF WICKETS

	SA	A	SA	A
Wkt	*1st*	*1st*	*2nd*	*2nd*
1st	0	158	35	52
2nd	20	167	45	52
3rd	20	168	295	144
4th	32	181	324	146
5th	81	181	346	196
6th	152	202	352	246
7th	175	203	468	262
8th	223	232	540	280
9th	227	243	–	345
10th	242	244	–	361

Umpires: Alim Dar (*Pakistan*) (106) and N.J.Llong (*England*) (38).
Referee: A.J.Pycroft (*Zimbabwe*) (49). **Test No. 2230/92 (A791/SA403)**

AUSTRALIA v SOUTH AFRICA (2nd Test)

At Bellerive Oval, Hobart, on 12, 13 (*no play*), 14, 15 November 2016.
Toss: South Africa. Result: **SOUTH AFRICA** won by an innings and 80 runs.
Debuts: Australia – C.J.Ferguson, J.M.Mennie.

AUSTRALIA

D.A.Warner	c de Kock b Philander	1	(2)	b Abbott	45
J.A.Burns	lbw b Abbott	1	(1)	c de Kock b Abbott	0
U.T.Khawaja	c Amla b Philander	4		c de Kock b Abbott	64
*S.P.D.Smith	not out	48		c de Kock b Rabada	31
A.C.Voges	c de Kock b Philander	0		c Duminy b Abbott	2
C.J.Ferguson	run out	3		c Elgar b Rabada	1
†P.M.Nevill	lbw b Rabada	3		c Duminy b Rabada	6
J.M.Mennie	b Philander	10		lbw b Rabada	0
M.A.Starc	c Duminy b Abbott	4		c de Kock b Abbott	0
J.R.Hazlewood	c Amla b Abbott	8		not out	6
N.M.Lyon	c de Kock b Philander	2		c Philander b Abbott	4
Extras	(LB 1)	1		(LB 1, NB 1)	2
Total	**(32.5 overs)**	**85**		**(60.1 overs)**	**161**

SOUTH AFRICA

S.C.Cook	c Nevill b Starc	23
D.Elgar	lbw b Starc	17
H.M.Amla	c Nevill b Hazlewood	47
J.P.Duminy	c Smith b Starc	1
*F.du Plessis	lbw b Hazlewood	7
T.Bavuma	c Lyon b Mennie	74
†Q.de Kock	b Hazlewood	104
V.D.Philander	c Nevill b Hazlewood	32
K.A.Maharaj	b Hazlewood	1
K.J.Abbott	lbw b Hazlewood	3
K.Rabada	not out	5
Extras	(B 3, LB 8, NB 1)	12
Total	**(100.5 overs)**	**326**

SOUTH AFRICA	O	M	R	W		O	M	R	W
Philander	10.1	5	21	5	(2)	16	6	31	0
Abbott	12.4	3	41	3	(1)	23.1	3	77	6
Rabada	6	0	20	1	(4)	17	5	34	4
Maharaj	4	2	2	0	(5)	3	0	10	0
Duminy					(3)	1	0	8	0
AUSTRALIA									
Starc	24	1	79	3					
Hazlewood	30.5	10	89	6					
Mennie	28	5	85	1					
Lyon	17	2	57	0					
Smith	1	0	5	0					

FALL OF WICKETS

	A	SA	A
Wkt	*1st*	*1st*	*2nd*
1st	2	43	0
2nd	2	44	79
3rd	8	46	129
4th	8	76	135
5th	17	132	140
6th	31	276	150
7th	59	292	150
8th	66	293	151
9th	76	297	151
10th	85	326	161

Umpires: Alim Dar (*Pakistan*) (107) and R.A.Kettleborough (*England*) (40).
Referee: A.J.Pycroft (*Zimbabwe*) (50). **Test No. 2231/93 (A792/SA404)**

AUSTRALIA v SOUTH AFRICA (3rd Test)

At Adelaide Oval, on 24, 25, 26, 27 November 2016 (day/night).
Toss: South Africa. Result: **AUSTRALIA** won by seven wickets.
Debuts: Australia – P.S.P.Handscomb, N.J.Maddinson, M.T.Renshaw; South Africa – T.Shamsi.

SOUTH AFRICA

S.C.Cook	c Smith b Starc	40		b Starc	104
D.Elgar	c Khawaja b Starc	5		c Smith b Starc	0
H.M.Amla	c Renshaw b Hazlewood	5		c Wade b Hazlewood	45
J.P.Duminy	c Wade b Hazlewood	5		b Lyon	26
*F.du Plessis	not out	118		c Handscomb b Starc	12
T.Bavuma	c Wade b Bird	8		c Smith b Lyon	21
†Q.de Kock	c Wade b Hazlewood	24	(8)	lbw b Bird	5
V.D.Philander	c Wade b Hazlewood	4	(9)	lbw b Starc	17
K.J.Abbott	lbw b Bird	17	(7)	lbw b Lyon	0
K.Rabada	st Wade b Lyon	1		c Wade b Hazlewood	7
T.Shamsi	not out	18		not out	0
Extras	(B 3, LB 8, W 2, NB 1)	14		(LB 10, NB 3)	13
Total	**(9 wkts dec, 76 overs)**	**259**		**(85.2 overs)**	**250**

AUSTRALIA

U.T.Khawaja	lbw b Philander	145	(3)	lbw b Shamsi	0
M.T.Renshaw	c Elgar b Abbott	10	(1)	not out	34
D.A.Warner	c Elgar b Abbott	11	(2)	run out	47
*S.P.D.Smith	run out	59		c de Kock b Abbott	40
P.S.P.Handscomb	b Abbott	54		not out	1
N.J.Maddinson	b Rabada	0			
†M.S.Wade	c de Kock b Philander	4			
M.A.Starc	c and b Rabada	53			
J.R.Hazlewood	not out	11			
N.M.Lyon	c Amla b Shamsi	13			
J.M.Bird	c du Plessis b Rabada	6			
Extras	(B 3, LB 9, W 2 NB 3)	17		(LB 4, NB 1)	5
Total	**(121.1 overs)**	**383**		**(3 wkts; 40.5 overs)**	**127**

AUSTRALIA	O	M	R	W		O	M	R	W
Starc	23	5	78	2		23.2	5	80	4
Hazlewood	22	3	68	4		20	8	41	2
Bird	16	3	57	2		20	3	54	1
Lyon	15	1	45	1		21	4	60	3
Warner						1	0	5	0
SOUTH AFRICA									
Philander	29	5	100	2	(2)	7	2	20	0
Abbott	29	11	49	3	(1)	10	2	26	1
Rabada	25.1	4	84	3		9	4	28	0
Shamsi	29	4	101	1		14.5	4	49	1
Duminy	6	0	25	0					
Elgar	2	0	11	0					
Bavuma	1	0	1	0					

FALL OF WICKETS

	SA	A	SA	A
Wkt	*1st*	*1st*	*2nd*	*2nd*
1st	12	19	1	64
2nd	36	37	82	64
3rd	44	174	131	125
4th	95	273	154	–
5th	117	277	190	–
6th	149	283	194	–
7th	161	327	201	–
8th	215	357	235	–
9th	220	370	250	–
10th	–	383	250	–

Umpires: R.A.Kettleborough (*England*) (41) and N.J.Llong (*England*) (39).
Referee: A.J.Pycroft (*Zimbabwe*) (51). **Test No. 2232/94 (A793/SA405)**

INDIA v ENGLAND (1st Test)

At Saurashtra Cricket Association Stadium, Rajkot, on 9, 10, 11, 12, 13 November 2016.
Toss: England. Result: **MATCH DRAWN**.
Debut: England – H.Hameed.

ENGLAND

*A.N.Cook	lbw b Jadeja	21		c Jadeja b Ashwin	130
H.Hameed	lbw b Ashwin	31		c and b Mishra	82
J.E.Root	c and b Yadav	124		c Saha b Mishra	4
B.M.Duckett	c Rahane b Ashwin	13			
M.M.Ali	b Shami	117			
B.A.Stokes	c Saha b Yadav	128	(4)	not out	29
†J.M.Bairstow	c Saha b Shami	46			
C.R.Woakes	c Saha b Jadeja	4			
A.U.Rashid	c Yadav b Jadeja	5			
Z.S.Ansari	lbw b Mishra	32			
S.C.J.Broad	not out	6			
Extras	(B 5, LB 4, NB 1)	10		(B 11, LB 3, NB 1)	15
Total	**(159.3 overs)**	**537**		**(3 wkts dec; 75.3 overs)**	**260**

INDIA

M.Vijay	c Hameed b Rashid	126		c Hameed b Rashid	31
G.Gambhir	lbw b Broad	29		c Root b Woakes	0
C.A.Pujara	c Cook b Stokes	124		lbw b Rashid	18
*V.Kohli	hit wkt b Rashid	40		not out	49
A.Mishra	c Hameed b Ansari	0			
A.M.Rahane	b Ansari	13	(5)	b Ali	1
R.Ashwin	c Ansari b Ali	70	(6)	c Root b Ansari	32
†W.P.Saha	c Bairstow b Ali	35	(7)	c and b Rashid	9
R.A.Jadeja	c Hameed b Rashid	12	(8)	not out	32
U.T.Yadav	c Stokes b Rashid	5			
Mohammed Shami	not out	8			
Extras	(B 23, LB 2, W 1)	26			–
Total	**(162 overs)**	**488**		**(6 wkts; 52.3 overs)**	**172**

INDIA	O	M	R	W		O	M	R	W
Mohammed Shami	28.1	5	65	2		11	1	29	0
Yadav	31.5	3	112	2	(4)	13	2	47	0
Ashwin	46	3	167	2		23.3	4	63	1
Jadeja	30	4	86	3	(2)	15	1	47	0
Mishra	23.3	3	98	1		13	0	60	2
ENGLAND									
Broad	29	9	78	1		3	2	8	0
Woakes	31	6	57	0		4	1	6	1
Ali	31	7	85	2	(4)	19	5	47	1
Ansari	23	1	77	2	(3)	8	1	41	1
Rashid	31	1	114	4		14.3	1	64	3
Stokes	17	2	52	1		2	1	1	0
Root						2	0	5	0

FALL OF WICKETS

	E	I	E	I
Wkt	*1st*	*1st*	*2nd*	*2nd*
1st	47	68	180	0
2nd	76	277	192	47
3rd	102	318	260	68
4th	281	319	–	71
5th	343	349	–	118
6th	443	361	–	132
7th	451	425	–	–
8th	465	449	–	–
9th	517	459	–	–
10th	537	488	–	–

Umpires: H.D.P.K.Dharmasena (*Sri Lanka*) (42) and C.B.Gaffaney (*New Zealand*) (11).
Referee: R.S.Madugalle (*Sri Lanka*) (170). **Test No. 2233/113 (I503/E979)**

INDIA v ENGLAND (2nd Test)

At Dr Y.S.Rajasekhara Reddy ACA-VDCA Stadium, Visakhapatnam, on 17, 18, 19, 20, 21 November 2016.
Toss: India. Result: **INDIA** won by 246 runs.
Debut: India – J.Yadav.

INDIA

M.Vijay	c Stokes b Anderson	20	c Root b Broad	3
K.L.Rahul	c Stokes b Broad	0	c Bairstow b Broad	10
C.A.Pujara	c Bairstow b Anderson	119	b Anderson	1
*V.Kohli	c Stokes b Ali	167	c Stokes b Rashid	81
A.M.Rahane	c Bairstow b Anderson	23	c Cook b Broad	26
R.Ashwin	c Bairstow b Stokes	58	c Bairstow b Broad	7
†W.P.Saha	lbw b Ali	3	lbw b Rashid	2
R.A.Jadeja	lbw b Ali	0	c Ali b Rashid	14
J.Yadav	c Anderson b Rashid	35	not out	27
U.T.Yadav	c Ali b Rashid	13	c Bairstow b Rashid	0
Mohammed Shami	not out	7	st Bairstow b Ali	19
Extras	(B 4, LB 5, W 1)	10	(B 5, LB 8, W 1)	14
Total	**(129.4 overs)**	**455**	**(63.1 overs)**	**204**

ENGLAND

*A.N.Cook	b Shami	2	lbw b Jadeja	54
H.Hameed	run out	13	lbw b Ashwin	25
J.E.Root	c U.T.Yadav b Ashwin	53	lbw b Shami	25
B.M.Duckett	b Ashwin	5	c Saha b Ashwin	0
M.M.Ali	lbw b J.Yadav	1	c Kohli b Jadeja	2
B.A.Stokes	lbw b Ashwin	70	b J.Yadav	6
†J.M.Bairstow	b U.T.Yadav	53	not out	34
A.U.Rashid	not out	32	c Saha b Shami	4
Z.S.Ansari	lbw b Jadeja	4	b Ashwin	0
S.C.J.Broad	lbw b Ashwin	13	lbw b J.Yadav	5
J.M.Anderson	lbw b Ashwin	0	lbw b J.Yadav	0
Extras	(B 6, LB 3)	9	(LB 3)	3
Total	**(102.5 overs)**	**255**	**(97.3 overs)**	**158**

ENGLAND	O	M	R	W		O	M	R	W
Anderson	20	3	62	3		15	3	33	1
Broad	16	2	49	1		14	5	33	4
Stokes	20	4	73	1	(4)	7	0	34	0
Ansari	12	1	45	0					
Rashid	34.4	2	110	2	(3)	24	3	82	4
Ali	25	1	98	3	(5)	3.1	1	9	1
Root	2	0	9	0					
INDIA									
Mohammed Shami	14	5	28	1		14	3	30	2
U.T.Yadav	18	2	56	1		8	3	8	0
Jadeja	29	10	57	1	(4)	34	14	35	2
Ashwin	29.5	6	67	5	(3)	30	11	52	3
J.Yadav	12	3	38	1		11.3	4	30	3

FALL OF WICKETS

	I	E	I	E
Wkt	*1st*	*1st*	*2nd*	*2nd*
1st	6	4	16	75
2nd	22	51	17	87
3rd	248	72	40	92
4th	316	79	117	101
5th	351	80	127	115
6th	363	190	130	115
7th	363	225	151	129
8th	427	234	162	143
9th	440	255	162	158
10th	455	255	204	158

Umpires: H.D.P.K.Dharmasena (*Sri Lanka*) (43) and R.J.Tucker (*Australia*) (49).
Referee: R.S.Madugalle (*Sri Lanka*) (171). **Test No. 2234/114 (I504/E980)**

INDIA v ENGLAND (3rd Test)

At Punjab CA I.S.Bindra Stadium, Mohali, Chandigarh, on 26, 27, 28, 29 November 2016.
Toss: England. Result: **INDIA** won by eight wickets.
Debut: India – K.K.Nair.

ENGLAND

*A.N.Cook	c Patel b Ashwin	27		b Ashwin	12
H.Hameed	c Rahane b U.T.Yadav	9	(8)	not out	59
J.E.Root	lbw b J.Yadav	15	(2)	c Rahane b Jadeja	78
M.M.Ali	c Vijay b Shami	16	(3)	c J.Yadav b Ashwin	5
†J.M.Bairstow	lbw b J.Yadav	89	(4)	c Patel b J.Yadav	15
B.A.Stokes	st Patel b Jadeja	29	(5)	lbw b Ashwin	5
J.C.Buttler	c Kohli b Jadeja	43		c Jadeja b J.Yadav	18
C.R.Woakes	b U.T.Yadav	25	(9)	c Patel b Shami	30
A.U.Rashid	c Patel b Shami	4	(10)	c U.T.Yadav b Shami	0
G.J.Batty	lbw b Shami	1	(6)	lbw b Jadeja	0
J.M.Anderson	not out	13		run out	5
Extras	(B 8, LB 3, NB 1)	12		(B 8, LB 1)	9
Total	**(93.5 overs)**	**283**		**(90.2 overs)**	**236**

INDIA

M.Vijay	c Bairstow b Stokes	12	c Root b Woakes	0
†P.A.Patel	lbw b Rashid	42	not out	67
C.A.Pujara	c Woakes b Rashid	51	c Root b Rashid	25
*V.Kohli	c Bairstow b Stokes	62	not out	6
A.M.Rahane	lbw b Rashid	0		
K.K.Nair	run out	4		
R.Ashwin	c Buttler b Stokes	72		
R.A.Jadeja	c Woakes b Rashid	90		
J.Yadav	c Ali b Stokes	55		
U.T.Yadav	c Bairstow b Stokes	12		
Mohammed Shami	not out	1		
Extras	(B 8, LB 4, W 3, NB 1)	16	(B 4, LB 1, NB 1)	6
Total	**(138.2 overs)**	**417**	**(2 wkts; 20.2 overs)**	**104**

INDIA	O	M	R	W		O	M	R	W
Mohammed Shami	21.5	5	63	3		14	3	37	2
U.T.Yadav	16	4	58	2		8	3	26	0
J.Yadav	15	5	49	2	(5)	12	2	21	2
Ashwin	18	1	43	1	(3)	26.2	4	81	3
Jadeja	23	4	59	2	(4)	30	12	62	2
ENGLAND									
Anderson	21	4	48	0		3	2	8	0
Woakes	24	7	86	0		2	0	16	1
Ali	13	1	33	0	(5)	3	0	13	0
Rashid	38	6	118	4	(3)	5	0	28	1
Stokes	26.2	5	73	5	(4)	4	0	16	0
Batty	16	0	47	0		3.2	0	18	0

FALL OF WICKETS

	E	I	E	I
Wkt	*1st*	*1st*	*2nd*	*2nd*
1st	32	39	27	7
2nd	51	73	39	88
3rd	51	148	70	–
4th	87	152	78	–
5th	144	156	78	–
6th	213	204	107	–
7th	258	301	152	–
8th	266	381	195	–
9th	268	414	195	–
10th	283	417	236	–

Umpires: M.Erasmus (*South Africa*) (37) and C.B.Gaffaney (*New Zealand*) (12).
Referee: R.S.Madugalle (*Sri Lanka*) (172). **Test No. 2235/115 (I505/E981)**

INDIA v ENGLAND (4th Test)

At Wankhede Stadium, Mumbai, on 8, 9, 10, 11, 12 December 2016.
Toss: England. Result: **INDIA** won by an innings and 36 runs.
Debut: England – K.K.Jennings.

ENGLAND

*A.N.Cook	st Patel b Jadeja	46		lbw b Jadeja	18
K.K.Jennings	c Pujara b Ashwin	112		lbw b Kumar	0
J.E.Root	c Kohli b Ashwin	21		lbw b J.Yadav	77
M.M.Ali	c Nair b Ashwin	50		c Vijay b Jadeja	0
†J.M.Bairstow	c U.T.Yadav b Ashwin	14		lbw b Ashwin	51
B.A.Stokes	c Kohli b Ashwin	31		c Vijay b Ashwin	18
J.C.Buttler	b Jadeja	76	(8)	not out	6
C.R.Woakes	c Patel b Jadeja	11	(9)	b Ashwin	0
A.U.Rashid	b Jadeja	4	(10)	c Rahul b Ashwin	2
J.T.Ball	c Patel b Ashwin	31	(7)	c Patel b Ashwin	2
J.M.Anderson	not out	0		c U.T.Yadav b Ashwin	2
Extras	(B 1, LB 2, NB 1)	4		(B 15, LB 2, NB 2)	19
Total	**(130.1 overs)**	**400**		**(55.3 overs)**	**195**

INDIA

K.L.Rahul	b Ali	24
M.Vijay	c and b Rashid	136
C.A.Pujara	b Ball	47
*V.Kohli	c Anderson b Woakes	235
K.K.Nair	lbw b Ali	13
†P.A.Patel	c Bairstow b Root	15
R.Ashwin	c Jennings b Root	0
R.A.Jadeja	c Buttler b Rashid	25
J.Yadav	st Bairstow b Rashid	104
B.Kumar	c Woakes b Rashid	9
U.T.Yadav	not out	7
Extras	(B 5, LB 8, W 3)	16
Total	**(182.3 overs)**	**631**

INDIA	O	M	R	W		O	M	R	W
Kumar	13	0	49	0		4	1	11	1
U.T.Yadav	11	2	38	0		3	0	10	0
Ashwin	44	4	112	6	(4)	20.3	3	55	6
J.Yadav	25	3	89	0	(5)	6	0	39	1
Jadeja	37.1	5	109	4	(3)	22	3	63	2
ENGLAND									
Anderson	20	5	63	0					
Woakes	16	2	79	1					
Ali	53	5	174	2					
Rashid	55.3	5	192	4					
Ball	18	5	47	1					
Stokes	10	2	32	0					
Root	10	2	31	2					

FALL OF WICKETS

	E	I	E
Wkt	*1st*	*1st*	*2nd*
1st	99	39	1
2nd	136	146	43
3rd	230	262	49
4th	230	279	141
5th	249	305	180
6th	297	307	182
7th	320	364	185
8th	334	605	189
9th	388	615	193
10th	400	631	195

Umpires: M.Erasmus (*South Africa*) (38), B.N.J.Oxenford (*Australia*) (35) and P.R.Reiffel (*Australia*) (28).
Referee: J.J.Crowe (*New Zealand*) (80). **Test No. 2236/116 (I506/E982)**
M.Erasmus replaced P.R.Reiffel as umpire after Reiffel was hit on the head by a ball.

INDIA v ENGLAND (5th Test)

At M.A.Chidambaram Stadium, Chepauk, Chennai, on 16, 17, 18, 19, 20 December 2016.
Toss: England. Result: **INDIA** won by an innings and 75 runs.
Debut: England – L.A.Dawson.

ENGLAND

*A.N.Cook	c Kohli b Jadeja	10	c Rahul b Jadeja	49
K.K.Jennings	c Patel b Sharma	1	c and b Jadeja	54
J.E.Root	c Patel b Jadeja	88	lbw b Jadeja	6
M.M.Ali	c Jadeja b Yadav	146	c Ashwin b Jadeja	44
†J.M.Bairstow	c Rahul b Jadeja	49	c Jadeja b Sharma	1
B.A.Stokes	c Patel b Ashwin	6	c Nair b Jadeja	23
J.C.Buttler	lbw b Sharma	5	not out	6
L.A.Dawson	not out	66	b Mishra	0
A.U.Rashid	c Patel b Yadav	60	c Jadeja b Yadav	2
S.C.J.Broad	run out	19	c Pujara b Jadeja	1
J.T.Ball	b Mishra	12	c Nair b Jadeja	0
Extras	(B 4, LB 5, W 1, Pen 5)	15	(B 12, LB 8, W 1)	21
Total	**(157.2 overs)**	**477**	**(88 overs)**	**207**

INDIA

K.L.Rahul	c Buttler b Rashid	199
†P.A.Patel	c Buttler b Ali	71
C.A.Pujara	c Cook b Stokes	16
*V.Kohli	c Jennings b Broad	15
K.K.Nair	not out	303
M.Vijay	lbw b Dawson	29
R.Ashwin	c Buttler b Broad	67
R.A.Jadeja	c Ball b Dawson	51
U.T.Yadav	not out	1
A.Mishra		
I.Sharma		
Extras	(B 2, LB 4, W 1)	7
Total	**(7 wkts dec; 190.4 overs)**	**759**

INDIA	O	M	R	W		O	M	R	W
Yadav	21	3	73	2	(4)	14	1	36	1
Sharma	21	6	42	2	(1)	10	2	17	1
Jadeja	45	9	106	3		25	5	48	7
Ashwin	44	3	151	1	(2)	25	6	56	0
Mishra	25.2	5	87	1		14	4	30	1
Nair	1	0	4	0					
ENGLAND									
Broad	27	6	80	2					
Ball	23	2	93	0					
Ali	41	1	190	1					
Stokes	20	2	76	1					
Rashid	29.4	1	153	1					
Dawson	43	4	129	2					
Root	2	0	12	0					
Jennings	5	1	20	0					

FALL OF WICKETS

	E	I	E
Wkt	*1st*	*1st*	*2nd*
1st	7	152	103
2nd	21	181	110
3rd	167	211	126
4th	253	372	129
5th	287	435	192
6th	300	616	193
7th	321	754	196
8th	429	–	200
9th	455	–	207
10th	477	–	207

Umpires: M.Erasmus (*South Africa*) (39) and S.D.Fry (*Australia*) (5).
Referee: J.J.Crowe (*New Zealand*) (81). **Test No. 2237/117 (I507/E983)**

NEW ZEALAND v PAKISTAN (1st Test)

At Hagley Oval, Christchurch, on 17 (*no play*), 18, 19, 20 November 2016.
Toss: New Zealand. Result: **NEW ZEALAND** won by eight wickets.
Debuts: New Zealand – C.de Grandhomme, J.A.Raval.

PAKISTAN

Sami Aslam	c Raval b Southee	19	c Watling b de Grandhomme	7
Azhar Ali	b de Grandhomme	15	b Boult	31
Babar Azam	c Taylor b de Grandhomme	7	c Watling b Wagner	29
Younus Khan	c Raval b de Grandhomme	2	c Watling b Wagner	1
*Misbah-ul-Haq	c Williamson b Boult	31	c Boult b Southee	13
Asad Shafiq	c Raval b de Grandhomme	16	c Raval b Wagner	17
†Sarfraz Ahmed	c Astle b Southee	7	b Boult	2
Mohammad Amir	b Boult	3	c Astle b Boult	6
Sohail Khan	c Latham b de Grandhomme	9	c de Grandhomme b Southee	40
Yasir Shah	not out	4	not out	6
Rahat Ali	c Watling b de Grandhomme	0	c Latham b Southee	2
Extras	(B 8, LB 12)	20	(B 5, LB 7, W 5)	17
Total	**(55.5 overs)**	**133**	**(78.4 overs)**	**171**

NEW ZEALAND

T.W.M.Latham	lbw b Amir	1		c Shafiq b Amir	9
J.A.Raval	c Aslam b Amir	55		not out	36
*K.S.Williamson	c Aslam b Sohail	4		c Aslam b Azhar	61
L.R.P.L.Taylor	c Ahmed b Rahat	11			
H.M.Nicholls	lbw b Sohail	30	(4)	not out	0
C.de Grandhomme	c Rahat b Sohail	29			
†B.J.Watling	c Younus b Rahat	18			
T.D.Astle	c Shafiq b Rahat	0			
T.G.Southee	c Ahmed b Amir	22			
N.Wagner	c Shafiq b Rahat	21			
T.A.Boult	not out	3			
Extras	(LB 1, W 1, NB 4)	6		(NB 2)	2
Total	**(59.5 overs)**	**200**		**(2 wkts; 31.3 overs)**	**108**

NEW ZEALAND	O	M	R	W		O	M	R	W
Southee	19	11	20	2	(2)	23.4	10	53	3
Boult	16	5	39	2	(1)	17	5	37	3
De Grandhomme	15.5	5	41	6		14	4	23	1
Wagner	5	0	13	0		20	6	34	3
Astle						4	0	12	0
PAKISTAN									
Mohammad Amir	18	4	43	3		7	2	12	1
Sohail Khan	22	5	78	3		6	1	21	0
Rahat Ali	15.5	2	62	4		6	0	24	0
Yasir Shah	4	0	16	0		9.3	1	45	0
Azhar Ali						3	1	6	1

FALL OF WICKETS

	P	NZ	P	NZ
Wkt	*1st*	*1st*	*2nd*	*2nd*
1st	31	6	21	19
2nd	53	15	58	104
3rd	53	40	64	–
4th	56	105	93	–
5th	88	109	93	–
6th	101	146	95	–
7th	114	146	105	–
8th	129	171	158	–
9th	129	177	166	–
10th	133	200	171	–

Umpires: I.J.Gould (*England*) (56) and S.Ravi (*India*) (16).
Referee: R.B.Richardson (*West Indies*) (5). **Test No. 2238/54 (NZ416/P402)**

NEW ZEALAND v PAKISTAN (2nd Test)

At Seddon Park, Hamilton, on 25, 26, 27, 28, 29 November 2016.
Toss: Pakistan. Result: **NEW ZEALAND** won by 138 runs.
Debut: Pakistan – Mohammad Rizwan.

NEW ZEALAND

J.A.Raval	c Rizwan b Imran	55		lbw b Amir	2
T.W.M.Latham	c Aslam b Amir	0		c Ahmed b Riaz	80
*K.S.Williamson	c Ahmed b Sohail	13		c Ahmed b Imran	42
L.R.P.L.Taylor	c Ahmed b Sohail	37		not out	102
H.M.Nicholls	c Ahmed b Riaz	13		c Ahmed b Imran	26
C.de Grandhomme	c Ahmed b Imran	37		c Ali b Imran	32
†B.J.Watling	not out	49		not out	15
M.J.Santner	c Younus b Sohail	16			
T.G.Southee	b Sohail	29			
M.J.Henry	c Sohail b Amir	15			
N.Wagner	c Younus b Imran	1			
Extras	(W 5, NB 1)	6		(LB 6, W 6, NB 2)	14
Total	**(83.4 overs)**	**271**		**(5 wkts dec; 85.3 overs)**	**313**

PAKISTAN

Sami Aslam	c Raval b Southee	5		c Williamson b Southee	91
*Azhar Ali	c Watling b Southee	1		b Santner	58
Babar Azam	not out	90		b Santner	16
Younus Khan	c Watling b Southee	2	(5)	lbw b Southee	11
Asad Shafiq	b Wagner	23	(6)	c Nicholls b Henry	0
Mohammad Rizwan	c Henry b Wagner	0	(7)	not out	13
†Sarfraz Ahmed	c Raval b Wagner	41	(4)	run out	19
Sohail Khan	c Watling b Southee	37		c Nicholls b de Grandhomme	8
Wahab Riaz	lbw b de Grandhomme	0	(10)	c Watling b Wagner	0
Mohammad Amir	c Raval b Southee	5	(9)	c Watling b Wagner	0
Imran Khan	c Watling b Southee	6		c Latham b Wagner	0
Extras	(B 4, LB 1, NB 1)	6		(B 4, LB 3, W 6, NB 1)	14
Total	**(67 overs)**	**216**		**(92.1 overs)**	**230**

PAKISTAN	O	M	R	W		O	M	R	W
Mohammad Amir	19	2	59	2		22	4	86	1
Sohail Khan	25	6	99	4		17	2	69	0
Imran Khan	20.4	5	52	3		20.3	4	76	3
Wahab Riaz	18	4	57	1		19	3	53	1
Azhar Ali	1	0	4	0		6	0	19	0
Asad Shafiq						1	0	4	0
NEW ZEALAND									
Southee	21	4	80	6		24	6	60	2
Henry	19	5	30	0		19	5	38	1
De Grandhomme	9	2	29	1	(5)	12	5	17	1
Wagner	14	2	59	3	(3)	20.1	4	57	3
Santner	4	0	13	0	(4)	16	2	49	2
Williamson						1	0	2	0

FALL OF WICKETS

	NZ	P	NZ	P
Wkt	*1st*	*1st*	*2nd*	*2nd*
1st	5	7	11	131
2nd	39	8	107	159
3rd	90	12	159	181
4th	113	51	219	199
5th	119	51	254	204
6th	170	125	–	218
7th	203	192	–	229
8th	239	193	–	230
9th	270	206	–	230
10th	271	216	–	230

Umpires: S.D.Fry (*Australia*) (4) and S.Ravi (*India*) (17).
Referee: R.B.Richardson (*West Indies*) (6). **Test No. 2239/55 (NZ417/P403)**

AUSTRALIA v PAKISTAN (1st Test)

At Woolloongabba, Brisbane, on 15, 16, 17, 18, 19 December 2016 (day/night).
Toss: Australia. Result: **AUSTRALIA** won by 39 runs.
Debuts: None.

AUSTRALIA

M.T.Renshaw	c Ahmed b Riaz	71	(2)	c Khan b Rahat	6
D.A.Warner	lbw b Amir	32	(1)	c Riaz b Amir	12
U.T.Khawaja	c Misbah b Shah	4		c Misbah b Rahat	74
*S.P.D.Smith	c Ahmed b Riaz	130		c Rahat b Shah	63
P.S.P.Handscomb	b Riaz	105		not out	35
N.J.Maddinson	c Ahmed b Riaz	1		c Azam b Riaz	4
†M.S.Wade	c Azhar b Amir	7		not out	1
M.A.Starc	c Shafiq b Amir	10			
J.R.Hazlewood	c Shafiq b Amir	8			
N.M.Lyon	c Shafiq b Shah	29			
J.M.Bird	not out	19			
Extras	(LB 5, W 1, NB 7)	13		(B 2, LB 4, NB 1)	7
Total	**(130.1 overs)**	**429**		**(5 wkts dec; 39 overs)**	**202**

PAKISTAN

Sami Aslam	c Wade b Bird	22		c Renshaw b Starc	15
Azhar Ali	c Khawaja b Starc	5		c Wade b Starc	71
Babar Azam	c Smith b Hazlewood	19		c Smith b Lyon	14
Younus Khan	c Wade b Hazlewood	0		c Smith b Lyon	65
*Misbah-ul-Haq	c Renshaw b Bird	4		c Wade b Bird	5
Asad Shafiq	c Khawaja b Starc	2		c Warner b Starc	137
†Sarfraz Ahmed	not out	59		b Starc	24
Wahab Riaz	c and b Hazlewood	1	(9)	c Smith b Bird	30
Yasir Shah	c Khawaja b Starc	1	(10)	run out	33
Mohammad Amir	c Wade b Bird	21	(8)	c Wade b Bird	48
Rahat Ali	run out	4		not out	1
Extras	(LB 3, W 1)	4		(LB 5, W 2)	7
Total	**(55 overs)**	**142**		**(145 overs)**	**450**

PAKISTAN	O	M	R	W	O	M	R	W
Mohammad Amir	31	7	97	4	8	0	37	1
Rahat Ali	22	5	74	0	10	1	40	2
Yasir Shah	43.1	6	129	2	10	1	45	1
Wahab Riaz	26	4	89	4	7	1	47	1
Azhar Ali	8	0	35	0	4	0	27	0
AUSTRALIA								
Starc	18	2	63	3	38	10	119	4
Hazlewood	14	1	22	3	42	11	99	0
Bird	12	6	23	3	33	6	110	3
Lyon	11	2	31	0	29	3	108	2
Maddinson					3	0	9	0

FALL OF WICKETS

	A	P	A	P
Wkt	*1st*	*1st*	*2nd*	*2nd*
1st	70	6	12	31
2nd	75	43	24	54
3rd	151	43	135	145
4th	323	48	188	165
5th	334	54	199	173
6th	342	56	–	220
7th	354	66	–	312
8th	380	67	–	378
9th	380	121	–	449
10th	429	142	–	450

Umpires: I.J.Gould (*England*) (57) and R.K.Illingworth (*England*) (24).
Referee: R.S.Madugalle (*Sri Lanka*) (173). **Test No. 2240/60 (A794/P404)**

AUSTRALIA v PAKISTAN (2nd Test)

At Melbourne Cricket Ground, on 26, 27, 28, 29, 30 December 2016.
Toss: Pakistan. Result: **AUSTRALIA** won by an innings and 18 runs.
Debuts: None.

PAKISTAN

Sami Aslam	c Smith b Lyon	9	b Hazlewood	2
Azhar Ali	not out	205	lbw b Hazlewood	43
Babar Azam	c Smith b Hazlewood	23	lbw b Starc	3
Younus Khan	b Bird	21	c Handscomb b Lyon	24
*Misbah-ul-Haq	c Maddinson b Bird	11	c Maddinson b Lyon	0
Asad Shafiq	c Smith b Bird	50	c Handscomb b Lyon	16
†Sarfraz Ahmed	c Renshaw b Hazlewood	10	b Starc	43
Mohammad Amir	c Wade b Starc	29	b Bird	11
Sohail Khan	run out	65	not out	10
Wahab Riaz	c and b Hazlewood	1	b Starc	0
Yasir Shah			c Bird b Starc	0
Extras	(B 4, LB 9, W 5, NB 1)	19	(B 4, LB 5, W 2)	11
Total	**(9 wkts dec; 126.3 overs)**	**443**	**(53.2 overs)**	**163**

AUSTRALIA

M.T.Renshaw	b Shah	10
D.A.Warner	c Ahmed b Riaz	144
U.T.Khawaja	c Ahmed b Riaz	97
*S.P.D.Smith	not out	165
P.S.P.Handscomb	c Aslam b Sohail	54
N.J.Maddinson	b Shah	22
†M.S.Wade	c Shafiq b Sohail	9
M.A.Starc	c Shafiq b Sohail	84
N.M.Lyon	c and b Shah	12
J.R.Hazlewood		
J.M.Bird		
Extras	(B 1, LB 12, W 1, NB 13)	27
Total	**(8 wkts dec; 142 overs)**	**624**

AUSTRALIA	O	M	R	W	O	M	R	W
Starc	31	6	125	1	15.2	4	36	4
Hazlewood	32.3	11	50	3	13	3	39	2
Bird	34	5	113	3	11	2	46	1
Lyon	23	1	115	1	14	4	33	3
Smith	3	0	9	0				
Maddinson	3	0	18	0				
PAKISTAN								
Mohammad Amir	33	6	91	0				
Sohail Khan	31	7	131	3				
Yasir Shah	41	2	207	3				
Wahab Riaz	32	5	147	2				
Azhar Ali	5	0	35	0				

FALL OF WICKETS	P	A	P
Wkt	*1st*	*1st*	*2nd*
1st	18	46	3
2nd	60	244	6
3rd	111	282	63
4th	125	374	63
5th	240	433	89
6th	268	454	101
7th	317	608	143
8th	435	624	153
9th	443	–	159
10th	–	–	163

Umpires: I.J.Gould (*England*) (58) and S.Ravi (*India*) (18).
Referee: R.S.Madugalle (*Sri Lanka*) (174). **Test No. 2241/61 (A795/P405)**

AUSTRALIA v PAKISTAN (3rd Test)

At Sydney Cricket Ground, on 3, 4, 5, 6, 7 January 2017.
Toss: Australia. Result: **AUSTRALIA** won by 220 runs.
Debuts: Australia – H.W.R Cartwright, Pakistan – Sharjeel Khan. ‡ (J.M.Bird)

AUSTRALIA

M.T.Renshaw	b Imran	184			
D.A.Warner	c Ahmed b Riaz	113	(1)	b Riaz	55
U.T.Khawaja	c Ahmed b Riaz	13	(2)	not out	79
*S.P.D.Smith	c Ahmed b Shah	24	(3)	c Ahmed b Shah	59
P.S.P.Handscomb	hit wkt b Riaz	110	(4)	not out	40
H.W.R.Cartwright	b Imran	37			
†M.S.Wade	c Azam b Ali	29			
M.A.Starc	c sub (Mohammad Rizwan) b Ali	16			
S.N.J.O'Keefe	not out	0			
J.R.Hazlewood					
N.M.Lyon					
Extras	(B 5, LB 1, W 2, NB 4)	12		(B 3, LB 3, W 1, NB 1)	8
Total	**(8 wkts dec; 135 overs)**	**538**		**(2 wkts dec; 32 overs)**	**241**

PAKISTAN

Azhar Ali	run out	71		c and b Hazlewood	11
Sharjeel Khan	c Renshaw b Hazlewood	4		c Warner b Lyon	40
Babar Azam	lbw b Hazlewood	0	(4)	lbw b Hazlewood	9
Younus Khan	not out	175	(5)	c Hazlewood b Lyon	13
*Misbah-ul-Haq	c sub‡ b Lyon	18	(6)	c Lyon b O'Keefe	38
Asad Shafiq	c Smith b O'Keefe	4	(7)	b Starc	30
†Sarfraz Ahmed	c sub‡ b Starc	18	(8)	not out	72
Mohammad Amir	c Warner b Lyon	4	(10)	run out	5
Wahab Riaz	b Lyon	8		c Wade b O'Keefe	12
Yasir Shah	c Smith b Hazlewood	10	(3)	c sub‡ b O'Keefe	13
Imran Khan	b Hazlewood	0		c sub‡ b Hazlewood	0
Extras	(B 3)	3		(NB 1)	1
Total	**(110.3 overs)**	**315**		**(80.2 overs)**	**244**

PAKISTAN	O	M	R	W		O	M	R	W
Mohammad Amir	24	2	83	0					
Imran Khan	27	4	111	2	(1)	6	2	43	0
Wahab Riaz	28	4	89	3		7	0	28	1
Yasir Shah	40	2	167	1	(2)	14	0	124	1
Azhar Ali	14	0	70	2	(4)	5	0	40	0
Asad Shafiq	2	0	12	0					
AUSTRALIA									
Starc	26	7	77	1		17	2	57	1
Hazlewood	27.3	7	55	4		18.2	7	29	3
O'Keefe	20	3	50	1	(4)	17	4	53	3
Lyon	33	3	115	3	(3)	27	6	100	2
Cartwright	4	0	15	0					
Smith					(5)	1	0	5	0

FALL OF WICKETS				
	A	P	A	P
Wkt	*1st*	*1st*	*2nd*	*2nd*
1st	151	6	71	51
2nd	203	6	174	55
3rd	244	152	–	67
4th	386	178	–	82
5th	477	197	–	96
6th	516	239	–	136
7th	532	244	–	188
8th	538	264	–	202
9th	–	315	–	224
10th	–	315	–	244

Umpires: R.K.Illingworth (*England*) (25) and S.Ravi (*India*) (19).
Referee: R.S.Madugalle (*Sri Lanka*) (175). **Test No. 2242/62 (A796/P406)**

SOUTH AFRICA v SRI LANKA (1st Test)

At St George's Park, Port Elizabeth, on 26, 27, 28, 29, 30 December 2016.
Toss: South Africa. Result: **SOUTH AFRICA** won by 206 runs.
Debuts: None.

SOUTH AFRICA

S.C.Cook	c Chandimal b Lakmal	59	c Chandimal b Chameera	117
D.Elgar	c Chandimal b Lakmal	45	c Mathews b Lakmal	52
H.M.Amla	c Chandimal b Lakmal	20	lbw b Fernando	48
J.P.Duminy	lbw b Herath	63	c Mathews b de Silva	25
*F.du Plessis	c Karunaratne b Lakmal	37	not out	67
T.Bavuma	lbw b Herath	3	c Mendis b de Silva	8
†Q.de Kock	b Fernando	37	not out	69
V.D.Philander	c Chameera b Fernando	13		
K.A.Maharaj	c Chandimal b Lakmal	0		
K.J.Abbott	run out	0		
K.Rabada	not out	0		
Extras	(LB 3, W 1, NB 5)	9	(B 5, LB 2, W 3, NB 10)	20
Total	**(98.5 overs)**	**286**	**(6 wkts dec; 90.5 overs)**	**406**

SRI LANKA

F.D.M.Karunaratne	b Abbott	5	run out	43
J.K.Silva	lbw b Philander	16	lbw b Rabada	48
M.D.K.J.Perera	c de Kock b Philander	7	c de Kock b Maharaj	6
B.K.G.Mendis	c de Kock b Abbott	0	c de Kock b Rabada	58
*A.D.Mathews	c Elgar b Rabada	39	lbw b Abbott	59
†L.D.Chandimal	lbw b Philander	28	c Rabada b Maharaj	8
D.M.de Silva	c de Kock b Philander	43	lbw b Abbott	22
H.M.R.K.B.Herath	lbw b Maharaj	24	c and b Philander	3
P.V.D.Chameera	c Amla b Abbott	19	c de Kock b Rabada	0
R.A.S.Lakmal	c Abbott b Philander	4	not out	19
A.N.P.R.Fernando	not out	8	b Maharaj	4
Extras	(LB 4, W 5 NB 3)	12	(B 4, LB 3, W 3, NB 1)	11
Total	**(64.5 overs)**	**205**	**(96.3 overs)**	**281**

SRI LANKA	O	M	R	W	O	M	R	W
Lakmal	27	9	63	5	18	2	64	1
Fernando	21.5	5	66	2	14	0	65	1
Mathews	13	5	26	0	4	0	10	0
Chameera	14	1	68	0	15	0	85	1
Herath	20	4	48	2	24.5	1	84	1
De Silva	3	0	12	0	15	0	91	2
SOUTH AFRICA								
Philander	20	7	45	5	22	5	65	1
Abbott	21.5	4	63	3	20	6	38	2
Rabada	13	3	63	1	21	4	77	3
Maharaj	10	3	30	1	30.3	7	86	3
Duminy					3	0	8	0

FALL OF WICKETS

	SA	SL	SA	SL
Wkt	*1st*	*1st*	*2nd*	*2nd*
1st	104	10	116	87
2nd	105	19	221	93
3rd	178	22	245	118
4th	213	61	267	193
5th	225	94	277	225
6th	253	121	406	246
7th	276	157	–	258
8th	276	181	–	258
9th	281	185	–	274
10th	286	205	–	281

Umpires: Alim Dar (*Pakistan*) (108) and B.N.J.Oxenford (*Australia*) (36).
Referee: D.C.Boon (*Australia*) (36). **Test No. 2243/23 (SA406/SL254)**

SOUTH AFRICA v SRI LANKA (2nd Test)

At Newlands, Cape Town, on 2, 3, 4, 5 January 2017.
Toss: Sri Lanka. Result: **SOUTH AFRICA** won by 282 runs.
Debuts: None.

SOUTH AFRICA					
S.C.Cook	c Mendis b Lakmal	0		c Karunaratne b Lakmal	30
D.Elgar	c Mendis b Lakmal	129		c Mathews b Herath	55
H.M.Amla	b Kumara	29		c Chandimal b Lakmal	0
J.P.Duminy	c Mendis b Kumara	0		lbw b Lakmal	30
*F.du Plessis	c Mathews b Herath	38		c Chandimal b Lakmal	41
T.Bavuma	c Tharanga b Kumara	10		run out	0
†Q.de Kock	c Chandimal b Kumara	101		c Chandimal b Kumara	29
K.J.Abbott	c Chandimal b Herath	16			
V.D.Philander	c Chandimal b Kumara	20		not out	15
K.A.Maharaj	not out	32	(8)	not out	20
K.Rabada	c Chandimal b Kumara	8			
Extras	(LB 3, W 5, NB 1)	9		(W 1, NB 3)	4
Total	**(116 overs)**	**392**		**(7 wkts dec; 51.5 overs)**	**224**

SRI LANKA				
F.D.M.Karunaratne	c Bavuma b Rabada	24	b Philander	6
J.K.Silva	b Rabada	11	c Cook b Rabada	29
B.K.G.Mendis	c Duminy b Maharaj	11	c Elgar b Philander	4
D.M.de Silva	lbw b Maharaj	16	lbw b Rabada	22
*A.D.Mathews	c du Plessis b Rabada	2	c de Kock b Rabada	49
†L.D.Chandimal	c de Kock b Rabada	4	c Cook b Rabada	30
W.U.Tharanga	not out	26	c de Kock b Rabada	12
H.M.R.K.B.Herath	lbw b Philander	1	not out	35
R.A.S.Lakmal	c Amla b Philander	0	c de Kock b Rabada	10
C.B.R.L.S.Kumara	b Philander	4	st de Kock b Maharaj	9
A.N.P.R.Fernando	c du Plessis b Philander	0	b Philander	5
Extras	(LB 5, W 5 NB 1)	11	(B 6, LB 5, NB 2)	13
Total	**(43 overs)**	**110**	**(62 overs)**	**224**

SRI LANKA	O	M	R	W		O	M	R	W
Lakmal	27	4	93	2		19.5	2	69	4
Fernando	15.4	3	46	0		11	0	46	0
Mathews	17	3	41	0					
Kumara	25	1	122	6	(3)	12	0	62	1
Herath	23.2	4	57	2		6	0	32	1
De Silva	8	0	30	0	(4)	3	0	15	0
SOUTH AFRICA									
Philander	12	4	27	4	(2)	14	1	48	3
Abbott	8	3	9	0	(1)	15	3	46	0
Rabada	12	2	37	4		17	3	55	6
Maharaj	11	1	32	2		16	3	64	1

FALL OF WICKETS	SA	SL	SA	SL
Wkt	*1st*	*1st*	*2nd*	*2nd*
1st	0	31	64	11
2nd	66	56	64	25
3rd	66	56	110	66
4th	142	60	136	69
5th	169	78	137	144
6th	272	78	170	165
7th	303	100	192	166
8th	336	100	–	178
9th	376	110	–	211
10th	392	110	–	224

Umpires: Alim Dar (*Pakistan*) (109) and R.J.Tucker (*Australia*) (50).
Referee: D.C.Boon (*Australia*) (37). **Test No. 2244/24 (SA407/SL255)**

SOUTH AFRICA v SRI LANKA (3rd Test)

At New Wanderers Stadium, Johannesburg, on 12, 13, 14 January 2017.
Toss: South Africa. Result: **SOUTH AFRICA** won by an innings and 118 runs.
Debut: South Africa – D.Olivier.

SOUTH AFRICA

S.C.Cook	lbw b Mendis	10
D.Elgar	c Karunaratne b Kumara	27
H.M.Amla	c Chandimal b Fernando	134
J.P.Duminy	c Mendis b Kumara	155
D.Olivier	c Chandimal b Mathews	3
*F.du Plessis	c Mendis b Fernando	16
T.Bavuma	c Silva b Fernando	0
†Q.de Kock	c de Silva b Kumara	34
V.D.Philander	c Chandimal b Fernando	0
W.D.Parnell	c Tharanga b Kumara	23
K.Rabada	not out	0
Extras	(B 11, LB 8, W 4, NB 1)	24
Total	**(124.1 overs)**	**426**

SRI LANKA

F.D.M.Karunaratne	c de Kock b Philander	0	b Rabada	50
J.K.Silva	c de Kock b Rabada	13	c de Kock b Rabada	0
B.K.G.Mendis	c Duminy b Rabada	41	b Parnell	24
D.M.de Silva	c Bavuma b Philander	10	c du Plessis b Olivier	12
*A.D.Mathews	c de Kock b Rabada	19	c du Plessis b Olivier	10
†L.D.Chandimal	c de Kock b Philander	5	c Amla b Philander	10
W.U.Tharanga	c Elgar b Olivier	24	c Duminy b Parnell	26
H.M.R.K.B.Herath	c Cook b Olivier	8	c Bavuma b Parnell	10
R.A.S.Lakmal	c Rabada b Parnell	4	c Philander b Parnell	31
C.B.R.L.S.Kumara	not out	1	c Cook b Olivier	0
A.N.P.R.Fernando	c and b Parnell	4	not out	0
Extras	(LB 2)	2	(LB 2, W 1, NB 1)	4
Total	**(45.4 overs)**	**131**	**(42.3 overs)**	**177**

SRI LANKA	O	M	R	W		O	M	R	W
Lakmal	30	8	81	0					
Fernando	27	8	78	4					
Mathews	20	6	52	2					
Kumara	25.1	2	107	4					
Herath	14	0	67	0					
De Silva	8	1	22	0					
SOUTH AFRICA									
Philander	14	5	28	3		10	1	35	1
Parnell	10.4	2	38	2	(3)	10.3	1	51	4
Olivier	9	3	19	2	(4)	9	2	38	3
Rabada	12	3	44	3	(2)	12	3	50	2
Duminy						1	0	1	0

FALL OF WICKETS

	SA	SL	SL
Wkt	*1st*	*1st*	*2nd*
1st	45	0	2
2nd	45	47	39
3rd	337	62	59
4th	346	70	87
5th	364	90	108
6th	364	100	108
7th	367	108	134
8th	378	126	177
9th	425	126	177
10th	426	131	177

Umpires: B.N.J.Oxenford (*Australia*) (37) and R.J.Tucker (*Australia*) (51).
Referee: D.C.Boon (*Australia*) (38). **Test No. 2245/25 (SA408/SL256)**

NEW ZEALAND v BANGLADESH (1st Test)

At Basin Reserve, Wellington, on 12, 13, 14, 15, 16 January 2017.
Toss: New Zealand. Result: **NEW ZEALAND** won by seven wickets.
Debuts: Bangladesh – Subashis Roy, Taskin Ahmed.

BANGLADESH

Tamim Iqbal	lbw b Boult	56		b Santner	25
Imrul Kayes	c Boult b Southee	1		not out	36
Mominul Haque	c Watling b Southee	64		c de Grandhomme b Wagner	23
Mahmudullah	c Watling b Wagner	26		c Watling b Wagner	5
Shakib Al Hasan	b Wagner	217	(6)	c Williamson b Santner	0
†*Mushfiqur Rahim	c Watling b Boult	159	(8)	retired hurt	13
Sabbir Rahman	not out	54		c Watling b Boult	50
Mehedi Hasan	c Southee b Wagner	0	(5)	run out	1
Taskin Ahmed	c Southee b Wagner	3		b Boult	5
Kamrul Islam	not out	6		c de Grandhomme b Southee	1
Subashis Roy				b Boult	0
Extras	(B 2, LB 6, NB 1)	9		(NB 1)	1
Total	**(8 wkts dec; 152 overs)**	**595**		**(57.5 overs)**	**160**

NEW ZEALAND

J.A.Raval	c Imrul b Kamrul	27	(2)	c and b Mehedi	13
T.W.M.Latham	lbw b Shakib	177	(1)	b Mehedi	16
*K.S.Williamson	c Imrul b Taskin	53		not out	104
L.R.P.L.Taylor	c Mahmudullah b Kamrul	40		c Mehedi b Subashis	60
H.M.Nicholls	c Mehedi b Shakib	53		not out	4
C.de Grandhomme	c Imrul b Subashis	14			
†B.J.Watling	c Imrul b Mahmudullah	49			
M.J.Santner	b Subashis	73			
T.G.Southee	lbw b Mahmudullah	1			
N.Wagner	c Imrul b Kamrul	18			
T.A.Boult	not out	4			
Extras	(B 10, LB 3, W 16, NB 1)	30		(B 14, LB 6)	20
Total	**(148.2 overs)**	**539**		**(3 wkts; 39.4 overs)**	**217**

NEW ZEALAND	O	M	R	W		O	M	R	W
Boult	34	5	131	2		13.5	3	53	3
Southee	34	5	158	2		13	5	34	1
De Grandhomme	20	2	65	0					
Wagner	44	8	151	4		15	3	37	2
Santner	17	2	62	0	(3)	16	5	36	2
Williamson	3	0	20	0					
BANGLADESH									
Mehedi Hasan	37	5	116	0	(2)	11.4	0	66	2
Subashis Roy	26.2	6	89	2	(5)	5	0	32	1
Taskin Ahmed	29	4	141	1	(4)	6	0	38	0
Kamrul Islam	26	4	87	3	(1)	7	0	31	0
Shakib Al Hasan	27	2	78	2	(3)	10	0	30	0
Mahmudullah	3	0	15	2					

FALL OF WICKETS

	B	NZ	B	NZ
Wkt	*1st*	*1st*	*2nd*	*2nd*
1st	16	54	50	32
2nd	60	131	63	39
3rd	145	205	66	202
4th	160	347	66	–
5th	519	366	96	–
6th	536	398	137	–
7th	542	471	148	–
8th	566	473	152	–
9th	–	504	160	–
10th	–	539	–	–

Umpires: M.Erasmus (*South Africa*) (40) and P.R.Reiffel (*Australia*) (29).
Referee: J.Srinath (*India*) (34). **Test No. 2246/12 (NZ418/B96)**

Imrul Kayes retired hurt on 24* at 46-0 and resumed at 148-7; Mushfiqur Rahim retired hurt at 114-5.

NEW ZEALAND v BANGLADESH (2nd Test)

At Hagley Oval, Christchurch, on 20, 21, 22, 23 January 2017.
Toss: New Zealand. Result: **NEW ZEALAND** won by nine wickets.
Debuts: Bangladesh – Nazmul Hossain, Nurul Hasan.

BANGLADESH

*Tamim Iqbal	c Watling b Southee	5		c Santner b Southee	8
Soumya Sarkar	c de Grandhomme b Boult	86		c Raval b de Grandhomme	36
Mahmudullah	c Watling b Boult	19		b Wagner	38
Shakib Al Hasan	c Watling b Southee	59		c de Grandhomme b Southee	8
Sabbir Rahman	c Southee b Boult	7	(6)	c Watling b Wagner	0
Nazmul Hossain	c Raval b Southee	18	(5)	b Boult	12
†Nurul Hasan	c Watling b Boult	47		c Watling b Wagner	0
Mehedi Hasan	b Wagner	10		c Latham b Boult	4
Taskin Ahmed	c Williamson b Southee	8		b Boult	33
Kamrul Islam	lbw b Southee	2		not out	25
Rubel Hossain	not out	16		c Watling b Southee	7
Extras	(B 4, LB 2, W 5, NB 1)	12		(LB 2)	2
Total	**(84.3 overs)**	**289**		**(52.5 overs)**	**173**

NEW ZEALAND

J.A.Raval	b Kamrul	16		b Kamrul	33
T.W.M.Latham	c Nurul b Taskin	68		not out	41
*K.S.Williamson	c Nurul b Kamrul	2			
L.R.P.L.Taylor	c sub (Taijul Islam) b Mehedi	77			
H.M.Nicholls	b Mehedi	98			
M.J.Santner	lbw b Shakib	29			
†B.J.Watling	b Shakib	1			
C.de Grandhomme	b Shakib	0	(3)	not out	33
T.G.Southee	c Mehedi b Shakib	17			
N.Wagner	run out	26			
T.A.Boult	not out	7			
Extras	(LB 6, W 4, NB 3)	13		(B 1, W 1, NB 2)	4
Total	**(148.2 overs)**	**354**		**(1 wkt; 18.4 overs)**	**111**

NEW ZEALAND	O	M	R	W		O	M	R	W
Boult	24	4	87	4		17	3	52	3
Southee	28.3	7	94	5		12.5	2	48	3
De Grandhomme	14	4	58	0		11	3	27	1
Wagner	18	1	44	1		12	3	44	3
BANGLADESH									
Taskin Ahmed	22	2	86	1		5	0	21	0
Mehedi Hasan	19	3	59	2		6	0	27	0
Rubel Hossain	17	2	65	0					
Kamrul Islam	19	4	78	2	(3)	3	0	21	1
Shakib Al Hasan	12.4	1	50	4	(4)	4	0	28	0
Soumya Sarkar	3	0	10	0					
Nazmul Hossain					(5)	0.4	0	13	0

FALL OF WICKETS

	B	NZ	B	NZ
Wkt	*1st*	*1st*	*2nd*	*2nd*
1st	7	45	17	56
2nd	38	47	58	–
3rd	165	153	73	–
4th	177	177	92	–
5th	179	252	100	–
6th	232	256	100	–
7th	248	256	106	–
8th	257	286	115	–
9th	273	343	166	–
10th	289	354	173	–

Umpires: N.J.Llong (*England*) (40) and P.R.Reiffel (*Australia*) (30).
Referee: J.Srinath (*India*) (35). **Test No. 2247/13 (NZ419/B97)**

INDIA v BANGLADESH (Only Test)

At Rajiv Gandhi International Stadium, Uppal, Hyderabad, on 9, 10, 11, 12, 13 February 2017.
Toss: India. Result: **INDIA** won by 208 runs.
Debuts: Bangladesh – Nazmul Hossain, Nurul Hasan.

INDIA				
K.L.Rahul	b Taskin	2	(2) c Mushfiqur b Taskin	10
M.Vijay	b Taijul	108	(1) c Mushfiqur b Taskin	7
C.A.Pujara	c Mushfiqur b Mehedi	83	not out	54
*V.Kohli	lbw b Taijul	204	c Mahmudullah b Shakib	38
A.M.Rahane	c Mehedi b Taijul	82	b Shakib	28
†W.P.Saha	not out	106		
R.Ashwin	c Soumya b Mehedi	34		
R.A.Jadeja	not out	60	(6) not out	16
B.Kumar				
U.T.Yadav				
I.Sharma				
Extras	(LB 5, W 1, NB 2)	8	(LB 5, W 1)	6
Total	**(6 wkts dec; 166 overs)**	**687**	**(4 wkts dec; 29 overs)**	**159**

BANGLADESH				
Tamim Iqbal	run out	24	c Kohli b Ashwin	3
Soumya Sarkar	c Saha b Yadav	15	c Rahane b Jadeja	42
Mominul Haque	lbw b Yadav	12	c Rahane b Ashwin	27
Mahmudullah	lbw b Sharma	28	c Kumar b Sharma	64
Shakib Al Hasan	c Yadav b Ashwin	82	c Pujara b Jadeja	22
†*Mushfiqur Rahim	c Saha b Ashwin	127	c Jadeja b Ashwin	23
Sabbir Rahman	lbw b Jadeja	16	lbw b Sharma	22
Mehedi Hasan	b Kumar	51	c Saha b Jadeja	23
Taijul Islam	c Saha b Yadav	10	(10) c Rahul b Jadeja	6
Taskin Ahmed	c Rahane b Jadeja	8	(11) lbw b Ashwin	1
Kamrul Islam	not out	0	(9) not out	3
Extras	(LB 15)	15	(B 4, LB 7, NB 3)	14
Total	**(127.5 overs)**	**388**	**(100.3 overs)**	**250**

BANGLADESH	O	M	R	W		O	M	R	W
Taskin Ahmed	25	2	127	1	(2)	7	0	43	2
Kamrul Islam	19	1	100	0					
Soumya Sarkar	1	0	4	0					
Mehedi Hasan	42	0	165	2		7	0	32	0
Shakib Al Hasan	24	4	104	0	(3)	9	0	50	2
Taijul Islam	47	6	156	3	(1)	6	1	29	0
Sabbir Rahman	3	0	10	0					
Mahmudullah	5	0	16	0					
INDIA									
Kumar	21	7	52	1		8	4	15	0
Sharma	20	5	69	1	(3)	13	3	40	2
Ashwin	28.5	7	98	2	(2)	30.3	10	73	4
Yadav	25	6	84	3		12	2	33	0
Jadeja	33	8	70	2		37	15	78	4

FALL OF WICKETS	I	B	I	B
Wkt	*1st*	*1st*	*2nd*	*2nd*
1st	2	38	12	11
2nd	180	44	23	71
3rd	234	64	90	75
4th	456	109	128	106
5th	495	216	–	162
6th	569	235	–	213
7th	–	322	–	225
8th	–	339	–	242
9th	–	378	–	249
10th	–	388	–	250

Umpires: M.Erasmus (*South Africa*) (41) and J.S.Wilson (*West Indies*) (4).
Referee: A.J.Pycroft (*Zimbabwe*) (52). **Test No. 2248/9 (I508/B98)**

INTERNATIONAL UMPIRES AND REFEREES 2017

ELITE PANEL OF UMPIRES 2017

The Elite Panel of ICC Umpires and Referees was introduced in April 2002 to raise standards and guarantee impartial adjudication. Two umpires from this panel stand in Test matches while one officiates with a home umpire from the Supplementary International Panel in limited-overs internationals.

Full Names	*Birthdate*	*Birthplace*	*Tests*	*Debut*	*LOI*	*Debut*
ALIM Sarwar DAR	06.06.68	Jhang, Pakistan	109	2003-04	182	1999-00
DHARMASENA, H.D.P.Kumar	24.04.71	Colombo, Sri Lanka	43	2010-11	76	2008-09
ERASMUS, Marais	27.02.64	George, South Africa	41	2009-10	67	2007-08
GAFFANEY, Christopher Blair	30.11.75	Dunedin, New Zealand	12	2014	48	2010
GOULD, Ian James	19.08.57	Taplow, England	58	2008-09	114	2006
ILLINGWORTH, Richard Keith	23.08.63	Bradford, England	25	2012-13	51	2010
KETTLEBOROUGH, Richard Allan	15.03.73	Sheffield, England	41	2010-11	68	2009
LLONG, Nigel James	11.02.69	Ashford, England	40	2007-08	107	2006
OXENFORD, Bruce Nicholas James	05.03.60	Southport, Australia	37	2010-11	80	2007-08
RAVI, Sundaram	22.04.66	Bangalore, India	19	2013-14	27	2011-12
REIFFEL, Paul Ronald	19.04.66	Box Hill, Australia	30	2012	46	2008-09
TUCKER, Rodney James	28.08.64	Sydney, Australia	51	2009-10	64	2008-09

ELITE PANEL OF REFEREES 2017

Full Names	*Birthdate*	*Birthplace*	*Tests*	*Debut*	*LOI*	*Debut*
BOON, David Clarence	29.12.60	Launceston, Australia	38	2011	88	2011
BROAD, Brian Christopher	29.09.57	Bristol, England	82	2003-04	281	2003-04
CROWE, Jeffrey John	14.09.58	Auckland, New Zealand	81	2004-05	250	2003-04
MADUGALLE, Ranjan Senerath	22.04.59	Kandy, Sri Lanka	175	1993-94	304	1993-94
PYCROFT, Andrew John	06.06.56	Harare, Zimbabwe	52	2009	126	2009
RICHARDSON, Sir Richard Benjamin	12.01.62	Five Islands, Antigua	6	2016	19	2016
SRINATH, Javagal	31.08.69	Mysore, India	35	2006	192	2006-07

INTERNATIONAL UMPIRES PANEL 2017

Nominated by their respective cricket boards, members from this panel officiate in home LOIs and supplement the Elite panel for Test matches. Specialist third umpires have been selected to undertake adjudication involving television replays. The number of Test matches/LOI in which they have stood is shown in brackets.

			Third Umpire
Australia	M.D.Martell (-/8)	S.D.Fry (5/31)	S.J.Nogajski (-/-) P.Wilson (-/6)
Bangladesh	Anisur Rahman (-/5)	Sharfuddoula (-/30)	Masudur Rahman (-/-)
England	R.J.Bailey (-/16)	M.A.Gough (4/31)	R.T.Robinson (-/10)
India	C.Shamshuddin (-/21)	A.K.Chaudhary (-/9)	C.K.Nandan (-/2) N.N.Menon (-/-)
New Zealand	W.J.Knights (-/2)	C.M.Brown (-/3)	S.B.Haig (-/-)
Pakistan	Shozab Raza (-/14)	Ahsan Raza (-/22)	Ahmed Shahab (-/4)
South Africa	A.T.Holdstock (-/8)	S.George (-/20)	P.B.Jele (-/-)
Sri Lanka	R.E.J.Martinesz (8/39)	R.S.A.Palliyaguruge (-/39)	R.R.Wimalasiri (-/7)
West Indies	G.O.Brathwaite (-/20)	J.S.Wilson (4/34)	L.S.Reifer (-/-) N.Duguid (-/-)
Zimbabwe	R.B.Tiffin (44/151)	T.J.Matibiri (-/20)	L.Rusere (-/3)

Test Match and LOI statistics to 18 February 2017.

TEST MATCH CAREER RECORDS

These records, complete to 22 February 2017, contain all players registered for county cricket in 2017 at the time of going to press, plus those who have played Test cricket since 10 December 2015 (Test No. 2191 and 2193).

ENGLAND – BATTING AND FIELDING

	M	*I*	*NO*	*HS*	*Runs*	*Avge*	*100*	*50*	*Ct/St*
M.M.Ali	37	62	7	155*	1927	35.03	5	9	19
T.R.Ambrose	11	16	1	102	447	29.80	1	3	31
J.M.Anderson	122	168	61	81	1093	10.21	–	1	77
Z.S.Ansari	3	5	–	32	49	9.80	–	–	1
J.M.Bairstow	38	65	6	167*	2435	41.27	3	14	93/5
J.T.Ball	3	6	–	31	52	8.66	–	–	1
G.S.Ballance	21	38	2	156	1413	39.25	4	7	20
G.J.Batty	9	12	2	38	149	14.90	–	–	3
I.R.Bell	118	205	24	235	7727	42.69	22	46	100
R.S.Bopara	13	19	1	143	575	31.94	3	–	6
S.G.Borthwick	1	2	–	4	5	2.50	–	–	2
T.T.Bresnan	23	26	4	91	575	26.13	–	3	8
S.C.J.Broad	102	145	19	169	2691	21.35	1	10	32
J.C.Buttler	18	30	5	85	784	31.36	–	6	54
M.A.Carberry	6	12	–	60	345	28.75	–	1	7
R.Clarke	2	3	–	55	96	32.00	–	1	1
P.D.Collingwood	68	115	10	206	4259	40.56	10	20	96
N.R.D.Compton	16	30	3	117	775	28.70	2	2	7
A.N.Cook	140	253	15	294	11057	46.45	30	53	141
L.A.Dawson	1	2	1	66*	66	66.00	–	1	–
B.M.Duckett	4	7	–	56	110	15.71	–	1	1
S.T.Finn	36	47	22	56	279	11.16	–	1	8
J.S.Foster	7	12	3	48	226	25.11	–	–	17/1
A.D.Hales	11	21	–	94	573	27.28	–	5	8
H.Hameed	3	6	1	82	219	43.80	–	2	4
K.K.Jennings	2	4	–	112	167	41.75	1	1	2
C.J.Jordan	8	11	1	35	180	18.00	–	–	14
S.C.Kerrigan	1	1	1	1*	1	–	–	–	–
A.Lyth	7	13	–	107	265	20.38	1	–	8
E.J.G.Morgan	16	24	1	130	700	30.43	2	3	11
G.Onions	9	10	7	17*	30	10.00	–	–	–
S.R.Patel	6	9	–	42	151	16.77	–	–	3
K.P.Pietersen	104	181	8	227	8181	47.28	23	35	62
L.E.Plunkett	13	20	5	55*	238	15.86	–	1	3
W.B.Rankin	1	2	–	13	13	6.50	–	–	–
A.U.Rashid	10	18	2	61	295	18.43	–	2	3
C.M.W.Read	15	23	4	55	360	18.94	–	1	48/6
S.D.Robson	7	11	–	127	336	30.54	1	1	5
J.E.Root	53	98	11	254	4594	52.80	11	27	65
A.Shahzad	1	1	–	5	5	5.00	–	–	2
R.J.Sidebottom	22	31	11	31	313	15.65	–	–	5
B.A.Stokes	32	57	1	258	1902	33.96	4	8	22
J.C.Tredwell	2	2	–	37	45	22.50	–	–	2
M.E.Trescothick	76	143	10	219	5825	43.79	14	29	95
I.J.L.Trott	49	87	6	226	3763	46.45	9	18	29
J.M.Vince	7	11	–	42	212	19.27	–	–	3
C.R.Woakes	17	28	8	66	591	29.55	–	2	9
M.A.Wood	8	14	5	32*	185	20.55	–	–	2

TESTS

ENGLAND – BOWLING

	O	M	R	W	Avge	Best	5wI	10wM
M.M.Ali	1111	160	4138	98	42.22	6- 67	2	–
J.M.Anderson	4473.2	1097	13310	467	28.50	7- 43	21	3
Z.S.Ansari	68	3	275	5	55.00	2- 76	–	–
J.T.Ball	76	19	228	2	114.00	1- 47	–	–
G.S.Ballance	2	1	5	0	–	–	–	–
G.J.Batty	285.4	38	914	15	60.93	3- 55	–	–
I.R.Bell	18	3	76	1	76.00	1- 33	–	–
R.S.Bopara	72.2	10	290	1	290.00	1- 39	–	–
S.G.Borthwick	13	0	82	4	20.50	3- 33	–	–
T.T.Bresnan	779	185	2357	72	32.73	5- 48	1	–
S.C.J.Broad	3500	787	10503	368	28.54	8- 15	15	2
R.Clarke	29	11	60	4	15.00	2- 7	–	–
P.D.Collingwood	317.3	51	1018	17	59.88	3- 23	–	–
A.N.Cook	3	0	7	1	7.00	1- 6	–	–
L.A.Dawson	43	4	129	2	64.50	2-129	–	–
S.T.Finn	1068.4	190	3800	125	30.40	6- 79	5	–
A.D.Hales	3	1	2	0	–	–	–	–
K.K.Jennings	5	1	20	0	–	–	–	–
C.J.Jordan	255	74	752	21	35.80	4- 18	–	–
S.C.Kerrigan	8	0	53	0	–	–	–	–
A.Lyth	1	1	0	0	–	–	–	–
G.Onions	267.4	50	957	32	29.90	5- 38	1	–
S.R.Patel	143	23	421	7	60.14	2- 27	–	–
K.P.Pietersen	218.3	15	886	10	88.60	3- 52	–	–
L.E.Plunkett	443.1	71	1536	41	37.46	5- 64	1	–
W.B.Rankin	20.5	0	81	1	81.00	1- 47	–	–
A.U.Rashid	424	32	1626	38	42.78	5- 64	1	–
J.E.Root	237.5	55	721	15	48.06	2- 9	–	–
A.Shahzad	17	4	63	4	15.75	3- 45	–	–
R.J.Sidebottom	802	188	2231	79	28.24	7- 47	5	1
B.A.Stokes	799.1	141	2723	79	34.46	6- 36	3	–
J.C.Tredwell	131	39	321	11	29.18	4- 47	–	–
M.E.Trescothick	50	6	155	1	155.00	1- 34	–	–
I.J.L.Trott	117	11	398	5	79.60	1- 5	–	–
J.M.Vince	4	1	13	0	–	–	–	–
C.R.Woakes	458.2	112	1408	48	29.33	6- 70	2	1
M.A.Wood	254.3	59	860	25	34.40	3- 39	–	–

AUSTRALIA – BATTING AND FIELDING

	M	I	NO	HS	Runs	Avge	100	50	Ct/St
J.M.Bird	8	8	6	19*	39	19.50	–	–	2
J.A.Burns	13	23	–	170	873	37.95	3	4	15
H.W.R.Cartwright	1	1	–	37	37	37.00	–	–	–
C.J.Ferguson	1	2	–	3	4	2.00	–	–	–
P.S.P.Handscomb	4	7	3	110	399	99.75	2	2	3
J.R.Hazlewood	26	28	12	39	253	15.81	–	–	12
M.C.Henriques	4	8	1	81*	164	23.42	–	2	1
J.M.Holland	2	4	3	1	1	1.00	–	–	–
U.T.Khawaja	23	40	4	174	1726	47.94	5	8	18
N.M.Lyon	63	75	28	40*	640	13.61	–	–	31
C.J.McKay	1	1	–	10	10	10.00	–	–	1
N.J.Maddinson	3	4	–	22	27	6.75	–	–	2
M.R.Marsh	19	31	4	87	626	23.18	–	2	9
S.E.Marsh	19	34	1	182	1325	40.15	4	5	16
J.M.Mennie	1	2	–	10	10	5.00	–	–	–
P.M.Nevill	17	23	2	66	468	22.28	–	3	61/2
S.N.J.O'Keefe	4	5	2	23	33	11.00	–	–	–
J.L.Pattinson	17	19	7	42	332	27.66	–	–	4

AUSTRALIA – BATTING AND FIELDING (continued)

	M	I	NO	HS	Runs	Avge	100	50	Ct/St
M.T.Renshaw	4	6	1	184	315	63.00	1	1	5
P.M.Siddle	62	86	14	51	1063	14.76	–	2	16
S.P.D.Smith	50	92	13	215	4752	60.15	17	20	67
M.A.Starc	34	51	12	99	949	24.33	–	8	15
A.C.Voges	20	31	7	269*	1485	61.87	5	4	15
M.S.Wade	16	27	5	106	673	30.59	2	3	47/4
D.A.Warner	60	111	4	253	5261	49.16	18	23	43

AUSTRALIA – BOWLING

	O	M	R	W	Avge	Best	5wI	10wM
J.M.Bird	292.2	75	934	34	27.47	5-59	1	–
H.W.R.Cartwright	4	0	15	0	–	–	–	–
J.R.Hazlewood	954.4	240	2702	109	24.78	6-70	4	–
M.C.Henriques	55	12	164	2	82.00	1-48	–	–
J.M.Holland	82	13	274	5	54.80	2-72	–	–
N.M.Lyon	2427.5	452	7769	228	34.07	7-94	7	1
C.J.McKay	28	5	101	1	101.00	1-56	–	–
N.J.Maddinson	6	0	27	0	–	–	–	–
M.R.Marsh	311.1	59	1081	29	37.27	4-61	–	–
J.M.Mennie	28	5	85	1	85.00	1-85	–	–
S.N.J.O'Keefe	146.5	26	459	14	32.78	3-53	–	–
J.L.Pattinson	546.3	116	1831	70	26.15	5-27	4	–
P.M.Siddle	2156.5	575	6314	211	29.92	6-54	8	–
S.P.D.Smith	207.1	19	891	17	52.41	3-18	–	–
M.A.Starc	1183.5	237	4046	143	28.29	6-50	7	1
A.C.Voges	12.4	1	44	0	–	–	–	–
M.S.Wade	1	1	0	0	–	–	–	–
D.A.Warner	57	1	269	4	67.25	2-45	–	–

SOUTH AFRICA – BATTING AND FIELDING

	M	I	NO	HS	Runs	Avge	100	50	Ct/St
K.J.Abbott	11	14	–	17	95	6.78	–	–	4
H.M.Amla	100	169	13	311*	7799	49.99	26	31	88
T.Bavuma	17	25	3	102*	660	30.00	1	4	8
S.C.Cook	9	15	–	117	615	41.00	3	2	6
Q de Kock	16	25	3	129*	1123	51.04	3	7	63/3
A.B.de Villiers	106	176	16	278*	8074	50.46	21	39	197/5
F.du Plessis	37	58	7	137	2228	43.68	6	9	22
J.P.Duminy	42	66	9	166	1982	34.77	6	8	33
D.Elgar	32	50	5	129	1737	38.60	6	5	35
S.R.Harmer	5	6	1	13	58	11.60	–	–	1
Imran Tahir	20	23	9	29*	130	9.28	–	–	8
R.K.Kleinveldt	4	5	2	17*	27	9.00	–	–	2
R.McLaren	2	3	1	33*	47	23.50	–	–	–
K.A.Maharaj	4	6	3	41*	110	36.66	–	–	–
M.Morkel	71	82	15	40	775	11.56	–	–	19
C.H.Morris	2	3	–	69	98	32.66	–	1	2
D.Olivier	1	1	–	3	3	3.00	–	–	–
W.D.Parnell	5	4	–	23	67	16.75	–	–	2
V.D.Philander	40	51	11	74	939	23.47	–	5	11
D.L.Piedt	7	8	1	19	48	6.85	–	–	4
K.Rabada	14	18	9	32*	127	14.11	–	–	5
J.A.Rudolph	48	83	9	222*	2622	35.43	6	11	29
T.Shamsi	1	2	2	18*	18	–	–	–	–
D.W.Steyn	85	105	22	76	1162	14.00	–	2	22
S.van Zyl	12	17	2	101*	395	26.33	1	–	6
D.J.Vilas	6	9	–	26	94	10.44	–	–	13
G.C.Viljoen	1	2	1	20*	26	26.00	–	–	–

SOUTH AFRICA – BOWLING

	O	M	R	W	Avge	Best	5wI	10wM
K.J.Abbott	346.5	95	886	39	22.71	7- 29	3	–
H.M.Amla	9	0	37	0	–	–	–	–
T.Bavuma	8	1	30	1	30.00	1- 29	–	–
S.C.Cook	2	0	16	0	–	–	–	–
A.B.de Villiers	34	6	104	2	52.00	2- 49	–	–
F.du Plessis	13	0	69	0	–	–	–	–
J.P.Duminy	416	43	1473	38	38.76	4- 73	–	–
D.Elgar	149.5	10	541	13	41.61	4- 22	–	–
S.R.Harmer	191.2	34	588	20	29.40	4- 61	–	–
Imran Tahir	654.1	86	2294	57	40.24	5- 32	2	–
R.K.Kleinveldt	111.1	21	422	10	42.20	3- 65	–	–
R.McLaren	44	8	162	3	54.00	2- 72	–	–
K.A.Maharaj	133	31	374	11	34.00	3- 56	–	–
M.Morkel	2273.2	490	7098	242	29.33	6- 23	6	–
C.H.Morris	61	10	253	4	63.25	1- 8	–	–
D.Olivier	18	5	57	5	11.40	3- 38	–	–
W.D.Parnell	80.4	10	347	13	26.69	4- 51	–	–
V.D.Philander	1241.2	301	3403	159	21.40	6- 44	11	2
D.L.Piedt	250	39	865	24	36.04	5-153	1	–
K.Rabada	383.2	78	1371	63	21.76	7-112	5	2
J.A.Rudolph	110.4	13	432	4	108.00	1- 1	–	–
T.Shamsi	43.5	8	150	2	75.00	1- 49	–	–
D.W.Steyn	2881	622	9303	417	22.30	7- 51	26	5
S.van Zyl	67.1	15	148	6	24.66	3- 20	–	–
G.C.Viljoen	19	2	94	1	94.00	1- 79	–	–

WEST INDIES – BATTING AND FIELDING

	M	I	NO	HS	Runs	Avge	100	50	Ct/St
D.Bishoo	21	35	11	45	406	16.91	–	–	12
J.Blackwood	22	39	3	112*	1128	31.33	1	9	19
C.R.Brathwaite	3	5	1	69	181	45.25	–	3	–
K.C.Brathwaite	34	64	5	212	2214	37.52	5	12	17
D.M.Bravo	49	89	4	218	3400	40.00	8	16	47
S.Chanderpaul	164	280	49	203*	11867	51.37	30	66	66
R.Chandrika	5	10	–	37	140	14.00	–	–	2
R.L.Chase	7	12	1	137*	325	29.54	1	1	1
M.L.Cummins	5	7	2	24*	30	6.00	–	–	–
S.O.Dowrich	8	14	2	74	409	34.08	–	4	8/3
F.H.Edwards	55	88	28	30	394	6.56	–	–	10
S.T.Gabriel	23	30	11	20*	112	5.89	–	–	10
C.H.Gayle	103	182	11	333	7214	42.18	15	37	96
J.O.Holder	20	34	6	103*	801	28.60	1	4	16
S.D.Hope	7	13	–	41	223	17.15	–	–	4
L.R.Johnson	9	16	–	66	403	25.18	–	2	7
A.S.Joseph	2	3	–	6	6	2.00	–	–	1
D.Ramdin	74	126	14	166	2898	25.87	4	15	205/12
K.A.J.Roach	37	59	10	41	509	10.38	–	–	10
M.N.Samuels	71	127	7	260	3917	32.64	7	24	28
J.E.Taylor	46	73	7	106	856	12.96	1	1	8
J.A.Warrican	4	7	6	21*	65	65.00	–	–	1

WEST INDIES – BOWLING

	O	M	R	W	Avge	Best	5wI	10wM
D.Bishoo	881	116	2849	77	37.00	8-49	3	1
J.Blackwood	40	4	165	2	82.50	2-14	–	–
C.R.Brathwaite	68	9	242	1	242.00	1-30	–	–
K.C.Brathwaite	179	18	611	12	50.91	6-29	1	–
D.M.Bravo	1	0	2	0	–	–	–	–

WEST INDIES – BOWLING (continued)

	O	M	R	W	Avge	Best	5wI	10wM
S.Chanderpaul	290	50	883	9	98.11	1- 2	–	–
R.L.Chase	207.1	26	643	11	58.45	5-121	1	–
M.L.Cummins	118.2	16	408	10	40.80	6- 48	1	–
F.H.Edwards	1600.2	183	6249	165	37.87	7- 87	12	–
S.T.Gabriel	540.4	94	1868	49	38.12	5- 96	1	–
C.H.Gayle	1184.5	230	3120	73	42.73	5- 34	2	–
J.O.Holder	478.4	117	1271	31	41.00	5- 30	1	–
L.R.Johnson	4	0	9	0	–	–	–	–
A.S.Joseph	58.5	14	190	5	38.00	3- 69	–	–
K.A.J.Roach	1129.5	214	3689	122	30.23	6- 48	6	1
M.N.Samuels	732	79	2445	41	59.63	4- 13	–	–
J.E.Taylor	1292.5	258	4480	130	34.46	6- 47	4	–
J.A.Warrican	122	8	509	11	46.27	4- 67	–	–

NEW ZEALAND – BATTING AND FIELDING

	M	I	NO	HS	Runs	Avge	100	50	Ct/St
C.J.Anderson	13	22	1	116	683	32.52	1	4	7
T.D.Astle	2	3	–	35	38	12.66	–	–	2
T.A.Boult	49	65	33	52*	472	14.75	–	1	22
D.A.J.Bracewell	27	45	4	47	568	13.85	–	–	10
M.D.Craig	15	25	9	67	589	36.81	–	3	14
C.de Grandhomme	4	6	1	37	145	29.00	–	–	5
J.E.C.Franklin	31	46	7	122*	808	20.71	1	2	12
M.J.Guptill	47	89	1	189	2586	29.38	3	17	50
M.J.Henry	7	12	3	66	200	22.22	–	1	4
T.W.M.Latham	29	55	2	177	2140	40.37	6	12	30
B.B.McCullum	101	176	9	302	6453	38.64	12	31	198/11
J.D.S.Neesham	10	19	1	137*	683	37.94	2	4	7
H.M.Nicholls	11	17	2	98	470	31.33	–	4	6
J.S.Patel	21	34	7	47	343	12.70	–	–	12
J.A.Raval	4	8	1	55	237	33.85	–	2	0
L.Ronchi	4	8	–	88	319	39.87	–	2	3
M.J.Santner	13	16	–	73	423	26.43	–	2	6
I.S.Sodhi	14	19	3	63	365	22.81	–	2	8
T.G.Southee	56	84	6	77*	1300	16.66	–	3	34
L.R.P.L.Taylor	80	145	17	290	6015	46.99	16	27	122
N.Wagner	29	37	9	37	352	12.57	–	–	5
B.J.Watling	49	80	13	142*	2565	38.28	6	12	161/6
K.S.Williamson	58	106	10	242*	4807	50.07	15	25	51

NEW ZEALAND – BOWLING

	O	M	R	W	Avge	Best	5wI	10wM
C.J.Anderson	217	34	659	16	41.18	3- 47	–	–
T.D.Astle	35	6	109	1	109.00	1- 56	–	–
T.A.Boult	1792.3	391	5366	185	29.00	6- 40	5	1
D.A.J.Bracewell	830.4	147	2796	72	38.83	6- 40	2	–
M.D.Craig	611.3	100	2326	50	46.52	7- 94	1	1
C.de Grandhomme	95.5	25	260	10	26.00	6- 41	1	–
J.E.C.Franklin	794.3	143	2786	82	33.97	6-119	3	–
M.J.Guptill	71.2	8	298	8	37.25	3- 11	–	–
M.J.Henry	289.1	52	954	17	56.11	4- 93	–	–
B.B.McCullum	29.1	5	88	1	88.00	1- 1	–	–
J.D.S.Neesham	151.5	14	552	12	46.00	3- 42	–	–
J.S.Patel	870.1	172	2812	58	48.48	5-110	1	–
M.J.Santner	379.3	75	1122	29	36.68	3- 60	–	–
I.S.Sodhi	471	72	1774	38	46.68	4- 60	–	–
T.G.Southee	2070.2	456	6323	201	31.45	7- 64	6	1

NEW ZEALAND – BOWLING (continued)

	O	M	R	W	Avge	Best	5wI	10wM
L.R.P.L.Taylor	16	3	48	2	24.00	2- 4	–	–
N.Wagner	1055.5	216	3373	118	28.58	6-41	4	–
K.S.Williamson	337.3	46	1129	29	38.93	4-44	–	–

INDIA – BATTING AND FIELDING

	M	I	NO	HS	Runs	Avge	100	50	Ct/St
R.Ashwin	45	63	10	124	1850	34.90	4	10	18
S.Dhawan	23	39	1	187	1464	38.52	4	3	18
G.Gambhir	58	104	5	206	4154	41.95	9	22	38
R.A.Jadeja	26	40	8	90	924	28.87	–	5	24
V.Kohli	54	92	6	235	4451	51.75	16	14	51
B.Kumar	17	22	3	63*	430	22.63	–	3	6
A.Mishra	22	32	2	84	648	21.60	–	4	8
Mohammed Shami	22	29	11	51*	233	12.94	–	1	4
K.K.Nair	3	3	1	303*	320	160.00	1	–	3
P.A.Patel	23	34	8	71	878	33.76	–	6	52/10
C.A.Pujara	44	74	7	206*	3393	50.64	10	13	31
A.M.Rahane	33	57	7	188	2382	47.64	8	10	40
K.L.Rahul	13	21	–	199	807	38.42	4	1	20
W.P.Saha	21	31	5	106*	839	32.26	2	4	35/7
I.Sharma	74	101	38	31*	550	8.73	–	–	14
R.G.Sharma	21	36	4	177	1184	37.00	2	7	22
M.Vijay	48	82	1	167	3295	40.67	9	14	37
J.Yadav	3	4	1	104	221	73.66	1	1	1
U.T.Yadav	27	30	10	30	175	8.75	–	–	11

INDIA – BOWLING

	O	M	R	W	Avge	Best	5wI	10wM
R.Ashwin	2181.2	439	6362	254	25.04	7-59	24	7
S.Dhawan	9	2	18	0	–	–	–	–
G.Gambhir	2	0	4	0	–	–	–	–
R.A.Jadeja	1245.1	339	2820	117	24.10	7-48	6	1
V.Kohli	25	2	70	0	–	–	–	–
B.Kumar	433.3	103	1277	43	29.69	6-82	4	–
A.Mishra	850.3	123	2715	76	35.72	5-71	1	–
Mohammed Shami	717.4	114	2478	76	32.60	5-47	2	–
K.K.Nair	1	0	4	0	–	–	–	–
C.A.Pujara	1	0	2	0	–	–	–	–
I.Sharma	2384.3	463	7842	215	36.47	7-74	7	1
R.G.Sharma	55.4	3	202	2	101.00	1-26	–	–
M.Vijay	51	5	147	1	147.00	1-12	–	–
J.Yadav	81.3	17	266	9	29.55	3-30	–	–
U.T.Yadav	746.5	131	2765	71	38.94	5-93	1	–

PAKISTAN – BATTING AND FIELDING

	M	I	NO	HS	Runs	Avge	100	50	Ct/St
Asad Shafiq	53	88	6	137	3364	41.02	10	18	47
Azhar Ali	57	108	8	302*	4707	47.07	12	25	55
Babar Azam	6	12	1	90*	300	27.27	–	2	3
Iftikhar Ahmed	1	1	–	4	4	4.00	–	–	1
Imran Khan	9	8	2	6	6	1.00	–	–	–
Junaid Khan	22	28	11	17	122	7.17	–	–	4
Misbah-ul-Haq	72	126	18	161*	4951	45.84	10	36	49
Mohammad Amir	25	48	8	48	546	13.65	–	–	1
Mohammad Hafeez	50	96	8	224	3452	39.22	9	12	43
Mohammad Nawaz	3	4	–	25	50	12.50	–	–	2
Mohammad Rizwan	1	2	1	13*	13	13.00	–	–	1
Rahat Ali	20	30	12	35*	136	7.55	–	–	9

PAKISTAN – BATTING AND FIELDING (continued)

	M	I	NO	HS	Runs	Avge	100	50	Ct/St
Sami Aslam	11	21	1	91	665	33.25	–	6	7
Sarfraz Ahmed	33	58	12	112	1948	42.34	3	11	86/17
Shan Masood	9	18	–	125	432	24.00	1	2	6
Sharjeel Khan	1	2	–	40	44	22.00	–	–	–
Sohail Khan	9	12	2	65	252	25.20	–	1	2
Wahab Riaz	24	37	4	39	273	8.27	–	–	4
Yasir Shah	23	32	4	33	332	11.85	–	–	16
Younus Khan	115	207	19	313	9977	53.06	34	32	129
Zulfiqar Babar	15	18	9	56	144	16.00	–	1	4

PAKISTAN – BOWLING

	O	M	R	W	Avge	Best	5wI	10wM
Asad Shafiq	18	0	69	1	69.00	1- 32	–	–
Azhar Ali	129.3	7	567	7	81.00	2- 35	–	–
Iftikhar Ahmed	4.2	1	13	1	13.00	1- 13	–	–
Imran Khan	248.4	47	844	28	30.14	5- 58	1	–
Junaid Khan	767.3	157	2253	71	31.73	5- 38	5	–
Mohammad Amir	882.1	179	2732	81	33.72	6- 84	3	–
Mohammad Hafeez	658.5	113	1763	52	33.90	4- 16	–	–
Mohammad Nawaz	63.5	12	147	5	29.40	2- 32	–	–
Rahat Ali	674.3	124	2171	58	37.43	6-127	2	–
Shan Masood	3	0	19	0	–	–	–	–
Sohail Khan	304.4	55	1125	27	41.66	5- 68	2	–
Wahab Riaz	745.2	101	2585	76	34.01	5- 63	2	–
Yasir Shah	1206	176	3908	124	31.51	7- 76	8	2
Younus Khan	134	18	491	9	54.55	2- 23	–	–
Zulfiqar Babar	746.2	143	2129	54	39.42	5- 74	2	–

SRI LANKA – BATTING AND FIELDING

	M	I	NO	HS	Runs	Avge	100	50	Ct/St
P.V.D.Chameera	6	11	1	19	61	6.10	–	–	3
L.D.Chandimal	34	61	4	162*	2342	41.08	7	10	67/10
D.M.de Silva	8	16	1	129	675	45.00	2	2	6
R.M.S.Eranga	19	26	11	45*	193	12.86	–	–	5
A.N.P.R.Fernando	24	42	17	17*	121	4.84	–	–	4
M.V.T.Fernando	1	2	1	0*	0	0.00	–	–	–
D.A.S.Gunaratne	2	4	1	116	225	75.00	1	1	2
H.M.R.K.B.Herath	78	119	24	80*	1396	14.69	–	2	22
M.D.U.S.Jayasundera	2	4	–	26	30	7.50	–	–	2
F.D.M.Karunaratne	36	70	3	186	2200	32.83	4	11	28
C.B.R.L.S.Kumara	4	6	2	9	21	5.25	–	–	–
R.A.S.Lakmal	34	52	17	31	312	8.91	–	–	8
A.D.Mathews	65	114	17	160	4470	46.08	7	26	49
B.K.G.Mendis	14	28	1	176	852	31.55	1	3	21
M.D.K.Perera	14	24	1	95	331	14.39	–	2	8
M.D.K.J.Perera	10	18	–	110	565	31.38	1	3	16/8
S.Prasanna	1	1	–	5	5	5.00	–	–	–
P.A.D.L.R.Sandakan	3	5	3	19*	33	16.50	–	–	1
K.C.Sangakkara	134	233	17	319	12400	57.40	38	52	182/20
M.D.Shanaka	1	2	–	4	4	2.00	–	–	–
J.K.Silva	35	66	–	139	1991	30.16	3	12	30/1
T.A.M.Siriwardana	5	9	–	68	298	33.11	–	2	3
W.U.Tharanga	25	46	3	165	1412	32.83	2	6	19
H.D.R.L.Thirimanne	26	50	6	155*	1056	24.00	1	4	11
K.D.K.Vithanage	10	16	2	103*	370	26.42	1	1	10

SRI LANKA – BOWLING

	O	M	R	W	Avge	Best	5wI	10wM
P.V.D.Chameera	172.5	10	726	22	33.00	5- 47	1	–
D.M.de Silva	69	9	257	5	51.40	2- 91	–	–
R.M.S.Eranga	648.3	125	2138	57	37.50	4- 49	–	–
A.N.P.R.Fernando	738	117	2622	61	42.98	4- 62	–	–
M.V.T.Fernando	2	0	16	1	16.00	1- 16	–	–
D.A.S.Gunaratne	5	0	28	0	–	–	–	–
H.M.R.K.B.Herath	3643	697	10108	357	28.31	9-127	28	7
M.D.U.S.Jayasundera	7	0	45	0	–	–	–	–
F.D.M.Karunaratne	2	0	5	0	–	–	–	–
C.B.R.L.S.Kumara	126.1	9	528	15	35.20	6-122	1	–
R.A.S.Lakmal	1084.1	196	3563	79	45.10	5- 63	1	–
A.D.Mathews	638	154	1737	33	52.66	4- 44	–	–
B.K.G.Mendis	6	1	18	1	18.00	1- 10	–	–
M.D.K.Perera	619.1	105	1866	67	27.85	6- 70	4	1
S.Prasanna	23	3	80	0	–	–	–	–
P.A.D.L.R.Sandakan	71.4	12	207	9	23.00	4- 58	–	–
K.C.Sangakkara	14	0	49	0	–	–	–	–
M.D.Shanaka	13	3	46	3	15.33	3- 46	–	–
T.A.M.Siriwardana	68.5	6	257	11	23.36	3- 25	–	–
H.D.R.L.Thirimanne	14	1	51	0	–	–	–	–
K.D.K.Vithanage	29	1	133	1	133.00	1- 73	–	–

A.N.P.R.Fernando is also known as N.Pradeep.

ZIMBABWE – BATTING AND FIELDING

	M	I	NO	HS	Runs	Avge	100	50	Ct/St
R.W.Chakabva	9	18	1	101	506	29.76	1	3	9
B.B.Chari	5	10	–	80	141	14.10	–	1	5
C.J.Chibhabha	2	4	–	60	103	25.75	–	1	–
M.T.Chinouya	2	4	2	1	1	0.50	–	–	–
A.G.Cremer	15	30	3	102*	411	15.22	1	–	9
C.R.Ervine	11	22	2	146	670	33.50	1	3	10
S.M.Ervine	5	8	–	86	261	32.62	–	3	7
K.M.Jarvis	8	14	6	25*	58	7.25	–	–	3
H.Masakadza	32	64	2	158	1794	28.93	4	6	22
P.S.Masvaure	2	4	–	42	55	13.75	–	–	–
T.M.K.Mawoyo	11	22	1	163*	615	29.28	1	3	7
P.J.Moor	3	6	–	79	211	35.16	–	2	6/1
C.B.Mpofu	11	21	7	20	49	3.50	–	–	2
C.T.Mumba	2	4	1	10*	14	4.66	–	–	1
J.C.Nyumbu	3	6	1	14	38	7.60	–	–	2
Sikandar Raza	6	12	–	82	389	32.41	–	4	–
B.R.M.Taylor	23	46	3	171	1493	34.72	4	7	23
D.T.Tiripano	5	10	3	49*	173	24.71	–	–	2
M.N.Waller	11	22	1	72*	436	20.76	–	3	10
S.C.Williams	6	12	–	119	364	30.33	1	1	6

ZIMBABWE – BOWLING

	O	M	R	W	Avge	Best	5wI	10wM
B.B.Chari	3	0	12	0	–	–	–	–
C.J.Chibhabha	30	3	111	1	111.00	1- 44	–	–
M.T.Chinouya	57	14	188	3	62.66	1- 45	–	–
A.G.Cremer	487	45	1924	37	52.00	4- 4	–	–
S.M.Ervine	95	18	388	9	43.11	4-116	–	–
K.M.Jarvis	261.3	47	952	30	31.73	5- 54	2	–
T.Kamungozi	26	6	58	1	58.00	1- 51	–	–
H.Masakadza	188	48	473	16	29.56	3- 24	–	–
P.S.Masvaure	14	0	61	0	–	–	–	–

ZIMBABWE – BOWLING (continued)

	O	*M*	*R*	*W*	*Avge*	*Best*	*5wI*	*10wM*
C.B.Mpofu	332.2	63	1170	25	46.80	4- 92	–	–
C.T.Mumba	77.5	12	298	8	37.25	4- 50	–	–
J.C.Nyumbu	110.3	11	379	5	75.80	5-157	1	–
Sikandar Raza	111.5	8	426	6	71.00	3-123	–	–
B.R.M.Taylor	7	0	38	0	–	–	–	–
D.T.Tiripano	162	32	472	9	52.44	3- 91	–	–
M.N.Waller	69	8	197	8	24.62	4- 59	–	–
S.C.Williams	74.2	5	286	5	57.20	2- 95	–	–

BANGLADESH – BATTING AND FIELDING

	M	*I*	*NO*	*HS*	*Runs*	*Avge*	*100*	*50*	*Ct/St*
Imrul Kayes	27	52	2	150	1432	28.64	3	4	27
Kamrul Islam	5	10	4	25*	44	7.33	–	–	–
Mahmudullah	32	60	2	115	1801	31.05	1	13	31/1
Mehedi Hasan	5	10	–	51	94	9.40	–	1	5
Mominul Haque	21	38	4	181	1676	49.29	4	11	17
Mushfiqur Rahim	52	96	7	200	3072	34.51	5	15	85/11
Mustafizur Rahman	2	1	–	3	3	3.00	–	–	–
Nazmul Hossain	1	2	–	18	30	15.00	–	–	–
Nurul Hasan	1	2		47	47	23.50	–	–	2
Rubel Hossain	24	41	18	45*	220	9.56		–	11
Sabbir Rahman	5	10	2	64*	247	30.87	–	3	2
Shafiul Islam	9	17	1	53	185	11.56	–	1	2
Shakib Al Hasan	47	88	7	217	3317	40.95	4	21	19
Shuvagata Hom	8	15	4	50	244	22.18	–	1	8
Soumya Sarkar	5	9	–	86	286	31.77	–	1	1
Subashis Roy	1	1	0	0	0	0.00	–	–	–
Taijul Islam	12	20	4	32	182	11.37	–	–	6
Tamim Iqbal	47	90	1	206	3470	38.98	8	20	12
Taskin Ahmed	3	6	–	33	58	9.66	–		

BANGLADESH – BOWLING

	O	*M*	*R*	*W*	*Avge*	*Best*	*5wI*	*10wM*
Imrul Kayes	4	0	12	0	–	–	–	–
Kamrul Islam	93	9	398	7	56.85	3- 87	–	–
Mahmudullah	502.3	50	1734	39	44.46	5- 51	1	–
Mehedi Hasan	232	20	762	25	30.48	6- 77	3	1
Mominul Haque	54.1	2	192	1	192.00	1- 10	–	–
Mustafizur Rahman	22.4	6	58	4	14.50	4- 37	–	–
Nazmul Hossain	0.4	0	13	0	–	–	–	–
Rubel Hossain	639	66	2494	32	77.93	5-166	1	–
Sabbir Rahman	11	0	33	0	–	–	–	–
Shafiul Islam	245	38	801	15	53.40	3- 86	–	–
Shakib Al Hasan	1798	333	5458	167	32.68	7- 36	15	1
Shuvagata Hom	141	10	506	8	63.25	2- 66	–	–
Soumya Sarkar	34.4	1	129	1	129.00	1- 45	–	–
Subashis Roy	31.2	6	121	3	40.33	2- 89	–	–
Taijul Islam	497.4	78	1567	46	34.06	8- 39	3	–
Tamim Iqbal	5	0	20	0	–	–	–	–
Taskin Ahmed	94	8	456	5	91.20	2- 43	–	–

INTERNATIONAL TEST MATCH RESULTS

Complete to 22 February 2017.

	Opponents	*Tests*	*Won by*										*Tied*	*Drawn*
			E	*A*	*SA*	*WI*	*NZ*	*I*	*P*	*SL*	*Z*	*B*		
England	Australia	341	108	140	–	–	–	–	–	–	–	–	–	93
	South Africa	145	58	–	32	–	–	–	–	–	–	–	–	55
	West Indies	151	46	–	–	54	–	–	–	–	–	–	–	51
	New Zealand	101	48	–	–	–	9	–	–	–	–	–	–	44
	India	117	43	–	–	–	–	25	–	–	–	–	–	49
	Pakistan	81	24	–	–	–	–	–	20	–	–	–	–	37
	Sri Lanka	31	12	–	–	–	–	–	–	8	–	–	–	11
	Zimbabwe	6	3	–	–	–	–	–	–	–	0	–	–	3
	Bangladesh	10	9	–	–	–	–	–	–	–	–	1	–	0
Australia	South Africa	94	–	51	23	–	–	–	–	–	–	–	–	20
	West Indies	116	–	58	–	32	–	–	–	–	–	–	1	25
	New Zealand	57	–	31	–	–	8	–	–	–	–	–	–	18
	India	90	–	40	–	–	–	24	–	–	–	–	1	25
	Pakistan	62	–	31	–	–	–	–	14	–	–	–	–	17
	Sri Lanka	29	–	17	–	–	–	–	–	4	–	–	–	8
	Zimbabwe	3	–	3	–	–	–	–	–	–	0	–	–	0
	Bangladesh	4	–	4	–	–	–	–	–	–	–	0	–	0
South Africa	West Indies	28	–	–	18	3	–	–	–	–	–	–	–	7
	New Zealand	42	–	–	24	–	4	–	–	–	–	–	–	14
	India	33	–	–	13	–	–	10	–	–	–	–	–	10
	Pakistan	23	–	–	12	–	–	–	4	–	–	–	–	7
	Sri Lanka	25	–	–	14	–	–	–	–	5	–	–	–	6
	Zimbabwe	8	–	–	7	–	–	–	–	–	0	–	–	1
	Bangladesh	10	–	–	8	–	–	–	–	–	–	0	–	2
West Indies	New Zealand	45	–	–	–	13	13	–	–	–	–	–	–	19
	India	94	–	–	–	30	–	18	–	–	–	–	–	46
	Pakistan	49	–	–	–	16	–	–	18	–	–	–	–	15
	Sri Lanka	17	–	–	–	3	–	–	–	8	–	–	–	6
	Zimbabwe	8	–	–	–	6	–	–	–	–	0	–	–	2
	Bangladesh	12	–	–	–	8	–	–	–	–	–	2	–	2
New Zealand	India	57	–	–	–	–	10	21	–	–	–	–	–	26
	Pakistan	55	–	–	–	–	10	–	24	–	–	–	–	21
	Sri Lanka	32	–	–	–	–	14	–	–	8	–	–	–	10
	Zimbabwe	17	–	–	–	–	11	–	–	–	0	–	–	6
	Bangladesh	13	–	–	–	–	10	–	–	–	–	0	–	3
India	Pakistan	59	–	–	–	–	–	9	12	–	–	–	–	38
	Sri Lanka	38	–	–	–	–	–	16	–	7	–	–	–	15
	Zimbabwe	11	–	–	–	–	–	7	–	–	2	–	–	2
	Bangladesh	9	–	–	–	–	–	7	–	–	–	0	–	2
Pakistan	Sri Lanka	51	–	–	–	–	–	–	19	14	–	–	–	18
	Zimbabwe	17	–	–	–	–	–	–	10	–	3	–	–	4
	Bangladesh	10	–	–	–	–	–	–	9	–	–	0	–	1
Sri Lanka	Zimbabwe	17	–	–	–	–	–	–	–	12	0	–	–	5
	Bangladesh	16	–	–	–	–	–	–	–	14	–	0	–	2
Zimbabwe	Bangladesh	14	–	–	–	–	–	–	–	–	6	5	–	3
		2248	351	375	151	165	89	137	130	80	11	8	2	749

	Tests	Won	Lost	Drawn	Tied	Toss Won
England	983	351	289	343	–	474
Australia	797†	376†	213	206	2	400†
South Africa	408	151	135	122	–	197
West Indies	520	165	181	173	1	270
New Zealand	419	89	169	161	–	209
India	507	136	157	213	1	257
Pakistan	407	130	119	158	–	194
Sri Lanka	256	80	95	81	–	140
Zimbabwe	101	11	64	26	–	57
Bangladesh	97	8	74	15	–	50

† total includes Australia's victory against the ICC World XI.

INTERNATIONAL TEST CRICKET RECORDS

(To 22 February 2017)

TEAM RECORDS

HIGHEST INNINGS TOTALS

952-6d	Sri Lanka v India	Colombo (RPS)	1997-98
903-7d	England v Australia	The Oval	1938
849	England v West Indies	Kingston	1929-30
790-3d	West Indies v Pakistan	Kingston	1957-58
765-6d	Pakistan v Sri Lanka	Karachi	2008-09
760-7d	Sri Lanka v India	Ahmedabad	2009-10
759-7d	India v England	Chennai	2016-17
758-8d	Australia v West Indies	Kingston	1954-55
756-5d	Sri Lanka v South Africa	Colombo (SSC)	2006
751-5d	West Indies v England	St John's	2003-04
749-9d	West Indies v England	Bridgetown	2008-09
747	West Indies v South Africa	St John's	2004-05
735-6d	Australia v Zimbabwe	Perth	2003-04
730-6d	Sri Lanka v Bangladesh	Dhaka	2013-14
729-6d	Australia v England	Lord's	1930
726-9d	India v Sri Lanka	Mumbai	2009-10
713-3d	Sri Lanka v Zimbabwe	Bulawayo	2003-04
710-7d	England v India	Birmingham	2011
708	Pakistan v England	The Oval	1987
707	India v Sri Lanka	Colombo (SSC)	2010
705-7d	India v Australia	Sydney	2003-04
701	Australia v England	The Oval	1934
699-5	Pakistan v India	Lahore	1989-90
695	Australia v England	The Oval	1930
692-8d	West Indies v England	The Oval	1995
690	New Zealand v Pakistan	Sharjah	2014-15
687-8d	West Indies v England	The Oval	1976
687-6d	India v Bangladesh	Hyderabad	2016-17
682-6d	South Africa v England	Lord's	2003
681-8d	West Indies v England	Port-of-Spain	1953-54
680-8d	New Zealand v India	Wellington	2013-14
679-7d	Pakistan v India	Lahore	2005-06
676-7	India v Sri Lanka	Kanpur	1986-87
675-5d	India v Pakistan	Multan	2003-04
674	Australia v India	Adelaide	1947-48
674-6	Pakistan v India	Faisalabad	1984-85

674-6d	Australia v England	Cardiff	2009
671-4	New Zealand v Sri Lanka	Wellington	1990-91
668	Australia v West Indies	Bridgetown	1954-55
664	India v England	The Oval	2007
660-5d	West Indies v New Zealand	Wellington	1994-95
659-8d	Australia v England	Sydney	1946-47
659-4d	Australia v India	Sydney	2011-12
658-8d	England v Australia	Nottingham	1938
658-9d	South Africa v West Indies	Durban	2003-04
657-8d	Pakistan v West Indies	Bridgetown	1957-58
657-7d	India v Australia	Calcutta	2000-01
656-8d	Australia v England	Manchester	1964
654-5	England v South Africa	Durban	1938-39
653-4d	England v India	Lord's	1990
653-4d	Australia v England	Leeds	1993
652-8d	West Indies v England	Lord's	1973
652	Pakistan v India	Faisalabad	1982-83
652-7d	England v India	Madras	1984-85
652-7d	Australia v South Africa	Johannesburg	2001-02
651	South Africa v Australia	Cape Town	2008-09
650-6d	Australia v West Indies	Bridgetown	1964-65

The highest for Zimbabwe is 563-9d (v WI, Harare, 2001), and for Bangladesh 638 (v SL, Galle, 2012-13).

LOWEST INNINGS TOTALS

† One batsman absent

26	New Zealand v England	Auckland	1954-55
30	South Africa v England	Port Elizabeth	1895-96
30	South Africa v England	Birmingham	1924
35	South Africa v England	Cape Town	1898-99
36	Australia v England	Birmingham	1902
36	South Africa v Australia	Melbourne	1931-32
42	Australia v England	Sydney	1887-88
42	New Zealand v Australia	Wellington	1945-46
42†	India v England	Lord's	1974
43	South Africa v England	Cape Town	1888-89
44	Australia v England	The Oval	1896
45	England v Australia	Sydney	1886-87
45	South Africa v Australia	Melbourne	1931-32
45	New Zealand v South Africa	Cape Town	2012-13
46	England v West Indies	Port-of-Spain	1993-94
47	South Africa v England	Cape Town	1888-89
47	New Zealand v England	Lord's	1958
47	West Indies v England	Kingston	2003-04
47	Australia v South Africa	Cape Town	2011-12
49	Pakistan v South Africa	Johannesburg	2012-13

The lowest for Sri Lanka is 71 (v P, Kandy, 1994-95), for Zimbabwe 51 (v NZ, Napier, 2011-12), and for Bangladesh 62 (v SL, Colombo PPS, 2006-07).

BATTING RECORDS
5000 RUNS IN TESTS

Runs			*M*	*I*	*NO*	*HS*	*Avge*	*100*	*50*
15921	S.R.Tendulkar	I	200	329	33	248*	53.78	51	68
13378	R.T.Ponting	A	168	287	29	257	51.85	41	62
13289	J.H.Kallis	SA/ICC	166	280	40	224	55.37	45	58
13288	R.S.Dravid	I/ICC	164	286	32	270	52.31	36	63
12400	K.C.Sangakkara	SL	134	233	17	319	57.40	38	52

Runs			M	I	NO	HS	Avge	100	50
11953	B.C.Lara	WI/ICC	131	232	6	400*	52.88	34	48
11867	S.Chanderpaul	WI	164	280	49	203*	51.37	30	66
11814	D.P.M.D.Jayawardena	SL	149	252	15	374	49.84	34	50
11174	A.R.Border	A	156	265	44	205	50.56	27	63
11057	A.N.Cook	E	140	253	15	294	46.45	30	53
10927	S.R.Waugh	A	168	260	46	200	51.06	32	50
10122	S.M.Gavaskar	I	125	214	16	236*	51.12	34	45
9977	Younus Khan	P	115	207	19	313	53.06	34	32
9265	G.C.Smith	SA/ICC	117	205	13	277	48.25	27	38
8900	G.A.Gooch	E	118	215	6	333	42.58	20	46
8832	Javed Miandad	P	124	189	21	280*	52.57	23	43
8830	Inzamam-ul-Haq	P/ICC	120	200	22	329	49.60	25	46
8781	V.V.S.Laxman	I	134	225	34	281	45.97	17	56
8643	M.J.Clarke	A	115	198	22	329*	49.10	28	27
8625	M.L.Hayden	A	103	184	14	380	50.73	30	29
8586	V.Sehwag	I/ICC	104	180	6	319	49.34	23	32
8540	I.V.A.Richards	WI	121	182	12	291	50.23	24	45
8463	A.J.Stewart	E	133	235	21	190	39.54	15	45
8231	D.I.Gower	E	117	204	18	215	44.25	18	39
8181	K.P.Pietersen	E	104	181	8	227	47.28	23	35
8114	G.Boycott	E	108	193	23	246*	47.72	22	42
8074	A.B.de Villiers	SA	106	176	16	278*	50.46	21	39
8032	G.St A.Sobers	WI	93	160	21	365*	57.78	26	30
8029	M.E.Waugh	A	128	209	17	153*	41.81	20	47
7799	H.M.Amla	SA	100	169	13	311*	49.99	26	31
7728	M.A.Atherton	E	115	212	7	185*	37.70	16	46
7727	I.R.Bell	E	118	205	24	235	42.69	22	46
7696	J.L.Langer	A	105	182	12	250	45.27	23	30
7624	M.C.Cowdrey	E	114	188	15	182	44.06	22	38
7558	C.G.Greenidge	WI	108	185	16	226	44.72	19	34
7530	Mohammad Yousuf	P	90	156	12	223	52.29	24	33
7525	M.A.Taylor	A	104	186	13	334*	43.49	19	40
7515	C.H.Lloyd	WI	110	175	14	242*	46.67	19	39
7487	D.L.Haynes	WI	116	202	25	184	42.29	18	39
7422	D.C.Boon	A	107	190	20	200	43.65	21	32
7289	G.Kirsten	SA	101	176	15	275	45.27	21	34
7249	W.R.Hammond	E	85	140	16	336*	58.45	22	24
7214	C.H.Gayle	WI	103	182	11	333	42.18	15	37
7212	S.C.Ganguly	I	113	188	17	239	42.17	16	35
7172	S.P.Fleming	NZ	111	189	10	274*	40.06	9	46
7110	G.S.Chappell	A	87	151	19	247*	53.86	24	31
7037	A.J.Strauss	E	100	178	6	177	40.91	21	27
6996	D.G.Bradman	A	52	80	10	334	99.94	29	13
6973	S.T.Jayasuriya	SL	110	188	14	340	40.07	14	31
6971	L.Hutton	E	79	138	15	364	56.67	19	33
6868	D.B.Vengsarkar	I	116	185	22	166	42.13	17	35
6806	K.F.Barrington	E	82	131	15	256	58.67	20	35
6744	G.P.Thorpe	E	100	179	28	200*	44.66	16	39
6453	B.B.McCullum	NZ	101	176	9	302	38.64	12	31
6361	P.A.de Silva	SL	93	159	11	267	42.97	20	22
6235	M.E.K.Hussey	A	79	137	16	195	51.52	19	29
6227	R.B.Kanhai	WI	79	137	6	256	47.53	15	28
6215	M.Azharuddin	I	99	147	9	199	45.03	22	21
6167	H.H.Gibbs	SA	90	154	7	228	41.95	14	26
6149	R.N.Harvey	A	79	137	10	205	48.41	21	24
6080	G.R.Viswanath	I	91	155	10	222	41.93	14	35

Runs			M	I	NO	HS	Avge	100	50
6015	L.R.P.L.Taylor	NZ	80	145	17	290	46.99	16	27
5949	R.B.Richardson	WI	86	146	12	194	44.39	16	27
5842	R.R.Sarwan	WI	87	154	8	291	40.01	15	31
5825	M.E.Trescothick	E	76	143	10	219	43.79	14	29
5807	D.C.S.Compton	E	78	131	15	278	50.06	17	28
5768	Salim Malik	P	103	154	22	237	43.69	15	29
5764	N.Hussain	E	96	171	16	207	37.19	14	33
5762	C.L.Hooper	WI	102	173	15	233	36.46	13	27
5719	M.P.Vaughan	E	82	147	9	197	41.44	18	18
5570	A.C.Gilchrist	A	96	137	20	204*	47.60	17	26
5515	M.V.Boucher	SA/ICC	147	206	24	125	30.30	5	35
5502	M.S.Atapattu	SL	90	156	15	249	39.02	16	17
5492	T.M.Dilshan	SL	87	145	11	193	40.98	16	23
5462	T.T.Samaraweera	SL	81	132	20	231	48.76	14	30
5444	M.D.Crowe	NZ	77	131	11	299	45.36	17	18
5410	J.B.Hobbs	E	61	102	7	211	56.94	15	28
5357	K.D.Walters	A	74	125	14	250	48.26	15	33
5345	I.M.Chappell	A	75	136	10	196	42.42	14	26
5334	J.G.Wright	NZ	82	148	7	185	37.82	12	23
5312	M.J.Slater	A	74	131	7	219	42.84	14	21
5261	D.A.Warner	A	60	111	4	253	49.16	18	23
5248	Kapil Dev	I	131	184	15	163	31.05	8	27
5234	W.M.Lawry	A	67	123	12	210	47.15	13	27
5200	I.T.Botham	E	102	161	6	208	33.54	14	22
5138	J.H.Edrich	E	77	127	9	310*	43.54	12	24
5105	A.Ranatunga	SL	93	155	12	135*	35.69	4	38
5062	Zaheer Abbas	P	78	124	11	274	44.79	12	20

The most for Zimbabwe is 4794 by A.Flower (112 innings), and for Bangladesh 3470 by Tamim Iqbal (90 innings).

750 RUNS IN A SERIES

Runs			Series	M	I	NO	HS	Avge	100	50
974	D.G.Bradman	A v E	1930	5	7	–	334	139.14	4	–
905	W.R.Hammond	E v A	1928-29	5	9	1	251	113.12	4	–
839	M.A.Taylor	A v E	1989	6	11	1	219	83.90	2	5
834	R.N.Harvey	A v SA	1952-53	5	9	–	205	92.66	4	3
829	I.V.A.Richards	WI v E	1976	4	7	–	291	118.42	3	2
827	C.L.Walcott	WI v A	1954-55	5	10	–	155	82.70	5	2
824	G.St A.Sobers	WI v P	1957-58	5	8	2	365*	137.33	3	3
810	D.G.Bradman	A v E	1936-37	5	9	–	270	90.00	3	1
806	D.G.Bradman	A v SA	1931-32	5	5	1	299*	201.50	4	–
798	B.C.Lara	WI v E	1993-94	5	8	–	375	99.75	2	2
779	E.de C.Weekes	WI v I	1948-49	5	7	–	194	111.28	4	2
774	S.M.Gavaskar	I v WI	1970-71	4	8	3	220	154.80	4	3
769	S.P.D.Smith	A v I	2014-15	4	8	2	192	128.16	4	2
766	A.N.Cook	E v A	2010-11	5	7	1	235*	127.66	3	2
765	B.C.Lara	WI v E	1995	6	10	1	179	85.00	3	3
761	Mudassar Nazar	P v I	1982-83	6	8	2	231	126.83	4	1
758	D.G.Bradman	A v E	1934	5	8	–	304	94.75	2	1
753	D.C.S.Compton	E v SA	1947	5	8	–	208	94.12	4	2
752	G.A.Gooch	E v I	1990	3	6	–	333	125.33	3	2

HIGHEST INDIVIDUAL INNINGS

400*	B.C.Lara	WI v E	St John's	2003-04
380	M.L.Hayden	A v Z	Perth	2003-04
375	B.C.Lara	WI v E	St John's	1993-94

374	D.P.M.D.Jayawardena	SL v SA	Colombo (SSC)	2006
365*	G.St A.Sobers	WI v P	Kingston	1957-58
364	L.Hutton	E v A	The Oval	1938
340	S.T.Jayasuriya	SL v I	Colombo (RPS)	1997-98
337	Hanif Mohammed	P v WI	Bridgetown	1957-58
336*	W.R.Hammond	E v NZ	Auckland	1932-33
334*	M.A.Taylor	A v P	Peshawar	1998-99
334	D.G.Bradman	A v E	Leeds	1930
333	G.A.Gooch	E v I	Lord's	1990
333	C.H.Gayle	WI v SL	Galle	2010-11
329*	M.J.Clarke	A v I	Sydney	2011-12
329	Inzamam-ul-Haq	P v NZ	Lahore	2001-02
325	A.Sandham	E v WI	Kingston	1929-30
319	V.Sehwag	I v SA	Chennai	2007-08
319	K.C.Sangakkara	SL v B	Chittagong	2013-14
317	C.H.Gayle	WI v SA	St John's	2004-05
313	Younus Khan	P v SL	Karachi	2008-09
311*	H.M.Amla	SA v E	The Oval	2012
311	R.B.Simpson	A v E	Manchester	1964
310*	J.H.Edrich	E v NZ	Leeds	1965
309	V.Sehwag	I v P	Multan	2003-04
307	R.M.Cowper	A v E	Melbourne	1965-66
304	D.G.Bradman	A v E	Leeds	1934
303*	K.K.Nair	I v E	Chennai	2016-17
302*	Azhar Ali	P v WI	Dubai (DSC)	2016-17
302	L.G.Rowe	WI v E	Bridgetown	1973-74
302	B.B.McCullum	NZ v I	Wellington	2013-14
299*	D.G.Bradman	A v SA	Adelaide	1931-32
299	M.D.Crowe	NZ v SL	Wellington	1990-91
294	A.N.Cook	E v I	Birmingham	2011
293	V.Sehwag	I v SL	Mumbai	2009-10
291	I.V.A.Richards	WI v E	The Oval	1976
291	R.R.Sarwan	WI v E	Bridgetown	2008-09
290	L.R.P.L.Taylor	NZ v A	Perth	2015-16
287	R.E.Foster	E v A	Sydney	1903-04
287	K.C.Sangakkara	SL v SA	Colombo (SSC)	2006
285*	P.B.H.May	E v WI	Birmingham	1957
281	V.V.S.Laxman	I v A	Calcutta	2000-01
280*	Javed Miandad	P v I	Hyderabad	1982-83
278*	A.B.de Villiers	SA v P	Abu Dhabi	2010-11
278	D.C.S.Compton	E v P	Nottingham	1954
277	B.C.Lara	WI v A	Sydney	1992-93
277	G.C.Smith	SA v E	Birmingham	2003
275*	D.J.Cullinan	SA v NZ	Auckland	1998-99
275	G.Kirsten	SA v E	Durban	1999-00
275	D.P.M.D.Jayawardena	SL v I	Ahmedabad	2009-10
274*	S.P.Fleming	NZ v SL	Colombo (SSC)	2002-03
274	R.G.Pollock	SA v A	Durban	1969-70
274	Zaheer Abbas	P v E	Birmingham	1971
271	Javed Miandad	P v NZ	Auckland	1988-89
270*	G.A.Headley	WI v E	Kingston	1934-35
270	D.G.Bradman	A v E	Melbourne	1936-37
270	R.S.Dravid	I v P	Rawalpindi	2003-04
270	K.C.Sangakkara	SL v Z	Bulawayo	2004
269*	A.C.Voges	A v WI	Hobart	2015-16
268	G.N.Yallop	A v P	Melbourne	1983-84
267*	B.A.Young	NZ v SL	Dunedin	1996-97

267	P.A.de Silva	SL v NZ	Wellington	1990-91
267	Younus Khan	P v I	Bangalore	2004-05
266	W.H.Ponsford	A v E	The Oval	1934
266	D.L.Houghton	Z v SL	Bulawayo	1994-95
263	A.N.Cook	E v P	Abu Dhabi	2015-16
262*	D.L.Amiss	E v WI	Kingston	1973-74
262	S.P.Fleming	NZ v SA	Cape Town	2005-06
261*	R.R.Sarwan	WI v B	Kingston	2004
261	F.M.M.Worrell	WI v E	Nottingham	1950
260	C.C.Hunte	WI v P	Kingston	1957-58
260	Javed Miandad	P v E	The Oval	1987
260	M.N.Samuels	WI v B	Khulna	2012-13
259*	M.J.Clarke	A v SA	Brisbane	2012-13
259	G.M.Turner	NZ v WI	Georgetown	1971-72
259	G.C.Smith	SA v E	Lord's	2003
258	T.W.Graveney	E v WI	Nottingham	1957
258	S.M.Nurse	WI v NZ	Christchurch	1968-69
258	B.A.Stokes	E v SA	Cape Town	2015-16
257*	Wasim Akram	P v Z	Sheikhupura	1996-97
257	R.T.Ponting	A v I	Melbourne	2003-04
256	R.B.Kanhai	WI v I	Calcutta	1958-59
256	K.F.Barrington	E v A	Manchester	1964
255*	D.J.McGlew	SA v NZ	Wellington	1952-53
254	D.G.Bradman	A v E	Lord's	1930
254	V.Sehwag	I v P	Lahore	2005-06
254	J.E.Root	E v P	Manchester	2016
253*	H.M.Amla	SA v I	Nagpur	2009-10
253	S.T.Jayasuriya	SL v P	Faisalabad	2004-05
253	D.A.Warner	A v NZ	Perth	2015-16
251	W.R.Hammond	E v A	Sydney	1928-29
250	K.D.Walters	A v NZ	Christchurch	1976-77
250	S.F.A.F.Bacchus	WI v I	Kanpur	1978-79
250	J.L.Langer	A v E	Melbourne	2002-03

The highest for Bangladesh is 217 by Shakib Al Hasan (v NZ, Wellington, 2016-17).

20 HUNDREDS

					Opponents									
			200	*Inn*	*E*	*A*	*SA*	*WI*	*NZ*	*I*	*P*	*SL*	*Z*	*B*
51	S.R.Tendulkar	I	6	329	7	11	7	3	4	–	2	9	3	5
45	J.H.Kallis	SA	2	280	8	5	–	8	6	7	6	1	3	1
41	R.T.Ponting	A	6	287	8	–	8	7	2	8	5	1	1	1
38	K.C.Sangakkara	SL	11	233	3	1	3	3	4	5	10	–	2	7
36	R.S.Dravid	I	5	286	7	2	2	5	6	–	5	3	3	3
34	Younus Khan	P	6	207	4	4	4	3	2	5	–	8	1	3
34	S.M.Gavaskar	I	4	214	4	8	–	13	2	–	5	2	–	–
34	B.C.Lara	WI	9	232	7	9	4	–	1	2	4	5	1	1
34	D.P.M.D.Jayawardena	SL	7	252	8	2	6	1	3	6	2	–	1	5
32	S.R.Waugh	A	1	260	10	–	2	7	2	2	3	3	1	2
30	M.L.Hayden †	A	2	184	5	–	6	5	1	6	1	3	2	–
30	A.N.Cook	E	3	253	–	4	2	5	3	6	5	3	–	2
30	S.Chanderpaul	WI	2	280	5	5	5	–	2	7	1	–	1	4
29	D.G.Bradman	A	12	80	19	–	4	2	–	4	–	–	–	–
28	M.J.Clarke	A	4	198	7	–	5	1	4	7	1	3	–	–
27	G.C.Smith	SA	5	205	7	3	–	7	2	–	4	–	1	3
27	A.R.Border	A	2	265	8	–	–	3	5	4	6	1	–	–
26	G.St A.Sobers	WI	2	160	10	4	–	–	1	8	3	–	–	–
26	H.M.Amla	SA	4	169	6	5	–	1	4	5	2	2	–	1

					Opponents									
			200	*Inn*	*E*	*A*	*SA*	*WI*	*NZ*	*I*	*P*	*SL*	*Z*	*B*
25	Inzamam-ul-Haq	P	2	200	5	1	–	4	3	3	–	5	2	2
24	G.S.Chappell	A	4	151	9	–	–	5	3	1	6	–	–	–
24	Mohammad Yousuf	P	4	156	6	1	–	7	1	4		1	2	2
24	I.V.A.Richards	WI	3	182	8	5	–	–	1	8	2	–	–	–
23	V.Sehwag	I	6	180	2	3	5	2	2	–	4	5	–	–
23	K.P.Pietersen	E	3	181	–	4	3	3	2	6	2	3	–	–
23	J.L.Langer	A	3	182	5	–	2	3	4	3	4	2	–	–
23	Javed Miandad	P	6	189	2	6	–	2	7	5	–	1	–	–
22	W.R.Hammond	E	7	140	–	9	6	1	4	2	–	–	–	–
22	M.Azharuddin	I	–	147	6	2	4	–	2	–	3	5	–	–
22	M.C.Cowdrey	E	–	188	–	5	3	6	2	3	3	–	–	–
22	G.Boycott	E	1	193	–	7	1	5	2	4	3	–	–	–
22	I.R.Bell	E	1	205	–	4	2	2	1	4	4	2	–	3
21	R.N.Harvey	A	2	137	6	–	8	3	–	4	–	–	–	–
21	A.B.de Villiers	SA	2	176	2	5	–	6	–	3	4	1	–	–
21	G.Kirsten	SA	3	176	5	2	–	3	2	3	2	1	1	2
21	A.J.Strauss	E		178	–	4	3	6	3	3	2	–	–	–
21	D.C.Boon	A	1	190	7	–	–	3	3	6	1	1	–	–
20	K.F.Barrington	E	1	131	–	5	2	3	3	3	4	–	–	–
20	P.A.de Silva	SL	2	159	2	1	–	–	2	5	8	–	1	1
20	M.E.Waugh	A	–	†209	6	–	4	4	1	1	3	1	–	–
20	G.A.Gooch	E	2	215	–	4	–	5	4	5	1	1		–

† Includes century scored for Australia v ICC in 2005-06.

The most for New Zealand is 17 by M.D.Crowe (131 innings), for Zimbabwe 12 by A.Flower (112), and for Bangladesh 8 by Tamim Iqbal (88 innings).

The most double hundreds by batsmen not included above are 6 by M.S.Atapattu (16 hundreds for Sri Lanka), 4 by L.Hutton (19 for England), 4 by C.G.Greenidge (19 for West Indies), 4 by V.Kohli (16 for India), 4 by Zaheer Abbas (12 for Pakistan), and 4 by B.B.McCullum (12 for New Zealand).

HIGHEST PARTNERSHIP FOR EACH WICKET

1st	415	N.D.McKenzie/G.C.Smith	SA v B	Chittagong	2007-08
2nd	576	S.T.Jayasuriya/R.S.Mahanama	SL v I	Colombo (RPS)	1997-98
3rd	624	K.C.Sangakkara/D.P.M.D.Jayawardena	SL v SA	Colombo (SSC)	2006
4th	449	A.C.Voges/S.E.Marsh	A v WI	Hobart	2015-16
5th	405	S.G.Barnes/D.G.Bradman	A v E	Sydney	1946-47
6th	399	B.A.Stokes/J.M.Bairstow	E v SA	Cape Town	2015-16
7th	347	D.St E.Atkinson/C.C.Depeiza	WI v A	Bridgetown	1954-55
8th	332	I.J.L.Trott/S.C.J.Broad	E v P	Lord's	2010
9th	195	M.V.Boucher/P.L.Symcox	SA v P	Johannesburg	1997-98
10th	198	J.E.Root/J.M.Anderson	E v I	Nottingham	2014

BOWLING RECORDS
200 WICKETS IN TESTS

Wkts			*M*	*Balls*	*Runs*	*Avge*	*5 wI*	*10 wM*
800	M.Muralitharan	SL/ICC	133	44039	18180	22.72	67	22
708	S.K.Warne	A	145	40705	17995	25.41	37	10
619	A.Kumble	I	132	40850	18355	29.65	35	8
563	G.D.McGrath	A	124	29248	12186	21.64	29	3
519	C.A.Walsh	WI	132	30019	12688	24.44	22	3
467	J.M.Anderson	E	122	26840	13310	28.50	21	3
434	Kapil Dev	I	131	27740	12867	29.64	23	2
431	R.J.Hadlee	NZ	86	21918	9612	22.30	36	9
421	S.M.Pollock	SA	108	24453	9733	23.11	16	1
417	D.W.Steyn	SA	85	17286	9303	22.30	26	5

Wkts			M	Balls	Runs	Avge	5 wI	10 wM
417	Harbhajan Singh	I	103	28580	13537	32.46	25	5
414	Wasim Akram	P	104	22627	9779	23.62	25	5
405	C.E.L.Ambrose	WI	98	22104	8500	20.98	22	3
390	M.Ntini	SA	101	20834	11242	28.82	18	4
383	I.T.Botham	E	102	21815	10878	28.40	27	4
376	M.D.Marshall	WI	81	17584	7876	20.94	22	4
373	Waqar Younis	P	87	16224	8788	23.56	22	5
368	S.C.J.Broad	E	102	21000	10503	28.54	15	2
362	Imran Khan	P	88	19458	8258	22.81	23	6
362	D.L.Vettori	NZ/ICC	113	28814	12441	34.36	20	3
357	H.M.R.K.B.Herath	SL	78	21858	10108	28.31	28	7
355	D.K.Lillee	A	70	18467	8493	23.92	23	7
355	W.P.J.U.C.Vaas	SL	111	23438	10501	29.58	12	2
330	A.A.Donald	SA	72	15519	7344	22.25	20	3
325	R.G.D.Willis	E	90	17357	8190	25.20	16	–
313	M.G.Johnson	A	73	16001	8891	28.40	12	3
311	Z.Khan	I	92	18785	10247	32.94	11	1
310	B.Lee	A	76	16531	9554	30.81	10	–
309	L.R.Gibbs	WI	79	27115	8989	29.09	18	2
307	F.S.Trueman	E	67	15178	6625	21.57	17	3
297	D.L.Underwood	E	86	21862	7674	25.83	17	6
292	J.H.Kallis	SA/ICC	166	20232	9535	32.65	5	–
291	C.J.McDermott	A	71	16586	8332	28.63	14	2
266	B.S.Bedi	I	67	21364	7637	28.71	14	1
261	Danish Kaneria	P	61	17697	9082	34.79	15	2
259	J.Garner	WI	58	13169	5433	20.97	7	–
259	J.N.Gillespie	A	71	14234	6770	26.13	8	–
255	G.P.Swann	E	60	15349	7642	29.96	17	3
254	R.Ashwin	I	45	13088	6362	25.04	24	7
252	J.B.Statham	E	70	16056	6261	24.84	9	1
249	M.A.Holding	WI	60	12680	5898	23.68	13	2
248	R.Benaud	A	63	19108	6704	27.03	16	1
248	M.J.Hoggard	E	67	13909	7564	30.50	7	1
246	G.D.McKenzie	A	60	17681	7328	29.78	16	3
242	M.Morkel	SA	71	13640	7098	29.33	6	–
242	B.S.Chandrasekhar	I	58	15963	7199	29.74	16	2
236	A.V.Bedser	E	51	15918	5876	24.89	15	5
236	J.Srinath	I	67	15104	7196	30.49	10	1
236	Abdul Qadir	P	67	17126	7742	32.80	15	5
235	G.St A.Sobers	WI	93	21599	7999	34.03	6	–
234	A.R.Caddick	E	62	13558	6999	29.91	13	1
233	C.S.Martin	NZ	71	14026	7878	33.81	10	1
229	D.Gough	E	58	11821	6503	28.39	9	–
228	R.R.Lindwall	A	61	13650	5251	23.03	12	–
228	N.M.Lyon	A	63	14567	7769	34.07	7	1
226	S.J.Harmison	E/ICC	63	13375	7192	31.82	8	1
226	A.Flintoff	E/ICC	79	14951	7410	32.78	3	–
218	C.L.Cairns	NZ	62	11698	6410	29.40	13	1
216	C.V.Grimmett	A	37	14513	5231	24.21	21	7
216	H.H.Streak	Z	65	13559	6079	28.14	7	–
215	I.Sharma	I	74	14307	7842	36.47	7	1
212	M.G.Hughes	A	53	12285	6017	28.38	7	1
211	P.M.Siddle	A	62	12941	6314	29.92	8	–
208	S.C.G.MacGill	A	44	11237	6038	29.02	12	2
208	Saqlain Mushtaq	P	49	14070	6206	29.83	13	3
202	A.M.E.Roberts	WI	47	11136	5174	25.61	11	2
202	J.A.Snow	E	49	12021	5387	26.66	8	1
201	T.G.Southee	NZ	56	12422	6323	31.45	6	1
200	J.R.Thomson	A	51	10535	5601	28.00	8	–

The most for Bangladesh is 167 in 47 Tests by Shakib Al Hasan.

35 OR MORE WICKETS IN A SERIES

Wkts			Series	M	Balls	Runs	Avge	5 wI	10 wM
49	S.F.Barnes	E v SA	1913-14	4	1356	536	10.93	7	3
46	J.C.Laker	E v A	1956	5	1703	442	9.60	4	2
44	C.V.Grimmett	A v SA	1935-36	5	2077	642	14.59	5	3
42	T.M.Alderman	A v E	1981	6	1950	893	21.26	4	–
41	R.M.Hogg	A v E	1978-79	6	1740	527	12.85	5	2
41	T.M.Alderman	A v E	1989	6	1616	712	17.36	6	1
40	Imran Khan	P v I	1982-83	6	1339	558	13.95	4	2
40	S.K.Warne	A v E	2005	5	1517	797	19.92	3	2
39	A.V.Bedser	E v A	1953	5	1591	682	17.48	5	1
39	D.K.Lillee	A v E	1981	6	1870	870	22.30	2	1
38	M.W.Tate	E v A	1924-25	5	2528	881	23.18	5	1
37	W.J.Whitty	A v SA	1910-11	5	1395	632	17.08	2	–
37	H.J.Tayfield	SA v E	1956-57	5	2280	636	17.18	4	1
37	M.G.Johnson	A v E	2013-14	5	1132	517	13.97	3	–
36	A.E.E.Vogler	SA v E	1909-10	5	1349	783	21.75	4	1
36	A.A.Mailey	A v E	1920-21	5	1465	946	26.27	4	2
36	G.D.McGrath	A v E	1997	6	1499	701	19.47	2	–
35	G.A.Lohmann	E v SA	1895-96	3	520	203	5.80	4	2
35	B.S.Chandrasekhar	I v E	1972-73	5	1747	662	18.91	4	–
35	M.D.Marshall	WI v E	1988	5	1219	443	12.65	3	1

The most for New Zealand is 33 by R.J.Hadlee (3 Tests v A, 1985-86), for Sri Lanka 30 by M.Muralitharan (3 Tests v Z, 2001-02), for Zimbabwe 22 by H.H.Streak (3 Tests v P, 1994-95), and for Bangladesh 19 by Mehedi Hasan (2 Tests v E, 2016-17).

15 OR MORE WICKETS IN A TEST († *On debut*)

19- 90	J.C.Laker	E v A	Manchester	1956
17-159	S.F.Barnes	E v SA	Johannesburg	1913-14
16-136†	N.D.Hirwani	I v WI	Madras	1987-88
16-137†	R.A.L.Massie	A v E	Lord's	1972
16-220	M.Muralitharan	SL v E	The Oval	1998
15- 28	J.Briggs	E v SA	Cape Town	1888-89
15- 45	G.A.Lohmann	E v SA	Port Elizabeth	1895-96
15- 99	C.Blythe	E v SA	Leeds	1907
15-104	H.Verity	E v A	Lord's	1934
15-123	R.J.Hadlee	NZ v A	Brisbane	1985-86
15-124	W.Rhodes	E v A	Melbourne	1903-04
15-217	Harbhajan Singh	I v A	Madras	2000-01

The best analysis for South Africa is 13-132 by M.Ntini (v WI, Port-of-Spain, 2004-05), for West Indies 14-149 by M.A.Holding (v E, The Oval, 1976), for Pakistan 14-116 by Imran Khan (v SL, Lahore, 1981-82), for Zimbabwe 11-257 by A.G.Huckle (v NZ, Bulawayo, 1997-98), and for Bangladesh 12-159 by Mehedi Hasan (v E, Dhaka, 2016-17).

NINE OR MORE WICKETS IN AN INNINGS

10-53	J.C.Laker	E v A	Manchester	1956
10-74	A.Kumble	I v P	Delhi	1998-99
9-28	G.A.Lohmann	E v SA	Johannesburg	1895-96
9-37	J.C.Laker	E v A	Manchester	1956
9-51	M.Muralitharan	SL v Z	Kandy	2001-02
9-52	R.J.Hadlee	NZ v A	Brisbane	1985-86
9-56	Abdul Qadir	P v E	Lahore	1987-88
9-57	D.E.Malcolm	E v SA	The Oval	1994
9-65	M.Muralitharan	SL v E	The Oval	1998
9-69	J.M.Patel	I v A	Kanpur	1959-60

9- 83	Kapil Dev	I v WI	Ahmedabad	1983-84
9- 86	Sarfraz Nawaz	P v A	Melbourne	1978-79
9- 95	J.M.Noreiga	WI v I	Port-of-Spain	1970-71
9-102	S.P.Gupte	I v WI	Kanpur	1958-59
9-103	S.F.Barnes	E v SA	Johannesburg	1913-14
9-113	H.J.Tayfield	SA v E	Johannesburg	1956-57
9-121	A.A.Mailey	A v E	Melbourne	1920-21
9-127	H.M.R.K.B.Herath	SL v P	Colombo (SSC)	2014

The best analysis for Zimbabwe is 8-109 by P.A.Strang (v NZ, Bulawayo, 2000-01), and for Bangladesh 8-39 by Taijul Islam (v Z, Dhaka, 2014-15).

HAT-TRICKS

F.R.Spofforth	Australia v England	Melbourne	1878-79
W.Bates	England v Australia	Melbourne	1882-83
J.Briggs[7]	England v Australia	Sydney	1891-92
G.A.Lohmann	England v South Africa	Port Elizabeth	1895-96
J.T.Hearne	England v Australia	Leeds	1899
H.Trumble	Australia v England	Melbourne	1901-02
H.Trumble	Australia v England	Melbourne	1903-04
T.J.Matthews (2)[2]	Australia v South Africa	Manchester	1912
M.J.C.Allom[1]	England v New Zealand	Christchurch	1929-30
T.W.J.Goddard	England v South Africa	Johannesburg	1938-39
P.J.Loader	England v West Indies	Leeds	1957
L.F.Kline	Australia v South Africa	Cape Town	1957-58
W.W.Hall	West Indies v Pakistan	Lahore	1958-59
G.M.Griffin[7]	South Africa v England	Lord's	1960
L.R.Gibbs	West Indies v Australia	Adelaide	1960-61
P.J.Petherick[1/7]	New Zealand v Pakistan	Lahore	1976-77
C.A.Walsh[3]	West Indies v Australia	Brisbane	1988-89
M.G.Hughes[3/7]	Australia v West Indies	Perth	1988-89
D.W.Fleming[1]	Australia v Pakistan	Rawalpindi	1994-95
S.K.Warne	Australia v England	Melbourne	1994-95
D.G.Cork	England v West Indies	Manchester	1995
D.Gough[7]	England v Australia	Sydney	1998-99
Wasim Akram[4]	Pakistan v Sri Lanka	Lahore	1998-99
Wasim Akram[4]	Pakistan v Sri Lanka	Dhaka	1998-99
D.N.T.Zoysa[5]	Sri Lanka v Zimbabwe	Harare	1999-00
Abdul Razzaq	Pakistan v Sri Lanka	Galle	2000-01
G.D.McGrath	Australia v West Indies	Perth	2000-01
Harbhajan Singh	India v Australia	Calcutta	2000-01
Mohammad Sami[7]	Pakistan v Sri Lanka	Lahore	2001-02
J.J.C.Lawson[7]	West Indies v Australia	Bridgetown	2002-03
Alok Kapali[7]	Bangladesh v Pakistan	Peshawar	2003
A.M.Blignaut	Zimbabwe v Bangladesh	Harare	2003-04
M.J.Hoggard	England v West Indies	Bridgetown	2003-04
J.E.C.Franklin	New Zealand v Bangladesh	Dhaka	2004-05
I.K.Pathan[6/7]	India v Pakistan	Karachi	2005-06
R.J.Sidebottom[7]	England v New Zealand	Hamilton	2007-08
P.M.Siddle	Australia v England	Brisbane	2010-11
S.C.J.Broad	England v India	Nottingham	2011
Sohag Gazi	Bangladesh v New Zealand	Chittagong	2013-14
S.C.J.Broad[7]	England v Sri Lanka	Leeds	2014
H.M.R.K.B.Herath	Sri Lanka v Australia	Galle	2016

[1] On debut. [2] Hat-trick in each innings. [3] Involving both innings. [4] In successive Tests. [5] His first 3 balls (second over of the match). [6] The fourth, fifth and sixth balls of the match. [7] On losing side.

WICKET-KEEPING RECORDS
150 DISMISSALS IN TESTS†

Total			*Tests*	*Ct*	*St*
555	M.V.Boucher	South Africa/ICC	147	532	23
416	A.C.Gilchrist	Australia	96	379	37
395	I.A.Healy	Australia	119	366	29
355	R.W.Marsh	Australia	96	343	12
294	M.S.Dhoni	India	90	256	38
270	B.J.Haddin	Australia	66	262	8
270†	P.J.L.Dujon	West Indies	79	265	5
269	A.P.E.Knott	England	95	250	19
256	M.J.Prior	England	79	243	13
241†	A.J.Stewart	England	82	227	14
228	Wasim Bari	Pakistan	81	201	27
219	R.D.Jacobs	West Indies	65	207	12
219	T.G.Evans	England	91	173	46
217	D.Ramdin	West Indies	74	205	12
206	Kamran Akmal	Pakistan	53	184	22
201†	A.C.Parore	New Zealand	67	194	7
198	S.M.H.Kirmani	India	88	160	38
189	D.L.Murray	West Indies	62	181	8
187	A.T.W.Grout	Australia	51	163	24
178†	B.B.McCullum	New Zealand	52	168	11
176	I.D.S.Smith	New Zealand	63	168	8
174	R.W.Taylor	England	57	167	7
165	R.C.Russell	England	54	153	12
157	B.J.Watling	New Zealand	49	151	6
156	H.A.P.W.Jayawardena	Sri Lanka	58	124	32
152	D.J.Richardson	South Africa	42	150	2
151†	K.C.Sangakkara	Sri Lanka	48	131	20
151†	A.Flower	Zimbabwe	55	142	9

The most for Bangladesh is 95 (84 ct, 11 st) by Mushfiqur Rahim in 51 Tests.

† *Excluding catches taken in the field*

25 OR MORE DISMISSALS IN A SERIES

29	B.J.Haddin	Australia v England	2013
28	R.W.Marsh	Australia v England	1982-83
27 (inc 2st)	R.C.Russell	England v South Africa	1995-96
27 (inc 2st)	I.A.Healy	Australia v England (6 Tests)	1997
26 (inc 3st)	J.H.B.Waite	South Africa v New Zealand	1961-62
26	R.W.Marsh	Australia v West Indies (6 Tests)	1975-76
26 (inc 5st)	I.A.Healy	Australia v England (6 Tests)	1993
26 (inc 1st)	M.V.Boucher	South Africa v England	1998
26 (inc 2st)	A.C.Gilchrist	Australia v England	2001
26 (inc 2st)	A.C.Gilchrist	Australia v England	2006-07
25 (inc 2st)	I.A.Healy	Australia v England	1994-95
25 (inc 2st)	A.C.Gilchrist	Australia v England	2002-03
25	A.C.Gilchrist	Australia v India	2007-08

TEN OR MORE DISMISSALS IN A TEST

11	R.C.Russell	England v South Africa	Johannesburg	1995-96
11	A.B.de Villiers	South Africa v Pakistan	Johannesburg	2012-13
10	R.W.Taylor	England v India	Bombay	1979-80
10	A.C.Gilchrist	Australia v New Zealand	Hamilton	1999-00

SEVEN DISMISSALS IN AN INNINGS

7	Wasim Bari	Pakistan v New Zealand	Auckland	1978-79
7	R.W.Taylor	England v India	Bombay	1979-80

7	I.D.S.Smith	New Zealand v Sri Lanka	Hamilton	1990-91
7	R.D.Jacobs	West Indies v Australia	Melbourne	2000-01

FIVE STUMPINGS IN AN INNINGS

5	K.S.More	India v West Indies	Madras	1987-88

FIELDING RECORDS
100 CATCHES IN TESTS

Total			*Tests*	*Total*			*Tests*
210	R.S.Dravid	India/ICC	164	122	I.V.A.Richards	West Indies	121
205	D.P.M.D.Jayawardena	Sri Lanka	149	121	A.J.Strauss	England	100
200	J.H.Kallis	South Africa/ICC	166	120	I.T.Botham	England	102
196	R.T.Ponting	Australia	168	120	M.C.Cowdrey	England	114
181	M.E.Waugh	Australia	128	115	C.L.Hooper	West Indies	102
171	S.P.Fleming	New Zealand	111	115	S.R.Tendulkar	India	200
169	G.C.Smith	South Africa/ICC	117	112	S.R.Waugh	Australia	168
164	B.C.Lara	West Indies/ICC	131	110	R.B.Simpson	Australia	62
157	M.A.Taylor	Australia	104	110	W.R.Hammond	England	85
156	A.R.Border	Australia	156	109	G.St A.Sobers	West Indies	93
141	A.N.Cook	England	140	108	S.M.Gavaskar	India	125
135	V.V.S.Laxman	India	134	105	I.M.Chappell	Australia	75
134	M.J.Clarke	Australia	115	105	M.Azharuddin	India	99
129	Younus Khan	Pakistan	115	105	G.P.Thorpe	England	100
128	M.L.Hayden	Australia	103	104†	A.B.de Villiers	South Africa	82
125	S.K.Warne	Australia	145	103	G.A.Gooch	England	118
122	L.R.P.L.Taylor	New Zealand	80	100	I.R.Bell	England	118
122	G.S.Chappell	Australia	87				

The most for Zimbabwe is 60 by A.D.R.Campbell (60) and for Bangladesh 31 by Mahmudullah (32).

† *Excluding catches taken when wicket-keeping.*

15 CATCHES IN A SERIES

15	J.M.Gregory	Australia v England	1920-21

SEVEN OR MORE CATCHES IN A TEST

8	A.M.Rahane	India v Sri Lanka	Galle	2015
7	G.S.Chappell	Australia v England	Perth	1974-75
7	Yajurvindra Singh	India v England	Bangalore	1976-77
7	H.P.Tillekeratne	Sri Lanka v New Zealand	Colombo (SSC)	1992-93
7	S.P.Fleming	New Zealand v Zimbabwe	Harare	1997-98
7	M.L.Hayden	Australia v Sri Lanka	Galle	2003-04

FIVE CATCHES IN AN INNINGS

5	V.Y.Richardson	Australia v South Africa	Durban	1935-36
5	Yajurvindra Singh	India v England	Bangalore	1976-77
5	M.Azharuddin	India v Pakistan	Karachi	1989-90
5	K.Srikkanth	India v Australia	Perth	1991-92
5	S.P.Fleming	New Zealand v Zimbabwe	Harare	1997-98
5	G.C.Smith	South Africa v Australia	Perth	2012-13
5	D.J.G.Sammy	West Indies v India	Mumbai	2013-14
5	D.M.Bravo	West Indies v Bangladesh	Kingstown	2014
5	A.M.Rahane	India v Sri Lanka	Galle	2015
5	J.Blackwood	West Indies v Sri Lanka	Colombo (PSS)	2015-16

APPEARANCE RECORDS
100 TEST MATCH APPEARANCES

			Opponents									
			E	*A*	*SA*	*WI*	*NZ*	*I*	*P*	*SL*	*Z*	*B*
200	S.R.Tendulkar	India	32	39	25	21	24	–	18	25	9	7
168†	R.T.Ponting	Australia	35	–	26	24	17	29	15	14	3	4
168	S.R.Waugh	Australia	46	–	16	32	23	18	20	8	3	2
166†	J.H.Kallis	South Africa/ICC	31	28	–	24	18	18	19	15	6	6
164	S.Chanderpaul	West Indies	35	20	24	–	21	25	14	7	8	10
164†	R.S.Dravid	India/ICC	21	32	21	23	15	–	15	20	9	7
156	A.R.Border	Australia	47	–	6	31	23	20	22	7	–	–
149	D.P.M.D.Jayawardena	Sri Lanka	23	16	18	11	13	18	29	–	8	13
147†	M.V.Boucher	South Africa/ICC	25	20	–	24	17	14	15	17	6	8
145†	S.K.Warne	Australia	36	–	24	19	20	14	15	13	1	2
140	A.N.Cook	England	–	30	15	17	13	25	18	16	–	6
134	V.V.S.Laxman	India	17	29	19	22	10	–	15	13	6	3
134	K.C.Sangakkara	Sri Lanka	22	11	17	12	12	17	23	–	5	15
133†	M.Muralitharan	Sri Lanka/ICC	16	12	15	12	14	22	16	–	14	11
133	A.J.Stewart	England	–	33	23	24	16	9	13	9	6	–
132	A.Kumble	India	19	20	21	17	11	–	15	18	7	4
132	C.A.Walsh	West Indies	36	38	10	–	10	15	18	3	2	–
131	Kapil Dev	India	27	20	4	25	10	–	29	14	2	–
131†	B.C.Lara	West Indies/ICC	30	30	18	–	11	17	12	8	2	2
128	M.E.Waugh	Australia	29	–	18	28	14	14	15	9	1	–
125	S.M.Gavaskar	India	38	20	–	27	9	–	24	7	–	–
124	Javed Miandad	Pakistan	22	24	–	17	18	28	–	12	3	–
124†	G.D.McGrath	Australia	30	–	17	23	14	11	17	8	1	2
122	J.M.Anderson	England	–	26	20	14	12	22	13	11	2	2
121	I.V.A.Richards	West Indies	36	34	–	–	7	28	16	–	–	–
120†	Inzamam-ul-Haq	Pakistan/ICC	19	13	13	15	12	10	–	20	11	6
119	I.A.Healy	Australia	33	–	12	28	11	9	14	11	1	–
118	I.R.Bell	England	–	33	11	12	13	20	13	10	–	6
118	G.A.Gooch	England	–	42	3	26	15	19	10	3	–	–
117	D.I.Gower	England	–	42	–	19	13	24	17	2	–	–
117†	G.C.Smith	South Africa/ICC	21	21	–	14	13	15	16	7	2	8
116	D.L.Haynes	West Indies	36	33	1	–	10	19	16	1	–	–
116	D.B.Vengsarkar	India	26	24		25	11	–	22	8	–	–
115	M.A.Atherton	England	–	33	18	27	11	7	11	4	4	–
115†	M.J.Clarke	Australia	35	–	14	12	11	22	10	8	–	2
115	Younus Khan	Pakistan	17	11	14	12	11	9	–	29	5	7
114	M.C.Cowdrey	England	–	43	14	21	18	8	10	–	–	–
113	S.C.Ganguly	India	12	24	17	12	8	–	12	14	9	5
113†	D.L.Vettori	New Zealand/ICC	17	18	14	10	–	15	9	11	9	9
111	S.P.Fleming	New Zealand	19	14	15	11	–	13	9	13	11	6
111	W.P.J.U.C.Vaas	Sri Lanka	15	12	11	9	10	14	18	–	15	7
110	S.T.Jayasuriya	Sri Lanka	14	13	15	10	13	10	17	–	13	5
110	C.H.Lloyd	West Indies	34	29	–	–	8	28	11	–	–	–
108	G.Boycott	England	–	38	7	29	15	13	6	–	–	–
108	C.G.Greenidge	West Indies	29	32	–	–	10	23	14	–	–	–
108	S.M.Pollock	South Africa	23	13	–	16	11	12	12	13	5	3
107	D.C.Boon	Australia	31	–	6	22	17	11	11	9	–	–
106	A.B.de Villiers	South Africa	20	20	–	13	10	17	12	7	3	4
105†	J.L.Langer	Australia	21	–	11	18	14	14	13	8	3	2
104	K.P.Pietersen	England	–	27	10	14	8	16	14	11	–	4
104†	V.Sehwag	India/ICC	17	23	15	10	12	–	9	11	3	4
104	M.A.Taylor	Australia	33	–	11	20	11	9	12	8	–	–
104	Wasim Akram	Pakistan	18	13	4	17	9	12	–	19	10	2
103	C.H.Gayle	West Indies	20	8	16	–	12	14	8	10	8	7

			Opponents									
			E	*A*	*SA*	*WI*	*NZ*	*I*	*P*	*SL*	*Z*	*B*
103	Harbhajan Singh	India	14	18	11	11	13	–	9	16	7	4
103†	M.L.Hayden	Australia	20	–	19	15	11	18	6	7	2	4
103	Salim Malik	Pakistan	19	15	1	7	18	22	–	15	6	–
102	I.T.Botham	England	–	36	–	20	15	14	14	3	–	–
102	S.C.J.Broad	England	–	22	14	12	12	15	14	10	–	3
102	C.L.Hooper	West Indies	24	25	10	–	2	19	14	6	2	–
101	G.Kirsten	South Africa	22	18	–	13	13	10	11	9	3	2
101	B.B.McCullum	New Zealand	16	16	13	13	–	10	8	12	4	9
101	M.Ntini	South Africa	18	15	–	15	11	10	9	12	3	8
100	H.M.Amla	South Africa	17	17	–	9	11	18	11	10	1	6
100	G.P.Thorpe	England	–	16	16	27	13	5	8	9	2	4
100	A.J.Strauss	England	–	20	16	18	9	12	13	8	–	4

† Includes appearance in the Australia v ICC 'Test' in 2005-06. The most for Zimbabwe is 67 by G.W.Flower, and for Bangladesh 61 by Mohammad Ashraful.

100 CONSECUTIVE TEST APPEARANCES

153	A.R.Border	Australia	March 1979 to March 1994
138	A.N.Cook	England	May 2006 to December 2016
107	M.E.Waugh	Australia	June 1993 to October 2002
106	S.M.Gavaskar	India	January 1975 to February 1987
101	B.B.McCullum	New Zealand	March 2004 to February 2016

50 TESTS AS CAPTAIN

			Won	*Lost*	*Drawn*	*Tied*
109	G.C.Smith	South Africa	53	29	27	–
93	A.R.Border	Australia	32	22	38	1
80	S.P.Fleming	New Zealand	28	27	25	–
77	R.T.Ponting	Australia	48	16	13	–
74	C.H.Lloyd	West Indies	36	12	26	–
60	M.S.Dhoni	India	27	18	15	–
59	A.N.Cook	England	24	22	13	–
57	S.R.Waugh	Australia	41	9	7	–
56	A.Ranatunga	Sri Lanka	12	19	25	–
54	M.A.Atherton	England	13	21	20	–
53	W.J.Cronje	South Africa	27	11	15	–
53	Misbah-ul-Haq	Pakistan	24	18	11	–
51	M.P.Vaughan	England	26	11	14	–
50	I.V.A.Richards	West Indies	27	8	15	–
50	M.A.Taylor	Australia	26	13	11	–
50	A.J.Strauss	England	24	11	15	–

The most for Zimbabwe is 21 by A.D.R.Campbell and H.H.Streak, and for Bangladesh 28 by Mushfiqur Rahim.

50 TEST UMPIRING APPEARANCES

128	S.A.Bucknor	(West Indies)	28.04.1989 to 22.03.2009
109	Alim Dar	(Pakistan)	21.10.2003 to 05.01.2017
108	R.E.Koertzen	(South Africa)	26.12.1992 to 24.07.2010
95	D.J.Harper	(Australia)	28.11.1998 to 23.06.2011
92	D.R.Shepherd	(England)	01.08.1985 to 07.06.2005
84	B.F.Bowden	(New Zealand)	11.03.2000 to 03.05.2015
78	D.B.Hair	(Australia)	25.01.1992 to 08.06.2008
74	S.J.A.Taufel	(Australia)	26.12.2000 to 20.08.2012
73	S.Venkataraghavan	(India)	29.01.1993 to 20.01.2004
66	H.D.Bird	(England)	05.07.1973 to 24.06.1996
58	I.J.Gould	(England)	19.11.2008 to 30.12.2016
57	S.J.Davis	(Australia)	27.11.1997 to 25.04.2015
51	R.J.Tucker	(Australia)	15.02.2010 to 14.01.2017

THE FIRST-CLASS COUNTIES REGISTER, RECORDS AND 2016 AVERAGES

All statistics are to 12 March 2017.

ABBREVIATIONS – General

*	not out/unbroken partnership
b	born
BB	Best innings bowling analysis
Cap	Awarded 1st XI County Cap
f-c	first-class
HS	Highest Score
IT20	International Twenty20
l-o	limited-overs
LOI	Limited-Overs Internationals
Tests	International Test Matches
F-c Tours	Overseas tours involving first-class appearances

Awards

PCA 2016	Professional Cricketers' Association Player of 2016
Wisden 2015	One of *Wisden Cricketers' Almanack*'s Five Cricketers of 2015
YC 2016	Cricket Writers' Club Young Cricketer of 2016

ECB Competitions

BHC	Benson & Hedges Cup (1972-2002)
CB40	Clydesdale Bank 40 (2010-12)
CC	Specsavers County Championship
C>	Cheltenham & Gloucester Trophy (2001-06)
FPT	Friends Provident Trophy (2007-09)
NL	National League (1999-2005)
NWT	NatWest Trophy (1981-2000)
P40	NatWest PRO 40 League (2006-09)
RLC	Royal London One-Day Cup (2014-16)
SL	Sunday League (1969-98)
T20	Twenty20 Competition
Y40	Yorkshire Bank 40 (2013)

Education

Ac	Academy
BHS	Boys' High School
C	College
CS	Comprehensive School
GS	Grammar School
HS	High School
I	Institute
S	School
SFC	Sixth Form College
SS	Secondary School
TC	Technical College
U	University
UWIC	University of Wales Institute, Cardiff

Playing Categories

LBG	Bowls right-arm leg-breaks and googlies
LF	Bowls left-arm fast
LFM	Bowls left-arm fast-medium
LHB	Bats left-handed
LM	Bowls left-arm medium pace
LMF	Bowls left-arm medium fast
OB	Bowls right-arm off-breaks
RF	Bowls right-arm fast
RFM	Bowls right-arm fast-medium
RHB	Bats right-handed
RM	Bowls right-arm medium pace
RMF	Bowls right-arm medium-fast
SLA	Bowls left-arm leg-breaks
SLC	Bowls left-arm 'Chinamen'
WK	Wicket-keeper

Teams (see also p 226)

AS	Adelaide Strikers
BH	Brisbane Heat
CC&C	Combined Campuses & Colleges
CD	Central Districts
CSK	Chennai Super Kings
DC	Deccan Chargers
DD	Delhi Daredevils
EL	England Lions
EP	Eastern Province
GL	Gujarat Lions
GW	Griqualand West
HB	Habib Bank Limited
HH	Hobart Hurricanes
KKR	Kolkata Knight Riders
KRL	Khan Research Laboratories
KXIP	Kings XI Punjab
KZN	KwaZulu-Natal Inland
ME	Mashonaland Eagles
MI	Mumbai Indians
MR	Melbourne Renegades
MS	Melbourne Stars
MT	Matabeleland Tuskers
MWR	Mid West Rhinos
NBP	National Bank of Pakistan
ND	Northern Districts
NSW	New South Wales
NT	Northern Transvaal
NW	North West
(O)FS	(Orange) Free State
PDSC	Prime Doleshwar Sporting Club
PIA	Pakistan International Airlines
PS	Perth Scorchers
PT	Pakistan Television
PTC	Pakistan Telecommunication Co
PW	Pune Warriors
Q	Queensland
RCB	Royal Challengers Bangalore
RPS	Rising Pune Supergiants
RR	Rajasthan Royals
SH	Sunrisers Hyderabad
SJD	Sheikh Jamal Dhanmondi
SNGPL	Sui Northern Gas Pipelines Limited
SR	Southern Rocks
SS	Sydney Sixers
SSGC	Sui Southern Gas Corporation
ST	Sydney Thunder
Tas	Tasmania
T&T	Trinidad & Tobago
TU	Tamil Union
Vic	Victoria
WA	Western Australia
WAPDA	Water & Power Development Authority
WP	Western Province
ZTB	Zarai Taraqiati Bank Limited

DERBYSHIRE

Formation of Present Club: 4 November 1870
Inaugural First-Class Match: 1871
Colours: Chocolate, Amber and Pale Blue
Badge: Rose and Crown
County Champions: (1) 1936
NatWest Trophy Winners: (1) 1981
Benson and Hedges Cup Winners: (1) 1993
Sunday League Winners: (1) 1990
Twenty20 Cup Winners: (0) best – Quarter-Finalist 2005

Chief Executive: Simon Storey, Derbyshire County Cricket Club, The 3aaa County Ground, Nottingham Road, Derby, DE21 6DA • Tel: 01332 388101 • Fax: 0844 500 8322 • Email: info@derbyshireccc.com • Web: www. derbyshireccc.com • Twitter: @DerbyshireCCC (27,852 followers)

Director of Cricket: Kim Barnett. **T20 Head Coach**: John Wright. **Captain**: B.A.Godleman. **Vice-Captain**: G.C.Wilson. **Overseas Players**: Imran Tahir and B.M.A.J.Mendis. **2017 Testimonial**: W.L.Madsen. **Head Groundsman**: Neil Godrich. **Scorer**: John Brown. ‡ New registration. NQ Not qualified for England.

CORK, Gregory Teodor Gerald (Denstone C), b Derby 29 Sep 1994. Son of D.G.Cork (Derbyshire, Lancashire, Hampshire and England 1990-2011). 6'2". RHB, LMF. Squad No 14. Debut (Derbyshire) 2016. Derbyshire 2nd XI debut 2011. HS 49 and BB – v Worcs (Worcester) 2016. LO HS 8 v Sri Lanka A (Derby) 2016. LO BB 2-17 v Somerset (Taunton) 2015 (RLC). T20 HS 13*. T20 BB 2-36.

COTTON, Benjamin David (Clayton Hall C; Stoke-on-Trent SFC), b Stoke-on-Trent, Staffs 13 Sep 1993. 6'4". RHB, RMF. Squad No 36. Debut (Derbyshire) 2014. Derbyshire 2nd XI debut 2011. HS 43 v Leics (Derby) 2015. BB 4-20 v Leics (Derby) 2014. LO HS 18* v Yorks (Scarborough) 2014 (RLC). LO BB 4-43 v Worcs (Worcester) 2016 (RLC). T20 HS 8. T20 BB 2-19.

CRITCHLEY, Matthew James John (St Michael's HS, Chorley), b Preston, Lancs 13 Aug 1996. 6'2". RHB, LB. Squad No 20. Debut (Derbyshire) 2015. Derbyshire 2nd XI debut 2014. HS 137* v Northants (Derby) 2015. BB 3-50 v Lancs (Southport) 2015. LO HS 43 v Notts (Mkt Warsop) 2016 (RLC). LO BB 4-48 v Northants (Derby) 2015 (RLC). T20 HS 10. T20 BB 3-36.

DAVIS, William Samuel (Stafford GS), b 6 Mar 1996. 6'1". RHB, RFM. Squad No 44. Debut (Derbyshire) 2015. Derbyshire 2nd XI debut 2013. HS 15 v Leics (Derby) 2016. BB 7-146 v Glamorgan (Colwyn Bay) 2016. LO HS – .

GODLEMAN, Billy Ashley (Islington Green S), b Islington, London 11 Feb 1989. 6'3". LHB, LB. Squad No 1. Middlesex 2005-09. Essex 2010-12. Derbyshire debut 2013; cap 2015; captain 2016 to date. 1000 runs (1): 1069 (2015). HS 204 v Worcs (Derby) 2016. BB – . LO HS 109* v Northants (Derby) 2015 (RLC). T20 HS 69.

HEMMINGS, Robert Philip (Sir Thomas Boughey S, Stoke-on-Trent; Denstone C), b Newcastle-under-Lyme, Staffs 28 Feb 1996. 6'4". RHB, RM. Squad No 24. Debut (Derbyshire) 2016. Derbyshire 2nd XI debut 2015. BB – . LO HS 25* v Sri Lanka A (Derby) 2016. LO –.

‡[NQ]**HENRY, Matt**hew James, b Christchurch, New Zealand 14 Dec 1991. RHB, RFM. Squad No 21. Canterbury 2010-11 to date. Worcestershire 2016. **Tests** (NZ): 7 (2015 to 2016-17); HS 66 v A (Christchurch) 2015-16; BB 4-93 v E (Lord's) 2015. **LOI** (NZ): 30 (2013-14 to 2016-17); HS 48* v P (Wellington) 2015-16; BB 5-30 v P (Abu Dhabi) 2014-15. **IT20** (NZ): 6 (2014-15 to 2016-17); HS 10 v P (Auckland) 2015-16; BB 3-44 v SL (Mt Maunganui) 2015-16. F-c Tours (NZ): E 2014 (NZ A), 2015; A 2015-16; I 2016-17; SL 2013-14 (NZ A). HS 75* Canterbury v CD (Rangiora) 2015-16. CC HS 49* Wo v Leics (Leicester) 2016. BB 5-18 NZ A v Surrey (Oval) 2014. CC BB 5-36 Wo v Northants (Northampton) 2016. LO HS 48* (*see LOI*). LO BB 6-45 Canterbury v Auckland (Auckland) 2012-13. T20 HS 42. T20 BB 4-43.

HOSEIN, Harvey Richard (Denstone C), b Chesterfield 12 Aug 1996. 5'10". RHB, WK. Squad No 16. Debut (Derbyshire) 2014, taking seven catches in an innings and UK record-equalling 11 in match v Surrey (The Oval). Derbyshire 2nd XI debut 2010, aged 13y 287d. HS 108 v Worcs (Worcester) 2016. LO HS 40 v Notts (Mkt Warsop) 2016 (RLC). T20 HS 0*.

HUGHES, Alex Lloyd (Ounsdale HS, Wolverhampton), b Wordsley, Staffs 29 Sep 1991. 5'10". RHB, RM. Squad No 18. Debut (Derbyshire) 2013. HS 140 v Glos (Derby) 2016. BB 4-46 v Glamorgan (Derby) 2014. LO HS 59* v Essex (Leek) 2013 (Y40). LO BB 3-31 v Leics (Derby) 2015 (RLC). T20 HS 43*. T20 BB 3-23.

‡[NQ]**IMRAN TAHIR,** Mohammad (Government Pakistan Angels HS and MAO College, Lahore), b Lahore, Pakistan 4 Jun 1979. 5'11". RHB, LB. Squad No 99. Lahore City 1996-97 to 1997-98. WAPDA 1998-99. REDCO 1999-00. Lahore Whites 2000-01. SNGPL 2001-02 to 2003-04. Sialkot 2002-03. Middlesex 2003. Lahore Blues 2004-05. PIA 2004-05 to 2006-07. Lahore Ravi 2005-06. Yorkshire (1 match) 2007. Titans 2007-08 to 2009-10. Hampshire 2008-14; cap 2009. Easterns 2008-09 to 2009-10. Warwickshire 2010; cap 2010. Dolphins 2010-11 to date. Lions 2012-13 to 2013-14. Nottinghamshire 2015-16; cap 2015. Staffordshire 2004-05. Qualified for SA on 1 Apr 2009. IPL: DD 2014 to 2016. **Tests** (SA): 20 (2011-12 to 2015-16); HS 29* v SL (Centurion) 2011-12; BB 5-32 v P (Dubai) 2013-14. **LOI** (SA): 74 (2010-11 to 2016-17); HS 29 v WI (Bridgetown) 2016; LO BB 7-45 v WI (Basseterre) 2016. **IT20** (SA): 31 (2013 to 2016-17); HS 9* v Netherlands (Chittagong) 2013-14, BB 5-24 v NZ (Auckland) 2016-17. F-c Tours (SA): E 2012; A 2012-13; NZ 2011-12; I 2015-16; SL 2004-05 (Pak A), 2014; UAE 2013-14 (v P). HS 77* H v Somerset (Southampton) 2009. 50 wkts (2+2); most – 74 (2004-05). BB 8-42 (12-133 match) Dolphins v Knights (Kimberley) 2015-16. UK BB 7-66 (12-189 match) H v Lancs (Manchester) 2008. LO HS 41* Staffs v Lancs (Stone) 2004 (CGT). LO BB 7-45 (*see LOI*). T20 HS 17*. T20 BB 5-24.

MacDONELL, Charles Michael (Wellingborough S; Collingwood C, Durham U), b Basingstoke, Hants 23 Feb 1995. RHB, RFM. Squad No 3. Durham MCCU 2015-16. Derbyshire debut 2016. Northamptonshire 2nd XI 2014-15. MCC Univs 2015. Durham 2nd XI 2015. Derbyshire 2nd XI 2016. Buckinghamshire 2014-15. HS 91 v Glos (Bristol) 2016. BB – . LO HS 19 v Sri Lanka A (Derby) 2016.

MADSEN, Wayne Lee (Kearsney C, Durban; U of South Africa), b Durban, South Africa 2 Jan 1984. Nephew of M.B.Madsen (Natal 1967-68 to 1978-79), T.R.Madsen (Natal 1976-77 to 1989-90) and H.R.Fotheringham (Natal, Transvaal 1971-72 to 1989-90), cousin of G.S.Fotheringham (KwaZulu-Natal 2008-09 to 2009-10). 5'11". RHB, OB. Squad No 77. KwaZulu-Natal 2003-04 to 2007-08. Dolphins 2006-07 to 2007-08. Derbyshire debut 2009, scoring 170 v Glos (Cheltenham); cap 2011; captain 2012-15; testimonial 2017. Qualified for England by residence in February 2015. 1000 runs (4); most – 1292 (2016). HS 231* v Northants (Northampton) 2012. BB 3-45 KZN v EP (Pt Elizabeth) 2007-08. De BB 2-9 v Sussex (Hove) 2013. LO HS 138 v Hants (Derby) 2014 (RLC). LO BB 3-27 v Durham (Derby) 2013 (Y40). T20 HS 65. T20 BB 1-7.

‡[NQ]**MENDIS**, Balapuwaduge Mankulasuriya Amith **Jeevan** (St Thomas C), b Colombo, Sri Lanka 15 Jan 1983. 5'8". LHB, LB. Squad No 88. Bloomfield 2000-01. Sinhalese 2002-03 to 2007-08. Tamil Union 2008-09 to date. Kandurata 2009-10. IPL: DD 2013. Big Bash: SS 2012-13. Joins Derbyshire for the first half of 2017. **LOI** (SL): 54 (2010 to 2014-15); HS 72 v I (Pallekele) 2012; BB 3-15 v NZ (Hambantota) 2012-13. **IT20** (SL): 16 (2011 to 2013); HS 43* and BB 3-24 v Z (Hambantota) 2012-13. F-c Tours (SLA): E 2004; A 2010; WI 2006-07; P 2002-03; B 2005-06. HS 206* Tamil v Colombo (Colombo CC) 2012-13. BB 6-37 (and 109) Tamil v Saracens (Colombo, PSS) 2011. LO HS 99* SL v Worcs (Worcester) 2011. LO BB 5-12 Tamil v Chilaw Marians (Colombo, PSS) 2013-14. T20 HS 67. T20 BB 4-14.

MILNES, Thomas Patrick (Heart of England S, Coventry), b Stourbridge, Worcs 6 Oct 1992. 5'11". RHB, RMF. Squad No 8. Warwickshire 2011-15. Derbyshire debut 2015. England U19 2010-11. HS 56 v Glos (Derby) 2016. BB 7-39 Wa v Oxford MCCU (Oxford) 2013. CC BB 6-93 v Essex (Derby) 2016. LO HS 16 Wa v Worcs (Birmingham) 2013 (Y40). LO BB 2-73 Wa v Northants (Birmingham) 2013 (Y40). T20 HS 0. T20 BB – .

PALLADINO, Antonio Paul (Cardinal Pole SS; Anglia Polytechnic U), b Tower Hamlets, London 29 Jun 1983. 6'0". RHB, RMF. Squad No 28. Cambridge UCCE 2003-05. Essex 2003-10. Namibia 2009-10. Derbyshire debut 2011; cap 2012. HS 106 v Australia A (Derby) 2012. CC HS 68 v Warwks (Birmingham) 2013. 50 wkts (2); most – 56 (2012). BB 7-53 v Kent (Derby) 2012. Hat-trick v Leics (Leicester) 2012. LO HS 31 Namibia v Boland (Windhoek) 2009-10. LO BB 5-49 v Lancs (Derby) 2014 (RLC). T20 HS 14*. T20 BB 4-21.

‡**REECE, Luis** Michael (St Michael's HS, Chorley; Leeds Met U), b Taunton, Somerset 4 Aug 1990. 6'1". LHB, LM. Squad No 10. Leeds/Bradford MCCU 2012-13. Lancashire 2013-15, no f-c appearances in 2016. MCC 2014. Unicorns 2011-12. HS 114* and BB 4-28 LBU v Leics (Leicester) 2013. CC HS 97 La v Glos (Bristol) 2013. CC BB 1-20 La v Hants (Southport) 2013. LO HS 59 Unicorns v Derbys (Chesterfield) 2012 (CB40). LO BB 4-35 Unicorns v Glos (Exmouth) 2011 (CB40). T20 HS 32. T20 BB 2-29.

SLATER, Benjamin Thomas (Netherthorpe S; Leeds Met U), b Chesterfield 26 Aug 1991. 5'10". LHB, OB. Squad No 26. Debut (Leeds/Bradford MCCU) 2012. Southern Rocks 2012-13. Derbyshire debut 2013. HS 119 v Leics (Derby) 2014, also scored 104 in same match. BB – . LO HS 148* v Northants (Northampton) 2016 (RLC). T20 HS 57.

[NQ]**SMIT, Daryn** (Northwood S; U of SA), b Durban, South Africa 28 Jan 1984. RHB, LB, occ WK. KwaZulu Natal 2004-05 to date. Dolphins 2005-06 to date. Joins Derbyshire on a two-year deal, and qualifies as a non-overseas player. 1000 runs (0+1): 1081 (2015-16). HS 156* KZN v NW (Durban) 2015-16. BB 7-27 KZN v SW Districts (Durban) 2013-14. LO HS 109 Dolphins v Warriors (East London) 2011-12. LO BB 4-39 KZN v GW (Kimberley) 2013-14. T20 HS 57. T20 BB 3-19.

TAYLOR, Thomas Alex Ian (Trentham HS, Stoke-on-Trent), b Stoke-on-Trent, Staffs 21 Dec 1994. 6'2". RHB, RMF. Squad No 15. Debut (Derbyshire) 2014. Derbyshire 2nd XI debut 2011. HS 80 v Kent (Derby) 2016. BB 6-61 v Lancs (Derby) 2015. LO HS – . LO BB 3-48 v Worcs (Worcester) 2014 (RLC).

THAKOR, Shivsinh Jaysinh (Loughborough GS; Uppingham S), b Leicester 22 Oct 1993. 6'1". RHB, RM. Squad No 57. Leicestershire 2011-13. No f-c appearances in 2014. Derbyshire debut 2015. Leicestershire 2nd XI debut 2008, aged 14y 218d. England U19 2010-11. HS 134 Le v Loughborough MCCU (Leicester) 2011 – on debut. CC HS 130 and BB 5-63 v Kent (Derby) 2016. LO HS 83* Le v Lancs (Leicester) 2012 (CB40). LO BB Le 4-49 v Worcs (Leicester) 2014 (RLC). T20 HS 42. T20 BB 3-17.

‡[NQ]**VILJOEN**, GC ('**Hardus**') b Witbank, South Africa 6 Mar 1989. RHB, RF. Squad No 7. Easterns 2008-09 to 2011-12. Titans 2009-10 to 2011-12. Lions 2012-13 to date. Kent 2016. Kolpak signing for 2017. **Tests** (SA): 1 (2015-16); HS 20* and BB 1-79 v E (Johannesburg) 2015-16. F-c Tours (SA A): A 2014, 2016; I 2015; Z 2016. HS 72 Lions v Titans (Centurion) 2015-16. CC HS 63 K v Northants (Beckenham) 2016. 50 wkts (0+1): 68 (2010-11). BB 8-105 Easterns v Northerns (Benoni) 2010-11. CC BB 5-55 K v Glos (Bristol) 2016. LO HS 54* Easterns v Boland (Paarl) 2011-12. LO BB 6-19 Lions v Titans (Centurion) 2012-13. T20 HS 41*. T20 BB 5-16.

‡[NQ]**WILSON, Gary** Craig (Methodist C, Belfast; Manchester Met U), b Dundonald, N Ireland 5 Feb 1986. 5'10". RHB, WK. Squad No 9. Ireland 2005 to date. Surrey 2010-16; cap 2014. MCC YC 2005. **LOI** (Ire): 73 (2007 to 2016-17); HS 113 v Netherlands (Dublin) 2010. **IT20** (Ire): 51 (2008 to 2016-17); HS 65* v Scotland (Dubai, DSC) 2016-17. HS 160* Sy v Leics (Oval) 2014. BB – . LO HS 113 (*see LOI*). T20 HS 65*.

WOOD, Thomas Anthony (Heanor Gate Science C), b Derby 11 May 1994. RHB, RM. Squad No 23. Debut (Derbyshire) 2016. Derbyshire 2nd XI debut 2014. HS 14 v Leics (Derby) 2016. LO HS 44 v Sri Lanka A (Derby) 2016.

RELEASED/RETIRED

(Having made a County 1st XI appearance in 2016)

[NQ]**BROOM, Neil** Trevor, b Christchurch, New Zealand 20 Nov 1983. Older brother of D.J.Broom (Otago 2009-10 to 2012-13). RHB, RM. Canterbury 2002-03 to 2014-15. Otago 2005-06 to date. Derbyshire 2016. **LOI** (NZ): 30 (2008-09 to 2009-10); HS 109* v B (Nelson) 2016-17. **IT20** (NZ): 11 (2008-09 to 2016-17); HS 36 v A (Sydney) 2008-09. F-c Tours (NZ A): I 2008 09, 2013-14. HS 203* Otago v ND (Queenstown) 2010-11. De HS 96 v Kent (Derby) 2016. BB 1-8 Canterbury v Otago (Christchurch) 2002-03. De BB 1-9 v Leics (Leicester) 2016. LO HS 164 Otago v Canterbury (Timaru) 2009-10. LO BB 2-59 NZ A v India A (Chennai) 2008-09. T20 HS 117*. T20 BB 2-19.

CARTER, Andrew (Lincoln C), b Lincoln 27 Aug 1988. 6'4". RHB, RM. Nottinghamshire 2009-15. Essex 2010 (on loan). Glamorgan 2015 (on loan). Derbyshire 2016. Hampshire (on loan) 2016. Lincolnshire 2007-10. HS 39 v Glamorgan (Derby) 2016. BB 5-40 Ex v Kent (Canterbury) 2010. De BB 3-114 v Northants (Northampton) 2016. LO HS 12 v Sussex (Hove) 2009 (P40). LO BB 4-45 v Durham (Nottingham) 2012 (CB40). T20 HS 5*. T20 BB 4-20.

DURSTON, Wesley John (Millfield S; University C, Worcester), b Taunton, Somerset 6 Oct 1980. 5'10". RHB, OB. Somerset 2002-09. Derbyshire 2010-16; cap 2012. Unicorns 2010 (l-o only). 1000 runs (1): 1138 (2011). HS 151 v Glos (Derby) 2011. BB 6-109 v Leics (Derby) 2015. LO HS 134 v Hants (Derby) 2014 (RLC). LO BB 3-7 v Worcs (Derby) 2011 (CB40). T20 HS 111 v Notts (Nottingham) 2010 – De record. T20 BB 3-14.

HUGHES, Chesney Francis (Albena Lake Hodge CS, Anguilla), b Anguilla 20 January 1991. 6'2". LHB, SLA. UK passport. Derbyshire 2010-16. Leeward Is 2015-16 to date. HS 270* v Yorks (Leeds) 2013. BB 3-87 v Glos (Bristol) 2016. LO HS 81 Leeward Is v Windward Is (Kingston) 2010-11. LO BB 5-29 v Unicorns (Wormsley) 2012 (CB40). T20 HS 65. T20 BB 4-23.

MELLOR, Alexander James (Westwood C, Leek; Staffs U), b Stoke-on-Trent, Staffs 22 Jul 1991. LHB, WK. Derbyshire 2016. Staffordshire 2014-15. Has played for seven different counties in 2nd XI championship. HS 44 v Essex (Derby) 2016. LO HS – . T20 HS 10*.

RELEASED/RETIRED continued on p 96

DERBYSHIRE 2016

RESULTS SUMMARY

	Place	Won	Lost	Drew	Aband	NR
Specsavers County Champ (2nd Division)	9th		5	10	1	
All First-Class Matches			5	10	1	
Royal London One-Day Cup (North Group)	7th	2	3			3
NatWest t20 Blast (North Group)	7th	5	7			2

SPECSAVERS COUNTY CHAMPIONSHIP AVERAGES
BATTING AND FIELDING

Cap		*M*	*I*	*NO*	*HS*	*Runs*	*Avge*	*100*	*50*	*Ct/St*
	H.R.Hosein	4	8	4	108	423	105.75	1	4	9
	S.J.Thakor	9	13	4	130	606	67.33	2	2	–
2011	W.L.Madsen	15	26	4	163	1292	58.72	6	3	11
	C.F.Hughes	11	19	4	137*	806	53.73	3	4	8
2015	B.A.Godleman	13	24	–	204	934	38.91	3	2	6
	A.L.Hughes	5	9	–	140	299	33.22	1	1	7
	B.T.Slater	9	15	1	110	393	28.07	1	1	3
	H.D.Rutherford	10	17	1	78	441	27.56	–	3	8
	N.T.Broom	14	22	1	96	530	25.23	–	2	7
	T.A.I.Taylor	3	6	–	80	147	24.50	–	1	–
	M.J.J.Critchley	7	12	1	70*	263	23.90	–	1	3
	A.Carter	4	4	1	39	68	22.66	–	–	2
	T.P.Milnes	5	9	–	56	188	20.88	–	1	1
	T.Poynton	9	11	2	53	167	18.55	–	1	15/1
2012	A.P.Palladino	14	20	5	49	268	17.86	–	–	2
	C.F.Parkinson	4	7	2	48*	80	16.00	–	–	–
2012	W.J.Durston	4	4	–	43	63	15.75	–	–	3
	B.D.Cotton	8	11	3	26	102	12.75	–	–	1
	L.J.Fletcher	4	4	–	14	34	8.50	–	–	1
	T.A.Wood	2	4	–	14	32	8.00	–	–	1
	W.S.Davis	6	8	1	15	34	4.85	–	–	–

Also played: G.T.G.Cork (1 match) 49, 4; R.P.Hemmings (1) did not bat (1 ct); C.M.MacDonell (1) 21, 35*; A.J.Mellor (2) 27, 44, 0 (7 ct).

BOWLING

	O	*M*	*R*	*W*	*Avge*	*Best*	*5wI*	*10wM*
A.P.Palladino	453.5	110	1201	39	30.79	5- 74	2	–
S.J.Thakor	188	24	687	22	31.22	5- 63	1	–
T.P.Milnes	172	37	509	15	33.93	6- 93	1	–
W.S.Davis	170.2	20	733	21	34.90	7-146	1	–
C.F.Parkinson	170.4	28	531	14	37.92	4- 90	–	–
B.D.Cotton	202.3	50	661	14	47.21	4- 28	–	–
Also bowled:								
W.J.Durston	101.4	14	397	9	44.11	3-149	–	–
C.F.Hughes	106.3	11	430	9	47.77	3- 87	–	–
A.Carter	101	12	440	6	73.33	3-114	–	–
W.L.Madsen	165.1	21	527	7	75.28	2- 24	–	–

N.T.Broom 17-2-64-3; G.T.G.Cork 17-2-70-0; M.J.J.Critchley 122.2-3-639-4; L.J.Fletcher 99-25-276-4; R.P.Hemmings 19-5-58-0; A.L.Hughes 53-10-169-1; H.D.Rutherford 2-0-8-0; B.T.Slater 13-0-71-0; T.A.I.Taylor 63-13-250-4.

Derbyshire played no first-class fixtures outside the County Championship in 2016. The First-Class Averages (pp 226–242) give the records of Derbyshire players in all first-class county matches, with the exception of A.Carter, L.J.Fletcher, C.M.MacDonell and A.J.Mellor, whose first-class figures for Derbyshire are as above.

DERBYSHIRE RECORDS

FIRST-CLASS CRICKET

Highest Total	For	801-8d		v	Somerset	Taunton	2007
	V	677-7d		by	Yorkshire	Leeds	2013
Lowest Total	For	16		v	Notts	Nottingham	1879
	V	23		by	Hampshire	Burton upon T	1958
Highest Innings	For	274	G.A.Davidson	v	Lancashire	Manchester	1896
	V	343*	P.A.Perrin	for	Essex	Chesterfield	1904

Highest Partnership for each Wicket

1st	322	H.Storer/J.Bowden	v	Essex	Derby	1929
2nd	417	K.J.Barnett/T.A.Tweats	v	Yorkshire	Derby	1997
3rd	316*	A.S.Rollins/K.J.Barnett	v	Leics	Leicester	1997
4th	328	P.Vaulkhard/D.Smith	v	Notts	Nottingham	1946
5th	302*†	J.E.Morris/D.G.Cork	v	Glos	Cheltenham	1993
6th	212	G.M.Lee/T.S.Worthington	v	Essex	Chesterfield	1932
7th	258	M.P.Dowman/D.G.Cork	v	Durham	Derby	2000
8th	198	K.M.Krikken/D.G.Cork	v	Lancashire	Manchester	1996
9th	283	A.Warren/J.Chapman	v	Warwicks	Blackwell	1910
10th	132	A.Hill/M.Jean-Jacques	v	Yorkshire	Sheffield	1986

† *346 runs were added for this wicket in two separate partnerships*

Best Bowling	For	10- 40	W.Bestwick	v	Glamorgan	Cardiff	1921
(Innings)	V	10- 45	R.L.Johnson	for	Middlesex	Derby	1994
Best Bowling	For	17-103	W.Mycroft	v	Hampshire	Southampton	1876
(Match)	V	16-101	G.Giffen	for	Australians	Derby	1886

Most Runs – Season	2165	D.B.Carr	(av 48.11)	1959
Most Runs – Career	23854	K.J.Barnett	(av 41.12)	1979-98
Most 100s – Season	8	P.N.Kirsten		1982
Most 100s – Career	53	K.J.Barnett		1979-98
Most Wkts – Season	168	T.B.Mitchell	(av 19.55)	1935
Most Wkts – Career	1670	H.L.Jackson	(av 17.11)	1947-63
Most Career W-K Dismissals	1304	R.W.Taylor	(1157 ct; 147 st)	1961-84
Most Career Catches in the Field	563	D.C.Morgan		1950-69

LIMITED-OVERS CRICKET

Highest Total	**50ov**	366-4		v	Comb Univs	Oxford	1991
	40ov	321-5		v	Essex	Leek	2013
	T20	222-5		v	Yorkshire	Leeds	2010
Lowest Total	**50ov**	73		v	Lancashire	Derby	1993
	40ov	60		v	Kent	Canterbury	2008
	T20	72		v	Leics	Derby	2013
Highest Innings	**50ov**	173*	M.J.Di Venuto	v	Derbys CB	Derby	2000
	40ov	141*	C.J.Adams	v	Kent	Chesterfield	1992
	T20	111	W.J.Durston	v	Notts	Nottingham	2010
Best Bowling	**50ov**	8-21	M.A.Holding	v	Sussex	Hove	1988
	40ov	6- 7	M.Hendrick	v	Notts	Nottingham	1972
	T20	5-27	T.Lungley	v	Leics	Leicester	2009

DURHAM

Formation of Present Club: 23 May 1882
Inaugural First-Class Match: 1992
Colours: Navy Blue, Yellow and Maroon
Badge: Coat of Arms of the County of Durham
County Champions: (3) 2008, 2009, 2013
Friends Provident Trophy Winners: (1) 2007
Royal London One-Day Cup Winners: (1) 2014
Twenty20 Cup Winners: (0); best – Finalist 2016

Chief Executive: David Harker, Emirates Riverside, Chester-le-Street, Co Durham DH3 3QR • Tel: 0191 387 1717 • Fax: 0191 387 1616 • Email: marketing@durhamccc.co.uk • Web: www.durhamccc.co.uk • Twitter: @DurhamCricket (39,506 followers)

Head Coach: Jon Lewis. **Bowling Coach**: Alan Walker. **Captains**: P.D.Collingwood (f-c) and K.K.Jennings (l-o). **Vice-Captain**: P.Coughlin. **Overseas Players**: S.C.Cook and T.W.M.Lathan. **2017 Testimonial**: P.D.Collingwood. **Head Groundsman**: Vic Demain. **Scorer**: William Dobson. ‡ New registration. NQ Not qualified for England.

Durham initially awarded caps immediately after their players joined the staff but revised this policy in 1998, again capping players on merit, past 'awards' having been nullified. Durham abolished both their capping and 'awards' systems after the 2005 season.

ARSHAD, Usman (Beckfoot GS, Bingley), b Bradford, Yorks 9 Jan 1993. 5'11". RHB, RMF. Squad No 78. Debut (Durham) 2013. Northumberland 2011. HS 84 v Yorks (Chester-le-St) 2016. BB 4-78 v Northants (Northampton) 2014. LO HS 25 v Surrey (Chester-le-St) 2015 (RLC). LO BB 3-50 v Warwicks (Gosforth) 2016 (RLC). T20 HS 43. T20 BB 3-18.

BURNHAM, Jack Tony Arthur (Deerness Valley CS, Durham), b Durham 18 Jan 1997. 6'1". RHB, RM. Squad No 8. Debut (Durham) 2015. Durham 2nd XI debut 2014. Northumberland 2015. HS 135 v Surrey (Oval) 2016. LO HS 26 v Northants (Northampton) 2016 (RLC). T20 HS 17.

CARSE, Brydon Alexander (Pearson HS, Pt Elizabeth), b Port Elizabeth, South Africa 31 Jul 1995. Son of J.A.Carse (Rhodesia, W Province, E Province, Northants, Border, Griqualand W 1977-78 to 1992-93). 6'1½". RHB, RF. Debut (Durham) 2016. Durham 2nd XI debut 2015. HS 47 v Notts (Nottingham) 2016. BB 3-38 v Lancs (Chester-le-St) 2016. T20 HS 1. T20 BB 1-11.

CLARK, Graham (St Benedict's Catholic HS, Whitehaven), b Whitehaven, Cumbria 16 Mar 1993. Younger brother of J.Clark (*see LANCASHIRE*). 6'1". RHB, LB. Squad No 7. Debut (Durham) 2015. Durham 2nd XI debut 2011. MCC YC 2013. HS 58 v Hants (Southampton) 2016. LO HS 42 v Yorks (Chester-le-St) 2015 (RLC). T20 HS 91* v Yorks (Leeds) 2015 – Du record. T20 BB – .

COLLINGWOOD, Paul David (Blackfyne CS; Derwentside C), b Shotley Bridge 26 May 1976. 5'11". RHB, RM. Squad No 5. Debut (Durham) 1996 v Northants (Chester-le-St) taking wicket of D.J.Capel with his first ball before scoring 91 and 16; cap 1998; benefit 2007; captain 2012 (*part*) to date; testimonial 2017. IPL: DD 2009-10. MBE 2005. *Wisden* 2007. **Tests**: 68 (2003-04 to 2010-11); 1000 runs (1): 1121 (2006); HS 206 v A (Adelaide) 2006-07; BB 3-23 v NZ (Wellington) 2007-08. **LOI**: 197 (2001 to 2010-11, 25 as captain); 1000 runs (1): 1064 (2007); HS 120* v A (Melbourne) 2006-07; BB 6-31 v B (Nottingham) 2005 – record analysis for E, and first to score a hundred (112*) and take six wickets in same LOI. **IT20**: 35 (2005 to 2010-11, 30 as captain); HS 79 v WI (Oval) 2007; BB 4-22 v SL (Southampton) 2006. F-c Tours: A 2006-07, 2010-11; SA 2009-10; WI 2003-04, 2008-09; NZ 2007-08; I 2005-06, 2008-09; P 2005-06; SL 2003-04, 2007-08; B 2009-10. 1000 runs (2); most – 1120 (2005). HS 206 (*see Tests*). Du HS 190 v SL (Chester-le-St) 2002 and 190 v Derbys (Derby) 2005, sharing Du record 4th wkt partnership of 250 with D.M.Benkenstein. BB 5-52 v Somerset (Stockton) 2005. LO HS 132 v Northants (Northampton) 2015 (RLC). LO BB 6-31 (*see LOI*). T20 HS 79. T20 BB 5-6 v Northants (Chester-le-St) 2011 – Du record.

‡[NQ]**COOK, Stephen** Craig, b Johannesburg, South Africa 29 Nov 1982. Son of S.J.Cook (Transvaal, Somerset & South Africa, 1972-73 to 1994-95). RHB, RM. Gauteng 2000-01 to 2014-15. Lions 2004-05 to date. North West 2015-16. **Tests** (SA): 9 (2015-16 to 2016-17); HS 117 v SL (Pt Elizabeth) 2016-17. F-c Tours (SA A)(C=Captain): A 2016C, 2016-17 (SA); SL 2010; Z 2016C. 1000 runs (0+4); most – 1642 (2009-10). HS 390 Lions v Warriors (East London) 2009-10 – record score in SA. BB 3-42 Lions v Dolphins (Durban) 2008-09. LO HS 127* Lions v Cobras (Johannesburg) 2015-16. LO BB 1-2 Lions v Titans (Johannesburg) 2008-09. T20 HS 66.

COUGHLIN, Josh (St Robert of Newminster Catholic CS, Washington), b Sunderland 29 Sep 1997. Younger brother of P.Coughlin (*see below*); nephew of T.Harland (Durham 1974-78). 6'4". LHB, RM. Debut (Durham) 2016. Durham 2nd XI debut 2015. England U19 2016. HS 0 and BB 1-10 v Sri Lanka A (Chester-le-St) 2016 – only 1st XI appearance.

COUGHLIN, Paul (St Robert of Newminster Catholic CS, Washington), b Sunderland 23 Oct 1992. Elder brother of J.Coughlin (*see above*); nephew of T.Harland (Durham 1974-78). 6'3". RHB, RM. Squad No 29. Debut (Durham) 2012. Northumberland 2011. No 1st XI appearances in 2013. HS 85 v Lancs (Chester-le-St) 2014, sharing Du record 9th wkt partnership of 150 with P.Mustard. BB 4-10 v Somerset (Chester-le-St) 2015. LO HS 17 v Northants (Northampton) 2016 (RLC). LO BB 1-34 v Surrey (Chester-le-St) 2014 (RLC). T20 HS 26*. T20 BB 5-42.

HICKEY, Adam James (Biddick S Sports C, Washington), b Darlington 1 Mar 1997. Son of D.J.Hickey (Cumberland 2010). 6'3". LHB, OB. Squad No 21. Debut (Durham) 2016. Durham 2nd XI debut 2014. HS 36* and BB 2-19 v Somerset (Taunton) 2016.

JENNINGS, Keaton Kent (King Edward VII S, Johannesburg), b Johannesburg, South Africa 19 Jun 1992. Son of R.V.Jennings (Transvaal 1973-74 to 1992-93), brother of D.Jennings (Gauteng and Easterns 1999 to 2003-04), nephew of K.E.Jennings (Northern Transvaal 1981-82 to 1982-83). 6'4". LHB, RMF. Squad No 1. Gauteng 2011-12. Durham debut 2012; captain 2017 (l-o only). **Tests**: 2 (2016-17); HS 112 v I (Mumbai), on debut; BB – . F-c Tours: I 2016-17; SL 2016-17 (Eng A). 1000 runs (1): 1602 (2016), inc seven hundreds (Du record). HS 221* v Yorks (Chester-le-St) 2016. BB 2-8 Gauteng v WP (Cape Town) 2011-12. Du BB 2-26 v Lancs (Southport) 2016. LO HS 101* EL v UAE (Dubai, DSC) 2016-17. LO BB 1-9 v Surrey (Chester-le-St) 2014 (RLC). T20 HS 88. T20 BB 4-37.

‡[NQ]**LATHAM, Thomas** William Maxwell, b Christchurch, New Zealand 2 Apr 1992. Son of R.T.Latham (Canterbury and New Zealand 1980-81 to 1994-95). 5'9". LHB, RM, WK. Canterbury 2010-11 to date. Kent 2016. **Tests** (NZ): 29 (2013-14 to 2016-17); HS 177 v B (Wellington) 2016-17. **LOI** (NZ): 54 (2011-12 to 2016-17); HS 137 v B (Christchurch) 2016-17. **IT20** (NZ): 12 (2012 to 2015); HS 26 v P (Dubai, DSC) 2014-15. F-c Tours (NZ): E 2013, 2014 (NZ A), 2015; A 2015-16; SA 2016; WI 2014; I 2013-14 (NZ A), 2016-17; SL 2013-14 (NZ A); Z 2016; UAE 2014-15 (v P). HS 261 Cant v CD (Napier) 2013-14. CC HS 90 K v Glos (Canterbury) 2016. BB 1-7 NZ v Cricket Australia (Sydney) 2015-16. LO HS 137 (*see LOI*). T20 HS 82.

[NQ]**McCARTHY, Barry** John (St Michael's C, Dublin; Dublin U), b Dublin, Ireland 13 Sep 1992. 5'11". RHB, RMF. Squad No 60. Debut (Durham) 2015. Durham 2nd XI debut 2014. **LOI** (Ire): 8 (2016 to 2016-17); HS 13 v A (Benoni) 2016-17; BB 4-59 v Afghanistan (Belfast) 2016. HS 51* v Hants (Chester-le-St) 2016. BB 5-70 v Lancs (Chester-le-St) 2016. LO HS 13 (*see LOI*). LO BB 4-59 (*see LOI*). T20 HS 2*. T20 BB 3-23.

MAIN, Gavin Thomas, b Lanark, Scotland 28 Feb 1995. 6'2". RHB, RMF. Squad No 20. Debut (Durham) 2014. Durham 2nd XI debut 2013. **IT20** (Scot): 3 (2015); HS – ; BB 1-21 v Ireland (Bready) 2015. HS 0*. BB 3-72 v Notts (Nottingham) 2014 – only 1st XI appearance.

ONIONS, Graham (St Thomas More RC S, Blaydon), b Gateshead 9 Sep 1982. 6'1". RHB, RFM. Squad No 9. Debut (Durham) 2004; benefit 2015. Dolphins 2013-14. MCC 2007-08, 2015-16. *Wisden* 2009. Missed entire 2010 season through back injury. **Tests**: 9 (2009 to 2012); HS 17* v A (Lord's) 2009; BB 5-38 v WI (Lord's) 2009 – on debut. **LOI**: 4 (2009 to 2009-10); HS 1 v A (Centurion) 2009-10; BB 2-58 v SL (Johannesburg) 2009-10. F-c Tours: SA 2009-10; NZ 2012-13; I 2007-08 (EL), 2012-13; SL 2013-14; B 2006-07 (Eng A); UAE 2011-12 (*part*). HS 65 v Notts (Chester-le-St) 2016. 50 wkts (7); most – 73 (2013). BB 9-67 v Notts (Nottingham) 2012. LO HS 19 v Derbys (Derby) 2008 (FPT). LO BB 4-45 v Lancs (Chester-le-St) 2013 (Y40). T20 HS 31. T20 BB 3-15.

[NQ]**POYNTER, Stuart** William (Teddington S), b Hammersmith, London 18 Oct 1990. Younger brother of A.D.Poynter (Middlesex and Ireland 2005 to date). 5'9". RHB, WK. Squad No 90. Middlesex 2010. Ireland 2011 to date. Warwickshire 2013. Durham debut 2016. No 1st XI appearances for Durham in 2015. **LOI** (Ire): 12 (2014 to 2016-17); HS 36 v SL (Dublin) 2016. **IT20** (Ire): 14 (2015 to 2016-17); HS 39 v Scotland (Dubai, DSC) 2016-17. F-c Tour (Ire): Z 2015-16. HS 125 Ire v Zimbabwe A (Harare) 2015-16. CC HS 42 v Notts (Chester-le-St) 2016. LO HS 109 Ire v Sri Lanka A (Belfast) 2014. T20 HS 39.

PRINGLE, Ryan David (Durham SFC), b Sunderland 17 Apr 1992. 6'0". RHB, OB. Squad No 17. Debut (Durham) 2014. Northumberland 2011-12. HS 99 v Hants (Chester-le-St) 2015. BB 7-107 (10-260 match) v Hants (Southampton) 2016. LO HS 125 v Derbys (Derby) 2016 (RLC). LO BB 2-39 v Northants (Northampton) 2016 (RLC). T20 HS 33. T20 BB 2-13.

RICHARDSON, Michael John (Rondebosch HS; Stonyhurst C, Nottingham U), b Pt Elizabeth, South Africa 4 Oct 1986. Son of D.J.Richardson (South Africa, EP and NT 1977-78 to 1997-98), grandson of J.H.Richardson (NE Transvaal and Transvaal B 1952-53 to 1960-61), nephew of R.P.Richardson (WP 1984-85 to 1988-89). 5'10". RHB, WK. Squad No 18. Debut (Durham) 2010. Colombo CC 2014-15. MCC YC 2008-09. 1000 runs (1): 1007 (2015). HS 148 v Yorks (Chester-le-St) 2014. LO HS 64 v Notts (Chester-le-St) 2016 (RLC). T20 HS 37.

RUSHWORTH, Christopher (Castle View CS, Sunderland), b Sunderland 11 Jul 1986. Cousin of P.Mustard (*see GLOUCESTERSHIRE*). 6'2". RHB, RMF. Squad No 22. Debut (Durham) 2010. MCC 2013, 2015. Northumberland 2004-05. PCA 2015. HS 46 v Somerset (Taunton) 2014. 50 wkts (2); most – 88 (2015). BB 9-52 (15-95 match) v Northants (Chester-le-St) 2014. Hat-trick v Hants (Southampton) 2015. LO HS 38* v Derbys (Chester-le-St) 2015 (RLC). LO BB 5-31 v Notts (Chester-le-St) 2010 (CB40). T20 HS 5. T20 BB 3-14.

STEEL, Cameron Tate (Scotch C, Perth, Australia; Millfield S; Durham U), b San Francisco, USA 13 Sep 1995. 5'10". RHB, LB. Durham MCCU 2014-16. Middlesex 2nd XI 2013-16. Somerset 2nd XI 2013. Durham 2nd XI debut 2016. Awaiting 1st XI debut. HS 80 DU v Somerset (Taunton Vale) 2015. BB 1-39 DU v Durham (Chester-le-St) 2014.

STOKES, Benjamin Andrew (Cockermouth S), b Christchurch, Canterbury, New Zealand 4 Jun 1991. 6'1". LHB, RFM. Squad No 38. Debut (Durham) 2010. Big Bash: MR 2014-15. YC 2013. **ECB Test & LO Central Contract 2016-17. Tests**: 32 (2013-14 to 2016-17); HS 258 v SA (Cape Town) 2015-16, setting E record fastest double century in 163 balls; BB 6-36 v A (Nottingham) 2015. **LOI**: 52 (2011 to 2016-17); HS 101 v B (Dhaka) 2016-17; BB 5-61 v A (Southampton) 2013. **IT20**: 21 (2011 to 2016-17); HS 38 v I (Nagpur) 2016-17; BB 3-26 v NZ (Delhi) 2015-16. F-c Tours: A 2013-14; SA 2015-16; WI 2010-11 (EL), 2014-15; I 2016-17; B 2016-17; UAE 2015-16 (v P). HS 258 (*see Tests*). Du HS 185 v Lancs (Chester-le-St) 2011, sharing Du record 4th wkt partnership of 331 with D.M.Benkenstein. BB 7-67 (10-121 match) v Sussex (Chester-le-St) 2014. LO HS 164 v Notts (Chester-le-St) 2014 (RLC) – Du record. LO BB 5-61 (*see LOI*). T20 HS 77. T20 BB 3-26.

WEIGHELL, William **James** (Stokesley S), b Middlesbrough, Yorks 28 Jan 1994. 6'4". LHB, RMF. Squad No 28. Debut (Durham) 2015. Durham 2nd XI debut 2012. Northumberland 2012 to date. HS 25 v Middx (Chester-le-St) 2015. BB 5-33 v Warwks (Birmingham) 2016.

WOOD, Mark Andrew (Ashington HS; Newcastle C), b Ashington 11 Jan 1990. 5'11". RHB, RF. Squad No 33. Debut (Durham) 2011. Northumberland 2008-10. **ECB Test Central Contract 2016-17. Tests**: 8 (2015 to 2015-16); HS 32* v A (Cardiff) 2015; BB 3-39 v P (Dubai, DSC) 2015-16. **LOI**: 11 (2015 to 2016); HS 13 v A (Manchester) 2015; BB 3-46 v P (Lord's) 2016. **IT20**: 1 (2015); HS – ; BB 3-26 v NZ (Manchester) 2015. F-c Tours (EL): SA 2014-15; SL 2013-14; UAE 2015-16 (v P). HS 66 v Notts (Chester-le-St) 2015. BB 5-32 EL v Sri Lanka A (Colombo, RPS) 2013-14. Du BB 5-37 v Somerset (Taunton) 2014. LO HS 15* v Lancs (Chester-le-St) 2013 (Y40). LO BB 3-23 v Scotland (Chester-le-St) 2013 (Y40). T20 HS 12. T20 BB 4-25.

RELEASED/RETIRED

(Having made a County 1st XI appearance in 2016)

BORTHWICK, S.G. – *see SURREY*.

HARRISON, Jamie (Sedburgh S), b Whiston, Lancs 19 Nov 1990. 6'0". RHB, LMF. Durham 2012-15. HS 65 v Northants (Northampton) 2014. BB 5-31 v Surrey (Chester-le-St) 2013. LO HS 7* v Somerset (Chester-le-St) 2012 (CB40). LO BB 4-40 v Leics (Leicester) 2016 (RLC). T20 BB 2-47.

[NQ]**NEESHAM, James** Douglas Sheahan, b Auckland, New Zealand 17 Sep 1990. LHB, RMF. Auckland 2009-10 to 2010-11. Otago 2011-12 to date. Derbyshire 2016 (l-o only). IPL: DD 2014. **Tests** (NZ): 10 (2013-14 to 2016-17); HS 137* v I (Wellington) 2013-14, on debut; BB 3-42 v SL (Wellington) 2014-15. **LOI** (NZ): 35 (2012-13 to 2016-17); HS 74 v A (Canberra) 2016-17; BB 4-42 v B (Dhaka) 2013-14. **IT20** (NZ): 15 (2012-13 to 2016-17); HS 28 v SA (Centurion) 2015; BB 3-16 v WI (Auckland) 2013-14. F-c Tours (NZ): A 2015-16; WI 2014; I 2013-14 (NZ A), 2016-17; UAE 2014-15 (v P). HS 147 Otago v CD (Nelson) 2013-14. BB 5-65 Otago v ND (Whangarei) 2013-14. LO HS 74 (*see LOI*). LO BB 5-44 Otago v Wellington (Wellington) 2011-12. T20 HS 59*. T20 BB 4-35.

[NQ]**MacLEOD, Calum** Scott (Hillpark S, Glasgow), b Glasgow, Scotland 15 Nov 1988. 6'0". RHB, RMF. Scotland 2007 to date. Warwickshire 2008-09. Durham 2014-16. **LOI** (Scot): 40 (2008 to 2016-17); HS 175 v Canada (Christchurch) 2013-14; BB 2-26 v Kenya (Aberdeen) 2013. **IT20** (Scot): 28 (2009 to 2016-17); HS 60 v Hong Kong (Abu Dhabi) 2016-17; BB 2-17 v Kenya (Aberdeen) 2013. F-c Tours (Scot): UAE 2011-12, 2012-13; Namibia 2011-12. HS 84 v Lancs (Manchester) 2014. BB 4-66 Sc v Canada (Aberdeen) 2009. LO HS 175 (*see LOI*). LO BB 3-37 Sc v UAE (Queenstown) 2013-14. T20 HS 104*. T20 BB 2-17.

MUCHALL, Gordon James (Durham S), b Newcastle upon Tyne, Northumb 2 Nov 1982. 6'0". RHB, RM. Northumberland 1999. Older brother of P.B.Muchall (Gloucestershire 2012). Durham 2002-16; cap 2005; benefit 2014. No f-c appearances in 2013. F-c Tour: SL 2002-03 (ECB Acad). HS 219 v Kent (Canterbury) 2006, sharing Du record 6th wkt partnership of 249 with P.Mustard. BB 3-26 v Yorks (Leeds) 2003. LO HS 101* v Yorks (Leeds) 2005 (NL). LO BB 1-15 v Sussex (Hove) 2003 (NL). T20 HS 66*. T20 BB 1-8.

MUSTARD, P. – *see GLOUCESTERSHIRE.*

RANDHAWA, Gurman Singh (Newsome HS; Huddersfield New C), b Huddersfield, Yorks 25 Jan 1992. 5'10". LHB, SLA. Yorkshire 2011. Durham 2016. Shropshire 2014-15. HS 5 and BB 2-54 Y v Durham MCCU (Durham) 2011. Du BB 1-60 v Sri Lanka A (Chester-le-St) 2016.

STONEMAN, M.D. – *see SURREY.*

DERBYSHIRE RELEASED/RETIRED (continued from p 89)

PARKINSON, C.F. – *see LEICESTERSHIRE.*

POYNTON, Thomas (John Taylor HS, Barton-under-Needwood; Repton S), b Burton upon Trent, Staffs 25 Nov 1989. 5'10". RHB, WK. Derbyshire 2007-16 No f-c appearances in 2009 and 2011. Missed entire 2014 season after suffering serious injury in a car crash. HS 106 v Northants (Northampton) 2012. BB 2-96 v Glamorgan (Cardiff) 2010. LO HS 40 v Middx (Chesterfield) 2011 (CB40). T20 HS 37*.

[NQ]**RUTHERFORD, Hamish** Duncan, b Dunedin, New Zealand 27 Apr 1989. Son of K.R.Rutherford (Gauteng, Otago, Transvaal & New Zealand 1982-83 to 1999-00). Nephew of I.A.Rutherford (C Districts, Otago & Worcestershire 1974-75 to 1983-84). LHB, SLA. Otago 2008-09 to date. Essex 2013. Derbyshire 2015-16. **Tests** (NZ): 16 (2012-13 to 2014-15); HS 171 v E (Dunedin) 2012-13 – on debut. **LOI** (NZ): 4 (2012-13 to 2013-14); HS 11 v E (Napier) 2012-13. **IT20** (NZ): 7 (2012-13 to 2013-14); HS 62 v E (Oval) 2013. F-c Tours (NZ): E 2013, 2014 (NZ A); WI 2014; B 2013-14. 1000 runs (0+1): 1077 (2012-13). HS 239 Otago v Wellington (Dunedin) 2011-12. De HS 108 v Kent (Chesterfield) 2015. BB – . LO HS 126 Otago v Wellington (Invercargill) 2015-16. LO BB – . T20 HS 106.

S.L.Elstone, T.C.Knight and H.J.White left the staff without making a County 1st XI appearance in 2016.

DURHAM 2016

RESULTS SUMMARY

	Place	Won	Lost	Drew	NR
Specsavers County Champ (1st Division)	4th	5	3	8	
All First-Class Matches		5	3	10	
Royal London One-Day Cup (North Group)	5th	4	3		1
NatWest t20 Blast (North Group)	Finalist	8	7		2

SPECSAVERS COUNTY CHAMPIONSHIP AVERAGES

BATTING AND FIELDING

Cap		*M*	*I*	*NO*	*HS*	*Runs*	*Avge*	*100*	*50*	*Ct/St*
	K.K.Jennings	16	28	4	221*	1548	64.50	7	2	18
	M.D.Stoneman	16	28	1	141*	1234	45.70	2	5	8
	S.G.Borthwick	16	28	2	188*	1060	40.76	3	5	25
1998	P.D.Collingwood	14	24	6	106*	595	33.05	1	3	12
	B.A.Carse	8	8	2	47	176	29.33	–	–	2
	G.Clark	3	6	–	58	170	28.33	–	2	–
	B.A.Stokes	6	9	1	51	226	28.25	–	2	1
	J.T.A.Burnham	14	24	1	135	630	27.39	1	3	6
	R.D.Pringle	10	12	2	57*	243	24.30	–	1	9
	G.Onions	16	19	7	65	282	23.50	–	1	2
	M.J.Richardson	15	24	2	99*	510	23.18	–	3	33/1
	B.J.McCarthy	7	10	2	51*	176	22.00	–	1	2
	M.A.Wood	3	6	–	36	130	21.66	–	–	–
	A.J.Hickey	3	6	3	36*	64	21.33	–	–	1
	P.Coughlin	6	10	–	39	198	19.80	–	–	3
	W.J.Weighell	3	4	1	22	53	17.66	–	–	1
	S.W.Poynter	4	7	–	42	119	17.00	–	–	12
	C.Rushworth	13	16	5	31*	114	10.36	–	–	3

Also batted: U.Arshad (2 matches) 32, 3, 84; G.J.Muchall (1 – cap 2005) 13, 17 (1 ct).

BOWLING

	O	*M*	*R*	*W*	*Avge*	*Best*	*5wI*	*10wM*
W.J.Weighell	112.5	22	329	16	20.56	5- 33	1	–
M.A.Wood	78	7	275	11	25.00	3- 24	–	–
B.A.Stokes	183.3	36	560	18	31.11	4- 54	–	–
G.Onions	544	95	1688	54	31.25	5- 90	1	–
B.J.McCarthy	177.1	25	632	20	31.60	5- 70	1	–
C.Rushworth	343.2	68	1049	32	32.78	5- 93	1	–
B.A.Carse	148.2	21	569	17	33.47	3- 38	–	–
P.Coughlin	137.3	26	395	10	39.50	2- 31	–	–
R.D.Pringle	201.2	24	804	19	42.31	7-107	1	1
S.G.Borthwick	310.3	33	1194	23	51.91	5- 79	1	–
Also bowled:								
A.J.Hickey	47.5	6	143	6	23.83	2- 19	–	–
K.K.Jennings	55	14	159	6	26.50	2- 26	–	–

U.Arshad 30-4-103-0; P.D.Collingwood 39.1-6-127-1; M.D.Stoneman 5-1-28-0.

The First-Class Averages (pp 226–242) give the records of Durham players in all first-class county matches (Durham's other opponents being Durham MCCU and Sri Lanka A), with the exception of B.A.Stokes, whose first-class figures for Durham are as above.

DURHAM RECORDS

FIRST-CLASS CRICKET

Highest Total	For 648-5d		v	Notts	Chester-le-St[2]	2009
	V 810-4d		by	Warwicks	Birmingham	1994
Lowest Total	For 67		v	Middlesex	Lord's	1996
	V 18		by	Durham MCCU	Chester-le-St[2]	2012
Highest Innings	For 273	M.L.Love	v	Hampshire	Chester-le-St[2]	2003
	V 501*	B.C.Lara	for	Warwicks	Birmingham	1994

Highest Partnership for each Wicket

1st	334*	S.Hutton/M.A.Roseberry	v	Oxford U	Oxford	1996
2nd	274	M.D.Stoneman/S.G.Borthwick	v	Middlesex	Chester-le-St[2]	2014
3rd	212	M.J.Di Venuto/D.M.Benkenstein	v	Essex	Chester-le-St[2]	2010
4th	331	B.A.Stokes/D.M.Benkenstein	v	Lancashire	Chester-le-St[2]	2011
5th	247	G.J.Muchall/I.D.Blackwell	v	Worcs	Worcester	2011
6th	249	G.J.Muchall/P.Mustard	v	Kent	Canterbury	2006
7th	315	D.M.Benkenstein/O.D.Gibson	v	Yorkshire	Leeds	2006
8th	147	P.Mustard/L.E.Plunkett	v	Yorkshire	Leeds	2009
9th	150	P.Mustard/P.Coughlin	v	Lancashire	Chester-le-St[2]	2014
10th	103	M.M.Betts/D.M.Cox	v	Sussex	Hove	1996

Best Bowling	For	10- 47	O.D.Gibson	v	Hampshire	Chester-le-St[2]	2007
(Innings)	V	9- 34	J.A.R.Harris	for	Middlesex	Lord's	2015
Best Bowling	For	14-177	A.Walker	v	Essex	Chelmsford	1995
(Match)	V	13-103	J.A.R.Harris	for	Middlesex	Lord's	2015

Most Runs – Season	1654	M.J.Di Venuto	(av 78.76)	2009
Most Runs – Career	10644	P.D.Collingwood	(av 34.11)	1996-2016
Most 100s – Season	7	K.K.Jennings		2016
Most 100s – Career	22	P.D.Collingwood		1996-2016
Most Wkts – Season	80	O.D.Gibson	(av 20.75)	2007
Most Wkts – Career	518	S.J.E.Brown	(av 28.30)	1992-2002
Most Career W-K Dismissals	638	P.Mustard	(619 ct; 19 st)	2002-16
Most Career Catches in the Field	212	P.D.Collingwood		1996-2016

LIMITED-OVERS CRICKET

Highest Total	**50ov**	353-8		v	Notts	Chester-le-St[2]	2014
	40ov	325-9		v	Surrey	The Oval	2011
	T20	225-2		v	Leics	Chester-le-St[2]	2010
Lowest Total	**50ov**	82		v	Worcs	Chester-le-St[1]	1968
	40ov	72		v	Warwicks	Birmingham	2002
	T20	93		v	Kent	Canterbury	2009
Highest Innings	**50ov**	164	B.A.Stokes	v	Notts	Chester-le-St[2]	2014
	40ov	150*	B.A.Stokes	v	Warwicks	Birmingham	2011
	T20	91*	G.Clark	v	Yorkshire	Leeds	2015
Best Bowling	**50ov**	7-32	S.P.Davis	v	Lancashire	Chester-le-St[1]	1983
	40ov	6-31	N.Killeen	v	Derbyshire	Derby	2000
	T20	5- 6	P.D.Collingwood	v	Northants	Chester-le-St[2]	2011

[1] Chester-le-Street CC (Ropery Lane) [2] Emirates Durham International Cricket Ground

ESSEX

Formation of Present Club: 14 January 1876
Inaugural First-Class Match: 1894
Colours: Blue, Gold and Red
Badge: Three Seaxes above Scroll bearing 'Essex'
County Champions: (6) 1979, 1983, 1984, 1986, 1991, 1992
NatWest/Friends Prov Trophy Winners: (3) 1985, 1997, 2008
Benson and Hedges Cup Winners: (2) 1979, 1998
Pro 40/National League (Div 1) Winners: (2) 2005, 2006
Sunday League Winners: (3) 1981, 1984, 1985
Twenty20 Cup Winners: (0); best – Semi-Finalist 2006, 2008, 2010

Chief Executive: Derek Bowden, The Cloudfm County Ground, New Writtle Street, Chelmsford CM2 0PG • Tel: 01245 252420 • Fax: 01245 254030 • Email: administration@essexcricket.org.uk • Web: www.essexcricket.org.uk • Twitter: @EssexCricket (46,999 followers)

Head Coach: Chris Silverwood. **Assistant Head Coach**: Anthony McGrath. **Captain**: R.N.ten Doeschate. **Vice-Captain**: T.Westley. **Overseas Players**: Mohammad Amir and N.Wagner. **2017 Testimonial**. None. **Head Groundsman**. Stuart Kerrison. **Scorer**. Tony Choat. ‡ New registration. [NQ] Not qualified for England.

Syed ASHAR Ahmed **ZAIDI**, b Karachi, Pakistan 13 Jul 1981. LHB, SLA. Squad No 99. UK citizen. Islamabad 1999-00 to 2009-10. PTC 2003-04 to 2005-06. Rawalpindi 2003-04 to 2004-05. KRL 2006-07. Federal Areas 2007-08. Sussex 2013-15. Essex debut 2016. HS 202 Islamabad v Sialkot (Sialkot) 2009-10. CC HS 106 Sx v Warwks (Birmingham) 2015. Ex HS 37 v Glos (Cheltenham) 2016. BB 4-50 Islamabad v Hyderabad (Islamabad) 2009-10. CC BB 4-57 Sx v Yorks (Hove) 2013. Ex BB 0-1 v Northants (Northampton) 2016. LO HS 141 Rupganj v Old DOHS (Mirpur) 2014-15. LO BB 4-39 Gazi Tank v PDSC (Mirpur) 2013-14. T20 HS 59*. T20 BB 4-11.

BEARD, Aaron Paul (Boswells S, Chelmsford), b Chelmsford 15 Oct 1997. LHB, RFM. Squad No 14. Debut (Essex) 2016. England U19 2016 to 2016-17. HS 0*. BB 4-62 v Sri Lankans (Chelmsford) 2016. CC BB 2-67 v Derbys (Chelmsford) 2016.

BOPARA, Ravinder Singh (Brampton Manor S; Barking Abbey Sports C), b Newham, London 4 May 1985. 5'8". RHB, RM. Squad No 25. Debut (Essex) 2002; cap 2005; benefit 2015; captain (l-o only) 2016. Auckland 2009-10. Dolphins 2010-11. IPL: KXIP 2009 to 2009-10. SH 2015. Big Bash: SS 2013-14. MCC 2006, 2008. YC 2008. **Tests**: 13 (2007-08 to 2012); HS 143 v WI (Lord's) 2009; BB 1-39 v SL (Galle) 2007-08. **LOI**: 120 (2006-07 to 2014-15); HS 101* v Ireland (Dublin) 2013; BB 4-38 v B (Birmingham) 2010. **IT20**: 38 (2008 to 2014); HS 65* v A (Hobart) 2013-14; BB 4-10 v WI (Oval) 2011 – E record. F-c Tours: WI 2008-09, 2010-11 (EL); SL 2007-08, 2011-12. 1000 runs (1): 1256 (2008). HS 229 v Northants (Chelmsford) 2007. BB 5-49 v Derbys (Chelmsford) 2016. LO HS 201* v Leics (Leicester) 2008 (FPT) – Ex record. LO BB 5-63 Dolphins v Warriors (Pietermaritzburg) 2010-11. T20 HS 105*. T20 BB 6-16.

BROWNE, Nicholas Lawrence Joseph (Trinity Catholic HS, Woodford Green), b Leytonstone 24 Mar 1991. 6'3½". LHB, LB. Squad No 10. Debut (Essex) 2013; cap 2015. MCC 2016. 1000 runs (2); most – 1262 (2016). HS 255 v Derbys (Chelmsford) 2016. BB – . LO HS 99 v Glamorgan (Chelmsford) 2016 (RLC). T20 HS 38.

CHOPRA, Varun (Ilford County HS), b Barking, Essex 21 Jun 1987. 6'1". RHB, LB. Squad No 6. Debut (Essex) 2006, scoring 106 v Glos (Chelmsford) on CC debut. Rejoined the county in 2016. Warwickshire 2010-16; cap 2012; captain 2015. Tamil Union 2011-12. F-c Tour (EL): SL 2013-14. 1000 runs (3); most – 1203 (2011). HS 233* TU v Sinhalese (Colombo, PSS) 2011-12. CC HS 228 Wa v Worcs (Worcester) 2011 (in 2nd CC game of season, having scored 210 v Somerset in 1st). Ex HS 155 v Glos (Bristol) 2008. BB – . LO HS 115 Wa v Leics (Birmingham) 2011 (CB40). T20 HS 97*.

COOK, Alastair Nathan (Bedford S), b Gloucester 25 Dec 1984. 6'3". LHB, OB. Squad No 26. Debut (Essex) 2003; cap 2005; benefit 2014. MCC 2004-07, 2015. YC 2005. *Wisden* 2011. **ECB Test Central Contract 2016-17. Tests**: 140 (2005-06 to 2016-17, 59 as captain); 1000 runs (5); most – 1364 (2015); HS 294 v I (Birmingham) 2011. Scored 60 and 104* v I (Nagpur) 2005-06 on debut. Third, after D.G.Bradman and S.R.Tendulkar, to score seven Test hundreds before his 23rd birthday. Second, after M.A.Taylor, to score 1000 runs in the calendar year of his debut. BB 1-6 v I (Nottingham) 2014. **LOI**: 92 (2006 to 2014-15, 69 as captain); HS 137 v P (Abu Dhabi) 2011-12. **IT20**: 4 (2007 to 2009-10); HS 26 v SA (Centurion) 2009-10. F-c Tours (C=Captain): A 2006-07, 2010-11, 2013-14C; SA 2009-10, 2015-16C; WI 2005-06 (Eng A), 2008-09, 2014-15C; NZ 2007-08, 2012-13C; I 2005-06, 2008-09, 2012-13C, 2016-17C; SL 2004-05 (Eng A), 2007-08, 2011-12; B 2009-10C, 2016-17C; UAE 2011-12 (v P), 2015-16C (v P). 1000 runs (6+1); most – 1466 (2005). HS 294 (*see Tests*). CC HS 195 v Northants (Northampton) 2005. BB 3-13 v Northants (Chelmsford) 2005. LO HS 137 (*see LOI*). BB – . T20 HS 100*.

COOK, Samuel James (Great Baddow HS & SFC; Loughborough U), b Chelmsford 4 Jul 1997. RHB, RFM. Squad No 16. Loughborough MCCU 2016. Essex 2nd XI debut 2014. Awaiting 1st XI debut. HS 0. BB 3-64 LU v Kent (Canterbury) 2016.

NQ**DIXON, Matt**hew William, b Subiaco, W Australia 12 Jun 1992. RHB, RF. Squad No 30. W Australia 2010-11 to 2015-16. Essex debut 2016. UK passport. HS 22 WA v Q (Perth) 2011-12. Ex HS 14 and BB 5-124 v Kent (Canterbury) 2016. LO HS 12 Cricket Australia XI v WA (Sydney) 2015-16. LO BB 3-40 CA v Tas (Sydney) 2015-16. T20 HS 1. T20 BB 3-32.

FOSTER, James Savin (Forest S, Snaresbrook; Collingwood C, Durham U), b Whipps Cross 15 Apr 1980. 6'0". RHB, WK. Squad No 7. British U 2000-01. Essex debut 2000; cap 2001; captain 2010 (*part*) to 2015; benefit 2011. Durham UCCE 2001. MCC 2004, 2008-10. **Tests**: 7 (2001-02 to 2002-03); HS 48 v I (Bangalore) 2001-02. **LOI**: 11 (2001-02); HS 13 v I (Bombay) 2001-02. **IT20**: 5 (2009); HS 14* v P (Oval) 2009. F-c Tours: A 2002-03; WI 2000-01 (Eng A); NZ 2001-02; I 2001-02, 2007-08 (Eng A). 1000 runs (1): 1037 (2004). HS 212 v Leics (Chelmsford) 2004. BB 1-122 v Northants (Northampton) 2008 – in contrived circumstances. LO HS 83* v Durham, inc 5 sixes in 5 balls off S.G.Borthwick (Chester-le-St) 2009 (P40). T20 HS 65*.

‡NQ**HARMER, Simon** Ross, b Pretoria, South Africa 10 Feb 1993. RHB, OB. Squad No 11. Eastern Province 2009-10 to 2011-12. Warriors 2010-11 to date. Joins Essex in 2017 (Kolpak). **Tests** (SA): 5 (2014-15 to 2015-16); HS 13 v I (Nagpur) 2015-16; BB 4-61 v I (Mohali) 2015-16. F-c Tours (SA): A 2014 (SA A); I 2015-16; B 2015; Ire 2012 (SA A). HS 100* EP v Border (East London) 2011-12. 50 wkts (0+1): 53 (2011-12). BB 8-60 Warriors v Cobras (Port Elizabeth) 2015-16. LO HS 43* Warriors v Titans (Centurion) 2013-14. LO BB 4-42 Warriors v Lions (Potchefstroom) 2011-12. T20 HS 43. T20 BB 3-28.

KHUSHI, Feroze Isa Nazir (Kelmscott S, Walthamstow; Leyton SFC), b Whipps Cross 23 Jun 1999. RHB. OB. Squad No 23. Essex 2nd XI debut 2015. Awaiting 1st XI debut.

LAWRENCE, Daniel William (Trinity Catholic HS, Woodford Green), b Whipps Cross 12 Jul 1997. 6'2". RHB, LB. Squad No 28. Debut (Essex) 2015. Essex 2nd XI debut 2013, aged 15y 321d. England U19 2015. 1000 runs (1): 1070 (2016). HS 161 v Surrey (Oval) 2015. BB 1-5 v Kent (Chelmsford) 2016. LO HS 35 v Kent (Chelmsford) 2016 (RLC). LO BB 3-35 v Middx (Lord's) 2016 (RLC). T20 HS 36. T20 BB 2-11.

‡[NQ]**MOHAMMAD AMIR**, b Gujar Khan, Punjab, Pakistan 13 Apr 1992. LHB, LF. Squad No 5. Federal Areas 2008-09. National Bank 2008-09 to 2009-10. SSGC 2015-16. Joins Essex for second half of 2017. **Tests** (P): 25 (2009 to 2016-17); HS 48 v A (Brisbane) 2016-17; BB 6-84 v E (Lord's) 2010. **LOI** (P): 29 (2009 to 2016-17); HS 73* v NZ (Abu Dhabi) 2009-10); BB 4-28 v SL (Colombo, RPS) 2009. **IT20** (P): 31 (2009 to 2016-17); HS 21* v A (Birmingham) 2010; BB 3-18 v I (Dhaka) 2015-16. F-c Tours (P): E 2010, 2016; A 2009-10, 2016-17; NZ 2009-10, 2016-17; SL 2009. HS 66 SSGC v Lahore Blues (Lahore) 2015-16. 50 wkts (0+1): 56 (2008-09). BB 7-61 (10-97 match) NBP v Lahore Shalimar (Lahore) 2008-09. LO HS 73* (*see LOI*). LO BB 5-36 Sindh v Islamabad (Faisalabad) 2016. T20 HS 21*. T20 BB 4-20.

NIJJAR, Aron Stuart Singh (Ilford County HS), b Goodmayes 24 Sep 1994. LHB, SLA. Squad No 19. Debut (Essex) 2015. Essex 2nd XI debut 2013. Suffolk 2014. No 1st XI appearances in 2016. HS 53 v Northants (Chelmsford) 2015. BB 2-33 v Lancs (Chelmsford) 2015. LO HS 21 v Yorks (Chelmsford) 2015 (RLC). LO BB 1-39 v Sussex (Hove) 2015 (RLC).

PORTER, James Alexander (Oak Park HS, Newbury Park; Epping Forest C), b Leytonstone 25 May 1993. 5'11½". RHB, RMF. Squad No 44. Debut (Essex) 2014, taking a wkt with his 5th ball; cap 2015. MCC YCs 2011-13. Essex 2nd XI debut 2014. HS 34 v Glamorgan (Cardiff) 2015. 50 wkts (2); most – 59 (2016). BB 5-46 v Northants (Chelmsford) 2016. LO HS 5* v Yorks (Chelmsford) 2015 (RLC). LO BB 3-39 v Hants (Southampton) 2015 (RLC).

[NQ]**QUINN, Matthew** Richard, b Auckland, New Zealand 28 Feb 1993. RHB, RMF. Squad No 94. Auckland 2012-13 to date. Essex debut 2016. UK passport. HS 50 v Auckland v Canterbury (Auckland) 2013-14. Ex HS 10 v Leics (Chelmsford) 2016. BB 7-76 (11-163 match) v Glos (Cheltenham) 2016. LO HS 36 Auckland v CD (Auckland) 2013-14. LO BB 4-71 v Sussex (Hove) 2016 (RLC). T20 HS 8*. T20 BB 4-35.

TAYLOR, Callum John (Cromer Ac; Eastern C, Norwich), b Norwich, Norfolk 26 Jun 1997. 5'11". RHB, RM. Squad No 67. Debut (Essex) 2015. Essex 2nd XI debut 2013. Norfolk 2013. England U19 2014-15 to 2015. HS 26 v Glamorgan (Cardiff) 2015. BB 1-6 v Cambridge MCCU (Cambridge) 2016. T20 HS 14.

[NQ]**Ten DOESCHATE, Ryan** Neil (Fairbairn C; Cape Town U), b Port Elizabeth, South Africa 30 Jun 1980. 5'10½". RHB, RMF. Squad No 27. Debut (Essex) 2003; cap 2006; captain (l-o) 2014-15; captain 2016 to date. EU passport – Dutch ancestry. Netherlands 2005 to 2009-10. Otago 2012-13. IPL: KKR 2011-15. Big Bash: AS 2014-15. **LOI** (Ne): 33 (2006 to 2010-11); HS 119 v E (Nagpur) 2010-11; BB 4-31 v Canada (Nairobi) 2006-07. **IT20** (Ne): 9 (2008 to 2009-10); HS 56 v Kenya (Belfast) 2008; BB 3-23 v Scotland (Belfast) 2008. F-c Tours (Ne): SA 2006-07, 2007-08; K 2005-06, 2009-10; Ireland 2005. 1000 runs (1): 1226 (2016). HS 259* and BB 6-20 (9-112 match) Netherlands v Canada (Pretoria) 2006. Ex HS 164 v Sri Lankans (Chelmsford) 2011. CC HS 159* v Surrey (Guildford) 2009. Ex BB 6-57 v New Zealanders (Chelmsford) 2008. CC BB 5-13 v Hants (Chelmsford) 2010. LO HS 180 v Scotland (Chelmsford) 2013 (Y40) – Ex 40-over record, inc 15 sixes. LO BB 5-50 v Glos (Bristol) 2007 (FPT). T20 HS 121*. T20 BB 4-24.

VELANI, Kishen Shailesh (Brentwood S), b Newham, London 2 Sep 1994. 5'10". RHB, RM. Squad No 8. Debut (Essex) 2013. Essex 2nd XI debut 2012. England U19 2012-13. HS 58 v Glos (Chelmsford) 2015. BB – . LO HS 27 v Northants (Northampton) 2014 (RLC). T20 HS 34.

‡[NQ]**WAGNER, Neil**, b Pretoria, South Africa 13 Mar 1986. LHB, LMF. Squad No 13. Northerns 2005-06 to 2007-08. Titans 2006-07 to 2007-08. Otago 2008-09 to date. Northamptonshire 2014. Lancashire 2016. Joins Essex for first half of 2017. **Tests** (NZ): 29 (2012 to 2016-17); HS 37 v WI (Dunedin) 2013-14; BB 6-41 v Z (Bulawayo) 2016. F-c Tours (NZ): E 2013, 2015; SA 2012-13, 2016; WI 2012, 2014; I 2016-17; Z 2007 (SA Acad), 2016; B 2013-14. HS 70 Otago v Wellington (Queenstown) 2009-10. CC HS 37 La v Hants (Manchester) 2016. 50 wkts (0+2); most – 51 (2010-11, 2012-13). BB 7-46 Otago v Wellington (Dunedin) 2011-12. CC BB 6-66 (11-111 match) La v Notts (Manchester) 2016. LO HS 42 Otago v CD (Dunedin) 2014-15. LO BB 5-34 Otago v Wellington (Wellington) 2008-09. T20 HS 14. T20 BB 4-33.

WALTER, Paul Ian (Billericay S), b Basildon 28 May 1994. LHB, LM. Squad No 22. Debut (Essex) 2016. Essex 2nd XI debut 2015. HS 47 and BB 3-44 v Derbys (Derby) 2016. T20 HS 8. T20 BB 3-26.

WESTLEY, Thomas (Linton Village C; Hills Road SFC), b Cambridge 13 March 1989. 6'2". RHB, OB. Squad No 21. Debut (Essex) 2007; cap 2013. MCC 2007, 2009, 2016. Durham MCCU 2010-11. Cambridgeshire 2005. 1000 runs (1): 1435 (2016). HS 254 v Worcs (Chelmsford) 2016. BB 4-55 DU v Durham (Durham) 2010. CC BB 4-75 v Surrey (Colchester) 2015. LO HS 111* v Yorks (Scarborough) 2014 (RLC). LO BB 4-60 v Northants (Northampton) 2014 (RLC). T20 HS 109*. T20 BB 2-27.

WHEATER, Adam Jack Aubrey (Millfield S), b Whipps Cross 13 Feb 1990. 5'6". RHB, WK. Squad No 31. Debut (Essex) 2008, returned in 2016. Cambridge MCCU 2010. Matabeleland Tuskers 2010-11 to 2012-13. Badureliya Sports Club 2011-12. Northern Districts 2012-13. Hampshire 2013-16; cap 2016. HS 204* H v Warwks (Birmingham) 2016. Ex HS 164 v Northants (Chelmsford) 2011, sharing Ex record 6th wkt partnership of 253 with J.S.Foster. BB 1-86 v Leics (Leicester) 2012 – in contrived circumstances. LO HS 135 v Essex (Chelmsford) 2014 (RLC). T20 HS 78.

RELEASED/RETIRED

(Having made a County 1st XI appearance in 2016)

[NQ]**CROSS, Matthew** Henry (Robert Gordon C, Aberdeen; Loughborough U), b Aberdeen, Scotland 15 Oct 1992. RHB, WK. Loughborough MCCU 2013. Scotland 2013 to date. Essex 2016 – 1 game (did not bat). Nottinghamshire 2nd XI 2011-14. Leicestershire 2nd XI 2015. **LOI** (Scot): 26 (2013-14 to 2016-17); HS 55 v Kenya (Christchurch) 2013-14. **IT20** (Scot): 23 (2013 to 2016-17); HS 60 v Ireland (Bready) 2015. HS 30 Scot v Afghan (Stirling) 2015. LO HS 88 Scot v UAE (Queenstown) 2013-14. T20 HS 60.

MASTERS, David Daniel (Fort Luton HS; Mid Kent CHE), b Chatham, Kent 22 Apr 1978. Son of K.D.Masters (Kent 1983-84), elder brother of D.Masters (Leicestershire 2009-10). 6'4". RHB, RMF. Kent 2000-02. Leicestershire 2003-07; cap 2007. Essex 2008-16; cap 2008; benefit 2013. HS 119 Le v Sussex (Hove) 2003. Ex HS 67 v Leics (Chelmsford) 2009. 50 wkts (4); most – 93 (2011). BB 8-10 v Leics (Southend) 2011. LO HS 39 Le v Glos (Cheltenham) 2006 (P40). LO BB 5-17 v Surrey (Oval) 2008 (FPT). T20 HS 14. T20 BB 3-7.

MICKLEBURGH, Jaik Charles (Bungay HS), b Norwich, Norfolk 30 Mar 1990. 5'10". RHB, RM. Essex 2008-16; cap 2013. Mid West Rhinos 2012-13. Norfolk 2007. HS 243 v Leics (Chelmsford) 2013. BB – . LO HS 73 MWR v ME (Kwekwe) 2012-13. T20 HS 47*.

MOORE, Thomas Cambridge (St Martin's S, Brentwood; Brentwood S), b Basildon 29 Mar 1992. 6'5". RHB, RMF. Essex 2014-16. HS 17 and BB 4-78 v Glamorgan (Chelmsford) 2014. T20 HS – .

NAPIER, Graham Richard (The Gilberd S, Colchester), b Colchester 6 Jan 1980. 5'9½". RHB, RM. Essex 1997-2016; cap 2003; benefit 2012. Wellington 2008-09. IPL: MI 2009. MCC 2004. F-c Tour (Eng A): I 2003-04. HS 196 v Surrey (Croydon) 2011, hitting a then world record-equalling 16 sixes and being dismissed just 28 balls after reaching his century. Won 2008 Walter Lawrence Trophy with 44-ball hundred v Sussex (Chelmsford). Won 2012 Walter Lawrence Trophy with 48-ball hundred v Cambridge MCCU (Cambridge). 50 wkts (3); most – 69 (2016). BB 7-21 v Cambridge MCCU (Cambridge) 2014. CC BB 7-90 v Leics (Leicester) 2013. LO HS 79 Essex CB v Lancs CB (Chelmsford) 2000 (NWT). LO BB 7-32 v Surrey (Chelmsford) 2013 (Y40). T20 HS 152* v Sussex (Chelmsford) 2008 – Ex record. T20 BB 4-10.

NQ**RYDER, Jesse** Daniel (Napier BHS), b Masterton, Wairarapa, New Zealand 6 Aug 1984. LHB, RM. C Districts 2002-03 to date. Wellington 2004-05 to 2012-13. Otago 2013-14 to 2014-15. Essex 2014-16; cap 2014. IPL: RCB 2009. PW 2011-12. **Tests** (NZ): 18 (2008-09 to 2011-12); HS 201 v I (Napier) 2008-09; BB 2-7 v A (Brisbane) 2008-09. **LOI** (NZ): 48 (2007-08 to 2013-14); HS 107 v P (Auckland) 2010-11; BB 3-29 v I (Auckland) 2008-09. **IT20** (NZ): 22 (2007-08 to 2013-14); HS 62 v WI (Hamilton) 2008-09; BB 1-2 v E (Auckland) 2007-08. F-c Tours (NZ): A 2008-09, 2011-12; I 2010-11; SL 2005-06 (NZ A) 2009, B 2008-09. HS 236 Wellington v CD (Palmerston N) 2004-05. Ex HS 133 v Glos (Chelmsford) 2014. BB 6-47 (10-100 match) v Glamorgan (Chelmsford) 2015. LO HS 136 CD v Canterbury (Christchurch) 2015-16. LO BB 4-39 Wellington v ND (Wellington) 2005-06. T20 HS 107*. T20 BB 5-27.

NQ**WAHAB RIAZ**, b Lahore, Pakistan 28 Jun 1985. RHB, LFM. Lahore 2001-02 to 2006-07. Karachi Port Trust 2003-04. Hyderabad 2003-04 to 2004-05. National Bank 2007-08 to 2014-15. Kent 2011. Lahore Shalimar 2012-13. Essex 2016 (T20 only). **Tests** (P): 24 (2010 to 2016-17); HS 39 v E (Manchester) 2016; BB 5-63 v E (Oval) 2010. **LOI** (P): 77 (2007-08 to 2016-17); HS 54* v Z (Brisbane) 2014-15; BB 5-46 v I (Mohali) 2010-11. **IT20** (P): 23 (2007-08 to 2016-17); HS 30* v NZ (Auckland) 2010-11; BB 3-18 v E (Manchester) 2016. F-c Tours (P): E 2010, 2016; A 2009 (P A), 2016-17; WI 2011; NZ 2010-11, 2016-17; SL 2009 (P A), 2014, 2015; B 2014-15. HS 84 NBP v WAPDA (Lahore) 2011-12. CC HS 34 K v Surrey (Canterbury) 2011. 50 wkts (0+2); most – 68 (2007-08). BB 9-59 (12-120 match) Lahore S v Lahore Ravi (Lahore) 2012-13. CC BB 4-94 K v Leics (Leicester) 2011. LO HS 77 NBP v PT (Rawalpindi) 2013-14. LO BB 5-24 NBP v SNGPL (Sargodha) 2008-09. T20 HS 32*. T20 BB 5-17.

J.R.Winslade left the staff without making a County 1st XI appearance in 2016.

ESSEX 2016

RESULTS SUMMARY

	Place	Won	Lost	Tied	Drew	NR
Specsavers County Champ (2nd Division)	**1st**	6	3		7	
All First-Class Matches		7	3		8	
Royal London One-Day Cup (South Group)	QF	4	3	1		1
NatWest t20 Blast (South Group)	QF	7	7			1

SPECSAVERS COUNTY CHAMPIONSHIP AVERAGES

BATTING AND FIELDING

Cap		*M*	*I*	*NO*	*HS*	*Runs*	*Avge*	*100*	*50*	*Ct/St*
2005	A.N.Cook	7	11	4	142	643	91.85	3	2	8
2006	R.N.ten Doeschate	15	21	3	145	1157	64.27	4	6	12
2013	T.Westley	16	23	–	254	1217	52.91	3	7	17
2015	N.L.J.Browne	16	25	3	255	1046	47.54	2	5	13
	D.W.Lawrence	15	21	–	154	902	42.95	3	4	12
2001	J.S.Foster	15	20	3	113	677	39.82	1	3	48/1
2005	R.S.Bopara	15	21	1	99	750	37.50	–	6	4
2013	J.C.Mickleburgh	8	12	–	103	314	26.16	1	1	9
2014	J.D.Ryder	7	10	1	51	234	26.00	–	2	4
	Ashar Zaidi	3	5	–	37	120	24.00	–	–	–
2003	G.R.Napier	14	15	2	124	298	22.92	1	–	2
2008	D.D.Masters	9	10	5	47*	105	21.00	–	–	–
2015	J.A.Porter	14	12	7	20*	56	11.20	–	–	7
	M.R.Quinn	4	6	1	10	29	5.80	–	–	1

Also batted: P.A.Beard (2 matches) 0* (1 ct); V.Chopra (2) 1, 79, 25 (4 ct); M.W.Dixon (3) 8, 1, 14; T.C.Moore (1) 0, 4* (3 ct); W.M.H.Rhodes (4) 1, 0, 3 (1 ct); K.S.Velani (2) 19, 22; P.I.Walter (2) 47, 28; A.J.A.Wheater (2) 59, 18, 21 (6 ct).

BOWLING

	O	*M*	*R*	*W*	*Avge*	*Best*	*5wI*	*10wM*
D.D.Masters	325.1	92	824	40	20.60	7- 52	1	–
M.R.Quinn	142	24	473	22	21.50	7- 76	1	1
G.R.Napier	451.3	96	1460	63	23.17	5- 59	4	–
R.S.Bopara	336.3	65	1110	42	26.42	5- 49	2	–
J.A.Porter	456.2	74	1613	55	29.32	5- 46	2	–
R.N.ten Doeschate	118	14	430	11	39.09	4- 31	–	–
Also bowled:								
W.M.H.Rhodes	87	23	278	9	30.88	2- 34	–	–
M.W.Dixon	84.1	12	386	9	42.88	5-124	1	–
T.Westley	109.5	18	351	8	43.87	2- 13	–	–

Ashar Zaidi 19.5-3-61-2; P.A.Beard 54.2-6-219-4; N.L.J.Browne 1-0-8-0; D.W.Lawrence 25-2-129-3; T.C.Moore 24-7-73-1; J.D.Ryder 75-15-254-1; K.S.Velani 3-0-41-0; P.I.Walter 50-7-214-4.

The First-Class Averages (pp 226–242) give the records of Essex players in all first-class county matches (Essex's other opponents being Cambridge MCCU and the Sri Lankans), with the exception of A.N.Cook, V.Chopra, W.M.H.Rhodes and A.J.A.Wheater, whose first-class figures for Essex are as above.

ESSEX RECORDS

FIRST-CLASS CRICKET

Highest Total	For 761-6d		v	Leics	Chelmsford	1990
	V 803-4d		by	Kent	Brentwood	1934
Lowest Total	For 20		v	Lancashire	Chelmsford	2013
	V 14		by	Surrey	Chelmsford	1983
Highest Innings	For 343*	P.A.Perrin	v	Derbyshire	Chesterfield	1904
	V 332	W.H.Ashdown	for	Kent	Brentwood	1934

Highest Partnership for each Wicket

1st	316	G.A.Gooch/P.J.Prichard	v	Kent	Chelmsford	1994
2nd	403	G.A.Gooch/P.J.Prichard	v	Leics	Chelmsford	1990
3rd	347*	M.E.Waugh/N.Hussain	v	Lancashire	Ilford	1992
4th	314	Salim Malik/N.Hussain	v	Surrey	The Oval	1991
5th	339	J.C.Mickleburgh/J.S.Foster	v	Durham	Chester-le-St[2]	2010
6th	253	A.J.A.Wheater/J.S.Foster	v	Northants	Chelmsford	2011
7th	261	J.W.H.T.Douglas/J.Freeman	v	Lancashire	Leyton	1914
8th	263	D.R.Wilcox/R.M.Taylor	v	Warwicks	Southend	1946
9th	251	J.W.H.T.Douglas/S.N.Hare	v	Derbyshire	Leyton	1921
10th	218	F.H.Vigar/T.P.B.Smith	v	Derbyshire	Chesterfield	1947

Best Bowling	For	10- 32	H.Pickett	v	Leics	Leyton	1895
(Innings)	V	10- 40	E.G.Dennett	for	Glos	Bristol	1906
Best Bowling	For	17-119	W.Mead	v	Hampshire	Southampton	1895
(Match)	V	17- 56	C.W.L.Parker	for	Glos	Gloucester	1925

Most Runs – Season	2559	G.A.Gooch	(av 67.34)	1984
Most Runs – Career	30701	G.A.Gooch	(av 51.77)	1973-97
Most 100s – Season	9	J.O'Connor		1929, 1934
	9	D.J.Insole		1955
Most 100s – Career	94	G.A.Gooch		1973-97
Most Wkts – Season	172	T.P.B Smith	(av 27.13)	1947
Most Wkts – Career	1610	T.P.B.Smith	(av 26.68)	1929-51
Most Career W-K Dismissals	1231	B.Taylor	(1040 ct; 191 st)	1949-73
Most Career Catches in the Field	519	K.W.R.Fletcher		1962-88

LIMITED-OVERS CRICKET

Highest Total	**50ov**	391-5		v	Surrey	The Oval	2008
	40ov	368-7		v	Scotland	Chelmsford	2013
	T20	242-3		v	Sussex	Chelmsford	2008
Lowest Total	**50ov**	57		v	Lancashire	Lord's	1996
	40ov	69		v	Derbyshire	Chesterfield	1974
	T20	74		v	Middlesex	Chelmsford	2013
Highest Innings	**50ov**	201*	R.S.Bopara	v	Leics	Leicester	2008
	40ov	180	R.N.ten Doeschate	v	Scotland	Chelmsford	2013
	T20	152*	G.R.Napier	v	Sussex	Chelmsford	2008
Best Bowling	**50ov**	5- 8	J.K.Lever	v	Middlesex	Westcliff	1972
		5- 8	G.A.Gooch	v	Cheshire	Chester	1995
	40ov	8-26	K.D.Boyce	v	Lancashire	Manchester	1971
	T20	6-16	T.G.Southee	v	Glamorgan	Chelmsford	2011

GLAMORGAN

Formation of Present Club: 6 July 1888
Inaugural First-Class Match: 1921
Colours: Blue and Gold
Badge: Gold Daffodil
County Champions: (3) 1948, 1969, 1997
Pro 40/National League (Div 1) Winners: (2) 2002, 2004
Sunday League Winners: (1) 1993
Twenty20 Cup Winners: (0); best – Semi-Finalist 2004

Chief Executive: Hugh Morris, The SSE SWALEC, Cardiff, CF11 9XR • Tel: 02920 409380 • Fax: 02920 419389 • email: info@glamorgancricket.co.uk • Web: www.glamorgancricket.com • Twitter: @GlamCricket (30,567 followers)

Head Coach: Robert Croft. **2nd XI Coach**: Steve Watkin. **Player Development Manager**: Richard Almond. **Captain**: J.A.Rudolph. **Overseas Player**: J.A.Rudolph. **2017 Testimonial**: None. **Head Groundsman**: Robin Saxton. **Scorer**: Andrew K.Hignell. ‡ New registration. NQ Not qualified for England.

BRAGG, William David (Rougemont S, Newport; UWIC), b Newport, Monmouthshire 24 Oct 1986. 5'9". LHB, RM. Squad No 22. Debut (Glamorgan) 2007; cap 2015. No f-c appearances in 2008. Wales MC 2004-09. 1000 runs (3); most – 1126 (2016). HS 161* v Essex (Cardiff) 2016. BB 2-10 v Worcs (Cardiff) 2013. LO HS 88 v Surrey (Guildford) 2014 (RLC). LO BB 1-11 v Glos (Cardiff) 2013 (Y40). T20 HS 15.

BULL, Kieran Andrew (Q Elizabeth HS, Haverfordwest; Cardiff Met U), b Haverfordwest 5 Apr 1995. 6'2". RHB, OB. Squad No 11. Debut (Glamorgan) 2014. Cardiff MCCU 2015. Wales MC 2012-13. No 1st XI appearances in 2016. HS 31 v Glos (Swansea) 2015. BB 4-62 v Kent (Canterbury) 2014. LO HS – . LO BB 1-40 v Middx (Lord's) 2015 (RLC).

CAREY, Lukas John (Pontarddulais CS; Gower SFC), b Carmarthen 17 Jul 1997. RHB, RFM. Squad No 17. Debut (Glamorgan) 2016. Glamorgan 2nd XI debut 2014. Wales MC 2016. HS 11 v Worcs (Worcester) 2016. BB 4-92 v Northants (Swansea) 2016.

CARLSON, Kiran Shah (Whitchurch HS), b Cardiff 16 May 1998. RHB, OB. Squad No 5. Glamorgan 2nd XI debut 2015. Wales MC 2014. Debut (Glamorgan) 2016. HS 119 v Essex (Chelmsford) 2016. BB 5-28 v Northants (Northampton) 2016 – on debut. Youngest ever to score a century & take five wkts in an innings in a f-c career, aged 18y 119d. LO HS 17 v Pakistan A (Newport) 2016.

COOKE, Christopher Barry (Bishops S, Cape Town; U of Cape Town), b Johannesburg, South Africa 30 May 1986. 5'11". RHB, WK. Squad No 46. W Province 2009-10. Glamorgan debut 2013; cap 2016. HS 171 v Kent (Canterbury) 2014. LO HS 137* v Somerset (Taunton) 2012 (CB40). T20 HS 65*.

DONALD, Aneurin Henry Thomas (Pontarddulais CS), b Swansea 20 Dec 1996. RHB, OB. Squad No 12. Debut (Glamorgan) 2014. Glamorgan 2nd XI debut 2012, aged 15y 189d. Wales MC 2012. HS 234 v Derbys (Colwyn Bay) 2016, in 123 balls equalling world record for fastest 200, inc 15 sixes, going from 0-127* between lunch and tea, and 127-234 after tea. LO HS 53 v Sussex (Cardiff) 2016 (RLC). T20 HS 55.

HOGAN, Michael Garry, b Newcastle, New South Wales, Australia 31 May 1981. British passport. 6'5". RHB, RFM. Squad No 31. W Australia 2009-10 to 2015-16. Glamorgan debut/cap 2013. Big Bash: HH 2011-13. HS 57 v Lancs (Colwyn Bay) 2015. 50 wkts (2); most – 67 (2013). BB 7-92 v Glos (Bristol) 2013. LO HS 27 WA v Vic (Melbourne) 2011-12. LO BB 5-44 WA v Vic (Melbourne) 2010-11. T20 HS 13. T20 BB 4-26.

[NQ]**INGRAM, Colin** Alexander, b Port Elizabeth, South Africa 3 Jul 1985. LHB, LB. Squad No 41. Free State 2004-05 to 2005-06. Eastern Province 2005-06 to 2008-09. Warriors 2006-07 to date. Somerset 2014. Glamorgan debut 2015 (Kolpak signing). IPL: DD 2011. **LOI** (SA): 31 (2010-11 to 2013-14); HS 124 v Z (Bloemfontein) 2010-11 – on debut; BB – . **IT20** (SA): 9 (2010-11 to 2011-12), HS 78 v I (Johannesburg) 2011-12. HS 190 EP v KZN (Port Elizabeth) 2008-09. Gm HS 105 v Kent (Cardiff) 2015. BB 4-16 EP v Boland (Port Elizabeth) 2005-06. Gm BB 3-90 v Essex (Chelmsford) 2015. LO HS 130 v Essex (Cardiff) 2015. LO BB 3-38 v Middx (Cardiff) 2016 (RLC). T20 HS 101. T20 BB 4-32.

LAWLOR, Jeremy Lloyd (Monmouth S; Cardiff Met U), b Cardiff 4 Nov 1995. Son of P.J.Lawlor (Glamorgan 1981). 6'0". RHB, RM. Squad No 6. Cardiff MCCU 2015-16. Glamorgan debut 2015. Glamorgan 2nd XI debut 2012. Wales MC 2013. No 1st XI appearances in 2016. HS 81 CfU v Hants (Southampton) 2016. Gm HS 0. BB – .

LLOYD, David Liam (Darland HS; Shrewsbury S), b St Asaph, Denbighs 15 May 1992. 5'9". RHB, RM. Squad No 14. Debut (Glamorgan) 2012. Glamorgan 2nd XI debut 2008. Wales MC 2010-11. HS 107 v Kent (Canterbury) 2016. BB 3-36 v Northants (Swansea) 2016. LO HS 65 v Kent (Canterbury) 2016 (RLC). BB 4-10 v Durham (Cardiff) 2014 (RLC). T20 HS 97*. T20 BB 2-13.

MESCHEDE, Craig Anthony Joseph (King's C, Taunton), b Johannesburg, South Africa 21 Nov 1991. 6'1". RHB, RMF. Squad No 44. Somerset 2011-14. Glamorgan debut 2015. HS 107 v Northants (Cardiff) 2015. BB 5-84 v Essex (Chelmsford) 2016. LO HS 45 v Hants (Swansea) 2016 (RLC). LO BB 4-5 Sm v Leics (Taunton) 2013 (Y40). T20 HS 53. T20 BB 3-9.

MORGAN, Alan Owen (Ysgol Gyfun yr Strade, Llanelli; Cardiff U), b Swansea 14 Apr 1994. RHB, SLA. Squad No 29. Cardiff MCCU 2014. Glamorgan debut 2016. MCC Univs 2013. Glamorgan 2nd XI debut 2014. Wales MC 2012 to date. HS 103* v Worcs (Worcester) 2016. BB 2-37 v Northants (Northampton) 2016. LO HS 29 and LO BB 2-49 v Pakistan A (Newport) 2016.

MURPHY, Jack Roger (Greenhill S, Tenby; Cardiff Met U), b Haverfordwest 15 Jul 1995. LHB, LFM. Squad No 7. Debut (Cardiff MCCU) 2015. Glamorgan 2nd XI debut 2011. Wales MC 2011-13. HS 22 and BB 2-90 CfU v Glamorgan (Cardiff) 2015. LO HS 6 v Pakistan A (Newport) 2016. LO BB – .

[NQ]**RUDOLPH**, Jacobus Andries ('**Jacques**') (Afrikaanse Hoer Seunskool), b Springs, Transvaal, South Africa 4 May 1981. Elder brother of G.J.Rudolph (Limpopo and Namibia 2006-07 to 2012-13). 5'11". LHB, LBG. Squad No 4. Northerns 1997-98 to 2003-04. Titans 2004-05 to 2014-15. Eagles 2005-06 to 2007-08. Yorkshire 2007-11 (Kolpak registration); scored 122 v Surrey (Oval) on debut; cap 2007. Surrey 2012. Glamorgan debut/cap 2014; captain 2015 to date. **Tests** (SA): 48 (2003 to 2012-13); HS 222* v B (Chittagong) 2003 – on debut; BB 1-1 v E (Leeds) 2003. **LOI** (SA): 45 (2003 to 2005-06); HS 81 v B (Dhaka) 2003. **IT20** (SA): 1 (2005-06); HS 6* v A (Brisbane) 2005-06. F-c Tours (SA): E 2003, 2012; A 2001-02, 2005-06, 2012-13; WI 2004-05; NZ 2003-04, 2011-12; I 2004-05; SL 2004, 2005-06, 2006; B 2003. 1000 runs (4+1); most – 1375 (2010). HS 228* Y v Durham (Leeds) 2010. Gm HS 139 v Glos (Bristol) 2014. BB 5-80 Eagles v Cape Cobras (Cape Town) 2007-08. CC BB 1-5 v Glos (Bristol) 2016. LO HS 169* v Sussex (Hove) 2014 – Gm record. LO BB 4-41 SA A v New Zealand A (Colombo) 2005-06. T20 HS 101*. T20 BB 3-16.

SALTER, Andrew Graham (Milford Haven SFC; Cardiff Met U), b Haverfordwest 1 Jun 1993. 5'9". RHB, OB. Squad No 21. Cardiff MCCU 2012-14. Glamorgan debut 2013. Glamorgan 2nd XI debut 2010. Wales MC 2010-11. HS 73 v Glos (Swansea) 2015. BB 3-5 v Northants (Cardiff) 2015. LO HS 51 v Pakistan A (Newport) 2016. LO BB 2-41 v Notts (Nottingham) 2012 (CB40) and 2-41 v Notts (Lord's) 2013 (Y40). T20 HS 17*. T20 BB 2-19.

SELMAN, Nicholas James (Matthew Flinders Anglican C, Buderim), b Brisbane, Australia 18 Oct 1995. RHB, RM. Squad No 9. Debut (Glamorgan) 2016. Kent 2nd XI debut 2014. Gloucestershire 2nd XI 2015. HS 122* v Northants (Swansea) 2016. BB – . LO HS 6 v Pakistan A (Newport) 2016.

NQ**SMITH, Ruaidhri** Alexander James (Llandaff Cathedral S; Shrewsbury S; Bristol U), b Glasgow, Scotland 5 Aug 1994. 6'1". RHB, RM. Squad No 20. Debut (Glamorgan) 2013. Wales MC 2010-11. Glamorgan 2nd XI debut 2011. Scotland (l-o only) 2013. **LOI** (Scot): 2 (2016); HS 10 and BB 1-34 v Afghanistan (Edinburgh) 2016. HS 57* v Glos (Bristol) 2014. BB 3-23 v Derbys (Chesterfield) 2015. LO HS 10 (*see LOI*). LO BB 4-76 v Pakistan A (Newport) 2016. T20 HS 16*. T20 BB 1-11.

NQ**van der GUGTEN, Timm**, b Hornsby, Sydney, Australia 25 Feb 1991. 6'1½". RHB, RFM. Squad No 64. New South Wales 2011-12. Netherlands 2012 to date. Glamorgan debut 2016. Big Bash: HH 2014-15. **LOI** (Neth): 4 (2011-12 to 2013); HS 2 (twice); BB 5-24 v Canada (King City, NW) 2013. **IT20** (Neth): 20 (2011-12 to 2015-16); HS 12* v Nepal (Rotterdam) 2015; BB 3-18 v B (The Hague) 2012. HS 57 Neth v Papua New Guinea (Amstelveen) 2015. Gm HS 36 v Derbys (Derby) 2016. 50 wkts (1): 56 (2016). BB 7-68 (10-121 match) Neth v Namibia (Windhoek) 2013. Gm BB 5-52 v Leics (Leicester) 2016. LO HS 23 Neth v Nepal (Amstelveen) 2016; LO BB 5-24 (*see LOI*). T20 HS 13. T20 BB 5-21.

WAGG, Graham Grant (Ashlawn S, Rugby), b Rugby, Warwks 28 Apr 1983. 6'0". RHB, LM. Squad No 8. Warwickshire 2002-04. Derbyshire 2006-10; cap 2007. Glamorgan debut 2011; cap 2013. F-c Tour (Eng A): I 2003-04. HS 200 v Surrey (Guildford) 2015. 50 wkts (2); most – 59 (2008). BB 6-29 v Surrey (Oval) 2014. LO HS 62* v Essex (Cardiff) 2015 (RLC). LO BB 4-35 De v Durham (Derby) 2008 (FPT). T20 HS 62. T20 BB 5-14 v Worcs (Worcester) 2013 – Gm record.

RELEASED/RETIRED
(Having made a County 1st XI appearance in 2016)

COSKER, Dean Andrew (Millfield S), b Weymouth, Dorset 7 Jan 1978. 5'11". RHB, SLA. Glamorgan 1996-2015; cap 2000; benefit 2010. MCC 2010. F-c Tours (Eng A): SA 1998-99; SL 1997-98; Z 1998-99; K 1997-98. HS 69 v Kent (Canterbury) 2015. 50 wkts (1): 51 (2010). BB 6-91 (11-126 match) v Essex (Cardiff) 2009. LO HS 50* v Northants (Northampton) 2009 (FPT). LO BB 5-54 v Essex (Chelmsford) 2003 (NL). T20 HS 21*. T20 BB 4-25.

HERRING, Cameron Lee (Tredegar CS; Cardiff Met U), b Abergavenny, Monmouthshire 15 July 1994. 5'6". RHB, WK. Gloucestershire 2013-14; cap 2013. Cardiff MCCU 2016. Glamorgan (l-o only) 2016. Gloucestershire 2nd XI 2011-15. HS 114* Gs v Cardiff MCCU (Bristol) 2014. CC HS 43 Gs v Northants (Bristol) 2013. LO HS 6 v Pakistan A (Newport) 2016. T20 HS 23*.

KETTLEBOROUGH, James Michael (Bedford S), b Huntingdon 22 Oct 1992. 5'11". RHB, OB. Northamptonshire 2014. Glamorgan 2015-16. Northamptonshire 2nd XI debut 2012. Middlesex 2nd XI 2011-12. Bedfordshire 2009-13. HS 81 v Glos (Bristol) 2015. LO HS 26 Nh v Lancs (Manchester) 2014 (RLC).

PENRHYN JONES, Dewi (Ellesmere S), b Wrexham, Denbighs 9 Sep 1994. 6'1". RHB, RFM. Glamorgan 2015. Glamorgan 2nd XI debut 2013. Wales MC 2012-14. HS 17 and BB 3-55 v Northants (Northampton) 2015. LO HS 0* v Middx (Lord's) 2015 (RLC). LO BB 1-22 v Middx (Cardiff) 2014 (RLC).

SMITH, Thomas Frederick (Clifton C), b Bristol, Glos 21 May 1996. RHB, OB. Gloucestershire 2nd XI 2013-14. MCC YC 2015-16. Glamorgan 2nd XI debut 2015. Awaiting f-c debut. LO HS 6 v Pakistan A (Newport) 2016.

RELEASED/RETIRED continued on p 114

GLAMORGAN 2016

RESULTS SUMMARY

	Place	Won	Lost	Drew	NR
Specsavers County Champ (2nd Division)	8th	3	8	5	
All First-Class Matches		3	8	6	
Royal London One-Day Cup (South Group)	7th	2	5		1
NatWest t20 Blast (South Group)	QF	8	4		3

SPECSAVERS COUNTY CHAMPIONSHIP AVERAGES

BATTING AND FIELDING

Cap		M	I	NO	HS	Runs	Avge	100	50	Ct/St
2016	C.B.Cooke	7	12	0	63	[illegible]	[illegible]		2	6
2013	G.G.Wagg	13	22	3	106	693	36.47	1	5	5
2015	W.D.Bragg	16	31	1	161*	1088	36.26	2	8	10
	A.H.T.Donald	16	30	1	234	983	33.89	1	5	12
	K.S.Carlson	4	8	1	119	227	32.42	1	1	1
	A.O.Morgan	9	17	3	103*	406	29.00	1	1	3
2003	M.A.Wallace	14	26	4	78	611	27.77	–	5	53/1
	N.J.Selman	10	19	2	122*	470	27.64	2	2	7
	D.L.Lloyd	15	27	1	107	712	27.38	2	2	5
2014	J.A.Rudolph	15	29	2	87	659	24.40		3	10
	C.A.J.Meschede	13	22	4	78	431	23.94	–	3	3
	A.G.Salter	7	11	3	45*	171	21.37	–	–	5
	J.M.Kettleborough	3	6	–	42	107	17.83	–	–	2
2013	M.G.Hogan	15	22	6	30	191	11.93	–	–	8
	T.van der Gugten	13	20	4	36	159	9.93	–	–	2
	H.W.Podmore	2	4	1	16*	24	8.00	–	–	–
	L.J.Carey	3	5	1	11	12	3.00	–	–	1

Also batted: R.A.J.Smith (1 match) 25, 0 (1 ct).

BOWLING

	O	M	R	W	Avge	Best	5wI	10wM
L.J.Carey	84.4	13	330	13	25.38	4-92	–	–
T.van der Gugten	450	72	1458	56	26.03	5-52	5	–
M.G.Hogan	500.4	139	1287	49	26.26	5-36	2	–
G.G.Wagg	421	69	1397	37	37.75	5-90	1	–
C.A.J.Meschede	351.5	65	1168	27	43.25	5-84	1	–
A.O.Morgan	232	34	740	13	56.92	2-37	–	–
D.L.Lloyd	149.1	17	583	10	58.30	3-36	–	–
Also bowled:								
K.S.Carlson	45	7	178	6	29.66	5-28	1	–
H.W.Podmore	54.3	5	225	6	37.50	3-59	–	–
A.G.Salter	136	13	492	7	70.28	3-56	–	–

W.D.Bragg 9-1-29-0; J.A.Rudolph 25.5-4-58-2; N.J.Selman 3-1-8-0; R.A.J.Smith 14-3-51-1.

The First-Class Averages (pp 226–242) give the records of Glamorgan players in all first-class county matches (Glamorgan's other opponents being Cardiff MCCU), with the exception of H.W.Podmore, whose first-class figures for Glamorgan are as above.

GLAMORGAN RECORDS

FIRST-CLASS CRICKET

Highest Total	For	718-3d		v	Sussex	Colwyn Bay	2000
	V	712		by	Northants	Northampton	1998
Lowest Total	For	22		v	Lancashire	Liverpool	1924
	V	33		by	Leics	Ebbw Vale	1965
Highest Innings	For	309*	S.P.James	v	Sussex	Colwyn Bay	2000
	V	322*	M.B.Loye	for	Northants	Northampton	1998

Highest Partnership for each Wicket

1st	374	M.T.G.Elliott/S.P.James	v	Sussex	Colwyn Bay	2000
2nd	252	M.P.Maynard/D.L.Hemp	v	Northants	Cardiff	2002
3rd	313	D.E.Davies/W.E.Jones	v	Essex	Brentwood	1948
4th	425*	A.Dale/I.V.A.Richards	v	Middlesex	Cardiff	1993
5th	264	M.Robinson/S.W.Montgomery	v	Hampshire	Bournemouth	1949
6th	240	J.Allenby/M.A.Wallace	v	Surrey	The Oval	2009
7th	211	P.A.Cottey/O.D.Gibson	v	Leics	Swansea	1996
8th	202	D.Davies/J.J.Hills	v	Sussex	Eastbourne	1928
9th	203*	J.J.Hills/J.C.Clay	v	Worcs	Swansea	1929
10th	143	T.Davies/S.A.B.Daniels	v	Glos	Swansea	1982

Best Bowling	For	10- 51	J.Mercer	v	Worcs	Worcester	1936
(Innings)	V	10- 18	G.Geary	for	Leics	Pontypridd	1929
Best Bowling	For	17-212	J.C.Clay	v	Worcs	Swansea	1937
(Match)	V	16- 96	G.Geary	for	Leics	Pontypridd	1929

Most Runs – Season	2276	H.Morris	(av 55.51)	1990
Most Runs – Career	34056	A.Jones	(av 33.03)	1957-83
Most 100s – Season	10	H.Morris		1990
Most 100s – Career	54	M.P.Maynard		1985-2005
Most Wkts – Season	176	J.C.Clay	(av 17.34)	1937
Most Wkts – Career	2174	D.J.Shepherd	(av 20.95)	1950-72
Most Career W-K Dismissals	933	E.W.Jones	(840 ct; 93 st)	1961-83
Most Career Catches in the Field	656	P.M.Walker		1956-72

LIMITED-OVERS CRICKET

Highest Total	**50ov**	429		v	Surrey	The Oval	2002
	40ov	328-4		v	Lancashire	Colwyn Bay	2011
	T20	240-3		v	Surrey	The Oval	2015
Lowest Total	**50ov**	68		v	Lancashire	Manchester	1973
	40ov	42		v	Derbyshire	Swansea	1979
	T20	94-9		v	Essex	Cardiff	2010
Highest Innings	**50ov**	169*	J.A.Rudolph	v	Sussex	Hove	2014
	40ov	155*	J.H.Kallis	v	Surrey	Pontypridd	1999
	T20	116*	I.J.Thomas	v	Somerset	Taunton	2004
Best Bowling	**50ov**	6-20	S.D.Thomas	v	Comb Univs	Cardiff	1995
	40ov	7-16	S.D.Thomas	v	Surrey	Swansea	1998
	T20	5-14	G.G.Wagg	v	Worcs	Worcester	2013

GLOUCESTERSHIRE

Formation of Present Club: 1871
Inaugural First-Class Match: 1870
Colours: Blue, Gold, Brown, Silver, Green and Red
Badge: Coat of Arms of the City and County of Bristol
County Champions (since 1890): (0); best – 2nd 1930, 1931, 1947, 1959, 1969, 1986
Gillette/NatWest/C&G Trophy Winners: (5) 1973, 1999, 2000, 2003, 2004
Benson and Hedges Cup Winners: (3) 1977, 1999, 2000
Pro 40/National League (Div 1) Winners: (1) 2000
Royal London One-Day Cup Winners: (1) 2015
Twenty20 Cup Winners: (0); best – Finalist 2007

Chief Executive: Will Brown, The Brightside Ground, Nevil Road, Bristol BS7 9EJ • Tel: 0117 910 8000 • Fax: 0117 924 1193 • Email: info@glosccc.co.uk • Web: www.glosccc.co.uk • Twitter: @Gloscricket (27,733 followers)

Head Coach: Richard Dawson. **Asst Head Coach**: Ian Harvey. **Captains**: G.H.Roderick (f-c) and M.Klinger (l-o). **Overseas Players**: C.T.Bancroft, M.Klinger and A.J.Tye (T20 only). **2017 Testimonial**: None. **Head Groundsman**: Sean Williams. **Scorer**: Adrian Bull. ‡ New registration. [NQ] Not qualified for England.

Gloucestershire revised their capping policy in 2004 and now award players with their County Caps when they make their first-class debut.

[NQ]**BANCROFT, Cameron** Timothy (Aquinas C, Perth), b Attadale, Perth, Australia 19 Nov 1992. 6'0". RHB, RM, WK. Squad No 43. W Australia 2013-14 to date. Gloucestershire debut/cap 2016. Big Bash: PS 2014-15 to date. Australia U19 2011. **IT20** (A): 1 (2015-16); HS 0* v I (Sydney) 2015-16. F-c Tours (Aus A): I 2015. HS 211 WA v NSW (Perth) 2014-15. Gs HS 70 v Glamorgan (Bristol) 2016. LO HS 176 WA v S Aus (Sydney Hurtsville) 2015-16. T20 HS 72.

BRACEY, James Robert (Filton CS), b Bristol 3 May 1997. Younger brother of S.N.Bracey (Cardiff MCCU 2014-15). LHB, WK. Debut (Gloucestershire) 2016; cap 2016. Gloucestershire 2nd XI debut 2015. HS 12 v Sussex (Bristol) 2016 – only 1st XI appearance.

COCKBAIN, Ian Andrew (Maghull HS), b Bootle, Liverpool 17 Feb 1987. Son of I.Cockbain (Lancs and Minor Cos 1979-94). 6'0". RHB, RM. Squad No 28. Debut (Gloucestershire) 2011; cap 2011. MCC YC 2008-10. HS 151* v Surrey (Bristol) 2014. BB 1-23 v Durham MCCU (Bristol) 2016. LO HS 98* v Worcs (Worcester) 2014 (RLC). T20 HS 91*.

DENT, Christopher David James (Backwell CS; Alton C), b Bristol 20 Jan 1991. 5'9". LHB, WK, occ SLA. Squad No 15. Debut (Gloucestershire) 2010; cap 2010. 1000 runs (3); most – 1336 (2016). HS 268 v Glamorgan (Bristol) 2015. BB 2-21 v Sussex (Hove) 2016. LO HS 151* v Glamorgan (Cardiff) 2013 (Y40). LO BB 4-43 v Leics (Bristol) 2012 (CB40). T20 HS 63*. T20 BB 1-4.

GILMOUR, Brandon Stuart (Park House S), b Bulawayo, Zimbabwe 11 Apr 1996. 5'10". LHB, RM. Squad No 55. Gloucestershire 2nd XI debut 2014. Awaiting 1st XI debut.

GRIESHABER, Patrick James (Sheldon S, Chippenham), b Bath, Somerset 24 Nov 1996. 5'9". RHB, WK. Debut (Gloucestershire) 2014; cap 2014. Gloucestershire 2nd XI debut 2012, aged 15y 180d. Wiltshire 2015-16. HS 10 v Glamorgan (Bristol) 2014. LO HS 20 v Sussex (Cheltenham) 2016 (RLC). T20 HS 9.

HAMMOND, Miles Arthur Halhead (St Edward's S, Oxford), b Cheltenham 11 Jan 1996. 5'11". LHB, OB. Squad No 88. Debut (Gloucestershire) 2013; cap 2013. England U19 2012-13. Gloucestershire 2nd XI debut 2010, aged 14y 120d. HS 30 v Glamorgan (Swansea) 2015. BB 1-96 v Glamorgan (Bristol) 2013. LO HS 0. LO BB 2-18 v Northants (Northampton) 2015 (RLC). T20 HS and BB – .

HANKINS, George Thomas (Millfield S), b Bath, Somerset 4 Jan 1997. 6'1½". RHB, OB. Squad No 21. Debut (Gloucestershire) 2016; cap 2016. Gloucestershire 2nd XI debut 2014. England U19 2016. HS 116 v Northants (Northampton) 2016.

HOWELL, Benny Alexander Cameron (The Oratory S), b Bordeaux, France 5 Oct 1988. Son of J.B.Howell (Warwickshire 2nd XI 1978). 5'11". RHB, RM. Squad No 13. Hampshire 2011. Gloucestershire debut/cap 2012. Berkshire 2007. HS 102 v Leics (Cheltenham) 2015. BB 5-57 v Leics (Leicester) 2013. LO HS 122 v Surrey (Croydon) 2011 (CB40). LO BB 3-37 v Yorks (Leeds) 2015 (RLC). T20 HS 57. T20 BB 4-26.

NQ**KLINGER, Michael** (Scopus Memorial C, Kew), b Kew, Melbourne, Australia 4 Jul 1980. 5'10½". RHB. Squad No 2. Victoria 1999-00 to 2007-08. S Australia 2008-09 to 2013-14. Worcestershire 2012; cap 2012. Gloucestershire debut/cap 2013; captain 2013-15; l-o captain 2016 to date. W Australia 2014-15 to date. Big Bash: AS 2011-12 to 2013-14. PS 2014-15 to date. **IT20** (A): 3 (2016-17); HS 62 v SL (Adelaide) 2016-17. 1000 runs (1+2); most – 1203 (2008-09). HS 255 S Aus v WA (Adelaide) 2008-09. Gs HS 163 v Hants (Bristol) 2013. LO HS 166* v Hants (Bristol) 2016 (RLC). T20 HS 126* v Essex (Bristol) 2015 – Gs record.

LIDDLE, Christopher John (Nunthorpe CS; Teesside Tertiary C), b Middlesbrough, Yorks 1 Feb 1984. 6'5". RHB, LFM. Squad No 23. Leicestershire 2005-06. Sussex 2007-15. Awaiting f-c debut for Gloucestershire having joined in 2016. HS 53 Sx v Worcs (Hove) 2007. BB 3-42 Le v Somerset (Leicester) 2006. LO HS 18 Sx v Warwks (Rugby) 2015 (RLC). LO BB 5-18 v Netherlands (Amstelveen) 2011 (CB40). T20 HS 16. T20 BB 5-17.

MILES, Craig Neil (Bradon Forest S, Swindon; Filton C, Bristol), b Swindon, Wilts 20 July 1994. Brother of A.J.Miles (Cardiff MCCU 2012). 6'4". RHB, RMF. Squad No 34. Debut (Gloucestershire) 2011; cap 2011. Gloucestershire 2nd XI debut 2009, aged 14y 318d. HS 62* v Worcs (Cheltenham) 2014. 50 wkts (2); most – 57 (2016). BB 6-63 v Northants (Northampton) 2015. LO HS 16 v Somerset (Taunton) 2016 (RLC). LO BB 4-29 v Yorks (Scarborough) 2015 (RLC). T20 HS 3*. T20 BB 3-25.

MUSTARD, Philip (Usworth CS), b Sunderland, Co Durham 8 Oct 1982. Cousin of C.Rushworth (*see DURHAM*). 5'11". LHB, WK. Durham 2002-16; captain 2010 (*part*) to 2012 (*part*). Mountaineers 2011-12. Auckland 2012-13. Lancashire 2015 (on loan). Gloucestershire debut/cap 2016 (on loan). **LOI**: 10 (2007-08); HS 83 v NZ (Napier) 2007-08. **IT20**: 2 (2007-08); HS 40 v NZ (Christchurch) 2007-08. HS 130 Du v Kent (Canterbury) 2006. Gs HS 107* v Derbys (Derby) 2016. BB 1-9 Du v Sussex (Hove) 2013. LO HS 143 Du v Surrey (Chester-le-St) 2012 (CB40). T20 HS 97*.

NQ**NOEMA-BARNETT, Kieran**, b Dunedin, New Zealand 4 Jun 1987. 6'1". LHB, RM. Squad No 11. Central Districts 2008-09 to date. Gloucestershire debut/cap 2015. HS 107 CD v Auckland (Auckland) 2011-12. Gs HS 84 v Worcs (Bristol) 2016. BB 4-20 CD v Otago (Dunedin) 2010-11. Gs BB 3-28 v Glamorgan (Swansea) 2015. LO HS 74 CD v ND (New Plymouth) 2016-17. LO BB 3-42 CD v Auckland (Auckland) 2013-14. T20 HS 57*. T20 BB 2-13.

NORWELL, Liam Connor (Redruth SS), b Bournemouth, Dorset 27 Dec 1991. 6'3". RHB, RMF. Squad No 24. Debut (Gloucestershire) 2011, taking 6-46 v Derbys (Bristol); cap 2011. HS 102 v Derbys (Bristol) 2016. 50 wkts (1): 68 (2015). BB 6-33 (10-65 match) v Essex (Chelmsford) 2015. LO HS 10 v Glamorgan (Cardiff) 2016 (RLC). LO BB 6-52 v Leics (Leicester) 2012 (CB40). T20 HS 2*. T20 BB 3-27.

PAYNE, David Alan (Lytchett Minster S), b Poole, Dorset, 15 Feb 1991. 6'2". RHB, LMF. Squad No 14. Debut (Gloucestershire) 2011; cap 2011. Dorset 2009. HS 67* v Glamorgan (Cardiff) 2016. BB 6-26 v Leics (Bristol) 2011. LO HS 23 v Kent (Canterbury) 2016 (RLC). LO BB 7-29 v Essex (Chelmsford) 2010 (CB40), inc 4 wkts in 4 balls and 6 wkts in 9 balls – Gs record. T20 HS 10. T20 BB 5-24 v Middx (Richmond) 2015 – Gs record.

[NQ]**RODERICK, Gareth** Hugh (Maritzburg C), b Durban, South Africa 29 Aug 1991. 6'0". RHB, WK. Squad No 27. UK passport. KZN 2010-11 to 2011-12. Gloucestershire debut/cap 2013; captain 2016 to date. HS 171 v Leics (Bristol) 2014. LO HS 104 v Leics (Leicester) 2015 (RLC). T20 HS 32.

SMITH, Thomas Michael John (Seaford Head Community C; Sussex Downs C), b Eastbourne, Sussex 29 Aug 1987. 5'9". RHB, SLA. Squad No 6. Sussex 2007-09. Surrey 2009 (l-o only). Middlesex 2010-13. Gloucestershire debut/cap 2013. HS 80 v Surrey (Bristol) 2014. BB 4-35 v Kent (Canterbury) 2014. LO HS 65 Sy v Leics (Leicester) 2009 (P40). LO BB 4-26 v Sussex (Cheltenham) 2016 (RLC). T20 HS 36*. T20 BB 5-24.

TAVARÉ, William Andrew (Bristol GS; Loughborough U), b Bristol 1 Jan 1990. Nephew of C.J.Tavaré (Kent, Somerset & England 1974-93). 6'0". RHB, RM. Squad No 4. Loughborough MCCU 2010-12. Gloucestershire debut/cap 2014. 1000 runs (1); 1014 (2014). HS 139 v Hants (Bristol) 2014 – on CC debut. BB – . LO HS 77 v Hants (Bristol) 2014 (RLC) – on l-o debut.

TAYLOR, Jack Martin Robert (Chipping Norton S), b Banbury, Oxfordshire 12 Nov 1991. Elder brother of M.D.Taylor (*see below*). 5'11". RHB, OB. Squad No 10. Debut (Gloucestershire) 2010; cap 2010. Oxfordshire 2009-11. HS 156 v Northants (Cheltenham) 2015. BB 4-16 v Glamorgan (Bristol) 2016. LO HS 53 v Derbys (Derby) 2014 (RLC). LO BB 4-38 v Hants (Bristol) 2014 (RLC). T20 HS 80. T20 BB 4-16.

TAYLOR, Matthew David (Chipping Norton S), b Banbury, Oxfordshire 8 Jul 1994. Younger brother of J.M.R.Taylor (*see above*). 6'0". RHB, LM. Squad No 36. Debut (Gloucestershire) 2013; cap 2013. Gloucestershire 2nd XI debut 2011. Oxfordshire 2011-12. HS 32* v Essex (Chelmsford) 2014. BB 5-75 v Hants (Bristol) 2014. LO HS 16 v Kent (Canterbury) 2016 (RLC). LO BB 2-33 v Sussex (Cheltenham) 2016 (RLC). T20 HS 5*. T20 BB 3-16.

[NQ]**TYE, Andrew** James (Padbury Senior HS, WA), b Perth, Australia 12 Dec 1986. 6'4". RHB, RMF. Squad No 68. W Australia 2014-15 to date. Big Bash: ST 2013-14. PS 2014-15 to date. Gloucestershire debut 2016 (T20 only). **IT20** (A): 5 (2015-16 to 2016-17); HS 4 v I (Melbourne) 2015-16; BB 3-37 v SL (Geelong) 2016-17. HS 10 WA v Tas (Hobart) 2014-15. BB 3-47 WA v Q (Brisbane) 2014-15. LO HS 28* WA v NSW (Sydney) 2013-14. LO BB 5-46 WA v Tas (Sydney) 2013-14. T20 HS 42. T20 BB 4-18.

[NQ]**van BUUREN, Graeme** Lourens, b Pretoria, South Africa 22 Aug 1990. 5'6". RHB, SLA. Squad No 12. Northerns 2009-10 to 2015-16. Titans 2012-13 to 2014-15. Gloucestershire debut/cap 2016. Non-overseas player due to his wife's UK passport. HS 235 Northerns v EP (Centurion) 2014-15. Gs HS 172* v Worcs (Worcester) 2016. BB 4-12 Northerns v SW Districts (Oudtshoorn) 2012-13. Gs BB 3-15 v Glamorgan (Bristol) 2016. LO HS 119* Northerns v EP (Pt Elizabeth, Grey HS) 2013-14. LO BB 5-35 Northerns v SW Districts (Pretoria) 2011-12. T20 HS 64. T20 BB 5-8.

RELEASED/RETIRED

(Having made a County 1st XI appearance in 2016)

HAMPTON, Thomas Robert Garth (John Hampden S, High Wycombe), b Kingston-upon-Thames, Surrey 5 Oct 1990. 6'0". RHB, RMF. Middlesex 2010. Gloucestershire debut/cap 2015. MCC YCs 2011-12. Buckinghamshire 2014-15. HS 1* and BB 1-15 M v Oxford MCCU (Oxford) 2010. CC HS 0*. CC BB 1-73 v Essex (Chelmsford) 2016.

MARSHALL, Hamish John Hamilton (Mahurangi C, Warkworth; King C, Auckland), b Warkworth, New Zealand 15 Feb 1979. Twin brother of J.A.H.Marshall (ND and NZ 1997-98 to 2011-12). Irish passport, qualified to play in April 2011. 5'9". RHB, RM. N Districts 1998-99 to 2011-12. Gloucestershire 2006-16, scoring 102 v Worcs on UK debut; cap 2006; benefit 2015. Wellington 2016-17. MCC 2012. Buckinghamshire 2003. **Tests** (NZ): 13 (2000-01 to 2005-06); HS 160 v SL (Napier) 2004-05. **LOI** (NZ): 66 (2003-04 to 2006-07); HS 101* v P (Faisalabad) 2003-04. **IT20** (NZ): 3 (2004-05 to 2005-06); HS 8 v A (Auckland) 2004-05. F-c Tours (NZ): A 2004-05; SA 2000-01, 2005-06; Z 2005; B 2004-05. 1000 runs (3); most – 1218 (2006). HS 170 ND v Canterbury (Rangiora) 2009-10. Gs HS 168 v Leics (Cheltenham) 2006. BB 4-24 v Leics (Leicester) 2009. LO HS 122 v Sussex (Hove) 2007 (P40). LO BB 2-21 v Hants (Southampton) 2009 (P40). T20 HS 102.

GLAMORGAN RELEASED/RETIRED (continued from p 108)

[NQ]**STEYN, Dale** Willem, b Phalaborwa, South Africa 27 Jun 1983. RHB, RF. Northerns 2003-04 to 2005-06. Titans 2004-05 to 2009-10. Essex 2005. Warwickshire 2007; cap 2007. IPL: RCB 2007-08 to 2009-10. DC 2011-12. SH 2013-15. GL 2016. Glamorgan 2016 (T20 only). *Wisden* 2012. **Tests** (SA): 85 (2004-05 to 2016-17); HS 76 v A (Melbourne) 2008-09; BB 7-51 v I (Nagpur) 2009-10. **LOI** (SA): 114 (+2 for Africa XI) (2005 to 2016-17); HS 35 v I (Jaipur) 2009-10; BB 6-39 v P (Port Elizabeth) 2013-14. **IT20** (SA): 42 (2007-08 to 2015-16); HS 5 v E (Bridgetown) 2010 and 5 v Neth (Chittagong) 2013-14; BB 4-9 v WI (Port Elizabeth) 2007-08. F-c Tours (SA): E 2008, 2012; A 2008-09, 2012-13, 2016-17; WI 2010; NZ 2011-12; I 2007-08 (SA A), 2009-10, 2015-16; P 2007-08; SL 2005-06 (SA A), 2006, 2014; Z 2014; B 2007-08, 2015; UAE 2010-11 (v P), 2013-14 (v P). HS 82 Ex v Durham (Chester-le-St) 2005. 50 wkts (0+2); most – 69 (2005-06). BB 8-41 (14-110 match) Titans v Eagles (Bloemfontein) 2007-08. CC BB 5-49 Wa v Worcs (Worcester) 2007. LO HS 35 (*see LOI*). LO BB 6-39 (*see LOI*). T20 HS 27*. T20 BB 4-9.

[NQ]**TAIT, Shaun** William (Oakwood Area State S, S Aus), b Bedford Park, Adelaide, S Australia 22 Feb 1983. 6'4". RHB, RF. S Aus 2002-03 to 2008-09. Durham 2004. Glamorgan 2010-16 (T20 only). IPL: RR 2009-13. Big Bash: MR 2011-12. AS 2012-13 to 2014-15. HH 2015-16 to date. **Tests** (A): 3 (2005 to 2007-08); HS 8 v I (Perth) 2007-08; BB 3-97 v E (Nottingham) 2005. **LOI** (A): 35 (2006-07 to 2010-11); HS 11 v E (Sydney) 2006-07; BB 4-39 v SA (Gros Islet) 2006-07. **IT20** (A): 21 (2007-08 to 2015-16); HS 6 v P (Birmingham) 2010; BB 3-13 v P (Melbourne) 2009-10. F-c Tour (A): E 2005. HS 68 S Aus v Vic (Adelaide) 2005-06. CC HS 4. BB 7-29 (10-98 match) S Aus v Q (Brisbane) 2007-08. CC BB – . LO HS 22* Aus A v Z (Perth) 2003-04. LO BB 8-43 inc hat-trick S Aus v Tas (Adelaide) 2003-04, 8th best analysis in all l-o cricket. T20 HS 26. T20 BB 5-32.

WALLACE, Mark Alexander (Crickhowell HS), b Abergavenny, Monmouthshire 19 Nov 1981. 5'9". LHB, WK. Glamorgan 1999-2016; cap 2003; captain 2012-14; benefit 2013. F-c Tour (ECB Acad): SL 2002-03. 1000 runs (1): 1020 (2011). HS 139 v Surrey (Oval) 2009, sharing Gm record 6th wkt partnership of 240 with J.Allenby. LO HS 118* v Glos (Cardiff) 2013 (Y40). T20 HS 69*.

GLOUCESTERSHIRE 2016

RESULTS SUMMARY

	Place	*Won*	*Lost*	*Drew*	*NR*
Specsavers County Champ (2nd Division)	6th	4	5	7	
All First-Class Matches		4	5	8	
Royal London One-Day Cup (South Group)	8th	2	5		1
NatWest t20 Blast (South Group)	QF	10	4		1

SPECSAVERS COUNTY CHAMPIONSHIP AVERAGES

BATTING AND FIELDING

Cap†		*M*	*I*	*NO*	*HS*	*Runs*	*Avge*	*100*	*50*	*Ct/St*
2013	M.Klinger	7	12	4	140	589	73.62	3	2	8
2016	P.Mustard	6	10	2	107*	447	55.87	1	3	23
2010	C.D.J.Dent	16	29	3	180	1243	47.80	3	7	17
2016	G.L.van Buuren	7	12	2	172*	459	45.90	2	–	4
2006	H.J.H.Marshall	16	26	–	135	1022	39.30	4	5	13
2010	J.M.R.Taylor	16	26	2	107*	860	35.83	2	4	10
2013	G.H.Roderick	14	25	3	102	725	32.95	1	6	25/2
2011	D.A.Payne	14	18	4	67*	389	27.78	–	3	9
2011	C.N.Miles	13	20	4	60*	407	25.43	–	3	3
2016	G.T.Hankins	9	15	–	116	374	24.93	1	1	6
2016	C.T.Bancroft	5	9	–	70	192	21.33	–	1	3
2011	I.A.Cockbain	4	7	–	67	147	21.00	–	1	1
2015	K.Noema-Barnett	8	12	–	84	245	20.41	–	2	6
2012	B.A.C.Howell	5	7	1	41	113	18.83	–	–	–
2011	L.C.Norwell	11	15	3	102	224	18.66	1	–	1
2013	M.D.Taylor	5	8	5	9*	42	14.00	–	–	1
2014	W.A.Tavaré	6	10	–	36	112	11.20	–	–	6
2016	J.Shaw	12	16	4	29	125	10.41	–	–	3

Also batted (one match each): J.R.Bracey (cap 2016) 2, 12; T.R.G.Hampton (cap 2015) 0, 0*.

BOWLING

	O	*M*	*R*	*W*	*Avge*	*Best*	*5wI*	*10wM*
L.C.Norwell	377.5	87	1167	39	29.92	4-65	–	–
C.N.Miles	381	55	1581	52	30.40	5-54	2	–
D.A.Payne	451.4	83	1380	43	32.09	5-36	1	–
J.Shaw	326.5	59	1258	34	37.00	5-79	1	–
M.D.Taylor	143	15	543	13	41.76	4-56	–	–
J.M.R.Taylor	293.5	52	998	22	45.36	4-16	–	–
K.Noema-Barnett	192.4	43	551	11	50.09	3-56	–	–
Also bowled:								
G.L.van Buuren	84	17	219	7	31.28	3-15	–	–

I.A.Cockbain 2.5-0-20-0; C.D.J.Dent 48.4-8-151-3; T.R.G.Hampton 21-1-107-1; B.A.C.Howell 46.1-11-150-1; H.J.H.Marshall 9-0-58-0.

The First-Class Averages (pp 226–242) give the records of Gloucestershire players in all first-class county matches (Gloucestershire's other opponents being Durham MCCU), with the exception of P.Mustard, whose first-class figures for Gloucestershire are as above, and: J.Shaw 13-17-5-29-137-11.41-0-0-4ct. 359.5-65-1360-36-37.77-5/79-1-0.

† Gloucestershire revised their capping policy in 2004 and now award players with their County Caps when they make their first-class debut.

GLOUCESTERSHIRE RECORDS

FIRST-CLASS CRICKET

Highest Total	For 695-9d		v	Middlesex	Gloucester	2004
	V 774-7d		by	Australians	Bristol	1948
Lowest Total	For 17		v	Australians	Cheltenham	1896
	V 12		by	Northants	Gloucester	1907
Highest Innings	For 341	C.M.Spearman	v	Middlesex	Gloucester	2004
	V 319	C.J.L.Rogers	for	Northants	Northampton	2006

Highest Partnership for each Wicket

1st	395	D.M.Young/R.B.Nicholls	v	Oxford U	Oxford	1962
2nd	256	C.T.M.Pugh/T.W.Graveney	v	Derbyshire	Chesterfield	1960
3rd	392	G.H.Roderick/A.P.R.Gidman	v	Leics	Bristol	2014
4th	321	W.R.Hammond/W.L.Neale	v	Leics	Gloucester	1937
5th	261	W.G.Grace/W.O.Moberley	v	Yorkshire	Cheltenham	1876
6th	320	G.L.Jessop/J.H.Board	v	Sussex	Hove	1903
7th	248	W.G.Grace/E.L.Thomas	v	Sussex	Hove	1896
8th	239	W.R.Hammond/A.E.Wilson	v	Lancashire	Bristol	1938
9th	193	W.G.Grace/S.A.P.Kitcat	v	Sussex	Bristol	1896
10th	137	C.N.Miles/L.C.Norwell	v	Worcs	Cheltenham	2014

Best Bowling (Innings)	For	10-40	E.G.Dennett	v	Essex	Bristol	1906
	V	10-66	A.A.Mailey	for	Australians	Cheltenham	1921
		10-66	K.Smales	for	Notts	Stroud	1956
Best Bowling (Match)	For	17-56	C.W.L.Parker	v	Essex	Gloucester	1925
	V	15-87	A.J.Conway	for	Worcs	Moreton-in-M	1914

Most Runs – Season	2860	W.R.Hammond	(av 69.75)	1933
Most Runs – Career	33664	W.R.Hammond	(av 57.05)	1920-51
Most 100s – Season	13	W.R.Hammond		1938
Most 100s – Career	113	W.R.Hammond		1920-51
Most Wkts – Season	222	T.W.J.Goddard	(av 16.80)	1937
	222	T.W.J.Goddard	(av 16.37)	1947
Most Wkts – Career	3170	C.W.L.Parker	(av 19.43)	1903-35
Most Career W-K Dismissals	1054	R.C.Russell	(950 ct; 104 st)	1981-2004
Most Career Catches in the Field	719	C.A.Milton		1948-74

LIMITED-OVERS CRICKET

Highest Total	**50ov**	401-7		v	Bucks	Wing	2003
	40ov	344-6		v	Northants	Cheltenham	2001
	T20	254-3		v	Middlesex	Uxbridge	2011
Lowest Total	**50ov**	82		v	Notts	Bristol	1987
	40ov	49		v	Middlesex	Bristol	1978
	T20	68		v	Hampshire	Bristol	2010
Highest Innings	**50ov**	177	A.J.Wright	v	Scotland	Bristol	1997
	40ov	153	C.M.Spearman	v	Warwicks	Gloucester	2003
	T20	126*	M.Klinger	v	Essex	Bristol	2015
Best Bowling	**50ov**	6-13	M.J.Proctor	v	Hampshire	Southampton	1977
	40ov	7-29	D.A.Payne	v	Essex	Chelmsford	2010
	T20	5-24	D.A.Payne	v	Middlesex	Richmond	2015

HAMPSHIRE

Formation of Present Club: 12 August 1863
Inaugural First-Class Match: 1864
Colours: Blue, Gold and White
Badge: Tudor Rose and Crown
County Champions: (2) 1961, 1973
NatWest/C&G/FP Trophy Winners: (3) 1991, 2005, 2009
Benson and Hedges Cup Winners: (2) 1988, 1992
Sunday League Winners: (3) 1975, 1978, 1986
Clydesdale Bank Winners: (1) 2012
Twenty20 Cup Winners: (2) 2010, 2012

Chairman: Rod Bransgrove, The Ageas Bowl, Botley Road, West End, Southampton SO30 3XH • Tel. 023 8047 2002 • Fax: 023 8047 2122 • Email: enquiries@ageasbowl.com • Web: www.ageasbowl.com • Twitter:@hantscricket (37,216 followers)

CEO: David Mann. **Cricket Operations Manager**: Tim Tremlett. **Director of Cricket**: Giles White. **1st XI Coach**: Craig White. **Batting Coach**: Tony Middleton. **Captain**: J.M.Vince. **Vice-Captain**: n/a. **Overseas Player**: G.J.Bailey. **2017 Testimonial**: None. **Head Groundsman**: Karl McDermott. **Scorer**: Kevin Baker. ‡ New registration. NQ Not qualified for England.

NQ**ABBOTT**, Kyle John, b Empangeni, South Africa 18 Jun 1987. RHB, RFM. Squad No 87. KwaZulu-Natal 2008-09 to 2009-10. Dolphins 2008-09 to date. Hampshire 2014, rejoins in 2017 on a Kolpak deal. Worcestershire 2016. **Tests** (SA): 11 (2012-13 to 2016-17); HS 17 v A (Adelaide) 2016-17; BB 7-29 v P (Centurion) 2012-13. **LOI** (SA): 28 (2012-13 to 2016-17); HS 23 v Z (Bulawayo) 2014; BB 4-21 v Ireland (Canberra) 2014-15. **IT20** (SA): 21 (2012-13 to 2015-16); HS 9* v NZ (Centurion) 2015; BB 3-20 v B (Dhaka) 2015. F-c Tours (SA): A 2016-17; I 2015-16. HS 80 Dolphins v Titans (Benoni) 2010-11. CC HS 40 H v Leics (Leicester) 2014. 50 wkts (0+1): 65 (2012-13). BB 8-45 (12-96 match) Dolphins v Cobras (Cape Town) 2012-13. CC BB 5-44 H v Essex (Southampton) 2014. LO HS 15* Dolphins v Titans (Durban) 2013-14. LO BB 4-21 (*see LOI*). T20 HS 16*. T20 BB 5-14.

ADAMS, James Henry Kenneth (Sherborne S; University C, London; Loughborough U), b Winchester 23 Sep 1980. 6'2". LHB, LM. Squad No 4. British U 2002-04. Hampshire debut 2002; cap 2006; captain 2012-15; benefit 2015. Loughborough UCCE 2003-04 – scoring 107 v Somerset (Taunton) on debut. MCC 2013. Dorset 1998. F-c Tour (EL): WI 2010-11. 1000 runs (5); most – 1351 (2009). HS 262* v Notts (Nottingham) 2006. BB 2-16 v Durham (Chester-le-St) 2004. LO HS 131 v Warwks (Birmingham) 2010 (CB40). LO BB 1-34 v Essex (Chelmsford) 2007 (FPT). T20 HS 101*. T20 BB – .

ALSOP, Thomas Philip (Lavington S), b High Wycombe, Bucks 26 Nov 1995. Younger brother of O.J.Alsop (Wiltshire 2010-12). 5'11". LHB, WK, occ SLA. Squad No 9. Debut (Hampshire) 2014. England Lions 2016-17. Hampshire 2nd XI debut 2013. England U19 2014 to 2015. No 1st XI appearances in 2015. HS 117 v Surrey (The Oval) 2016. LO HS 116 v Surrey (Southampton) 2016 (RLC). T20 HS 85.

NQ**BAILEY, George** John, b Launceston, Tasmania, Australia 7 Sep 1982. 5'10". RHB, RM. Squad No 10. Tasmania 2004-05 to date. Hampshire debut 2013, rejoins in 2017 on a two-year contract. Middlesex 2016. Sussex 2015 (l-o and T20 only) IPL: CSK 2009 to 2009-10. KXIP 2014-15. RPS 2016. Big Bash: MS 2011-12. HH 2012-13 to date. **Tests** (A): 5 (2013-14); HS 53 v E (Adelaide) 2013-14. **LOI** (A): 90 (2011-12 to 2016-17); HS 156 v I (Nagpur) 2013-14. **IT20** (A): 29 (2011-12 to 2016); HS 63 v WI (Colombo, RPS) 2012-13. F-c Tours (Aus A): E 2012; I 2008-09. HS 200* Tas v NSW (Wollongong) 2016-17. UK HS 110* M v Surrey (Lord's) 2016. H HS 93 v Leics (Southampton) 2013. BB – . LO HS 156 (*see LOI*). LO BB 1-19 Tas v Vic (Melbourne) 2004-05. T20 HS 76.

BERG, Gareth Kyle (South African College S), b Cape Town, South Africa 18 Jan 1981. 6'0". RHB, RMF. Squad No 13. England qualified through residency. Middlesex 2008-14; cap 2010. Hampshire debut 2015; cap 2016. Italy (T20 only) 2011-12 to date. HS 130* M v Leics (Leicester) 2011, sharing M record 9th wkt partnership of 172 with T.J.Murtagh. H HS 99 v Sussex (Hove) 2015. BB 6-56 v Yorks (Southampton) 2016. LO HS 75 M v Glamorgan (Lord's) 2013 (Y40). LO BB 4-24 M v Worcs (Worcester) 2011 (CB40). T20 HS 90. T20 BB 4-20.

CARBERRY, Michael Alexander (St John Rigby Catholic C), b Croydon, Surrey 29 Sep 1980. 6'0". LHB, RM. Squad No 15. Surrey 2001-02. Kent 2003-05. Hampshire debut/cap 2006. MCC 2008, 2015. Big Bash: PS 2014-15. **Tests**: 6 (2009-10 to 2013-14); HS 60 v A (Adelaide) 2013-14. **LOI**: 6 (2013 to 2014); HS 63 v A (Cardiff) 2013. **IT20**: 1 (2014); HS 7 v SL (Oval) 2014. F-c Tours: A 2013-14; B 2006-07 (Eng A), 2009-10. 1000 runs (4); most – 1275 (2015). HS 300* v Yorks (Southampton) 2011, sharing in UK 3rd highest and UK record 3rd-wkt partnership of 523 with N.D.McKenzie. BB 2-85 v Durham (Chester-le-St) 2006. LO HS 150* v Lancs (Southampton) 2013 (Y40). LO BB 3-37 v Derbys (Derby) 2013 (Y40). T20 HS 100*. T20 BB 1-16.

CRANE, Mason Sydney (Lancing C), b Shoreham-by-Sea, Sussex 18 Feb 1997. 5'7". RHB, LB. Squad No 32. Debut (Hampshire) 2015. NSW 2016-17. Hampshire 2nd XI debut 2013. HS 24* v Cardiff MCCU (Southampton) 2016. CC HS 22 v Warwks (Birmingham) 2016. BB 5-35 v Warwks (Southampton) 2015. LO HS 16* v Kent (Canterbury) 2015 (RLC). LO BB 4-30 v Middx (Southampton) 2015 (RLC). T20 HS 2*. T20 BB 2-35.

DAWSON, Liam Andrew (John Bentley S, Calne), b Swindon, Wilts 1 Mar 1990. 5'8". RHB, SLA. Squad No 8. Debut (Hampshire) 2007; cap 2013. Mountaineers 2011-12. Essex 2015 (on loan). Wiltshire 2006-07. **Tests**: 1 (2016-17); HS 66* and BB 2-129 v I (Chennai) 2016-17. **LOI**: 1 (2016); HS 10 and BB 2-70 v P (Cardiff) 2016. **IT20**: 2 (2016 to 2016-17); HS – ; BB 3-27 v SL (Southampton) 2016. F-c Tour: I 2016-17. HS 169 v Somerset (Southampton) 2011. BB 7-51 Mountaineers v ME (Mutare) 2011-12 (also scored 110* in same match). BB 5-29 v Leics (Southampton) 2012. LO HS 113* SJD v Kalabagan (Savar) 2014-15. LO BB 6-47 v Sussex (Southampton) 2015 (RLC). T20 HS 76*. T20 BB 5-17.

‡**DICKINSON, Calvin** Miles (St Edward's S, Oxford; Oxford Brookes U), b Durban, South Africa 3 Nov 1996. RHB, WK. UK passport. Oxford MCCU 2016. Worcestershire 2nd XI 2015. Essex 2nd XI 2016. HS 62 OU v Northants (Oxford) 2016.

DUGGAN, Benjamin Jason (Cowes Enterprise C), b Newport, IoW 28 Mar 1998. LHB, SLA. Hampshire 2nd XI debut 2015. Awaiting 1st XI debut.

NQ**EDWARDS, Fidel** Henderson (St James's SS), b Gays, St Peter, Barbados 6 Feb 1982. 5'11". RHB, RFM. Squad No 82. Half-brother of P.T.Collins (Barbados, Surrey, Middlesex & West Indies 1996-97 to 2011-12). Barbados 2001-02 to 2013-14. Hampshire debut 2015. Kolpak signing. IPL: DC 2009 to 2009-10. Big Bash: ST 2011-12. **Tests** (WI): 55 (2003 to 2012-13); HS 30 v I (Roseau) 2011; BB 7-87 v NZ (Napier) 2008-09. **LOI** (WI): 50 (2003-04 to 2009); HS 13 v NZ (Wellington) 2008-09; BB 6-22 v Z (Harare) 2003-04 – on debut. **IT20** (WI): 20 (2007-08 to 2012-13); HS 7* v E (Oval) 2011; BB 3-23 v A (Bridgetown) 2011-12. F-c Tours (WI): E 2004, 2007, 2009, 2012; A 2005-06; SA 2003-04, 2007-08; NZ 2005-06, 2008-09; I 2011-12, 2013-14 (WI A); P 2006-07; Z 2003-04; B 2011-12, 2012-13. HS 40 Bar v Jamaica (Bridgetown) 2007-08. H HS 17* v Warwks (Southampton) 2015. BB 7-87 (*see Tests*). H BB 6-88 (10-145 match) v Notts (Nottingham) 2015. LO HS 21* Bar v Jamaica (Providence) 2007-08. LO BB 6-22 (*see LOI*). T20 HS 11*. T20 BB 5-22.

ERVINE, Sean Michael (Lomagundi C, Chinhoyi), b Harare, Zimbabwe 6 Dec 1982. Elder brother of C.R.Ervine (Midlands, SR 2003-04 to date); son of R.M.Ervine (Rhodesia 1977-78); grandson of M.A.Den (Rhodesia 1935-36); nephew of N.B.Ervine (Rhodesia 1977-78) and G.M.Den (Rhodesia and Eastern Province 1963-64 to 1969-70). 6'2". LHB, RMF. Squad No 7. CFX Academy 2000-01 to 2001. Midlands 2001-02 to 2003-04. Hampshire debut/cap 2005; qualified for England in 2013 season; benefit 2016. W Australia 2006-07 to 2007-08. Southern Rocks 2009-10. Matabeleland Tuskers 2011-12 to 2012-13. **Tests** (Z): 5 (2003 to 2003-04); HS 86 v B (Harare) 2003-04; BB 4-146 v A (Perth) 2003-04. **LOI** (Z): 42 (2001-02 to 2003-04); HS 100 v I (Adelaide) 2003-04; BB 3-29 v P (Sharjah) 2001-02. F-c Tours (Z): E 2003; A 2003-04. 1000 runs (1): 1090 (2016). HS 237* v Somerset (Southampton) 2010. BB 6-82 Midlands v Mashonaland (Kwekwe) 2002-03. H BB 5-60 v Glamorgan (Cardiff) 2005. LO HS 167* v Ireland (Southampton) 2009 (FPT). LO BB 5-50 v Glamorgan (Cardiff) 2005 (CGT). T20 HS 82. T20 BB 4-12.

GOODWIN, Jake (Kingsdown S), b Swindon, Wilts 19 Jan 1998. RHB, RM. Hampshire 2nd XI debut 2015. Awaiting f-c debut. T20 HS 32.

‡**HART, Asher** Hale-Bopp Joseph Arthur (Ullswater Community C), b Carlisle 30 Mar 1997. RHB, RMF. Durham 2nd XI 2016. Northumberland 2016. Awaiting 1st XI debut.

HAY, Fraser Steven (Trinity C, Perth; U of WA), b Perth, Australia 9 Jul 1996. RHB, RM. Hampshire 2nd XI debut 2016. Awaiting 1st XI debut. UK passport.

McCOY, Joshua Ian (Millfield S), b Portsmouth 2 Mar 1998. RHB, RMF. Hampshire 2nd XI debut 2016. England U19 2016. Awaiting 1st XI debut.

McMANUS, Lewis David (Clayesmore S, Bournemouth), b Poole, Dorset 9 Oct 1994. 5'10". RHB, WK. Squad No 18. Debut (Hampshire) 2015. Hampshire 2nd XI debut 2011. Dorset 2011-13. HS 132* v Surrey (Southampton) 2016. LO HS 35 v Somerset (Southampton) 2016 (RLC). T20 HS 41.

‡[NQ]**ROSSOUW, Rilee** Roscoe, b Bloemfontein, South Africa, 9 Oct 1989. LHB, OB. Squad No 27. Free State 2007-08 to 2012-13. Eagles 2008-09 to 2009-10. Knights 2010-11 to date. Joins Hampshire in 2017 on three year Kolpak deal. IPL: RCB 2014-15. **LOI** (SA): 36 (2014 to 2016-17); HS 132 v WI (Centurion) 2014-15; BB 1-17 v Z (Harare) 2014. **IT20** (SA): 15 (2014-15 to 2015-16); HS 78 v A (Adelaide) 2014-15. F-c Tours (SA A): A 2014; SL 2010; B 2010. 1000 runs (0+1): 1261 (2009-10). HS 319 Eagles v Titans (Centurion) 2009-10, sharing in 3rd highest 2nd wkt partnership in all f-c cricket of 480 with D.Elgar. BB 1-1 Knights v Cobras (Cape Town) 2013-14. LO HS 137 SA A v India A (Darwin) 2014. LO BB 1-17 (*see LOI*). T20 HS 78. T20 BB 1-8.

SMITH, William Rew (Bedford S; Collingwood C, Durham U), b Luton, Beds 28 Sep 1982. 5'9". RHB, OB. Squad No 2. Nottinghamshire 2002-06. Durham UCCE 2003-05; captain 2004-05. British U 2004-05. Durham 2007-13; captain 2009-10 (*part*). Hampshire debut 2014; cap 2015. Bedfordshire 1999-2002. 1000 runs (1): 1187 (2014). HS 210 v Lancs (Southampton) 2016. BB 3-34 DU v Leics (Leicester) 2005. H BB 2-27 v Kent (Southampton) 2014. LO HS 120* Du v Surrey (Chester-le-St) 2013 (Y40). LO BB 2-19 Du v Derbys (Derby) 2013 (Y40). T20 HS 55. T20 BB 3-15.

STEVENSON, Ryan Anthony (King Edward VI Community C), b Torquay, Devon 2 Apr 1992. 6'2". RHB, RMF. Squad No 47. Debut (Hampshire) 2015. Devon 2015. HS 30 v Durham (Chester-le-St) 2015. BB 1-15 v Notts (Nottingham) 2015. LO HS 0. LO BB 1-28 v Essex (Southampton) 2016 (RLC). T20 HS 3. T20 BB 2-40.

TAYLOR, Bradley Jacob (Eggar's S, Alton), b Winchester 14 Mar 1997. 5'11". RHB, OB. Squad No 93. Debut (Hampshire) 2013. Hampshire 2nd XI debut 2013. England U19 2014 to 2014-15. No 1st XI appearances in 2015. HS 36 v Cardiff MCCU (Southampton) 2016. CC HS 20 and BB 4-64 v Lancs (Southport) 2013. LO HS 2* and LO BB 2-23 v Bangladesh A (Southampton) 2013. T20 HS 9*. T20 BB 2-20.

TOPLEY, Reece James William (Royal Hospital S, Ipswich), b Ipswich, Suffolk 21 February 1994. Son of T.D.Topley (Surrey, Essex, GW 1985-94) and nephew of P.A.Topley (Kent 1972-75). 6'7". RHB, LMF. Squad No 6. Essex 2011-15; cap 2013. Hampshire 2016 – missed all bar one game due to injuries. Essex 2nd XI debut 2010, aged 16y 156d. England U19 2012-13. **LOI**: 10 (2015 to 2015-16); HS 6 v A (Manchester) 2015; BB 4-50 v SA (Pt Elizabeth) 2015-16. **IT20**: 4 (2015 to 2015-16); HS 1* v SA (Johannesburg) 2015-16; BB 3-24 v P (Dubai, DSC) 2015-16. F-c Tour (EL): SL 2013-14. HS 15 v Warwks (Southampton) 2016. BB 6-29 (11-85 match) Ex v Worcs (Chelmsford) 2013. LO HS 19 Ex v Somerset (Taunton) 2011 (CB40). LO BB 4-26 Ex v Derbys (Colchester) 2013 (Y40). T20 HS 5*. T20 BB 4-26.

VINCE, James Michael (Warminster S), b Cuckfield, Sussex 14 Mar 1991. 6'2". RHB, RM. Squad No 14. Debut (Hampshire) 2009; cap 2013; captain 2016 to date. Wiltshire 2007-08. Big Bash: ST 2016-17. **Tests**: 7 (2016); HS 42 (twice) v P (Lord's & Birmingham) 2016; BB – . **LOI**: 5 (2015 to 2016-17); HS 51 v SL (Cardiff) 2016. **IT20**: 5 (2015-16 to 2016); HS 46 v P (Sharjah) 2015-16. F-c Tours (EL): SA 2014-15; SL 2013-14. 1000 runs (2); most – 1525 (2014). HS 240 v Essex (Southampton) 2014. BB 5-41 v Loughborough MCCU (Southampton) 2013. CC BB 2-2 v Lancs (Southport) 2013. LO HS 131 v Scotland (Southampton) 2011 (CB40). LO BB 1-18 EL v Australia A (Sydney) 2012-13. T20 HS 107*. T20 BB 1-5.

WEATHERLEY, Joe James (King Edward VI S, Southampton), b Winchester 19 Jan 1997. 6'1". RHB, OB. Squad No 5. Debut (Hampshire) 2016. Hampshire 2nd XI debut 2014. England U19 2014-15. Moves to Kent on loan for 2017. HS 83 v Cardiff MCCU (Southampton) 2016. CC HS 9 v Middx (Northwood) 2016. BB – . LO HS 27 v Glamorgan (Swansea) 2016 (RLC). LO BB – . T20 HS 43. T20 BB – .

[NQ]**WHEAL, Brad**ley Thomas James (Clifton C), b Durban, South Africa 28 Aug 1996. 5'9". RHB, RMF. Squad No 58. Debut (Hampshire) 2015. **LOI** (Scot): 5 (2015-16 to 2016-17); HS 2* v Hong Kong (Mong Kok) 2015-16; BB 2-31 v Afghanistan (Edinburgh) 2016. **IT20** (Scot): 5 (2015-16 to 2016-17); HS 2* and BB 3-20 v Hong Kong (Mong Kok) 2015-16. HS 14 v Surrey (Southampton) 2016. BB 6-51 v Notts (Nottingham) 2016. LO HS 13 v Somerset (Southampton) 2016 (RLC). LO BB 4-38 v Kent (Southampton) 2016 (RLC). T20 HS 16. T20 BB 3-20.

WOOD, Christopher Philip (Alton C), b Basingstoke 27 June 1990. 6'2". RHB, LM. Squad No 25. Debut (Hampshire) 2010. Missed most of 2016 due to knee ligament injury. HS 105* v Leics (Leicester) 2012. BB 5-39 v Kent (Canterbury) 2014. LO HS 41 v Essex (Southampton) 2013 (Y40). LO BB 5-22 v Glamorgan (Cardiff) 2012 (CB40). T20 HS 27. T20 BB 4-16.

RELEASED/RETIRED

(Having made a County 1st XI appearance in 2016)

ANDREW, Gareth Mark (Ansford Community S; Richard Huish C), b Yeovil, Somerset 27 Dec 1983. 6'0". LHB, RMF. Somerset 2003-05. Worcestershire 2008-15. Canterbury 2012-13. Hampshire 2016. HS 180* Canterbury v Auckland (Auckland) 2012-13. CC HS 92* Wo v Notts (Worcester) 2009. H HS 25 v Surrey (The Oval) 2016. 50 wkts (1): 52 (2011). BB 5-40 v Glamorgan (Cardiff) 2014. H BB 3-104 v Durham (Chester-le-St) 2016. LO HS 104 v Surrey (Oval) 2010 (CB40). LO BB 5-31 v Yorks (Worcester) 2009 (P40). T20 HS 65*. T20 BB 4-22.

[NQ]**BEST, Tino** la Bertram, b Richmond Gap, St Michael, Barbados 26 Aug 1981. RHB, RF. Barbados 2001-02 to 2015-16. Yorkshire 2010. Hampshire 2016. **Tests** (WI): 25 (2002-03 to 2013-14); HS 95 v E (Birmingham) 2012; BB 6-40 v B (Khulna) 2012-13. **LOI** (WI): 26 (2003-04 to 2013-14); HS 24 v I (Dambulla) 2005; BB 4-35 v B (Kingstown) 2003-04 – on LOI debut. **IT20** (WI): 6 (2012-13 to 2013-14); HS 17* v P (Kingstown) 2013; BB 3-18 v Z (North Sound) 2012-13. F-c Tours (WI): E 2002 (WI A), 2004, 2006 (WI A), 2012; A 2005-06; I 2013-14; NZ 2013-14; SL 2005; B 2012-13. HS 95 (*see Tests*). H HS 23* v Middx (Southampton) 2016. BB 7-33 (11-66 match) Barbados v Windward Is (Crab Hill) 2003-04. H BB 5-90 v Lancs (Manchester) 2016. LO HS 24 (*see LOI*). LO BB 5-24 Barbados v Guyana (Kingston) 2010-11. T20 HS 17*. T20 BB 4-19.

CARTER, A. – *see DERBYSHIRE.*

GRIFFITHS, G.T. – *see LEICESTERSHIRE.*

HAMZA ALI (City Ac, Bristol; Filton SFC), b Bristol, Glos 8 Aug 1995; d Bristol 9 Jun 2016. RHB, RMF. Hampshire 2016. Hampshire 2nd XI debut 2015. HS – . BB 2-47 v Cardiff MCCU (Southampton) 2016. LO HS 13 and LO BB 3-39 Rawalpindi Rams v NBP (Karachi) 2014-15.

[NQ]**McLAREN, R.** – *see LANCASHIRE.*

[NQ]**SAMMY, Darren** Julius Garvey, b Micoud, St Lucia, 20 Dec 1983. RHB, RM. Windward Is 2002-03 to 2012-13. Glamorgan (T20 only) 2014. Nottinghamshire (T20 only) 2015. Hampshire (T20 only) 2016. IPL: SH 2013-14. RCB 2015. Big Bash: HH 2014-15 to 2015-16. **Tests** (WI): 38 (2007 to 2013-14, 30 as captain); HS 106 v E (Nottingham) 2012; BB 7-66 v E (Manchester) 2007. **LOI** (WI): 126 (2004 to 2014-15, 51 as captain); HS 89 v Ireland (Nelson) 2014-15; BB 4-26 v Z (Kingstown) 2009-10. **IT20** (WI): 66 (2007 to 2015-16, 47 as captain); HS 42* v P (Dhaka) 2013-14; BB 5-26 v Z (Port of Spain) 2009-10. F-c Tours (WI)(C=Captain): E 2006 (WI A), 2007, 2009, 2012C, A 2009-10; SA 2007-08; NZ 2013-14C; I 2011-12C, 2013-14C; SL 2005 (WI A), 2010-11C; B 2011-12C, 2012-13C. HS 121 Windward Is v Barbados (Bridgetown) 2008-09. BB 7-66 (*see Tests*). LO HS 89 (*see LOI*). LO BB 4-16 WI A v Sri Lanka A (Gros Islet) 2006-07. T20 HS 71*. T20 BB 5-26.

[NQ]**SHAHID KHAN AFRIDI**, Sahibzada Mohammad (Ibrahim Alibhai B, Islamia Science C, Karachi) b Kohat, Pakistan, 1 Mar 1980. Brother of Tariq Afridi (Karachi 1999-00) and Ashfaq Afridi (Karachi Blues 2008-09). RHB, LBG. Debut Combined XI v Eng A 1995-96. Karachi 1995-96 to 2003-04. HB 1997-98 to date. Leicestershire 2001; cap 2001. Derbyshire 2003. GW 2003-04. Sind 2007-08 to 2008-09. MCC 2001. Hampshire 2016 (l-o only). IPL: DC 2007-08. Big Bash: MR 2011-12. **Tests** (P): 27 (1998-99 to 2010, 1 as captain); HS 156 v I (Faisalabad) 2005-06; BB 5-52 v A (Karachi) 1998-99 – on debut. **LOI** (P): 398 (1996-97 to 2014-15, 38 as captain); HS 124 v B (Dambulla) 2010; BB 7-12 v WI (Providence) 2013, 2nd best analysis in all LOIs. Scored a 37-ball hundred which included then joint record 11 sixes v SL (Nairobi) 1996-97 in his first LOI innings. **IT20** (P): 98 (2006-07 to 2015-16, 39 as captain); HS 54* v SL (Lord's) 2009; BB 4-11 v Netherlands (Lord's) 2009. F-c Tours (P): E 2006, 2010; A 1996-97, 2004-05; WI 1999-00, 2005; I 1998-99, 2004-05; SL 2005-06; Z 2002-03; B 1998-99. HS 164 Le v Northants (Northampton) 2001. BB 6-101 HB v KRL (Rawalpindi) 1997-98. UK BB 5-84 Le v Essex (Chelmsford) 2001. LO HS 124 (*see LOI*). LO BB 7-12 (*see LOI*). T20 HS 80. T20 BB 5-7.

TOMLINSON, James Andrew (Harrow Way S, Andover; Cardiff U), b Winchester 12 Jun 1982. 6'1". LHB, LMF. British U 2002-03. Hampshire 2002-16; cap 2008. Wiltshire 2001. HS 51 v Glos (Southampton) 2014. 50 wkts (2); most – 67 (2008). BB 8-46 (10-194 match) v Somerset (Taunton) 2008. LO HS 14 v Durham (Chester-le-St) 2010 (CB40). LO BB 4-47 v Glamorgan (Southampton) 2006 (CGT). T20 HS 5. T20 BB 1-20.

RELEASED/RETIRED continued on p 127

HAMPSHIRE 2016

RESULTS SUMMARY

	Place	*Won*	*Lost*	*Drew*	*NR*
Specsavers County Champ (1st Division)	8th	2	4	10	
All First-Class Matches		2	4	11	
Royal London One-Day Cup (South Group)	5th	4	4		
NatWest t20 Blast (South Group)	8th	4	8		2

SPECSAVERS COUNTY CHAMPIONSHIP AVERAGES

BATTING AND FIELDING

Cap		*M*	*I*	*NO*	*HS*	*Runs*	*Avge*	*100*	*50*	*Ct/St*
2005	S.M.Ervine	12	21	4	158*	1050	61.76	4	5	9
	R.McLaren	15	24	9	100	832	55.46	1	6	6
2016	A.J.A.Wheater	12	21	4	204*	802	47.17	2	3	16/1
2006	J.H.K.Adams	14	25	–	99	897	35.88	–	8	13
	L.D.McManus	10	13	1	132*	425	35.41	1	2	20/6
2013	L.A.Dawson	12	20	1	116	644	33.89	1	5	2
2013	J.M.Vince	8	14	–	119	473	33.78	1	2	5
	T.P.Alsop	12	20	–	117	655	32.75	1	5	12
2015	W.R.Smith	16	28	–	210	827	29.53	1	3	11
2006	M.A.Carberry	8	15	1	107	411	29.35	1	1	4
2016	G.K.Berg	10	13	3	56	288	28.80	–	1	3
2008	J.A.Tomlinson	6	9	4	23*	75	15.00	–	–	2
	G.M.Andrew	6	7	1	25	85	14.16	–	–	2
	M.S.Crane	12	17	4	22	101	7.76	–	–	4
	B.T.J.Wheal	8	9	4	14	37	7.40	–	–	1
	T.L.Best	6	8	1	23*	49	7.00	–	–	3

Also batted: A.Carter (2 matches) 4, 4 (1 ct); F.H.Edwards (2) 4; R.J.W.Topley (1) 15; D.J.Wainwright (1) 35*, 1*; J.J.Weatherley (1) 4, 9; C.P.Wood (2) 31, 6.

BOWLING

	O	*M*	*R*	*W*	*Avge*	*Best*	*5wI*	*10wM*
J.A.Tomlinson	151.3	40	483	14	34.50	4- 74	–	–
B.T.J.Wheal	211	36	720	20	36.00	6- 51	1	–
G.K.Berg	251.2	73	694	19	36.52	6- 56	1	–
R.McLaren	382	81	1242	32	38.81	5-104	1	–
T.L.Best	136.5	20	554	14	39.57	5- 90	1	–
L.A.Dawson	306.5	56	877	20	43.85	4-100	–	–
M.S.Crane	372	49	1409	31	45.45	3- 19	–	–
Also bowled:								
A.Carter	42	8	126	6	21.00	4- 52	–	–
G.M.Andrew	129	25	439	7	62.71	3-104	–	–
W.R.Smith	126.1	20	401	5	80.20	1- 1	–	–

T.P.Alsop 10-0-66-2; F.H.Edwards 45-6-247-3; S.M.Ervine 61-10-216-2; J.M.Vince 15.2-1-72-2; D.J.Wainwright 31-4-112-2; C.P.Wood 51-19-139-3.

The First-Class Averages (pp 226–242) give the records of Hampshire players in all first-class county matches (Hampshire's other opponents being Cardiff MCCU), with the exception of A.Carter and J.M.Vince, whose first-class figures for Hampshire are as above, and:
A.J.A.Wheater 13-22-4-204*-850-47.22-2-3-17/1.

HAMPSHIRE RECORDS

FIRST-CLASS CRICKET

Highest Total	For 714-5d		v	Notts	Southampton	2005
	V 742		by	Surrey	The Oval	1909
Lowest Total	For 15		v	Warwicks	Birmingham	1922
	V 23		by	Yorkshire	Middlesbrough	1965
Highest Innings	For 316	R.H.Moore	v	Warwicks	Bournemouth	1937
	V 303*	G.A.Hick	for	Worcs	Southampton	1997

Highest Partnership for each Wicket

1st	347	V.P.Terry/C.L.Smith	v	Warwicks	Birmingham	1987
2nd	373	J.H.K.Adams/M.A.Carberry	v	Somerset	Taunton	2011
3rd	523	M.A.Carberry/N.D.McKenzie	v	Yorkshire	Southampton	2011
4th	278	J.H.K.Adams/J.M.Vince	v	Yorkshire	Scarborough	2010
5th	235	G.Hill/D.F.Walker	v	Sussex	Portsmouth	1937
6th	411	R.M.Poore/E.G.Wynyard	v	Somerset	Taunton	1899
7th	325	G.Brown/C.H.Abercrombie	v	Essex	Leyton	1913
8th	257	N.Pothas/A.J.Bichel	v	Glos	Cheltenham	2005
9th	230	D.A.Livingstone/A.T.Castell	v	Surrey	Southampton	1962
10th	192	H.A.W.Bowell/W.H.Livsey	v	Worcs	Bournemouth	1921

Best Bowling	For	9- 25	R.M.H.Cottam	v	Lancashire	Manchester	1965
(Innings)	V	10- 46	W.Hickton	for	Lancashire	Manchester	1870
Best Bowling	For	16- 88	J.A.Newman	v	Somerset	Weston-s-Mare	1927
(Match)	V	17-103	W.Mycroft	for	Derbyshire	Southampton	1876

Most Runs – Season	2854	C.P.Mead	(av 79.27)	1928
Most Runs – Career	48892	C.P.Mead	(av 48.84)	1905-36
Most 100s – Season	12	C.P.Mead		1928
Most 100s – Career	138	C.P.Mead		1905-36
Most Wkts – Season	190	A.S.Kennedy	(av 15.61)	1922
Most Wkts – Career	2669	D.Shackleton	(av 18.23)	1948-69
Most Career W-K Dismissals	700	R.J.Parks	(630 ct; 70 st)	1980-92
Most Career Catches in the Field	629	C.P.Mead		1905-36

LIMITED-OVERS CRICKET

Highest Total	**50ov**	371-4		v	Glamorgan	Southampton	1975
	40ov	353-8		v	Middlesex	Lord's	2005
	T20	225-2		v	Middlesex	Southampton	2006
Lowest Total	**50ov**	50		v	Yorkshire	Leeds	1991
	40ov	43		v	Essex	Basingstoke	1972
	T20	85		v	Sussex	Southampton	2008
Highest Innings	**50ov**	177	C.G.Greenidge	v	Glamorgan	Southampton	1975
	40ov	172	C.G.Greenidge	v	Surrey	Southampton	1987
	T20	124*	M.J.Lumb	v	Essex	Southampton	2009
Best Bowling	**50ov**	7-30	P.J.Sainsbury	v	Norfolk	Southampton	1965
	40ov	6-20	T.E.Jesty	v	Glamorgan	Cardiff	1975
	T20	5-14	A.D.Mascarenhas	v	Sussex	Hove	2004

KENT

Formation of Present Club: 1 March 1859
Substantial Reorganisation: 6 December 1870
Inaugural First-Class Match: 1864
Colours: Maroon and White
Badge: White Horse on a Red Ground
County Champions: (6) 1906, 1909, 1910, 1913, 1970, 1978
Joint Champions: (1) 1977
Gillette Cup Winners: (2) 1967, 1974
Benson and Hedges Cup Winners: (3) 1973, 1976, 1978
Pro 40/National League (Div 1) Winners: (1) 2001
Sunday League Winners: (4) 1972, 1973, 1976, 1995
Twenty20 Cup Winners: (1) 2007

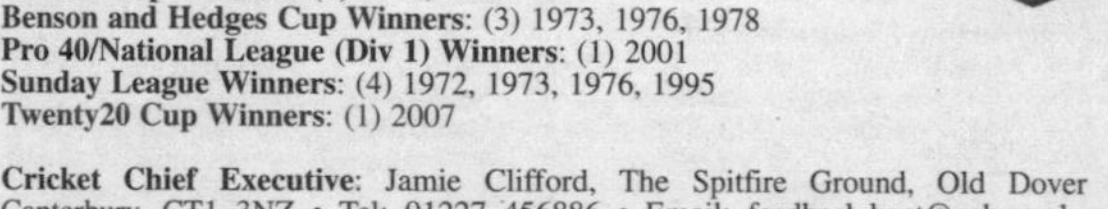

Cricket Chief Executive: Jamie Clifford, The Spitfire Ground, Old Dover Road, Canterbury, CT1 3NZ • Tel: 01227 456886 • Email: feedback.kent@ecb.co.uk • Web: www.kentcricket.co.uk • Twitter: @kentcricket (35,277 followers)

Head Coach: Matt Walker. **Assistant Coach**: Allan Donald. **Captain**: S.A.Northeast. **Overseas Player**: tba. **2017 Testimonial**: J.C.Tredwell. **Head Groundsman**: Simon Williamson. **Scorer**: Lorne Hart. ‡ New registration. [NQ] Not qualified for England.

BALL, Adam James (Beths GS, Bexley) b Greenwich, London 1 March 1993. 6'2". RHB, LFM. Squad No 24. Debut (Kent) 2011. Kent 2nd XI debut 2009, aged 16y 117d. England U19 2010 to 2010-11. HS 69 v Lancs (Canterbury) 2013. BB 3-36 v Leics (Leicester) 2011. LO HS 40* v Windward Is (Coolidge) 2016-17. LO BB 3-36 v Sussex (Horsham) 2013 (Y40). T20 HS 18. T20 BB 2-18.

BELL-DRUMMOND, Daniel James (Millfield S), b Lewisham, London 4 Aug 1993. 5'10". RHB, RMF. Squad No 23. Debut (Kent) 2011; cap 2015. MCC 2014. Kent 2nd XI debut 2009, aged 16y 21d. England U19 2010 to 2010-11. 1000 runs (1): 1058 (2014). HS 206* v Loughborough MCCU (Canterbury) 2016. CC 153 v Hants (Southampton) 2014. BB – . LO HS 171* EL v Sri Lanka A (Canterbury) 2016. LO BB – . T20 HS 112*.

BERNARD, Hugh Robert (Archbishop's S, Canterbury), Canterbury 14 Sep 1996. 5'10". RHB, RMF. Squad No 27. Debut (Kent) 2016. Kent 2nd XI debut 2014. HS 14 and BB 2-68 v Glamorgan (Canterbury) 2016. LO HS 7 v Windward Is (Coolidge) 2016-17. LO BB 1-40 v Leeward Is (Coolidge) 2016-17.

BILLINGS, Samuel William (Haileybury S; Loughborough U), b Pembury 15 Jun 1991. 5'11". RHB, WK. Squad No 7. Loughborough MCCU 2011, scoring 131 v Northants (Loughborough) on f-c debut. Kent debut 2011; cap 2015. MCC 2015. **LOI**: 9 (2015 to 2016-17); HS 62 v B (Chittagong) 2016-17. **IT20**: 10 (2015 to 2016-17); HS 53 v P (Dubai, DSC) 2015-16. HS 171 v Glos (Bristol) 2016. LO HS 175 EL v Pakistan A (Canterbury) 2016. T20 HS 78*.

BLAKE, Alexander James (Hayes SS; Leeds Met U), b Farnborough 25 Jan 1989. 6'1". LHB, RMF. Squad No 10. Debut (Kent) 2008. Leeds/Bradford UCCE 2009-11 (not f-c). HS 105* v Yorks (Leeds) 2010. BB 2-9 v Pakistanis (Canterbury) 2010. CC BB 1-60 v Hants (Southampton) 2010. LO HS 89 v Lancs (Canterbury) 2015 (RLC). LO BB 2-13 v Yorks (Leeds) 2011 (CB40). T20 HS 71*.

CLAYDON, Mitchell Eric (Westfield Sports HS, Sydney), b Fairfield, NSW, Australia 25 Nov 1982. 6'4". LHB, RMF. Squad No 8. Yorkshire 2005-06. Durham 2007-13. Canterbury 2010-11. Kent debut 2013; cap 2016. HS 77 v Leics (Leicester) 2014. 50 wkts (2); most – 59 (2014). BB 6-104 Du v Somerset (Taunton) 2011. K BB 5-42 v Worcs (Canterbury) 2016. LO HS 19 Du v Glos (Bristol) 2009 (FPT). LO BB 4-39 Cant v Otago (Timaru) 2010-11. T20 HS 19. T20 BB 5-26.

COLES, Matthew Thomas (Maplesden Noakes S; Mid-Kent C), b Maidstone 26 May 1990. 6'3". LHB, RFM. Squad No 26. Debut (Kent) 2009; cap 2012. Hampshire 2013-14. HS 103* v Yorks (Leeds) 2012. 50 wkts (2); most – 67 (2015). BB 6-51 v Northants (Northampton) 2012. LO HS 100 v Surrey (Oval) 2015 (RLC). LO BB 6-32 v Yorks (Leeds) 2012 (CB40). T20 HS 54. T20 BB 4-27.

COWDREY, Fabian Kruuse (Tonbridge S), b Canterbury 30 Jan 1993. Son of C.S.Cowdrey (Kent, Glamorgan, England 1977-92), grandson of M.C.Cowdrey (Kent, Oxford U, England 1950-76), nephew of G.R.Cowdrey (Kent 1984-97). 6'0". RHB, SLA. Squad No 30. Cardiff MCCU 2013. Kent debut 2014. Kent 2nd XI debut 2009, aged 16y 207d. HS 62 CfU v Glamorgan (Cardiff) 2013. K HS 54 v Glamorgan (Canterbury) 2015. BB 3-59 v Hants (Canterbury) 2014. LO HS 75 v Surrey (Oval) 2014 (RLC). LO BB 3-32 v Hants (Canterbury) 2015 (RLC). T20 HS 71. T20 BB 3-18.

CRAWLEY, Zak (Tonbridge S), b Bromley 3 Feb 1998. 6'6". RHB, RM. Squad No 16. Kent 2nd XI debut 2013, aged 15y 199d. Awaiting 1st XI debut.

DENLY, Joseph Liam (Chaucer TC), b Canterbury 16 Mar 1986. 6'0". RHB, LB. Squad No 6. Kent debut 2004; cap 2008. Middlesex 2012-14; cap 2012. MCC 2013. **LOI**: 9 (2009 to 2009-10); HS 67 v Ireland (Belfast) 2009 – on debut. **IT20**. 5 (2009 to 2009-10); HS 14 and BB 1-9 v SA (Centurion) 2009-10. F-c Tours (Eng A): NZ 2008-09; I 2007-08. 1000 runs (3); most – 1081 (2015). HS 206* v Northants (Northampton) 2016. BB 3-43 v Surrey (Oval) 2011. LO HS 115 v Warwks (Birmingham) 2009 (FPT). LO BB 3-19 Brothers v Abahani (Fatullah) 2014-15. T20 HS 100. T20 BB 1-9.

[NQ]**DICKSON, Sean** Robert, b Johannesburg, South Africa 2 Sep 1991. 5'10". RHB, RM. Squad No 58. Northerns 2013-14 to 2014-15. Kent debut 2015. UK passport holder. HS 207* v Derbys (Derby) 2016. BB 1-15 Northerns v GW (Centurion) 2014-15. K BB – . LO HS 99 v Middx (Lord's) 2016 (RLC). T20 HS 53. T20 BB 1-9.

GIDMAN, William Robert Simon (Wycliffe C; Berkshire C of Agriculture), b High Wycombe, Bucks 14 Feb 1985. Younger brother of A.P.R.Gidman (Gloucestershire, Worcestershire 2002-15). 6'2". LHB, RM. Squad No 42. Durham 2007. No f-c appearances in 2008-10. Gloucestershire 2011-14; cap 2011, becoming first player for Gs to score 1000 runs and take 50 wkts in debut season. Nottinghamshire 2015. Kent debut 2016. MCC YC 2004-06. 1000 runs (1): 1006 (2011). HS 143 and BB 6-15 (10-43 match) Gs v Leics (Bristol) 2013 – only the fifth Gs player to score a century and take ten wkts in a match. K HS 99* v Sussex (Hove) 2016. 50 wkts (2); most – 55 (2013). K BB 2-21 v Worcs (Canterbury) 2016. LO HS 94 v Windward Is (Coolidge) 2016-17. LO BB 4-36 Du v Hants (Chester-le-St) 2010 (CB40). T20 HS 40*. T20 BB 2-23.

HAGGETT, Calum John (Millfield S), b Taunton, Somerset 30 Oct 1990. 6'3". LHB, RMF. Squad No 25. Debut (Kent) 2013. HS 80 v Surrey (Oval) 2015. BB 4-15 v Derbys (Derby) 2016. LO HS 45 v Leeward Is (Coolidge) 2016-17. LO BB 4-59 v Windward Is (Coolidge) 2016-17. T20 HS 11. T20 BB 2-12.

HARTLEY, Charles Frederick (Millfield S), b Redditch, Worcs 4 Jan 1994. 6'2". RHB, RMF. Squad No 22. Debut (Kent) 2014. Kent 2nd XI debut 2013. No 1st XI appearances in 2015. HS 2 and BB 2-40 v Leics (Leicester) 2014. LO HS 15 and LO BB 2-23 v Glos (Canterbury) 2016 (RLC).

HUNN, Matthew David (St Joseph's C, Ipswich), b Colchester, Essex 22 Mar 1994. 6'4". RHB, RMF. Squad No 14. Debut (Kent) 2013. Essex 2nd XI 2012. Suffolk 2011-13. HS 32* v Glos (Canterbury) 2016. BB 5-99 v Australians (Canterbury) 2015. CC BB 4-47 v Essex (Tunbridge W) 2015. LO HS 5* v Lancs (Canterbury) 2015 (RLC). LO BB 2-31 v Sussex (Canterbury) 2015 (RLC). T20 HS – . T20 BB 3-30.

IMRAN QAYYUM (Villiers HS, Southall; Greenford SFC; City U), b Ealing, Middx 23 May 1993. 6'0". RHB, SLA. Squad No 11. Debut (Kent) 2016. Kent 2nd XI debut 2013. Northamptonshire 2nd XI 2013. HS 0*. BB 3-158 v Northants (Northampton) 2016. LO HS 18 v Leeward Is (Coolidge) 2016-17. LO BB 3-42 v Windward Is (Coolidge) 2016-17.

NORTHEAST, Sam Alexander (Harrow S), b Ashford 16 Oct 1989. 5'11". RHB, LB. Squad No 17. Debut (Kent) 2007; cap 2012; captain 2016 to date. MCC 2013. 1000 runs (2); most – 1402 (2016). HS 191 v Derbys (Canterbury) 2016. BB 1-60 v Glos (Cheltenham) 2013. LO HS 132 v Somerset (Taunton) 2014 (RLC). T20 HS 114 v Somerset (Taunton) 2015 – K record.

RILEY, Adam Edward Nicholas (Beths GS, Bexley; Loughborough U), b Sidcup 23 Mar 1992. 6'2". RHB, OB. Squad No 33. Debut (Kent) 2011. Loughborough MCCU 2012-14. MCC 2015. F-c Tour (EL): SA 2014-15. HS 34 v Derbys (Canterbury) 2015. 50 wkts (1): 57 (2014). BB 7-150 v Hants (Southampton) 2013. LO HS 21* v Leeward Is (Coolidge) 2016-17. LO BB 2-30 v West Indies U19 (North Sound) 2016-17. T20 HS 5*. T20 BB 4-22.

ROBINSON, Oliver Graham (Hurtsmere S, Greenwich), b Sidcup 1 Dec 1998. RHB, WK, occ RM. Kent 2nd XI debut 2015. Awaiting f-c debut. LO HS – .

ROUSE, Adam Paul (Perrins Community Sports C; Peter Symonds C, Winchester), b Harare, Zimbabwe 30 Jun 1992. 5'10". RHB, WK. Squad No 12. Hampshire 2013. Gloucestershire 2014; cap 2014. Kent debut 2016. Hampshire 2nd XI debut 2008, aged 15y 331d. England U19 2010. HS 65 v Glamorgan (Cardiff) 2016. LO HS 61* v West Indies U19 (North Sound) 2016-17. T20 HS 35*.

STEVENS, Darren Ian (Hinckley C), b Leicester 30 Apr 1976. 5'11". RHB, RM. Squad No 3. Leicestershire 1997-2004; cap 2002. MCC 2002. Kent debut/cap 2005; benefit 2016. F-c Tour (ECB Acad): SL 2002-03. 1000 runs (3); most – 1304 (2013). HS 208 v Glamorgan (Canterbury) 2005 and 208 v Middx (Uxbridge) 2009. 50 wkts (2); most – 61 (2015). BB 7-21 (11-70 match) v Surrey (Canterbury) 2011. LO HS 133 Le v Northumb (Jesmond) 2000 (NWT). LO BB 5-32 v Scotland (Edinburgh) 2005 (NL). T20 HS 90. T20 BB 4-14.

THOMAS, Ivan Alfred Astley (John Roan S, Blackheath; Leeds U), b Greenwich, London 25 Sep 1991. 6'4". RHB, RMF. Squad No 5. Leeds/Bradford MCCU 2012-14. Kent debut 2012. HS 13 v Australians (Canterbury) 2015. CC HS 7* v Glos (Bristol) 2015. BB 4-48 v Leics (Canterbury) 2015. LO HS 5* v Windward Is (Coolidge) 2016-17. LO BB 4-51 v T&T (North Sound) 2016-17. T20 HS 3*. T20 BB 2-42.

TREDWELL, James Cullum (Southlands Community CS, New Romney), b Ashford 27 Feb 1982. 6'0". LHB, OB. Squad No 15. Debut (Kent) 2001; cap 2007; captain 2013; testimonial 2017. Sussex (on loan) 2014. MCC 2004, 2008, 2016. **Tests**: 2 (2009-10 to 2014-15); HS 37 v B (Dhaka) 2009-10; BB 4-47 v WI (North Sound) 2014-15. **LOI**: 45 (2009-10 to 2014-15); HS 30 v I (Nottingham) 2014; BB 4-41 v Scotland (Aberdeen) 2014. **IT20**: 17 (2012-13 to 2014); HS 22 and BB 1-16 v WI (Bridgetown) 2013-14. F-c Tours: WI 2014-15; NZ 2012-13 (*part*); I 2003-04 (Eng A, captain); B 2009-10. HS 124 v Essex (Chelmsford) 2016, sharing K record 8th wkt partnership of 222 with S.A.Northeast. 50 wkts (1): 69 (2009). BB 8-66 (11-120 match) v Glamorgan (Canterbury) 2009. LO HS 88 v Surrey (Oval) 2007 (FPT). LO BB 6-27 v Middx (Southgate) 2009 (FPT). T20 HS 34*. T20 BB 4-21.

RELEASED/RETIRED

(Having made a County 1st XI appearance in 2016)

GRIFFITHS, David Andrew (Sandown HS, IoW), b Newport, IoW 10 Sep 1985. 6'1". LHB, RFM. Hampshire 2006-13. Kent 2014. HS 31* H v Surrey (Southampton) 2007. K HS 12 and BB 6-63 v Glos (Canterbury) 2014. LO HS 12* v Warwks (Birmingham) 2014 (RLC). LO BB 4-29 H v Glos (Southampton) 2009 (P40). T20 HS 18*. T20 BB 4-22.

JACKSON, Callum Frederick (St Bede's S, Upper Dicker), b Eastbourne, E.Sussex 7 Sep 1994. 5'11". RHB, WK. Sussex 2013. Kent 2016. Sussex 2nd XI debut 2011, aged 16y 225d. England U19 2012-13. No f-c appearances in 2014-15. HS 38 v Sussex (Tunbridge W) 2016. LO HS 34* Sx v Essex (Hove) 2015 (RLC). T20 HS 3.

LATHAM, T.W.M. – *see DURHAM.*

[NQ]**RABADA, Kagiso**, b Johannesburg, South Africa 25 May 1995. 6'3". LHB, RF. Gauteng 2013-14. Lions 2013-14 to 2014-15. Kent 2016. **Tests** (SA): 14 (2015-16 to 2016-17); HS 32* v NZ (Durban) 2016; BB 7-112 (13-144 match) v E (Centurion) 2015-16. **LOI** (SA): 34 (2015 to 2016-17); HS 19* v I (Indore) 2015-16; BB 6-16 v B (Dhaka) 2015 – on debut. **IT20** (SA): 16 (2014-15 to 2015-16); HS 5* and BB 3-30 v NZ (Centurion) 2015. F-c Tours (SA): A 2014 (SA A), 2016-17; NZ 2016-17; I 2015-16. HS 48* Lions v Titans (Johannesburg) 2014-15. K HS 14 and K BB 4-118 v Essex (Chelmsford) 2016. BB 9-33 (14-105 match) Lions v Dolphins (Johannesburg) 2014-15. LO HS 22 Lions v Knights (Johannesburg) 2014-15. LO BB 6-16 (*see LOI*). T20 HS 8*. T20 BB 3-12.

VILJOEN, G.C. – *see DERBYSHIRE.*

R.W.T.Key left the staff at the beginning of the 2016 season without making a County 1st XI appearance.

HAMPSHIRE RELEASED/RETIRED (continued from p 121)

WAINWRIGHT, David John (Hemsworth HS and SFC; Loughborough U); b Pontefract, Yorks 21 Mar 1985. 5'9". LHB, SLA. Yorkshire 2004-11; cap 2010. Loughborough UCCE 2005-06. British U 2006. Police Sports Club 2011-12. Derbyshire 2012-15; cap 2012. Hampshire 2016. Shropshire 2016. HS 109 De v Leics (Leicester) 2014. 50 wkts (1): 50 (2012). BB 6-33 De v Northants (Derby) 2012. H HS 35* and H BB 2-112 v Somerset (Taunton) 2016. LO HS 41 De v Notts (Nottingham) 2014 (RLC). LO BB 4-11 De v Durham (Derby) 2013 (Y40). T20 HS 20*. T20 BB 3-6.

WHEATER, A.J.A. – *see ESSEX.*

C.A.Young left the staff without making a County 1st XI appearance in 2016.

KENT 2016

RESULTS SUMMARY

	Place	Won	Lost	Drew	Aband	NR
Specsavers County Champ (2nd Division)	2nd	5	2	8	1	
All First-Class Matches		5	2	9	1	
Royal London One-Day Cup (South Group)	QF	5	4			
NatWest t20 Blast (South Group)	7th	6	8			

SPECSAVERS COUNTY CHAMPIONSHIP AVERAGES

BATTING AND FIELDING

Cap		*M*	*I*	*NO*	*HS*	*Runs*	*Avge*	*100*	*50*	*Ct/St*
	W.R.S.Gidman	5	7	4	99*	362	120.66	–	5	5
2012	S.A.Northeast	15	22	6	191	1337	83.56	5	3	5
2015	D.J.Bell-Drummond	12	19	5	124	747	53.35	1	6	1
2005	D.I.Stevens	14	16	–	140	782	48.87	2	5	8
2015	S.W.Billings	7	7	–	171	329	47.00	1	1	25/1
	T.W.M.Latham	6	9	1	90	374	46.75	–	4	9
	S.R.Dickson	14	20	3	207*	675	39.70	1	4	8
2008	J.L.Denly	15	21	2	206*	733	38.57	1	4	7
	A.J.Blake	7	10	3	89*	268	38.28	–	2	4
2012	M.T.Coles	10	9	–	70	273	30.33	–	2	5
2007	J.C.Tredwell	11	12	2	124	291	29.10	1	–	14
	A.P.Rouse	6	6	–	65	164	27.33	–	1	28/1
	A.J.Ball	4	6	–	66	141	23.50	–	1	2
	C.J.Haggett	6	5	1	33*	87	21.75	–	–	1
	G.C.Viljoen	4	4	–	63	80	20.00	–	1	1
2016	M.E.Claydon	14	15	3	55	187	15.58	–	1	1
	C.F.Jackson	3	4	–	38	61	15.25	–	–	9

Also batted: H.R.Bernard (1 match) 14; F.K.Cowdrey (1) 3, 15; M.D.Hunn (4) 32*, 3, 0* (2 ct); Imran Qayyum (2) 0, 0* (1 ct); K.Rabada (2) 14, 5, 6; A.E.N.Riley (3) 5*, 32*.

BOWLING

	O	*M*	*R*	*W*	*Avge*	*Best*	*5wI*	*10wM*
G.C.Viljoen	103.5	12	385	20	19.25	5- 55	1	–
M.T.Coles	291.5	51	1059	37	28.62	5-116	1	–
D.I.Stevens	401.1	104	1131	37	30.56	4- 74	–	–
M.E.Claydon	399.4	75	1519	48	31.64	5- 42	2	–
C.J.Haggett	158.4	30	529	15	35.26	4- 15	–	–
J.C.Tredwell	299	61	921	22	41.86	4- 45	–	–
Also bowled:								
K.Rabada	77	21	232	7	33.14	4-118	–	–
M.D.Hunn	87	8	335	8	41.87	2- 33	–	–
Imran Qayyum	78.2	14	283	6	47.16	3-158	–	–

A.J.Ball 42-2-159-3; H.R.Bernard 22-3-105-3; J.L.Denly 66.3-4-222-3; S.R.Dickson 1-0-4-0; W.R.S.Gidman 44-15-123-4; T.W.M.Latham 2-0-5-0; S.A.Northeast 1.4-0-2-0; A.E.N.Riley 26-1-146-0.

The First-Class Averages (pp 226–242) give the records of Kent players in all first-class county matches (Kent's other opponents being Loughborough MCCU).

KENT RECORDS

FIRST-CLASS CRICKET

Highest Total	For 803-4d		v	Essex	Brentwood	1934
	V 676		by	Australians	Canterbury	1921
Lowest Total	For 18		v	Sussex	Gravesend	1867
	V 16		by	Warwicks	Tonbridge	1913
Highest Innings	For 332	W.H.Ashdown	v	Essex	Brentwood	1934
	V 344	W.G.Grace	for	MCC	Canterbury	1876

Highest Partnership for each Wicket

1st	300	N.R.Taylor/M.R.Benson	v	Derbyshire	Canterbury	1991
2nd	366	S.G.Hinks/N.R.Taylor	v	Middlesex	Canterbury	1990
3rd	323	R.W.T.Key/M.van Jaarsveld	v	Surrey	Tunbridge Wells	2005
4th	368	P.A.de Silva/G.R.Cowdrey	v	Derbyshire	Maidstone	1995
5th	277	F.E.Woolley/L.E.G.Ames	v	N Zealanders	Canterbury	1931
6th	315	P.A.de Silva/M.A.Ealham	v	Notts	Nottingham	1995
7th	248	A.P.Day/E.Humphreys	v	Somerset	Taunton	1908
8th	222	S.A.Northeast/J.C.Tredwell	v	Essex	Chelmsford	2016
9th	171	M.A.Ealham/P.A.Strang	v	Notts	Nottingham	1997
10th	235	F.E.Woolley/A.Fielder	v	Worcs	Stourbridge	1909

Best Bowling	For	10- 30	C.Blythe	v	Northants	Northampton	1907
(Innings)	V	10- 48	C.H.G.Bland	for	Sussex	Tonbridge	1899
Best Bowling	For	17- 48	C.Blythe	v	Northants	Northampton	1907
(Match)	V	17-106	T.W.J.Goddard	for	Glos	Bristol	1939

Most Runs – Season	2894	F.E.Woolley	(av 59.06)	1928
Most Runs – Career	47868	F.E.Woolley	(av 41.77)	1906-38
Most 100s – Season	10	F.E.Woolley		1928, 1934
Most 100s – Career	122	F.E.Woolley		1906-38
Most Wkts – Season	262	A.P.Freeman	(av 14.74)	1933
Most Wkts – Career	3340	A.P.Freeman	(av 17.64)	1914-36
Most Career W-K Dismissals	1253	F.H.Huish	(901 ct; 352 st)	1895-1914
Most Career Catches in the Field	773	F.E.Woolley		1906-38

LIMITED-OVERS CRICKET

Highest Total	**50ov**	384-6		v	Berkshire	Finchampstead	1994
	40ov	337-7		v	Sussex	Canterbury	2013
	T20	231-7		v	Surrey	The Oval	2015
Lowest Total	**50ov**	60		v	Somerset	Taunton	1979
	40ov	83		v	Middlesex	Lord's	1984
	T20	72		v	Hampshire	Southampton	2011
Highest Innings	**50ov**	143	C.J.Tavaré	v	Somerset	Taunton	1985
	40ov	146	A.Symonds	v	Lancashire	Tunbridge Wells	2004
	T20	114	S.A.Northeast	v	Somerset	Taunton	2015
Best Bowling	**50ov**	8-31	D.L.Underwood	v	Scotland	Edinburgh	1987
	40ov	6- 9	R.A.Woolmer	v	Derbyshire	Chesterfield	1979
	T20	5-17	Wahab Riaz	v	Glos	Beckenham	2011

LANCASHIRE

Formation of Present Club: 12 January 1864
Inaugural First-Class Match: 1865
Colours: Red, Green and Blue
Badge: Red Rose
County Champions (since 1890): (8) 1897, 1904, 1926, 1927, 1928, 1930, 1934, 2011
Joint Champions: (1) 1950
Gillette/NatWest Trophy Winners: (7) 1970, 1971, 1972, 1975, 1990, 1996, 1998
Benson and Hedges Cup Winners: (4) 1984, 1990, 1995, 1996
Pro 40/National League (Div 1) Winners: (1) 1999.
Sunday League Winners: (4) 1969, 1970, 1989, 1998
Twenty20 Cup Winners: (1) 2015

Chief Executive: Daniel Gidney, Emirates Old Trafford, Talbot Road, Manchester M16 0PX • Tel: 0161 868 6700 • Email: enquiries@lccc.co.uk • Web: www.lccc.co.uk • Twitter: @LancsCCC (52,405 followers)

Head Coach: Glen Chapple. **Assistant Coach**: Mark Chilton. **Captain**: S.J.Croft. **Overseas Players**: Junaid Khan (T20 only) and R.McLaren. **2017 Testimonial**: None. **Head Groundsman**: Matthew Merchant. **Scorer**: Chris Rimmer. ‡ New registration. NQ Not qualified for England.

ANDERSON, James Michael (St Theodore RC HS and SFC, Burnley), b Burnley 30 Jul 1982. 6'2". LHB, RFM. Squad No 9. Debut (Lancashire) 2002; cap 2003; benefit 2012. YC 2003. *Wisden* 2008. **ECB Test Central Contract 2016-17. Tests**: 122 (2003 to 2016-17); HS 81 v I (Nottingham) 2014, sharing a world Test record 10th wkt partnership of 198 with J.E.Root; 50 wkts (2); most – 57 (2010); BB 7-43 v NZ (Nottingham) 2008. **LOI**: 194 (2002-03 to 2014-15); HS 28 v NZ (Southampton) 2013; BB 5-23 v SA (Port Elizabeth) 2009-10. Hat-trick v P (Oval) 2003 – 1st for E in 373 LOI. **IT20**: 19 (2006-07 to 2009-10); HS 1* v A (Sydney) 2006-07; BB 3-23 v Netherlands (Lord's) 2009. F-c Tours: A 2006-07, 2010-11, 2013-14; SA 2004-05, 2009-10, 2015-16; WI 2003-04, 2005-06 (Eng A) (*part*), 2008-09, 2014-15; NZ 2007-08, 2012-13; I 2005-06 (*part*), 2008-09, 2012-13, 2016-17; SL 2003-04, 2007-08, 2011-12; UAE 2011-12 (v P), 2015-16 (v P). HS 81 (*see Tests*). La HS 42 v Surrey (Manchester) 2015. 50 wkts (3); most – 60 (2005). BB 7-43 (*see Tests*). La BB 7-77 v Essex (Chelmsford) 2015. Hat-trick v Essex (Manchester) 2003. LO HS 28 (*see LOI*). LO BB 5-23 (*see LOI*). T20 HS 16. T20 BB 3-23.

BAILEY, Thomas Ernest (Our Lady's Catholic HS, Preston), b Preston 21 Apr 1991. 6'4". RHB, RMF. Squad No 8. Debut (Lancashire) 2012. HS 53 v Middx (Manchester) 2016. BB 5-12 v Leics (Leicester) 2015. LO HS 5* and LO BB 3-31 v Middx (Blackpool) 2015 (RLC). T20 HS 0*. T20 BB 2-24.

BOHANNON, Joshua James (Harper Green HS), b Bolton 9 Apr 1997. RHB. Lancashire 2nd XI debut 2014. Awaiting 1st XI debut. Scholarship contract for 2017.

BROWN, Karl Robert (Hesketh Fletcher HS, Atherton), b Bolton 17 May 1988. 5'10". RHB, RMF. Squad No 14. Debut (Lancashire) 2006; cap 2015. Moors Sports Club 2011-12. HS 132 v Glamorgan (Manchester) 2015. BB 2-30 v Notts (Nottingham) 2009. LO HS 129 v Yorks (Manchester) 2014 (RLC). T20 HS 69.

BUTTLER, Joseph Charles (King's C, Taunton), b Taunton, Somerset 8 Sep 1990. 6'0". RHB, WK. Squad No 6. Somerset 2009-13; cap 2013. Lancashire debut 2014. Big Bash: MR 2013-14. **ECB L-O Central Contract 2016-17. Tests**: 18 (2014 to 2016-17); HS 85 v I (Southampton) 2014. **LOI**: 87 (2011-12 to 2016-17); HS 129 v NZ (Birmingham) 2015. **IT20**. 53 (2011 to 2016-17); HS 73* v SL (Southampton) 2016. HS 144 Sm v Hants (Southampton) 2010. La HS 100* v Durham (Chester-le-St) 2014. BB – . LO HS 129 (*see LOI*). T20 HS 73*.

[NQ]**CHANDERPAUL, Shivnarine** (Cove and John SS, Unity Village), b Unity Village, Demerara, Guyana 16 Aug 1974. 5'6". LHB, LB. Guyana 1991-92 to date. Durham 2007-09. Lancashire 2010; cap 2010, returning in 2017 as a Kolpak signing. Warwickshire 2011. Derbyshire 2013-14; cap 2014. IPL: RCB 2007-08. *Wisden* 2007. **Tests** (WI): 164 (1993-94 to 2015, 14 as captain); 1000 runs (1): 1065 (2002); HS 203* v SA (Georgetown) 2004-05; BB 1-2 v A (Adelaide) 1996-97. **LOI** (WI): 268 (1994-95 to 2010-11, 16 as captain); HS 150 v SA (E London) 1998-99; BB 3-18 v I (Sharjah) 1997-98. **IT20** (WI): 22 (2005-06 to 2010); HS 41 v E (Oval) 2007. F-c Tours (WI) (C=Captain): E 1995, 2000, 2004, 2007, 2009, 2012; A 1995-96, 1996-97, 2000-01, 2005-06C, 2009-10; SA 1998-99, 2003-04, 2007-08, 2014-15; NZ 1994-95, 1999-00, 2005-06C, 2008-09, 2013-14; I 1994-95, 2002-03, 2011-12, 2013-14; P 1997-98, 2001-02 (Sharjah), 2006-07; SL 2005C, 2010-11; Z 2001, 2003-04; B 1999-00, 2002-03, 2011-12, 2012-13; K 2001. 1000 runs (1+1); most – 1107 (2004-05). HS 303* Guyana v Jamaica (Kingston) 1995-96. CC HS 201* Du v Worcs (Worcester) 2009. La HS 120 v Kent (Canterbury) 2010. BB 4-48 Guyana v Leeward Is (Basseterre) 1992-93. LO HS 150 (*see LOI*). LO BB 4-22 Guyana v Trinidad (Hampton Court) 1995-96. T20 HS 87*.

CHAPPLE, Glen (West Craven HS; Nelson & Colne C), b Skipton, Yorks 23 Jan 1974. 6'1". RHB, RMF. Debut (Lancashire) 1992; cap 1994; benefit 2004; captain 2009-14. *Wisden* 2011. **LOI:** 1 (2006); HS 14 and BB - v Ireland (Belfast) 2006. F-c Tours (Eng A): A 1996-97; WI 1995-96 (La); I 1994-95. HS 155 v Somerset (Manchester) 2001. Scored 100 off 27 balls in contrived circumstances v Glamorgan (Manchester) 1993. 50 wkts (7); most – 57 (2011). BB 7-53 v Durham (Blackpool) 2007. LO HS 81* v Derbys (Manchester) 2002 (CGT). LO BB 6-18 v Essex (Lord's) 1996 (NWT) – La record. T20 HS 55*. T20 BB 3-36.

CLARK, Jordan (Sedbergh S), b Whitehaven, Cumbria 14 Oct 1990. Elder brother of G.Clark (*see DURHAM*). 6'4". RHB, RMF, occ WK. Squad No 16. Debut (Lancashire) 2015. HS 84* v Yorks (Manchester) 2016. BB 4-101 v Northants (Northampton) 2015. LO HS 72 v Durham (Chester-le-St) 2013 (Y40). LO BB 2-27 v Kent (Canterbury) 2015 (RLC). T20 HS 44. T20 BB 4-22.

CROFT, Steven John (Highfield HS, Blackpool; Myerscough C), b Blackpool 11 Oct 1984. 5'10". RHB, OB. Squad No 15. Debut (Lancashire) 2005, cap 2010, captain 2017. Auckland 2008-09. HS 156 v Northants (Manchester) 2014. BB 6-41 v Worcs (Manchester) 2012. LO HS 107 v Somerset (Taunton) 2011 (CB40). LO BB 4-24 v Scotland (Manchester) 2008 (FPT). T20 HS 94*. T20 BB 3-6.

DAVIES, Alexander Luke (Queen Elizabeth GS, Blackburn), b Darwen 23 Aug 1994. 5'7". RHB, WK. Squad No 17. Debut (Lancashire) 2012, without batting or bowling. Lancashire 2nd XI debut 2011. HS 99 v Kent (Manchester) 2015. LO HS 73* v Warwks (Manchester) 2015 (RLC). T20 HS 47.

GUEST, Brooke David (Kent Street Senior HS, Perth, WA; Murdoch U, Perth), b Whitworth Park, Manchester 14 May 1997. RHB, WK. Squad No 29. Lancashire 2nd XI debut 2016. Awaiting 1st XI debut. Summer contract.

HAMEED, Haseeb (Bolton S), b Bolton 17 Jan 1997. 6'2". RHB, LB. Squad No 23. Debut (Lancashire) 2015; cap 2016. Lancashire 2nd XI debut 2013. England U19 2014-15 to 2015. **Tests**: 3 (2016-17); HS 82 v I (Rajkot) 2016-17 – on debut. F-c Tours: I 2016-17; SL 2016-17 (EL). 1000 runs (1): 1198 (2016). HS 122 v Notts (Nottingham) 2016. BB – .

NQ**JARVIS, Kyle** Malcolm (St John's C, Harare), b Harare, Zimbabwe 16 Feb 1989. Son of M.P.Jarvis (Zimbabwe 1979-80 to 1994-95). 6'4". RHB, RFM. Squad No 27. Mashonaland Eagles 2009-10 to 2012-13. C Districts 2011-12 to 2012-13. Lancashire debut 2013; cap 2015. **Tests** (Z): 8 (2011 to 2013); HS 25* v P (Bulawayo) 2011; BB 5-54 v WI (Bridgetown) 2012-13. **LOI** (Z): 24 (2009-10 to 2013); HS 13 v SA (Centurion) 2009-10; BB 3-36 v Kenya (Harare) 2009-10. **IT20** (Z): 9 (2011 to 2012-13); HS 9* v SA (Hambantota) 2012-13; BB 3-15 v P (Harare) 2011. F-c Tour (Z): WI 2012-13. HS 57 v Yorks (Manchester) 2016. 50 wkts (2); most – 62 (2015). BB 7-35 ME v MT (Bulawayo) 2012-13. La BB 6-70 (11-119 match) v Surrey (Manchester) 2016. LO HS 33* MWR v Mountaineers (Kwekwe) 2014-15. LO BB 4-31 v Derbys (Derby) 2016 (RLC). T20 HS 10. T20 BB 3-15.

JONES, Robert Peter (Bridgewater HS), b Warrington, Cheshire 3 Nov 1995. RHB, LB. Squad No 12. Debut (Lancashire) 2016. Lancashire 2nd XI debut 2013. Cheshire 2014. England U19 2014. HS 106* v Middx (Manchester) 2016.

NQ**JUNAID KHAN**, Mohammad, b Matra, NW Frontier, Pakistan 24 Dec 1989. RHB, LMF. Abbottabad 2006-07 to 2011-12. NW Frontier Province 2008-09. KRL 2008-09. Lancashire 2011-14, returns for T20 only. WAPDA 2012-13 to date. **Tests** (P): 22 (2011 to 2015); HS 17 v Z (Harare) 2013; BB 5-38 v SL (Abu Dhabi) 2011-12. **LOI** (P): 56 (2011 to 2016-17); HS 25 v SA (Benoni) 2012-13; BB 4-12 v Ireland (Belfast) 2011. **IT20** (P): 9 (2011 to 2013-14): HS 3* v WI (Gros Islet) 2011; BB 3-24 v Afghanistan (Sharjah) 2013-14. F-c Tours (P): SA 2012-13; WI 2010-11; SL 2010 (P A), 2012, 2014, 2015; Z 2011, 2013; B 2015; UAE 2011-12 (v E), 2013-14 (v SA), 2013-14 (v SL). HS 71 Abbottabad v Rawalpindi (Abbottabad) 2007-08. La HS 16 v Durham (Liverpool) 2011. BB 7-46 (13-77 match) Abbottabad v Peshawar (Peshawar) 2007-08. La BB 3-84 v Middx (Manchester) 2014. LO HS 32 P A v South Africa A (Colombo, PSS) 2010. LO BB 5-45 Fighters v Warriors (Karachi) 2014-15. T20 HS 36. T20 BB 4-12.

KERRIGAN, Simon Christopher (Corpus Christi RC HS, Preston), b Preston 10 May 1989. 5'9". RHB, SLA. Squad No 10. Debut (Lancashire) 2010; cap 2013. MCC 2013. **Tests**: 1 (2013); HS 1* and BB – v A (Oval) 2013. F-c Tour (EL): SL 2013-14. HS 62* v Hants (Southport) 2013. 50 wkts (2); most – 58 (2013). BB 9-51 (12-192 match) v Hants (Liverpool) 2011. LO HS 10 v Middx (Lord's) 2012 (CB40). LO BB 3-21 EL v Sri Lanka A (Northampton) 2011. T20 HS 4*. T20 BB 3-17.

LAMB, Daniel John (St Michael's HS, Chorley; Cardinal Newman C, Preston), b Preston 7 Sep 1995. RHB, RM. Squad No 26. Lancashire 2nd XI debut 2013. Awaiting 1st XI debut.

LESTER, Toby James (Rossall S; Loughborough U), b Blackpool 5 Apr 1993. 6'4". LHB, LFM. Squad No 5. Loughborough MCCU 2012-14. Lancashire debut 2015. MCC Univs 2012-14. Worcestershire 2nd XI 2014. Lancashire 2nd XI debut 2014. HS 2* LU v Sussex (Hove) 2014. La HS 1 v Middx (Manchester) 2016. BB 3-50 v Essex (Manchester) 2015.

LILLEY, Arron Mark (Mossley Hollins HS; Ashton SFC), b Tameside 1 Apr 1991. 6'1". RHB, OB. Squad No 19. Debut (Lancashire) 2013. HS 63 and BB 5-23 v Derbys (Southport) 2015. LO HS 10 v Hants (Manchester) 2013 (Y40). LO BB 4-30 v Derbys (Manchester) 2013 (Y40). T20 HS 22*. T20 BB 3-31.

LIVINGSTONE, Liam Stephen (Chetwynde S, Barrow-in-Furness), b Barrow-in-Furness, Cumberland 4 Aug 1993. 6'1". RHB, LB. Squad No 7. Debut (Lancashire) 2016. Lancashire 2nd XI debut 2012. F-c Tour (EL): SL 2016-17. HS 140* (and 105) EL v Sri Lanka A (Dambulla) 2016-17. La HS 108* v Somerset (Taunton) 2016. BB 1-19 v Hants (Manchester) 2016. LO HS 98 v Derbys (Derby) 2016 (RLC). LO BB 3-51 v Yorks (Manchester) 2016 (RLC). T20 HS 55. T20 BB 1-9.

‡NQ**McLAREN, Ryan** (Grey C, Bloemfontein; Free State U), b Kimberley, South Africa 9 Feb 1983. 6'4". Son of P.McLaren (GW 1977-78 to 1994-95), nephew of Keith McLaren (GW 1971-72 to 1984-85), cousin of A.P.McLaren (GW 1998-99 to 2011-12, Eagles 2007-08 to 2008-09, Knights 2010-11, SW Districts 2012-13 to 2013-14, Warriors 2012-13). LHB, RFM. Squad No 35. FS 2003-04 to 2004-05. Eagles 2004-05 to 2009-10. Kent 2007-09 (Kolpak registration); cap 2007. Knights 2010-11 to 2013-14. Dolphins 2014-15. Hampshire 2015-16. IPL: MI 2009-10. KXIP 2011. KKR 2013. **Tests** (SA): 2 (2009-10 to 2013-14); HS 33* v E (Johannesburg) 2009-10; BB 2-72 v A (Centurion) 2013-14. **LOI** (SA): 54 (2009-10 to 2014-15); HS 71* v I (Cardiff) 2013; BB 4-19 v P (Birmingham) 2013. **IT20** (SA): 12 (2009-10 to 2014-15); HS 6* and BB 5-19 (SA record analysis) v WI (North Sound) 2009-10. F-c Tour (SA A): Ire 2012. HS 140 Eagles v Warriors (Bloemfontein) 2005-06. UK HS 100 H v Surrey (Oval) 2016. 50 wkts (1+1); most – 54 (2006-07). BB 8-38 Eagles v Cobras (Stellenbosch) 2006-07. UK BB 6-75 K v Notts (Nottingham) 2008. LO HS 88 Knights v Cobras (Bloemfontein) 2013-14. LO BB 5-38 Knights v Warriors (Kimberley) 2012-13. T20 HS 51*. T20 BB 5-19.

MAHMOOD, Saqib (Matthew Moss HS, Rochdale), b Birmingham 25 Feb 1997. 6'3". RHB, RFM. Squad No 25. Debut (Lancashire) 2016. England U19 2014. HS 0* and BB 1-121 v Hants (Southampton) 2016. LO HS 6* and LO BB 3-55 v Northants (Northampton) 2016 (RLC). T20 HS [illegible]. T20 BB 3-12.

PARKINSON, Matthew William (Bolton S), b Bolton 24 Oct 1996. Twin brother of C.F.Parkinson (*see LEICESTERSHIRE*). 6'0". RHB, LB. Squad No 28. Debut (Lancashire) 2016. Lancashire 2nd XI debut 2013. Staffordshire 2014. England U19 2015. HS 9 and BB 5-49 v Warwks (Manchester) 2016 – on debut.

PARRY, Stephen David (Audenshaw HS), b Manchester 12 Jan 1986. 6'0". RHB, SLA. Squad No 4. Debut (Lancashire) 2007, taking 5-23 v Durham U (Durham); cap 2015. Cumberland 2005-06. Big Bash: BH 2014-15. **LOI**: 2 (2013-14); HS – ; BB 3-32 v WI (North Sound) 2013-14. **IT20**: 5 (2013-14 to 2015-16); HS 1 v Netherlands (Chittagong) 2013-14; BB 2-33 v P (Dubai, DSC) 2015-16. HS 37 v Durham (Manchester) 2014. CC BB 3-51 v Kent (Canterbury) 2013. BB 5-23 (*see above*). LO HS 31 v Essex (Chelmsford) 2009 (FPT). LO BB 5-17 v Surrey (Manchester) 2013 (Y40). T20 HS 15. T20 BB 5-13 v Worcs (Manchester) 2016 – La record.

PROCTER, Luke Anthony (Counthill S, Oldham), b Oldham 24 June 1988. 5'11". LHB, RM. Squad No 2. Debut (Lancashire) 2010. Cumberland 2007. HS 137 v Hants (Manchester) 2016. BB 7-71 v Surrey (Liverpool) 2012. LO HS 97 v West Indies A (Manchester) 2010. LO BB 3-29 v Unicorns (Colwyn Bay) 2010 (CB40). T20 HS 25*. T20 BB 3-22.

‡NQ**VILAS, Dane** James, b Johannesburg, South Africa 10 Jun 1985. RHB, WK. Squad No 33. Gauteng 2006-07 to 2009-10. Lions 2008-09 to 2009-10. W Province 2010-11. Cape Cobras 2011-12 to date. Joins Lancashire in 2017 on Kolpak contract. **Tests** (SA): 6 (2015 to 2015-16); HS 26 v E (Johannesburg) 2015-16. **IT20** (SA): 1 (2011-12); HS – . F-c Tours (SA): A 2016 (SA A), I 2015 (SA A), 2015-16; Z 2016 (SA A), B 2015. HS 216* Cobras v Lions (Paarl) 2015-16. LO HS 120 Gauteng v Namibia (Windhoek) 2009-10 and 120 WP v Namibia (Windhoek) 2010-11. T20 HS 71*

RELEASED/RETIRED

(Having made a County 1st XI appearance in 2016)

BUCK, N.L. – *see NORTHAMPTONSHIRE.*

EDWARDS, George Alexander (St Joseph C, Croydon), b King's College H, Camberwell, London 29 Jul 1992. 6'3". RHB, RMF. Surrey 2011-13. Joined Lancashire in 2015, but played T20 only. HS 19 Sy v Cambridge MCCU (Cambridge) 2011. CC HS 17 and BB 4-44 Sy v Worcs (Worcester) 2012. LO HS 8* Sy v Glamorgan (Guildford) 2014 (RLC). LO BB 1-29 Sy v Durham (Chester-le-St) 2014 (RLC). T20 HS 2*. T20 BB 4-20.

GRIFFITHS, G.T. – *see LEICESTERSHIRE.*

NQ**GUPTILL, Martin** James (Avondale C), b Auckland, New Zealand 30 Sep 1986. 6'3". RHB, OB. Auckland 2005-06 to date. Derbyshire 2011-15; cap 2012. Lancashire l-o and T20 only 2016. IPL: MI 2016. Big Bash: ST 2012-13. **Tests** (NZ): 47 (2008-09 to 2016-17); HS 189 v B (Hamilton) 2009-10; BB 3-11 v Z (Bulawayo) 2016. **LOI** (NZ): 143 (2008-09 to 2016-17); 1000 runs (1): 1489 (2015); HS 237* v WI (Wellington) 2014-15, 2nd highest score in all LOI; BB 2-6 v I (Delhi) 2016-17. **IT20** (NZ): 61 (2008-09 to 2015-16); HS 101* v SA (East London) 2012-13; BB – . F-c Tours (NZ): E 2013, 2015; A 2011-12, 2015-16; SA 2012-13, 2016; WI 2012; I 2008-09 (NZ A), 2010-11, 2012, 2016-17; SL 2009, 2012-13; Z 2010-11 (NZ A), 2011-12, 2016. HS 227 De v Glos (Bristol) 2015. BB 3-11 (*see Tests*). LO HS 237* (*see LOI*). LO BB 2-6 (*see LOI*). T20 HS 120*. T20 BB – .

NQ**PETERSEN, Alviro** Nathan, b Port Elizabeth, South Africa 25 November 1980. RHB, RM/OB. Northerns 2000-01 to 2005-06. Titans 2004-05 to 2005-06. Lions 2005-06 to 2015-16. North West 2008-09. Glamorgan 2011; cap/captain 2011. Essex 2012. Somerset 2013-14; cap 2013. Lancashire 2015-16; cap 2016. **Tests** (SA): 36 (2009-10 to 2014-15); HS 182 v E (Leeds) 2012; scored 100 v I (Kolkata) on debut; BB 1-2 v WI (Port of Spain) 2010. **LOI** (SA): 21 (2006-07 to 2013); HS 80 v Z (Potchefstroom) 2006-07; BB – . **IT20** (SA): 2 (2010); HS 8 v WI (North Sound) 2010. F-c Tours (SA): E 2012; A 2012-13; WI 2010; NZ 2011-12; I 2007-08 (SA A), 2009-10; SL 2014; Z 2007 (SA A), 2014; B 2010 (SA A); UAE (v P) 2010-11, 2013-14. 1000 runs (2+2); most – 1376 (2008-09). HS 286 v Glamorgan (Colwyn Bay) 2015, sharing La record partnership of 501 with A.G.Prince. BB 3-58 Lions v Warriors (Port Elizabeth) 2013-14. CC BB 1-27 Sm v Sussex (Taunton) 2013. LO HS 145* Lions v Dolphins (Potchefstroom) 2011-12. LO BB 2-48 Lions v Cape Cobras (Johannesburg) 2011-12. T20 HS 103* v Leics (Leicester) 2016 – La record. T20 BB 1-4.

REECE, L.M. – *see DERBYSHIRE.*

SMITH, Thomas Christopher (Parkland HS, Chorley; Runshaw C, Leyland), b Liverpool 26 Dec 1985. 6'3". LHB, RMF. Lancashire 2005-16; cap 2010; captain 2015-16. Leicestershire (on loan) 2008. F-c Tour (Eng A): B 2006-07. HS 128 v Hants (Southampton) 2010. 50 wkts (1): 54 (2014). BB 6-46 v Yorks (Manchester) 2009. LO HS 117 and LO BB 4-48 v Notts (Nottingham) 2011 (CB40). T20 HS 92*. T20 BB 3-12.

WAGNER, N. – *see ESSEX.*

LANCASHIRE 2016

RESULTS SUMMARY

	Place	Won	Lost	Drew	NR
Specsavers County Champ (1st Division)	7th	3	5	8	
All First-Class Matches		3	5	8	
Royal London One-Day Cup (North Group)	9th	2	4		2
NatWest t20 Blast (North Group)	5th	6	7		1

SPECSAVERS COUNTY CHAMPIONSHIP AVERAGES

BATTING AND FIELDING

Cap		*M*	*I*	*NO*	*HS*	*Runs*	*Avge*	*100*	*50*	*Ct/St*
	L.S.Livingstone	15	23	7	108*	815	50.93	2	6	26
2016	H.Hameed	16	27	3	122	1198	49.91	4	7	6
2016	A.N.Petersen	15	24	1	191	1134	49.30	3	6	8
	R.P.Jones	4	7	2	106*	212	42.40	1	–	3
	L.A.Procter	16	25	1	137	822	34.25	2	3	5
2010	T.C.Smith	8	13	–	87	417	32.07	–	4	9
	N.L.Buck	3	4	2	27*	63	31.50	–	–	–
	A.L.Davies	5	6	–	55	187	31.16	–	1	17/1
2010	S.J.Croft	16	25	1	100	713	29.70	1	4	30
	J.Clark	7	10	1	84*	225	25.00	–	2	1
	A.M.Lilley	4	7	1	45	129	21.50	–	–	1
2013	S.C.Kerrigan	13	18	7	48	225	20.45	–	–	6
2015	K.R.Brown	10	17	–	61	337	19.82	–	2	6
2015	K.M.Jarvis	16	23	4	57	338	17.78	–	1	3
	T.E.Bailey	6	9	1	53	91	11.37	–	1	–
	N.Wagner	9	12	–	37	111	9.25	–	–	2
2003	J.M.Anderson	4	4	1	8	14	4.66	–	–	1
	M.W.Parkinson	4	5	1	9	16	4.00	–	–	1

Also batted: J.C.Buttler (1 match) 16, 26 (1 ct); T.J.Lester (2) 0*, 1; S.Mahmood (1) 0*; T.J.Moores (2) 25, 35, 18 (7 ct).

BOWLING

	O	*M*	*R*	*W*	*Avge*	*Best*	*5wI*	*10wM*
J.M.Anderson	137.5	46	307	15	20.46	3- 29	–	–
T.C.Smith	133	31	374	15	24.93	5- 25	1	–
T.E.Bailey	215.4	51	592	22	26.90	5-110	2	–
N.Wagner	286.4	52	937	32	29.28	6- 66	2	1
K.M.Jarvis	545.2	130	1673	51	32.80	6- 70	2	1
M.W.Parkinson	114.1	23	363	10	36.30	5- 49	1	–
S.C.Kerrigan	498.4	106	1326	35	37.88	6- 86	2	1
J.Clark	132	23	456	11	41.45	3- 20	–	–
L.A.Procter	152.5	28	505	10	50.50	3- 14	–	–
Also bowled:								
A.M.Lilley	105.3	21	333	8	41.62	5-130	1	–

N.L.Buck 63-12-210-2; S.J.Croft 46-7-155-2; H.Hameed 2-0-3-0; T.J.Lester 29-3-119-0; L.S.Livingstone 51-7-166-1; S.Mahmood 33-5-121-1.

Lancashire played no first-class fixtures outside the County Championship in 2016. The First-Class Averages (pp 226–242) give the records of their players in all first-class county matches, with the exception of J.M.Anderson and T.J.Moores, whose first-class figures for Lancashire are as above.

LANCASHIRE RECORDS

FIRST-CLASS CRICKET

Highest Total	For 863		v	Surrey	The Oval	1990
	V 707-9d		by	Surrey	The Oval	1990
Lowest Total	For 25		v	Derbyshire	Manchester	1871
	V 20		by	Essex	Chelmsford	2013
Highest Innings	For 424	A.C.MacLaren	v	Somerset	Taunton	1895
	V 315*	T.W.Hayward	for	Surrey	The Oval	1898

Highest Partnership for each Wicket

1st	368	A.C.MacLaren/R.H.Spooner	v	Glos	Liverpool	1903
2nd	371	F.B.Watson/G.E.Tyldesley	v	Surrey	Manchester	1928
3rd	501	A.N.Petersen/A.G.Prince	v	Glamorgan	Colwyn Bay	2015
4th	358	S.P.Titchard/G.D.Lloyd	v	Essex	Chelmsford	1996
5th	360	S.G.Law/C.L.Hooper	v	Warwicks	Birmingham	2003
6th	278	J.Iddon/H.R.W.Butterworth	v	Sussex	Manchester	1932
7th	248	G.D.Lloyd/I.D.Austin	v	Yorkshire	Leeds	1997
8th	158	J.Lyon/R.M.Ratcliffe	v	Warwicks	Manchester	1979
9th	142	L.O.S.Poidevin/A.Kermode	v	Sussex	Eastbourne	1907
10th	173	J.Briggs/R.Pilling	v	Surrey	Liverpool	1885

Best Bowling	For	10-46	W.Hickton	v	Hampshire	Manchester	1870
(Innings)	V	10-40	G.O.B.Allen	for	Middlesex	Lord's	1929
Best Bowling	For	17-91	H.Dean	v	Yorkshire	Liverpool	1913
(Match)	V	16-65	G.Giffen	for	Australians	Manchester	1886

Most Runs – Season	2633	J.T.Tyldesley	(av 56.02)	1901
Most Runs – Career	34222	G.E.Tyldesley	(av 45.20)	1909-36
Most 100s – Season	11	C.Hallows		1928
Most 100s – Career	90	G.E.Tyldesley		1909-36
Most Wkts – Season	198	E.A.McDonald	(av 18.55)	1925
Most Wkts – Career	1816	J.B.Statham	(av 15.12)	1950-68
Most Career W-K Dismissals	925	G.Duckworth	(635 ct; 290 st)	1923-38
Most Career Catches in the Field	556	K.J.Grieves		1949-64

LIMITED-OVERS CRICKET

Highest Total	**50ov**	381-3		v	Herts	Radlett	1999
	40ov	324-4		v	Worcs	Worcester	2012
	T20	231-4		v	Yorkshire	Manchester	2015
Lowest Total	**50ov**	59		v	Worcs	Worcester	1963
	40ov	68		v	Yorkshire	Leeds	2000
		68		v	Surrey	The Oval	2002
	T20	91		v	Derbyshire	Manchester	2003
Highest Innings	**50ov**	162*	A.R.Crook	v	Bucks	Wormsley	2005
	40ov	143	A.Flintoff	v	Essex	Chelmsford	1999
	T20	103*	A.N.Petersen	v	Leics	Leicester	2016
Best Bowling	**50ov**	6-10	C.E.H.Croft	v	Scotland	Manchester	1982
	40ov	6-25	G.Chapple	v	Yorkshire	Leeds	1998
	T20	5-13	S.D.Parry	v	Worcs	Manchester	2016

LEICESTERSHIRE

Formation of Present Club: 25 March 1879
Inaugural First-Class Match: 1894
Colours: Dark Green and Scarlet
Badge: Gold Running Fox on Green Ground
County Champions: (3) 1975, 1996, 1998
Benson and Hedges Cup Winners: (3) 1972, 1975, 1985
Sunday League Champions: (2) 1974, 1977
Twenty20 Cup Winners: (3) 2004, 2006, 2011

Chief Executive: Wasim Khan, Fischer County Ground, Grace Road, Leicester LE2 8EB • Tel: 0116 283 2128 • Fax: 0116 244 0363 • Email: enquiries@leicestershireccc.co.uk • Web: www.leicestershireccc.co.uk • Twitter: @leicsccc (25,720 followers)

Head Coach: Pierre de Bruyn. **Assistant Coach**: Graeme Welch. **Captains**: M.J.Cosgrove (f-c) and C.J.McKay (l-o). **Overseas Players**: C.N.Ackermann and C.J.McKay. **2017 Testimonial**: None. **Head Groundsman**: Andy Ward. **Scorer**: Paul Rogers. ‡ New registration. NQ Not qualified for England.

‡NQ**ACKERMANN, Colin** Niel (Grey HS, Port Elizabeth; U of SA), b George, South Africa 4 Apr 1991. RHB, OB. Squad No 84. Eastern Province 2010-11 to 2015-16. Warriors 2013-14 to date. Joins Leicestershire in 2017 on a two-year contract. 1000 runs (0+1): 1200 (2013-14). HS 150 Warriors v Titans (Benoni) 2016-17. BB 3-85 EP v FS (Bloemfontein) 2012-13. LO HS 92 Warriors v Cobras (Port Elizabeth) 2015-16. LO BB 3-35 EP v Easterns (Benoni) 2011-12. T20 HS 79*. T20 BB 3-23.

ALI, Aadil Masud (Lancaster S, Leicester; Q Elizabeth C), b Leicester 29 Dec 1994. 5'11". RHB, OB. Squad No 14. Debut (Leicestershire) 2015. Leicestershire 2nd XI debut 2013. HS 80 v Glos (Leicester) 2015. BB – . LO HS 84 v Glos (Leicester) 2015 (RLC). LO BB – T20 HS 26.

†**BURKE, James** Edward (Plymouth C), b Plymouth, Devon 25 Jan 1991. 6'2". RHB, RMF. Squad No 58. Somerset 2012. Surrey 2015-16. Devon 2008-13. Joins Leicestershire in 2017 on one-year loan. HS 79 Sy v Derbys (Oval) 2015. BB 4-19 Sy v Leics (Leicester) 2015. LO HS 26* Sy v Northants (Oval) 2015 (RLC). LO BB 5-28 Sy v Derbys (Guildford) 2015 (RLC). T20 HS 8. T20 BB 3-23.

CHAPPELL, Zachariah John ('**Zak**') (Stamford S), b Grantham, Lincs 21 Aug 1996. 6'4". RHB, RFM. Squad No 32. Debut (Leicestershire) 2015. HS 96 v Derbys (Derby) 2015. BB 2-44 v Kent (Leicester) 2016. LO HS 31 and LO BB 1-28 v Worcs (Worcester) 2015 (RLC). T20 BB – .

NQ**COSGROVE, Mark** James, b Elizabeth, Adelaide, S Australia 14 Jun 1984. 5'9". LHB, RM. Squad No 55. S Australia 2002-03 to 2015-16. Glamorgan 2006-10; cap 2006. Tasmania 2010-11 to 2013-14. Leicestershire debut/cap 2015; captain 2015 to date. Big Bash: HH 2011-12. ST 2012-13 to 2014-15. SS 2013-14. **LOI** (A): 3 (2005-06 to 2006-07); HS 74 v B (Fatullah) 2005-06 – on debut; BB 1-1 v WI (Kuala Lumpur) 2006-07. 1000 runs (3); most – 1279 (2016). HS 233 Gm v Derbys (Derby) 2006. Le HS 156 v Derbys (Derby) 2015. BB 3-3 S Aus v Tas (Adelaide) 2006-07. CC BB Gm 3-30 v Derbys (Derby) 2009. Le BB 2-14 v Worcs (Worcester) 2016. LO HS 121 S Aus v WA (Perth) 2005-06. LO BB 2-21 S Aus v Q (Brisbane) 2005-06. T20 HS 89. T20 BB 2-11.

DEARDEN, Harry Edward (Tottington HS), b Bury, Lancs 7 May 1997. LHB, OB. Squad No 5. Debut (Leicestershire) 2016. Lancashire 2nd XI 2014-15. Cheshire 2016. HS 16 v Derbys (Derby) 2016.

DELPORT, Cameron Scott (Kloof Senior S, Durban; Westville BHS), b Durban, South Africa 12 May 1989. 5'10". LHB, RM. Squad No 89. KwaZulu-Natal 2008-09 to date. Dolphins 2008-09 to 2011-12. Big Bash: ST 2014-15. Joined Leicestershire in 2016 for l-o and T20 only, qualifies as non-overseas player. HS 163 KZN v Northerns (Centurion) 2010-11. BB 2-10 KZN v Northern Cape (Chatsworth) 2016-17. LO HS 169* Dolphins v Knights (Bloemfontein) 2014-15. LO BB 4-42 Dolphins v Titans (Durban) 2011-12. T20 HS 103*. T20 BB 4-17.

DEXTER, Neil John (Northwood HS, Durban; Varsity C; U of South Africa), b Johannesburg, South Africa 21 Aug 1984. 6'0". RHB, RMF. Squad No 17. Kent 2005-08. Essex 2008. Middlesex 2009-15; cap 2010; captain 2010 (*part*) to 2013. Leicestershire debut 2016. Qualified for England in 2010. HS 163* M v Northants (Northampton) 2014. Le HS 136 v Glos (Leicester) 2016. BB 6-63 M v Lancs (Lord's) 2014. Le BB 5-52 v Sussex (Leicester) 2016. LO HS 135* K v Glamorgan (Cardiff) 2006 (CGT). LO BB 4-2 v Lancs (Leicester) 2016 (RLC). T20 HS 73. T20 BB 4-21.

ECKERSLEY, Edmund John Holden ('**Ned**') (St Benedict's GS, Ealing), b Oxford 9 Aug 1989. 6'0". RHB, WK, occ OB. Squad No 33. Debut (Leicestershire) 2011; cap 2013. Mountaineers 2011-12. MCC 2013. 1000 runs (1): 1302 (2013). HS 147 v Essex (Chelmsford) 2013 and 147 v Glamorgan (Leicester) 2015. BB 2-29 v Lancs (Manchester) 2013. LO HS 108 v Yorks (Leicester) 2013 (Y40). T20 HS 43.

FAZAKERLEY, William Nicholas. (Lancing C), b Guernsey 19 Jun 1998. 6'3". RHB, RFM. Squad No 35. Leicestershire 2nd XI debut 2016. Awaiting 1st XI debut.

GRIFFITHS, Gavin Timothy (St Mary's C, Crosby), b Ormskirk, Lancs 19 Nov 1993. 6'2". RHB, RMF. Squad No 7. Lancashire (l-o) 2014-15. Hampshire (T20) 2016. Lancashire 2nd XI debut 2011. Awaiting f-c debut. England U19 2012-13. LO HS 5* La v Kent (Canterbury) 2015 (RLC). LO BB 3-41 La v Notts (Liverpool) 2015 (RLC). T20 HS 4*. T20 BB 3-33.

HILL, Lewis John (Hastings HS, Hinckley; John Cleveland C), b Leicester 5 Oct 1990. 5'7½". RHB, WK, occ RM. Squad No 23. Debut (Leicestershire) 2015. Unicorns 2012-13. HS 126 v Surrey (Oval) 2015. LO HS 86 v Durham (Leicester) 2015 (RLC). T20 HS 31*.

HORTON, Paul James (St Margaret's HS, Liverpool), b Sydney, Australia 20 Sep 1982. 5'10". RHB, RM. Squad No 2. UK resident since 1997. Lancashire 2003-15; cap 2007. Matabeleland Tuskers 2010-11 to 2011-12. Leicestershire debut 2016. 1000 runs (3); most – 1116 (2007). HS 209 MT v SR (Masvingo) 2010-11. CC HS 173 La v Somerset (Taunton) 2009. Le HS 117* v Worcs (Worcester) 2016. BB 2-6 v Sussex (Leicester) 2016. LO HS 111* La v Derbys (Manchester) 2009 (FPT). LO BB 1-7 v Lancs (Leicester) 2016 (RLC). T20 HS 71*.

JONES, Richard Alan (Grange HS and King Edward VI C, Stourbridge; Loughborough U), b Wordsley, Stourbridge, Worcs 6 Nov 1986. 6'2". RHB, RMF. Squad No 25. Worcestershire 2007-13; cap 2007. Matabeleland Tuskers 2011-12. Warwickshire 2014-15. Leicestershire debut 2014 (on loan). HS 62 MT v SR (Bulawayo) 2011-12. UK HS 53* Wo v Durham (Worcester) 2009. Le HS 33 v Worcs (Worcester) 2016. BB 7-115 Wo v Sussex (Hove) 2010. Le BB 2-41 v Glos (Cheltenham) 2016. LO HS 26 Wa v Notts (Nottingham) 2016 (RLC). LO BB 1-25 MT v ME (Bulawayo) 2011-12. T20 HS 9. T20 BB 5-34.

^NQ^KLEIN, Dieter (Hoerskool, Lichtenburg), b Lichtenburg, South Africa 31 Oct 1988. 5'10". RHB, LMF. Squad No 77. North West 2007-08 to 2015-16. Lions 2012-13 to 2013-14. Leicestershire debut 2016. HS 66 NW v Border (E London) 2014-15. Le HS 16* and Le BB 4-107 v Essex (Leicester) 2016. BB 8-72 NW v Northerns (Potchefstroom) 2014-15. LO HS 17 NW v Northerns (Potchefstroom) 2014-15. LO BB 5-35 NW v Northerns (Pretoria) 2012-13. T20 HS 16. T20 BB 3-27.

[NQ]**McKAY, Clinton** James, b Melbourne, Australia 22 Feb 1983. 6'4". RHB, RFM. Squad No 27. Victoria 2006-07 to 2015-16. Leicestershire debut/cap 2015; captain 2017 (l-o only). IPL: MI 2012. Big Bash: MS 2011-12 to 2014-15. ST 2015-16 to date. **Tests** (A): 1 (2009-10); HS 10 and BB 1-56 v WI (Perth) 2009-10. **LOI** (A): 59 (2009-10 to 2013-14); HS 30 v SL (Oval) 2013; BB 5-28 v SL (Adelaide) 2011-12. **IT20** (A): 6 (2010-11 to 2013-14); HS 7 and BB 2-24 v WI (Bridgetown) 2011-12. HS 65 Vic v WA (Melbourne) 2012-13 and 65 v Glamorgan (Cardiff) 2016. 50 wkts (2); most – 58 (2015). BB 6-40 Vic v Tas (Melbourne) 2011-12. Le BB 6-54 v Kent (Canterbury) 2015. LO HS 57 Vic v Tas (Brisbane) 2014-15. LO BB 5-28 (*see LOI*). T20 HS 21*. T20 BB 4-24.

PARKINSON, Callum Francis (Bolton S), b Bolton, Lancs 24 Oct 1996. Twin brother of M.W.Parkinson (*see LANCASHIRE*). RHB, SLA. Squad No 10. Derbyshire 2016. Staffordshire 2015-16. HS 48* and BB 4-90 v Leics (Leicester) 2016.

PETTINI, Mark Lewis (Comberton Village C; Hills Road SFC, Cambridge; Cardiff U), b Brighton, Sussex 7 Aug 1983. 5'10". RHB, RM. Squad No 6. Essex 2001-15; cap 2006; captain 2007 (*part*) to 2010 (*part*). Mountaineers 2011-12 to 2014-15. Mashonaland Eagles 2015-16. Leicestershire debut 2016; captain (l-o only) 2016. MCC 2005. 1000 runs (1): 1218 (2006). HS 209 Mountaineers v MT (Bulawayo) 2013-14. CC HS 208* Ex v Derbys (Chelmsford) 2006. Le HS 142* v Sussex (Hove) 2016. BB 1-72 Ex v Leics (Leicester) 2012 – in contrived circumstances. LO HS 144 Ex v Surrey (Oval) 2007 (FPT). T20 HS 95*.

RAINE, Benjamin Alexander (St Aidan's RC SS, Sunderland) b Sunderland, Co Durham 14 Sep 1991. 6'0". LHB, RMF. Squad No 44. Durham 2011. Leicestershire debut 2013. HS 72 v Lancs (Manchester) 2013. 50 wkts (1): 61 (2015). BB 5-43 v Glamorgan (Cardiff) 2015. LO HS 43 v Yorks (Leicester) 2014 (RLC). LO BB 3-62 v Derbys (Derby) 2016 (RLC). T20 HS 48. T20 BB 3-7.

ROBSON, Angus James (Marcellin C, Randwick; Australian C of PE), b Darlinghurst, Sydney, Australia 19 Feb 1992. Younger brother of S.D.Robson (*see MIDDLESEX*). 5'9". RHB, LB. Squad No 8. Debut (Leicestershire) 2013. 1000 runs (2), most – 1086 (2014). HS 120 v Essex (Chelmsford) 2015. BB – . LO HS 90 v Yorks (Leeds) 2015 (RLC).

[NQ]**RONCHI, Luke**, b Dannevirke, Manawatu, New Zealand 23 Apr 1981. 5'11". RHB, WK. W Australia 2002-03 to 2011-12. Wellington 2011-12 to date. Somerset 2015. Warwickshire 2016 (T20 only). IPL: MI 2007-08 to 2009. Big Bash: PS 2011-12 to 2012-13. **Tests** (NZ): 4 (2015 to 2016-17); HS 88 v E (Leeds) 2015. **LOI** (A/NZ): 78 (4 for A 2008; 74 for NZ 2013 to 2016-17); HS 170* v SL (Dunedin) 2014-15. **IT20** (A/NZ): 32 (3 for A 2008 to 2008-09, 29 for NZ 2013-14 to 2016-17); HS 51* v WI (Wellington) 2013-14. F-c Tours: E 2015 (NZ); I 2008-09 (Aus A), 2013 (NZ A), 2016-17 (NZ); P 2007-08 (Aus A); SL 2013-14 (NZ A). HS 148 WA v NSW (Sydney) 2009-10. CC HS 51 Sm v Warwks (Taunton) 2015. LO HS 170* (*see LOI*). T20 HS 79.

SAYER, Robert John (Ramsey Abbey C; Leeds Beckett U), b Huntingdon, Cambridgeshire 25 Jan 1995. 6'3". RHB, OB. Squad No 12. Debut (Leicestershire) 2015. Leicestershire 2nd XI debut 2013. Cambridgeshire 2013. HS 34 v Glos (Leicester) 2015. BB 2-41 v Sri Lankans (Leicester) 2016. CC BB 2-59 v Derbys (Leicester) 2015. LO HS 26 v Notts (Leicester) 2016 (RLC). LO BB 1-31 v Lancs (Leicester) 2016 (RLC). T20 HS 9. T20 BB 2-16.

SHRECK, Charles Edward (Truro S), b Truro, Cornwall 6 Jan 1978. 6'7". RHB, RFM. Squad No 4. Nottinghamshire 2003-11; cap 2006. Wellington 2005-06 to 2007-08. Kent 2012-13. Leicestershire debut 2014. MCC 2008. Cornwall 1997-2002. HS 56 v Surrey (Oval) 2014. 50 wkts (4); most – 61 (2006, 2008). BB 8-31 (12-129 match) Nt v Middx (Nottingham) 2006. Le BB 5-71 v Essex (Chelmsford) 2015. Hat-trick Nt v Middx (Lord's) 2006. LO HS 9* Wellington v CD (Palmerston N) 2005-06. LO BB 5-19 Cornwall v Worcs (Truro) 2002 (CGT). T20 HS 10. T20 BB 4-22.

SYKES, James Stuart (St Ives S, Huntingdon), b Hinchingbrooke, Cambs 26 Apr 1992. 6'2". LHB, SLA. Squad No 60. Debut (Leicestershire) 2013. Cambridgeshire 2010. HS 34 v Lancs (Manchester) 2013. BB 4-176 v Essex (Chelmsford) 2013 – on debut. LO HS 15 v Glos (Bristol) 2013 (Y40). LO BB 3-34 v Hants (Southampton) 2014 (RLC). T20 HS 2*. T20 BB 2-24.

WELLS, Thomas Joshua (Gartree HS; Beauchamp C, Leicester), b Grantham, Lincs 15 Mar 1993. Father, John Wells, played rugby for Leicester. 6'2". RHB, RMF. Squad No 48. Debut (Leicestershire) 2013. Leicestershire 2nd XI debut 2010. HS 87* v Sri Lankans (Leicester) 2016. CC HS 82 v Hants (Leicester) 2013. BB 3-68 v Lancs (Leicester) 2015. LO HS 32* v Glamorgan (Swansea) 2013 (Y40). LO BB 2-45 v Glos (Leicester) 2015 (RLC). T20 HS 64*. T20 BB 1-17.

RELEASED/RETIRED

(Having made a County 1st XI appearance in 2016)

NQ**BEHARDIEN, Farhaan**, b Johannesburg, South Africa 9 Oct 1983. RHB, RFM. W Province 2004-05. Titans 2006-07 to date. Northerns 2007-08 to 2008-09. IPL: KXIP 2016. Leicestershire (T20 only) 2016. **LOI** (SA): 55 (2012-13 to 2016-17); HS 70 v NZ (Potchefstroom) 2015; BB 3-19 v SL (Pallekele) 2013. **IT20** (SA): 29 (2011-12 to 2016-17); HS 36 v NZ (Centurion) 2015; BB 2-15 v SL (Delhi) 2015-16. F-c Tours (SA A): A 2014; Ire 2012 (v SL A). HS 150* Titans v Eagles (Benoni) 2008-09. BB 3-48 WP v E Province (Port Elizabeth) 2004-05 – on debut. LO HS 113* Titans v Lions (Centurion) 2013-14. LO BB 3-16 Northerns v KZN (Pretoria) 2008-09. T20 HS 72*. T20 BB 2-15.

BURGESS, Michael Gregory Kerran (Cranleigh S; Loughborough U), b Epsom, Surrey 8 Jul 1994. RHB, RM, occ WK. Loughborough MCCU 2014-15. Leicestershire 2016. Surrey 2nd XI 2011-13. HS 98 v Sri Lankans (Leicester) – only fc game for Le. LO HS 49 v Glos (Leicester) 2015 (RLC).

FRECKINGHAM, Oliver Henry (K Edward S, Melton Mowbray), b Oakham, Rutland 12 Nov 1988. 6'1". RHB, RFM. Leicestershire 2013-15. HS 34* v Derbys (Derby) 2015. BB 6-125 v Northants (Northampton) 2013. LO HS 5* v Notts (Leicester) 2016 (RLC). LO BB 2-38 v Worcs (Leicester) 2014 (RLC). T20 HS 4*. T20 BB 2-21.

NAIK, Jigar Kumar Hakumatrai (Rushey Mead SS; Gateway SFC; Nottingham Trent U; Loughborough U), b Leicester 10 Aug 1984. 6'2". RHB, OB. Leicestershire 2006-16; cap 2013. Loughborough UCCE 2007. Colombo CC 2010-11. HS 109* v Derbys (Leicester) 2009. BB 8-179 v Lancs (Manchester) 2015. LO HS 36* v Derbys (Leicester) 2014 (RLC). LO BB 3-21 v Lancs (Leicester) 2009 (P40). T20 HS 16*. T20 BB 3-3.

NQ**O'BRIEN, Kevin** Joseph (Marian C, Dublin; Tallaght I of Tech), b Dublin, Ireland 4 Mar 1984. RHB, RM. Squad No 31. Son of B.A.O'Brien (Ireland 1966-81) and younger brother of N.J.O'Brien (*see below*). Ireland 2006-07 to date. Nottinghamshire 2009. Surrey 2014. Leicestershire 2015-16 (l-o and T20 only). **LOI** (Ire): 105 (2006 to 2016-17); HS 142 v Kenya (Nairobi) 2006-07; BB 4-13 v Netherlands (Amstelveen) 2013. **IT20** (Ire): 58 (2008 to 2016-17); HS 42* v Netherlands (Sylhet) 2013-14; BB 3-8 v Nepal (Belfast) 2015. HS 171* Ire v Kenya (Nairobi) 2008-09. CC HS 17 Sy v Hants (Oval) 2014. BB 5-39 Ire v Canada (Toronto) 2010. LO HS 142 (*see LOI*). LO BB 4-13 (*see LOI*). T20 HS 119. T20 BB 4-22.

NQ**O'BRIEN, Niall** John (Marian C, Dublin), b Dublin, Ireland 8 Nov 1981. Son of B.A.O'Brien (Ireland 1966-81); elder brother of K.J.O'Brien (*see above*). 5'6". LHB, WK. Kent 2004-06. Ireland 2005-06 to date. Northamptonshire 2007-12; cap 2011. Leicestershire 2013-16. MCC 2012. **LOI** (Ire): 77 (2006 to 2016-17); HS 80* v Scotland (Dubai, DSC) 2014-15. **IT20** (Ire): 30 (2008 to 2015-16); HS 50 v Canada (Colombo, SSC) 2009-10. HS 182 Nh v Glamorgan (Cardiff) 2012. Le HS 133 v Glamorgan (Leicester) 2013. BB 1-4 K v Cambridge UCCE (Cambridge) 2006. LO HS 121 Nh v Hants (Southampton) 2011 (CB40). T20 HS 84.

SHEIKH, Atif (Bluecoat S), b Nottingham 18 Feb 1991. 6'0". RHB, LFM. Derbyshire 2010. Leicestershire 2014-16. HS 12 v Essex (Leicester) 2014. BB 4-97 v Glos (Bristol) 2014, inc hat-trick. LO HS 22 and LO BB 3-49 v Australians (Leicester) 2015. T20 HS 14. T20 BB 2-11.

NQ**TAYLOR, Robert** Meadows Lombe (Harrow S; Loughborough U), b Northampton 21 Dec 1989. 6'3". LHB, LMF. Loughborough MCCU 2010-12. Leicestershire 2011-16. **LOI** (Scot): 15 (2012-13 to 2015-16); HS 46* v Kenya (Christchurch) 2013-14; BB 3-39 v Kenya (Aberdeen) 2013. **IT20** (Scot): 9 (2013-14 to 2015-16); HS 41* v Netherlands (Dubai) 2013-14; BB 3-17 v Hong Kong (Dublin) 2015. HS 101* LU v Leics (Leicester) 2011. Le HS 98 v Kent (Leicester) 2014. BB 5-55 v Glos (Leicester) 2014. LO HS 62 v Warwks (Birmingham) 2016 (RLC). LO BB 4-58 v Durham (Leicester) 2016 (RLC). T20 HS 41*. T20 BB 4-11.

NQ**UMAR AKMAL**, b Lahore, Pakistan 26 May 1990. Younger brother of Kamran Akmal (Lahore City, NBP, Lahore Whites & Pakistan 1997-98 to date) and Adnan Akmal (ZTB, Lahore, Multan, SNGPL & Pakistan 2003-04 to date). RHB, WK, occ OB. SNGPL 2007-08 to 2015-16. Lahore Shalimar 2012-13. Leicestershire 2015; cap 2015 – played T20 only in 2016. Lahore Whites 2016-17 **Tests** (P): 16 (2009-10 to 2011); HS 129 v NZ (Dunedin) 2009-10 – on debut. **LOI** (P): 116 (2009 to 2016-17); HS 102* v SL (Colombo, RPS) 2009 and 102* v Afghan (Fatullah) 2013-14. **IT20** (P): 82 (2009 to 2016-17); HS 94 v A (Dhaka) 2013-14. F-c Tours (P): E 2010; A 2009 (Pak A), 2009-10; WI 2011; NZ 2009-10; Z 2011; UAE 2010-11 (v SA). HS 248 SNGPL v Karachi Blues (Karachi) 2007-08. Le HS 20 v Lancs (Manchester) 2015. BB 2-24 Lahore S v Hyderabad (Lahore) 2012-13. LO HS 104 Pak A v Aus A (Brisbane) 2009. LO BB 1-7 SNGPL v WAPDA (Faisalabad) 2013-14. T20 HS 115*. T20 BB 1-36.

WHITE, Wayne Andrew (John Port S, Etwall; Nottingham Trent U), b Derby 22 Apr 1985. 6'2". RHB, RMF. Derbyshire 2005-15. Leicestershire 2009-16; cap 2012. Lancashire 2013-14. HS 101* v Derbys (Derby) 2010. BB 6-25 De v Kent (Canterbury) 2015. Le BB 5-51 v Northants (Northampton) 2015. LO HS 46* v Glamorgan (Leicester) 2009 (P40). LO BB 6-29 v Notts (Leics) 2010 (CB40). T20 HS 26. T20 BB 3-21.

L.J.Hurt left the staff without making a 1st XI appearance in 2016.

COUNTY CAPS AWARDED IN 2016

Derbyshire	–
Durham	–
Essex	–
Glamorgan	C.B.Cooke
Gloucestershire	C.T.Bancroft, J.R.Bracey, G.T.Hankins, P.Mustard, I.Shaw, G.L.van Buuren
Hampshire	G.K.Berg, A.J.A.Wheater
Kent	M.E.Claydon
Lancashire	H.Hameed, A.N.Petersen
Leicestershire	–
Middlesex	N.R.T.Gubbins, P.R.Stirling, A.C.Voges
Northamptonshire	B.M.Duckett, R.K.Kleinveldt
Nottinghamshire	J.T.Ball, J.M.Bird, D.T.Christian
Somerset	T.D.Groenewald, C.Overton
Surrey	T.K.Curran, B.T.Foakes, A.Harinath
Sussex	L.W.P.Wells, D.Wiese
Warwickshire	–
Worcestershire (colours)	K.J.Abbott, M.L.Cummins, M.J.Henry, G.H.Rhodes, M.J.Santner
Yorkshire	Azeem Rafiq, A.J.Hodd, J.A.Leaning, D.J.Willey

Durham abolished their capping system after 2005. Gloucestershire award caps on first-class debut. Worcestershire award club colours on Championship debut. Glamorgan's capping system is now based on a player's number of appearances and not on his performances.

LEICESTERSHIRE 2016

RESULTS SUMMARY

	Place	*Won*	*Lost*	*Drew*	*NR*
Specsavers County Champ (2nd Division)	7th	4	4	8	
All First-Class Matches		4	4	9	
Royal London One-Day Cup (North Group)	8th	2	3		3
NatWest t20 Blast (North Group)	9th	4	8		2

SPECSAVERS COUNTY CHAMPIONSHIP AVERAGES

BATTING AND FIELDING

Cap		*M*	*I*	*NO*	*HS*	*Runs*	*Avge*	*100*	*50*	*Ct/St*
2012	W.A.White	4	4	2	58	103	51.50	–	1	1
2015	M.J.Cosgrove	16	27	1	146	1279	49.19	5	5	10
	N.J.O'Brien	9	14	3	93	432	39.27	–	2	30
2013	E.J.H.Eckersley	11	18	2	117	624	39.00	3	1	29
	N.J.Dexter	16	27	1	136	958	36.84	3	4	4
	P.J.Horton	16	28	2	117*	908	34.92	2	6	8
	M.L.Pettini	16	26	2	142*	694	28.91	2	1	3
	A.J.Robson	16	28	1	84	732	27.11	–	9	14
	R.A.Jones	6	9	2	33	127	18.14	–	–	2
	R.J.Sayer	2	4	2	32*	36	18.00	–	–	–
	B.A.Raine	14	19	1	64	321	17.83	–	1	2
2015	C.J.McKay	15	20	1	65	300	15.78	–	2	–
	R.M.L.Taylor	3	4	–	21	50	12.50	–	–	2
	L.J.Hill	2	4	–	36	46	11.50	–	–	–
	D.Klein	2	4	1	16*	31	10.33	–	–	–
	A.M.Ali	4	7	–	30	71	10.14	–	–	1
	H.E.Dearden	2	4	–	16	36	9.00	–	–	2
	C.E.Shreck	16	20	12	20	51	6.37	–	–	6

Also batted: Z.J.Chappell (2 matches) 7, 10, 0; J.K.H.Naik (2 – cap 2013) 26*, 8* (2 ct); J.S.Sykes (1) 12*; T.J.Wells (1) 18, 0.

BOWLING

	O	*M*	*R*	*W*	*Avge*	*Best*	*5wI*	*10wM*
C.J.McKay	411.1	78	1260	56	22.50	6- 73	1	–
W.A.White	64.1	13	225	10	22.50	4- 24	–	–
N.J.Dexter	261.5	50	824	29	28.41	5- 52	1	–
B.A.Raine	338	77	1108	35	31.65	5- 66	1	–
C.E.Shreck	442.3	85	1455	44	33.06	4- 33	–	–
Also bowled:								
D.Klein	44	5	211	9	23.44	4-107	–	–
R.A.Jones	115	20	446	7	63.71	2- 41	–	–

A.M.Ali 3-1-21-0; Z.J.Chappell 20.2-2-98-3; M.J.Cosgrove 29.4-2-112-3; E.J.H.Eckersley 2-0-7-0; P.J.Horton 13-3-43-2; J.K.H.Naik 30-6-67-0; A.J.Robson 8-1-32-0; R.J.Sayer 67-6-273-4; R.M.L.Taylor 48.3-9-187-2.

The First-Class Averages (pp 226–242) give the records of Leicestershire players in all first-class county matches (Leicestershire's other opponents being the Sri Lankans).

LEICESTERSHIRE RECORDS

FIRST-CLASS CRICKET

Highest Total	For 701-4d		v	Worcs	Worcester	1906
	V 761-6d		by	Essex	Chelmsford	1990
Lowest Total	For 25		v	Kent	Leicester	1912
	V 24		by	Glamorgan	Leicester	1971
	24		by	Oxford U	Oxford	1985
Highest Innings	For 309*	H.D.Ackerman	v	Glamorgan	Cardiff	2006
	V 355*	K.P.Pietersen	for	Surrey	The Oval	2015

Highest Partnership for each Wicket

1st	390	B.Dudleston/J.F.Steele	v	Derbyshire	Leicester	1979
2nd	289*	J.C.Balderstone/D.I.Gower	v	Essex	Leicester	1981
3rd	436*	D.L.Maddy/B.J.Hodge	v	L'boro UCCE	Leicester	2003
4th	360*	J.W.A.Taylor/A.B.McDonald	v	Middlesex	Leicester	2010
5th	330	J.W.A.Taylor/S.J.Thakor	v	L'boro MCCU	Leicester	2011
6th	284	P.V.Simmons/P.A.Nixon	v	Durham	Chester-le-St[2]	1996
7th	219*	J.D.R.Benson/P.Whitticase	v	Hampshire	Bournemouth	1991
8th	195	J.W.A.Taylor/J.K.H.Naik	v	Derbyshire	Leicester	2009
9th	160	R.T.Crawford/ W.W.Odell	v	Worcs	Leicester	1902
10th	228	R.Illingworth/K.Higgs	v	Northants	Leicester	1977

Best Bowling	For	10- 18	G.Geary	v	Glamorgan	Pontypridd	1929
(Innings)	V	10- 32	H.Pickett	for	Essex	Leyton	1895
Best Bowling	For	16- 96	G.Geary	v	Glamorgan	Pontypridd	1929
(Match)	V	16-102	C.Blythe	for	Kent	Leicester	1909

Most Runs – Season	2446	L.G.Berry	(av 52.04)	1937
Most Runs – Career	30143	L.G.Berry	(av 30.32)	1924-51
Most 100s – Season	7	L.G.Berry		1937
	7	W.Watson		1959
	7	B.F.Davison		1982
Most 100s – Career	45	L.G.Berry		1924-51
Most Wkts – Season	170	J.E.Walsh	(av 18.96)	1948
Most Wkts – Career	2131	W.E.Astill	(av 23.18)	1906-39
Most Career W-K Dismissals	905	R.W.Tolchard	(794 ct; 111 st)	1965-83
Most Career Catches in the Field	426	M.R.Hallam		1950-70

LIMITED-OVERS CRICKET

Highest Total	**50ov**	406-5		v	Berkshire	Leicester	1996
	40ov	344-4		v	Durham	Chester-le-St[2]	1996
	T20	221-3		v	Yorkshire	Leeds	2004
Lowest Total	**50ov**	56		v	Northants	Leicester	1964
		56		v	Minor Cos	Wellington	1982
	40ov	36		v	Sussex	Leicester	1973
	T20	90		v	Notts	Nottingham	2014
Highest Innings	**50ov**	201	V.J.Wells	v	Berkshire	Leicester	1996
	40ov	154*	B.J.Hodge	v	Sussex	Horsham	2004
	T20	111	D.L.Maddy	v	Yorkshire	Leeds	2004
Best Bowling	**50ov**	6-16	C.M.Willoughby	v	Somerset	Leicester	2005
	40ov	6-17	K.Higgs	v	Glamorgan	Leicester	1973
	T20	5-13	A.B.McDonald	v	Notts	Nottingham	2010

MIDDLESEX

Formation of Present Club: 2 February 1864
Inaugural First-Class Match: 1864
Colours: Blue
Badge: Three Seaxes
County Champions (since 1890): (11) 1903, 1920, 1921, 1947, 1976, 1980, 1982, 1985, 1990, 1993, 2016
Joint Champions: (2) 1949, 1977
Gillette/NatWest Trophy Winners: (4) 1977, 1980, 1984, 1988
Benson and Hedges Cup Winners: (2) 1983, 1986
Sunday League Winners: (1) 1992
Twenty20 Cup Winners: (1) 2008

Chief Executive: Richard Goatley, Lord's Cricket Ground, London NW8 8QN • Tel: 020 7289 1300 • Fax: 020 7289 5831 • Email: enquiries@middlesexccc.com • Web: www.middlesexccc.com • Twitter: @Middlesex_CCC (32,505 followers)

Managing Director of Cricket: Angus Fraser. **Head Coach**: Richard Scott. **Assistant Coach**: Richard Johnson. **T20 Coach**: Daniel Vettori. **Captains**: J.E.C.Franklin (f-c & l-o), D.J.Malan (T20). **Overseas Players**: B.B.MCullum (T20 only) and A.C.Voges. **2017 Testimonial**: None. **Head Groundsman**: Mick Hunt. **Scorer**: Don Shelley. ‡ New registration. [NQ] Not qualified for England.

ANDERSSON, Martin Kristoffer (Reading Blue Coat S), b Reading, Berks 6 Sep 1996. 6'1". RHB, RM. Squad No 24. Middlesex 2nd XI debut 2013. Berkshire 2015-16. Awaiting 1st XI debut.

COMPTON, Nicholas Richard Denis (Harrow S; Durham U), b Durban, South Africa 26 Jun 1983. Son of R.Compton (Natal 1978-79 to 1980-81), grandson of D.C.S.Compton (Middlesex, England, Holkar, Europeans, Commonwealth and Cavaliers 1936-64), great-nephew of L.H.Compton (Middlesex 1938-56). 6'1". RHB, OB. Squad No 3. Middlesex debut 2004; cap 2006. Somerset 2010-14; cap 2011. Mashonaland Eagles 2010-11. Worcestershire (1 game) 2013. MCC 2007, 2015. PCA 2012. *Wisden* 2012. **Tests**: 16 (2012-13 to 2016); HS 117 v NZ (Dunedin) 2012-13. F-c Tours: SA 2015-16; NZ 2012-13; I 2012-13; B 2006-07 (Eng A). 1000 runs (6); most – 1494 (2012). Scored 685 runs in April 2012 – a record for April. HS 254* Sm v Durham (Chester-le-St) 2011. M HS 190 v Durham (Lord's) 2006. BB 1-1 Sm v Hants (Southampton) 2010. M BB 1-94 v Sussex (Southgate) 2007. LO HS 131 v Kent (Canterbury) 2009 (FPT). LO BB 1-0 v Scotland (Lord's) 2009 (FPT). T20 HS 78.

[NQ]**ESKINAZI, Stephen** Sean (Christ Church GS, Claremont; U of WA), b Johannesburg, South Africa 28 Mar 1994. 6'2". RHB, WK. Squad No 28. Debut (Middlesex) 2015. Middlesex 2nd XI debut 2013. UK passport. HS 157 v Yorks (Scarborough) 2016. LO HS 29 v Glos (Bristol) 2016 (RLC).

FINN, Steven Thomas (Parmiter's S, Garston), b Watford, Herts 4 Apr 1989. 6'7½". RHB, RFM. Squad No 9. Debut (Middlesex) 2005; cap 2009. Otago 2011-12. YC 2010. **ECB Test Central Contract 2016-17. Tests**: 36 (2009-10 to 2016-17); HS 56 v NZ (Dunedin) 2012-13; BB 6-79 v A (Birmingham) 2015. **LOI**: 68 (2010-11 to 2016-17); HS 35 v A (Brisbane) 2010-11; BB 5-33 v I (Brisbane) 2014-15. **IT20**: 21 (2011 to 2015); HS 8* v I (Colombo, RPS) 2012-13; BB 3-16 v NZ (Pallekele) 2012-13. F-c Tours: A 2010-11, 2013-14; SA 2015-16; NZ 2012-13; I 2012-13; SL 2011-12; B 2009-10, 2016-17; UAE 2011-12 (v P). HS 56 (*see Tests*). M HS 41* v Oxford MCCU (Oxford) 2015. CC HS 37* v Warwks (Birmingham) 2014. 50 wkts (2); most – 64 (2010). BB 9-37 (14-106 match) v Worcs (Worcester) 2010. LO HS 42* v Glamorgan (Cardiff) 2014 (RLC). LO BB 5-33 v Derbys (Lord's) 2011 (CB40). T20 HS 8*. T20 BB 4-28.

[NQ]**FRANKLIN, James** Edward Charles (Wellington C; Victoria U), Wellington, New Zealand 7 Nov 1980. 6'4½". LHB, LM. Squad No 74. Irish passport. Wellington 1998-99 to 2014-15. Gloucestershire 2004-10; cap 2004. Glamorgan 2006; cap 2006. Nottinghamshire 2014; cap 2014. Middlesex debut/cap 2015; captain (f-c & l-o) 2017 (l-o only in 2016). IPL: MI 2011-12. Big Bash: AS 2011-12. **Tests** (NZ): 31 (2000-01 to 2012-13); HS 122* v SA (Cape Town) 2006-07; BB 6-119 v A (Auckland) 2004-05. Hat-trick v B (Dhaka) 2004-05. **LOI** (NZ): 110 (2000-01 to 2013); HS 98* v I (Bangalore) 2010-11; BB 5-42 v E (Chester-le-St) 2004. **IT20** (NZ): 38 (2005-06 to 2013); HS 60 v Z (Hamilton) 2011-12; BB 4-15 v E (Hamilton) 2012-13. F-c Tours (NZ): E 2004; A 2004-05; SA 2004-05 (NZ A), 2005-06, 2012-13; I 2012; SL 2012-13; Z 2005, 2010-11 (NZ A); B 2004-05. HS 219 Wellington v Auckland (Auckland) 2008-09. HS 135 v Worcs (Uxbridge) 2015. BB 7-14 Gs v Derbys (Bristol) 2010. M BB 3-26 v Durham (Lord's) 2016. Hat-tricks (*see above*) and Gs v Derbys (Cheltenham) 2009, also scoring 109 in same match. LO HS 133* Gs v Derbys (Bristol) 2010 (CB40). LO BB 5-42 (*see LOI*). T20 HS 90. T20 BB 5-21.

FULLER, James Kerr (Otago U, NZ), b Cape Town, South Africa 24 Jan 1990. UK passport. 6'3". RHB, RFM. Squad No 26. Otago 2009-10 to 2012-13. Gloucestershire 2011-15; cap 2011. Middlesex debut 2016. HS 93 v Somerset (Taunton) 2016. BB 6-24 (10-79 match) Otago v Wellington (Dunedin) 2012-13. CC BB 6-47 Gs v Surrey (Oval) 2014. M BB 5-70 v Hants (Northwood) 2016. Hat-trick v Worcs (Cheltenham) 2013. LO HS 45 Gs v Surrey (Bristol) 2015 (RLC). LO BB 6-35 v Netherlands (Amstelveen) 2012 (CB40). T20 HS 36. T20 BB 4-24.

GODSAL, Arthur (Chiswick S), b Chiswick 23 Sep 1997. RHB, RMF. Middlesex 2nd XI debut 2013. England U19 2016-17. Awaiting 1st XI debut. Summer contract.

GUBBINS, Nicholas Richard Trail (Radley C; Leeds U), b Richmond, Surrey 31 Dec 1993. 6'0½". LHB, LB. Squad No 18. Leeds/Bradford MCCU 2013-15. Middlesex debut 2014; cap 2016. Middlesex 2nd XI debut 2012. F-c Tours (EL): SL 2016-17; UAE 2016-17 (v Afghan). 1000 runs (1): 1409 (2016). HS 201* v Lancs (Lord's) 2016. LO HS 141 v Sussex (Hove) 2015 (RLC). T20 HS 46.

HARRIS, James Alexander Russell (Pontardulais CS; Gorseinon C), b Morriston, Swansea, Glamorgan 16 May 1990. 6'0". RHB, RMF. Squad No 5. Glamorgan 2007-12, making debut aged 16y 351d – youngest Gm player to take an f-c wicket; cap 2010. Middlesex debut 2013; cap 2015. Loaned to Glamorgan during 2014. MCC 2016. Wales MC 2005-08. F-c Tours (EL): WI 2010-11; SL 2013-14. HS 87* Gm v Notts (Swansea) 2007. M HS 78 v Somerset (Taunton) 2015. 50 wkts (2); most – 73 (2015). BB 9-34 (13-103 match) v Durham (Lord's) 2015 – record innings and match analysis v Durham. Took 12-118 in match for Gm v Glos (Bristol) 2007 – youngest (17y 3d) to take 10 wickets in any CC match. LO HS 32 v Hants (Southampton) 2015 (RLC). LO BB 4-38 v Glamorgan (Lord's) 2015 (RLC). T20 HS 18. T20 BB 4-23.

HELM, Thomas George (Misbourne S, Gt Missenden), b Stoke Mandeville Hospital, Bucks 7 May 1994. 6'4". RHB, RMF. Squad No 7. Debut (Middlesex) 2013. Glamorgan 2014 (on loan). Middlesex 2nd XI debut 2011. Buckinghamshire 2011. F-c Tour (EL): SL 2016-17. HS 27 v Oxford MCCU (Oxford) 2015. CC HS 18 and BB 3-46 v Yorks (Leeds) 2013. LO HS 13* EL v Sri Lanka A (Kurunegala) 2016-17. LO BB 5-33 EL v Sri Lanka A (Colombo, CCC) 2016-17. T20 HS – . T20 BB 1-29.

HIGGINS, Ryan Francis (Bradfield C), b Harare, Zimbabwe 6 Jan 1995. 5'10". RHB, OB. Squad No 11. Middlesex 2nd XI debut 2012. Awaiting f-c debut. LO HS 39 and LO BB 1-53 v Somerset (Taunton) 2016 (RLC). T20 HS 57*. T20 BB 5-13 v Hants (Southampton) 2016 – M record.

HOLDEN, Max David Edward (Sawston Village C; Hills Road SFC, Cambridge), b Cambridge 18 Dec 1997. 5'11". LHB, OB. Squad No 4. Middlesex 2nd XI debut 2013. England U19 2014-15 to 2016-17. Awaiting 1st XI debut. On loan to Northamptonshire until end June 2017.

LACE, Thomas Cresswell (Millfield S), b Hammersmith 27 May 1998. RHB, WK. Middlesex 2nd XI debut 2015. Awaiting 1st XI debut. Summer contract.

[NQ]**McCULLUM, Brendon** Barrie, b Dunedin, New Zealand 27 Sep 1981. Son of S.J.McCullum (Otago 1976-77 to 1990-91), younger brother of N.L.McCullum (Otago and Glamorgan 1999-00 to date). RHB, RM, WK. Squad No 42. Otago 1999-00 to 2014-15. Canterbury 2003-04 to 2006-07. Glamorgan 2006; cap 2006. Middlesex debut 2016 (T20 only). IPL: KKR 2007-08 to 2013. CSK 2014 to 2015. GL 2016. Big Bash: BH 2011-12 to date. **Tests** (NZ): 101 (2003-04 to 2015-16, 31 as captain); 1000 runs (1): 1164 (2014); HS 302 v I (Wellington) 2013-14 – NZ record; BB 1-1 v P (Dubai) 2014-15. Scored fastest Test century (54 balls) in final Test, v A (Christchurch) 2015-16. **LOI** (NZ): 260 (2001-02 to 2015-16, 62 as captain); HS 166 v Ireland (Aberdeen) 2008. **IT20** (NZ): 71 (2004-05 to 2015, 28 as captain); HS 123 v B (Pallekele) 2012-13. F-c Tours (NZ)(C=Captain): E 2004, 2008, 2013C, 2015C; A 2004-05, 2008-09, 2011-12, 2015-16C; SA 2005-06, 2007-08, 2012-13C; WI 2012, 2014C; I 2010-11, 2012; SL 2009, 2012-13; Z 2005, 2011-12; B 2004-05, 2008-09, 2013-14C; UAE (v P) 2014-15C. HS 302 (*see Tests*). CC HS 160 Gm v Leics (Cardiff) 2006 – on Gm debut. BB 1-1 (*see Tests*). LO HS 170 Otago v Auckland (Auckland) 2007-08. T20 HS 158* Wa v Derbys (Birmingham) 2015 – UK record & joint 3rd highest score in all T20 cricket, and 158* KKR v RCB (Bangalore) 2007-08.

MALAN, Dawid Johannes (Paarl HS), b Roehampton, Surrey 3 Sep 1987. Son of D.J.Malan (WP B and Transvaal B 1978-79 to 1981-82), elder brother of C.C.Malan (Loughborough MCCU 2009-10). 6'0". LHB, LB. Squad No 29. Boland 2005-06. MCC YC 2006-07. Middlesex debut 2008, scoring 132* v Northants (Uxbridge); cap 2010; T20 captain 2016 to date. MCC 2010-11, 2013. 1000 runs (2); most – 1137 runs (2014). HS 182* v Notts (Nottingham) 2015. BB 5-61 v Lancs (Liverpool) 2012. LO HS 185* EL v Sri Lanka A (Northampton) 2016. LO BB 4-25 PDSC v Partex (Savar) 2014-15. T20 HS 115*. T20 BB 2-10.

MORGAN, Eoin Joseph Gerard (Catholic University S), b Dublin, Ireland 10 Sep 1986. 6'0". LHB, RM. Squad No 16. UK passport. Ireland 2004 to 2007-08. Middlesex debut 2006; cap 2008; l-o captain 2014-15. IPL: RCB 2009-10. KKR 2011-13. SH 2015-16. Big Bash: ST 2013-14 to date. *Wisden* 2010. **ECB L-O Central Contract 2016-17. Tests**: 16 (2010 to 2011-12); HS 130 v P (Nottingham) 2010. **LOI** (E/Ire): 176 (23 for Ire 2006 to 2008-09; 153 for E 2009 to 2016-17, 54 as captain); HS 124* v Ireland (Dublin) 2013. **IT20**: 67 (2009 to 2016-17, 24 as captain); HS 85* v SA (Johannesburg) 2009-10. F-c Tours (Ire): A 2010-11 (E); NZ 2008-09 (Eng A); Namibia 2005-06; UAE 2006-07, 2007-08, 2011-12 (v P). 1000 runs (1): 1085 (2008). HS 209* Ire v UAE (Abu Dhabi) 2006-07. M HS 191 v Notts (Nottingham) 2014. BB 2-24 v Notts (Lord's) 2007. LO HS 161 v Kent (Canterbury) 2009 (FPT). LO BB – . T20 HS 85*.

[NQ]**MURTAGH, Timothy** James (John Fisher S; St Mary's C), b Lambeth, London 2 Aug 1981. Elder brother of C.P.Murtagh (Loughborough UCCE and Surrey 2005-09), nephew of A.J.Murtagh (Hampshire and EP 1973-77). 6'0". LHB, RFM. Squad No 34. British U 2000-03. Surrey 2001-06. Middlesex debut 2007; cap 2008; benefit 2015. Ireland 2012-13 to date. MCC 2010. **LOI** (Ire): 23 (2012 to 2016-17); HS 23* v Scotland (Belfast) 2013; BB 4-32 v Z (Harare) 2015-16. **IT20** (Ire): 14 (2012 to 2015-16); HS 12* v UAE (Abu Dhabi) 2015-16; BB 3-23 v PNG (Townsville) 2015-16. HS 74* Sy v Middx (Oval) 2004 and 74* Sy v Warwks (Croydon) 2005. M HS 55 v Leics (Leicester) 2011, sharing M record 9th wkt partnership of 172 with G.K.Berg. 50 wkts (6); most – 85 (2011). BB 7-82 v Derbys (Derby) 2009. LO HS 35* v Surrey (Lord's) 2008 (FPT). LO BB 4-14 Sy v Derbys (Derby) 2005 (NL). T20 HS 40*. T20 BB 6-24 Sy v Middx (Lord's) 2005 – Sy record and 4th best UK figs.

PATEL, Ravi Hasmukh (Merchant Taylors' S, Northwood; Loughborough U), b Harrow 4 Aug 1991. 5'8". RHB, SLA. Squad No 36. Debut (Middlesex) 2010. Loughborough MCCU 2011. Essex (on loan) 2015. HS 26* v Warwks (Uxbridge) 2013. BB 5-69 v Cambridge MCCU (Cambridge) 2013. CC BB 4-42 v Sussex (Lord's) 2015. LO HS 0*. LO BB 3-71 EL v Sri Lanka A (Taunton) 2014. T20 HS 11*. T20 BB 4-18.

PODMORE, Harry William (Twyford HS), b Hammersmith, London 23 Jul 1994. 6'3". RHB, RM. Squad No 23. Glamorgan 2016 (on loan). Middlesex debut 2016. Middlesex 2nd XI debut 2011. MCC YC 2013. HS 21 v Warwks (Birmingham) 2016. BB 4-54 v Somerset (Taunton) 2016. LO HS 1* v Notts (Lord's) 2014 (RLC). LO BB 2-46 v Somerset (Lord's) 2014 (RLC). T20 HS 9. T20 BB 3-13.

RAYNER, Oliver Philip (St Bede's S, Upper Dicker), b Fallingbostel, W Germany, 1 Nov 1985. 6'5". RHB, OB. Squad No 2. Sussex 2006-11, scoring 101 v Sri Lankans (Hove) – first hundred on debut for Sussex since 1920. Middlesex debut 2011; cap 2015. MCC 2014. F-c Tours (EL): SL 2013-14, 2016-17; UAE 2016-17 (v Afghan). HS 143* v Notts (Nottingham) 2012. 50 wkts (1): 51 (2016). BB 8-46 (15-118 match) v Surrey (Oval) 2013. LO HS 61 Sx v Lancs (Hove) 2006 (P40). LO BB 4-35 v Notts (Lord's) 2015 (RLC). T20 HS 41*. T20 BB 5-18.

ROBSON, Sam David (Marcellin C, Randwick), b Paddington, Sydney, Australia 1 Jul 1989. Elder brother of A.J.Robson (*see LEICESTERSHIRE*). 6'0". RHB, LB. Squad No 12. Qualified for England in April 2013. Debut (Middlesex) 2009; cap 2013. **Tests**: 7 (2014); HS 127 v SL (Leeds) 2014. F-c Tours (EL): SA 2014-15; SL 2013-14. 1000 runs (2); most – 1180 (2013). HS 231* v Warwks (Lord's) 2013. BB 1-4 EL v Sri Lanka A (Dambulla) 2013-14. M BB – . LO HS 88 v Notts (Lord's) 2015 (RLC). T20 HS 28*.

ROLAND-JONES, Tobias Skelton ('Toby') (Hampton S; Leeds U), b Ashford 29 Jan 1988. 6'4". RHB, RMF. Squad No 21. Debut (Middlesex) 2010; cap 2012. MCC 2011. Leeds/Bradford UCCE 2009 (not f-c). F-c Tours (EL): SL 2016-17; UAE 2016-17 (v Afghan). HS 103* v Yorks (Lord's) 2015. 50 wkts (2); most – 64 (2012). BB 6-50 (12-105 match) v Northants (Northampton) 2014. Hat-tricks (2): v Derbys (Lord's) 2013, and v Yorks (Lord's) 2016 – at end of match to secure the Championship. LO HS 31* v Kent (Radlett) 2015. LO BB 4-40 v Essex (Lord's) 2016 (RLC). T20 HS 30. T20 BB 4-25.

SCOTT, George Frederick Buchan (Beechwood Park S; St Albans S; Leeds U), b Hemel Hempstead, Herts 6 Nov 1995. Younger brother of J.E.B.Scott (Hertfordshire 2013 to date). 6'2". RHB, RM. Squad No 17. Leeds/Bradford MCCU 2015-16. Middlesex 2nd XI debut 2013. Hertfordshire 2011-14. Awaiting Middlesex f-c debut. HS 16* LBU v Sussex (Hove) 2016. BB 2-67 LBU v Sussex (Hove) 2015. LO HS 4 v Notts (Lord's) 2015 (RLC). LO BB – . T20 HS 20.

SIMPSON, John Andrew (St Gabriel's RC HS), b Bury, Lancs 13 Jul 1988. 5'10". LHB, WK. Squad No 20. Debut (Middlesex) 2009; cap 2011. Cumberland 2007. MCC YCs 2008. HS 143 v Surrey (Lord's) 2011. LO HS 82 v Glos (Cheltenham) 2010 (CB40). T20 HS 84*.

NQ**SOWTER, Nathan** Adam (Hill Sport HS, NSW), b Penrith, NSW, Australia 12 Oct 1992. 5'10". RHB, LB. Squad No 72. Middlesex 2nd XI debut 2014. Signed l-o contract in 2016. Awaiting f-c debut. LO HS 0. LO BB – . T20 HS 4. T20 BB 2-2.

NQ**STIRLING, Paul** Robert (Belfast HS), b Belfast, N Ireland 3 Sep 1990. Father Brian Stirling was an international rugby referee. 5'10". RHB, OB. Squad No 39. Ireland 2007-08 to date. Middlesex debut 2013; cap 2016. **LOI** (Ire): 73 (2008 to 2016-17); HS 177 v Canada (Toronto) 2010; BB 4-11 v Netherlands (Amstelveen) 2010. **IT20** (Ire): 43 (2009 to 2016-17); HS 79 v Afghanistan (Dubai, DSC) 2011-12; BB 3-21 v B (Belfast) 2012. F-c Tours (Ire): WI 2009-10; Kenya 2011-12; Z 2015-16; UAE 2013-14. HS 115 Ire v UAE (Dublin) 2015. M HS 85 v Somerset (Lord's) 2016. BB 2-27 Ire v Namibia (Windhoek) 2015-16. M BB 2-31 v Oxford MCCU (Oxford) 2015. CC BB 2-43 v Surrey (Lord's) 2013. LO HS 177 (*see LOI*). LO BB 4-11 (*see LOI*). T20 HS 90. T20 BB 4-10.

[NQ]**VOGES, Adam** Charles (Edith Cowan U, Perth), b Perth, Australia 4 Oct 1979. 6'0". RHB, SLA. Squad No 32. W Australia 2002-03 to date. Nottinghamshire 2008-12; cap 2008. Middlesex debut 2013; captain 2015-16; cap 2016. IPL: RR 2009-10. Big Bash: MS: 2011-12. PS 2012-13 to date. **Tests** (A): 20 (2015 to 2016-17); 1000 runs (1): 1028 (2015) – becoming only the 3rd batsman to score 1000 runs in the year of his debut; HS 269* v WI (Hobart) 2015-16; scored a record 614 Test runs between dismissals (269*, 106* and 239 v WI); BB – . **LOI** (A): 31 (2006-07 to 2013-14); HS 112* v WI (Melbourne) 2012-13. BB 1-3 v E (Birmingham) 2013. **IT20** (A): 7 (2007-08 to 2012-13); HS 51 v WI (Brisbane) 2012-13; BB 2-5 v I (Melbourne) 2007-08. F-c Tours (A): E 2015; WI 2015; NZ 2015-16; I 2008-09 (Aus A); P 2007-08 (Aus A); SL 2016. 1000 runs (0+1): 1132 (2014-15). HS 269* (*see Tests*). UK HS 165 Nt v Oxford MCCU (Oxford) 2011. M HS 160* v Hants (Northwood) 2016. BB 4-92 WA v S Aus (Adelaide) 2006-07. UK BB 3-21 Nt v Durham (Nottingham) 2008. M BB 2-20 v Durham (Lord's) 2015. LO HS 112* (*see LOI*). LO BB 3-20 WA v Q (Sydney) 2015-16. T20 HS 82*. T20 BB 2-4.

WHITE, Robert George (Harrow S; Loughborough U), b 15 Sep 1995. RHB, WK, occ RM. Squad No 14. Loughborough MCCU 2015-16. Middlesex 2nd XI debut 2013. Awaiting 1st XI debut. HS 30 LU v Kent (Canterbury) 2016.

RELEASED/RETIRED

(Having made a County 1st XI appearance in 2016)

[NQ]**BAILEY, G.J.** – *see HAMPSHIRE.*

[NQ]**McCLENAGHAN, Mitchell** John, b Hastings, Hawke's Bay, New Zealand 11 Jun 1986. LHB, LMF. C Districts 2007-08 to 2010-11. Auckland 2011-12 to date. Worcestershire 2014. Middlesex (T20 only) 2015-16. IPL: MI 2015-16. **LOI** (NZ): 48 (2012-13 to 2015-16); HS 34* v SA (Mt Maunganui) 2014-15; BB 5-58 v WI (Auckland) 2013-14. **IT20** (NZ): 28 (2012-13 to 2015-16); HS 6* v E (Auckland) 2012-13; BB 3-17 v A (Dharamsala) 2015-16. HS 34 v Auckland v CD (Napier) 2011-12. CC HS 27 and CC BB 5-78 Wo v Derbys (Derby) 2014. BB 8-23 Auckland v Otago (Auckland) 2011-12. LO HS 34* (*see LOI*). LO BB 6-41 Auckland v Wellington (Auckland) 2011-12. T20 HS 20. T20 BB 5-29.

A.Balbirnie and C.T.Steel left the staff without making a County 1st XI appearance in 2016.

NORTHAMPTONSHIRE RELEASED/RETIRED (continued from p 153)

STONE, O.P. – *see WARWICKSHIRE.*

TERRY, Sean Paul (Aquinas C, Perth; Notre Dame U, Perth, Australia), b Southampton 1 Aug 1991. Son of V.P.Terry (Hampshire and England 1978-96). 5'11". RHB, OB. Hampshire 2012-15. Northamptonshire 2016. **LOI** (Ire): 5 (2016 to 2016-17); HS 16 v SA (Benoni) 2016-17. **IT20** (Ire): 1 (2016); HS 4 v Hong Kong (Bready) 2016. HS 62* H v Sussex (Hove) 2015. Nh HS 54 v Sussex (Arundel) 2016. LO HS 63 v Leics (Southampton) 2014 (RLC). T20 HS 4.

MIDDLESEX 2016

RESULTS SUMMARY

	Place	Won	Lost	Drew	NR
Specsavers County Champ (1st Division)	**1st**	6		10	
All First-Class Matches		6		10	
Royal London One-Day Cup (South Group)	6th	4	4		
NatWest t20 Blast (South Group)	QF	7	7		1

SPECSAVERS COUNTY CHAMPIONSHIP AVERAGES

BATTING AND FIELDING

Cap		M	I	NO	HS	Runs	Avge	100	50	Ct/St
2016	A.C.Voges	6	6	1	160*	388	77.60	1	2	5
	G.J.Bailey	3	5	1	110*	284	71.00	1	2	2
2016	N.R.T.Gubbins	16	24	1	201*	1409	61.26	4	9	6
2013	S.D.Robson	14	21	1	231	899	44.95	3	4	16
	S.S.Eskinazi	9	15	1	157	609	43.50	2	2	4
2011	J.A.Simpson	16	23	5	100*	779	43.27	1	7	45/1
2010	D.J.Malan	15	23	1	147	951	43.22	3	5	6
2015	J.E.C.Franklin	14	19	4	99	641	42.73	–	4	10
2015	J.A.R.Harris	7	9	3	78	203	33.83	–	2	2
2016	P.R.Stirling	9	7	1	85	199	33.16	–	1	3
2012	T.S.Roland-Jones	13	14	3	79*	319	29.00	–	2	4
2006	N.R.D.Compton	10	17	1	131	436	27.25	1	2	9
2008	T.J.Murtagh	14	12	4	47	168	21.00	–	–	4
2015	O.P.Rayner	13	13	3	26	100	10.00	–	–	18
2009	S.T.Finn	8	7	1	22*	50	8.33	–	–	1

Also batted: J.K.Fuller (3 matches) 93, 36 (3 ct); R.H.Patel (1) 4*; H.W.Podmore (3) 2*, 21 (1 ct).

BOWLING

	O	M	R	W	Avge	Best	5wI	10wM
H.W.Podmore	90	21	240	11	21.81	4-54	–	–
O.P.Rayner	444.5	108	1202	51	23.56	6-79	3	–
T.S.Roland-Jones	482.2	95	1524	54	28.22	6-54	2	1
T.J.Murtagh	457.2	116	1227	43	28.53	5-53	1	–
S.T.Finn	259	41	912	31	29.41	4-54	–	–
J.K.Fuller	100	17	393	12	32.75	5-70	1	–
J.A.R.Harris	228.2	34	807	16	50.43	3-67	–	–
J.E.C.Franklin	205	39	646	11	58.72	3-26	–	–

Also bowled: N.R.T.Gubbins 7-0-38-0; D.J.Malan 29-4-87-2; R.H.Patel 37-7-94-3; P.R.Stirling 53-6-138-0; A.C.Voges 15-0-65-0.

Middlesex played no first-class fixtures outside the County Championship in 2016. The First-Class Averages (pp 226–242) give the records of their players in all first-class county matches, with the exception of N.R.D.Compton, S.T.Finn and H.W.Podmore, whose first-class figures for Middlesex are as above.

MIDDLESEX RECORDS

FIRST-CLASS CRICKET

Highest Total	For 642-3d		v	Hampshire	Southampton	1923
	V 850-7d		by	Somerset	Taunton	2007
Lowest Total	For 20		v	MCC	Lord's	1864
	V 31		by	Glos	Bristol	1924
Highest Innings	For 331*	J.D.B.Robertson	v	Worcs	Worcester	1949
	V 341	C.M.Spearman	for	Glos	Gloucester	2004

Highest Partnership for each Wicket

1st	372	M.W.Gatting/J.L.Langer	v	Essex	Southgate	1998
2nd	380	F.A.Tarrant/J.W.Hearne	v	Lancashire	Lord's	1914
3rd	424*	W.J.Edrich/D.C.S.Compton	v	Somerset	Lord's	1948
4th	325	J.W.Hearne/E.H.Hendren	v	Hampshire	Lord's	1919
5th	338	R.S.Lucas/T.C.O'Brien	v	Sussex	Hove	1895
6th	270	J.D.Carr/P.N.Weekes	v	Glos	Lord's	1994
7th	271*	E.H.Hendren/F.T.Mann	v	Notts	Nottingham	1925
8th	182*	M.H.C.Doll/H.R.Murrell	v	Notts	Lord's	1913
9th	172	G.K.Berg/T.J.Murtagh	v	Leics	Leicester	2011
10th	230	R.W.Nicholls/W.Roche	v	Kent	Lord's	1899

Best Bowling	For	10- 40	G.O.B.Allen	v	Lancashire	Lord's	1929
(Innings)	V	9- 38	R.C.R-Glasgow†	for	Somerset	Lord's	1924
Best Bowling	For	16-114	G.Burton	v	Yorkshire	Sheffield	1888
(Match)		16-114	J.T.Hearne	v	Lancashire	Manchester	1898
	V	16-100	J.E.B.B.P.Q.C.Dwyer	for	Sussex	Hove	1906

Most Runs – Season	2669	E.H.Hendren	(av 83.41)	1923
Most Runs – Career	40302	E.H.Hendren	(av 48.81)	1907-37
Most 100s – Season	13	D.C.S.Compton		1947
Most 100s – Career	119	E.H.Hendren		1907-37
Most Wkts – Season	158	F.J.Titmus	(av 14.63)	1955
Most Wkts – Career	2361	F.J.Titmus	(av 21.27)	1949-82
Most Career W-K Dismissals	1223	J.T.Murray	(1024 ct; 199 st)	1952-75
Most Career Catches in the Field	561	E.H.Hendren		1907-37

LIMITED-OVERS CRICKET

Highest Total	**50ov**	367-6		v	Sussex	Hove	2015
	40ov	350-6		v	Lancashire	Lord's	2012
	T20	221-2		v	Sussex	Hove	2015
Lowest Total	**50ov**	41		v	Essex	Westcliff	1972
	40ov	23		v	Yorkshire	Leeds	1974
	T20	92		v	Surrey	Lords	2013
Highest Innings	**50ov**	163	A.J.Strauss	v	Surrey	The Oval	2008
	40ov	147*	M.R.Ramprakash	v	Worcs	Lord's	1990
	T20	129	D.T.Christian	v	Kent	Canterbury	2014
Best Bowling	**50ov**	7-12	W.W.Daniel	v	Minor Cos E	Ipswich	1978
	40ov	6- 6	R.W.Hooker	v	Surrey	Lord's	1969
	T20	5-13	M.Kartik	v	Essex	Lord's	2007
		5-13	R.F.Higgins	v	Hampshire	Southampton	2016

† R.C.Robertson-Glasgow

NORTHAMPTONSHIRE

Formation of Present Club: 31 July 1878
Inaugural First-Class Match: 1905
Colours: Maroon
Badge: Tudor Rose
County Champions: (0); best – 2nd 1912, 1957, 1965, 1976
Gillette/NatWest/C&G/FP Trophy Winners: (2) 1976, 1992
Benson and Hedges Cup Winners: (1) 1980
Twenty20 Cup Winners: (2) 2013, 2016

Chief Executive: Ray Payne, County Ground, Abington Avenue, Northampton, NN1 4PR • Tel: 01604 514455 • Fax: 01604 609288 • Email: post@nccc.co.uk • Web: www.nccc.co.uk • Twitter: @NorthantsCCC (31,739 followers)

Head Coach: David Ripley. **Captain**: A.G.Wakely. **Overseas Players**: R.K.Kleinveldt and S.Prasanna (T20 only). **2017 Testimonial**: None. **Head Groundsman**: Craig Harvey. **Scorer**: Tony Kingston. ‡ New registration. NQ Not qualified for England.

AZHARULLAH, Mohammad, b Burewala, Punjab, Pakistan 25 Dec 1983. 5'7". RHB, RFM. Squad No 92. Multan 2004-05 to 2006-07. WAPDA 2004-05 to 2012-13. Quetta 2005-06. Baluchistan 2007-08 to 2008-09. Northamptonshire debut 2013; cap 2015. UK qualified through residency and British wife. HS 58* v Kent (Canterbury) 2015. BB 7-74 Quetta v Lahore Ravi (Quetta) 2005-06. Nh BB 7-76 (10-158 match) v Sussex (Northampton) 2014. LO HS 9 (twice). LO BB 5-38 v Hants (Southampton) 2014 (RLC). T20 HS 6*. T20 BB 4-14.

‡**BUCK, Nathan** Liam (Newbridge HS; Ashby S), b Leicester 26 Apr 1991. 6'2". RHB, RMF. Squad No 11. Leicestershire 2009-14; cap 2011. Lancashire 2015-16. F-c Tour (EL): WI 2010-11. HS 29* Le v Worcs (Worcester) 2014. BB 5-76 Le v Essex (Chelmsford) 2014. LO HS 21 Le v Glamorgan (Leicester) 2009 (P40). LO BB 4-39 EL v Sri Lanka A (Dambulla) 2011-12. T20 HS 8*. T20 BB 3-16.

COBB, Joshua James (Oakham S), b Leicester 17 Aug 1990. Son of R.A.Cobb (Leics and N Transvaal 1980-89). 5'11½". RHB, LB. Squad No 4. Leicestershire 2007-14; l-o captain 2014. Northamptonshire debut 2015. HS 148* Le v Middx (Lord's) 2008. Nh HS 95 v Derbys (Derby) 2015. BB 2-11 Le v Glos (Leicester) 2008. Nh BB 1-19 v Oxford MCCU (Oxford) 2016. LO HS 137 Le v Lancs (Manchester) 2012 (CB40). LO BB 3-34 Le v Glos (Leicester) 2013 (Y40). T20 HS 84. T20 BB 4-22.

CROOK, Steven Paul (Rostrevor C; Magill U), b Modbury, S Australia 28 May 1983. Younger brother of A.R.Crook (S Australia, Aus Academy, Lancashire, Northamptonshire 1998-99 to 2008). 5'11". RHB, RFM. Squad No 25. UK passport. Lancashire 2003-05. Northamptonshire debut 2005; cap 2013. Middlesex 2011-12. Aus Academy 2001-02. HS 145 v Worcs (Worcester) 2016. BB 5-48 M v Lancs (Lord's) 2012. Nh BB 5-71 v Essex (Northampton) 2009. LO HS 100 SJD v PDSC (Savar) 2013-14. LO BB 5-36 v Warwks (Northampton) 2013 (Y40). T20 HS 63. T20 BB 3-19.

DUCKETT, Ben Matthew (Stowe S), b Farnborough, Kent 17 Oct 1994. 5'7". LHB, WK, occ OB. Squad No 17. Debut (Northamptonshire) 2013; cap 2016. Northamptonshire 2nd XI debut 2011. England U19 2012-13. PCA 2016. YC 2016. **Tests**: 4 (2016-17); HS 56 v B (Dhaka) 2016-17. F-c Tours: I 2016-17; B 2016-17. 1000 runs (2); most – 1338 (2016). HS 282* v Sussex (Northampton) 2016. LO HS 220* EL v Sri Lanka A (Canterbury) 2016. T20 HS 84.

GLEESON, Richard James, b Blackpool, Lancs 2 Dec 1987. RHB, RM. Squad No 33. Debut (Northamptonshire) 2015. Cumberland 2010-15. HS 31 v Glos (Bristol) 2016. BB 4-105 v Essex (Northampton) 2016. LO HS 4* v Lancs (Northampton) 2016 (RLC). LO BB 5-47 v Worcs (Worcester) 2016 (RLC). T20 HS 7*. T20 BB 3-12.

KEOGH, Robert Ian (Queensbury S; Dunstable C), b Luton, Beds 21 Oct 1991. 5'11". RHB, OB. Squad No 14. Debut (Northamptonshire) 2012. Bedfordshire 2009-10. HS 221 v Hants (Southampton) 2013. BB 9-52 (13-125 match) v Glamorgan (Northampton) 2016. LO HS 134 v Durham (Northampton) 2016 (RLC). LO BB 1-49 v Somerset (Northampton) 2015 (RLC). T20 HS 28. T20 BB – .

NQ**KLEINVELDT, Rory** Keith, b Cape Town, South Africa 15 Mar 1983. Cousin of M.C.Kleinveldt (W Province 2010-11 to date). Nephew of J.Kleinveldt (W Province and Transvaal 1979-80 to 1982-83). 6'2". RHB, RFM. Squad No 6. W Province 2002-03 to 2005-06. Cape Cobras 2005-06 to date. Hampshire 2008 (1 game). Northamptonshire debut 2015; cap 2016. **Tests** (SA): 4 (2012-13); HS 17* v A (Brisbane) 2012-13; BB 3-65 v A (Adelaide) 2012-13. **LOI** (SA): 10 (2012-13 to 2013); HS 43 v E (Oval) 2013; BB 4-22 v P (Bloemfontein) 2012-13. **IT20** (SA): 6 (2008-09 to 2012-13); HS 22 v P (Centurion) 2012-13; BB 3-18 v NZ (Durban) 2012-13. F-c Tours (SA A): A 2012-13 (SA); I 2007-08; SL 2010. HS 115* WP v KZN (Chatsworth) 2005-06. Nh HS 97 v Derbys (Northampton) 2016. 50 wkts (1): 57 (2015). BB 8-47 Cobras v Warriors (Stellenbosch) 2005-06. Nh BB 5-41 v Kent (Northampton) 2015. LO HS 128 v Notts (Nottingham) 2016 (RLC). LO BB 4-22 (*see LOI*). T20 HS 46. T20 BB 3-14.

NQ**LEVI, Richard** Ernst, b Johannesburg, South Africa 14 Jan 1988. 5'11". RHB, RM. Squad No 88. W Province 2006-07 to date. Cape Cobras 2008-09 to date. Northamptonshire debut 2014 (Kolpak signing). **IT20** (SA): 13 (2011-12 to 2012-13); HS 117* v NZ (Hamilton) 2011-12. HS 168 v Essex (Northampton) 2015. LO HS 166 Cobras v Titans (Paarl) 2012-13. T20 HS 117*.

NQ**MURPHY, David** (Richard Hale S, Hertford; Loughborough U), b Welwyn Garden City, Herts 24 June 1989. 5'11". RHB, WK. Squad No 19. Loughborough MCCU 2009-11. Northamptonshire debut 2009. **LOI** (Scot): 8 (2012-13 to 2013); HS 20* v Ireland (Belfast) 2013. **IT20** (Scot): 4 (2012-13 to 2013-14); HS 20 v Kenya (Dubai) 2013-14. HS 135* v Surrey (Oval) 2015. BB 1-40 v Leics (Northampton) 2016. LO HS 31* v Netherlands (Northampton) 2010 (CB40). T20 HS 20.

NEWTON, Robert Irving (Framlingham C), b Taunton, Somerset 18 Jan 1990. 5'8". RHB, OB. Squad No 10. Debut (Northamptonshire) 2010. HS 202* v Leics (Northampton) 2016. BB – . LO HS 88* v Kent (Tunbridge W) 2013 (Y40). T20 HS 38.

NQ**PRASANNA, Seekkuge** (Rewatha C), b Balapitiya, Sri Lanka 27 Jun 1985. 5'9". RHB, LB. Squad No 41. Sri Lanka Army 2006-07 to date. Kandurata 2008-09 to 2009-10. Northamptonshire debut 2016. **Tests** (SL): 1 (2011); HS 5 and BB – v A (Pallekele) 2011. **LOI** (SL): 34 (2011 to 2016); HS 95 v Ireland (Dublin) 2016; BB 3-32 v A (Colombo, RPS) 2011. **IT20** (SL): 14 (2013-14 to 2016-17); HS 37* v SA (Cape Town) 2016-17; BB 2-45 v P (Dubai, DSC) 2013-14. F-c Tour (SL A): E 2011. HS 81 SL Army v Colts (Panagoda) 2012-13. Nh HS 31 v Worcs (Northampton) 2016. 50 wkts (0+4); most – 71 (2008-09). BB 8-59 (12-95 match) SL Army v Bloomfield (Panagoda) 2008-09. NH BB 5-97 v Glos (Bristol) 2016. LO HS 95 (*see LOI*). LO BB 6-23 SL A v England Lions (Worcester) 2011. T20 HS 53. T20 BB 4-19.

ROSSINGTON, Adam Matthew (Mill Hill S), b Edgware, Middx 5 May 1993. 5'11". RHB, WK. Squad No 7. Middlesex 2010-14. Northamptonshire debut 2014. Middlesex 2nd XI debut 2010. England U19 2010-11, scoring 113 v SL on debut. HS 138* v Sussex (Arundel) 2016. Won 2013 Walter Lawrence Trophy with 55-ball century v Cambridge MCCU (Cambridge). LO HS 97 v Notts (Nottingham) 2016 (RLC). T20 HS 85.

SANDERSON, Ben William (Ecclesfield CS; Sheffield C), b Sheffield, Yorks 3 Jan 1989. 6'0". RHB, RMF. Squad No 26. Yorkshire 2008-10. Northamptonshire debut 2015. Shropshire 2013-15. HS 42 v Kent (Canterbury) 2015. 50 wkts (1): 55 (2016). BB 8-73 v Glos (Northampton) 2016. LO HS 12* Y v Essex (Leeds) 2010 (CB40). LO BB 2-17 Y v Derbys (Leeds) 2010 (CB40). T20 HS 1*. T20 BB 4-21.

WAKELY, Alexander George (Bedford S), b Hammersmith, London 3 Nov 1988. 6'2". RHB, RM. Squad No 8. Debut (Northamptonshire) 2007; cap 2012; captain 2015 to date. Missed entire 2014 season due to ruptured Achilles. Bedfordshire 2004-05. HS 123 v Leics (Northampton) 2015. BB 2-62 v Somerset (Taunton) 2007. LO HS 102 v Kent (Tunbridge W) 2013 (Y40). LO BB 2-14 v Lancs (Northampton) 2007 (P40). T20 HS 64. T20 BB – .

WHITE, Graeme Geoffrey (Stowe S), b Milton Keynes, Bucks 18 Apr 1987. 5'11". RHB, SLA. Squad No 87. Debut (Northamptonshire) 2006. Nottinghamshire 2010-13. HS 65 v Glamorgan (Colwyn Bay) 2007. BB 6-44 v Glamorgan (Northampton) 2016. LO HS 40 v Notts (Nottingham) 2016 (RLC). LO BB 6-37 v Lancs (Northampton) 2016 (RLC). T20 HS 34. T20 BB 5-22 Nt v Lancs (Nottingham) 2013 – Nt record.

ZAIB, Saif Ali (RGS High Wycombe), b High Wycombe, Bucks 22 May 1998. LHB, SLA. Squad No 5. Debut (Northamptonshire) 2015. Northamptonshire 2nd XI debut 2013, aged 15y 90d. HS 65* v Glamorgan (Swansea) 2016. BB 5-148 v Leics (Northampton) 2016. LO HS 16 v Leics (Northampton) 2015 (RLC). LO BB – .

RELEASED/RETIRED

(Having made a County 1st XI appearance in 2016, even if not formally contracted. Some may return in 2017.)

ASHRAF, Moin Aqeeb (Dixons City Academy, Bradford), b Bradford, Yorks 5 Jan 1992. 6'4". RHB, RMF. Yorkshire 2010-13. Leeds/Bradford MCCU 2016. Northamptonshire (T20 only) 2016. HS 10 and BB 5-32 Y v Kent (Leeds) 2010. LO HS 3* Y v Kent (Leeds) 2012 (CB40). LO BB 3-38 Y v Glamorgan (Leeds) 2013 (Y40). T20 HS 4. T20 BB 4-18.

BARRETT, Chad Anthony (King Edward VII S, Johannesburg), b Johannesburg, South Africa 22 May 1989. 6'2". RHB, RMF. Northamptonshire 2011-16. HS 114* and BB 1-29 v Worcs (Worcester) 2016.

PANESAR, Mudhsuden Singh ('**Monty**') (Stopsley HS; Bedford Modern S; Loughborough U), b Luton, Beds 25 Apr 1982. 6'0". LHB, SLA. Northamptonshire 2001-16; cap 2006. British U 2002-05. Loughborough UCCE 2004. Lions 2009-10. Sussex 2010-13; cap 2010. Essex 2013-15. MCC 2006, 2014. Bedfordshire 1998-99. *Wisden* 2007. **Tests**: 50 (2005-06 to 2013-14); HS 26 v SL (Nottingham) 2006; BB 6-37 v NZ (Manchester) 2008. **LOI**: 26 (2006-07 to 2007-08); HS 13 v WI (Nottingham) 2007; BB 3-25 v B (Bridgetown) 2006-07. **IT20**: 1 (2006-07); HS 1 and BB 2-40 v A (Sydney) 2006-07. F-c Tours: A 2006-07, 2010-11, 2013-14; WI 2008-09; NZ 2007-08, 2012-13; I 2005-06, 2008-09, 2012-13; SL 2002-03 (ECB Acad), 2007-08, 2011-12; UAE 2011-12 (v P). HS 46* Sx v Middx (Hove) 2010. Nh HS 39* v Worcs (Northampton) 2005. 50 wkts (6); most – 71 (2006). BB 7-60 (13-137 match) Sx v Somerset (Taunton) 2012. Nh BB 7-181 v Essex (Chelmsford) 2005. LO HS 17* Nh v Leics (Northampton) 2008 (FPT). LO BB 5-20 ECB Acad v SL Acad XI (Colombo) 2002-03. T20 HS 3*. T20 BB 3-14.

RELEASED/RETIRED continued on p 148

NORTHAMPTONSHIRE 2016

RESULTS SUMMARY

	Place	Won	Lost	Drew	Aband	NR
Specsavers County Champ (2nd Division)	5th	4	3	8	1	
All First-Class Matches		4	3	9	1	
Royal London One-Day Cup (North Group)	5th	4	4			1
NatWest t20 Blast (North Group)	**Winners**	10	5			2

SPECSAVERS COUNTY CHAMPIONSHIP AVERAGES

BATTING AND FIELDING

Cap		*M*	*I*	*NO*	*HS*	*Runs*	*Avge*	*100*	*50*	*Ct/St*
2016	B.M.Duckett	14	24	2	282*	1338	60.81	4	5	9/1
	R.I.Newton	10	19	3	202*	810	50.62	3	2	4
	J.D.Libby	5	7	1	102	293	48.83	1	1	1
	A.M.Rossington	12	17	4	138*	556	42.76	1	3	11/3
2013	S.P.Crook	10	15	3	145	484	40.33	2	1	1
2012	A.G.Wakely	12	19	3	104	630	39.37	1	4	11
	S.A.Zaib	3	5	1	65*	127	31.75	–	1	3
	R.I.Keogh	11	17	–	154	519	30.52	1	2	3/1
	R.E.Levi	10	14	–	104	427	30.50	1	1	11
2016	R.K.Kleinveldt	11	15	2	97	391	30.07	–	3	11
	D.Murphy	11	17	4	60*	355	27.30	–	1	33/2
	R.J.Gleeson	6	6	2	31	89	22.25	–	–	1
	J.J.Cobb	6	8	–	49	160	20.00	–	–	–
	S.Prasanna	2	4	–	31	70	17.50	–	–	2
	G.G.White	5	5	–	33	73	14.60	–	–	3
2006	M.S.Panesar	3	4	2	17*	28	14.00	–	–	2
2015	M.Azharullah	12	15	3	14*	72	6.00	–	–	1
	B.W.Sanderson	14	15	3	19	58	4.83	–	–	1

Also batted: C.A.Barrett (2 matches) 114*, 4* (3 ct); L.J.Evans (1) 74, 73 (2 ct); O.P.Stone (3) 4, 60, 19 (3 ct); S.P.Terry (2) 54, 6, 35 (1 ct).

BOWLING

	O	*M*	*R*	*W*	*Avge*	*Best*	*5wI*	*10wM*
B.W.Sanderson	408.5	95	1157	55	21.03	8- 73	4	1
G.G.White	107	24	281	13	21.61	6- 44	1	–
R.I.Keogh	242.2	42	828	31	26.70	9- 52	1	1
R.K.Kleinveldt	302.1	60	930	26	35.76	5- 53	1	–
M.Azharullah	277.2	46	987	25	39.48	6- 68	1	–
R.J.Gleeson	147.5	25	505	10	50.50	4-105	–	–
S.P.Crook	139.2	18	578	10	57.80	2- 7	–	–
Also bowled:								
S.Prasanna	53.2	13	165	9	18.33	5- 97	1	–
S.A.Zaib	32	2	174	5	34.80	5-148	1	–
O.P.Stone	87.4	8	282	6	47.00	4- 56	–	–
M.S.Panesar	112	16	425	5	85.00	3-122	–	–

C.A.Barrett 20-0-100-2; J.J.Cobb 39-6-94-0; B.M.Duckett 0.5-0-8-0; J.D.Libby 21-3-71-2; D.Murphy 5-0-40-1; A.M.Rossington 2-0-12-0; A.G.Wakely 5-1-12-0.

The First-Class Averages (pp 226–242) give the records of Northamptonshire players in all first-class county matches (Northamptonshire's other opponents being Oxford MCCU), with the exception of L.J.Evans and J.D.Libby, whose first-class figures for Northamptonshire are as above.

NORTHAMPTONSHIRE RECORDS

FIRST-CLASS CRICKET

Highest Total	For 781-7d		v	Notts	Northampton	1995
	V 673-8d		by	Yorkshire	Leeds	2003
Lowest Total	For 12		v	Glos	Gloucester	1907
	V 33		by	Lancashire	Northampton	1977
Highest Innings	For 331*	M.E.K.Hussey	v	Somerset	Taunton	2003
	V 333	K.S.Duleepsinhji	for	Sussex	Hove	1930

Highest Partnership for each Wicket

1st	375	R.A.White/M.J.Powell	v	Glos	Northampton	2002
2nd	344	G.Cook/R.J.Boyd-Moss	v	Lancashire	Northampton	1986
3rd	393	A.Fordham/A.J.Lamb	v	Yorkshire	Leeds	1990
4th	370	R.T.Virgin/P.Willey	v	Somerset	Northampton	1976
5th	401	M.B.Loye/D.Ripley	v	Glamorgan	Northampton	1998
6th	376	R.Subba Row/A.Lightfoot	v	Surrey	The Oval	1958
7th	293	D.J.G.Sales/D.Ripley	v	Essex	Northampton	1999
8th	179	A.J.Hall/J.D.Middlebrook	v	Surrey	The Oval	2011
9th	156	R.Subba Row/S.Starkie	v	Lancashire	Northampton	1955
10th	148	B.W.Bellamy/J.V.Murdin	v	Glamorgan	Northampton	1925

Best Bowling	For 10-127	V.W.C.Jupp	v	Kent	Tunbridge W	1932
(Innings)	V 10- 30	C.Blythe	for	Kent	Northampton	1907
Best Bowling	For 15- 31	G.E.Tribe	v	Yorkshire	Northampton	1958
(Match)	V 17- 48	C.Blythe	for	Kent	Northampton	1907

Most Runs – Season	2198	D.Brookes	(av 51.11)	1952
Most Runs – Career	28980	D.Brookes	(av 36.13)	1934-59
Most 100s – Season	8	R.A.Haywood		1921
Most 100s – Career	67	D.Brookes		1934-59
Most Wkts – Season	175	G.E.Tribe	(av 18.70)	1955
Most Wkts – Career	1102	E.W.Clark	(av 21.26)	1922-47
Most Career W-K Dismissals	810	K.V.Andrew	(653 ct; 157 st)	1953-66
Most Career Catches in the Field	469	D.S.Steele		1963-84

LIMITED-OVERS CRICKET

Highest Total	**50ov**	425		v	Notts	Nottingham	2016
	40ov	324-6		v	Warwicks	Birmingham	2013
	T20	224-5		v	Glos	Milton Keynes	2005
Lowest Total	**50ov**	62		v	Leics	Leicester	1974
	40ov	41		v	Middlesex	Northampton	1972
	T20	47		v	Durham	Chester-le-St[2]	2011
Highest Innings	**50ov**	161	D.J.G.Sales	v	Yorkshire	Northampton	2006
	40ov	172*	W.Larkins	v	Warwicks	Luton	1983
	T20	111*	L.Klusener	v	Worcs	Kidderminster	2007
Best Bowling	**50ov**	7-10	C.Pietersen	v	Denmark	Brondby	2005
	40ov	7-39	A.Hodgson	v	Somerset	Northampton	1976
	T20	6-21	A.J.Hall	v	Worcs	Northampton	2008

NOTTINGHAMSHIRE

Formation of Present Club: March/April 1841
Substantial Reorganisation: 11 December 1866
Inaugural First-Class Match: 1864
Colours: Green and Gold
Badge: Badge of City of Nottingham
County Champions (since 1890): (6) 1907, 1929, 1981, 1987, 2005, 2010
NatWest Trophy Winners: (1) 1987
Benson and Hedges Cup Winners: (1) 1989
Sunday League Winners: (1) 1991
Yorkshire Bank 40 Winners: (1) 2013
Twenty20 Cup Winners: (0); best – Finalist 2006

Chief Executive: Lisa Pursehouse, Trent Bridge, West Bridgford, Nottingham NG2 6AG • Tel: 0115 982 3000 • Fax: 0115 982 3037 • Email: administration@nottsccc.co.uk • Web: www.trentbridge.co.uk • Twitter: @TrentBridge (40,668 followers)

Director of Cricket: Mick Newell. **Head Coach**: Peter Moores. **Assistant Head Coach**: Paul Franks. **Bowling Coach**: Andy Pick. **Captains**: C.M.W.Read (f-c & l-o) and D.T.Christian (T20). **Overseas Players**: D.T.Christian and I.S.Sodhi (T20 only). **2017 Testimonial**: S.R.Patel. **Head Groundsman**: Steve Birks. **Scorer**: Roger Marshall. ‡ New registration. [NQ] Not qualified for England.

BALL, Jacob Timothy ('**Jake**') (Meden CS), b Mansfield 14 Mar 1991. Nephew of B.N.French (Notts and England 1976-95). 6'0". RHB, RFM. Squad No 28. Debut (Nottinghamshire) 2011; cap 2016. MCC 2016. **Tests**: 3 (2016 to 2016-17); HS 31 and BB 1-47 v I (Mumbai) 2016-17. **LOI**: 6 (2016-17); HS 28 v B (Dhaka) 2016-17; BB 5-51 v B (Dhaka) 2016-17 – different games. F-c Tour: I 2016-17. HS 49* v Warwks (Nottingham) 2015. 50 wkts (1): 54 (2016). BB 6-49 v Sussex (Nottingham) 2015. Hat-trick v Middx (Nottingham) 2016. LO HS 28 (*see LOI*). BB 5-51 (*see LOI*). T20 HS 8*. T20 BB 3-36.

BROAD, Stuart Christopher John (Oakham S), b Nottingham 24 Jun 1986. 6'6". LHB, RFM. Squad No 16. Son of B.C.Broad (Glos, Notts, OFS and England 1979-94). Debut (Leicestershire) 2005; cap 2007. Nottinghamshire debut/cap 2008. YC 2006. *Wisden* 2009. **ECB Test Central Contract 2016-17. Tests**: 102 (2007-08 to 2016-17); HS 169 v P (Lord's) 2010, sharing in record Test and UK f-c 8th wkt partnership of 332 with I.J.L.Trott; 50 wkts (2); most – 62 (2013); BB 8-15 v A (Nottingham) 2015. Hat-tricks (2): v I (Nottingham) 2011, and v SL (Leeds) 2014. **LOI**: 121 (2006 to 2015-16, 3 as captain); HS 45* v I (Manchester) 2007; BB 5-23 v SA (Nottingham) 2008. **IT20**: 56 (2006 to 2013-14, 27 as captain); HS 18* v SA (Chester-le-St) 2012 and 18* v A (Melbourne) 2013-14; BB 4-24 v NZ (Auckland) 2012-13. F-c Tours: A 2010-11, 2013-14; SA 2009-10, 2015-16; WI 2005-06 (Eng A), 2008-09, 2014-15; NZ 2007-08, 2012-13; I 2008-09, 2012-13, 2016-17; SL 2007-08, 2011-12; B 2006-07 (Eng A), 2009-10, 2016-17; UAE 2011-12 (v P), 2015-16 (v P). HS 169 (*see Tests*). CC HS 91* Le v Derbys (Leicester) 2007. Nt HS 60 v Worcs (Nottingham) 2009. BB 8-15 (*see Tests*). CC BB 8-52 (11-131 match) Nt v Warwks (Birmingham) 2010. LO HS 45* (*see LOI*). LO BB 5-23 (*see LOI*). T20 HS 18*. T20 BB 4-24.

CARTER, Matthew (Branston S), b Lincoln 26 May 1996. Younger brother of A.Carter (*see DERBYSHIRE*). RHB, OB. Debut (Nottinghamshire) 2015, taking 7-56 v Somerset (Taunton) – the best debut figures for Nt since 1914. Nottinghamshire 2nd XI debut 2013. Lincolnshire 2013-16. HS 11 and BB 7-56 (10-195 match) v Somerset (Taunton) 2015.

[NQ]**CHRISTIAN, Daniel** Trevor, b Camperdown, NSW, Australia 4 May 1983. RHB, RFM. S Australia 2007-08 to 2012-13. Hampshire 2010. Gloucestershire 2013; cap 2013. Victoria 2013-14 to date. Nottinghamshire debut/cap 2016, having joined in 2015 for l-o and T20 only; captain 2016 to date (T20 only). IPL: DC 2011-12. RCB 2013. Big Bash BH 2011-12 to 2014-15. HH 2015-16 to date. **LOI** (A): 19 (2011-12 to 2013-14); HS 39 v I (Adelaide) 2011-12; BB 5-31 v SL (Melbourne) 2011-12. **IT20** (A): 15 (2009-10 to 2013-14); HS 6* v E (Hobart) 2013-14; BB 3-27 v WI (Gros Islet) 2011-12. HS 131* S Aus v NSW (Adelaide) 2011-12. CC HS 36 and CC BB 2-115 H v Somerset (Taunton) 2010. Nt HS 31 v Hants (Southampton) 2016. BB 5-24 (9-87 match) S Aus v WA (Perth) (2009-10). Nt BB 1-22 v Warwks (Birmingham) 2016. LO HS 117 Vic v NSW (Sydney) 2013-14. LO BB 6-48 S Aus v Vic (Geelong) 2010-11. T20 HS 129 M v Kent (Canterbury) 2014 – M record. T20 BB 5-14.

FLETCHER, Luke Jack (Henry Mellish S, Nottingham), b Nottingham 18 Sep 1988. 6'6". RHB, RMF. Squad No 19. Debut (Nottinghamshire) 2008; cap 2014. Surrey 2015 (on loan). Derbyshire 2016 (on loan). HS 92 v Hants (Southampton) 2009. BB 5-52 v Warwks (Nottingham) 2013. LO HS 40* v Durham (Chester-le-St) 2009 (P40). LO BB 4-44 v Warwks (Nottingham) 2014 (RLC). T20 HS 8. T20 BB 4-30.

GURNEY, Harry Frederick (Garendon HS; Loughborough GS; Leeds U), b Nottingham 25 Oct 1986. 6'2". RHB, LFM. Squad No 11. Leicestershire 2007-11. Nottinghamshire debut 2012; cap 2014. MCC 2014. Bradford/Leeds UCCE 2006-07 (not f-c). **LOI**: 10 (2014 to 2014-15); HS 6* v SL (Colombo, RPS) 2014-15; BB 4-55 v SL (Lord's) 2014. **IT20**: 2 (2014); BB 2-26 v SL (Oval) 2014. HS 27* v Cambridge MCCU (Cambridge) 2016. CC HS 24* Le v Middx (Leicester) 2009. BB 6-61 v Durham (Chester-le-St) 2016. Hat-trick v Sussex (Hove) 2013. LO HS 13* v Durham (Chester-le-St) 2012 (CB40). LO BB 5-24 Le v Hants (Leicester) 2010 (CB40). T20 HS 5*. T20 BB 4-20.

HALES, Alexander Daniel (Chesham HS), b Hillingdon, Middx 3 Jan 1989. 6'5". RHB, OB, occ WK. Squad No 10. Debut (Nottinghamshire) 2008; cap 2011. Worcestershire 2014 (1 game, on loan). Buckinghamshire 2006-07. MCC YCs 2006-07. Big Bash: MR 2012-13. AS 2013-14. HH 2014-15. **ECB L-O Central Contract 2016-17. Tests**: 11 (2015-16 to 2016); HS 94 v SL (Lord's) 2016; BB – . **LOI**: 41 (2014 to 2016-17); HS 171 v P (Nottingham) 2016 – E record. **IT20**: 45 (2011 to 2016); HS 116* v SL (Chittagong) 2013-14 – E record. 1000 runs (3); most – 1127 (2011). HS 236 v Notts (Nottingham) 2015. BB 2-63 v Yorks (Nottingham) 2009. LO HS 171 (see *LOI*). T20 HS 116*.

HUTTON, Brett Alan (Worksop C), b Doncaster, Yorks 6 Feb 1993. 6'2". RHB, RM. Squad No 26. Debut (Nottinghamshire) 2011. Nottinghamshire 2nd XI debut 2010. No 1st XI appearances in 2014. HS 74 v Durham (Nottingham) 2016. BB 5-29 (10-106 match) v Durham (Nottingham) 2015. LO HS 33* v Lancs (Liverpool) 2015 (RLC). LO BB 3-72 v Kent (Nottingham) 2015 (RLC). T20 HS 4*. T20 BB 1-24.

KITT, Benjamin Michael, b Plymouth, Devon 18 Jan 1995. RHB, RMF. Nottinghamshire 2nd XI debut 2012. Cornwall 2011-12. Awaiting 1st XI debut.

LIBBY, Jacob ('**Jake**') Daniel (Plymouth C; UWIC), b Plymouth, Devon 3 Jan 1993. 5'9". RHB, OB. Squad No 2. Cardiff MCCU 2014. Nottinghamshire debut 2014, scoring 108 v Sussex (Nottingham). Northamptonshire 2016 (on loan). Cornwall 2011-14. HS 144 v Durham (Chester-le-St) 2016. BB 1-13 Nh v Leics (Leicester) 2016.

LUMB, Michael John (St Stithians C, Johannesburg), b Johannesburg, South Africa 12 Feb 1980. Son of R.G.Lumb (Yorkshire 1970-84), nephew of A.J.S.Smith (SAU and Natal 1972-73 to 1983-84). 6'0". LHB, RM. Squad No 45. Yorkshire 2000-06; ECB qualified and CC debut 2001; cap 2003. Hampshire 2007-11; cap 2008. Nottinghamshire debut/cap 2012. IPL: RR 2009-10. DC 2011. Big Bash: SS 2011-12 to date. **LOI**: 3 (2013-14); HS 106 v WI (North Sound) 2013-14, becoming only the 2nd England player after D.L.Amiss to score a century on LOI debut. **IT20**: 27 (2009-10 to 2013-14); HS 63 v WI (Bridgetown) 2013-14. F-c Tour (Eng A): I 2003-04. 1000 runs (3); most – 1120 (2013). HS 221* v Derbys (Nottingham) 2013. BB 2-10 Y v Kent (Canterbury) 2001. LO HS 184 v Northants (Nottingham) 2016 – Nt record. LO BB – . T20 HS 124* H v Essex (Southampton) 2009 – H record. T20 BB 3-32.

MOORES, Thomas James (Loughborough GS), b Brighton, Sussex 4 Sep 1996. Son of P.Moores (Worcestershire, Sussex & OFS 1983-98); nephew of S.Moores (Cheshire 1995). LHB, WK. Lancashire 2016 (on loan). Nottinghamshire debut 2016. Nottinghamshire 2nd XI debut 2014. HS 41 v Yorks (Scarborough) 2016. LO HS 10 La v Leics (Leicester) 2016 (RLC). T20 HS 39*.

MULLANEY, Steven John (St Mary's RC S, Astley), b Warrington, Cheshire 19 Nov 1986. 5'9". RHB, RM. Squad No 5. Lancashire 2006-08. No f-c appearances in 2009. Nottinghamshire debut 2010, scoring 100* v Hants (Southampton); cap 2013. 1000 runs (1): 1148 (2016). HS 165* La v Durham UCCE (Durham) 2007. Nt HS 165 v Somerset (Nottingham) 2016. BB 4-31 v Essex (Nottingham) 2010. LO HS 89 v Yorks (Scarborough) 2016 (RLC). LO BB 4-29 v Kent (Nottingham) 2013 (Y40). T20 HS 53. T20 BB 4-19.

PATEL, Samit Rohit (Worksop C), b Leicester 30 Nov 1984. Elder brother of A.Patel (Derbyshire and Notts 2007-11). 5'8". RHB, SLA. Squad No 21. Debut (Nottinghamshire) 2002; cap 2008; testimonial 2017. MCC 2014, 2016. **Tests**: 6 (2011-12 to 2015-16); HS 42 v P (Sharjah) 2015-16; BB 2-27 v SL (Galle) 2011-12. **LOI**: 36 (2008 to 2012-13); HS 70* v I (Mohali) 2011-12; BB 5-41 v SA (Oval) 2008. **IT20**: 18 (2011 to 2012-13); HS 67 v SL (Pallekele) 2012-13; BB 2-6 v Afghanistan (Colombo, RPS) 2012-13. F-c Tours: NZ 2008-09 (Eng A); I 2012-13; SL 2011-12; UAE 2015-16 (v P). 1000 runs (2); most – 1125 (2014). HS 256 v Durham MCCU (Nottingham) 2013. CC HS 176 v Glos (Nottingham) 2007. BB 7-68 (11-111 match) v Hants (Southampton) 2011. LO HS 129* v Warwks (Nottingham) 2013 (Y40). LO BB 6-13 v Ireland (Dublin) 2009 (FPT). T20 HS 90*. T20 BB 4-20.

READ, Christopher Mark Wells (Torquay GS; Bath U), b Paignton, Devon 10 Aug 1978. 5'8". RHB, WK. Squad No 7. Gloucestershire (l-o only) 1997. Debut 1997-98 for England A in Kenya. Nottinghamshire debut 1998; cap 1999; captain 2008 to date; benefit 2009. MCC 2002. Devon 1995-97. *Wisden* 2010. **Tests**: 15 (1999 to 2006-07); HS 55 v P (Leeds) 2006. Made six dismissals twice in successive innings 2006-07 to establish an Ashes record. **LOI**: 36 (1999-00 to 2006-07); HS 30* v SA (Manchester) 2003. **IT20**: 1 (2006); HS 13 v P (Bristol) 2006. F-c Tours: A 2006-07; SA 1998-99 (Eng A), 1999-00; WI 2000-01 (Eng A), 2003-04, 2005-06 (Eng A); SL 1997-98 (Eng A), 2002-03 (ECB Acad), 2003-04; Z 1998-99 (Eng A); B 2003-04; K 1997-98 (Eng A). 1000 runs (3); most – 1203 (2009). HS 240 v Essex (Chelmsford) 2007. BB – . LO HS 135 v Durham (Nottingham) 2006 (CGT). T20 HS 58*.

ROOT, William Thomas (Worksop C; Leeds Beckett U), b Sheffield, Yorks 5 Aug 1992. Younger brother of J.E.Root (*see YORKSHIRE*). LHB, OB. Leeds/Bradford MCCU 2015-16. Nottinghamshire debut 2015. Yorkshire 2nd XI 2009-11. Nottinghamshire 2nd XI debut 2011. Suffolk 2014. HS 133 LBU v Sussex (Hove) 2016. CC HS 66* v Somerset (Taunton) 2016. BB – .

SMITH, Gregory Philip (Oundle S; St Hild & St Bede C, Durham U), b Leicester 16 Nov 1988. 6'0". RHB, LBG. Squad No 22. Leicestershire 2008-14, returned in 2015 on loan. Durham MCCU 2009-11. Badureliya 2013-14. Colombo CC 2014-15. Nottinghamshire debut 2015. HS 158* Le v Glos (Leicester) 2010. Nt HS 54 v Surrey (Nottingham) 2016. BB 1-64 Le v Glos (Leicester) 2008. LO HS 135* Le v Somerset (Leicester) 2013 (Y40). T20 HS 102.

‡NQ**SODHI**, Inderbir Singh ('**Ish**'), b Ludhiana, Punjab, India 31 Oct 1992. RHB, LBG. Northern Districts 2012-13 to date. Joins Nottinghamshire in 2017 for T20 only. Big Bash: AS 2016-17. **Tests** (NZ): 14 (2013-14 to 2016-17); HS 63 v P (Abu Dhabi) 2014-15; BB 4-60 v Z (Bulawayo) 2016. **LOI** (NZ): 15 (2015 to 2016-17); HS 5 v SA (Durban) 2015; BB 3-38 v Z (Harare) 2015. **IT20** (NZ): 12 (2014 to 2016-17); HS 0*; BB 3-18 v I (Nagpur) 2015-16. F-c Tours (NZ): WI 2014; I 2013-14, 2016-17; SL 2013-14 (NZ A); Z 2016; B 2013-14; UAE 2014-15 (v P). HS 82* ND v Otago (Dunedin) 2014-15. BB 7-102 ND v Otago (Dunedin) 2015-16. LO HS 35 ND v Wellington (Mt Maunganui) 2014-15. LO BB 4-10 NZ A v Sri Lanka A (Bristol) 2014. T20 HS 19. T20 BB 6-11 – 6th best analysis in all T20.

NQ**TAYLOR, Brendan** Ross Murray, b Harare, Zimbabwe 6 Feb 1986. RHB, WK, OB. Mashonaland 2001-02 to 2004-05. Northerns (Zim) 2007-08 to 2008-09. MRW 2009-10 to 2013-14. Nottinghamshire debut/cap 2015. **Tests** (Z): 23 (2004 to 2014-15, 13 as captain); HS 171 v B (Harare) 2013; BB – . **LOI** (Z): 167 (2004 to 2014-15, 34 as captain); HS 145* v SA (Bloemfontein) 2010-11; BB 3-54 v B (Dhaka) 2004-05. **IT20** (Z): 26 (2006-07 to 2013-14, 17 as captain); HS 75* v NZ (Hamilton) 2011-12; BB 1-16 v SA (Kimberley) 2010-11. F-c Tours (Z) (C=Captain): SA 2004-05, 2007-08; WI 2010, 2012-13C; NZ 2011-12C; I 2005-06; P 2004-05, 2007-08; B 2003-04 (ZA), 2004-05, 2014-15C. 1000 runs (1+1); most – 1070 (2015). HS 217 MWR v SR (Masvingo) 2009-10. Nt HS 152 v Somerset (Taunton) 2015. BB 2-36 Mashonaland v Manicaland (Mutare) 2003-04. LO HS 145* (*see LOI*). LO BB 5-28 Zim A v India A (Harare) 2004. T20 HS 101*. T20 BB 3-38.

WESSELS, Mattheus Hendrik ('**Riki**') (Woodridge C, Pt Elizabeth; Northampton U), b Marogudoore, Queensland, Australia 12 Nov 1985. Left Australia when 2 months old. Qualified for England after gaining a UK passport in July 2016. Son of K.C.Wessels (OFS, Sussex, WP, NT, Q, EP, GW, Australia and South Africa 1973-74 to 1999-00). 5'11". RHB, WK. Squad No 9. MCC 2004. Northamptonshire 2005-09. Nondescripts 2007-08. MWR 2009-10 to 2011-12. Nottinghamshire debut 2011; cap 2014. Big Bash: SS 2014-15. 1000 runs (2); most – 1213 (2014). HS 199 v Sussex (Hove) 2012. BB 1-10 MWR v MT (Bulawayo) 2009-10. LO HS 146 v Northants (Nottingham) 2016 (RLC). LO BB 1-0 MWR v MT (Bulawayo) 2009-10. T20 HS 97 v Durham (Chester-le-St) 2015 – Nt record.

WOOD, Luke (Portland CS, Worksop), b Sheffield, Yorks 2 Aug 1995. 5'9". LHB, LM. Squad No 14. Debut (Nottinghamshire) 2014. Nottinghamshire 2nd XI debut 2012. England U19 2014. HS 100 v Sussex (Nottingham) 2015. BB 5-40 v Cambridge MCCU (Cambridge) 2016. CC BB 3-27 v Sussex (Horsham) 2015. LO HS 52 and LO BB 2-44 v Leics (Leicester) 2016 (RLC). T20 HS 0. T20 BB – .

RELEASED/RETIRED

(Having made a County 1st XI appearance in 2016)

[NQ]**BIRD, Jackson** Munro (St Pius X C, Sydney; St Ignatius C, Riverview), b Paddington, Sydney, Australia 11 Dec 1986. RHB, RFM. Tasmania 2011-12 to date. Hampshire 2015. Nottinghamshire 2016; cap 2016. Big Bash: MS 2011-12 to 2014-15. SS 2015-16 to date. **Tests** (A): 8 (2012-13 to 2016-17); HS 19* v P (Brisbane) 2016-17; BB 5-59 v NZ (Christchurch) 2015-16. F-c Tours (A): E 2012 (Aus A), 2013, 2013; NZ 2015-16; I 2016-17 (Aus A). HS 39 Tas v SA (Adelaide) 2016-17. Nt HS 23 v Yorks (Nottingham) 2016. 50 wkts (0+1): 53 (2011-12). BB 7-45 (10-92 match) Tas v NSW (Hobart) 2015-16. Nt BB 4-56 v Surrey (Nottingham) 2016. LO HS 6 Tas v NSW (Sydney) 2016-17. LO BB 3-39 Tas v S Aus (Adelaide) 2011-12. T20 HS 14*. T20 BB 4-31.

IMRAN TAHIR – *see DERBYSHIRE.*

[NQ]**RUSSELL, Andre** Dwayne, b Jamaica 29 Apr 1988. RHB, RF. Jamaica 2006-07 to 2013-14. IPL: DD 2012-13, KKR 2014-16. Big Bash: MR 2014-15, ST 2015-16 to date. Nottinghamshire 2016 (T20 only). **Tests** (WI): 1 (2010-11); HS 2 and BB 1-73 v SL (Galle). **LOI** (WI): 51 (2010-11 to 2015-16); HS 92* v I (North Sound) 2011; BB 4-35 v I (Kingston) 2011. **IT20** (WI): 43 (2011 to 2016); HS 43* v I (Mumbai) 2015-16; BB 2-10 v B (Dhaka) 2013-14. F-c Tours (WI): E 2010 (WI A); SL 2010-11. HS 128 WI A v Bangladesh A (North Sound) 2011-12. BB 5-36 WI A v Bangladesh A (Gros Islet) 2011-12. LO HS 132* (in 56 balls, inc 13 sixes) Sagicor HPC v Bangladesh A (Bridgetown) 2014. LO BB 6-28 Sagicor HPC v Bangladesh A (Lucas Street) 2014. T20 HS 100. T20 BB 4-11.

TAYLOR, James William Arthur (Shrewsbury S), b Nottingham 6 Jan 1990. 5'6". RHB, LB. Leicestershire 2008-11; cap 2009. Nottinghamshire 2012-16; cap 2012; l-o captain 2014-15. Sussex (1 game) 2013. MCC 2010. Shropshire 2007. YC 2009. **Tests**: 7 (2012); HS 76 v P (Sharjah) 2015-16. **LOI**: 27 (2011 to 2015-16); HS 101 v A (Manchester) 2015. F-c Tours: SA 2015-16; WI 2010-11 (EL); SL 2013-14 (EL); UAE 2015-16 (v P). 1000 runs (5); most – 1602 (2011). HS 291 v Sussex (Horsham) 2015. BB – . LO HS 146* v Derbys (Nottingham) 2014 (RLC). LO BB 4-61 Le v Warwks (Leicester) 2010 (CB40). T20 HS 62*. T20 BB 1-10.

WOOD, Samuel Kenneth William (Colonel Frank Seely S, Nottingham), b Nottingham 3 Apr 1993. 5'11". LHB, OB. Nottinghamshire 2011-14. Nottinghamshire 2nd XI debut 2008, aged 15y 40d. England U19 2010-11. HS 45 and BB 3-64 v Surrey (Oval) 2012. LO HS 32 v Bangladesh A (Nottingham) 2013. LO BB 2-24 v Lancs (Manchester) 2011 (CB40). T20 HS 17. T20 BB 2-21.

W.R.S.Gidman left the staff without making a County 1st XI appearance in 2016.

NOTTINGHAMSHIRE 2016

RESULTS SUMMARY

	Place	Won	Lost	Drew	NR
Specsavers County Champ (1st Division)	9th	1	9	6	
All First-Class Matches		2	9	6	
Royal London One-Day Cup (North Group)	6th	3	4		1
NatWest t20 Blast (North Group)	SF	9	3		4

SPECSAVERS COUNTY CHAMPIONSHIP AVERAGES

BATTING AND FIELDING

Cap		*M*	*I*	*NO*	*HS*	*Runs*	*Avge*	*100*	*50*	*Ct/St*
2013	S.J.Mullaney	16	30	2	165	1009	36.03	3	3	19
2015	B.R.M.Taylor	13	24	2	114	759	34.50	2	3	10
2008	S.R.Patel	16	28	–	124	957	34.17	2	6	12
2008	S.C.J.Broad	4	6	–	55	191	31.83	–	1	3
	J.D.Libby	11	21	–	144	627	29.85	1	3	3
1999	C.M.W.Read	12	21	4	101	492	28.94	1	3	33/2
2012	M.J.Lumb	16	29	–	108	817	28.17	1	3	6
2014	M.H.Wessels	12	21	2	159*	489	25.73	1	3	21/2
2016	D.T.Christian	3	5	1	31	96	24.00			2
	G.P.Smith	7	12	–	54	257	21.41	–	1	3
	B.A.Hutton	12	19	3	74	337	21.06	–	2	3
	T.J.Moores	4	7		41	123	17.57	–	–	–
	Imran Tahir	7	12	4	25	127	15.87	–	–	3
	L.Wood	3	5	1	27	55	13.75	–	–	2
2014	L.J.Fletcher	6	10	2	32	88	11.00	–	–	3
2016	J.T.Ball	11	17	1	33	153	9.56			3
2016	J.M.Bird	5	8	–	23	51	6.37	–	–	1
	M.Carter	3	5	1	8	20	5.00	–	–	2
2014	H.F.Gurney	13	21	9	16	56	4.66	–	–	1

Also batted: A.D.Hales (2 matches – cap 2011) 36, 34, 73; W.T.Root (1) 10, 66*.

BOWLING

	O	*M*	*R*	*W*	*Avge*	*Best*	*5wI*	*10wM*
J.T.Ball	343	64	1133	49	23.12	6- 57	3	–
S.C.J.Broad	116	35	312	10	31.20	3- 50	–	–
L.J.Fletcher	183.1	48	469	15	31.26	4- 25	–	–
H.F.Gurney	412.3	76	1304	41	31.80	6- 61	2	–
S.R.Patel	351.5	64	1147	32	35.84	4- 71	–	–
Imran Tahir	288.4	51	930	25	37.20	7-112	1	–
J.M.Bird	157.3	27	558	15	37.20	4- 56	–	–
B.A.Hutton	268.3	47	1027	26	39.50	3- 54	–	–
S.J.Mullaney	139.5	36	430	10	43.00	3- 54	–	–

Also bowled: M.Carter 76-8-316-3; D.T.Christian 15-1-80-1; J.D.Libby 4-1-8-0; W.T.Root 2-0-5-0; L.Wood 80-13-297-4.

The First-Class Averages (pp 226–242) give the records of Nottinghamshire players in all first-class county matches (Nottinghamshire's other opponents being Cambridge MCCU), with the exception of S.C.J.Broad, L.J.Fletcher, A.D.Hales, J.D.Libby, T.J.Moores and W.T.Root, whose first-class figures for Nottinghamshire are as above, and:
J.T.Ball 12-18-2-33-171-10.68-0-0-1ct. 355-68-1169-53-22.05-6/57-3-0.

NOTTINGHAMSHIRE RECORDS

FIRST-CLASS CRICKET

Highest Total	For 791			v	Essex	Chelmsford	2007
	V 781-7d			by	Northants	Northampton	1995
Lowest Total	For 13			v	Yorkshire	Nottingham	1901
	V 16			by	Derbyshire	Nottingham	1879
	16			by	Surrey	The Oval	1880
Highest Innings	For 312*	W.W.Keeton		v	Middlesex	The Oval	1939
	V 345	C.G.Macartney		for	Australians	Nottingham	1921

Highest Partnership for each Wicket

1st	406*	D.J.Bicknell/G.E.Welton	v	Warwicks	Birmingham	2000
2nd	398	A.Shrewsbury/W.Gunn	v	Sussex	Nottingham	1890
3rd	367	W.Gunn/J.R.Gunn	v	Leics	Nottingham	1903
4th	361	A.O.Jones/J.R.Gunn	v	Essex	Leyton	1905
5th	359	D.J.Hussey/C.M.W.Read	v	Essex	Nottingham	2007
6th	372*	K.P.Pietersen/J.E.Morris	v	Derbyshire	Derby	2001
7th	301	C.C.Lewis/B.N.French	v	Durham	Chester-le-St[2]	1993
8th	220	G.F.H.Heane/R.Winrow	v	Somerset	Nottingham	1935
9th	170	J.C.Adams/K.P.Evans	v	Somerset	Taunton	1994
10th	152	E.B.Alletson/W.Riley	v	Sussex	Hove	1911
	152	U.Afzaal/A.J.Harris	v	Worcs	Nottingham	2000

Best Bowling	For	10-66	K.Smales	v	Glos	Stroud	1956
(Innings)	V	10-10	H.Verity	for	Yorkshire	Leeds	1932
Best Bowling	For	17-89	F.C.L.Matthews	v	Northants	Nottingham	1923
(Match)	V	17-89	W.G.Grace	for	Glos	Cheltenham	1877

Most Runs – Season	2620	W.W.Whysall	(av 53.46)	1929
Most Runs – Career	31592	G.Gunn	(av 35.69)	1902-32
Most 100s – Season	9	W.W.Whysall		1928
	9	M.J.Harris		1971
	9	B.C.Broad		1990
Most 100s – Career	65	J.Hardstaff jr		1930-55
Most Wkts – Season	181	B.Dooland	(av 14.96)	1954
Most Wkts – Career	1653	T.G.Wass	(av 20.34)	1896-1920
Most Career W-K Dismissals	957	T.W.Oates	(733 ct; 224 st)	1897-1925
Most Career Catches in the Field	466	A.O.Jones		1892-1914

LIMITED-OVERS CRICKET

Highest Total	**50ov**	445-8		v	Northants	Nottingham	2016
	40ov	296-7		v	Somerset	Taunton	2002
	T20	220-4		v	Leics	Leicester	2014
Lowest Total	**50ov**	74		v	Leics	Leicester	1987
	40ov	57		v	Glos	Nottingham	2009
	T20	91		v	Lancashire	Manchester	2006
Highest Innings	**50ov**	184	M.J.Lumb	v	Northants	Nottingham	2016
	40ov	150*	A.D.Hales	v	Worcs	Nottingham	2009
	T20	97	M.H.Wessels	v	Durham	Chester-le-St[2]	2015
Best Bowling	**50ov**	6-10	K.P.Evans	v	Northumb	Jesmond	1994
	40ov	6-12	R.J.Hadlee	v	Lancashire	Nottingham	1980
	T20	5-22	G.G.White	v	Lancashire	Nottingham	2013

SOMERSET

Formation of Present Club: 18 August 1875
Inaugural First-Class Match: 1882
Colours: Black, White and Maroon
Badge: Somerset Dragon
County Champions: (0); best – 2nd (Div 1) 2001, 2010, 2012, 2016
Gillette/NatWest/C&G Trophy Winners: (3) 1979, 1983, 2001
Benson and Hedges Cup Winners: (2) 1981, 1982
Sunday League Winners: (1) 1979
Twenty20 Cup Winners: (1) 2005

Chief Executive: Guy Lavender, Cooper Associates County Ground, Taunton TA1 1JT • Tel: 0845 337 1875 • Fax: 01823 332395 • Email: enquiries@somersetcountycc.co.uk • Web: www.somersetcricketclub.co.uk • Twitter: @SomersetCCC (56,769 followers)

Director of Cricket: Matt Maynard. **Assistant/Bowling Coach**: Jason Kerr. **Academy/2nd XI Coach**: Steve Snell. **Captains**: T.B.Abell (f-c) and J.Allenby (l-o). **Overseas Player**: D.Elgar. **2017 Testimonial**: J.C.Hildreth. **Groundsman**: Simon Lee. **Scorers**: Gerald Stickley and Polly Rhodes. ‡ New registration. [NQ] Not qualified for England.

ABELL, Thomas Benjamin (Taunton S; Exeter U), b Taunton 5 Mar 1994. 5'10". RHB, RM. Squad No 28. Debut (Somerset) 2014; captain 2017. Somerset 2nd XI debut 2010. HS 135 v Lancs (Manchester) 2016. BB 1-11 v Yorks (Taunton) 2015. LO HS 106 v Sussex (Taunton) 2016 (RLC). T20 HS 7.

ALLENBY, James (Christ Church GS, Perth), b Perth, W Australia 12 Sep 1982. 6'0". RHB, RM. Squad No 6. Leicestershire 2006-09. Glamorgan 2009-14; cap 2010; captain (T20) 2014. Somerset debut 2015; captain (l-o) 2016 to date. 1000 runs (1): 1202 (2013). HS 138* Le v Bangladesh A (Leicester) 2008 and 138* Gm v Leics (Leicester) 2013. Sm HS 64 v Notts (Nottingham) 2015. 50 wkts (1): 54 (2014). BB 6-54 (10-128 match) Gm v Hants (Cardiff) 2014. Sm BB 4-67 v Middx (Taunton) 2016. LO HS 91* Le v Middx (Lord's) 2007 (P40). LO BB 5-43 Le v Derbys (Leicester) 2007 (FPT). T20 HS 110. T20 BB 5-21 Le v Lancs (Manchester) 2008, inc 4 wkts in 4 balls.

BARTLETT, George Anthony (Millfield S), b Frimley, Surrey 14 Mar 1998. RHB, OB. Somerset 2nd XI debut 2015. England U19 2016 to 2016-17. Awaiting 1st XI debut.

BESS, Dominic Mark (Blundell's S), b Exeter, Devon 22 Jul 1997. Cousin of Z.G.G.Bess (Devon 2015 to date) and J.J.Bess (Devon 2007 to date). RHB, OB. Debut (Somerset) 2016. Somerset 2nd XI debut 2013. Devon 2015 to date. HS 41 v Notts (Taunton) 2016. BB 6-28 v Warwks (Taunton) 2016. T20 HS 1. T20 BB 1-31.

[NQ]**DAVEY, Josh**ua Henry (Culford S), b Aberdeen, Scotland 3 Aug 1990. RHB, RMF. Squad No 38. Middlesex 2010-12. Scotland 2011-12 to date. Somerset debut 2015. Suffolk 2014. **LOI** (Scot): 28 (2010 to 2016-17); HS 64 v Afghanistan (Sharjah) 2012-13; BB 6-28 v Afghanistan (Abu Dhabi) 2014-15. **IT20** (Scot): 14 (2012 to 2016-17); HS 24 v Z (Nagpur) 2015-16; BB 4-34 v Netherlands (Abu Dhabi) 2016-17. HS 72 M v Oxford MCCU (Oxford) 2010 – on debut. CC HS 61 M v Glos (Bristol) 2010. Sm HS 15 v New Zealanders (Taunton) 2015. BB 4-53 Scot v Afghanistan (Abu Dhabi) 2012-13. CC BB 2-39 v Durham (Chester-le-St) 2016. LO HS 91 Scot v Warwks (Birmingham) 2011 (CB40). LO BB 6-28 (*see LOI*). T20 HS 24. T20 BB 4-34.

DAVIES, Ryan Christopher (Sandwich TS), b Thanet, Kent 5 Nov 1996. 5'9". RHB, WK. Kent 2015. Kent 2nd XI debut 2013. England U19 2014-15 to 2015. HS 86 v Lancs (Manchester) 2016, sharing Sm record 8th wkt partnership of 236 with P.D.Trego. LO HS 46 v Warwks (Birmingham) 2016 (RLC). T20 HS 6.

‡**DAVIES, Steven** Michael (King Charles I S, Kidderminster), b Bromsgrove, Worcs 17 Jun 1986. 5'10". LHB, WK. Worcestershire 2005-09. Surrey 2010-16; cap 2011. MCC 2006-07, 2011. **LOI**: 8 (2009-10 to 2010-11); HS 87 v P (Chester-le-St) 2010. **IT20**: 5 (2008-09 to 2010-11); HS 33 v P (Cardiff) 2010. F-c Tours: A 2010-11; B 2006-07 (Eng A); UAE 2011-12 (v P). 1000 runs (6); most – 1147 (2016). HS 200* Sy v Glamorgan (Cardiff) 2015. LO HS 127* Sy v Hants (Oval) 2013 (Y40). T20 HS 99*.

NQ**ELGAR**, Dean, b Welkom, OFS, South Africa 11 Jun 1987. LHB, SLA. Free State 2005-06 to 2010-11. Eagles 2006-07 to 2009-10. Knights 2010-11 to 2013-14. Somerset 2013, returning in 2017. Titans 2014-15 to date. Surrey 2015. **Tests** (SA): 33 (2012-13 to 2016-17); HS 140 v NZ (Dunedin) 2016-17; BB 4-22 v I (Mohali) 2015-16. **LOI** (SA): 6 (2012 to 2015-16); HS 42 v E (Oval) 2012; BB 1-11 v E (Southampton) 2012. F-c Tours (SA): A 2012-13, 2016 (SA A), 2016-17; NZ 2016-17; I 2015-16; SL 2010 (SA A), 2014; Z 2014; B 2010 (SA A), 2015; UAE (v P) 2013-14; Ire 2012 (SA A). 1000 runs (0+1): 1193 (2009-10). HS 268 SA A v Australia A (Pretoria) 2013. Sy HS 98 v Glos (Oval) 2015. Sm HS 33 and CC BB 1-26 v Durham (Taunton) 2013. BB 4-22 (*see Tests*). LO HS 117 Knights v Dolphins (Pietermaritzburg) 2011-12. LO BB 3-43 Titans v Dolphins (Durban) 2014-15. T20 HS 72. T20 BB 4-23.

GREEN, Benjamin George Frederick (Exeter S), b Exeter, Devon 28 Sep 1997. RHB, RFM. Somerset 2nd XI debut 2014. Devon 2014-15. England U19 2014-15 to 2015. Awaiting f-c debut. T20 HS 12*.

GREGORY, Lewis (Hele's S, Plympton), b Plymouth, Devon 24 May 1992. 6'0". RHB, RMF. Squad No 24. Debut (Somerset) 2011; cap 2015. Devon 2008. HS 73* v Yorks (Leeds) 2016. BB 6-47 (11-122 match) v Northants (Northampton) 2014. LO HS 105* v Durham (Taunton) 2014 (RLC). LO BB 4-23 v Essex (Chelmsford) 2016 (RLC). T20 HS 37*. T20 BB 4-15.

GROENEWALD, Timothy Duncan (Maritzburg C; South Africa U), b Pietermaritzburg, South Africa 10 Jan 1984. 6'0". RHB, RFM. Squad No 5. Debut Cambridge UCCE 2006. Warwickshire 2006-08. Derbyshire 2009-14; cap 2011. Somerset debut 2014; cap 2016. HS 78 Wa v Bangladesh A (Birmingham) 2008. CC HS 76 Wa v Durham (Chester-le-St) 2006. Sm HS 47 and Sm BB 5-65 v New Zealanders (Taunton) 2015. BB 6-50 De v Surrey (Croydon) 2009. Hat-trick De v Essex (Chelmsford) 2014. LO HS 57 v Warwks (Birmingham) 2014 (RLC). LO BB 4-22 De v Worcs (Worcester) 2011 (CB40). T20 HS 41. T20 BB 4-21.

HILDRETH, James Charles (Millfield S), b Milton Keynes, Bucks 9 Sep 1984. 5'10", RHB, RMF. Squad No 25. Debut (Somerset) 2003; cap 2007; testimonial 2017. MCC 2015. F-c Tour (EL): WI 2010-11. 1000 runs (6); most – 1620 (2015). HS 303* v Warwks (Taunton) 2009. BB 2-39 v Hants (Taunton) 2004. LO HS 151 v Scotland (Taunton) 2009 (FPT). LO BB 2-26 v Worcs (Worcester) 2008 (FPT). T20 HS 107*. T20 BB 3-24.

HOSE, Adam John (Carisbrooke S), b Newport, IoW 25 Oct 1992. RHB, RMF. Squad No 21. Debut (Somerset) 2016. MCC YC 2011-14. Glamorgan 2nd XI 2012. Hampshire 2nd XI 2014. Kent 2nd XI 2014. HS 10 v Pakistanis (Taunton) 2016. LO HS 77 v Essex (Chelmsford) 2016 (RLC). T20 HS 20.

LEACH, Matthew **Jack** (Bishop Fox's Community S, Taunton; Richard Huish C; UWIC), b Taunton 22 Jun 1991. 6'0". LHB, SLA. Squad No 17. Cardiff MCCU 2012. Somerset debut 2012. Dorset 2011. F-c Tours (EL): SL 2016-17; UAE 2016-17 (v Afghan). HS 43 v Yorks (Leeds) 2014. 50 wkts (1): 68 (2016). BB 7-106 (11-180 match) v Warwks (Taunton) 2015. LO HS 18 v Surrey (Oval) 2014 (RLC). LO BB 3-7 EL v UAE (Dubai, DSC) 2016-17.

[NQ]**LEASK, Michael** Alexander, b Aberdeen, Scotland 29 Oct 1990. RHB, OB. Northamptonshire (l-o only) 2014. Somerset 2nd XI debut 2015. Awaiting f-c debut. **LOI** (Scot): 16 (2013-14 to 2016-17); HS 50 and BB 1-26 v Ireland (Dublin) 2014. **IT20** (Scot): 14 (2013 to 2016-17); HS 58 v Netherlands (Abu Dhabi) 2013-14; BB 3-20 v UAE (Edinburgh) 2015. LO HS 50 (*see LOI*). LO BB 2-23 Scot v Nepal (Ayr) 2015. T20 HS 58. T20 BB 3-20.

[NQ]**MYBURGH, Johannes** Gerhardus (Pretoria BHS; U of SA), b Pretoria, South Africa 22 Oct 1980. Elder brother of S.J.Myburgh (Northerns, KZN and Netherlands 2005-06 to date), brother-in-law of F.de Wet (Northerns, NW, Lions, Hampshire, Dolphins and South Africa 2001-02 to 2011-12). 5'7". RHB, OB. Squad No 9. Northerns 1997-98 to 2006-07. Titans 2004-05. Canterbury 2007-08 to 2009-10. Hampshire 2011. Durham 2012. Somerset debut 2014. EU qualified through wife's visa. HS 203 Northerns B v Easterns (Pretoria) 1997-98. Sm HS 150 v Durham MCCU (Taunton Vale) 2015. CC HS 118 v Durham (Taunton) 2015. BB 4-56 Canterbury v ND (Hamilton) 2008-09. Sm BB 3-57 v Yorks (Taunton) 2015. LO HS 112 Canterbury v Auckland (Christchurch) 2009-10. LO BB 2-22 Canterbury v CD (Christchurch) 2009-10. T20 HS 88. T20 BB 3-16.

OVERTON, Craig (West Buckland S), b Barnstaple, Devon 10 Apr 1994. Twin brother of Jamie Overton (*see below*). 6'5". RHB, RMF. Squad No 12. Debut (Somerset) 2012; cap 2016. Somerset 2nd XI debut 2011. Devon 2010-11. HS 138 v Hants (Taunton) 2016. BB 6-74 v Warwks (Birmingham) 2015. LO HS 60* EL v Sri Lanka A (Dambulla) 2016-17. LO BB 3-29 EL v UAE (Dubai, DSC) 2016-17. T20 HS 15. T20 BB 1-23.

OVERTON, Jamie (West Buckland S), b Barnstaple, Devon 10 Apr 1994. Twin brother of Carig Overton (*see above*). 6'5". RHB, RFM. Squad No 11. Debut (Somerset) 2012. Somerset 2nd XI debut 2011. Devon 2011. HS 56 v Warwks (Birmingham) 2014. BB 6-95 v Middx (Taunton) 2013. LO HS 40* v Glos (Taunton) 2016 (RLC). LO BB 4-42 v Durham (Chester-le-St) 2012 (CB40). T20 HS 31. T20 BB 4-22.

ROUSE, Timothy David (Kingswood S, Bath; Cardiff U), b Sheffield, Yorks 9 Apr 1996. Younger brother of H.P.Rouse (Leeds/Bradford MCCU 2013-15). RHB, OB. Cardiff MCCU 2015-16. Somerset debut 2016. Somerset 2nd XI debut 2012. HS 41 v Pakistanis (Taunton) 2016. BB 1-3 CfU v Glamorgan (Cardiff) 2015.

SALE, Oliver Richard Trethowan (Sherborne S), b Newcastle-under-Lyme, Staffs 30 Sep 1995. RHB, RFM. Somerset 2nd XI debut 2014. Awaiting f-c debut. T20 HS 1.

TREGO, Peter David (Wyvern CS, W-s M), b Weston-super-Mare 12 Jun 1981. 6'0". RHB, RMF. Squad No 7. Somerset 2000-02, 2006 to date; cap 2007; benefit 2015. Kent 2003. Middlesex 2005. C Districts 2013-14. MCC 2013. Herefordshire 2005. 1000 runs (1): 1070 (2016). HS 154* v Lancs (Manchester) 2016, sharing Sm record 8th wkt partnership of 236 with R.C.Davies. 50 wkts (1): 50 (2012). BB 7-84 (11-153 match) v Yorks (Leeds) 2014. LO HS 147 v Glamorgan (Taunton) 2010 (CB40). LO BB 5-40 EL v West Indies A (Worcester) 2010. T20 HS 94*. T20 BB 4-27.

TRESCOTHICK, Marcus Edward (Sir Bernard Lovell S), b Keynsham 25 Dec 1975. 6'2". LHB, RM, occ WK. Squad No 2. Debut (Somerset) 1993; cap 1999; joint captain 2002; benefit 2008; captain 2010-15. PCA 2000, 2009, 2011. *Wisden* 2004. MBE 2005. **Tests**: 76 (2000 to 2006, 2 as captain); HS 219 v SA (Oval) 2003; BB 1-34 v P (Karachi) 2000-01. **LOI**: 123 (2000 to 2006, 10 as captain); HS 137 v P (Lord's) 2001; BB 2-7 v Z (Manchester) 2000. **IT20**: 3 (2005 to 2006); HS 72 v SL (Southampton) 2006. F-c Tours: A 2002-03; SA 2004-05; WI 2003-04; NZ 1999-00 (Eng A), 2001-02; I 2001-02, 2005-06 (*part*); P 2000-01, 2005-06; SL 2000-01, 2003-04; B 1999-00 (Eng A), 2003-04. 1000 runs (8); most – 1817 (2009). HS 284 v Northants (Northampton) 2007. BB 4-36 (inc hat-trick) v Young A (Taunton) 1995. CC BB 4-82 v Yorks (Leeds) 1998. Hat-trick 1995 (*see above*). LO HS 184 v Glos (Taunton) 2008 (P40) – Sm l-o record. LO BB 4-50 v Northants (Northampton) 2000 (NL). T20 HS 108*.

[NQ]**VAN DER MERWE, Roelof** Erasmus, b Johannesburg, South Africa 31 Dec 1984. RHB, SLA. Northerns 2006-07 to 2013-14. Titans 2007-08 to 2014-15. Netherlands 2015 to date. Somerset debut 2016. IPL: RCB 2009 to 2009-10. DD 2011-13. Big Bash: BH 2011-12. **LOI** (SA): 13 (2008-09 to 2010); HS 12 v I (Gwalior) 2009-10; BB 3-27 v Z (Centurion) 2009-10. **IT20** (SA/Neth): 24 (13 for SA 2008-09 to 2010; 11 for Neth 2015 to 2016-17); HS 48 v A (Centurion) 2008-09; BB 2-3 v Ireland (Dharmasala) 2015-16. HS 205* Titans v Warriors (Benoni) 2014-15. Sm HS 102* v Hants (Taunton) 2016. BB 4-45 v Durham (Taunton) 2016. LO HS 93 Titans v Lions (Centurion) 2010-11. LO BB 5-26 Titans v Knights (Centurion) 2012-13. T20 HS 89*. T20 BB 3-16.

[NQ]**VAN MEEKEREN, Paul** Adriaan, b Amsterdam, Netherlands 15 Jan 1993. RHB, RMF. Netherlands 2013 to date. Somerset debut 2016. Glamorgan 2nd XI 2016. **LOI** (Neth); 2 (2013 to 2013-14); HS 15* and BB 1-54 v SA (Amstelveen) 2013. **IT20** (Neth): 18 (2013 to 2016-17); HS 18 v Hong Kong (Dubai, DSC) 2016-17; BB 4-11 v Ireland (Dharamsala) 2015-16. HS 34 and BB 3-44 Neth v PNG (Amstelveen) 2015. Sm HS 0 and Sm BB 3-78 v Pakistanis (Taunton) 2016. LO HS 15* (*see LOI*). LO BB 3-42 Neth v Kent (Deventer) 2013 (Y40). T20 HS 18. T20 BB 4-11.

WALLER, Maximilian Thomas Charles (Millfield S; Bournemouth U), b Salisbury, Wiltshire 3 March 1988. 6'0". RHB, LB. Squad No 10. Debut (Somerset) 2009. Dorset 2007-08. No f-c appearances since 2012. HS 28 v Hants (Southampton) 2009. BB 3-33 v Cardiff MCCU (Taunton Vale) 2012. CC BB 2-27 v Sussex (Hove) 2009. LO HS 25* v Glamorgan (Taunton) 2013 (Y40). LO BB 3-39 v Middx (Taunton) 2010 (Y40). T20 HS 11*. T20 BB 4-16.

RELEASED/RETIRED

(Having made a County 1st XI appearance in 2016)

BARROW, Alexander William Rodgerson (King's C, Taunton), b Frome 6 May 1992. 5'7". RHB, RM/OB. Somerset 2011-16. HS 88 v Northants (Taunton) 2014. BB 1-4 v Hants (Southampton) 2011. LO HS 72 v Durham (Chester-le-St) 2012 (CB40). T20 HS 17*.

[NQ]**GAYLE, Chris**topher Henry, b Kingston, Jamaica 21 Sep 1979. LHB, OB. Jamaica 1998-99 to 2012-13. Worcestershire 2005. Somerset 2015-16 (T20 only). IPL: KKR 2009 to 2009-10. RCB 2011 to date. Big Bash: ST 2011-12 to 2012-13. MR 2015-16. **Tests** (WI): 103 (1999-00 to 2014, 20 as captain); HS 333 v SL (Galle) 2010-11; BB 5-34 v E (Birmingham) 2004. **LOI** (WI): 266+3 for ICC (1999 to 2014-15, 53 as captain); HS 215 v Z (Canberra) 2014-15 – WI record and 4th highest in all LOI; BB 5-46 v A (St George's) 2003. **IT20** (WI): 50 (2005-06 to 2015-16, 17 as captain); HS 117 v SA (Johannesburg) 2007; BB 2-15 v A (Hobart) 2009-10. F-c Tours (WI)(C=captain): E 2000, 2002 (WI A), 2004, 2007, 2009C; A 2005-06, 2009-10C; SA 2003-04, 2007-08C; NZ 2005-06, 2008-09C; I 1998-99 (WI A), 2002-03, 2013-14; P 2006-07; SL 2001-02, 2010-11; Z 2001, 2003-04; B 2002-03, 2012-13; UAE 2001-02. 1000 runs (0+1): 1271 (2000-01). HS 333 (*see Tests*). CC HS 57 and CC BB 2-18 Wo v Leics (Worcester) 2005. BB 5-34 (*see Tests*). LO HS 215 (*see LOI*). LO BB 5-46 (*see LOI*). T20 HS 175* RCB v PW (Bangalore) 2013 – world record T20 score. T20 BB 4-22.

[NQ]**JAYAWARDENA**, Denagamage Proboth **Mahela** De Silva (Nalanda C, Colombo), b Colombo, Sri Lanka 27 May 1977. 5'9". RHB, RM. Sinhalese SC 1996-97 to 2012-13. Sussex 2015 (T20 only). Somerset 2016 (l-o & T20 only). IPL: KXIP 2007-10. DD 2012-13. Big Bash: AS 2015-16. *Wisden* 2006. **Tests** (SL): 149 (1997 to 2014, 38 as captain); 1000 runs (3); most – 1194 (2009); HS 374 v SA (Colombo) 2006; BB 2-32 v P (Galle) 2000-01. **LOI** (SL): 448 (1997-98 to 2014-15, 129 as captain); 1000 runs (4); most – 1260 (2001); HS 144 v E (Leeds) 2011; BB 2-56 v K (Southampton) 1999. **IT20** (SL): 55 (2006 to 2013-14); HS 100 v Z (Providence) 2010. F-c Tours (SL) (C=captain): E 1998, 2002, 2006C, 2011, 2014; A 2004, 2007-08C, 2012-13; SA 1997-98, 2000-01, 2002-03, 2011-12; WI 2003, 2007-08C; NZ 2004-05, 2006-07C; I 1997-98, 2005-06, 2009-10; P 1998-99, 1999-00, 2001-02, 2004-05, 2008-09C; Z 1999-00, 2004; B 1998-99, 2005-06C, 2008-09C, 2013-14; UAE 2011-12 (v P), 2013-14 (v P). 1000 runs (0+2); most 1426 (2001-02). HS 374 (*see Tests*). BB 5-72 Sinhalese v Colts (Colombo) 1996-97. LO HS 163* Sinhalese v Bloomfield (Colombo) 2010-11. LO BB 3-25 Sinhalese v Sebastianites (Colombo) 1998-99. T20 HS 116. T20 BB 2-22.

[NQ]**ROGERS, Christopher** John Llewellyn (Wesley C, Perth; Curtin U, Perth), b St George, Sydney, Australia 31 Aug 1977. Son of W.J.Rogers (NSW 1968-69 to 1969-70). 5'10". LHB, LBG. W Australia 1998-99 to 2007-08. Derbyshire 2004-10; cap 2008; captain 2008 (*part*) to 2010 (*part*). Leicestershire 2005. Northamptonshire 2006-07. Victoria 2008-09 to 2014-15. Middlesex 2011-14; cap 2011; captain 2013-14. Somerset 2016; captain 2016. MCC 2011. Big Bash: ST 2012-13. **Tests** (A): 25 (2007-08 to 2015), HS 173 v E (Lord's) 2015. F-c Tours (A): E 2013, 2015; SA 2013-14; P 2007-08 (Aus A); UAE 2014-15 (v P). 1000 runs (9+2); most – 1536 (2013). HS 319 Nh v Glos (Northampton) 2006. Sm HS 132 (and 100*) v Notts (Taunton) 2016. BB 1-16 Nh v Leics (Northampton) 2006. LO HS 140 Vic v S Aus (Melbourne) 2009-10. LO BB 2-22 Nh v Durham (Northampton) 2006. T20 HS 58.

[NQ]**YASIR ARAFAT** Satti (Gordon C, Rawalpindi), b Rawalpindi, Pakistan 12 Mar 1982. 5'9½". RHB, RFM. Rawalpindi 1997-98 to date. Pakistan Reserves 1999-00. KRL 2000-01 to 2014-15. NBP 2005-06. Sussex 2006-10; cap 2006. Kent 2007-08; cap 2007. Federal Areas 2007-08 to 2008-09. Surrey 2011. Somerset 2013-16 (T20 only). UK passport. Big Bash: PS 2013-14 to 2014-15. **Tests** (P): 3 (2007-08 to 2008-09); HS 50* v SL (Karachi) 2008-09; BB 5-161 v I (Bangalore) 2007-08 – on debut. **LOI** (P): 11 (1999-00 to 2009); HS 27 v SA (Chandigarh) 2006-07; BB 1-28 v SL (Karachi) 1999-00. **IT20** (P): 13 (2007-08 to 2012-13); HS 17 v Scotland (Durban) 2007-08; BB 3-18 v SL (Hambantota) 2012. F-c Tours (P): WI 2010-11 (Pak A); I 2007-08; SL 2001 (Pak A), 2004-05 (Pak A). HS 170 KRL v Multan (Multan) 2011-12. CC HS 122 K v Sussex (Canterbury) 2007. 50 wkts (0+4); most – 91 (2001-02). BB 9-35 KRL v SSGC (Rawalpindi) 2008-09. CC BB 6-86 K v Hants (Canterbury) 2008. LO HS 110* Otago v Auckland (Oamaru) 2009-10. LO BB 6-24 Pakistan A v England A (Colombo) 2004-05. T20 HS 49. T20 BB 4-5.

SOMERSET 2016

RESULTS SUMMARY

	Place	Won	Lost	Tied	Drew	NR
Specsavers County Champ (1st Division)	2nd	6	1		9	
All First-Class Matches		6	1		10	
Royal London One-Day Cup (South Group)	SF	7	2	1		
NatWest t20 Blast (South Group)	9th	3	10			1

SPECSAVERS COUNTY CHAMPIONSHIP AVERAGES

BATTING AND FIELDING

Cap		M	I	NO	HS	Runs	Avge	100	50	Ct/St
	J.G.Myburgh	3	5	1	110	234	58.50	1	2	–
1999	M.E.Trescothick	16	27	3	218	1239	51.62	4	4	33
2007	J.C.Hildreth	16	23	2	166	1012	48.19	4	2	9
2007	P.D.Trego	16	24	2	154*	1047	47.59	2	6	5
	C.J.L.Rogers	16	25	2	132	1010	43.91	3	6	8
2016	T.D.Groenewald	12	16	12	26*	138	34.50	–	–	1
2015	L.Gregory	12	16	4	73*	329	27.41	–	2	3
	J.Allenby	12	17	–	63	446	26.23	–	5	20
	T.B.Abell	13	22	1	135	538	25.61	2	1	10
2016	C.Overton	13	19	2	138	435	25.58	1	–	11
	J.Overton	6	9	2	51	161	23.00	–	1	1
	R.C.Davies	15	19	1	86	380	21.11	–	3	27/6
	R.E.van der Merwe	7	10	1	102*	180	20.00	1	–	3
	M.J.Leach	15	16	4	27*	121	10.08	–	–	5

Also batted: A.W.R.Barrow (1 match) 10, 21 (2 ct); D.M.Bess (2) 9, 25, 41 (4 ct); J.H.Davey (1) 10 (1 ct).

BOWLING

	O	M	R	W	Avge	Best	5wI	10wM
D.M.Bess	59.5	20	136	13	10.46	6-28	2	–
M.J.Leach	526.3	117	1422	65	21.87	6-42	5	–
J.Overton	133.3	27	382	17	22.47	5-42	1	–
T.D.Groenewald	347.2	85	1005	37	27.16	5-90	2	–
R.E.van der Merwe	203.4	40	614	22	27.90	4-45	–	–
J.Allenby	243.2	57	598	21	28.47	4-67	–	–
L.Gregory	276.5	61	894	29	30.82	4-58	–	–
C.Overton	380.5	83	1168	34	34.35	4-54	–	–
Also bowled:								
P.D.Trego	149.3	35	429	5	85.80	1-14	–	–

T.B.Abell 1-0-11-0; J.H.Davey 20-3-79-2; J.G.Myburgh 5-1-22-0; C.J.L.Rogers 1-0-4-0.

The First-Class Averages (pp 226–242) give the records of Somerset players in all first-class county matches (Somerset's other opponents being the Pakistanis).

SOMERSET RECORDS

FIRST-CLASS CRICKET

Highest Total	For 850-7d		v	Middlesex	Taunton	2007
	V 811		by	Surrey	The Oval	1899
Lowest Total	For 25		v	Glos	Bristol	1947
	V 22		by	Glos	Bristol	1920
Highest Innings	For 342	J.L.Langer	v	Surrey	Guildford	2006
	V 424	A.C.MacLaren	for	Lancashire	Taunton	1895

Highest Partnership for each Wicket

1st	346	L.C.H.Palairet/ H.T.Hewett	v	Yorkshire	Taunton	1892
2nd	450	N.R.D.Compton/J.C.Hildreth	v	Cardiff MCCU	Taunton Vale	2012
3rd	319	P.M.Roebuck/M.D.Crowe	v	Leics	Taunton	1984
4th	310	P.W.Denning/I.T.Botham	v	Glos	Taunton	1980
5th	320	J.D.Francis/I.D.Blackwell	v	Durham UCCE	Taunton	2005
6th	265	W.E.Alley/K.E.Palmer	v	Northants	Northampton	1961
7th	279	R.J.Harden/G.D.Rose	v	Sussex	Taunton	1997
8th	236	P.D.Trego/R.C.Davies	v	Lancashire	Manchester	2016
9th	183	C.H.M.Greetham/H.W.Stephenson	v	Leics	Weston-s-Mare	1963
	183	C.J.Tavaré/N.A.Mallender	v	Sussex	Hove	1990
10th	163	I.D.Blackwell/N.A.M.McLean	v	Derbyshire	Taunton	2003

Best Bowling (Innings)	For	10- 49	E.J.Tyler	v	Surrey	Taunton	1895
	V	10- 35	A.Drake	for	Yorkshire	Weston-s-Mare	1914
Best Bowling (Match)	For	16- 83	J.C.White	v	Worcs	Bath	1919
	V	17-137	W.Brearley	for	Lancashire	Manchester	1905

Most Runs – Season	2761	W.E.Alley	(av 58.74)	1961
Most Runs – Career	21142	H.Gimblett	(av 36.96)	1935-54
Most 100s – Season	11	S.J.Cook		1991
Most 100s – Career	49	H.Gimblett		1935-54
	49	M.E.Trescothick		1993-2016
Most Wkts – Season	169	A.W.Wellard	(av 19.24)	1938
Most Wkts – Career	2165	J.C.White	(av 18.03)	1909-37
Most Career W-K Dismissals	1007	H.W.Stephenson	(698 ct; 309 st)	1948-64
Most Career Catches in the Field	392	M.E.Trescothick		1993-2016

LIMITED-OVERS CRICKET

Highest Total	**50ov**	413-4		v	Devon	Torquay	1990
	40ov	377-9		v	Sussex	Hove	2003
	T20	250-3		v	Glos	Taunton	2006
Lowest Total	**50ov**	58		v	Middlesex	Southgate	2000
	40ov	58		v	Essex	Chelmsford	1977
	T20	82		v	Kent	Taunton	2010
Highest Innings	**50ov**	177	S.J.Cook	v	Sussex	Hove	1990
	40ov	184	M.E.Trescothick	v	Glos	Taunton	2008
	T20	151*	C.H.Gayle	v	Kent	Taunton	2015
Best Bowling	**50ov**	8-66	S.R.G.Francis	v	Derbyshire	Derby	2004
	40ov	6-16	Abdur Rehman	v	Notts	Taunton	2012
	T20	6- 5	A.V.Suppiah	v	Glamorgan	Cardiff	2011

SURREY

Formation of Present Club: 22 August 1845
Inaugural First-Class Match: 1864
Colours: Chocolate
Badge: Prince of Wales' Feathers
County Champions (since 1890): (18) 1890, 1891, 1892, 1894, 1895, 1899, 1914, 1952, 1953, 1954, 1955, 1956, 1957, 1958, 1971, 1999, 2000, 2002
Joint Champions: (1) 1950
NatWest Trophy Winners: (1) 1982
Benson and Hedges Cup Winners: (3) 1974, 1997, 2001
Pro 40/National League (Div 1) Winners: (1) 2003
Sunday League Winners: (1) 1996
Clydesdale Bank 40 Winners: (1) 2011
Twenty20 Cup Winners: (1) 2003

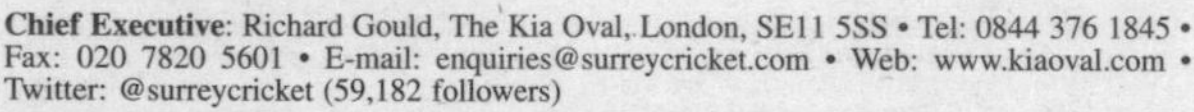

Chief Executive: Richard Gould, The Kia Oval, London, SE11 5SS • Tel: 0844 376 1845 • Fax: 020 7820 5601 • E-mail: enquiries@surreycricket.com • Web: www.kiaoval.com • Twitter: @surreycricket (59,182 followers)

Director of Cricket: Alec Stewart. **Head Coach**: Michael Di Venuto. **Captain**: G.J.Batty. **Vice-Captain**: R.J.Burns. **Overseas Players**: A.J.Finch (T20 only) and K.C.Sangakkara. **2017 Testimonial**: G.J.Batty. **Head Groundsman**: Lee Fortiss. **Scorer**: Keith Booth. ‡ New registration. [NQ] Not qualified for England.

ANSARI, Zafar Shahaan (Hampton S; Trinity Hall, Cambridge), b Ascot, Berks 10 Dec 1991. Younger brother of A.S.Ansari (Cambridge U 2008-13). 5'11". LHB, SLA. Squad No 22. Cambridge MCCU 2011-13. Surrey debut 2011; cap 2014. MCC 2015. **Tests**: 3 (2016-17); HS 32 v I (Rajkot) 2016-17; BB 2-76 v B (Dhaka) 2016-17. **LOI**: 1 (2015) did not bat or bowl. 1000 runs (1): 1029 (2014). HS 112 v Glamorgan (Colwyn Bay) 2014. BB 6-30 v Glos (Oval) 2015. LO HS 66* v Yorks (Oval) 2013 (RLC). LO BB 4-42 v Scotland (Oval) 2013 (Y40). T20 HS 67*. T20 BB 3-17.

BATTY, Gareth Jon (Bingley GS), b Bradford, Yorks 13 Oct 1977. Younger brother of J.D.Batty (Yorkshire and Somerset 1989-96). 5'11". RHB, OB. Squad No 13. Yorkshire 1997. Surrey 1999-2001, rejoined in 2010; cap 2011; captain 2015; testimonial 2017. Worcestershire 2002-09. MCC 2012. **Tests**: 9 (2003-04 to 2016-17); HS 38 v SL (Kandy) 2003-04; BB 3-55 v SL (Galle) 2003-04. Took wicket with his third ball in Test cricket. **LOI**: 10 (2002-03 to 2008-09); HS 17 v WI (Bridgetown) 2008-09; BB 2-40 v WI (Gros Islet, St Lucia) 2003-04. **IT20**: 1 (2008-09); HS 4 v WI (Port of Spain) 2008-09. F-c Tours: WI 2003-04, 2005-06; NZ 2008-09 (Eng A); I 2016-17; SL 2002-03 (ECB Acad), 2003-04; B 2003-04, 2016-17. HS 133 Wo v Surrey (Oval) 2004. Sy HS 110* v Hants (Southampton) 2016, sharing Sy record 8th wkt partnership of 222* with B.T.Foakes. 50 wkts (2); most – 60 (2003). BB 8-68 v Essex (Chelmsford) 2014. Hat-trick v Derbys (Oval) 2015. LO HS 83* v Yorks (Oval) 2001 (NL). LO BB 5-35 Wo v Hants (Southampton) 2009 (FPT). T20 HS 87. T20 BB 4-13.

‡**BORTHWICK, Scott** George (Farringdon Community Sports C, Sunderland), b Sunderland, Co Durham 19 Apr 1990. 5'9". LHB, LBG. Durham 2009-16. Wellington 2015-16 to date. **Tests**: 1 (2013-14); HS 4 and BB 3-33 v A (Sydney) 2013-14. **LOI**: 2 (2011 to 2011-12); HS 15 v Ireland (Dublin) 2011; BB – . **IT20**: 1 (2011); HS 14 and BB 1-15 v WI (Oval) 2011. F-c Tours: A 2013-14; SL 2013-14 (EL). 1000 runs (5); most – 1390 (2015). HS 216 Du v Middx (Chester-le-St) 2014, sharing Du record 2nd wkt partnership of 274 with M.D.Stoneman. BB 6-70 Du v Surrey (Oval) 2013. LO HS 87 and LO BB 5-38 Du v Leics (Leicester) 2015 (RLC). T20 HS 62. T20 BB 4-18.

BURNS, Rory Joseph (City of London Freemen's S), b Epsom 26 Aug 1990. 5'10". LHB, WK, occ RM. Squad No 17. Debut (Surrey) 2011; cap 2014. MCC 2016. MCC Univs 2010. 1000 runs (3); most – 1248 (2016). HS 199 v Glos (Bristol) 2014. BB 1-18 v Middx (Lord's) 2013. LO HS 95 v Glos (Bristol) 2015 (RLC). T20 HS 46*.

CURRAN, Samuel Matthew (Wellington C), b Northampton 3 Jun 1998. Son of K.M.Curran (Glos, Natal, Northants, Boland and Zimbabwe 1980-81 to 1999), grandson of K.P.Curran (Rhodesia 1947-48 to 1954-55), younger brother of T.K.Curran (*see below*). 5'8". LHB, LMF. Squad No 58. Debut (Surrey) 2015, taking 5-101 v Kent (Oval). Surrey 2nd XI debut 2013. F-c Tours (EL): SL 2016-17; UAE 2016-17 (v Afghan). HS 96 v Lancs (Oval) 2016. BB 7-58 v Durham (Chester-le-St) 2016. LO HS 57 v Glos (Oval) 2016 (RLC). LO BB 4-32 v Northants (Oval) 2015 (RLC). T20 HS 32. T20 BB 3-17.

CURRAN, Thomas Kevin (Hilton C, Durban), b Cape Town, South Africa 12 Mar 1995. Son of K.M.Curran (Glos, Natal, Northants, Boland and Zimbabwe 1980-81 to 1999), grandson of K.P.Curran (Rhodesia 1947-48 to 1954-55), elder brother of S.M.Curran (*see above*). 6'0". RHB, RMF. Squad No 59. Debut (Surrey) 2014; cap 2016. Surrey 2nd XI debut 2012. HS 60 v Leics (Leicester) 2015. 50 wkts (1): 76 (2015). BB 7-20 v Glos (Oval) 2015. LO HS 44 v Yorks (Oval) 2015 (RLC). LO BB 5-16 EL v UAE (Dubai, DSC) 2016-17. T20 HS 41. T20 BB 4-35.

DERNBACH, Jade Winston (St John the Baptist S), b Johannesburg, South Africa 3 Mar 1986. 6'1½". RHB, RFM. Squad No 16. Italian passport. UK resident since 1998. Debut (Surrey) 2003; cap 2011. **LOI**: 24 (2011 to 2013); HS 5 v SL (Leeds) 2011; BB 4-45 v P (Dubai) 2011-12. **IT20**: 34 (2011 to 2013-14); HS 12 v I (Colombo, RPS) 2012-13; BB 4-22 v I (Manchester) 2011. F-c Tour (EL): WI 2010-11. HS 56* v Northants (Northampton) 2010. 50 wkts (1): 51 (2010). BB 6-47 v Leics (Leicester) 2009. LO HS 31 v Somerset (Taunton) 2010 (CB40). LO BB 6-35 v Glos (Lord's) 2015 (RLC). T20 HS 24*. T20 BB 4-22.

DUNN, Matthew Peter (Bearwood C, Wokingham), b Egham 5 May 1992. 6'1". LHB, RFM. Squad No 4. Debut (Surrey) 2010. MCC 2015. HS 31* v Kent (Guildford) 2014. BB 5-48 v Glos (Oval) 2014. LO HS – . LO BB 2-32 England Dev XI v Sri Lanka A (Manchester) 2011. T20 HS 2. BB 3-8.

[NO]**FINCH, Aaron** James, b Colac, Victoria, Australia 17 Nov 1986. 5'9". RHB, SLA. Victoria 2007-08 to date. Yorkshire 2014-15. Surrey debut 2016. IPL: RR: 2009-10. DD 2011-12. PW 2013. SH 2014. MI 2015. GL 2016. Big Bash: MR 2011-12 to date. **LOI** (A): 79 (2012-13 to 2016-17); HS 148 v Scotland (Edinburgh) 2013; BB 1-2 v I (Pune) 2013-14. **IT20** (A): 31 (2010-11 to 2016-17); HS 156 v E (Southampton) 2013 – world record IT20 score. F-c Tours (Aus A): SA/Z 2013; Z 2011. HS 288* Cricket A v New Zealanders (Sydney) 2015-16. CC HS 110 Y v Warwks (Birmingham) 2014, and 110 v Warwks (Guildford) 2016. BB 1-0 Vic v WA (Perth) 2013-14. CC BB 1-20 Y v Sussex (Arundel) 2014. LO HS 154 Vic v Q (Brisbane) 2012-13. LO BB 2-44 Aus A v EL (Hobart) 2012-13. T20 HS 156. T20 BB 1-9.

FOAKES, Benjamin Thomas (Tendring TC), b Colchester, Essex 15 Feb 1993. 6'1". RHB, WK. Squad No 7. Essex 2011-14. Surrey debut 2015; cap 2016. MCC 2016. Essex 2nd XI debut 2008, aged 15y 172d. England U19 2010-11. F-c Tours (EL): SL 2013-14, 2016-17; UAE 2016-17 (v Afghan). HS 141* v Hants (Southampton) 2016, sharing Sy record 8th wkt partnership of 222* with G.J.Batty. LO HS 90 v Yorks (Leeds) 2016. T20 HS 49.

FOOTITT, Mark Harold Alan (Carlton le Willows S; West Notts C), b Nottingham 25 Nov 1985. 6'2". RHB, LFM. Squad No 6. Nottinghamshire 2005-09. MCC 2006. Derbyshire 2010-15; cap 2014. F-c Tour: SA 2015-16. HS 34 De v Leics (Leicester) 2015. Sy HS 16 v Warwks (Guildford) 2016. 50 wkts (2); most – 84 (2014). BB 7-62 v Lancs (Oval) 2016. LO HS 11* De v Notts (Nottingham) 2014 (RLC). LO BB 5-28 De v Scotland (Edinburgh) 2013 (Y40). T20 HS 2*. T20 BB 3-22.

HARINATH, Arun (Tiffin Boys GS; Loughborough U), b Sutton 26 Mar 1987. 5'11". LHB, OB. Squad No 10. Loughborough UCCE 2007-09. Surrey debut 2009; cap 2016. MCC 2008. Buckinghamshire 2007-08. HS 154 v Derbys (Derby) 2013. BB 2-1 v Glamorgan (Colwyn Bay) 2014. LO HS 52 v Derbys (Oval) 2013 (Y40). LO BB – .

McKERR, Conor (St John's C, Johannesburg), b 19 Jan 1998. 6'6". RHB, RFM. Squad No 83. SA U19 ODI 2014-15 to 2015. Surrey 2nd XI debut 2016. UK passport. Awaiting senior debut.

MEAKER, Stuart Christopher (Cranleigh S), b Durban, South Africa 21 Jan 1989. Moved to UK in 2001. 5'11". RHB, RFM. Squad No 18. Debut (Surrey) 2008; cap 2012. **LOI**: 2 (2011-12); HS 1 and BB 1-45 v I (Mumbai) 2011-12. **IT20**: 2 (2012-13); HS – ; BB 1-28 v I (Pune) 2013-14. F-c Tour: I 2012-13. HS 94 v Bangladeshis (Oval) 2010. CC HS 72 v Essex (Colchester) 2009. 50 wkts (1): 51 (2012). BB 8-52 (11-167 match) v Somerset (Oval) 2012. LO HS 21* v Glamorgan (Oval) 2012 (CB40). LO BB 4-38 EL v UAE (Dubai, DSC) 2016-17. T20 HS 17. T20 BB 4-30.

PIETERSEN, Kevin Peter (Maritzburg C; Natal U), b Pietermaritzburg, South Africa 27 Jun 1980. British passport (English mother) – qualified for England Oct 2004. 6'4". RHB, OB. Natal/KZN 1997-98 to 1999-00. Nottinghamshire 2001-04; cap 2002. Hampshire 2005-08; cap 2005 (no f-c appearances 2006-07, 2009-10). Surrey 2010-15, rejoins in 2017 for T20 only. Dolphins 2010-11. MCC 2004. IPL: RCB 2009-10. DD 2012-14. RPS 2016. Big Bash: MS 2014-15 to date. MBE 2005. *Wisden* 2005. **Tests**: 104 (2005 to 2013-14, 3 as captain); 1000 runs (4); most – 1343 (2006); HS 227 v A (Adelaide) 2010-11; BB 3-52 v SA (Leeds) 2012. **LOI**: 134 (2004-05 to 2013, 12 as captain; +2 for ICC World XI); HS 130 v P (Dubai) 2011-12; BB 2-22 v SA (Leeds) 2008. **IT20**: 37 (2005 to 2013); HS 79 v Z (Cape Town) 2007-08; BB 1-27 v SA (Centurion) 2009-10. F-c Tours: A 2006-07, 2010-11, 2013-14; SA 2009-10; WI 2008-09; NZ 2007-08, 2012-13; I 2003-04 (Eng A), 2005-06, 2008-09 (Captain), 2012-13; P 2005-06; SL 2007-08, 2011-12; B 2009-10; UAE 2011-12 (v P). 1000 runs (3); most – 1546 (2003). HS 355* v Leics (Oval) 2015 – record score v Le. BB 4-31 Nt v Durham U (Nottingham) 2003. CC BB 3-72 Nt v Hants (Nottingham) 2004. Sy BB 2-24 v Notts (Oval) 2012. LO HS 147 Nt v Somerset (Taunton) 2002 (NL). LO BB 3-14 Nt v Middx (Lord's) 2004 (NL). T20 HS 115*. T20 BB 3-33.

NQ**PILLANS, Mathew** William (Pretoria BHS; U of Pretoria), b Durban, South Africa 4 Jul 1991. 6'4". RHB, RF. Squad No 33. Northerns 2012-13. KwaZula Natal Inland 2013-14 to date. Dolphins 2013-14 to 2015-16. Surrey debut 2016. Somerset 2nd XI 2014. HS 49 KZN v Easterns (Benoni) 2015-16. Sy HS 34* v Somerset (Taunton) 2016. BB 6-67 (10-129 match) Dolphins v Knights (Durban) 2014-15. Sy BB – . LO HS 20* KZN v NW (Pietermaritzburg) 2013-14. LO BB 3-14 KZN v Namibia (Pietermaritzburg) 2015-16. T20 HS 23. T20 BB 3-15.

POPE, Oliver John Douglas (Cranleigh S), b Chelsea, Middx 2 Jan 1998. 5'9". RHB, WK. Squad No 32. Surrey 2nd XI debut 2015. England U19 2016 to 2016-17. Awaiting f-c debut. LO HS 20 v Yorks (Leeds) 2016 (RLC) – only 1st XI appearance.

NQ**RAMPAUL, Ravi**, b Preysal, Trinidad 15 Oct 1984. 6'1". LHB, RFM. Trinidad & Tobago 2001-02 to date. Surrey debut 2016. IPL: RCB 2013-14. **Tests** (WI): 18 (2009-10 to 2012-13); HS 40* v A (Adelaide) 2009-10; BB 4-48 v P (Providence) 2011. **LOI** (WI): 92 (2003-04 to 2015-16); HS 86* v I (Visakhapatnam) 2011-12; BB 5-49 v B (Khulna) 2012-13. **IT20** (WI): 23 (2007 to 2015-16); HS 8 v Ire (Providence) 2010; BB 3-16 v A (Colombo, RPS) 2012-13. F-c Tours (WI): E 2007, 2012; A 2009-10; SA 2003-04 (WI A); I 2011-12; B 2011-12, 2012-13. HS 64* WI A v Sri Lanka A (Basseterre) 2006-07. Sy HS 13* v Notts (Nottingham) 2016. BB 7-51 T&T v Barbados (Pointe-a-Pierre) 2006-07. Sy BB 5-85 v Somerset (Oval) 2016. LO HS 86* (*see LOI*). LO BB 5-49 (*see LOI*). T20 HS 23*. T20 BB 5-9.

ROY, Jason Jonathan (Whitgift S), b Durban, South Africa 21 Jul 1990. 6'0". RHB, RM. Squad No 20. Debut (Surrey) 2010; cap 2014. **ECB L-O Central Contract 2016-17. LOI**: 38 (2015 to 2016-17); HS 162 v SL (Oval) 2016. **IT20**: 19 (2014 to 2016-17); HS 78 v NZ (Delhi) 2015-16. 1000 runs (1): 1078 (2014). HS 143 v Lancs (Oval) 2015. BB 3-9 v Glos (Bristol) 2014. LO HS 162 (*see LOI*). LO BB – . T20 HS 122* v Somerset (Oval) 2015 – Sy record. T20 BB 1-23.

NQ**SANGAKKARA, Kumar** Chokshanada (Trinity C, Kandy; Colombo U), b Matale, Sri Lanka, 27 Oct 1977. 5'11". LHB, WK, occ OB. Squad No 11. Nondescripts 1997-98 to 2007-08. Central Province 2003-04 to 2004-05. Warwickshire 2007; cap 2007. Durham 2014. Surrey debut/cap 2015. IPL: KXIP 2007-10. DC 2011-12. SH 2013. Big Bash: HH 2015-16. *Wisden* 2011. **Tests** (SL): 134 (2000 to 2015, 15 as captain); 1000 runs (5); most – 1438 (2014); HS 319 v B (Chittagong) 2013-14 (also scored 105 to become only the 2nd man, after G.A.Gooch, to score a treble century and a century in the same match). Scored 287 v SA (Colombo, SSC) 2006, sharing in world record f-c partnership for any wkt of 624 with D.P.M.D.Jayawardena; BB – . **LOI** (SL): 397 (2000 to 2014-15, 45 as captain; +4 for Asia XI, +3 for ICC World XI); 1000 runs (6); most – 1333 (2006); HS 169 v SA (Colombo, RPS) 2013. **IT20** (SL): 56 (2006 to 2013-14, 22 as captain); HS 78 v I (Nagpur) 2009-10. F-c Tours (SL) (C=Captain): E 2002, 2006, 2011, 2014; A 2004, 2007-08, 2012-13; SA 1999-00 (SL A), 2000-01, 2002-03, 2011-12; WI 2003, 2007-08; NZ 2004-05, 2006-07, 2014-15; I 2005-06, 2009-10C; P 2001-02, 2004-05, 2008-09; Z 2004, 2008-09; B 2005-06, 2008-09, 2013-14; UAE 2011-12 (v P), 2013-14 (v P). 1000 runs (1+1): 1191 (2003-04). HS 319 (*see Tests*). CC HS 171 v Somerset (Oval) 2016. BB 1-13 SL v Zim A (Harare) 2004. LO HS 169 (*see LOI*). T20 HS 94.

SIBLEY, Dominic Peter (Whitgift S, Croydon), b Epsom 5 Sep 1995. 6'0". RHB, LB. Squad No 45. Debut (Surrey) 2013. Surrey 2nd XI debut 2011, aged 15y 302d. England U19 2012-13 to 2014. HS 242 v Yorks (Oval) 2013. BB 2-103 v Hants (Southampton) 2016. LO HS 37 v Durham (Chester-le-St) 2013 (Y40). LO BB 1-20 v Essex (Chelmsford) 2016 (RLC). T20 HS 74*. T20 BB 2-33.

‡**STONEMAN, Mark** Daniel (Whickham CS), b Newcastle upon Tyne, Northumb 26 Jun 1987. 5'11". LHB, OB. Durham 2007-16; captain (l-o only) 2015-16. 1000 runs (4); most – 1317 (2016). HS 187 Du v Middx (Chester-le-St) 2014, sharing Du record 2nd wkt partnership of 274 with S.G.Borthwick. BB – . LO HS 136* Du v Scotland (Chester-le-St) 2012 (CB40). T20 HS 89*.

VAN DEN BERGH, Frederick Oliver Edward (Whitgift S, Croydon; Hatfield C, Durham U), b Farnborough, Kent 14 Jun 1992. 6'0". RHB, SLA. Squad No 5. Debut (Surrey) 2011. Durham MCCU 2013-14. Surrey 2nd XI debut, aged 16y 326d. No 1st XI appearances in 2015 or 2016. HS 34 and BB 4-84 DU v Notts (Nottingham) 2013. Sy HS 16* v Leeds/Bradford MCCU (Oval) 2012. Sy BB 3-79 v Cambridge MCCU (Cambridge) 2011. LO HS 29* v Sussex (Oval) 2014 (RLC). LO BB – .

VIRDI, Guramar Singh ('**Amar**') (Guru Nanak Sikh Ac, Hayes), b Chiswick, Middx 19 Jul 1998. 5'10". RHB, OB. Squad No 19. Surrey 2nd XI debut 2016. England U19 2016. Awaiting 1st XI debut.

RELEASED/RETIRED

(Having made a County 1st XI appearance in 2016)

NQ**AZHAR MAHMOOD** Sagar (F.G. No. 1 HS, Islamabad), b Rawalpindi, Pakistan 28 Feb 1975. 6'0". RHB, RMF. Islamabad 1993-94 to 2006-07. United Bank 1995-96 to 1996-97. Rawalpindi 1998-99 to 2004-05. PIA 2001-02. Surrey debut 2002; cap 2004. HB 2006-07 to 2010-11. Kent 2008-12, (British passport holder) scoring 116 v Notts (Canterbury) on debut; cap 2008. MCC 2001. Returned to Surrey in 2015 for l-o and T20 only, player/coach in 2016. IPL: KXIP 2012-13. KKR 2015. Big Bash: ST 2012-13. **Tests** (P): 21 (1997-98 to 2001); HS 136 v SA (Johannesburg) 1997-98; BB 4-50 v E (Lord's) 2001. Scored 128* and 50* v SA (Rawalpindi) 1997-98 on debut. **LOI** (P): 143 (1996-97 to 2006-07); HS 67 v I (Adelaide) 1999-00; BB 6-18 v WI (Sharjah) 1999-00. F-c Tours (P): E 1997 (Pak A), 2001; A 1999-00; SA 1997-98; I 1998-99; SL 2000; Z 1997-98. HS 204* v Middx (Oval) 2005. 50 wkts (0+1): 59 (1996-97). BB 8-61 v Lancs (Oval) 2002. LO HS 101* v Glamorgan (Oval) 2006 (CGT). LO BB 6-18 (*see LOI*). T20 HS 106*. T20 BB 5-24.

NQ**BRAVO, Dwayne** John, b Santa Cruz, Trinidad 7 Oct 1983. Older half-brother of D.M.Bravo (Trinidad & Tobago, Nottinghamshire and WI 2006-07 to date). RHB, RMF. Trinidad & Tobago 2001-02 to 2012-13. Kent 2006. Surrey 2016 (T20 only). IPL: MI 2007-08 to 2009-10. CSK 2011-15. GL 2016. Big Bash: SS 2011-12. MR 2013-14 to date. **Tests** (WI): 40 (2004 to 2010-11, 1 as captain): HS 113 v A (Hobart) 2005-06; BB 6-55 v E (Manchester) 2004. **LOI** (WI): 164 (2004 to 2014-15, 37 as captain); HS 112* v E (Ahmedabad) 2006-07; BB 6-43 v Z (St George's) 2012-13. **IT20** (WI): 66 (2005-06 to 2016-17, 6 as captain); HS 66* v I (Lord's) 2009; BB 4-28 v SL (Colombo, RPS) 2015-16. F-c Tours (WI): E 2002 (WI A), 2004, 2007; A 2005-06, 2009-10; SA 2007-08; NZ 2005-06; P 2006-07; SL 2010-11. HS 197 T&T v West Indies B (Couva) 2003-04. CC HS 76 K v Lancs (Canterbury) 2006. BB 6-11 T&T v Windward Is (St George's) 2002-03. CC BB 6-112 K v Notts (Nottingham) 2006. LO HS 112* (*see LOI*). LO BB 6-43 (*see LOI*). T20 HS 70*. T20 BB 5-23.

BURKE, J.E. – *see LEICESTERSHIRE* (one-year loan).

DAVIES, S.M. – *see SOMERSET.*

NQ**MORRIS, Chris**topher Henry, b Pretoria, South Africa 20 Apr 1987. Son of W.F.Morris (N Transvaal 1979-80 to 1991-92). RHB, RFM. North West 2009-10 to 2011-12. Lions 2011-12 to 2014-15. Titans 2015-16 to date. Surrey 2016 (T20 only). IPL: CSK 2013. RR 2015. DD 2016. **Tests** (SA): 2 (2015-16); HS 69 v E (Cape Town) 2015-16 – on debut; BB 1-8 v E (Johannesburg) 2015-16. **LOI** (SA): 23 (2013 to 2016-17); HS 62 v E (Johannesburg) 2015-16; BB 4-31 v SL (Centurion) 2016-17. **IT20** (SA): 12 (2012-13 to 2016-17); HS 17* v E (Cape Town) 2015-16; BB 4-27 v Afghanistan (Mumbai) 2015-16. HS 154 NW v Easterns (Potchefstroom) 2010-11. BB 8-44 (12-101 match) Lions v Dolphins (Johannesburg) 2012-13. LO HS 90* NW v SW Districts (Potchefstroom) 2010-11. LO BB 4-30 NW v KZN (Durban) 2010-11. T20 HS 82*. T20 BB 4-9.

WILSON, G.C. – *see DERBYSHIRE.*

A.Kapil left the staff without making a County 1st XI appearance in 2016.

SURREY 2016

RESULTS SUMMARY

	Place	Won	Lost	Drew	NR
Specsavers County Champ (1st Division)	5th	4	6	6	
All First-Class Matches		4	6	7	
Royal London One-Day Cup (South Group)	Finalist	6	4		1
NatWest t20 Blast (South Group)	5th	7	7		

SPECSAVERS COUNTY CHAMPIONSHIP AVERAGES

BATTING AND FIELDING

Cap		*M*	*I*	*NO*	*HS*	*Runs*	*Avge*	*100*	*50*	*Ct/St*
2015	K.C.Sangakkara	12	22	1	171	1039	49.47	1	7	10
	A.J.Finch	4	6	–	110	292	48.66	1	2	2
2016	B.T.Foakes	15	24	6	141*	759	42.16	1	3	43/3
2014	R.J.Burns	16	30	2	122	1144	40.85	2	7	15
	S.M.Curran	9	14	2	96	472	39.33	–	5	3
2014	J.J.Roy	11	19	–	120	745	39.21	2	3	9
2011	S.M.Davies	15	26	2	117	923	38.45	1	5	10
2016	A.Harinath	11	21	1	137	707	35.35	1	4	5
	D.P.Sibley	7	13	2	99	377	34.27	–	3	6
2014	Z.S.Ansari	10	17	1	53	439	27.43	–	2	5
2011	G.J.Batty	16	25	4	110*	478	22.76	1	–	4
2016	T.K.Curran	15	26	1	54	427	17.08	–	3	5
	M.W.Pillans	4	6	1	34*	73	14.60	–	–	1
2012	S.C.Meaker	11	15	6	41	126	14.00	–	–	5
	R.Rampaul	5	7	4	13*	33	11.00	–	–	2
	J.E.Burke	3	5	–	31	38	7.60	–	–	–
2014	G.C.Wilson	2	4	–	12	27	6.75	–	–	1
	M.H.A.Footitt	8	11	3	16	49	6.12	–	–	3

Also batted: M.P.Dunn (2 matches) 6*, 5*, 2.

BOWLING

	O	*M*	*R*	*W*	*Avge*	*Best*	*5wI*	*10wM*
R.Rampaul	128.5	13	510	21	24.28	5-85	2	–
M.H.A.Footitt	248.3	44	913	34	26.85	7-62	3	–
S.M.Curran	215	49	752	27	27.85	7-58	2	–
S.C.Meaker	298.5	42	1145	37	30.94	4-40	–	–
G.J.Batty	434.1	93	1280	41	31.21	7-32	2	1
Z.S.Ansari	236.4	39	691	22	31.40	6-36	1	–
T.K.Curran	445.4	87	1494	33	45.27	4-58	–	–

Also bowled: J.E.Burke 37.3-4-184-4; R.J.Burns 3-1-7-0; M.P.Dunn 39-5-188-1; A.J.Finch 3-1-10-0; A.Harinath 18.2-1-59-0; M.W.Pillans 93-15-332-0; D.P.Sibley 36-6-133-2.

The First-Class Averages (pp 226–242) give the records of Surrey players in all first-class county matches (Surrey's other opponents being Loughborough MCCU).

SURREY RECORDS

FIRST-CLASS CRICKET

Highest Total	For 811		v	Somerset	The Oval	1899
	V 863		by	Lancashire	The Oval	1990
Lowest Total	For 14		v	Essex	Chelmsford	1983
	V 16		by	MCC	Lord's	1872
Highest Innings	For 357*	R.Abel	v	Somerset	The Oval	1899
	V 366	N.H.Fairbrother	for	Lancashire	The Oval	1990

Highest Partnership for each Wicket

1st	428	J.B.Hobbs/A.Sandham	v	Oxford U	The Oval	1926
2nd	371	J.B.Hobbs/E.G.Hayes	v	Hampshire	The Oval	1909
3rd	413	D.J.Bicknell/D.M.Ward	v	Kent	Canterbury	1990
4th	448	R.Abel/T.W.Hayward	v	Yorkshire	The Oval	1899
5th	318	M.R.Ramprakash/Azhar Mahmood	v	Middlesex	The Oval	2005
6th	298	A.Sandham/H.S.Harrison	v	Sussex	The Oval	1913
7th	262	C.J.Richards/K.T.Medlycott	v	Kent	The Oval	1987
8th	222*	B.T.Foakes/G.J.Batty	v	Hampshire	Southampton	2016
9th	168	E.R.T.Holmes/E.W.J.Brooks	v	Hampshire	The Oval	1936
10th	173	A.Ducat/A.Sandham	v	Essex	Leyton	1921

Best Bowling	For	10-43	T.Rushby	v	Somerset	Taunton	1921
(Innings)	V	10-28	W.P.Howell	for	Australians	The Oval	1899
Best Bowling	For	16-83	G.A.R.Lock	v	Kent	Blackheath	1956
(Match)	V	15-57	W.P.Howell	for	Australians	The Oval	1899

Most Runs – Season	3246	T.W.Hayward	(av 72.13)	1906
Most Runs – Career	43554	J.B.Hobbs	(av 49.72)	1905-34
Most 100s – Season	13	T.W.Hayward		1906
	13	J.B.Hobbs		1925
Most 100s – Career	144	J.B.Hobbs		1905-34
Most Wkts – Season	252	T.Richardson	(av 13.94)	1895
Most Wkts – Career	1775	T.Richardson	(av 17.87)	1892-1904
Most Career W-K Dismissals	1221	H.Strudwick	(1035 ct; 186 st)	1902-27
Most Career Catches in the Field	605	M.J.Stewart		1954-72

LIMITED-OVERS CRICKET

Highest Total	**50ov**	496-4		v	Glos	The Oval	2007
	40ov	386-3		v	Glamorgan	The Oval	2010
	T20	224-5		v	Glos	Bristol	2006
Lowest Total	**50ov**	74		v	Kent	The Oval	1967
	40ov	64		v	Worcs	Worcester	1978
	T20	88		v	Kent	The Oval	2012
Highest Innings	**50ov**	268	A.D.Brown	v	Glamorgan	The Oval	2002
	40ov	203	A.D.Brown	v	Hampshire	Guildford	1997
	T20	122*	J.J.Roy	v	Somerset	The Oval	2015
Best Bowling	**50ov**	7-33	R.D.Jackman	v	Yorkshire	Harrogate	1970
	40ov	7-30	M.P.Bicknell	v	Glamorgan	The Oval	1999
	T20	6-24	T.J.Murtagh	v	Middlesex	Lord's	2005

SUSSEX

Formation of Present Club: 1 March 1839
Substantial Reorganisation: August 1857
Inaugural First-Class Match: 1864
Colours: Dark Blue, Light Blue and Gold
Badge: County Arms of Six Martlets
County Champions: (3) 2003, 2006, 2007
Gillette/NatWest/C&G Trophy Winners: (5) 1963, 1964, 1978, 1986, 2006
Pro 40/National League (Div 1) Winners: (2) 2008, 2009
Sunday League Winners: (1) 1982
Twenty20 Cup Winners: (1) 2009

Chief Executive: Rob Andrew, The 1st Central County Ground, Eaton Road, Hove BN3 3AN • Tel: 0844 264 0202 • Fax: 01273 771549 • Email: info@sussexcricket.co.uk • Web: www.sussexcricket.co.uk • Twitter: @SussexCCC (43,440 followers)

Director of Cricket: Keith Greenfield. **Head Coach**: Mark J.G.Davis. **Asst Head Coach/ Bowling Coach**: Jon Lewis. **Batting Coach**: Michael Yardy. **Academy Director**: Carl Hopkinson. **Captain**: L.J.Wright. **Vice-Captain**: B.C.Brown. **Overseas Players**: V.D.Philander and L.R.P.L.Taylor. **2017 Testimonial**: C.D.Nash. **Head Groundsman**: Andy Mackay. **Scorer**: M.J. (Mike) Charman. ‡ New registration. NQ Not qualified for England.

NQ**ARCHER, Jofra** Chioke, b Bridgetown, Barbados 1 Apr 1995. 6'0". RHB, RFM. Squad No 22. Debut (Sussex) 2016. HS 73 v Essex (Colchester) 2016. BB 4-31 v Leics (Leicester) 2016. LO HS 35 and LO BB 5-42 v Somerset (Taunton) 2016 (RLC). T20 HS 12*. T20 BB 3-39.

BEER, William Andrew Thomas (Reigate GS; Collyer's C, Horsham), b Crawley 8 Oct 1988. 5'10". RHB, LB. Squad No 18. Debut (Sussex) 2008. HS 39 v Middx (Lord's) 2013. BB 3-31 v Worcs (Worcester) 2010. LO HS 45* v Durham (Hove) 2014 (RLC). LO BB 3-27 v Warwks (Hove) 2012 (CB40). T20 HS 37. T20 BB 3-14.

BRIGGS, Danny Richard (Isle of Wight C), b Newport, IoW 30 Apr 1991. 6'2". RHB, SLA. Squad No 21. Hampshire 2009-15; cap 2012. Sussex debut 2016. **LOI**: 1 (2011-12); HS – ; BB 2-39 v P (Dubai) 2011-12. **IT20**: 7 (2012 to 2013-14); HS 0*; BB 2-25 v A (Chester-le-St) 2013. F-c Tour (EL): WI 2010-11. HS 54 H v Glos (Bristol) 2013. Sx HS 49 v Essex (Colchester) 2016. BB 6-45 EL v Windward Is (Roseau) 2010-11. CC BB 6-65 H v Notts (Southampton) 2011. Sx BB 5-93 v Glos (Bristol) 2016. LO HS 25 and LO BB 4-32 H v Glamorgan (Cardiff) 2012 (CB40). T20 HS 13. T20 BB 5-19.

BROWN, Ben Christopher (Ardingly C), b Crawley 23 Nov 1988. 5'8". RHB, WK. Squad No 26. Debut (Sussex) 2007; cap 2014. 1000 runs (1): 1031 (2015). HS 163 v Durham (Hove) 2014. BB 1-48 v Essex (Colchester) 2016. LO HS 62 v Hants (Hove) 2016 (RLC). T20 HS 68.

‡EVANS, Laurie John (Whitgift S; The John Fisher S; St Mary's C, Durham U), b Lambeth, London 12 Oct 1987. 6'0". RHB, OB. Squad No 32. Durham UCCE 2007. MCC 2007. Surrey 2009-10. Warwickshire 2010-16. Northamptonshire 2016 (on loan). HS 213* and BB 1-29 Wa v Sussex (Birmingham) 2015, sharing Wa 6th wkt record partnership of 327 with T.R.Ambrose. LO HS 70* Wa v Essex (Birmingham) 2016 (RLC). LO BB – . T20 HS 69*. T20 BB 1-5.

FINCH, Harry Zachariah (St Richard's Catholic C, Bexhill; Eastbourne C), b Hastings 10 Feb 1995. 5'8". RHB, RMF. Squad No 6. Debut (Sussex) 2013. Sussex 2nd XI debut 2011, aged 16y 69d. England U19 2012-13. HS 135* and BB 1-9 v Leeds/Bradford MCCU (Hove) 2016. HS 66 v Kent (Tunbridge W) 2016. CC BB 1-30 v Northants (Arundel) 2016. LO HS 92* v Glamorgan (Hove) 2014 (RLC). LO BB – . T20 HS 35*.

CARTON, George Henry Simmons (Hurstpierpoint C), b Brighton 15 Apr 1997. 5'10½". LHB, LMF. Squad No 27. Debut (Sussex) 2016. Sussex 2nd XI debut 2014. HS 18* v Glamorgan (Cardiff) 2016. BB 3-93 v Northants (Northampton) 2016. LO HS 4 v Essex (Hove) 2016 (RLC). LO BB 4-43 EL v Sri Lanka A (Canterbury) 2016. T20 HS 2*. T20 BB 4-16.

HAINES, Thomas Jacob (Tanbridge House S, Horsham; Hurstpierpoint C), b Crawley 28 Oct 1998. LHB, RM. Debut (Sussex) 2016. Sussex 2nd XI debut 2014. HS 11 v Kent (Hove) 2016. BB – .

JORDAN, Christopher James (Comber Mere S, Barbados; Dulwich C), b Christ Church, Barbados 4 Oct 1988. 6'0". RHB, RFM. Squad No 8. Surrey 2007-12. Barbados 2011-12 to 2012-13. Sussex debut 2013; cap 2014. IPL: RCB 2016. Big Bash: AS 2016-17. **Tests**: 8 (2014 to 2014-15); HS 35 v SL (Lord's) 2014; BB 4-18 v I (Oval) 2014. **LOI**: 31 (2013 to 2016); HS 38* v SL (Oval) 2014; BB 5-29 v SL (Manchester) 2014. **IT20**: 22 (2013-14 to 2016-17); HS 27* v WI (Bridgetown) 2013-14; BB 4-28 v SL (Delhi) 2015-16. F-c Tour: WI 2014-15. HS 131 v Essex (Colchester) 2016. 50 wkts (1): 61 (2013). BB 7-43 Barbados v CC&C (Bridgetown) 2012-13. Sx BB 6-48 v Yorks (Leeds) 2013. LO HS 55 v Surrey (Guildford) 2016 (RLC). LO BB 5-28 v Middx (Hove) 2016 (RLC). T20 HS 45*. T20 BB 4-11.

NQ**JOYCE, Edmund** Christopher (Presentation C, Bray, Co Wicklow; Trinity C, Dublin), b Dublin, Ireland 22 Sep 1978. Brother of four Ireland cricketers: Augustine (2000), Dominick (2004-06), Cecilia (2001-07) and Isobel, her twin (1999-2007). 5'11". LHB, RM. Squad No 24. Ireland 1997-98 to date. Middlesex 1999-2008; cap 2002. Sussex debut/cap 2009; captain 2013-15. MCC 2006, 2008. **LOI** (E/Ire): 63 (17 for E 2006 to 2006-07; 46 for Ire 2010-11 to 2016); HS 160* Ire v Afghanistan (Belfast) 2016. **IT20** (E/Ire): 18 (2 for E 2006 to 2006-07; 16 for Ire 2011-12 to 2013-14); HS 78* Ire v Scotland (Dubai, DSC) 2011-12. F-c Tour (Eng A): WI 2005-06. 1000 runs (9); most – 1668 (2005). HS 250 v Derbys (Derby) 2016. BB M 2-34 v Cambridge U (Cambridge) 2004. CC BB 1-4 M v Glamorgan (Cardiff) 2005. Sx BB 1-9 v Hants (Southampton) 2009. LO HS 160* (*see LOI*). LO BB 2-10 M v Notts (Nottingham) 2003 (NL). T20 HS 78*.

MACHAN, Matthew William (Brighton C), b Brighton 15 Feb 1991. 5'8". LHB, RM. Squad No 15. Debut (Sussex) 2010. Scotland 2012-13 to date. **LOI** (Scot): 23 (2012-13 to 2015-16); HS 114 and BB 3-31 v Kenya (Aberdeen) 2013. **IT20** (Scot): 13 (2012-13 to 2015-16); HS 67* v Netherlands (Dubai) 2013-14; BB 3-23 v Afghanistan (Sharjah) 2012-13. HS 192 v Somerset (Taunton) 2015. BB 1-36 Sc v Australia A (Edinburgh) 2013. LO HS 126* v Unicorns (Hove) 2012 (CB40). BB 3-31 (*see LOI*). T20 HS 90*. T20 BB 3-23.

NQ**MAGOFFIN, Stephen** James (Indooropilly HS; Curtin U, Perth), b Corinda, Queensland, Australia 17 Dec 1979. 6'3". LHB, RFM. Squad No 64. W Australia 2004-05 to 2010-11. Surrey 2007 (one f-c match). Worcestershire 2008. Queensland 2011-12. Sussex debut 2012; cap 2013. HS 79 WA v Tas (Perth) 2008-09. UK HS 51 v Northants (Northampton) 2014. 50 wkts (5); most – 73 (2015). BB 8-20 (12-31 match) v Somerset (Horsham) 2013. LO HS 24* Wo v Hants (Southampton) 2008 (FPT). LO BB 4-58 Sy v Kent (Oval) 2007 (FPT). T20 HS 11*. T20 BB 2-15.

MILLS, Tymal Solomon (Mildenhall TC), b Dewsbury, Yorks 12 Aug 1992. 6'1". RHB, LF. Squad No 7. Essex 2011-14. Sussex debut 2015. Essex 2nd XI debut 2010. England U19 2010-11. Big Bash: BH 2016-17. **IT20**: 4 (2016 to 2016-17); HS 0; BB 1-27 v I (Kanpur) 2016-17. F-c Tour (EL): SL 2013-14. HS 31* EL v Sri Lanka A (Colombo, RPS) 2013-14. CC HS 30 Ex v Kent (Canterbury) 2014. Sx HS 8 v Worcs (Hove) 2015. BB 4-25 Ex v Glamorgan (Cardiff) 2012. Sx BB 2-28 v Hants (Southampton) 2015. LO HS 3* v Notts (Hove) 2015 (RLC). LO BB 3-23 Ex v Durham (Chelmsford) 2013 (Y40). T20 HS 8*. T20 BB 4-22.

NASH, Christopher David (Collyer's SFC; Loughborough U), b Cuckfield 19 May 1983. 5'11". RHB, OB. Squad No 23. Debut (Sussex) 2002; cap 2008; testimonial 2017. Loughborough UCCE 2003-04. British U 2004. 1000 runs (4); most – 1321 (2009). HS 184 v Leics (Leicester) 2010. BB 4-12 v Glamorgan (Cardiff) 2010. LO HS 124* v Kent (Canterbury) 2011 (CB40). LO BB 4-40 v Yorks (Hove) 2009 (FPT). T20 HS 112*. T20 BB 4-7.

NQ**PHILANDER, Vernon** Darryl, b Bellville, Cape Province, South Africa 24 Jun 1985. RHB, RMF. Western Province 2003-04 to 2015-16. WP Boland 2004-05. Cape Cobras 2005-06 to date. Middlesex 2008. Somerset 2012. Kent 2013. Nottinghamshire 2015; cap 2015. Devon 2004. **Tests** (SA): 41 (2011-12 to 2016-17); HS 74 v P (Centurion) 2012-13; BB 6-44 (10-114 match) v NZ (Hamilton) 2011-12. **LOI** (SA): 30 (2007 to 2015), HS 30* v NZ (Potchefstroom) 2015; BB 4-12 v Ireland (Belfast) 2007 – on debut. **IT20** (SA): 7 (2007-08); HS 6 v E (Cape Town) 2007-08; BB 2-23 v B (Cape Town) 2007-08. F-c Tours (SA): E 2012; A 2012-13, 2016-17; NZ 2011-12; I 2015-16; SL 2010 (SA A), 2014; Z 2014, 2016; B 2010 (SA A), 2015; UAE (v P) 2013-14. HS 168 WP v GW (Kimberley) 2004-05. CC HS 41 Nt v Durham (Chester-le-St) 2015. 50 wkts (0+2); most – 59 (2009-10). BB 7-61 Cobras v Knights (Cape Town) 2011-12. CC BB 5-43 Sm v Middx (Taunton) 2012. LO HS 79* SA A v Bangladesh A (East London) 2010-11. LO BB 4-12 (*see LOI*). T20 HS 56*. T20 BB 5-17.

RAWLINS, Delray Millard Wendell (Bede's S, Upper Dicker), b Bermuda 14 Sep 1997. 6'1". LHB, SLA. Squad No 9. Sussex 2nd XI debut 2015. England U19 2016-17. Awaiting 1st XI debut.

ROBINSON, Oliver Edward (King's S, Canterbury), b Margate, Kent 1 Dec 1993. 6'1". RHB, RM. Squad No 25. Debut (Sussex) 2015. Kent 2nd XI 2011-12. Leicestershire 2nd XI 2013. Yorkshire 2nd XI 2013-14. HS 110 v Durham (Chester-le-St) 2015, on debut, sharing Sx record 10th wkt partnership of 164 with M.E.Hobden. BB 6-33 v Warwks (Hove) 2015. LO HS 30 v Kent (Canterbury) 2015 (RLC). LO BB 2-61 v Middx (Hove) 2015 (RLC). T20 HS 10. T20 BB 3-16.

SAKANDE, Abidine (Ardingly C; St John's C, Oxford), b Chester 22 Sep 1994. 6'1". RHB, RFM. Squad No 11. Oxford U 2014-15. Oxford MCCU 2015-16. Sussex debut 2016. Sussex 2nd XI debut 2011. HS 33 OU v Cambridge U (Cambridge) 2015. BB 3-38 OU v Middx (Oxford) 2015. Sx BB – . LO HS – . LO BB 1-46 v Kent (Hove) 2016 (RLC).

SALT, Philip Dean (Reed's S, Cobham), b Bodelwyddan, Denbighs 28 Aug 1996. 5'10". RHB, OB. Squad No 28. Debut (Sussex) 2013. Sussex 2nd XI debut 2014. HS 42 v Glos (Bristol) 2016. LO HS 81 v Middx (Hove) 2016 (RLC).

SHAHZAD, Ajmal (Woodhouse Grove S; Bradford U), b Huddersfield, Yorks 27 Jul 1985. 6'0". RHB, RFM. Squad No 4. Yorkshire 2006-12 (first British-born Asian to play for Yorkshire); cap 2010. Lancashire 2012 (on loan). Nottinghamshire 2013-14. Sussex debut 2015. **Tests**: 1 (2010); HS 5 and BB 3-45 v B (Manchester) 2010. **LOI**: 11 (2009-10 to 2010-11); HS 9 v A (Brisbane) 2010-11; BB 3-41 v B (Bristol) 2010. **IT20**: 3 (2009-10 to 2010-11); HS 0*; BB 2-38 v P (Dubai) 2009-10. F-c Tours: A 2010-11; B 2009-10. HS 88 Y v Sussex (Hove) 2009. Sx HS 45* and BB 5-46 v Worcs (Hove) 2015. LO HS 59* Y v Kent (Leeds) 2011 (CB40). LO BB 5-51 Y v Sri Lanka A (Leeds) 2007. T20 HS 20. T20 BB 3-26.

[NQ]**TAYLOR,** Luteru **Ross** Poutoa Lote, b Lower Hutt, Wellington, New Zealand 8 Mar 1984. 6'0". RHB, OB. Squad No 16. Central Districts 2002-03 to date. Sussex debut 2016. IPL: RCB 2007-08 to 2009-10. RR 2011. DD 2012-14. PW 2013. **Tests** (NZ): 81 (2007-08 to 2016-17, 14 as captain); HS 290 v A (Perth) 2015-16; BB 2-4 v I (Ahmedabad) 2010-11. **LOI** (NZ): 183 (2005-06 to 2016-17, 20 as captain); 1000 runs (1): 1046 (2015); HS 131* v P (Pallekele) 2010-11; BB – . **IT20** (NZ): 73 (2006-07 to 2015-16, 13 as captain); HS 63 v WI (Auckland) 2008-09. F-c Tours (NZ) (C=Captain): E 2008, 2013, 2015; A 2008-09, 2011-12C, 2015-16; SA 2004 (NZ A), 2007-08, 2016; WI 2012C; I 2010-11, 2012C, 2014, 2016-17; SL 2009, 2012-13C; Z 2011-12C, 2016; B 2008-09, 2013-14; UAE 2014-15 (v P). HS 290 (*see Tests*). Sx HS 142* v Kent (Tunbridge W) 2016. BB 2-4 (*see Tests*). LO HS 132* CD v Otago (Dunedin) 2003-04. LO BB 1-13 CD v Canterbury (Christchurch) 2005-06. T20 HS 111*. T20 BB 3-28.

‡[NQ]**VAN ZYL, Stiaan**, b Cape Town, South Africa 19 Sep 1987. LHB, RM. Squad No 74. Boland 2006-07 to 2010-11. Cape Cobras 2007-08 to date. W Province 2014-15 to date. Joins Sussex in 2017 on three-year Kolpak deal. **Tests** (SA): 12 (2014-15 to 2016); HS 101* v WI (Centurion) 2014-15 – on debut; BB 3-20 v E (Durban) 2015-16. F-c Tours (SA): A 2016 (SA A), I 2015 (SA A), 2015-16; SL 2010 (SA A); B 2010 (SA A), 2015; Ire 2012 (SA A). HS 172 Cobras v Titans (Benoni) 2010-11. BB 5-32 Boland v Northerns (Paarl) 2010-11. LO HS 114* Cobras v Eagles (Kimberley) 2009-10. LO BB 4-24 Boland v Gauteng (Stellenbosch) 2010-11. T20 HS 86*. T20 BB 2-19.

WELLS, Luke William Peter (St Bede's S, Upper Dicker), b Eastbourne 29 Dec 1990. Son of A.P.Wells (Border, Kent, Sussex and England 1981-2000); nephew of C.M.Wells (Border, Derbyshire, Sussex and WP 1979-96). 6'4". LHB, LB. Squad No 31. Debut (Sussex) 2010; cap 2016. Colombo CC 2011-12. 1000 runs (1): 1016 (2014). HS 208 v Surrey (Oval) 2013. BB 3-35 v Durham (Arundel) 2015. LO HS 23 v Notts (Horsham) 2014 (RLC). BB 3-19 v Netherlands (Amstelveen) 2011 (CB40). T20 HS 11.

WHITTINGHAM, Stuart Gordon (Christ's Hospital, Horsham; Loughborough U), b Derby 10 Feb 1994. 6'0". RHB, RFM. Squad No 29. Loughborough MCCU 2015. Sussex debut 2016. Sussex 2nd XI debut 2014. MCC Universities 2013. HS 8* v Worcs (Worcester) 2016. BB 4-58 v Glamorgan (Hove) 2016.

[NQ]**WIESE, David** (Witbank HS), b Roodepoort, South Africa 18 May 1985. RHB, RMF. Squad No 96. Easterns 2005-06-2011-12. Titans 2009-10 to date. Sussex debut/cap 2016 (Kolpak deal). IPL: RCB 2015-16. **LOI** (SA): 6 (2015 to 2015-16); HS 41* and BB 3-50 v E (Cape Town) 2015-16. **IT20** (SA): 20 (2013 to 2015-16); HS 28 v WI (Nagpur) 2015-16; BB 5-23 v WI (Durban) 2014-15. F-c Tour (SA A): A 2014. HS 208 Easterns v GW (Benoni) 2008-09. Sx HS 70* and Sx BB 4-18 v Worcs (Hove) 2016. BB 6-58 Titans v Knights (Centurion) 2014-15. LO HS 106 Easterns v FS (Bloemfontein) 2007-08. LO BB 5-25 Easterns v Boland (Benoni) 2010-11. T20 HS 71*. T20 BB 5-19.

WRIGHT, Luke James (Belvoir HS; Ratcliffe C; Loughborough U), b Grantham, Lincs 7 Mar 1985. Younger brother of A.S.Wright (Leicestershire 2001-02). 5'11". RHB, RMF. Squad No 10. Leicestershire 2003 (one f-c match). Sussex debut 2004; cap 2007; T20 captain & benefit 2015; captain 2016 to date. IPL: PW 2012-13. Big Bash: MS 2011-12 to date. **LOI**: 50 (2007 to 2013-14); HS 52 v NZ (Birmingham) 2008; BB 2-34 v NZ (Bristol) 2008 and 2-34 v A (Southampton) 2010. **IT20**: 51 (2007-08 to 2013-14); HS 99* v Afghanistan (Colombo, RPS) 2012-13; BB 2-24 v NZ (Hamilton) 2012-13. F-c Tour (EL): NZ 2008-09. 1000 runs (1): 1220 (2015). HS 226* v Worcs (Worcester) 2015, sharing Sx record 6th wkt partnership of 335 with B.C.Brown. BB 5-65 v Derbys (Derby) 2010. LO HS 143* EL v Bangladesh A (Bristol) 2013. LO BB 4-12 v Middx (Hove) 2004 (NL). T20 HS 153* v Essex (Chelmsford) 2014 – Sx record. T20 BB 3-17.

RELEASED/RETIRED

(Having made a County 1st XI appearance in 2016)

CACHOPA, Craig (West Lake BHS), b Welkom, OFS, South Africa 17 Jan 1992. Younger brother of Carl Cachopa (Auckland, C Districts 2004-05 to 2014-15) and B.Cachopa (Auckland, Canterbury 2010-11 to date). RHB, RM, occ WK. Wellington 2011-12 to 2015-16. Auckland 2012-13 to 2014-15. Sussex 2014-16. Portuguese passport holder. HS 203 Auckland v Wellington (Auckland) 2013-14. Sx HS 84 v Warwks (Horsham) 2014 – on Sx debut. BB – . LO HS 121 Auckland v Canterbury (Christchurch) 2012-13. T20 HS 89*.

DAVIS, Christian Arthur Linghorne (Bedford S; Leeds U), b Milton Keynes, Bucks 11 Oct 1992. 6'2". RHB, LFM. Leeds/Bradford MCCU 2014-16. Sussex 2016. Northamptonshire 2nd XI 2010-13. MCC Univs 2014-16. Bedfordshire 2010-13. England U19 2010-11. HS 65 LBU v Sussex (Hove) 2016. Sx HS 12 v Glamorgan (Cardiff) 2016. LO HS 54 Nh v Kent (Northampton) 2012 (CB40). LO BB 1-25 v Kent (Hove) 2016 (RLC).

HATCHETT, Lewis James (Steyning GS), b Shoreham-by-Sea 21 Jan 1990. 6'3". LHB, LMF. Sussex 2010-16. HS 25 v Yorks (Leeds) 2015. BB 5-47 v Leics (Leicester) 2010. LO HS 5 v Kent (Canterbury) 2014 (RLC). LO BB 3-44 v Surrey (Oval) 2014 (RLC). T20 HS 0*. T20 BB 3-23.

HUDSON-PRENTICE, Fynn Jake (Warden Park S, Cuckfield; Bede's S, Upper Dicker), b Haywards Heath 12 Jan 1996. RHB, RMF. Sussex 2015-16. Sussex 2nd XI debut 2012. HS 20 v Kent (Hove) 2016 and 20 v Worcs (Hove) 2016. BB – . LO HS 48 v Kent (Hove) 2016 (RLC). LO BB – .

NQ**KULASEKARA**, Kulasekara Mudiyanselage Dinesh **Nuwan**, b Nittambuwa, Sri Lanka 22 Jul 1982. RHB, RFM. Galle CC 2002-03 to 2003-04. Colts CC 2004-05 to 2013-14. Basnahira North 2007-08 to 2009-10. Sussex 2016 (T20 only). IPL: CSK 2011 to 2012. **Tests** (SL): 21 (2004-05 to 2014); HS 64 v E (Lord's) 2006; BB 4-21 v P (Colombo, PSS) 2009. **LOI** (SL): 173 (2003-04 to 2015-16); HS 73 v A (Brisbane) 2011-12; BB 5-22 v A (Brisbane) 2012-13. **IT20** (SL): 56 (2008-09 to 2016-17); HS 31 v B (Chittagong) 2013-14; BB 4-31 v A (Geelong) 2016-17. F-c Tours (SL): E 2004 (SL A), 2006, 2014; A 2012-13; WI 2006-07 (SL A); NZ 2004-05; I 2009-10; Z 2007-08 (SL A). HS 95 Galle v Nondescripts (Colombo, NCC) 2003-04. 50 wkts (0+1): 61 (2002-03). BB 7-27 Colts v Bloomfield (Colombo, BCC) 2007-08. LO HS 84 Colts v Bloomfield (Colombo, CCC) 2007-08. LO BB 5-22 (*see LOI*). T20 HS 31. T20 BB 4-12.

NQ**MUSTAFIZUR RAHMAN**, b Khulna, Bangladesh 6 Sep 1995. 5'11". LHB, LMF. Squad No 90. Khulna 2013-14 to date. South Zone 2013-14 to 2014-15. Sussex 2016 (T20 only). **Tests** (B): 3 (2015 to 2016-17); HS 4 v SL (Galle) 2016-17; BB 4-37 v SA (Chittagong) 2015. **LOI** (B): 11 (2015 to 2016-17); HS 9 v I (Dhaka) 2015; BB 6-43 v I (Dhaka) 2015. **IT20** (B): 15 (2015 to 2016-17); HS 6 and BB 5-22 v NZ (Kolkata) 2015-16. HS 14 South Zone v East Zone (Chittagong) 2015. BB 5-28 Khulna v Chittagong (Savar) 2014-15. LO HS 9 (*see LOI*). LO BB 6-43 (*see LOI*). T20 HS 6. T20 BB 5-22.

J.E.Anyon left the staff at the beginning of the season without making a County 1st XI appearance in 2016.

SUSSEX 2016

RESULTS SUMMARY

	Place	Won	Lost	Drew	NR
Specsavers County Champ (2nd Division)	4th	4	2	10	
All First-Class Matches		4	2	12	
Royal London One-Day Cup (South Group)	9th	1	7		
NatWest t20 Blast (South Group)	6th	5	6		3

SPECSAVERS COUNTY CHAMPIONSHIP AVERAGES

BATTING AND FIELDING

Cap		*M*	*I*	*NO*	*HS*	*Runs*	*Avge*	*100*	*50*	*Ct/St*
2014	C.J.Jordan	5	7	2	131	323	64.60	1	3	6
2009	E.C.Joyce	12	17	1	250	1026	64.12	3	6	3
2008	C.D.Nash	15	24	1	144	1256	54.60	3	9	20
2014	B.C.Brown	16	22	5	159*	854	50.23	3	4	40
	L.R.P.L.Taylor	8	11	1	142*	478	47.80	1	4	6
2016	L.W.P.Wells	15	21	1	181	859	42.95	4	1	6
	O.E.Robinson	11	14	4	81	389	38.90	–	3	4
	M.W.Machan	7	9	–	66	249	27.66	–	1	6
2007	L.J.Wright	6	8	–	60	213	26.62	–	2	–
	H.Z.Finch	7	9	2	66	175	25.00	–	2	5
	J.C.Archer	6	8	–	73	195	24.37	–	1	4
	D.Wiese	6	9	2	70*	153	21.85	–	1	7
	D.R.Briggs	11	13	3	49	197	19.70	–	–	5
	A.Shahzad	7	8	1	26	109	15.57	–	–	1
	P.D.Salt	3	4	–	42	61	15.25	–	–	–
	Craig Cachopa	3	5	–	34	68	13.60	–	–	3
	G.H.S.Garton	4	5	2	18*	36	12.00	–	–	1
	F.J.Hudson-Prentice	4	6	–	20	69	11.50	–	–	–
2013	S.J.Magoffin	16	16	4	23*	122	10.16	–	–	4
	S.G.Whittingham	6	4	2	8*	20	10.00	–	–	1

Also batted (2 matches each): W.A.T.Beer 12*, 5 (2 ct); C.A.L.Davis 0, 2, 12 (2 ct); T.J.Haines 0, 11, 1 (1 ct); L.J.Hatchett 3, 17 (1 ct).

BOWLING

	O	*M*	*R*	*W*	*Avge*	*Best*	*5wI*	*10wM*
S.J.Magoffin	523.1	144	1249	62	20.14	5- 32	5	1
D.Wiese	152.2	34	456	19	24.00	4- 18	–	–
J.C.Archer	212.1	45	705	23	30.65	4- 31	–	–
S.G.Whittingham	153.4	18	576	18	32.00	4- 58	–	–
G.H.S.Garton	88.1	9	352	10	35.20	3- 93	–	–
C.J.Jordan	201	38	678	17	39.88	4- 36	–	–
A.Shahzad	184.5	25	673	16	42.06	3- 34	–	–
D.R.Briggs	345.5	64	1061	23	46.13	5- 93	2	–
O.E.Robinson	267.3	46	910	19	47.89	4-110	–	–
Also bowled:								
L.J.Hatchett	41	6	182	6	30.33	5- 58	1	–
L.W.P.Wells	153	13	558	9	62.00	3-105	–	–

W.A.T.Beer 48.3-5-164-1; B.C.Brown 3-0-48-1; H.Z.Finch 11-1-44-1; T.J.Haines 4-1-8-0; M.W.Machan 1-0-3-0; C.D.Nash 6-0-24-0.

The First-Class Averages (pp 226–242) give the records of Sussex players in all first-class county matches (Sussex's other opponents being Leeds/Bradford MCCU and the Pakistanis), with the exception of C.A.L.Davis, whose first-class figures for Sussex are as above.

SUSSEX RECORDS

FIRST-CLASS CRICKET

Highest Total	For	742-5d		v	Somerset	Taunton	2009
	V	726		by	Notts	Nottingham	1895
Lowest Total	For	19		v	Surrey	Godalming	1830
		19		v	Notts	Hove	1873
	V	18		by	Kent	Gravesend	1867
Highest Innings	For	344*	M.W.Goodwin	v	Somerset	Taunton	2009
	V	322	E.Paynter	for	Lancashire	Hove	1937

Highest Partnership for each Wicket

1st	490	E.H.Bowley/J.G.Langridge	v	Middlesex	Hove	1933
2nd	385	E.H.Bowley/M.W.Tate	v	Northants	Hove	1921
3rd	385*	M.H.Yardy/M.W.Goodwin	v	Warwicks	Hove	2006
4th	363	M.W.Goodwin/C.D.Hopkinson	v	Somerset	Taunton	2009
5th	297	J.H.Parks/H.W.Parks	v	Hampshire	Portsmouth	1937
6th	335	L.J.Wright/B.C.Brown	v	Durham	Hove	2014
7th	344	K.S.Ranjitsinhji/W.Newham	v	Essex	Leyton	1902
8th	291	R.S.C.Martin-Jenkins/M.J.G.Davis	v	Somerset	Taunton	2002
9th	178	H.W.Parks/A.F.Wensley	v	Derbyshire	Horsham	1930
10th	164	O.E.Robinson/M.E.Hobden	v	Durham	Chester-le-St[2]	2015

Best Bowling	For	10- 48	C.H.G.Bland	v	Kent	Tonbridge	1899
(Innings)	V	9- 11	A.P.Freeman	for	Kent	Hove	1922
Best Bowling	For	17-106	G.R.Cox	v	Warwicks	Horsham	1926
(Match)	V	17- 67	A.P.Freeman	for	Kent	Hove	1922

Most Runs – Season	2850	J.G.Langridge	(av 64.77)	1949
Most Runs – Career	34150	J.G.Langridge	(av 37.69)	1928-55
Most 100s – Season	12	J.G.Langridge		1949
Most 100s – Career	76	J.G.Langridge		1928-55
Most Wkts – Season	198	M.W.Tate	(av 13.47)	1925
Most Wkts – Career	2211	M.W.Tate	(av 17.41)	1912-37
Most Career W-K Dismissals	1176	H R Butt	(911 ct; 265 st)	1890-1912
Most Career Catches in the Field	779	J.G.Langridge		1928-55

LIMITED-OVERS CRICKET

Highest Total	**50ov**	384-9		v	Ireland	Belfast	1996
	40ov	399-4		v	Worcs	Horsham	2011
	T20	242-5		v	Glos	Bristol	2016
Lowest Total	**50ov**	49		v	Derbyshire	Chesterfield	1969
	40ov	59		v	Glamorgan	Hove	1996
	T20	67		v	Hampshire	Hove	2004
Highest Innings	**50ov**	158*	M.W.Goodwin	v	Essex	Chelmsford	2006
	40ov	163	C.J.Adams	v	Middlesex	Arundel	1999
	T20	153*	L.J.Wright	v	Essex	Chelmsford	2014
Best Bowling	**50ov**	6- 9	A.I.C.Dodemaide	v	Ireland	Downpatrick	1990
	40ov	7-41	A.N.Jones	v	Notts	Nottingham	1986
	T20	5-11	Mushtaq Ahmed	v	Essex	Hove	2005

WARWICKSHIRE

Formation of Present Club: 8 April 1882
Substantial Reorganisation: 19 January 1884
Inaugural First-Class Match: 1894
Colours: Dark Blue, Gold and Silver
Badge: Bear and Ragged Staff
County Champions: (7) 1911, 1951, 1972, 1994, 1995, 2004, 2012
Gillette/NatWest Trophy Winners: (5) 1966, 1968, 1989, 1993, 1995
Benson and Hedges Cup Winners: (2) 1994, 2002
Sunday League Winners: (3) 1980, 1994, 1997
Clydesdale Bank 40 Winners: (1) 2010
Royal London Cup Winners: (1) 2015
Twenty20 Cup Winners: (1) 2014

Chief Executive: Neil Snowball, County Ground, Edgbaston, Birmingham, B5 7QU • Tel: 0844 635 1902 • Fax: 0121 446 4544 • Email: info@edgbaston.com • Web: www.edgbaston.com • Twitter: @CricketingBears (34,910 followers)

Sport Director: Ashley Giles. **1st Team Coach**: Jim Troughton. **Batting Coach**: Tony Frost. **Bowling Coach**: Alan Richardson. **Captain**: I.R.Bell. **Overseas Players**: C.de Grandhomme (T20 only) and J.S.Patel. **2017 Testimonial**: None. **Head Groundsman**: Gary Barwell. **Scorer**: Mel Smith. ‡ New registration. NQ Not qualified for England.

ADAIR, Mark Richard (Sullivan Upper S, Hollywood), b Belfast, N Ireland 27 Mar 1996. 6'2". RHB, RFM. Squad No 27. Debut (Warwickshire) 2015. Warwickshire 2nd XI debut 2013. HS 32 v Notts (Birmingham) 2016. BB 1-61 v Somerset (Taunton) 2015. T20 HS 7. T20 BB 2-18.

AMBROSE, Timothy Raymond (Merewether HS, NSW; TAFE C), b Newcastle, NSW, Australia 1 Dec 1982. ECB qualified – British/EU passport. 5'7". RHB, WK. Squad No 11. Sussex 2001-05; cap 2003. Warwickshire debut 2006; cap 2007; benefit 2016. **Tests**: 11 (2007-08 to 2008-09); HS 102 v NZ (Wellington) 2007-08. **LOI**: 5 (2008); HS 6 v NZ (Oval) 2008. **IT20**: 1 (2008); HS – . F-c Tours: WI 2008-09; NZ 2007-08. HS 251* v Worcs (Worcester) 2007. LO HS 135 v Durham (Birmingham) 2007 (FPT). T20 HS 77.

BANKS, Liam (Newcastle-under-Lyme S & SFC), b Newcastle-under-Lyme, Staffs 3 Jun 1999. 5'10". RHB, OB. Warwickshire 2nd XI debut 2015. Awaiting 1st XI debut. Signed professional contract in June 2016.

BARKER, Keith Hubert Douglas (Moorhead HS; Fulwood C, Preston), b Manchester 21 Oct 1986. Son of K.H.Barker (British Guiana 1960-61 to 1963-64). Played football for Blackburn Rovers and Rochdale. 6'3". LHB, LMF. Squad No 13. Debut (Warwickshire) 2009; cap 2013. HS 125 v Surrey (Guildford) 2013. 50 wkts (3); most – 62 (2016). BB 6-40 v Somerset (Taunton) 2012. LO HS 56 v Scotland (Birmingham) 2011 (CB40). LO BB 4-33 v Scotland (Birmingham) 2010 (CB40). T20 HS 46. T20 BB 4-19.

BELL, Ian Ronald (Princethorpe C), b Walsgrave-on-Sowe 11 Apr 1982. 5'9". RHB, RM. Squad No 4. Debut (Warwickshire) 1999; cap 2001; benefit 2011; captain 2016 to date. MCC 2004, 2016. YC 2004. MBE 2005. *Wisden* 2007. **Tests**: 118 (2004 to 2015-16); 1000 runs (1): 1005 (2013); HS 235 v I (Oval) 2011; BB 1-33 v P (Faisalabad) 2005-06. **LOI**: 161 (2004-05 to 2014-15), 1000 runs (1): 1080 (2007); HS 141 v A (Hobart) 2014-15; BB 3-9 v Z (Bulawayo) 2004-05 – taking a wicket with his third ball in LOI. **IT20**: 8 (2006 to 2014); HS 60* v NZ (Manchester) 2008. F-c Tours: A 2006-07, 2010-11, 2013-14; SA 2009-10; WI 2000-01 (Eng A – *part*), 2008-09, 2014-15; NZ 2007-08, 2012-13; I 2005-06, 2008-09, 2012-13; P 2005-06; SL 2002-03 (ECB Acad), 2004-05, 2007-08, 2011-12; B 2009-10; UAE 2011-12 (v P), 2015-16 (v P). 1000 runs (4); most – 1714 (2004). HS 262* v Sussex (Horsham) 2004. BB 4-4 v Middx (Lord's) 2004. LO HS 158 EL v India A (Worcester) 2010. LO BB 5-41 v Essex (Chelmsford) 2003 (NL). T20 HS 90. T20 BB 1-12.

CLARKE, Rikki (Broadwater SS; Godalming C), b Orsett, Essex 29 Sep 1981. 6'4". RHB, RFM. Squad No 81. Surrey 2002-07, scoring 107* v Cambridge U (Cambridge) on debut; cap 2005. Derbyshire cap/captain 2008. Warwickshire debut 2008; cap 2011. MCC 2006, 2016. YC 2002. **Tests**: 2 (2003-04); HS 55 and BB 2-7 v B (Chittagong) 2003-04. **LOI**: 20 (2003 to 2006); HS 39 v P (Lord's) 2006; BB 2-28 v B (Dhaka) 2003-04. F-c Tours: WI 2003-04, 2005-06; SL 2002-03 (ECB Acad), 2004-05; B 2003-04. 1000 runs (1): 1027 (2006). HS 214 Sy v Somerset (Guildford) 2006. Wa HS 140 v Lancs (Liverpool) 2012. BB 6-63 v Kent (Canterbury) 2010. Took seven catches in an innings v Lancs (Liverpool) 2011 to equal world record. LO HS 98* Sy v Derbys (Derby) 2002 (NL). LO BB 5-26 v Worcs (Birmingham) 2016 (RLC). T20 HS 79*. T20 BB 3-11.

‡[NQ]**DE GRANDHOMME, Colin**, b Harare, Zimbabwe 22 Jul 1986. Son of L.L.de Grandhomme (Rhodesia B and Zimbabwe 1979-80 to 1987-88). RHB, RFM. Zimbabwe A 2005-06. Auckland 2006-07 to date. Joins Warwickshire for T20 only in 2017. **Tests** (NZ): 4 (2016-17); HS 37 v P (Hamilton) 2016-17; BB 6-41 v P (Christchurch) 2016-17 – on debut. **LOI** (NZ): 9 (2011-12 to 2016-17); HS 36 v SA (Auckland) 2011-12; BB 2-40 v SA (Wellington) 2016-17. **IT20** (NZ): 8 (2011-12 to 2016-17); HS 41* v B (Napier) 2016-17; BB 2-22 v SA (Auckland) 2016-17. F-c Tours: E 2014 (NZ A); SA 2005-06 (Z U23). HS 144* Auckland v Otago (Auckland) 2016-17. BB 6-24 Auckland v Wellington (Auckland) 2013-14. LO HS 151 NZ A v Northants (Northampton) 2014. LO BB 4-37 Auckland v Wellington (Wellington) 2015-16.

HAIN, Samuel Robert (Southport S, Gold Coast), b Hong Kong 16 July 1995. 5'10". RHB, OB. Squad No 16. Debut (Warwickshire) 2014. Warwickshire 2nd XI debut 2011. UK passport (British parents). HS 208 v Northants (Birmingham) 2014. LO HS 107 v Durham (Gosforth) 2016 (RLC). T20 HS 92*.

HANNON-DALBY, Oliver James (Brooksbank S; Leeds Met U), b Halifax, Yorks 20 Jun 1989. 6'7". LHB, RMF. Squad No 20. Yorkshire 2008-12. Warwickshire debut 2013. HS 40 v Somerset (Taunton) 2014. BB 5-68 Y v Warwks (Birmingham) and 5-68 Y v Somerset (Leeds) 2010 – in consecutive matches. Wa BB 4-50 v Oxford MCCU (Oxford) 2013. LO HS 21* Y v Warwks (Scarborough) 2012 (CB40). LO BB 5-27 v Glamorgan (Birmingham) 2015 (RLC). T20 HS 9. T20 BB 4-29.

JAVID, Ateeq (Aston Manor S), b Birmingham 15 Oct 1991. 5'8". RHB, OB. Squad No 17. Debut (Warwickshire) 2009. HS 133 v Somerset (Birmingham) 2013. BB 1-1 v Lancs (Manchester) 2014. LO HS 43 v Kent (Canterbury) 2013 (Y40). LO BB 4-42 v Yorks (Leeds) 2016 (RLC). T20 HS 51*. T20 BB 4-17.

LAMB, Matthew (North Bromsgrove HS; Bromsgrove S), b Wolverhampton, Staffs 19 July 1996. 6'1". RHB, RMF. Debut (Warwickshire) 2016. Warwickshire 2nd XI debut 2015. Signed professional contract in June 2016. HS 1 v Somerset (Taunton) 2016 – only 1st XI appearance.

MELLOR, Alexander James (Westwood C, Leek; Staffordshire U), b Stoke-on-Trent, Staffs 22 Jul 1991. 5'10". LHB, WK. Squad No 15. Derbyshire 2016. Warwickshire debut 2016. Somerset 2nd XI 2012-14. Warwickshire 2nd XI 2015. Staffordshire 2014-15. HS 44 De v Essex (Derby) 2016. Wa HS 27 v Lancs (Birmingham) 2016. LO HS – . T20 HS 10*.

PANAYI, George David (Shrewsbury S), b Enfield, Middx 23 Sep 1997. 6'3". RHB, RFM. Warwickshire 2nd XI debut 2015. Awaiting 1st XI debut. Signed professional contract in June 2016.

NQ**PATEL, Jeetan** Shashi, b Wellington, New Zealand 7 May 1980. 5'10". RHB, OB. Squad No 5. Wellington 1999-00 to date. Warwickshire debut 2009; cap 2012. *Wisden* 2014. **Tests** (NZ): 22 (2006-07 to 2016-17); HS 47 v I (Kolkata) 2016-17; BB 5-110 v WI (Napier) 2008-09. **LOI** (NZ): 42 (2005 to 2016-17); HS 34 v SL (Kingston) 2006-07; BB 3-11 v SA (Mumbai, BS) 2006-07. **IT20** (NZ): 11 (2005-06 to 2008-09); HS 5 v E (Auckland) 2007-08; BB 3-20 v SA (Johannesburg) 2005-06. F-c Tours (NZ): E 2008; SA 2005-06, 2012-13; I 2010-11, 2012, 2016-17; SL 2009, 2012-13; Z 2010-11, 2011-12; B 2008-09. HS 120 v Yorks (Birmingham) 2009. 50 wkts (5); most – 69 (2016). BB 7-38 v Somerset (Taunton) 2015. LO HS 50 v Kent (Birmingham) 2013 (Y40). LO BB 5-43 v Somerset (Birmingham) 2016 (RLC). T20 HS 34*. T20 BB 4-11.

NQ**PORTERFIELD, William** Thomas Stuart (Strabane GS; Leeds Met U), b Londonderry, N.Ireland 6 Sep 1984. 5'11". LHB, OB. Squad No 10. Ireland 2006-07 to 2008-09. Gloucestershire 2008-10; cap 2008. Warwickshire debut 2011; cap 2014. MCC 2007. **LOI** (Ire): 95 (2006 to 2016-17, 72 as captain); HS 112* v Bermuda (Nairobi) 2006-07. **IT20** (Ire): 56 (2008 to 2016-17, 56 as captain); HS 72 v UAE (Abu Dhabi) 2015-16. HS 186 Ire v Namibia (Windhoek) 2015-16. CC HS 175 Gs v Worcs (Cheltenham) 2010. Wa HS 118 v Somerset (Birmingham) 2014. BB 1-29 Ire v Jamaica (Spanish Town) 2009-10. UK BB 1-57 Gs v Loughborough UCCE (Bristol) 2008. LO HS 112* (*see LOI*). T20 HS 127*.

POYSDEN, Joshua Edward (Cardinal Newman S, Hove; Anglia RU), b Shoreham-by-Sea, Sussex 8 Aug 1991. 5'9". LHB, LB. Squad No 14. Cambridge MCCU 2011-13. Warwickshire debut 2015. Unicorns (l-o) 2013. HS 47 CU v Surrey (Cambridge) 2011. Wa HS 7* v Surrey (Guildford) 2016. BB 5-53 v Middx (Birmingham) 2016. LO HS 10* Unicorns v Glos (Wormsley) 2013 (Y40). LO BB 3-33 Unicorns v Middx (Lord's) 2013 (Y40). T20 BB 9*. T20 BB 4-51.

NQ**RANKIN,** William **Boyd** (Strabane GS; Harper Adams UC), b Londonderry, Co Derry, N Ireland 5 Jul 1984. Brother of R.J.Rankin (Ireland U19 2003-04). 6'8". LHB, RFM. Squad No 30. Ireland 2006-07 to 2008. Derbyshire 2007. Warwickshire debut 2008; cap 2013. Became available for England in 2012, before rejoining Ireland in 2015-16. **Tests**: 1 (2013-14); HS 13 and BB 1-47 v A (Sydney) 2013-14. **LOI** (E/Ire): 46 (39 for Ire 2006-07 to 2016, 7 for E 2013 to 2013-14); HS 18* Ire v SL (Dublin) 2016; BB 4-46 E v Ire (Dublin) 2013. **IT20** (E/Ire): 26 (24 for Ire 2009 to 2016-17, 2 for E 2013); HS 16* Ire v UAE (Abu Dhabi) 2015-16; BB 3-16 Ire v UAE (Dubai, DSC) 2016-17. F-c Tour: A 2013-14. HS 56* v Worcs (Birmingham) 2015. 50 wkts (1): 55 (2011). BB 6-55 v Yorks (Leeds) 2015. LO HS 18* v Northants (Northampton) 2013 (Y40) and *see LOI*. LO BB 4-34 v Kent (Birmingham) 2010 (CB40). T20 HS 16*. T20 BB 4-9.

SINGH, Sukhjit ('**Sunny**') (George Dixon International S, Birmingham; South & City C), b India 30 Mar 1966. 5'10". LHB, SLA. Squad No 58. Warwickshire 2nd XI debut. Awaiting 1st XI debut.

STONE, Oliver Peter (Thorpe St Andrew HS), b Norwich, Norfolk 9 Oct 1993. 6'1". RHB, RFM. Northamptonshire 2012-16. Northamptonshire 2nd XI debut 2010. Norfolk 2011. Captained England U19 2012-13. HS 60 Nh v Kent (Northampton) 2016. BB 5-44 Nh v Kent (Northampton) 2015. LO HS 24* Nh v Derbys (Derby) 2015 (RLC). LO BB 3-34 Nh v Glos (Northampton) 2015 (RLC). T20 HS 6*. T20 BB 2-18.

THOMASON, Aaron Dean (Barr Beacon S, Walsall), b Birmingham 26 Jun 1997. 5'10". RHB, RMF. Squad No 26. Warwickshire 2nd XI debut 2014. England U19 2015. Awaiting f-c debut. LO HS 0* and LO BB – v Middx (Lord's) 2014 (RLC). T20 HS 6. T20 BB 2-24.

TROTT, Ian **Jonathan** Leonard (Rondebosch BHC; Stellenbosch U), b Cape Town, South Africa 22 Apr 1981. Stepbrother of K.C.Jackson (WP and Boland 1988-89 to 2001-02). 6'0". RHB, RM. Squad No 9. Boland 2000-01. W Province 2001-02. EU/British passport. Warwickshire debut 2003, scoring 134 v Sussex (Birmingham); cap 2005; benefit 2014. Otago 2005-06. *Wisden* 2010. **Tests**: 52 (2009 to 2014-15); 1000 runs (2); most – 1325 (2010); HS 226 v B (Lord's) 2010; scored 119 v A (Oval) 2009 on debut. BB 1-5 v SL (Lord's) 2011. **LOI**: 68 (2009 to 2013); 1000 runs (1): 1315 (2011); HS 137 v A (Sydney) 2010-11; BB 2-31 v A (Adelaide) 2010-11. **IT20**: 7 (2007 to 2009-10); HS 51 v SA (Centurion) 2009-10. F-c Tours: A 2010-11, 2013-14 (*part*); SA 2009-10, 2014-15 (EL); WI 2014-15; NZ 2008-09 (EL), 2012-13; I 2007-08 (EL), 2012-13; SL 2011-12; B 2009-10; UAE 2011-12 (v P). 1000 runs (7); most – 1400 (2009). HS 226 (*see Tests*). Wa HS 219* v Middx (Lord's) 2016. BB 7-39 v Kent (Canterbury) 2003. LO HS 137 (*see LOI*). LO BB 4-55 v Hants (Lord's) 2005 (CGT). T20 HS 86*. T20 BB 2-19.

UMEED, Andrew Robert Isaac (High School of Glasgow), b Glasgow 19 Apr 1996. 6'1". RHB, LB. Squad No 23. Scotland 2015. Warwickshire debut 2016. Warwickshire 2nd XI debut 2014. HS 101 v Durham (Birmingham) 2016 – on Wa debut.

WESTWOOD, Ian James (Wheelers Lane S, Solihull SFC), b Birmingham 13 Jul 1982. 5'7½". LHB, OB. Squad No 22. Debut (Warwickshire) 2003; cap 2008; captain 2009-10; benefit 2015. HS 196 v Yorks (Leeds) 2015. BB 2-39 v Hants (Southampton) 2009. LO HS 65 v Northants (Northampton) 2008 (FPT). BB 1-28 Wa CB v Cambs (March) 2001 (CGT). T20 HS 49*. T20 BB 3-29.

WOAKES, Christopher Roger (Barr Beacon Language S, Walsall), b Birmingham 2 March 1989. 6'2". RHB, RFM. Squad No 19. Debut (Warwickshire) 2006; cap 2009. MCC 2009. Herefordshire 2006-07. **ECB Test & LO Central Contract 2016-17. Tests**: 17 (2013 to 2016-17); HS 66 v SL (Lord's) 2016; BB 6-70 v P (Lord's) 2016. **LOI**: 61 (2010-11 to 2016-17), HS 95* v SL (Nottingham) 2016; BB 6-45 v A (Brisbane) 2010-11. **IT20**: 8 (2010-11 to 2015-16); HS 37 v P (Sharjah) 2015-16, BB 2-40 v P (Dubai, DSC) 2015-16. F-c Tours: SA 2015-16; WI 2010-11 (EL); I 2016-17; SL 2013-14 (EL); B 2016-17; UAE 2015-16 (v P). HS 152* v Derbys (Derby) 2013. 50 wkts (3); most – 59 (2016). BB 9-36 v Durham (Birmingham) 2016. LO HS 95* (*see LOI*). LO BB 6-45 (*see LOI*). T20 HS 55*. T20 BB 4-21.

WRIGHT, Christopher Julian Clement (Eggars S, Alton; Anglia Ruskin U), b Chipping Norton, Oxon 14 Jul 1985. 6'3". RHB, RFM. Squad No 31. Cambridge UCCE 2004-05. Middlesex 2004-07. Tamil Union 2005-06. Essex 2008-11. Warwickshire debut 2011; cap 2013. HS 77 Ex v Cambridge MCCU (Cambridge) 2011. CC HS 71* Ex v Middx (Chelmsford) 2008. Wa HS 65 v Notts (Birmingham) 2014 and 65 v Sussex (Birmingham) 2015. 50 wkts (1): 67 (2012). BB 6-22 Ex v Leics (Leicester) 2008. Wa BB 6-31 v Durham (Birmingham) 2013. LO HS 42 Ex v Glos (Cheltenham) 2011 (CB40). LO BB 4-20 Ex v Unicorns (Chelmsford) 2011 (CB40). T20 HS 6*. T20 BB 4-24.

RELEASED/RETIRED continued on p 193

WARWICKSHIRE 2016

RESULTS SUMMARY

	Place	Won	Lost	Drew	NR
Specsavers County Champ (1st Division)	6th	3	4	9	
All First-Class Matches		3	4	10	
Royal London One-Day Cup (North Group)	**Winners**	7	3		1
NatWest t20 Blast (North Group)	6th	6	7		1

SPECSAVERS COUNTY CHAMPIONSHIP AVERAGES

BATTING AND FIELDING

Cap		*M*	*I*	*NO*	*HS*	*Runs*	*Avge*	*100*	*50*	*Ct/St*
2005	I.J.L.Trott	16	24	2	219*	975	44.31	2	6	3
2009	C.R.Woakes	5	7	1	121	252	42.00	1	1	1
2007	T.R.Ambrose	14	19	4	104	599	39.93	1	6	53/4
2012	V.Chopra	14	22	2	107	694	34.70	1	5	18
2001	I.R.Bell	15	22	2	174	678	33.90	1	3	7
2013	K.H.D.Barker	16	22	3	113	608	32.00	1	4	7
2008	I.J.Westwood	10	16	1	127	367	24.46	1	1	3
	A.J.Mellor	3	5	1	27	93	23.25	–	–	4
	S.R.Hain	15	21	1	135	455	22.75	1	1	19
2011	R.Clarke	15	20	3	74	384	22.58	–	4	30
2012	J.S.Patel	16	21	5	31	298	18.62	–	–	8
	A.R.I.Umeed	6	10	1	101	165	18.33	1	–	4
2013	C.J.C.Wright	9	15	2	45	207	15.92	–	–	2
	O.J.Hannon-Dalby	7	9	3	30	39	6.50	–	–	–
	L.J.Evans	2	4	–	9	26	6.50	–	–	3
2013	W.B.Rankin	7	6	1	16*	22	4.40	–	–	2
	J.E.Poysden	5	4	2	7*	8	4.00	–	–	–

Also batted (1 match each): M.R.Adair 32; M.Lamb 1, 1.

BOWLING

	O	*M*	*R*	*W*	*Avge*	*Best*	*5wI*	*10wM*
C.R.Woakes	128.1	30	409	23	17.78	9-36	1	–
J.E.Poysden	80.4	7	323	15	21.53	5-53	1	–
K.H.D.Barker	522.1	153	1365	59	23.13	5-53	1	–
J.S.Patel	616.4	168	1658	69	24.02	5-32	4	1
C.J.C.Wright	265.2	51	776	30	25.86	4-41	–	–
R.Clarke	415.3	99	1179	42	28.07	4-20	–	–
W.B.Rankin	169.2	23	514	18	28.55	3-33	–	–
Also bowled:								
O.J.Hannon-Dalby	153	26	524	8	65.50	2-39	–	–

M.R.Adair 15-4-47-0; T.R.Ambrose 1.5-1-0-1; I.R.Bell 8-2-17-0; V.Chopra 2-0-12-0; S.R.Hain 6-0-24-0; I.J.L.Trott 58-7-203-3; I.J.Westwood 5-0-16-0.

The First-Class Averages (pp 226–242) give the records of Warwickshire players in all first-class county matches (Warwickshire's other opponents being Leeds/Bradford MCCU), with the exception of L.J.Evans and A.J.Mellor, whose first-class figures for Warwickshire are as above, and:
V.Chopra 15-23-2-107-780-37.14-1-6-19ct. 2-0-12-0.
C.R.Woakes 6-9-3-121-285-47.50-1-1-2ct. 149.1-34-467-25-18.68-9/36-1-0.

WARWICKSHIRE RECORDS

FIRST-CLASS CRICKET

Highest Total	For 810-4d		v	Durham	Birmingham	1994
	V 887		by	Yorkshire	Birmingham	1896
Lowest Total	For 16		v	Kent	Tonbridge	1913
	V 15		by	Hampshire	Birmingham	1922
Highest Innings	For 501*	B.C.Lara	v	Durham	Birmingham	1994
	V 322	I.V.A.Richards	for	Somerset	Taunton	1985

Highest Partnership for each Wicket

1st	377*	N.F.Horner/K.Ibadulla	v	Surrey	The Oval	1960
2nd	465*	J.A.Jameson/R.B.Kanhai	v	Glos	Birmingham	1974
3rd	327	S.P.Kinneir/W.G.Quaife	v	Lancashire	Birmingham	1901
4th	470	A.I.Kallicharran/G.W.Humpage	v	Lancashire	Southport	1982
5th	335	J.O.Troughton/T.R.Ambrose	v	Hampshire	Birmingham	2009
6th	327	L.J.Evans/T.R.Ambrose	v	Sussex	Birmingham	2015
7th	289*	I.R.Bell/T.Frost	v	Sussex	Horsham	2004
8th	228	A.J.W.Croom/R.E.S.Wyatt	v	Worcs	Dudley	1925
9th	233	I.J.L.Trott/J.S.Patel	v	Yorkshire	Birmingham	2009
10th	214	N.V.Knight/A.Richardson	v	Hampshire	Birmingham	2002

Best Bowling	For	10-41	J.D.Bannister	v	Comb Servs	Birmingham	1959
(Innings)	V	10-36	H.Verity	for	Yorkshire	Leeds	1931
Best Bowling	For	15-76	S.Hargreave	v	Surrey	The Oval	1903
(Match)	V	17-92	A.P.Freeman	for	Kent	Folkestone	1932

Most Runs – Season	2417	M.J.K.Smith	(av 60.42)	1959
Most Runs – Career	35146	D.L.Amiss	(av 41.64)	1960-87
Most 100s – Season	9	A.I.Kallicharran		1984
	9	B.C.Lara		1994
Most 100s – Career	78	D.L.Amiss		1960-87
Most Wkts – Season	180	W.E.Hollies	(av 15.13)	1946
Most Wkts – Career	2201	W.E.Hollies	(av 20.45)	1932-57
Most Career W-K Dismissals	800	E.J.Smith	(662 ct; 138 st)	1904-30
Most Career Catches in the Field	422	M.J.K.Smith		1956-75

LIMITED-OVERS CRICKET

Highest Total	**50ov**	392-5		v	Oxfordshire	Birmingham	1984
	40ov	321-7		v	Leics	Birmingham	2010
	T20	242-2		v	Derbyshire	Birmingham	2015
Lowest Total	**50ov**	94		v	Glos	Bristol	2000
	40ov	59		v	Yorkshire	Leeds	2001
	T20	73		v	Somerset	Taunton	2013
Highest Innings	**50ov**	206	A.I.Kallicharran	v	Oxfordshire	Birmingham	1984
	40ov	137	I.R.Bell	v	Yorkshire	Birmingham	2005
	T20	158*	B.B.McCullum	v	Derbyshire	Birmingham	2015
Best Bowling	**50ov**	7-32	R.G.D.Willis	v	Yorkshire	Birmingham	1981
	40ov	6-15	A.A.Donald	v	Yorkshire	Birmingham	1995
	T20	5-19	N.M.Carter	v	Worcs	Birmingham	2005

WORCESTERSHIRE

Formation of Present Club: 11 March 1865
Inaugural First-Class Match: 1899
Colours: Dark Green and Black
Badge: Shield Argent a Fess between three Pears Sable
County Championships: (5) 1964, 1965, 1974, 1988, 1989
NatWest Trophy Winners: (1) 1994
Benson and Hedges Cup Winners: (1) 1991
Pro 40/National League (Div 1) Winners: (1) 2007
Sunday League Winners: (3) 1971, 1987, 1988
Twenty20 Cup Winners: (0); best – Quarter-Finalist 2004, 2007, 2012, 2014, 2015

Chief Executive: Tom Scott, County Ground, New Road, Worcester, WR2 4QQ • Tel: 01905 748474 • Fax: 01905 748005 • Email: info@wccc.co.uk • Web: www.wccc.co.uk • Twitter: @WorcsCCC (37,133 followers)

Director of Cricket: Steve Rhodes. **Bowling/Assistant Coach**: Matt Mason. **Captain**: J.Leach. **Overseas Players**: J.W.Hastings and M.J.Santner (T20 only). **2017 Testimonial**: None. **Head Groundsman**: Tim Packwood. **Scorer**: Dawn Pugh. ‡ New registration. [NQ] Not qualified for England.

Worcestershire revised their capping policy in 2002 and now award players with their County Colours when they make their Championship debut.

ALI, Moeen Munir (Moseley S), b Birmingham, Warwks 18 Jun 1987. Brother of A.K.Ali (Worcs, Glos and Leics 2000-12), cousin of Kabir Ali (Worcs, Rajasthan, Hants and Lancs 1999-2014). 6'0". LHB, OB. Squad No 8. Warwickshire 2005-06. Worcestershire debut 2007. Moors SC 2011-12. MT 2012-13. MCC 2012. PCA 2013. *Wisden* 2014. **ECB Test & L-O Central Contract 2016-17. Tests**: 37 (2014 to 2016-17); 1000 runs (1): 1078 (2016); HS 155* v SL (Chester-le-St) 2016; BB 6-67 v I (Southampton) 2014. **LOI**: 52 (2013-14 to 2016-17); HS 128 v Scotland (Christchurch) 2014-15; BB 3-32 v A (Manchester) 2015. **IT20**: 22 (2013-14 to 2016-17); HS 72* v A (Cardiff) 2015; BB 2-21 v I (Kanpur) 2016-17. F-c Tours: SA 2015-16; WI 2014-15; I 2016-17; SL 2013-14 (EL); B 2016-17; UAE 2015-16 (v P). 1000 runs (2); most – 1420 (2013). HS 250 v Glamorgan (Worcester) 2013. BB 6-29 (12-96 match) v Lancs (Manchester) 2012. LO HS 158 v Sussex (Horsham) 2011 (CB40). LO BB 3-28 v Notts (Nottingham) 2013 (Y40). T20 HS 90. T20 BB 5-34.

BARNARD, Edward George (Shrewsbury S), b Shrewsbury, Shrops 20 Nov 1995. Younger brother of M.R.Barnard (Oxford MCCU 2010). 6'1". RHB, RMF. Squad No 30. Debut (Worcestershire) 2015. Shropshire 2012. England U19 2012-13 to 2014. HS 73 v Derbys (Derby) 2016. BB 4-62 v Leics (Worcester) 2016. LO HS 51 v Somerset (Taunton) 2015 (RLC). LO BB 3-45 v Notts (Nottingham) 2016 (RLC). T20 HS 10. T20 BB 2-18.

CLARKE, Joe Michael (Llanfyllin HS), b Shrewsbury, Shrops 26 May 1996. 5'11". RHB, WK. Squad No 33. Debut (Worcestershire) 2015. Worcestershire 2nd XI debut 2013. Shropshire 2012-13. England U19 2014. F-c Tour (EL): UAE 2016-17 (v Afghan). 1000 runs (1): 1325 (2016). HS 194 v Derbys (Worcester) 2016. BB – . LO HS 131* v Glos (Worcester) 2015 (RLC). T20 HS 69*.

COX, Oliver **Ben** (Bromsgrove S), b Wordsley, Stourbridge 2 Feb 1992. 5'10". RHB, WK. Squad No 10. Debut (Worcestershire) 2009. HS 109 v Somerset (Worcester) 2015. LO HS 39 v Derbys (Worcester) 2014 (RLC). T20 HS 59*.

D'OLIVEIRA, Brett Louis (Worcester SFC), b Worcester 28 Feb 1992. Son of D.B.D'Oliveira (Worcs 1982-95), grandson of B.L.D'Oliveira (Worcs, EP and England 1964-80). 5'9". RHB, LB. Squad No 15. Debut (Worcestershire) 2012. HS 202* v Glamorgan (Cardiff) 2016. BB 5-48 v Durham (Chester-le-St) 2015. LO HS 42 v Yorks (Worcester) 2015 (RLC). LO BB 3-35 v Warwks (Worcester) 2013 (Y40). T20 HS 62*. T20 BB 3-20.

FELL, Thomas Charles (Oakham S; Oxford Brookes U), b Hillingdon, Middx 17 Oct 1993. 6'1". RHB, WK, occ OB. Squad No 29. Oxford MCCU 2013. Worcestershire debut 2013. Worcestershire 2nd XI debut 2010. 1000 runs (1): 1127 (2015). HS 171 v Middx (Worcester) 2015. LO HS 116* v Lancs (Worcester) 2016 (RLC).

NQ**HASTINGS, John** Wayne (St Dominic's Catholic C, Sydney; Australian C of PE), b Penrith, NSW, Australia 4 Nov 1985. 6'6". RHB, RFM. Victoria 2007-08 to date. Durham 2014-15. Joins Worcestershire in 2017, subject to injury concerns. IPL: CSK 2014. KKR 2016. Big Bash: MS 2012-13 to date. **Tests** (A): 1 (2012-13); HS 32 and BB 1-51 v SA (Perth) 2012-13. **LOI** (A): 28 (2010-11 to 2016-17), HS 51 v SA (Centurion) 2016-17; BB 6-45 v SL (Dambulla) 2016. **IT20** (A): 9 (2010-11 to 2016); HS 15 v SL (Perth) 2010-11; BB 3-14 v SL (Pallekele) 2011. HS 93 Vic v Tas (Hobart) 2009-10. CC HS 91 Du v Sussex (Arundel) 2015. BB 7-60 Du v Worcs (Worcester) 2015. LO HS 69* Vic v S Australia (Adelaide) 2012-13. LO BB 6-45 (*see LOI*). T20 HS 80*. T20 BB 4-26.

HEPBURN, Alex (Aquinas C, Perth), b Subiaco, W Australia 21 Dec 1995. 5'10". RHB, RM. Squad No 26. Worcestershire 2nd XI debut 2013. Awaiting f-c debut. LO HS 32 v Derbys (Derby) 2015 (RLC). LO BB 4-34 v Leics (Worcester) 2015 (RLC).

KERVEZEE, Alexei Nicolaas (Duneside HS, Namibia; Grenoobi HS, SA; Segbroek C, Holland), b Walvis Bay, Namibia 11 Sep 1989. 5'8". RHB, OB. Squad No 5. Netherlands 2005 to 2009-10. Worcestershire debut 2008. Now qualified for England. **LOI** (Neth): 39 (2006 to 2011-12); HS 92 v Kenya (Voorburg) 2010; BB – . **IT20** (Neth): 10 (2009 to 2011-12); HS 58* v Afghanistan (Dubai, DSC) 2011-12. 1000 runs (1): 1190 (2010). HS 155 v Derbys (Derby) 2010. BB 3-72 v Sussex (Hove) 2015. LO HS 121* Neth v Denmark (Potchefstroom) 2008-09. LO BB – . T20 HS 58*.

KOHLER-CADMORE, Tom (Malvern C), b Chatham, Kent 19 Aug 1994. 6'2". RHB, OB. Squad No 32. Debut (Worcestershire) 2014. Worcestershire 2nd XI debut 2010, aged 15y 342d. HS 169 v Glos (Worcester) 2016. LO HS 119 v Northants (Worcester) 2016 (RLC). T20 HS 127 v Durham (Worcester) 2016 – Wo record, winning Walter Lawrence Trophy for fastest 100 (43 balls).

LEACH, Joseph (Shrewsbury S; Leeds U), b Stafford 30 Oct 1990. Elder brother of S.G.Leach (Oxford MCCU 2014-16). 6'1". RHB, RMF. Squad No 23. Leeds/Bradford MCCU 2012. Worcestershire debut 2012; captain 2017. Staffordshire 2008-09. HS 114 v Glos (Cheltenham) 2013. 50 wkts (2); most – 67 (2016). BB 6-73 v Warwks (Birmingham) 2015. LO HS 63 v Yorks (Leeds) 2016 (RLC). LO BB 4-30 v Northants (Worcester) 2015 (RLC). T20 HS 20. T20 BB 5-33.

MITCHELL, Daryl Keith Henry (Prince Henry's HS; University C, Worcester), b Badsey, near Evesham 25 Nov 1983. 5'10". RHB, RM. Squad No 27. Debut (Worcestershire) 2005; captain 2011-16; benefit 2016. Mountaineers 2011-12. MCC 2015. 1000 runs (4); most – 1334 (2014). HS 298 v Somerset (Taunton) 2009. BB 4-49 v Yorks (Leeds) 2009. LO HS 107 v Sussex (Hove) 2013 (Y40). LO BB 4-19 v Northants (Milton Keynes) 2014 (RLC). T20 HS 68*. T20 BB 5-28 v Northants (Northampton) 2014 – Wo record.

MORRIS, Charles Andrew John (King's C, Taunton; Oxford Brookes U), b Hereford 6 Jul 1992. 6'0". RHB, RMF. Squad No 31. Oxford MCCU 2012-14. Worcestershire debut 2013. Worcestershire 2nd XI debut 2012. Kent 2nd XI 2012. MCC Univs 2012. Devon 2011-12. HS 33* OU v Warwks (Oxford) 2013. Wo HS 25* v Australians (Worcester) 2013. CC HS 24 v Glos (Worcester) 2014 and 24 v Sussex (Hove) 2015. 50 wkts (2); most – 56 (2014). BB 5-54 v Derbys (Derby) 2014. LO HS 16* v Northants (Milton Keynes) 2014 (RLC). LO BB 3-46 v Derbys (Derby) 2015 (RLC). T20 HS 3. T20 BB 2-30.

RHODES, George Harry (Chase HS & SFC, Malvern), b Birmingham 26 Oct 1993. Son of S.J.Rhodes (Yorkshire, Worcestershire & England 1981-2004) and grandson of W.E.Rhodes (Nottinghamshire 1961-64). RHB, OB. Squad No 34. Debut (Worcestershire) 2016. Worcestershire 2nd XI debut 2012. HS 59 v Essex (Chelmsford) 2016. BB 2-83 v Kent (Canterbury) 2016. LO HS 5* v Lancs (Worcester) 2016 (RLC). LO BB 2-34 v Yorks (Leeds) 2016 (RLC). T20 HS 8. T20 BB 4-13.

NQ**SANTNER, Mitchell** Josef, b Hamilton, New Zealand 5 Feb 1992. LHB, SLA. N Districts 2011-12 to date. Worcestershire debut 2016. Rejoins in 2017 for T20 only. **Tests** (NZ): 14 (2015-16 to 2016-17); HS 73 v B (Wellington) 2016-17; BB 3-60 v I (Kolkata) 2016-17. **LOI** (NZ): 32 (2015 to 2016-17); HS 48 v P (Wellington) 2015-16; BB 3-31 v E (Chester-le-St) 2015. **IT20** (NZ): 14 (2015 to 2016-17); HS 18 and BB 4-11 v I (Nagpur) 2015-16. F-c Tour (NZ): A 2015-16; SA 2016; I 2016-17; Z 2016. HS 118 ND v Canterbury (Gisborne) 2013-14. Wo HS 23* v Glamorgan (Cardiff) 2016. BB 3-51 ND v Auckland (Whangarei) 2014-15. LO HS 86 ND v CD (New Plymouth) 2014-15. LO BB 4-38 NZ A v Sri Lanka A (Christchurch) 2015-16. T20 HS 45*. T20 BB 4-11.

SCRIMSHAW, George Louis Sheridan (John Taylor HS, Burton), b Burton-on-Trent, Staffs 10 Feb 1998. 6'6". RHB, RMF. Squad No 9. Worcestershire 2nd XI debut 2016. Awaiting 1st XI debut.

SHANTRY, Jack David (Priory SS; Shrewsbury SFC; Liverpool U), b Shrewsbury, Shrops 29 Jan 1988. Son of B.K.Shantry (Gloucestershire 1978-79), brother of A.J.Shantry (Northants, Warwicks, Glamorgan 2003-11). 6'4". LHB, LM. Squad No 11. Debut (Worcestershire) 2009. Shropshire 2007-09. HS 106 v Glos (Worcester) 2016. 50 wkts (2); most – 67 (2015). BB 7-60 v Oxford MCCU (Oxford) 2013. CC BB 7-69 v Essex (Worcester) 2013. LO HS 31 v Somerset (Taunton) 2015 (RLC). LO BB 4-29 v Northants (Worcester) 2015 (RLC). T20 HS 12*. T20 BB 4-33.

TONGUE, Joshua Charles (King's S, Worcester; Worcester SFC), b Redditch 15 Nov 1997. 6'5". RHB, RM. Squad No 24. Debut (Worcestershire) 2016. Worcestershire 2nd XI debut 2015. HS – . BB 3-35 v Oxford MCCU (Oxford) 2016 – only 1st XI appearance.

TWOHIG, Benjamin Jake (Malvern C), b Dewsbury, Yorks 13 Apr 1998. 5'9". RHB, SLA. Squad No 42. Worcestershire 2nd XI debut 2014. Awaiting 1st XI debut.

WESTBURY, Oliver Edward (Ellowes Hall Sports C, Dudley; Shrewsbury S), b Dudley, Warwicks 2 Jul 1997. 5'10". RHB, OB. Squad No 19. Worcestershire 2nd XI debut 2015. England U19 2016. Awaiting 1st XI debut.

WHITELEY, Ross Andrew (Repton S), b Sheffield, Yorks 13 Sep 1988. 6'2". LHB, LM. Squad No 44. Derbyshire 2008-13. Worcestershire debut 2013. HS 130* De v Kent (Derby) 2011. Wo HS 101 v Yorks (Scarborough) 2015. BB 2-6 De v Hants (Derby) 2012. Wo BB 1-23 v Hants (Worcester) 2013. LO HS 77 v Yorks (Worcester) 2015 (RLC). LO BB 1-17 De v Unicorns (Wormsley) 2012 (CB40). T20 HS 91*. T20 BB 1-12.

RELEASED/RETIRED

(Having made a County 1st XI appearance in 2016)

ABBOTT, K.J. – *see HAMPSHIRE.*

[NQ]**CUMMINS, Miguel** Lamar, b St Michael, Barbados 5 Sep 1990. LHB, RF. Barbados 2011-12 to date. Worcestershire 2016. **Tests** (WI): 5 (2016 to 2016-17); HS 24* v I (Kingston) 2016; BB 6-48 v I (Gros Islet) 2016. **LOI** (WI): 2 (2013-14 to 2016-17); HS – ; BB 1-42 v Ireland (Kingston) 2013-14. HS 29* Barbados v Leeward Is (Basseterre) 2015-16. Wo HS 25 and Wo BB 7-84 (12-166 match) v Sussex (Hove) 2016. BB 7-45 Barbados v T&T (Port of Spain) 2012-13. LO HS 4* WI A v India A (Bangalore) 2013. LO BB 4-31 WI A v India A (Bangalore) 2013 – separate matches. T20 HS 10. T20 BB 1-24.

HENRY, M.J. – *see DERBYSHIRE.*

RUSSELL, Christopher James (Medina HS), b Newport, IoW 16 Feb 1989. 6'1". RHB, RMF. Worcestershire 2012-14. No f-c appearances 2015-16. HS 22 v Middx (Worcester) 2012. BB 4-43 v Warwks (Birmingham) 2012. LO HS 2 v Derbys (Worcester) 2016 (RLC). LO BB 4-32 v Netherlands (Rotterdam) 2013 (Y40). T20 HS 3*. T20 HS – . T20 BB 4-40.

WARWICKSHIRE RELEASED/RETIRED (continued from p 187)

(Having made a County 1st XI appearance in 2016)

CHOPRA, V. – *see ESSEX.*

EVANS, L.J. – *see SUSSEX.*

GORDON, Recordo Olton (Aston Manor S; Hamstead Hall SFC), b St Elizabeth, Jamaica 12 Oct 1991. RHB, RFM. Warwickshire 2013-14. No f-c appearances in 2015-16. HS 14* and BB 4-53 v Somerset (Taunton) 2014. LO HS 9* v Notts (Mkt Warsop) 2015 (RLC). LO BB 3-25 v Surrey (Birmingham) 2014 (RLC). T20 HS 18. T20 BB 4-20.

JONES, R.A. – *see LEICESTERSHIRE.*

RONCHI, L. – *see LEICESTERSHIRE.*

[NQ]**WADE, Matthew** Scott, b Hobart, Australia 26 Dec 1987. 5'7". LHB, WK, occ RM. Victoria 2007-08 to date. Warwickshire 2016 (T20 only). IPL: DD 2011. BB: MS 2011-12 to 2013-14. MR 2014-15 to 2015-16. **Tests** (A): 18 (2012 to 2016-17); HS 106 v WI (Roseau) 2012. **LOI** (A): 87 (2011-12 to 2016-17); HS 100* v P (Brisbane) 2016-17. **IT20** (A): 26 (2011-12 to 2016); HS 72 v I (Sydney) 2011-12. F-c Tours: E 2013; WI 2012; I 2012-13, 2015 (Aus A), 2016-17. HS 152 Vic v Q (Brisbane) 2014-15. BB 1-23 Vic v Q (Brisbane) 2013-14. LO HS 130 Aus A v South Africa A (Chennai) 2015. T20 HS 80.

F.R.J.Coleman and J.P.Webb left the staff without making a County 1st XI appearance in 2016.

WORCESTERSHIRE 2016

RESULTS SUMMARY

	Place	Won	Lost	Drew	Aband	NR
Specsavers County Champ (2nd Division)	3rd	6	4	5	1	
All First-Class Matches		7	4	5	1	
Royal London One-Day Cup (North Group)	8th	4	4			1
NatWest t20 Blast (North Group)	8th	5	7			2

SPECSAVERS COUNTY CHAMPIONSHIP AVERAGES

BATTING AND FIELDING

Cap†		*M*	*I*	*NO*	*HS*	*Runs*	*Avge*	*100*	*50*	*Ct/St*
2008	M.M.Ali	3	4	1	136*	273	91.00	1	2	–
2015	J.M.Clarke	15	26	1	194	1206	48.24	5	4	6
2016	M.J.Henry	6	6	2	49*	180	45.00	–	–	1
2012	J.Leach	15	21	5	107*	583	36.43	1	4	4
2009	O.B.Cox	15	23	2	75	757	36.04	–	6	32/2
2013	T.C.Fell	8	16	1	85	530	35.33	–	4	4
2005	D.K.H.Mitchell	15	27	2	107*	873	34.92	2	5	13
2012	B.L.D'Oliveira	14	25	1	202*	763	31.79	2	2	8
2016	G.H.Rhodes	6	11	2	59	274	30.44	–	2	2
2014	T.Kohler-Cadmore	13	21	1	169	561	28.05	2	1	18
2013	R.A.Whiteley	13	22	2	71	542	27.10	–	4	12
2015	E.G.Barnard	14	20	4	73	430	26.87	–	2	5
2009	J.D.Shantry	11	12	4	106	210	26.25	1	–	4
2009	A.N.Kervezee	4	7	1	41	151	25.16	–	–	1
2014	C.A.J.Morris	7	9	6	11	32	10.66	–	–	1
2016	M.L.Cummins	3	4	1	25	29	9.66	–	–	–

Also batted: K.J.Abbott (2 matches – cap 2016) 5, 3, 10; M.J.Santner (1 – cap 2016) 23*.

BOWLING

	O	*M*	*R*	*W*	*Avge*	*Best*	*5wI*	*10wM*
M.L.Cummins	96.2	12	377	15	25.13	7-84	2	1
M.J.Henry	234	48	716	27	26.51	5-36	1	–
J.Leach	495.4	74	1786	65	27.47	5-60	5	–
E.G.Barnard	358.2	66	1351	31	43.58	4-62	–	–
B.L.D'Oliveira	259.1	30	761	16	47.56	4-80	–	–
C.A.J.Morris	144.1	26	563	11	51.18	2-35	–	–
J.D.Shantry	358.2	87	1039	18	57.72	4-89	–	–

Also bowled: K.J.Abbott 75-17-249-1; M.M.Ali 42-5-161-1; J.M.Clarke 2-0-22-0; T.C.Fell 2.2-1-10-0; A.N.Kervezee 33-9-89-1; D.K.H.Mitchell 30.5-6-92-3; G.H.Rhodes 64.5-5-263-3.

The First-Class Averages (pp 226–242) give the records of Worcestershire players in all first-class county matches (Worcestershire's other opponents being Oxford MCCU), with the exception of M.M.Ali, whose first-class figures for Worcestershire are as above.

† Worcestershire revised their capping policy in 2002 and now award players with their County Colours when they make their Championship debut.

WORCESTERSHIRE RECORDS

FIRST-CLASS CRICKET

Highest Total	For 701-6d		v	Surrey	Worcester	2007
	V 701-4d		by	Leics	Worcester	1906
Lowest Total	For 24		v	Yorkshire	Huddersfield	1903
	V 30		by	Hampshire	Worcester	1903
Highest Innings	For 405*	G.A.Hick	v	Somerset	Taunton	1988
	V 331*	J.D.B.Robertson	for	Middlesex	Worcester	1949

Highest Partnership for each Wicket

1st	309	H.K.Foster/F.L.Bowley	v	Derbyshire	Derby	1901
2nd	316	S.C.Moore/V.S.Solanki	v	Glos	Cheltenham	2008
3rd	438*	G.A.Hick/T.M.Moody	v	Hampshire	Southampton	1997
4th	330	B.F.Smith/G.A.Hick	v	Somerset	Taunton	2006
5th	393	E.G.Arnold/W.B.Burns	v	Warwicks	Birmingham	1909
6th	265	G.A.Hick/S.J.Rhodes	v	Somerset	Taunton	1988
7th	256	D.A.Leatherdale/S.J.Rhodes	v	Notts	Nottingham	2002
8th	184	S.J.Rhodes/S.R.Lampitt	v	Derbyshire	Kidderminster	1991
9th	181	J.A.Cuffe/R.D.Burrows	v	Glos	Worcester	1907
10th	119	W.B.Burns/G.A.Wilson	v	Somerset	Worcester	1906

Best Bowling	For	9- 23	C.F.Root	v	Lancashire	Worcester	1931
(Innings)	V	10- 51	J.Mercer	for	Glamorgan	Worcester	1936
Best Bowling	For	15- 87	A.J.Conway	v	Glos	Moreton-in-M	1914
(Match)	V	17-212	J.C.Clay	for	Glamorgan	Swansea	1937

Most Runs – Season	2654	H.H.I.H.Gibbons	(av 52.03)	1934
Most Runs – Career	34490	D.Kenyon	(av 34.18)	1946-67
Most 100s – Season	10	G.M.Turner		1970
	10	G.A.Hick		1988
Most 100s – Career	106	G.A.Hick		1984-2008
Most Wkts – Season	207	C.F.Root	(av 17.52)	1925
Most Wkts – Career	2143	R.T.D.Perks	(av 23.73)	1930-55
Most Career W-K Dismissals	1095	S.J.Rhodes	(991 ct; 104 st)	1985-2004
Most Career Catches in the Field	528	G.A.Hick		1984-2008

LIMITED-OVERS CRICKET

Highest Total	**50ov**	404-3		v	Devon	Worcester	1987
	40ov	376-6		v	Surrey	Oval	2010
	T20	227-6		v	Northants	Kidderminster	2007
Lowest Total	**50ov**	58		v	Ireland	Worcester	2009
	40ov	86		v	Yorkshire	Leeds	1969
	T20	53		v	Lancashire	Manchester	2016
Highest Innings	**50ov**	180*	T.M.Moody	v	Surrey	The Oval	1994
	40ov	160	T.M.Moody	v	Kent	Worcester	1991
	T20	127	T.Kohler-Cadmore	v	Durham	Worcester	2004
Best Bowling	**50ov**	7-19	N.V.Radford	v	Beds	Bedford	1991
	40ov	6-16	Shoaib Akhtar	v	Glos	Worcester	2005
	T20	5-28	D.K.H.Mitchell	v	Northants	Northampton	2014

YORKSHIRE

Formation of Present Club: 8 January 1863
Substantial Reorganisation: 10 December 1891
Inaugural First-Class Match: 1864
Colours: Dark Blue, Light Blue and Gold
Badge: White Rose
County Championships (since 1890): (32) 1893, 1896, 1898, 1900, 1901, 1902, 1905, 1908, 1912, 1919, 1922, 1923, 1924, 1925, 1931, 1932, 1933, 1935, 1937, 1938, 1939, 1946, 1959, 1960, 1962, 1963, 1966, 1967, 1968, 2001, 2014, 2015
Joint Champions: (1) 1949
Gillette/C&G Trophy Winners: (3) 1965, 1969, 2002
Benson and Hedges Cup Winners: (1) 1987
Sunday League Winners: (1) 1983
Twenty20 Cup Winners: (0); best – Finalist 2012

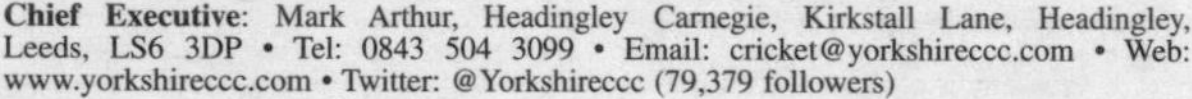

Chief Executive: Mark Arthur, Headingley Carnegie, Kirkstall Lane, Headingley, Leeds, LS6 3DP • Tel: 0843 504 3099 • Email: cricket@yorkshireccc.com • Web: www.yorkshireccc.com • Twitter: @Yorkshireccc (79,379 followers)

Director of Professional Cricket: Martyn Moxon. **1st XI Coach**: Andrew Gale. **YCCC Coach**: Ian Dews. **Captain**: G.S.Ballance. **Vice-Captain**: T.T.Bresnan. **Overseas Player**: P.S.P.Handscomb. **2017 Testimonials**: S.A.Patterson and R.J.Sidebottom (Aug-Sep). **Head Groundsman**: Andy Fogarty. **Scorer**: John Potter. ‡ New registration. [NQ] Not qualified for England.

AZEEM Muhammad **RAFIQ** (Holgate S Sports C; Barnsley C), b Karachi, Pakistan 27 Feb 1991. 5'11". RHB, OB. Squad No 30. Yorkshire debut 2009. Derbyshire (on loan) 2011. HS 100 v Worcs (Worcester) 2009. BB 5-50 v Essex (Chelmsford) 2012. LO HS 34* v Unicorns (Leeds) 2012 (CB40). LO BB 5-30 v Bangladesh A (Leeds) 2013. T20 HS 21*. T20 BB 3-15.

BAIRSTOW, Jonathan Marc (St Peter's S, York; Leeds Met U), b Bradford 26 Sep 1989. Son of D.L.Bairstow (Yorkshire, GW and England 1970-90); brother of A.D.Bairstow (Derbyshire 1995). 6'0". RHB, WK, occ RM. Squad No 21. Debut (Yorkshire) 2009; cap 2011. Inaugural winner of Young Wisden Schools Cricketer of the Year 2008. YC 2011. **ECB Test Central Contract 2016-17. Tests**: 38 (2012 to 2016-17); 1000 runs (1): 1470 (2016); HS 167* v SL (Lord's) 2016. Took a world record 70 dismissals in 2016, as well as scoring a record number of runs in a calendar year for a keeper. **LOI**: 23 (2011 to 2016-17); HS 83* v NZ (Chester-le-St) 2015. **IT20**: 20 (2011 to 2016): HS 60* v P (Dubai) 2011-12. F-c Tours: A 2013-14; SA 2014-15 (EL), 2015-16; WI 2010-11 (EL); I 2012-13, 2016-17; SL 2013-14 (EL); B 2016-17; UAE 2015-16 (v P). 1000 runs (3); most – 1286 (2016). HS 246 v Hants (Leeds) 2016. LO HS 123 EL v New Zealand A (Bristol) 2014. T20 HS 102*.

BALLANCE, Gary Simon (Peterhouse S, Marondera, Zimbabwe; Harrow S; Leeds Met U), b Harare, Zimbabwe 22 Nov 1989. Nephew of G.S.Ballance (Rhodesia B 1978-79) and D.L.Houghton (Rhodesia/Zimbabwe 1978-79 to 1997-98). 6'0". LHB, LB. Squad No 19. Debut (Yorkshire) 2008; cap 2012; captain 2017. MWR 2010-11 to 2011-12. *Wisden* 2014. **Tests**: 21 (2013-14 to 2016-17); HS 156 v I (Southampton) 2014; BB – . **LOI**: 16 (2013 to 2014-15); HS 79 v A (Melbourne) 2013-14. F-c Tours: A 2013-14; WI 2014-15; B 2016-17. 1000 runs (1+1); most – 1363 (2013). HS 210 MWR v SR (Masvingo) 2011-12. Y HS 174 v Northants (Leeds) 2014. BB – . LO HS 139 v Unicorns (Leeds) 2013. T20 HS 68.

BRESNAN, Timothy Thomas (Castleford HS and TC; Pontefract New C), b Pontefract 28 Feb 1985. 6'0". RHB, RFM. Squad No 16. Debut (Yorkshire) 2003; cap 2006; benefit 2014. MCC 2006, 2009. Big Bash: HH 2014-15. *Wisden* 2011. **Tests**: 23 (2009 to 2013-14); HS 91 v B (Dhaka) 2009-10; BB 5-48 v I (Nottingham) 2011. **LOI**: 85 (2006 to 2015); HS 80 v SA (Centurion) 2009-10; BB 5-48 v I (Bangalore) 2010-11. **IT20**: 34 (2006 to 2013-14); HS 47* v WI (Bridgetown) 2013-14; BB 3-10 v P (Cardiff) 2010. F-c Tours: A 2010-11, 2013-14; I 2012-13; SL 2011-12; B 2006-07 (Eng A), 2009-10. HS 169* v Durham (Chester-le-St) 2015, sharing Y record 7th wkt partnership of 366* with J.M.Bairstow. BB 5-36 v Notts (Scarborough) 2016. LO HS 95* v Notts (Scarborough) 2016 (RLC). BB 5-48 (*see LOI*). T20 HS 51. T20 BB 3-10.

BROOK, Harry Cherrington (Sedbergh S), b Keighley 22 Feb 1999. 5'11". RHB, RM. Debut (Yorkshire) 2016. Yorkshire 2nd XI debut 2015. England U19 2016-17. HS 0.

BROOKS, Jack Alexander (Wheatley Park S), b Oxford 4 Jun 1984. 6'2". RHB, RFM. Squad No 70. Northamptonshire 2009-12; cap 2012. Yorkshire debut 2013; cap 2013. Oxfordshire 2004-09. F-c Tour (EL): SA 2014-15. HS 53 Nh v Glos (Bristol) 2010. Y HS 50* v Middx (Lord's) 2015. 50 wkts (3); most – 71 (2014). BB 6-65 v Middx (Lord's) 2016. LO HS 10 Nh v Middx (Uxbridge) 2009 (P40). LO BB 3-30 v Hants (Southampton) 2014 (RLC). T20 HS 33*. T20 BB 5-21.

CALLIS, Elliot (Worksop C), b Doncaster 8 Nov 1994. 6'2". RHB, LB. Debut (Yorkshire) 2016. Yorkshire 2nd XI debut 2013. Bedfordshire 2015. HS 84 v Pakistan A (Leeds) 2016. LO HS 10 v Sri Lanka A (Leeds) 2014.

CARVER, Karl (Thirsk S & SFC), b Northallerton 26 Mar 1996. 5'10". LHB, SLA. Squad No 29. Debut (Yorkshire) 2014. Yorkshire 2nd XI debut 2013. HS 16 v Leeds/Bradford MCCU (Leeds) 2015. CC HS 5 v Worcs (Worcester) 2015. BB 4-106 v MCC (Abu Dhabi) 2015-16. CC BB – . LO HS 35* v Somerset (Scarborough) 2015 (RLC). LO BB 3-5 v Lancs (Manchester) 2016 (RLC). T20 HS 2. T20 BB 3-40.

COAD, Benjamin Oliver (Thirsk S & SFC), b Harrogate 10 Jan 1994. 6'2". RHB, RM. Squad No 10. Debut (Yorkshire) 2016. Yorkshire 2nd XI debut 2012. HS 17* and CC BB 1-70 v Durham (Chester-le-St) 2016. BB 1-57 v Pakistan A (Leeds) 2016. LO HS 2* v Sri Lanka A (Leeds) 2014. LO BB 1-34 v Glos (Bristol) 2013 (Y40). T20 HS 2*. T20 BB 2-24.

FISHER, Matthew David (Easingwold SS), b York 9 Nov 1997. 6'1". RHB, RFM. Squad No 7. Debut (Yorkshire) 2015. Yorkshire 2nd XI debut 2013, aged 15y 201d. England U19 2014. Missed almost all of 2016 season through injury. HS 0*. BB 2-61 v Hants (Southampton), 2015. LO HS 34 v Somerset (Scarborough) 2015 (RLC). LO BB 3-32 v Leics (Leeds) 2015 (RLC). T20 HS 0*. T20 BB 5-22.

GIBSON, Ryan (Fylinghall S), b Middlesbrough 22 Jan 1996. 6'4". RHB, RM. Squad No 24. Debut (Yorkshire) 2016. Yorkshire 2nd XI debut 2012. HS 0 and BB 1-42 v Pakistan A (Leeds) 2016. LO HS 9 v Sri Lanka A (Leeds) 2014. LO BB 1-17 v Bangladesh A (Leeds) 2013. T20 HS 18. T20 BB – .

‡[NQ]**HANDSCOMB, Peter** Stephen Patrick (Mt Waverley SC; Deakin U, Melbourne), b Melbourne, Australia 26 Apr 1991. RHB, WK. British passport (English parents). Victoria 2011-12 to date. Gloucestershire 2015; cap 2015. IPL: RPS 2016. Big Bash: MS 2012-13 to date. **Tests** (A): 6 (2016-17); HS 110 v P (Sydney) 2016-17. **LOI** (A): 5 (2016-17); HS 82 v P (Perth) 2016-17. F-c Tours (A): I 2015 (Aus A), 2016-17. HS 215 Vic v NSW (Sydney) 2016-17. CC HS 76 Gs v Lancs (Manchester) 2015. LO HS 82 (*see LOI*). T20 HS 103*.

HODD, Andrew John (Bexhill C; Loughborough U), b Chichester, Sussex 12 Jan 1984. 5'9". RHB, WK. Squad No 4. Sussex 2003-11. Surrey 2005 (1 match). Yorkshire debut 2012 (on loan); cap 2016. HS 123 Sx v Yorks (Hove) 2007. Y HS 96* v Notts (Scarborough) 2016. LO HS 91 Sx v Lancs (Hove) 2010 (CB40). T20 HS 70.

LEANING, Jack Andrew (Archbishop Holgate's S, York; York C), b Bristol, Glos 18 Oct 1993. 5'10". RHB, RMF. Squad No 34. Debut (Yorkshire) 2013; cap 2016. Yorkshire 2nd XI debut 2011. YC 2015. HS 123 v Somerset (Taunton) 2014. BB 1-82 v Notts (Nottingham) 2015. LO HS 131* v Leics (Leicester) 2016 (RLC). LO BB 5-22 v Unicorns (Leeds) 2013 (Y40). T20 HS 64. T20 BB – .

LEES, Alexander Zak (Holy Trinity SS, Halifax), b Halifax 14 Apr 1993. 6'3". LHB, LB. Squad No 14. Debut (Yorkshire) 2010; cap 2014; captain (l-o) 2016. Yorkshire 2nd XI debut 2010. YC 2014. 1000 runs (2); most – 1199 (2016). HS 275* v Derbys (Chesterfield) 2013. LO HS 102 v Northants (Northampton) 2014 (RLC). T20 HS 67*.

LYTH, Adam (Caedmon S, Whitby; Whitby Community C), b Whitby 25 Sep 1987. 5'8". LHB, RM. Squad No 9. Debut (Yorkshire) 2007; cap 2010. PCA 2014. *Wisden* 2014. **Tests**: 7 (2015); HS 107 v NZ (Leeds) 2015. F-c Tours (EL): SA 2014-15; WI 2010-11. 1000 runs (3); most – 1619 (2014). HS 251 v Lancs (Manchester) 2014, sharing in Y record 6th wicket partnership of 296 with A.U.Rashid. BB 2-9 v Middx (Scarborough) 2016. LO HS 136 v Lancs (Manchester) 2016 (RLC). LO BB 1-6 v Middx (Leeds) 2013 (Y40). T20 HS 87. T20 BB 2-5.

PATTERSON, Steven Andrew (Malet Lambert CS; St Mary's SFC, Hull; Leeds U), b Hull 3 Oct 1983. 6'4". RHB, RMF. Squad No 17. Debut (Yorkshire) 2005; cap 2012; testimonial 2017. Bradford/Leeds UCCE 2003 (not f-c). HS 63* v Warwks (Birmingham) 2016. 50 wkts (2); most – 53 (2012). BB 6-56 v Durham (Chester-le-St) 2016. LO HS 25* v Worcs (Leeds) 2006 (P40). LO BB 6-32 v Derbys (Leeds) 2010. T20 HS 3*. T20 BB 4-30.

PLUNKETT, Liam Edward (Nunthorpe SS; Teesside Tertiary C), b Middlesbrough 6 Apr 1985. 6'3". RHB, RFM. Squad No 28. Durham 2003-12. Dolphins 2007-08. Yorkshire debut 2013; cap 2013. **ECB L-O Central Contract 2016-17. Tests**: 13 (2005-06 to 2014); HS 55* v I (Lord's) 2014; BB 5-64 v SL (Leeds) 2014. **LOI**: 49 (2005-06 to 2016-17); HS 56 v P (Lahore) 2005-06; BB 4-40 v WI (North Sound) 2016-17. **IT20**: 11 (2006 to 2016-17); HS 4 v WI (Kolkata) 2015-16; BB 3-21 v P (Dubai, DSC) 2015-16. F-c Tours (EL): SA 2014-15; WI 2010-11; NZ 2008-09; I 2005-06 (E), 2007-08; P 2005-06 (E); SL 2013-14. HS 126 v Hants (Leeds) 2016. 50 wkts (3); most – 60 (2009). BB 6-33 v Leeds/Bradford MCCU (Leeds) 2013 on Y debut. CC BB 6-63 (11-119 match) Du v Worcs (Chester-le-St) 2009. LO HS 72 Du v Somerset (Chester-le-St) 2008 (P40). LO BB 4-15 Du v Essex (Chester-le-St) 2007 (FPT). T20 HS 41. T20 BB 5-31.

RASHID, Adil Usman (Belle Vue S, Bradford), b Bradford 17 Feb 1988. 5'8". RHB, LBG. Squad No 3. Debut (Yorkshire) 2006; cap 2008. MCC 2007-09. Big Bash: AS 2015-16. YC 2007. Match double (114, 48, 8-157 and 2-45) for England U19 v India U19 (Taunton) 2006. Tests: 10 (2015-16 to 2016-17); HS 61 v P (Dubai, DSC) 2015-16; BB 5-64 v P (Abu Dhabi) 2015-16 – on debut. **LOI**: 41 (2009 to 2016-17); HS 69 v NZ (Birmingham) 2015; BB 4-43 v B (Chittagong) 2016-17. **IT20**: 23 (2009 to 2016-17); HS 9* v SA (Nottingham) 2009; BB 2-18 v P (Dubai, DSC) 2015-16 and 2-18 v Afghanistan (Delhi) 2015-16. F-c Tours: WI 2010-11 (EL); I 2007-08 (EL), 2016-17; B 2006-07 (Eng A), 2016-17; UAE 2015-16 (v P). HS 180 v Somerset (Leeds) 2013. 50 wkts (2); most – 65 (2008). BB 7-107 v Hants (Southampton) 2008. LO HS 71 v Glos (Leeds) 2014 (RLC). LO BB 5-33 v Hants (Southampton) 2014 (RLC). T20 HS 36*. T20 BB 4-20.

READ, Jonathan (Lady Lumley's S & SFC), b Scarborough 2 Feb 1998. 5'7". RHB, WK. Debut (Yorkshire) 2016. Yorkshire 2nd XI debut 2015. HS 14 v Pakistan A (Leeds) 2016.

RHODES, William Michael Henry (Cottingham HS, Cottingham SFC, Hull), b Nottingham 2 Mar 1995. 6'2". LHB, RMF. Squad No 35. Debut (Yorkshire) 2014-15. Essex 2016 (on loan). Yorkshire 2nd XI debut 2012. England U19 2014. HS 95 v MCC (Abu Dhabi) 2015-16. CC HS 79 v Warwks (Birmingham) 2015. BB 3-42 v Middx (Leeds) 2015. LO HS 46 v Leics (Leeds) 2015 (RLC). LO BB 2-22 v Essex (Chelmsford) 2015 (RLC). T20 HS 45. T20 BB 3-27.

ROOT, Joseph Edward (King Ecgbert S, Sheffield; Worksop C), b Sheffield 30 Dec 1990. Elder brother of W.T.Root (*see NOTTINGHAMSHIRE*). 6'0". RHB, OB. Squad No 5. Debut (Yorkshire) 2010; cap 2012. YC 2012. **ECB Test & L-O Central Contract 2016-17. Tests**: 53 (2012-13 to 2016-17); 1000 runs (2); most – 1477 (2016); HS 254 v P (Manchester) 2016, BB 2-9 v A (Lord's) 2013. **LOI**: 83 (2012-13 to 2016-17); HS 125 v SA (Centurion) 2015-16; BB 2-15 v WI (North Sound) 2013-14. **IT20**: 24 (2012-13 to 2016-17); HS 90* v A (Southampton) 2013; BB 2-9 v WI (Kolkata) 2015-16. F-c Tours: A 2013-14; SA 2015-16; WI 2014-15; NZ 2012-13; I 2012-13, 2016-17; B 2016-17; UAE 2015-16 (v P). 1000 runs (3); most – 1228 (2013). HS 254 (*see Tests*). CC HS 236 v Derbys (Leeds) 2013. BB 3-33 v Warwks (Leeds) 2011. LO HS 125 (*see LOI*). LO BB 2-10 EL v Bangladesh A (Sylhet) 2011-12. T20 HS 92*. T20 BB 1-12.

SHAW, Joshua (Crofton HS, Wakefield; Skills Exchange C), b Wakefield, Yorks 3 Jan 1996. Son of C.Shaw (Yorkshire 1984-88). 6'1". RHB, RMF. Squad No 25. Gloucestershire 2016 (on season-long loan); cap 2016. Yorkshire 2016. Yorkshire 2nd XI debut 2012. England U19 2012-13 to 2014. HS 29 Gs v Leics (Cheltenham) 2016. Y HS 24 v Durham (Chester-le-St) 2016. BB 5-79 Gs v Sussex (Bristol) 2016. Y BB 3-58 v Pakistan A (Leeds) 2016. T20 HS 0*. T20 BB – .

SIDEBOTTOM, Ryan Jay (King James's GS, Almondbury), b Huddersfield 15 Jan 1978. Son of A.Sidebottom (Yorkshire, OFS and England 1973-91). 6'3". LHB, LFM. Squad No 11. Debut (Yorkshire) 1997; cap 2000; testimonial 2017. Nottinghamshire 2004-10; cap 2004; benefit 2010. *Wisden* 2007. **Tests**: 22 (2001 to 2009-10); HS 31 v SL (Kandy) 2007-08; BB 7-47 v NZ (Napier) 2007-08. Hat-trick v NZ (Hamilton) 2007-08. **LOI**: 25 (2001-02 to 2009-10); HS 24 v A (Southampton) 2009; BB 3-19 v SL (Dambulla) 2007-08. **IT20**: 18 (2007 to 2010); HS 5* and BB 3-16 v NZ (Auckland) 2007-08. F-c Tours: SA 2009-10; WI 2000-01 (Eng A), 2008-09; NZ 2007-08; SL 2007-08. HS 61 v Worcs (Worcester) 2011. 50 wkts (4); most – 62 (2011). BB 7-37 (11-98 match) v Somerset (Leeds) 2011. LO HS 32 Nt v Middx (Nottingham) 2005 (NL). LO BB 6-40 v Glamorgan (Cardiff) 1998 (SL). T20 HS 17*. T20 BB 4-25.

WAINMAN, James Charles (Leeds GS), b Harrogate 25 Jan 1993. 6'4". RHB, LMF. Squad No 15. Yorkshire 2nd XI debut 2010. Awaiting f-c debut. LO HS 33 and LO BB 3-51 v Sri Lanka A (Leeds) 2014. T20 HS 12*. T20 BB 1-27.

WAITE, Matthew James (Brigshaw HS), b Leeds 24 Dec 1995. 6'0". RHB, RFM. Squad No 6. Yorkshire 2nd XI debut 2014. Awaiting f-c debut. LO HS 38 and LO BB 3-48 v Surrey (Leeds) 2016 (RLC). T20 HS 19*. T20 BB 1-6.

WARNER, Jared David (Kettleborough Park HS; Silcoates SFC), b Wakefield 14 Nov 1995. 6'1". RHB, RFM. Squad No 45. Yorkshire 2nd XI debut 2015. England U19 2014-15 to 2015. Awaiting 1st XI debut.

WILLEY, David Jonathan (Northampton S), b Northampton 28 Feb 1990. Son of P.Willey (Northants, Leics and England 1966-91). 6'1". LHB, LFM. Squad No 72. Northamptonshire 2009-15; cap 2013. Yorkshire debut/cap 2016. Bedfordshire 2008. Big Bash: PS 2015-16 to date. **LOI**: 25 (2015 to 2016-17); HS 13* v SA (Centurion) 2015-16; BB 4-34 v SL (Cardiff) 2016. **IT20**: 12 (2015 to 2016); HS 21 and BB 3-20 v WI (Kolkata) 2015-16. HS 104* Nh v Glos (Northampton) 2015. Y HS 22 v Middx (Lord's) 2016. BB 5-29 (10-75 match) Nh v Glos (Northampton) 2011. Y BB 3-55 v Surrey (Leeds) 2016. LO HS 167 Nh v Warwks (Birmingham) 2013 (Y40). LO BB 5-62 EL v New Zealand A (Bristol) 2014. T20 HS 100. T20 BB 4-9.

RELEASED/RETIRED

(Having made a County 1st XI appearance in 2016)

GALE, Andrew William (Whitcliffe Mount S; Heckmondwike GS), b Dewsbury 28 Nov 1983. 6'2". LHB, LB. Yorkshire 2004-16; cap 2008; captain 2010-16; benefit 2016. F-c Tour (EL): WI 2010-11. 1000 runs (2); most – 1076 (2013). HS 272 v Notts (Scarborough) 2013. BB 1-33 v Loughborough UCCE (Leeds) 2007. LO HS 125* v Essex (Chelmsford) 2010 (CB40). T20 HS 91.

[NQ]**HEAD, Travis** Michael, b Adelaide, Australia 29 Dec 1993. LHB, OB. S Australia 2011-12 to date. Yorkshire 2016. IPL: RCB 2016. Big Bash: AS 2012-13 to date. MCC YC 2013. **LOI** (A): 22 (2016 to 2016-17); HS 128 v P (Adelaide) 2016-17; BB 2-22 v SL (Pallekele) 2016. **IT20** (A): 7 (2015-16 to 2016-17); HS 45 v SL (Pallekele) 2016; BB 1-16 v SL (Adelaide) 2016-17. F-c Tour (Aus A): I 2015. HS 192 S Aus v Tas (Adelaide) 2015-16. Y HS 54 v Warwks (Leeds) 2016. BB 3-42 S Aus v NSW (Adelaide) 2015-16. LO HS 202 S Aus v WA (Sydney) 2015-16. LO BB 2-9 S Aus v NSW (Brisbane) 2014-15. T20 HS 101*. T20 BB 3-16.

[NQ]**LEHMANN, Jake** Scott (Charles Campbell SS), b Melbourne, Australia 8 Jul 1992. Son of D.S.Lehmann (S Australia, Victoria, Yorkshire and Australia 1987-88 to 2007-08), nephew of C.White (Yorkshire, Victoria and England 1990-2007). LHB, SLA. S Australia 2014-15 to date. Yorkshire 2016. Big Bash: 2015-16 to date. HS 205 S Aus v Tas (Hobart) 2015-16. Y HS 116 v Somerset (Leeds) 2016. LO HS 58 S Aus v Vic (Sydney) 2015-16. T20 HS 24. T20 BB 1-5.

[NQ]**WILLIAMSON, Kane** Stuart (Tauranga Boys' C), b Tauranga, New Zealand 8 Aug 1990. Cousin of D.Cleaver (C Districts 2010-11 to date). 5'8". RHB, OB. N Districts 2007-08 to date. Gloucestershire 2011-12; cap 2011. Yorkshire 2013-16. IPL: SH 2015-16. **Tests** (NZ): 59 (2010-11 to 2016-17, 11 as captain); 1000 runs (1): 1172 (2015); HS 242* v SL (Wellington) 2014-15; scored 131 v I (Ahmedabad) 2010-11 on debut; BB 4-44 v E (Auckland) 2012-13. **LOI** (NZ): 111 (2010 to 2016-17, 37 as captain); 1000 runs (1): 1376 (2015); HS 145* v SA (Kimberley) 2012-13; BB 4-22 v SA (Paarl) 2012-13. **IT20** (NZ): 39 (2011-12 to 2016-17, 21 as captain); HS 73* v B (Napier) 2016-17; BB 2-16 v B (Mt Maunganui) 2016-17. F-c Tours (NZ)(C=Captain): E 2013, 2015; A 2011-12, 2015-16; SA 2012-13, 2016C; WI 2012, 2014; I 2010-11, 2012, 2016-17C; SL 2012-13; Z 2011-12, 2016C; B 2013-14; UAE 2014-15 (v P). HS 284* ND v Wellington (Lincoln) 2011-12). Y HS 189 v Sussex (Scarborough) 2014. BB 5-75 ND v Canterbury (Christchurch) 2008-09. CC BB 3-58 Gs v Northants (Northampton) 2012. Y BB 2-44 v Sussex (Hove) 2013. LO HS 145* (*see LOI*). LO BB 5-51 ND v Auckland (Auckland) 2009-10. T20 HS 101*. T20 BB 3-33.

YORKSHIRE 2016

RESULTS SUMMARY

	Place	*Won*	*Lost*	*Drew*	*NR*
Specsavers County Champ (1st Division)	3rd	5	3	8	
All First-Class Matches		5	3	9	
Royal London One-Day Cup (North Group)	SF	5	4		1
NatWest t20 Blast (North Group)	SF	8	6		2

SPECSAVERS COUNTY CHAMPIONSHIP AVERAGES

BATTING AND FIELDING

Cap		*M*	*I*	*NO*	*HS*	*Runs*	*Avge*	*100*	*50*	*Ct/St*
2011	J.M.Bairstow	4	6	–	246	533	88.83	2	–	5/1
	J.S.Lehmann	5	8	1	116	384	54.85	1	2	2
2006	T.T.Bresnan	11	19	4	142*	722	48.13	1	5	12
2013	L.E.Plunkett	8	13	3	126	449	44.90	1	3	3
2010	A.Lyth	16	30	2	202	1133	40.46	4	3	25
2014	A.Z.Lees	16	30	1	132	1165	40.17	3	7	12
2012	G.S.Ballance	13	25	2	132	780	33.91	2	4	8
2016	Azeem Rafiq	6	8	2	74	201	33.50	–	2	5
2008	A.U.Rashid	10	16	2	88	393	28.07	–	3	7
2013	J.A.Brooks	14	20	11	48	250	27.77	–	–	4
2016	A.J.Hodd	12	18	3	96*	391	26.06	–	2	35/3
2008	A.W.Gale	15	26	1	83	525	21.00	–	2	2
	W.M.H.Rhodes	2	4	–	20	73	18.25	–	–	1
2016	J.A.Leaning	9	15	2	51	233	17.92	–	1	8
2012	S.A.Patterson	15	20	1	63*	300	15.78	–	2	–
2016	D.J.Willey	4	5	–	22	58	11.60	–	–	–
	K.S.Williamson	2	4	–	28	42	10.50	–	–	3
2000	R.J.Sidebottom	9	11	3	23	75	9.37	–	–	1

Also batted: B.O.Coad (1 match) 17*; T.M.Head (1) 54, 2; J.E.Root (2 – cap 2012) 0, 27, 213 (5 ct); J.Shaw (1) 24 (1 ct).

BOWLING

	O	*M*	*R*	*W*	*Avge*	*Best*	*5wI*	*10wM*
R.J.Sidebottom	245	63	657	31	21.19	5-51	1	–
J.A.Brooks	432.2	105	1501	60	25.01	6-65	3	–
S.A.Patterson	440.5	138	1146	39	29.38	6-56	1	–
T.T.Bresnan	297.1	71	934	31	30.12	5-36	1	–
A.U.Rashid	293.2	36	1083	32	33.84	4-17	–	–
L.E.Plunkett	172.1	23	602	10	60.20	2-46	–	–
Also bowled:								
D.J.Willey	102	23	334	9	37.11	3-55	–	–
A.Lyth	79	10	322	7	46.00	2- 9	–	–

Azeem Rafiq 99.3-24-275-3; G.S.Ballance 1-0-11-0; B.O.Coad 35-10-108-1; T.M.Head 4-1-16-0; A.J.Hodd 1-0-14-0; J.A.Leaning 10-2-27-0; A.Z.Lees 4-0-51-2; W.M.H.Rhodes 41-5-137-3; J.E.Root 18-3-49-2; J.Shaw 29-3-119-2; K.S.Williamson 18-2-59-2.

The First-Class Averages (pp 226–242) give the records of Yorkshire players in all first-class county matches (Yorkshire's other opponents being Pakistan A), with the exception of J.M.Bairstow, G.S.Ballance and J.E.Root, whose first-class figures for Yorkshire are as above, and:

W.M.H.Rhodes 3-5-0-20-82-16.40-0-0-2ct. 57-8-174-4-43.50-2/67-0-0.
J.Shaw 2-2-1-24-31-31.00-0-0-1ct. 45.4-8-177-5-35.40-3/58-0-0.

YORKSHIRE RECORDS

FIRST-CLASS CRICKET

Highest Total	For 887		v	Warwicks	Birmingham	1896
	V 681-7d		by	Leics	Bradford	1996
Lowest Total	For 23		v	Hampshire	Middlesbrough	1965
	V 13		by	Notts	Nottingham	1901
Highest Innings	For 341	G.H.Hirst	v	Leics	Leicester	1905
	V 318*	W.G.Grace	for	Glos	Cheltenham	1876

Highest Partnership for each Wicket

1st	555	P.Holmes/H.Sutcliffe	v	Essex	Leyton	1932
2nd	346	W.Barber/M.Leyland	v	Middlesex	Sheffield	1932
3rd	346	J.J.Sayers/A.McGrath	v	Warwicks	Birmingham	2009
4th	372	J.E.Root/J.M.Bairstow	v	Surrey	Leeds	2016
5th	340	E.Wainwright/G.H.Hirst	v	Surrey	The Oval	1899
6th	296	A.Lyth/A.U.Rashid	v	Lancashire	Manchester	2014
7th	366*	J.M.Bairstow/T.T.Bresnan	v	Durham	Chester-le-St[2]	2015
8th	292	R.Peel/Lord Hawke	v	Warwicks	Birmingham	1896
9th	246	T.T.Bresnan/J.N.Gillespie	v	Surrey	The Oval	2007
10th	149	G.Boycott/G.B.Stevenson	v	Warwicks	Birmingham	1982

Best Bowling (Innings)	For	10-10	H.Verity	v	Notts	Leeds	1932
	V	10-37	C.V.Grimmett	for	Australians	Sheffield	1930
Best Bowling (Match)	For	17-91	H.Verity	v	Essex	Leyton	1933
	V	17-91	H.Dean	for	Lancashire	Liverpool	1913

Most Runs – Season	2883	H.Sutcliffe	(av 80.08)	1932
Most Runs – Career	38558	H.Sutcliffe	(av 50.20)	1919-45
Most 100s – Season	12	H.Sutcliffe		1932
Most 100s – Career	112	H.Sutcliffe		1919-45
Most Wkts – Season	240	W.Rhodes	(av 12.72)	1900
Most Wkts – Career	3597	W.Rhodes	(av 16.02)	1898-1930
Most Career W-K Dismissals	1186	D.Hunter	(863 ct; 323 st)	1888-1909
Most Career Catches in the Field	665	J.Tunnicliffe		1891-1907

LIMITED-OVERS CRICKET

Highest Total	**50ov**	411-6		v	Devon	Exmouth	2004
	40ov	352-6		v	Notts	Scarborough	2001
	T20	223-6		v	Durham	Leeds	2016
Lowest Total	**50ov**	76		v	Surrey	Harrogate	1970
	40ov	54		v	Essex	Leeds	2003
	T20	90-9		v	Durham	Chester-le-St[2]	2009
Highest Innings	**50ov**	175	T.M.Head	v	Leics	Leicester	2016
	40ov	191	D.S.Lehmann	v	Notts	Scarborough	2001
	T20	109	I.J.Harvey	v	Derbyshire	Leeds	2005
Best Bowling	**50ov**	7-27	D.Gough	v	Ireland	Leeds	1997
	40ov	7-15	R.A.Hutton	v	Worcs	Leeds	1969
	T20	5-16	R.M.Pyrah	v	Durham	Scarborough	2011

FIRST-CLASS UMPIRES 2017

† New appointment. See page 0 for key to abbreviations.

BAILEY, Robert John (Biddulph HS), b Biddulph, Staffs 28 Oct 1963. 6'3". RHB, OB. Northamptonshire 1982-99; cap 1985; benefit 1993; captain 1996-97. Derbyshire 2000-01; cap 2000. Staffordshire 1980. YC 1984. **Tests:** 4 (1988 to 1989-90); HS 43 v WI (Oval) 1988. **LOI**: 4 (1984-85 to 1989-90); HS 43* v SL (Oval) 1988. F-c Tours: SA 1991-92 (Nh); WI 1989-90; Z 1994-95 (Nh). 1000 runs (13); most – 1987 (1990). HS 224* Nh v Glamorgan (Swansea) 1986. BB 5-54 Nh v Notts (Northampton) 1993. F-c career: 374 matches; 21844 runs @ 40.52, 47 hundreds; 121 wickets @ 42.51; 272 ct. Appointed 2006. Umpired 16 LOI (2011 to 2016). **ICC International Panel 2011 to date.**

BAINTON, Neil Laurence, b Romford, Essex 2 October 1970. No f-c appearances. Appointed 2006.

BALDWIN, Paul Kerr, b Epsom, Surrey 18 Jul 1973. No f-c appearances. Umpired 18 LOI (2006 to 2009). Reserve List 2010 14. Appointed 2015.

BURNS, Michael (Walney CS), b Barrow-in-Furness, Lancs 6 Feb 1969. 6'0". RHB, RM, WK. Warwickshire 1992-96. Somerset 1997-2005; cap 1999; captain 2003-04. 1000 runs (2); most – 1133 (2003). HS 221 Sm v Yorks (Bath) 2001. BB 6-54 Sm v Leics (Taunton) 2001. F-c career: 154 matches; 7648 runs @ 32.68, 8 hundreds; 68 wickets @ 42.42; 142 ct, 7 st. Appointed 2016.

COOK, Nicholas Grant Billson (Lutterworth GS), b Leicester 17 Jun 1956. 6'0". RHB, SLA. Leicestershire 1978-85; cap 1982. Northamptonshire 1986-94; cap 1987; benefit 1995. **Tests:** 15 (1983 to 1989); HS 31 v A (Oval) 1989; BB 6-65 (11-83 match) v P (Karachi) 1983-84. **LOI:** 3 (1983-84 to 1989-90), HS – ; BB 2-18 v P (Peshawar) 1987-88. F-c Tours: NZ 1979-80 (DHR), 1983-84; P 1983-84, 1987-88; SL 1985-86 (Eng B); Z 1980-81 (Le), 1984-85 (EC). HS 75 Le v Somerset (Taunton) 1980. 50 wkts (8); most – 90 (1982). BB 7-34 (10-97 match) Nh v Essex (Chelmsford) 1992. F-c career: 356 matches; 3137 runs @ 11.66; 879 wickets @ 29.01; 197 ct. Appointed 2009.

COWLEY, Nigel Geoffrey Charles (Duchy Manor SS, Mere), b Shaftesbury, Dorset 1 Mar 1953. 5'7". RHB, OB. Dorset 1972. Hampshire 1974-89; cap 1978; benefit 1988. Glamorgan 1990. 1000 runs (1): 1042 (1984). HS 109* H v Somerset (Taunton) 1977. BB 6-48 H v Leics (Southampton) 1982. F-c career: 271 matches; 7309 runs @ 23.35, 2 hundreds; 437 wickets @ 34.04; 105 ct. Appointed 2000.

EVANS, Jeffery Howard, b Llanelli, Carms 7 Aug 1954. No f-c appearances. Appointed 2001. Umpired in Indian Cricket League 2007-08.

EVANS, Russell John (Colonel Frank Seely S), b Calverton, Notts 1 Oct 1965. Younger brother of K.P.Evans (Nottinghamshire 1984-99). 6'0". RHB, RM. Nottinghamshire 1987-90. Minor Cos 1994. Lincolnshire 1994-97. HS 59 MC v South Africans (Torquay) 1994. BB 3-40 Nt v OU (Oxford) 1988. F-c career: 7 matches; 201 runs @ 25.12; 3 wickets @ 32.33; 5 ct. Reserve List 2011-14. Appointed 2015.

GALE, Stephen Clifford, b Shrewsbury, Shropshire 3 Jun 1952. RHB, LB. No f-c appearances. Shropshire (list A only) 1976-85. Reserve List 2008-10. Appointed 2011.

GARRATT, Steven Arthur, b Nottingham 5 Jul 1953. No f-c appearances. Reserve List 2003-07. Appointed 2008.

GOUGH, Michael Andrew (English Martyrs RCS; Hartlepool SFC), b Hartlepool, Co Durham 18 Dec 1979. Son of M.P.Gough (Durham 1974-77). 6'5". RHB, OB. Durham 1998-2003. F-c Tours (Eng A): NZ 1999-00; B 1999-00. HS 123 Du v CU (Cambridge) 1998. CC HS 103 Du v Essex (Colchester) 2002. BB 5-56 Du v Middx (Chester-le-St) 2001. F-c career: 67 matches; 2952 runs @ 25.44, 2 hundreds; 30 wickets @ 45.00; 57 ct. Reserve List 2006-08. Appointed 2009. Umpired 4 Tests (2016 to 2016-17) and 31 LOI (2013 to 2016-17). **ICC International Panel 2012 to date.**

GOULD, Ian James (Westgate SS, Slough), b Taplow, Bucks 19 Aug 1957. 5'8". LHB, WK. Middlesex 1975 to 1980-81, 1996; cap 1977. Auckland 1979-80. Sussex 1981-90; cap 1981; captain 1987; benefit 1990. MCC YC. **LOI:** 18 (1982-83 to 1983); HS 42 v A (Sydney) 1982-83. F-c Tours: A 1982-83; P 1980-81 (Int); Z 1980-81 (M). HS 128 M v Worcs (Worcester) 1978. BB 3-10 Sx v Surrey (Oval) 1989. Middlesex coach 1991-2000. Reappeared in one match (v OU) 1996. F-c career: 298 matches; 8756 runs @ 26.05, 4 hundreds; 7 wickets @ 52.14; 603 dismissals (536 ct, 67 st). Appointed 2002. Umpired 58 Tests (2008-09 to 2016-17) and 114 LOI (2006 to 2016), including 2010-11 and 2014-15 World Cups. **ICC Elite Panel 2009 to date.**

HARTLEY, Peter John (Greenhead GS; Bradford C), b Keighley, Yorks 18 Apr 1960. 6'0". RHB, RMF. Warwickshire 1982. Yorkshire 1985-97; cap 1987; benefit 1996. Hampshire 1998-2000; cap 1998. F-c Tours (Y): SA 1991-92; WI 1986-87; Z 1995-96. HS 127* Y v Lancs (Manchester) 1988. 50 wkts (7); most – 81 (1995). BB 9-41 (inc hat-trick, 4 wkts in 5 balls and 5 in 9; 11-68 match) Y v Derbys (Chesterfield) 1995. Hat-trick 1995. F-c career: 232 matches; 4321 runs @ 19.91, 2 hundreds; 683 wickets @ 30.21; 68 ct. Appointed 2003. Umpired 6 LOI (2007 to 2009). **ICC International Panel 2006-09.**

ILLINGWORTH, Richard Keith (Salts GS), b Bradford, Yorks 23 Aug 1963. 5'11". RHB, SLA. Worcestershire 1982-2000; cap 1986; benefit 1997. Natal 1988-89. Derbyshire 2001. Wiltshire 2005. **Tests:** 9 (1991 to 1995-96); HS 28 v SA (Pt Elizabeth) 1995-96; BB 4-96 v WI (Nottingham) 1995. Took wicket of P.V.Simmons with his first ball in Tests – v WI (Nottingham) 1991. **LOI:** 25 (1991 to 1995-96); HS 14 v P (Melbourne) 1991-92; BB 3-33 v Z (Albury) 1991-92. F-c Tours: SA 1995-96; NZ 1991-92; P 1990-91 (Eng A); SL 1990-91 (Eng A); Z 1989-90 (Eng A), 1990-91 (Wo), 1993-94 (Wo), 1996-97 (Wo). HS 120* Wo v Warwks (Worcester) 1987 – as night-watchman. Scored 106 for England A v Z (Harare) 1989-90 – also as night-watchman. 50 wkts (5); most – 75 (1990). BB 7-50 Wo v OU (Oxford) 1985. F-c career: 376 matches; 7027 runs @ 22.45, 4 hundreds; 831 wickets @ 31.54; 161 ct. Appointed 2006. Umpired 25 Tests (2012-13 to 2016-17) and 51 LOI (2010 to 2016-17), including 2014-15 World Cup. **ICC Elite Panel 2013 to date.**

KETTLEBOROUGH, Richard Allan (Worksop C), b Sheffield, Yorks 15 Mar 1973. 6'0". LHB, RM. Yorkshire 1994-97. Middlesex 1998-99. F-c Tour (Y): Z 1995-96. HS 108 Y v Essex (Leeds) 1996. BB 2-26 Y v Notts (Scarborough) 1996. F-c career: 33 matches; 1258 runs @ 25.16, 1 hundred; 3 wickets @ 81.00; 20 ct. Appointed 2006. Umpired 41 Tests (2010-11 to 2016-17) and 68 LOI (2009 to 2016-17), including 2010-11 and 2014-15 World Cups. **ICC Elite Panel 2011 to date.**

LLONG, Nigel James (Ashford North S), b Ashford, Kent 11 Feb 1969. 6'0". LHB, OB. Kent 1990-98; cap 1993. F-c Tour (K): Z 1992-93. HS 130 K v Hants (Canterbury) 1996. BB 5-21 K v Middx (Canterbury) 1996. F-c career: 68 matches; 3024 runs @ 31.17, 6 hundreds; 35 wickets @ 35.97; 59 ct. Appointed 2002. Umpired 40 Tests (2007-08 to 2016-17) and 107 LOI (2006 to 2016-17), including 2010-11 and 2014-15 World Cups. **ICC Elite Panel 2012 to date.**

LLOYD, Graham David (Hollins County HS), b Accrington, Lancs 1 Jul 1969. Son of D.Lloyd (Lancs and England 1965-83). 5'9". RHB, RM. Lancashire 1988-2002; cap 1992; benefit 2001. **LOI:** 6 (1996 to 1998-99); HS 22 v A (Oval) 1997. F-c Tours: A 1992-93 (Eng A); WI 1995-96 (La). 1000 runs (5); most – 1389 (1992). HS 241 La v Essex (Chelmsford) 1996. BB 1-4. F-c career: 203 matches; 11279 runs @ 38.23, 24 hundreds; 2 wickets @ 220.00; 140 ct. Reserve List 2009-13. Appointed 2014.

LLOYDS, Jeremy William (Blundell's S), b Penang, Malaya 17 Nov 1954. 6'0". LHB, OB. Somerset 1979-84; cap 1982. Gloucestershire 1985-91; cap 1985. OFS 1983-84 to 1987-88. F-c Tour (Gl): SL 1986-87. 1000 runs (3); most – 1295 (1986). HS 132* Sm v Northants (Northampton) 1982. BB 7-88 Sm v Essex (Chelmsford) 1982. F-c career: 267 matches; 10679 runs @ 31.04, 10 hundreds; 333 wickets @ 38.86; 229 ct. Appointed 1998. Umpired 5 Tests (2003-04 to 2004-05) and 18 LOI (2000 to 2005-06). **ICC International Panel 2003-06**.

MALLENDER, Neil Alan (Beverley GS), b Kirk Sandall, Yorks 13 Aug 1961. 6'0". RHB, RFM. Northamptonshire 1980-86 and 1995-96; cap 1984. Somerset 1987-94; cap 1987; benefit 1994. Otago 1983-84 to 1992-93; captain 1990-91 to 1992-93. **Tests:** 2 (1992); HS 4 v P (Oval) 1992; BB 5-50 v P (Leeds) 1992 – on debut. F-c Tour (Nh): Z 1994-95. HS 100* Otago v CD (Palmerston N) 1991-92. UK HS 87* Sm v Sussex (Hove) 1990. 50 wkts (6); most – 56 (1983). BB 7-27 Otago v Auckland (Auckland) 1984-85. UK BB 7-41 Nh v Derbys (Northampton) 1982. F-c career: 345 matches; 4709 runs @ 17.18, 1 hundred; 937 wickets @ 26.31; 111 ct. Appointed 1999. Umpired 3 Tests (2003-04) and 22 LOI (2001 to 2003-04), including 2002-03 World Cup. **ICC Elite Panel 2004**.

MILLNS, David James (Garibaldi CS; N Notts C; Nottingham Trent U), b Clipstone, Notts 27 Feb 1965. 6'3". LHB, RF. Nottinghamshire 1988-89, 2000-01; cap 2000. Leicestershire 1990-99; cap 1991; benefit 1999. Tasmania 1994-95. Boland 1996-97. F-c Tours: A 1992-93 (Eng A); SA 1996-97 (Le). HS 121 Le v Northants (Northampton) 1997. 50 wkts (4); most – 76 (1994). BB 9-37 (12-91 match) Le v Derbys (Derby) 1991. F-c career: 171 matches; 3082 runs @ 22.01, 3 hundreds; 553 wickets @ 27.35; 76 ct. Reserve List 2007-08. Appointed 2009.

O'SHAUGHNESSY, Steven Joseph (Harper Green SS, Farnworth), b Bury, Lancs 9 Sep 1961. 5'10½". RHB, RM. Lancashire 1980-87; cap 1985. Worcestershire 1988-89. Scored 100 in 35 min to equal world record for La v Leics (Manchester) 1983. 1000 runs (1): 1167 (1984). HS 159* La v Somerset (Bath) 1984. BB 4-66 La v Notts (Nottingham) 1982. F-c career: 112 matches; 3720 runs @ 24.31, 5 hundreds; 114 wickets @ 36.03; 57 ct. Reserve List 2009-10. Appointed 2011.

ROBINSON, Robert Timothy (Dunstable GS; High Pavement SFC; Sheffield U), b Sutton in Ashfield, Notts 21 Nov 1958. 6'0". RHB, RM. Nottinghamshire 1978-99; cap 1983; captain 1988-95; benefit 1992. *Wisden* 1985. **Tests:** 29 (1984-85 to 1989); HS 175 v A (Leeds) 1985. **LOI**: 26 (1984-85 to 1988); HS 83 v P (Sharjah) 1986-87. F-c Tours: A 1987-88; SA 1989-90 (Eng XI), 1996-97 (Nt); NZ 1987-88; WI 1985-86; I/SL 1984-85; P 1987-88. 1000 runs (14) inc 2000 (1): 2032 (1984). HS 220* Nt v Yorks (Nottingham) 1990. BB 1-22. F-c career: 425 matches; 27571 runs @ 42.15, 63 hundreds; 4 wickets @ 72.25; 257 ct. Appointed 2007. Umpired 10 LOI (2013 to 2016). **ICC International Panel (Third Umpire) 2012 to date.**

SAGGERS, Martin John (Springwood HS, King's Lynn; Huddersfield U), b King's Lynn, Norfolk 23 May 1972. 6'2". RHB, RMF. Durham 1996-98. Kent 1999-2009; cap 2001; benefit 2009. MCC 2004. Essex 2007 (on loan). Norfolk 1995-96. **Tests**: 3 (2003-04 to 2004); HS 1 and BB 2-29 v B (Chittagong) 2003-04 – on debut. F-c Tour: B 2003-04. HS 64 K v Worcs (Canterbury) 2004. 50 wkts (4); most – 83 (2002). BB 7-79 K v Durham (Chester-le-St) 2000. F-c career: 119 matches; 1165 runs @ 11.20; 415 wickets @ 25.33; 27 ct. Reserve List 2010-11. Appointed 2012.

†**TAYLOR, Billy** Victor (Bitterne Park S, Southampton), b Southampton 11 Jan 1977. Younger brother of J.L.Taylor (Wiltshire 1998-2002). 6'3". LHB, RMF. Sussex 1999-2003. Hampshire 2004-09; cap 2006; testimonial 2010. Wiltshire 1996-98. HS 40 v Essex (Southampton) 2004. BB 6-32 v Middlesex (Southampton) 2006 (inc hat-trick). F-c career: 54 matches; 431 runs @10.26; 136 wickets @ 33.34; 6 ct. Reserve list 2011-16. Appointed 2017.

WHARF, Alexander George (Buttershaw Upper S; Thomas Danby C), b Bradford, Yorks 4 Jun 1975. 6'5". RHB, RMF. Yorkshire 1994-97. Nottinghamshire 1998-99. Glamorgan 2000-08, scoring 100* v OU (Oxford) on debut; cap 2000; benefit 2009. **LOI**: 13 (2004 to 2004-05); HS 9 v India (Lord's) 2004; BB 4-24 v Z (Harare) 2004-05. F-c Tour (Eng A): WI 2005-06. HS 128* Gm v Glos (Bristol) 2007. 50 wkts (1): 52 (2003). BB 6-59 Gm v Glos (Bristol) 2005. F-c career: 121 matches; 3570 runs @ 23.03, 6 hundreds; 293 wickets @ 37.34; 63 ct. Reserve List 2011-13. Appointed 2014.

RESERVE FIRST-CLASS LIST: Ian D.Blackwell, Ben J.Debenham, Tom Lungley, James D.Middlebrook, Mark Newell, Paul R.Pollard, Russell J.Warren, Christopher M.Watts.

Test Match and LOI statistics to 18 February 2017.

TOURING TEAMS REGISTER 2016

SRI LANKA

Full Names	*Birthdate*	*Birthplace*	*Team*	*Type*	*F-C Debut*
CHAMEERA, P.V.Dushmantha	11.01.92	Ragama	Nondescripts	RHB/RF	2011-12
CHANDIMAL, Lokuge Dinesh	18.11.89	Balapitiya	Nondescripts	RHB/WK	2009
DE SILVA, Dhananjaya Maduranga	06.09.91	Colombo	Tamil Union	RHB/OB	2011
DICKWELLA, D.P.D.Niroshan	23.06.93	Kandy	Nondescripts	LHB/WK	2012-13
ERANGA, R.M.Shaminda	23.06.86	Chilaw	Tamil Union	RHB/RFM	2006-07
FERNANDO, A.Nuwan Pradeep R.	19.10.86	Negombo	Sinhalese	RHB/RFM	2007-08
HERATH, H.M.Rangana K.B.	19.03.78	Kurunegala	Tamil Union	LHB/SLA	1996-97
KARUNARATNE, F.Dimuth M.	21.04.88	Colombo	Sinhalese	LHB/RM	2008-09
LAKMAL, R.A.Suranga	10.03.87	Matara	Tamil Union	RHB/RMF	2007-08
MATHEWS, Angelo Davis	02.06.87	Colombo	Colts	RHB/RM	2006-07
MENDIS, B.Kusal G.	02.02.95	Moratuwa	Colombo	RHB/WK	2014-15
PERERA, M.D.Kusal J.	17.08.90	Kalubowila	Colts	LHB/WK	2009-10
PRASAD, K.T.G.Dhammika	30.05.83	Ragama	Sinhalese	RHB/RFM	2001-02
SHANAKA, M.Dasun	09.09.91	Negombo	Sinhalese	RHB/RM	2011-12
SILVA, Jayan Kaushal	27.05.86	Colombo	Sinhalese	RHB/WK	2002-03
SIRIWARDANA, T.A.Milinda	04.12.85	Nagoda	Badureliya	LHB/SLA	2005-06
THIRIMANNE, H.D.R.Lahiru	08.09.89	Moratuwa	Ragama	LHB/RMF	2008-09

NB: A.N.P.R.Fernando is also known as Nuwan Pradeep.

PAKISTAN

Full Names	*Birthdate*	*Birthplace*	*Team*	*Type*	*F-C Debut*
ASAD SHAFIQ	28.01.86	Karachi	Habib Bank	RHB/LB	2007-08
AZHAR ALI	19.02.85	Lahore	Sui Northern	RHB/LB	2001-02
IFTIKHAR AHMED	03.09.85	Peshawar	Sui Northern	RHB/OB	2011-12
IMRAN KHAN, Mohammad	15.07.87	Lower Dir	Peshawar	RHB/RMF	2007-08
MISBAH-UL-HAQ Khan Niazi	28.05.74	Mianwali	Sui Northern	RHB/LB	1998-99
MOHAMMAD AMIR	13.04.92	Gujar Khan	Sui Southern	LHB/LF	2008-09
MOHAMMAD HAFEEZ	17.10.80	Sargodha	Sui Northern	RHB/OB	1998-99
RAHAT ALI	12.09.88	Multan	Khan Research	RHB/LFM	2007-08
SAMI ASLAM	12.12.95	Lahore	Lahore Whites	LHB/RM	2012-13
SARFRAZ AHMED	22.05.87	Karachi	PIA	RHB/WK	2005-06
SHAN MASOOD	14.10.89	Kuwait	United Bank	LHB/RM	2007-08
SOHAIL KHAN	06.03.84	Malakand	Sui Southern	RHB/RFM	2007-08
WAHAB RIAZ	28.06.85	Lahore	National Bank	RHB/LF	2001-02
YASIR SHAH	02.05.86	Swabi	Sui Northern	RHB/LB	2001-02
YOUNUS KHAN	29.11.77	Mardan	United Bank	RHB/LB	1998-99
ZULFIQAR BABAR	10.12.78	Okara	WAPDA	RHB/SLA	2001-02

SRI LANKA A

Full Names	*Birthdate*	*Birthplace*	*Team*	*Type*	*F-C Debut*
DE SILVA, Dhananjaya Maduranga	06.09.91	Colombo	Tamil Union	RHB/OB	2011
DICKWELLA, D.P.D.Niroshan	23.06.93	Kandy	Nondescripts	LHB/WK	2012-13
FERNANDO, Asitha Madusanka	31.07.97	Katuneriya	Chilaw	RHB/RMF	2016
FERNANDO, M.Vishwa T.	18.09.91	Colombo	Bloomfield	RHB/LMF	2011-12
GAMAGE, P.Lahiru S.	05.04.88	Maradana	Colombo	RHB/RFM	2006-07
JAYASUNDERA, M.D.Udara S.	03.01.91	Minuwangoda	Ragama	LHB/LB	2009-10
JAYASURIYA, N.G.R.Prabath	05.11.91	Matale	Colts	RHB/SLA	2011-12
PATHIRANA, Sachith Shanaka	21.03.89	Kandy	Colombo	LHB/SLA	2008-09
PRIYANJAN, S.M.Ashan	14.08.89	Colombo	Colombo	RHB/OB	2008-09
RAJITHA, C.A.Kasun	01.06.93	Matara	Saracens	RHB/RMF	2014-15
RANASINGHE, Minod Bhanuka	29.04.95		Sinhalese	LHB/WK	2014-15
SILVA, A.Roshen S.	17.11.88	Colombo	Ragama	RHB/OB	2006-07
UDAWATTE, Mahela Lakmal	19.07.86	Colombo	Chilaw	LHB/OB	2005-06
WARNAPURA, Madawa S.	04.06.88	Colombo	Colombo	RHB/RM	2008-09

PAKISTAN A

Full Names	*Birthdate*	*Birthplace*	*Team*	*Type*	*F-C Debut*
ABDUL REHMAN MUZAMMIL	31.07.89	Multan	Khan Research	RHB/OB	2013-14
AZIZULLAH	09.11.92	Peshawar	Sui Northern	RHB/RMF	2012-13
BABAR AZAM, Mohammad	15.10.94	Lahore	Sui Southern	RHB/OB	2010-11
BILAWAL BHATTI	17.09.91	Muridke	Sui Northern	RHB/RMF	2008-09
FAKHAR ZAMAN	10.04.90	Mardan	Habib Bank	LHB/SLA	2012-13
HASAN ALI	07.02.94	Punjab	Islamabad	RHB/RMF	2013-14
JAAHID Shaukat ALI	05.03.95	Karachi	Karachi B	RHB/OB	2013-14
MIR HAMZA	10.09.92	Karachi	United Bank	LHB/LM	2012-13
MOHAMMAD ASGHAR	28.12.98	Killa Abdullah	United Bank	RHB/SLA	2014-15
MOHAMMAD HASAN	04.10.90	Karachi	Karachi Whites	RHB/WK	2007-08
MOHAMMAD NAWAZ	21.03.94	Rawalpindi	National Bank	LHB/SLA	2012-13
SAUD SHAKEEL	05.09.95	Karachi	Karachi B	LHB/SLA	2015-16
SHADAB KHAN	04.10.98	Mianwali	Karachi Whites	RHB/LB	2016
SHARJEEL KHAN	14.08.89	Hyderabad	United Bank	LHB/LB	2009-10
UMAR SIDDIQ Khan	30.12.92	Lahore	United Bank	LHB/OB	2012-13

UNIVERSITIES REGISTER 2016

CAMBRIDGE († = Blue)

Full Names	*Birthdate*	*Birthplace*	*College*	*Bat/Bowl*	*F-C Debut*
†ABBOTT, James Barrington	25.05.94	Hammersmith	Magdalene	RHB/WK	2014
ALLCHIN, Alastair Thomas Arthur	12.11.91	Chelmsford	Anglia RU	RHB/RFM	2013
ARIF, Adil Tahir	06.11.94	Sharjah, UAE	Anglia RU	RHB/RM	2014
ARKSEY, Joshua Benjamin Thomas	20.12.94	Cambridge	Anglia RU	RHB/SLA	2015
†BARDOLIA, Shivaan	06.07.89	New Jersey, USA	Clare Hall	RHB/LB	2016
BARTON, Adam Paul	17.04.95	Epsom	Anglia RU	RHB/LMF	2014
BRIERLEY, Drew	26.02.97		Anglia RU	RHB	2016
BRYANT, Benjamin Joshua	15.12.94	Lambeth	Anglia RU	RHB/OB	2016
†CHOHAN, Darshan	04.11.95	Singapore	St Catharine's	LHB/SLA	2015
†COLVERD, Thomas Gerald Lancaster	13.11.95	Tokyo, Japan	Robinson	RHB/OB	2016
†CRICHARD, Ruari James	09.01.95	Hammersmith	St John's	RHB/RMF	2015
†DALGLEISH, Angus Duncan	01.02.96	London	Trinity Hall	RHB/LM	2016
ELLISON, Harry Richard Clive	22.02.93	Canterbury	Anglia RU	RHB/OB	2014
†EMERTON, Connor John	05.06.94	Hillingdon	Jesus	RHB/RM	2016
†HEARNE, Alexander Gordon	23.09.93	Kensington	St John's	RHB/LB	2013
PALMER, Harrison John			Anglia RU	RHB/WK	2016
†PATEL, Avish Rasiklal	31.07.94	Leicester	Robinson	RHB/LB	2015
TETLEY, Joseph William	14.04.95	Sheffield	Anglia RU	LHB/WK	2015
†TICE, Patrick James Aikman	30.06.94	Basingstoke	Fitzwilliam	RHB/WK	2015
†WAGHORN, Alexander Charles	09.01.95	Wandsworth	Pembroke	RHB/RMF	2016

CARDIFF

Full Names	*Birthdate*	*Birthplace*	*College*	*Bat/Bowl*	*F-C Debut*
BRAND, Neil	12.04.96	Johannesburg, SA	Cardiff Met	LHB/SLA	2015
CULLEN, Thomas Nicholas	04.01.92	Perth, Australia	Cardiff Met	RHB/WK	2015
EDWARDS, Richard Daniel	30.12.94	Neath	Cardiff Met	LHB/RM	2016
GRIFFITHS, Sean William	16.05.95	Neath	Cardiff Met	RHB/RM	2014
HERRING, Cameron Lee	15.07.94	Abergavenny	Cardiff Met	RHB/WK	2013
HOLMES, Gregory Clarke	22.09.93	Neath	Cardiff Met	RHB/RM	2016
LAWLOR, Jeremy Lloyd	04.11.95	Cardiff	Cardiff Met	RHB/RM	2015
LEVEROCK, Kamau Sadiki	19.10.94	Bermuda	Cardiff Met	LHB/RFM	2015
MILTON, Alexander Geoffrey	19.05.96	Surrey	Cardiff Met	RHB/WK	2016
ROUSE, Timothy David	09.04.96	Sheffield	Cardiff	RHB/OB	2015
SCRIVEN, Bradley	08.12.93	High Wycombe	Cardiff Met	RHB/RM	2014
THOMSON, Alexander Thomas	30.10.93	Stoke-on-Trent	Cardiff Met	RHB/OB	2014
TURPIN, James Ross	18.03.97	Fowey	Cardiff Met	RHB/RM	2016
WESTPHAL, Andrew Alexander	28.07.94	London	Cardiff Met	RHB/RMF	2014

DURHAM

Full Names	*Birthdate*	*Birthplace*	*College*	*Bat/Bowl*	*F-C Debut*
ALEXANDER, Timothy David	01.12.94	Norwich		RHB/RFM	2014
CLARK, Jack	26.09.94	Ashington	Grey	LHB/LM	2016
DEWES, Jonathan James Northam	19.08.95	Frimley		RHB/SLA	2016
DUNFORD, Jake Edward	24.06.94	Jersey		RHB/WK	2016
GIBSON, Robert Andrew Max	11.03.94	Emsworth	Hild Bede	RHB/LB	2015
JENKINS, William Henry	04.07.94	Yeovil	St Cuthbert's	RHB/RM	2014
KURTZ, Eben Everett	12.11.95	Camden	Hatfield	LHB/LM	2016
MacDONELL, Charles Michael	23.02.95	Basingstoke	Collingwood	RHB/RFM	2015
PHILLIPS, William David Beauclerk	12.04.93	Auckland, NZ	Grey	RHB/RM	2015
POLLOCK, Edward John	10.07.95	High Wycombe	Collingwood	LHB/OB	2015
STEEL, Cameron Tate	13.09.95	California, USA	Hild Bede	RHB/LB	2014
WOOD, Jack Michael	04.11.94	Reading	St Aidan's	RHB/RM	2015

LEEDS/BRADFORD

Full Names	*Birthdate*	*Birthplace*	*College*	*Bat/Bowl*	*F-C Debut*
ASHRAF, Moin Aqeeb	05.01.92	Bradford	Leeds Beckett	RHB/RMF	2010
BULLEN, Steven Frank Gregory	12.07.92	Watford	Leeds Beckett	RHB/WK	2015
DAVIS, Christian Arthur Linghorne	11.10.92	Milton Keynes	Leeds	RHB/LFM	2014
GOWERS, Ashley Mark	12.12.94	Bury	Leeds Beckett	RHB/WK	2016
HARWOOD, Christopher Samuel	01.10.94	Weymouth, USA	Leeds Beckett	RHB/RMF	2016
LILLEY, Alexander Edward	17.04.92	Halifax	Leeds	RHB/LM	2011
OGDEN, Archie	24.02.94	Rotherham	Leeds Beckett	LHB/LMF	2016
ROOT, William Thomas	05.08.92	Sheffield	Leeds Beckett	LHB/OB	2015
SCOTT, George Frederick Buchan	06.11.95	Hemel Hempstead	Leeds	RHB/RM	2015
THOMPSON, Henry Lester	01.12.92	Preston	Leeds	RHB/OB	2013
WATKINSON, Liam	27.07.91	Bolton	Leeds Beckett	RHB/RM	2015
WESTON, Logan Patrick	03.07.92	Bradford	Leeds Beckett	RHB/OB	2015

LOUGHBOROUGH

Full Names	*Birthdate*	*Birthplace*	*College*	*Bat/Bowl*	*F-C Debut*
AKRAM, Basil Mohammad Ramzan	23.02.93	Waltham Forest	Loughborough	RHB/RMF	2014
BURGESS, Michael Gregory Kerran	08.07.94	Epsom	Loughborough	RHB/WK	2014
COOK, Samuel James	04.08.97	Chelmsford	Loughborough	RHB/RFM	2016
GAMBLE, Robert Neil	25.01.95	Nottingham	Loughborough	RHB/RMF	2015
GRANT, Samuel Edward	30.08.95	Shoreham-by-Sea	Loughborough	LHB/LMF	2014
HALEY, Oliver Joseph Patrick	15.03.96	Solihull	Loughborough	RHB/OB	2016
HASAN AZAD, Mohammad	07.01.94	Karachi, Pakistan	Loughborough	LHB/OB	2015
KUMAR, Nitish Roenik	21.05.94	Scarborough, Can	Loughborough	RHB/OB	2009
LOWEN, Charles Timothy	12.09.92	Enfield	Loughborough	RHB/WK	2016
NURSE, Connor Jack	22.11.94	Camden	Loughborough	LHB/SLA	2016
THURSTON, Charles Oliver	17.08.96	Cambridge	Loughborough	RHB/RM	2016
WHITE, Robert George	15.09.95	Ealing	Loughborough	RHB/RFM	2015

OXFORD († = Blue)

Full Names	*Birthdate*	*Birthplace*	*College*	*Bat/Bowl*	*F-C Debut*
†BISHNOI, Bhavya	16.02.93	Delhi, India	St Antony's	RHB/RM	2016
BODENSTEIN, Cornelis Johannes	03.11.92	Pretoria, SA	Brookes U	LHB/LMF	2013
BROUGHTON, Bruno Miles	10.10.95	Lambeth	Brookes U	RHB/SLA	2016
†CLAUGHTON, Thomas Hugh	24.01.96	Slough	Magdalen	RHB/OB	2015
†DAWES, Michael James	23.02.92	Epsom		RHB/RM	2016
DICKINSON, Calvin Miles	03.11.96	Durban, SA	Brookes U	RHB/WK	2016
ELLIS, Edward John	09.05.95	Ascot	Brookes U	RHB/WK	2015
†ESCOTT, Daniel Alexander	26.09.96	Torbay	Lincoln	RHB/LB	2016
†GNODDE, James Spencer Drury	09.11.93	Westminster	Pembroke	LHB/SLA	2015
GRUNDY, Jack Oliver	25.06.94	Warwick	Brookes U	RHB/LMF	2015
HASSAM MUSHTAQ			Brookes U	RHB/LB	2016
†HEYWOOD, Robert Alistair	30.07.94	Basingstoke	Worcester	RHB	2016
†HUGHES, Matthew Stephen Turner	17.04.96	Manchester	Hertford	RHB	2015
†JONES, Owain James	24.09.92	Brighton	St Edmund Hall	LHB/RM	2015
LAIDMAN, Matthew John	20.10.92	Sutton	Brookes U	RHB/WK	2016
LAKE, Malcolm Blair	03.08.94	Harare, Zimbabwe	Brookes U	LHB/RM	2015
LEACH, Stephen Geoffrey	19.11.93	Stafford	Brookes U	LHB/LB	2014
McIVER, Jack Nathan	26.04.92	Hammersmith	Brookes U	RHB/OB	2015
†MARSDEN, Jonathan	07.04.93	Sevenoaks	St Hilda's	RHB/RFM	2013
PATERNOTT, Lloyd Christopher	15.01.92	Watford	Brookes U	RHB/RM	2014
SAKANDE, Abidine	22.09.94	Chester	St John's	RHB/RFM	2014
WELLER, Sam David	21.11.94	Chislehurst	Brookes U	RHB/RFM	2014
†WESTAWAY, Samuel Alexander	29.07.92	Welwyn Garden	Green Templeton	RHB/WK	2011
†WINTER, Matthew James	08.11.93	Crewe	Lady Margaret	RHB	2013

THE 2016 FIRST-CLASS SEASON STATISTICAL HIGHLIGHTS

FIRST TO INDIVIDUAL TARGETS

1000 RUNS	T.Westley	Essex	14 July
2000 RUNS	–	Most – 1602 K.K.Jennings (Durham)	
50 WICKETS	C.R.Woakes	Warwickshire & England	25 July
100 WICKETS	–	Most – 69 G.R.Napier (Essex) & J.S.Patel (Warwickshire)	

TEAM HIGHLIGHTS
HIGHEST INNINGS TOTALS

640-9d	Essex v Northamptonshire	Northampton
637-7d	Surrey v Hampshire	Southampton
607-7d	Durham v Surrey	The Oval
601-5d	Essex v Worcestershire	Chelmsford

HIGHEST FOURTH INNINGS TOTAL

404-8	Worcestershire (set 401) v Northamptonshire	Worcester

LOWEST INNINGS TOTALS

43	Leicestershire v Worcestershire	Leicester
52	Cambridge MCCU v Nottinghamshire	Cambridge
91	Sri Lanka v England (*1st Test*)	Leeds
94	Derbyshire v Kent	Derby
94	Nottinghamshire v Yorkshire	Scarborough
95	Glamorgan v Northamptonshire	Swansea
95	Somerset v Warwickshire	Taunton
96	Leicestershire v Glamorgan	Leicester

HIGHEST MATCH AGGREGATE

1432-30	Leicestershire (407 & 307-3d) v Worcs (349 & 369-7)	Worcester

LARGE MARGINS OF VICTORY

523 runs	Essex (416-4d & 409-7d) beat Cambridge MCCU (124 & 178)	Cambridge
This was Essex's largest ever winning margin by runs.		
517 runs	Notts (530-8d & 170-5d) beat Cambridge MCCU (52 & 131)	Cambridge
482 runs	Worcs (345-9d & 451-3d) beat Oxford MCCU (190 & 124)	Oxford
This was Worcestershire's largest ever winning margin by runs.		
Inns & 161 runs	Essex (601-5d) beat Worcestershire (230 & 210)	Chelmsford
Inns & 127 runs	Kent (496) beat Sussex (180 & 189)	Hove
Inns & 116 runs	Middlesex (467-3d) beat Hampshire (131 & 220)	Northwood

NARROW MARGINS OF VICTORY

1 wkt	Somerset (102 & 301-9) beat Surrey (264 & 138)	Taunton
11 runs	Glamorgan (286 & 296) beat Essex (319 & 252)	Chelmsford
11 runs	Worcestershire (306 & 194) beat Sussex (229 & 260)	Hove

SIX FIFTIES IN AN INNINGS

Durham (607-7d) v Surrey	The Oval
Essex (640-9d) v Northamptonshire	Northampton

ELEVEN BOWLERS IN AN INNINGS

Warwickshire v Middlesex (304-6d)	Lord's

MOST EXTRAS IN AN INNINGS

B	*LB*	*W*	*NB*		
60	4	28	–	28 Essex (441-8d) v Northamptonshire	Chelmsford
60	36	10	8	6 Leicestershire (332) v Northamptonshire	Leicester

Under ECB regulations, Test matches excluded, two penalty extras were scored for each no-ball.

BATTING HIGHLIGHTS
DOUBLE HUNDREDS

J.M.Bairstow	246	Yorkshire v Hampshire	Leeds
D.J.Bell-Drummond	206*	Kent v Loughborough MCCU	Canterbury
N.L.J.Browne (2)	255	Essex v Derbyshire	Chelmsford
	229*	Essex v Derbyshire	Derby
J.L.Denly	206*	Kent v Northamptonshire	Northampton
S.R.Dickson	207*	Kent v Derbyshire	Derby
B.L.D'Oliveira	202*	Worcestershire v Glamorgan	Cardiff
A.H.T.Donald	234	Glamorgan v Derbyshire	Colwyn Bay
B.M.Duckett (2)	282*	Northamptonshire v Sussex	Northampton
	208	Northamptonshire v Kent	Beckenham
B.A.Godleman	204	Derbyshire v Worcestershire	Derby
N.R.T.Gubbins	201*	Middlesex v Lancashire	Lord's
K.K.Jennings (2)	221*	Durham v Yorkshire	Chester-le-Street
	201*	Durham v Surrey	Chester-le-Street
E.C.Joyce	230	Sussex v Derbyshire	Derby
A.Lyth	202	Yorkshire v Surrey	The Oval
R.I.Newton	202*	Northamptonshire v Leicestershire	Northampton
S.D.Robson	231	Middlesex v Warwickshire	Lord's
J.E.Root (2)	213	Yorkshire v Surrey	Leeds
	254	England v Pakistan (*2nd Test*)	Manchester
W.R.Smith	210	Hampshire v Lancashire	Southampton
M.E.Trescothick	218	Somerset v Nottinghamshire	Nottingham
I.J.L.Trott	219*	Warwickshire v Middlesex	Lord's
T.Westley	254	Essex v Worcestershire	Chelmsford
A.J.A.Wheater	204*	Hampshire v Warwickshire	Birmingham
Younus Khan	218	Pakistan v England (*4th Test*)	The Oval

HUNDREDS IN THREE CONSECUTIVE INNINGS

E.J.H.Eckersley 117	104	Leicestershire v Derbyshire	Leicester
	107	Leicestershire v Northamptonshire	Northampton
J.C.Mickleburgh 125	102	Essex v Cambridge MCCU	Cambridge
	109	Essex v Sri Lankans	Chelmsford

DOUBLE HUNDRED AND A HUNDRED IN A MATCH

S.D.Robson	231	106	Middlesex v Warwickshire	Lord's

The most runs ever scored in a f-c match by a Middlesex batsman.

HUNDRED IN EACH INNINGS OF A MATCH

S.G.Borthwick	134	103*	Durham v Lancashire	Chester-le-Street
S.M.Davies	115	109	Surrey v Loughborough MCCU	The Oval
E.J.H.Eckersley	117	104	Leicestershire v Derbyshire	Leicester
S.M.Ervine	103	106	Hampshire v Somerset	Taunton
H.Hameed	114	100*	Lancashire v Yorkshire	Manchester
K.K.Jennings	116	105*	Durham v Somerset	Chester-le-Street

J.C.Mickleburgh	125	102	Essex v Cambridge MCCU	Cambridge
D.K.H.Mitchell	107*	103	Worcestershire v Northamptonshire	Worcester
C.J.L.Rogers	132	100*	Somerset v Nottinghamshire	Taunton
B.R.M.Taylor	114	105*	Nottinghamshire v Durham	Nottingham

FASTEST HUNDRED AGAINST GENUINE BOWLING

S.R.Patel (124)	68 balls	Nottinghamshire v Warwickshire	Nottingham

FASTEST DOUBLE HUNDRED AGAINST GENUINE BOWLING

A.H.T.Donald (234)	123 balls	Glamorgan v Derbyshire	Colwyn Bay

Equalled the world record, by R.Shastri in 1985, for the fastest 200.

MOST SIXES IN AN INNINGS

15	A.H.T.Donald (234)	Glamorgan v Derbyshire	Colwyn Bay

200 RUNS IN A DAY

A.H.T.Donald (0-234)	Glamorgan v Derbyshire	Colwyn Bay

Went from 0-127 between lunch and tea, and 127*-234 after tea.*

150 OR MORE RUNS FROM BOUNDARIES IN AN INNINGS

Runs	*6s*	*4s*			
194	15	26	A.H.T.Donald	Glamorgan v Derbyshire	Colwyn Bay
164	2	38	B.M.Duckett	Northamptonshire v Sussex	Northampton
152	–	38	T.Westley	Essex v Worcestershire	Chelmsford

HUNDRED ON FIRST-CLASS DEBUT

D.A.Escott	125	Oxford U v Cambridge U	Oxford

Also took 6-71 in the second innings.

HUNDRED ON FIRST-CLASS DEBUT IN BRITAIN

M.D.Shanaka	112	Sri Lankans v Leicestershire	Leicester

CARRYING BAT THROUGH COMPLETED INNINGS

K.K.Jennings	201*	Durham (401) v Surrey	Chester-le-Street
R.P.Jones	106*	Lancashire (259) v Middlesex	Manchester
N.J.Selman	122*	Glamorgan (236) v Northamptonshire	Swansea

60% OF A COMPLETED INNINGS TOTAL

71.67%	S.R.Patel	(124/173)	Nottinghamshire v Warwickshire	Nottingham

LONG INNINGS (Qualification 600 mins and/or 400 balls)

Mins	*Balls*				
552	445	N.L.J.Browne	(255)	Essex v Derbyshire	Chelmsford
562	417	N.L.J.Browne	(229*)	Essex v Derbyshire	Derby
578	416	K.K.Jennings	(221*)	Durham v Yorkshire	Chester-le-Street
614	406	J.E.Root	(254)	England v Pakistan (*2nd Test*)	Manchester
574	455	W.R.Smith	(210)	Hampshire v Lancashire	Southampton

UNUSUAL DISMISSAL – HANDLED THE BALL

S.R.Dickson	Kent v Leicestershire	Leicester

FIRST-WICKET PARTNERSHIP OF 100 IN EACH INNINGS

131/190*	D.J.Bell-Drummond/T.W.M.Latham	Kent v Glamorgan	Canterbury
123/100*	M.E.Trescothick/J.G.Myburgh	Somerset v Nottinghamshire	Nottingham
140/113	B.M.Duckett/R.I.Newton	Northants v Glamorgan	Northampton

OTHER NOTABLE PARTNERSHIPS († *Team record*)

Qualifications: 1st-4th wkts: 250 runs; 5th-6th: 225; 7th: 200; 8th: 175; 9th: 150; 10th: 100.

First Wicket

286	D.K.H.Mitchell/B.L.D'Oliveira	Worcestershire v Oxford MCCU	Oxford

Second Wicket

310	E.C.Joyce/L.W.P.Wells	Sussex v Derbyshire	Derby

Third Wicket

279	A.C.Voges/J.A.Simpson	Middlesex v Hampshire	Northwood
269	C.J.L.Rogers/J.C.Hildreth	Somerset v Nottinghamshire	Taunton
264	P.J.Horton/M.J.Cosgrove	Leicestershire v Worcestershire	Worcester
253	D.L.D'Oliveira/J.M.Clarke	Worcestershire v Glamorgan	Cardiff
251	B.A.Godleman/W.L.Madsen	Derbyshire v Worcestershire	Derby

Fourth Wicket

372†	J.E.Root/J.M.Bairstow	Yorkshire v Surrey	Leeds

Fifth Wicket

294	L.W.P.Wells/B.C.Brown	Sussex v Glamorgan	Hove
258*	B.C.Brown/H.Z.Finch	Sussex v Leeds/Bradford MCCU	Hove
258	S.W.Billings/D.I.Stevens	Kent v Gloucestershire	Bristol

Seventh Wicket

227	J.M.Bairstow/L.E.Plunkett	Yorkshire v Hampshire	Leeds
215	R.N.ten Doeschate/J.S.Foster	Essex v Northamptonshire	Northampton

Eighth Wicket

236†	P.D.Trego/R.C.Davies	Somerset v Lancashire	Manchester
222*†	B.T.Foakes/G.J.Batty	Surrey v Hampshire	Southampton
222†	S.A.Northeast/J.C.Tredwell	Kent v Essex	Chelmsford
217	R.E.van der Merwe/C.Overton	Somerset v Hampshire	Taunton

Ninth Wicket

174	M.D.Shanaka/H.M.R.K.B.Herath	Sri Lankans v Leicestershire	Leicester
162	J.A.R.Harris/J.K.Fuller	Middlesex v Somerset	Taunton

Tenth Wicket

107	J.Clark/K.M.Jarvis	Lancashire v Yorkshire	Manchester

BOWLING HIGHLIGHTS
EIGHT OR MORE WICKETS IN AN INNINGS

R.I.Keogh	9-52	Northamptonshire v Glamorgan	Northampton
B.W.Sanderson	8-73	Northamptonshire v Gloucestershire	Northampton
C.R.Woakes	9-36	Warwickshire v Durham	Birmingham

TEN OR MORE WICKETS IN A MATCH

J.M.Anderson	10- 45	England v Sri Lanka (*1st Test*)	Leeds
G.J.Batty	10-115	Surrey v Somerset	Taunton
M.L.Cummins	12-166	Worcestershire v Sussex	Hove
K.M.Jarvis	11-119	Lancashire v Surrey	Manchester
R.I.Keogh	13-125	Northamptonshire v Glamorgan	Northampton
S.C.Kerrigan	10-166	Lancashire v Middlesex	Manchester
S.J.Magoffin	10- 70	Sussex v Worcestershire	Hove
J.S.Patel	10-123	Warwickshire v Surrey	Guildford

R.D.Pringle	10-260	Durham v Hampshire	Southampton
M.R.Quinn	11-163	Essex v Gloucestershire	Cheltenham
T.S.Roland-Jones	10-127	Middlesex v Yorkshire	Lord's
B.W.Sanderson	10- 89	Northamptonshire v Glamorgan	Swansea
N.Wagner	11-111	Lancashire v Nottinghamshire	Manchester
C.R.Woakes	11-102	England v Pakistan (*1st Test*)	Lord's
Yasir Shah	10-141	Pakistan v England (*1st Test*)	Lord's

BOWLING UNCHANGED THROUGHOUT INNINGS

M.J.Henry (13-3-27-4)/J.Leach (12-7-10-4)	Worcestershire v Leics	Leicester

HAT-TRICKS

J.T.Ball	Nottinghamshire v Middlesex	Nottingham
T.S.Roland-Jones	Middlesex v Yorkshire	Lord's

Last three wickets of match to secure County Championship for Middlesex.

FOUR WICKETS IN FIVE DELIVERIES

M.V.T.Fernando	Sri Lanka A v Durham	Chester-le-Street

200 RUNS CONCEDED IN AN INNINGS

M.S.Crane	51-4-210-3	Hampshire v Surrey	Southampton
Yasir Shah	54-6-213-1	England v Pakistan (*2nd Test*)	Manchester

MOST OVERS BOWLED IN AN INNINGS

Yasir Shah	54-6-213-1	England v Pakistan (*2nd Test*)	Manchester

ALL-ROUND HIGHLIGHTS
MATCH DOUBLE (HUNDRED AND FIVE WICKETS IN AN INNINGS)

D.A.Escott (125 & 6-71)	Oxford U v Cambridge U	Oxford
S.J.Thakor (130 & 5-63)	Derbyshire v Kent	Derby
G.R.Napier (124 & 5-114)	Essex v Sussex	Colchester

MATCH DOUBLE (HUNDRED AND FIVE DISMISSALS IN AN INNINGS)

J.M.Bairstow (140 & 5ct)	England v Sri Lanka (*1st Test*)	Leeds

WICKET-KEEPING HIGHLIGHTS
SIX OR MORE WICKET-KEEPING DISMISSALS IN AN INNINGS

T.R.Ambrose	5ct, 1st	Warwickshire v Nottinghamshire	Birmingham
S.W.Billings	7ct	Kent v Worcestershire	Canterbury

NINE OR MORE WICKET-KEEPING DISMISSALS IN A MATCH

J.M.Bairstow	9ct	England v Sri Lanka (*1st Test*)	Leeds
S.W.Billings	8ct, 1st	Kent v Worcestershire	Canterbury
J.A.Simpson	9ct	Middlesex v Somerset	Taunton
M.A.Wallace (2)	9ct	Glamorgan v Derbyshire	Colwyn Bay
	9ct	Glamorgan v Worcestershire	Worcester

NO BYES CONCEDED IN AN INNINGS OF 600 OR MORE

D.Murphy	Essex (640-9d) v Northamptonshire	Northampton

FIELDING HIGHLIGHTS

SIX OR MORE CATCHES IN THE FIELD IN A MATCH

L.S.Livingstone	6ct	Lancashire v Durham	Chester-le-Street
M.E.Trescothick	7ct	Somerset v Warwickshire	Taunton

COUNTY CHAMPIONSHIP 2016
SPECSAVERS FINAL TABLES

DIVISION 1

	P	W	L	D	Bonus Points Bat	Bonus Points Bowl	Deduct Points	Total Points
1 **MIDDLESEX** (2)	16	6	–	10	48	40	4	230
2 Somerset (6)	16	6	1	9	44	41	–	226
3 Yorkshire (1)	16	5	3	8	49	42	–	211
4 Durham (4) (Rel)	16	5	3	8	39	41	–	200
5 Surrey (-)	16	4	6	6	46	42	–	182
6 Warwickshire (5)	16	3	4	9	39	44	–	176
7 Lancashire (-)	16	3	5	8	39	38	–	165
8 Hampshire (7)	16	2	4	10	41	35	3	155
9 Nottinghamshire (3)	16	1	9	6	34	44	–	124

DIVISION 2

	P	W	L	D	A	Bonus Points Bat	Bonus Points Bowl	Deduct Points	Total Points
1 Essex (3)	16	6	3	7	–	58	46	–	235
2 Kent (7)	16	5	2	8	1	49	38	–	212
3 Worcestershire (-)	16	6	4	5	1	42	35	–	203
4 Sussex (-)	16	4	2	10	–	40	38	–	192
5 Northamptonshire (5)	16	4	3	8	1	42	33	–	184
6 Gloucestershire (6)	16	4	5	7	–	44	40	–	183
7 Leicestershire (9)	16	4	4	8	–	39	40	1	182
8 Glamorgan (4)	16	3	8	5	–	34	42	1	148
9 Derbyshire (8)	16	–	5	10	1	32	32	–	119

Middlesex deducted 4 points for slow over rate.
Hampshire deducted 3 points for slow over rate in two games.
Glamorgan and Leicestershire each deducted 1 point for slow over rate.

After the season, the ECB relegated Durham to Division 2 as part of a package of ECB financial assistance to the county; Hampshire stayed in Division 1.

SCORING OF CHAMPIONSHIP POINTS 2016

(a) For a win, 16 points, plus any points scored in the first innings.

(b) In a tie, each side to score eight points, plus any points scored in the first innings.

(c) In a drawn match, each side to score five points, plus any points scored in the first innings (see also paragraph (e) below).

(d) If the scores are equal in a drawn match, the side batting in the fourth innings to score eight points plus any points scored in the first innings, and the opposing side to score three points plus any points scored in the first innings.

(e) **First Innings Points** (awarded only for performances **in the first 110 overs** of each first innings and retained whatever the result of the match).

(i) A maximum of five batting points to be available as under:
200 to 249 runs – 1 point; 250 to 299 runs – 2 points; 300 to 349 runs – 3 points; 350 to 399 runs – 4 points; 400 runs or over – 5 points.

(ii) A maximum of three bowling points to be available as under:
3 to 5 wickets taken – 1 point; 6 to 8 wickets taken – 2 points; 9 to 10 wickets taken – 3 points.

(f) If a match is abandoned without a ball being bowled, each side to score five points.

(g) The side which has the highest aggregate of points gained at the end of the season shall be the Champion County of their respective Division. Should any sides in the Championship table be equal on points, the following tie-breakers will be applied in the order stated: most wins, fewest losses, team achieving most points in contests between teams level on points, most wickets taken, most runs scored. At the end of the season, the top two teams from the Second Division will be promoted and the bottom two teams from the First Division will be relegated.

COUNTY CHAMPIONS

The English County Championship was not officially constituted until December 1889. Prior to that date there was no generally accepted method of awarding the title; although the 'least matches lost' method existed, it was not consistently applied. Rules governing playing qualifications were agreed in 1873 and the first unofficial points system 15 years later.

Research has produced a list of champions dating back to 1826, but at least seven different versions exist for the period from 1864 to 1889 (see *The Wisden Book of Cricket Records*). Only from 1890 can any authorised list of county champions commence.

That first official Championship was contested between eight counties: Gloucestershire, Kent, Lancashire, Middlesex, Nottinghamshire, Surrey, Sussex and Yorkshire. The remaining counties were admitted in the following seasons: 1891 – Somerset, 1895 – Derbyshire, Essex, Hampshire, Leicestershire and Warwickshire, 1899 – Worcestershire, 1905 – Northamptonshire, 1921 – Glamorgan, and 1992 – Durham.

The Championship pennant was introduced by the 1951 champions, Warwickshire, and the Lord's Taverners' Trophy was first presented in 1973. The first sponsors, Schweppes (1977-83), were succeeded by Britannic Assurance (1984-98), PPP Healthcare (1999-2000), CricInfo (2001), Frizzell (2002-05), Liverpool Victoria (2006-15) and Specsavers (from 2016). Based on their previous season's positions, the 18 counties were separated into two divisions in 2000. From 2000 to 2005 the bottom three Division 1 teams were relegated and the top three Division 2 sides promoted. This was reduced to two teams from the end of the 2006 season.

1890	Surrey
1891	Surrey
1892	Surrey
1893	Yorkshire
1894	Surrey
1895	Surrey
1896	Yorkshire
1897	Lancashire
1898	Yorkshire
1899	Surrey
1900	Yorkshire
1901	Yorkshire
1902	Yorkshire
1903	Middlesex
1904	Lancashire
1905	Yorkshire
1906	Kent
1907	Nottinghamshire
1908	Yorkshire
1909	Kent
1910	Kent
1911	Warwickshire
1912	Yorkshire
1913	Kent
1914	Surrey
1919	Yorkshire
1920	Middlesex
1921	Middlesex
1922	Yorkshire
1923	Yorkshire
1924	Yorkshire
1925	Yorkshire
1926	Lancashire
1927	Lancashire
1928	Lancashire
1929	Nottinghamshire
1930	Lancashire
1931	Yorkshire
1932	Yorkshire
1933	Yorkshire
1934	Lancashire
1935	Yorkshire
1936	Derbyshire
1937	Yorkshire
1938	Yorkshire
1939	Yorkshire
1946	Yorkshire
1947	Middlesex
1948	Glamorgan
1949	Middlesex Yorkshire
1950	Lancashire Surrey
1951	Warwickshire
1952	Surrey
1953	Surrey
1954	Surrey
1955	Surrey
1956	Surrey
1957	Surrey
1958	Surrey
1959	Yorkshire
1960	Yorkshire
1961	Hampshire
1962	Yorkshire
1963	Yorkshire
1964	Worcestershire
1965	Worcestershire
1966	Yorkshire
1967	Yorkshire
1968	Yorkshire
1969	Glamorgan
1970	Kent
1971	Surrey
1972	Warwickshire
1973	Hampshire
1974	Worcestershire
1975	Leicestershire
1976	Middlesex
1977	Kent Middlesex
1978	Kent
1979	Essex
1980	Middlesex
1981	Nottinghamshire
1982	Middlesex
1983	Essex
1984	Essex
1985	Middlesex
1986	Essex
1987	Nottinghamshire
1988	Worcestershire
1989	Worcestershire
1990	Middlesex
1991	Essex
1992	Essex
1993	Middlesex
1994	Warwickshire
1995	Warwickshire
1996	Leicestershire
1997	Glamorgan
1998	Leicestershire
1999	Surrey
2000	Surrey
2001	Yorkshire
2002	Surrey
2003	Sussex
2004	Warwickshire
2005	Nottinghamshire
2006	Sussex
2007	Sussex
2008	Durham
2009	Durham
2010	Nottinghamshire
2011	Lancashire
2012	Warwickshire
2013	Durham
2014	Yorkshire
2015	Yorkshire
2016	Middlesex

COUNTY CHAMPIONSHIP RESULTS 2016

DIVISION 1

	DURHAM	HANTS	LANCS	MIDDX	NOTTS	SOM'T	SURREY	WARWKS	YORKS
DURHAM		C-le-St	C-le-St	C-le-St	C-le-St	C-le-St	C-le-St	C-le-St	C-le-St
	–	Drawn	D 73	Drawn	Drawn	Drawn	D 21	Drawn	Drawn
HANTS	So'ton		So'ton	So'ton	So'ton	So'ton	So'ton	So'ton	So'ton
	D 6w	–	Drawn	Drawn	H 69	Drawn	Sy I/13	Drawn	Drawn
LANCS	S'port	Man		Man	Man	Man	Man	Man	Man
	D 2w	L I/94	–	Drawn	L 8w	Drawn	L I/96	Drawn	Drawn
MIDDX	Lord's	N'wood	Lord's		Lord's	Lord's	Lord's	Lord's	Lord's
	M I/80	M I/116	Drawn	–	Drawn	Drawn	Drawn	Drawn	M 61
NOTTS	N'ham	N'ham	N'ham	N'ham		N'ham	N'ham	N'ham	N'ham
	Drawn	H 176	Drawn	M 5w	–	Sm 10w	N 3w	W 53	Drawn
SOM'T	Taunton	Taunton	Taunton	Taunton	Taunton		Taunton	Taunton	Taunton
	Sm 39	Drawn	Drawn	M 2w	Sm 325	–	Sm 1w	Sm 31	Drawn
SURREY	Oval	Oval	Oval	Oval	Oval	Oval		G'ford	Oval
	Drawn	Drawn	Sy 10w	Drawn	Sy 228	Drawn	–	W 10w	Drawn
WARWKS	B'ham	B'ham	B'ham	B'ham	B'ham	B'ham	B'ham		B'ham
	D 4w	Drawn	W 237	Drawn	Drawn	Drawn	Sy 226	–	Drawn
YORKS	Leeds	Leeds	Leeds	Scar	Scar	Leeds	Leeds	Leeds	
	Y 228	Drawn	Y 175	M I/4	Y 305	Sm 10w	Y I/20	Y 48	–

DIVISION 2

	DERBYS	ESSEX	GLAM	GLOS	KENT	LEICS	N'HANTS	SUSSEX	WORCS
DERBYS		Derby	Derby	Derby	Derby	Derby	C'field	Derby	Derby
	–	E I/62	Drawn	Drawn	K 7w	Drawn	Aband	Drawn	Drawn
ESSEX	C'ford		C'ford	C'ford	C'ford	C'ford	C'ford	Colch'r	C'ford
	Drawn	–	Gm 11	E 10w	E 10w	L 4w	E I/92	Drawn	E I/161
GLAM	Col B	Cardiff		Cardiff	Cardiff	Cardiff	Swansea	Cardiff	Cardiff
	Gm 4w	Drawn	–	Gs 10w	Drawn	L 10w	N 251	S 2w	Drawn
GLOS	Bristol	Chelt'm	Bristol		Bristol	Chelt'm	Bristol	Bristol	Bristol
	Drawn	Gs 61	Gs 125	–	K I/69	L 6w	Drawn	Drawn	Drawn
KENT	Cant	Cant	Cant	Cant		Cant	Beck	Tun W	Cant
	Drawn	Drawn	K 10w	Drawn	–	Drawn	N 10w	Drawn	K 10w
LEICS	Leics	Leics	Leics	Leics	Leics		Leics	Leics	Leics
	Drawn	E I/10	L 26	Drawn	Drawn	–	Drawn	S I/59	W 7w
N'HANTS	No'ton	No'ton	No'ton	No'ton	No'ton	No'ton		No'ton	No'ton
	Drawn	Drawn	N 318	N 114	Drawn	Drawn	–	Drawn	W 311
SUSSEX	Hove	Hove	Hove	Hove	Hove	Hove	Arundel		Hove
	S 10w	Drawn	Drawn	S I/2	K I/127	Drawn	Drawn	–	W 11
WORCS	Worcs	Worcs	Worcs	Worcs	Worcs	Worcs	Worcs	Worcs	
	W 9w	Drawn	Gm 5w	Gs 5w	Aband	W 5w	W 2w	Drawn	–

COUNTY CHAMPIONSHIP FIXTURES 2017

DIVISION 1

	ESSEX	HANTS	LANCS	MIDDX	SOM'T	SURREY	WARWKS	YORKS
ESSEX		C'ford	C'ford	C'ford	C'ford	C'ford	C'ford	C'ford
	–							
HANTS	So'ton		So'ton	So'ton	So'ton	So'ton	So'ton	So'ton
		–						
LANCS	Man	Man		S'port	Man	Man	Man	Man
			–					
MIDDX	Lord's	Uxbridge	Lord's		Lord's	Lord's	Lord's	Lord's
				–				
SOM'T	Taunton	Taunton	Taunton	Taunton		Taunton	Taunton	Taunton
					–			
SURREY	G'ford	Oval	Oval	Oval	Oval		Oval	Oval
						–		
WARWKS	B'ham	B'ham	B'ham	B'ham	B'ham	B'ham		B'ham
							–	
YORKS	Scar	Leeds	Leeds	Leeds	Scar	Leeds	Leeds	
								–

DIVISION 2

	DERBYS	DURHAM	GLAM	GLOS	KENT	LEICS	N'HANTS	NOTTS	SUSSEX	WORCS
DERBYS		C'field	Derby		Derby	Derby	Derby	Derby		Derby
	–			–					–	
DURHAM	C-le-St		C-le-St		C-le-St		C-le-St	C-le-St	C-le-St	C-le-St
		–		–		–				
GLAM	Cardiff	Swansea		Cardiff			Cardiff	Cardiff	Col B	Cardiff
			–		–	–				
GLOS	Bristol	Bristol	Chelt'm		Bristol	Bristol		Bristol		Chelt'm
				–			–		–	
KENT	Cant	Cant	Cant	Cant		Cant	Beck'm		Tun W	
					–			–		–
LEICS		Leics	Leics	Leics	Leics		Leics	Leics	Leics	
	–					–				–
N'HANTS	No'ton		No'ton	No'ton		No'ton		No'ton	No'ton	No'ton
		–			–		–			
NOTTS	N'ham			N'ham	N'ham	N'ham	N'ham		N'ham	N'ham
		–	–					–		
SUSSEX	Hove	Hove		Hove	Hove	Arundel		Hove		Hove
			–				–		–	
WORCS		Worcs	Worcs	Worcs	Worcs	Worcs	Worcs		Worcs	
	–							–		–

ROYAL LONDON ONE-DAY CUP 2016

This latest format of limited-overs competition was launched in 2014, and is now the only List-A tournament played in the UK. The top four from each group went through to the quarter-finals, with the top team from each group having a home draw against the fourth team in the other group, and the second team in each group having a home draw against the third team in the other group. The winner is decided in the final at Lord's.

NORTH GROUP	*P*	*W*	*L*	*T*	*NR*	*Pts*	*Net RR*
1 Northamptonshire	8	4	3	–	1	9	+0.78
2 Warwickshire	8	4	3	–	1	9	+0.74
3 Yorkshire	8	4	3	–	1	9	+0.59
4 Worcestershire	8	4	3	–	1	9	+0.04
5 Durham	8	4	3	–	1	9	–0.63
6 Nottinghamshire	8	3	4	–	1	7	+0.22
7 Derbyshire	8	2	3	–	3	7	–0.33
8 Leicestershire	8	2	3	–	3	7	–0.48
9 Lancashire	8	2	4	–	2	6	–1.32

SOUTH GROUP	*P*	*W*	*L*	*T*	*NR*	*Pts*	*Net RR*
1 Somerset	8	6	1	1	–	13	–0.08
2 Kent	8	5	3	–	–	10	+0.58
3 Essex	8	4	2	1	1	10	–0.11
4 Surrey	8	4	3	–	1	9	+0.99
5 Hampshire	8	4	4	–	–	8	+0.39
6 Middlesex	8	4	4	–	–	8	+0.11
7 Glamorgan	8	3	4	–	1	7	–0.32
8 Gloucestershire	8	2	5	–	1	5	–0.70
9 Sussex	8	1	7	–	–	2	–0.67

Win = 2 points. Tie (T)/No Result (NR) = 1 point.

Positions of counties finishing equal on points are decided by most wins or, if equal, the team with the higher net run rate (ie deducting from the average runs per over scored by that team in matches where a result was achieved, the average runs per over scored against that team); if still equal, the team that achieved the most points in the matches played between them. In the even the teams still cannot be separated, the winner will be decided by drawing lots.

[illegible]

Highest total	445-8		Nottinghamshire v Northants	Nottingham
Biggest victory (runs)	242		Yorkshire beat Lancashire	Manchester
Biggest victory (wkts)	9		Warwickshire beat Leics	Birmingham
	9		Somerset beat Worcs	Taunton
Most runs	540 (ave 60.00)	S.R.Hain	(Warwickshire)	
Highest innings	184	M.J.Lumb	Nottinghamshire v Northants	Nottingham
Most sixes inns	9	R.K.Kleinveldt	Northants v Nottinghamshire	Nottingham
Highest partnership	342	M.J.Lumb/M.H.Wessels	Notts v Northants	Nottingham
Most wickets	24 (ave 17.41)	M.T.Coles	(Kent)	
Best bowling	6-37	G.G.White	Northamptonshire v Lancashire	Northampton
Most economical	10-0-25-4	G.K.Berg	Hampshire v Glamorgan	Swansea
Most expensive	10-0-101-1	M.J.J.Critchley	Derbyshire v Worcs	Worcester
Most w/k dismissals	14	B.T.Foakes	(Surrey)	
Most catches	8	R.S.Bopara (Essex), A.J.Blake (Kent), J.J.Roy (Surrey)		

2016 ROYAL LONDON ONE-DAY CUP FINAL
WARWICKSHIRE v SURREY

At Lord's, London, on 17 September.
Result: **WARWICKSHIRE** won by eight wickets.
Toss: Surrey. Award: I.J.L.Trott.

SURREY		**Runs**	**Balls**	**4/6**	**Fall**
J.J.Roy	c Evans b Wright	24	30	4	1- 45
S.M.Davies	st Ambrose b Javid	23	29	4	2- 50
K.C.Sangakkara	c Ambrose b Hannon-Dalby	21	39	–	3- 99
R.J.Burns	b Patel	40	83	2	9-129
† B.T.Foakes	lbw b Hannon-Dalby	0	4	–	4-101
Z.S.Ansari	c Evans b Patel	0	3	–	5-102
S.M.Curran	b Javid	13	19	2	6-118
T.K.Curran	run out	4	13	–	7-129
* G.J.Batty	b Woakes	0	4	–	8-129
S.C.Meaker	not out	0	9	–	
J.W.Dernbach	b Woakes	7	8	–/1	10-136
Extras	(LB 1, W 3)	4			
Total	(40.1 overs)	**136**			

WARWICKSHIRE		**Runs**	**Balls**	**4/6**	**Fall**
I.J.L.Trott	not out	82	100	10	
S.R.Hain	c S.M.Curran b Ansari	12	29	1	1-45
* I.R.Bell	c Foakes b Meaker	17	26	1	2-89
† T.R.Ambrose	not out	22	27	1	
L.J.Evans					
C.R.Woakes					
R.Clarke					
A.Javid					
J.S.Patel					
C.J.C.Wright					
O.J.Hannon-Dalby					
Extras	(LB 3, W 1)	4			
Total	(2 wkts; 30.2 overs)	**137**			

WARWICKSHIRE	**O**	**M**	**R**	**W**	**SURREY**	**O**	**M**	**R**	**W**
Clarke	3	0	24	0	Dernbach	6	0	27	0
Woakes	9.1	2	24	2	S.M.Curran	4.2	0	20	0
Wright	6	1	17	1	T.K.Curran	4	0	14	0
Javid	5	0	15	2	Meaker	4	0	25	1
Hannon-Dalby	8	0	27	2	Ansari	8	0	33	1
Patel	9	1	28	2	Batty	4	0	15	0

Umpires: D.J.Millns and R.T.Robinson

SEMI-FINALS

At Headingley, Leeds, on 28 August. Toss: Yorkshire. **SURREY** won by 19 runs. Surrey 255-7 (50; S.M.Davies 104, B.T.Foakes 90, M.J.Waite 3-48). Yorkshire 236 (48.5; T.T.Bresnan 68, S.C.Meaker 3-61). Award: S.M.Davies.

At Edgbaston, Birmingham, on 29 August. Toss: Warwickshire. **WARWICKSHIRE** won by 8 runs. Warwickshire 284-4 (50; I.R.Bell 94*, S.R.Hain 86). Somerset 276-9 (50; P.D.Trego 58, J.S.Patel 5-43). Award: J.S.Patel.

PRINCIPAL LIST A RECORDS 1963-2016

These records cover all the major limited-overs tournaments played by the counties since the inauguration of the Gillette Cup in 1963.

Highest Totals	496-4		Surrey v Glos	The Oval	2007
	445-8		Notts v Northants	Nottingham	2016
Highest Total Batting Second	429		Glamorgan v Surrey	The Oval	2002
Lowest Totals	23		Middlesex v Yorks	Leeds	1974
	36		Leics v Sussex	Leicester	1973
Largest Victory (Runs)	346		Somerset beat Devon	Torquay	1990
	304		Sussex beat Ireland	Belfast	1996
Highest Scores	268	A.D.Brown	Surrey v Glamorgan	The Oval	2002
	206	A.I.Kallicharran	Warwicks v Oxfords	Birmingham	1984
	203	A.D.Brown	Surrey v Hampshire	Guildford	1997
	201*	R.S.Bopara	Essex v Leics	Leicester	2008
	201	V.J.Wells	Leics v Berkshire	Leicester	1996
Fastest Hundred	36 balls	G.D.Rose	Somerset v Devon	Torquay	1990
	44 balls	M.A.Ealham	Kent v Derbyshire	Maidstone	1995
	44 balls	T.C.Smith	Lancashire v Worcs	Worcester	2012
	44 balls	D.I.Stevens	Kent v Sussex	Canterbury	2013
Most Sixes (Inns)	15	R.N.ten Doeschate	Essex v Scotland	Chelmsford	2013
Highest Partnership for each Wicket					
1st	342	M.J.Lumb/M.H.Wessels	Notts v Northants	Nottingham	2016
2nd	302	M.E.Trescothick/C.Kieswetter	Somerset v Glos	Taunton	2008
3rd	309*	T.S.Curtis/T.M.Moody	Worcs v Surrey	The Oval	1994
4th	234*	D.Lloyd/C.H.Lloyd	Lancashire v Glos	Manchester	1978
5th	221*	R.R.Sarwan/M.A.Hardinges	Glos v Lancashire	Manchester	2005
6th	226	N.J.Llong/M.V.Fleming	Kent v Cheshire	Bowdon	1999
7th	170	D.R.Brown/A.F.Giles	Warwicks v Essex	Birmingham	2003
8th	174	R.W.T.Key/J.C.Tredwell	Kent v Surrey	The Oval	2007
9th	155	C.M.W.Read/A.J.Harris	Notts v Durham	Nottingham	1984
10th	82	G.Chapple/P.J.Martin	Lancashire v Worcs	Manchester	1996
Best Bowling	8-21	M.A.Holding	Derbyshire v Sussex	Hove	1988
	8-26	K.D.Boyce	Essex v Lancashire	Manchester	1971
	8-31	D.L.Underwood	Kent v Scotland	Edinburgh	1987
	8-66	S.R.G.Francis	Somerset v Derbys	Derby	2004
Four Wkts in Four Balls		A.Ward	Derbyshire v Sussex	Derby	1970
		V.C.Drakes	Notts v Derbyshire	Nottingham	1999
		D.A.Payne	Gloucestershire v Essex	Chelmsford	2010
		G.R.Napier	Essex v Surrey	Chelmsford	2013
Most Economical Analyses					
	8-8-0-0	B.A.Langford	Somerset v Essex	Yeovil	1969
	8-7-1-1	D.R.Doshi	Notts v Northants	Northampton	1977
	12-9-3-1	J.Simmons	Lancashire v Suffolk	Bury St Eds	1985
	8-6-2-3	F.J.Titmus	Middlesex v Northants	Northampton	1972
Most Expensive Analyses					
	9-0-108-3	S.D.Thomas	Glamorgan v Surrey	The Oval	2002
	10-0-107-0	J.W.Dernbach	Surrey v Essex	The Oval	2008
	11-0-103-0	G.Welch	Warwicks v Lancs	Birmingham	1995
	10-0-101-1	M.J.J.Critchley	Derbyshire v Worcs	Worcester	2016
Century and Five Wickets in an Innings					
	154*, 5-26	M.J.Procter	Glos v Somerset	Taunton	1972
	206, 6-32	A.I.Kallicharran	Warwicks v Oxfords	Birmingham	1984
	103, 5-41	C.L.Hooper	Kent v Essex	Maidstone	1993
	125, 5-41	I.R.Bell	Warwicks v Essex	Chelmsford	2003
Most Wicket-Keeping Dismissals in an Innings					
	8 (8 ct)	D.J.S.Taylor	Somerset v British Us	Taunton	1982
	8 (8 ct)	D.J.Pipe	Worcs v Herts	Hertford	2001
Most Catches in an Innings by a Fielder					
	5	J.M.Rice	Hampshire v Warwicks	Southampton	1978
	5	D.J.G.Sales	Northants v Essex	Northampton	2007

NATWEST t20 BLAST 2016

In 2016, the Twenty20 competition was sponsored by NatWest. Between 2003 and 2009, three regional leagues competed to qualify for the knockout stages, but this was reduced to two leagues in 2010, before returning to the three-division format in 2012. In 2014, the competition reverted to two regional leagues. (2015's positions in brackets.)

NORTH GROUP

	P	*W*	*L*	*T*	*NR*	*Pts*	*Net RR*
Nottinghamshire (5)	14	8	2	–	4	20	+0.74
Northamptonshire (3)	14	7	5	–	2	16	+0.26
Yorkshire (8)	14	7	5	–	2	16	+0.22
Durham (6)	14	6	6	–	2	14	–0.05
Lancashire (4)	14	6	7	–	1	13	+0.20
Warwickshire (1)	14	6	7	–	1	13	–0.21
Derbyshire (9)	14	5	7	–	2	12	+0.02
Worcestershire (2)	14	5	7	–	2	12	–0.86
Leicestershire (7)	14	4	8	–	2	10	–0.18

SOUTH GROUP

	P	*W*	*L*	*T*	*NR*	*Pts*	*Net RR*
Gloucestershire (5)	14	10	3	–	1	21	+0.51
Glamorgan (6)	14	8	3	–	3	19	+1.00
Middlesex (9)	14	7	6	–	1	15	+0.39
Essex (4)	14	7	6	–	1	15	+0.17
Surrey (7)	14	7	7	–	–	14	+0.15
Sussex (2)	14	5	6	–	3	13	–0.05
Kent (1)	14	6	8	–	–	12	–0.64
Hampshire (3)	14	4	8	–	2	10	–0.69
Somerset (8)	14	3	10	–	1	7	–0.66

QUARTER-FINALS: NOTTINGHAMSHIRE beat Essex by 39 runs at Nottingham.
NORTHANTS beat Middlesex by seven wickets at Northampton.
DURHAM beat Gloucestershire by 19 runs at Bristol.
YORKSHIRE beat Glamorgan by 90 runs at Cardiff.

SEMI-FINALS: NORTHANTS beat Nottinghamshire by 8 runs at Birmingham.
DURHAM beat Yorkshire by 7 runs at Birmingham.

LEADING AGGREGATES AND RECORDS 2016

BATTING (500 runs)	*M*	*I*	*NO*	*HS*	*Runs*	*Avg*	*100*	*50*	*R/100b*	*Sixes*
M.Klinger (Glos)	15	14	3	101	548	49.81	1	4	134.6	16
C.A.Ingram (Glam)	14	14	2	101	502	41.83	1	4	164.5	29

BOWLING (20 wkts)	*O*	*M*	*R*	*W*	*Avge*	*BB*	*4w*	*R/Over*
B.A.C.Howell (Glos)	56.0	1	385	24	16.04	3-18	–	6.87
G.R.Napier (Essex)	43.2	–	369	22	16.77	3-28	–	8.51
T.T.Bresnan (Yorks)	44.0	2	353	21	16.80	3-15	–	8.02
J.Leach (Worcs)	43.2	–	402	20	20.10	5-33	1	9.27

Highest total	242-5		Sussex v Gloucestershire	Bristol
Highest innings	127	T.Kohler-Cadmore	Worcestershire v Durham	Worcester
Highest partnership	187	J.J.Roy/A.J.Finch	Surrey v Kent	The Oval
Best bowling	5-13	S.D.Parry	Lancashire v Worcs	Manchester
	5-13	R.F.Higgins	Middlesex v Hampshire	Southampton
Most economical	4-0-11-2	D.W.Lawrence	Essex v Surrey	The Oval
Most expensive	4-0-63-1	B.J.McCarthy	Durham v Worcestershire	Worcester
	4-0-63-0	U.Arshad	Durham v Yorkshire	Leeds
Most w/k dismissals	14	P.Mustard (Durham, Gloucestershire)		
Most dismissals (inns)	5	C.B.Cooke	Glamorgan v Surrey	Cardiff
Most catches	12	M.W.Machan (Sussex)		
Most catches (inns)	5	M.W.Machan	Sussex v Glamorgan	Hove

2016 NATWEST t20 BLAST FINAL
NORTHAMPTONSHIRE v DURHAM

At Edgbaston, Birmingham, on 20 August (floodlit).

Result: **NORTHAMPTONSHIRE** won by four wickets.

Toss: Durham. Award: J.J.Cobb.

DURHAM		**Runs**	**Balls**	**4/6**	**Fall**
M.D.Stoneman	c and b Azharullah	3	6	–	1- 16
K.K.Jennings	c Cobb b Kleinveldt	88	58	5/4	7-140
B.A.Stokes	c Keogh b Sanderson	18	8	4	2- 34
† M.J.Richardson	c Rossington b Crook	4	8	–	3- 43
J.T.A.Burnham	run out	0	3	–	4- 49
* P.D.Collingwood	c Crook b Sanderson	9	11	–	5- 89
R.D.Pringle	c Cobb b Sanderson	2	7	–	6-104
S.G.Borthwick	c Rossington b Kleinveldt	10	12	–	8-144
U.Arshad	not out	4	5	–	
M.A.Wood	not out	5	3	1	
C.Rushworth					
Extras	(LB 4, W 4, NB 2)	10			
Total	(8 wkts; 20 overs)	**153**			

NORTHAMPTONSHIRE		**Runs**	**Balls**	**4/6**	**Fall**
R.E.Levi	run out	2	3	–	2- 4
† A.M.Rossington	c Borthwick b Wood	2	4	–	1- 4
J.J.Cobb	c Richardson b Rushworth	80	48	10/3	5-148
B.M.Duckett	lbw b Rushworth	4	5	1	3- 9
* A.G.Wakely	run out	43	39	3/2	4-129
R.I.Keogh	not out	16	11	2	
S.P.Crook	run out	0	3	–	6-149
R.K.Kleinveldt	not out	2	3	–	
G.G.White					
B.W.Sanderson					
Azharullah					
Extras	(LB 1, W 3, NB 2)	6			
Total	(6 wkts; 19.1 overs)	**155**			

NORTHAMPTONSHIRE	**O**	**M**	**R**	**W**	**DURHAM**	**O**	**M**	**R**	**W**
Sanderson	4	0	31	3	Rushworth	4	0	22	2
Kleinveldt	4	0	40	2	Wood	4	0	25	1
Azharullah	4	0	21	1	Arshad	3.1	0	41	0
Crook	4	0	26	1	Jennings	4	0	34	0
Cobb	1	0	9	0	Borthwick	4	0	32	0
White	3	0	22	0					

Umpires: N.A.Mallender and R.T.Robinson

TWENTY20 CUP WINNERS

2003	Surrey	2008	Middlesex	2013	Northamptonshire
2004	Leicestershire	2009	Sussex	2014	Warwickshire
2005	Somerset	2010	Hampshire	2015	Lancashire
2006	Leicestershire	2011	Leicestershire	2016	Northamptonshire
2007	Kent	2012	Hampshire		

PRINCIPAL TWENTY20 CUP RECORDS 2003-16

Highest Total	254-3		Gloucestershire v Middx	Uxbridge	2011
Highest Total Batting 2nd	226-3		Sussex v Essex	Chelmsford	2014
Lowest Total	47		Northants v Durham	Chester-le-St	2011
Largest Victory (Runs)	143		Somerset v Essex	Chelmsford	2011
Largest Victory (Balls)	75		Hampshire v Glos	Bristol	2010
Highest Scores	158*	B.B.McCullum	Warwickshire v Derbys	Birmingham	2015
	153*	L.J.Wright	Sussex v Essex	Chelmsford	2014
	152*	G.R.Napier	Essex v Sussex	Chelmsford	2008
	151*	C.H.Gayle	Somerset v Kent	Taunton	2015
Fastest Hundred	34 balls	A.Symonds	Kent v Middlesex	Maidstone	2004
Most Sixes (Innings)	16	G.R.Napier	Essex v Sussex	Chelmsford	2008
Most Runs in Career	3212	P.Mustard	Durham, Gloucestershire		2003-16

Highest Partnership for each Wicket

1st	192	K.J.O'Brien/H.J.H.Marshall	Gloucestershire v Middx	Uxbridge	2011
2nd	186	J.L.Langer/C.L.White	Somerset v Glos	Taunton	2006
3rd	144*	J.H.K.Adams/S.M.Ervine	Hampshire v Surrey	Southampton	2010
4th	159*	L.J.Wright/M.W.Machan	Sussex v Essex	Chelmsford	2014
5th	117*	M.N.W.Spriegel/G.C.Wilson	Surrey v Middlesex	Lord's	2012
6th	126*	C.S.MacLeod/J.W.Hastings	Durham v Northants	Chester-le-St	2014
7th	80	D.T.Christian/T.S.Roland-Jones	Middlesex v Kent	Canterbury	2014
8th	71*	M.Klinger/J.K.Fuller	Gloucestershire v Essex	Chelmsford	2015
9th	59*	G.Chapple/P.J.Martin	Lancashire v Leics	Leicester	2003
9th	59*	D.J.Willey/J.A.Brooks	Northants v Warwickshire	Birmingham	2011
10th	59	H.H.Streak/J.E.Anyon	Warwickshire v Worcs	Birmingham	2005

Best Bowling	6- 5	A.V.Suppiah	Somerset v Glamorgan	Cardiff	2011
	6-16	T.G.Southee	Essex v Glamorgan	Chelmsford	2011
	6-21	A.J.Hall	Northants v Worcs	Northampton	2008
	6-24	T.J.Murtagh	Surrey v Middlesex	Lord's	2005
Most Wkts in Career	156	Yasir Arafat	Hants, Kent, Lancs, Somerset, Surrey, Sussex		2006-16

Most Economical Innings Analyses (Qualification: 4 overs)

4-2-5-2	A.C.Thomas	Somerset v Hampshire	Southampton	2010
4-0-5-3	D.R.Briggs	Hampshire v Kent	Catnerbury	2010
4-1-6-2	J.Louw	Northants v Warwicks	Birmingham	2004
4-0-6-1	M.W.Alleyne	Glos v Worcs	Worcester	2005

Most Maiden Overs in an Innings

4-2-9-1	M.Morkel	Kent v Surrey	Beckenham	2007
4-2-5-2	A.C.Thomas	Somerset v Hampshire	Southampton	2010

Most Expensive Innings Analyses

4-0-67-1	R.J.Kirtley	Sussex v Essex	Chelmsford	2008
4-0-65-2	M.J.Hoggard	Yorkshire v Lancs	Leeds	2005
4-0-64-0	Abdul Razzaq	Hampshire v Somerset	Taunton	2010
4-0-63-1	R.J.Kirtley	Sussex v Surrey	Hove	2004
4-0-63-1	B.J.McCarthy	Durham v Worcs	Worcester	2016

Most Wicket-Keeping Dismissals in Career

102	J.S.Foster	Essex		2003-16

Most Wicket-Keeping Dismissals in an Innings

5 (5 ct)	M.J.Prior	Sussex v Middlesex	Richmond	2006
5 (4 ct, 1 st)	G.L.Brophy	Yorkshire v Durham	Chester-le-St	2008
5 (3 ct, 2 st)	B.J.M.Scott	Worcs v Yorkshire	Worcester	2011
5 (4 ct, 1 st)	G.C.Wilson	Surrey v Hampshire	The Oval	2014
5 (5 ct)	N.J.O'Brien	Leics v Northants	Leicester	2014
5 (3 ct, 2 st)	J.A.Simpson	Middlesex v Surrey	Lord's	2014
5 (4 ct, 1 st)	C.B.Cooke	Glamorgan v Surrey	Cardiff	2016

Most Catches in Career

78	S.J.Croft	Lancashire		2006-16

Most Catches in an Innings by a Fielder

5	M.W.Machan	Sussex v Glamorgan	Hove	2016

YOUNG CRICKETER OF THE YEAR

This annual award, made by The Cricket Writers' Club, is currently restricted to players qualified for England, Andrew Symonds meeting that requirement at the time of his award, and under the age of 23 on 1st May. In 1986 their ballot resulted in a dead heat. Up to 6 April 2017 their selections have gained a tally of 2,573 international Test match caps (shown in brackets).

1950	R.Tattersall (16)	1973	M.Hendrick (30)	1995	A.Symonds (26 – Australia)
1951	P.B.H.May (66)	1974	P.H.Edmonds (51)	1996	C.E.W.Silverwood (6)
1952	F.S.Trueman (67)	1975	A.Kennedy	1997	B.C.Hollioake (2)
1953	M.C.Cowdrey (114)	1976	G.Miller (34)	1998	A.Flintoff (79)
1954	P.J.Loader (13)	1977	I.T.Botham (102)	1999	A.J.Tudor (10)
1955	K.F.Barrington (82)	1978	D.I.Gower (117)	2000	P.J.Franks
1956	B.Taylor	1979	P.W.G.Parker (1)	2001	O.A.Shah (6)
1957	M.J.Stewart (8)	1980	G.R.Dilley (41)	2002	R.Clarke (2)
1958	A.C.D.Ingleby-Mackenzie	1981	M.W.Gatting (79)	2003	J.M.Anderson (122)
1959	G.Pullar (28)	1982	N.G.Cowans (19)	2004	I.R.Bell (118)
1960	D.A.Allen (39)	1983	N.A.Foster (29)	2005	A.N.Cook (140)
1961	P.H.Parfitt (37)	1984	R.J.Bailey (4)	2006	S.C.J.Broad (102)
1962	P.J.Sharpe (12)	1985	D.V.Lawrence (5)	2007	A.U.Rashid (10)
1963	G.Boycott (108)	1986	A.A.Metcalfe	2008	R.S.Bopara (13)
1964	J.M.Brearley (39)	1986	J.J.Whitaker (1)	2009	J.W.A.Taylor (7)
1965	A.P.E.Knott (95)	1987	R.J.Blakey (2)	2010	S.T.Finn (36)
1966	D.L.Underwood (86)	1988	M.P.Maynard (4)	2011	J.M.Bairstow (38)
1967	A.W.Greig (58)	1989	N.Hussain (96)	2012	J.E.Root (53)
1968	R.M.H.Cottam (4)	1990	M.A.Atherton (115)	2013	B.A.Stokes (32)
1969	A.Ward (5)	1991	M.R.Ramprakash (52)	2014	A.Z.Lees
1970	C.M.Old (46)	1992	I.D.K.Salisbury (15)	2015	J.A.Leaning
1971	J.Whitehouse	1993	M.N.Lathwell (2)	2016	B.M.Duckett (4)
1972	D.R.Owen-Thomas	1994	J.P.Crawley (37)		

THE PROFESSIONAL CRICKETERS' ASSOCIATION

PLAYER OF THE YEAR

Founded in 1967, the Professional Cricketers' Association introduced this award, decided by their membership, in 1970. The award, now known as the Reg Hayter Cup, is presented at the PCA's Annual Awards Dinner in London.

1970	M.J.Procter	1985	N.V.Radford	2001	D.P.Fulton
1970	J.D.Bond	1986	C.A.Walsh	2002	M.P.Vaughan
1971	L.R.Gibbs	1987	R.J.Hadlee	2003	Mushtaq Ahmed
1972	A.M.E.Roberts	1988	G.A.Hick	2004	A.Flintoff
1973	P.G.Lee	1989	S.J.Cook	2005	A.Flintoff
1974	B.Stead	1990	G.A.Gooch	2006	M.R.Ramprakash
1975	Zaheer Abbas	1991	Waqar Younis	2007	O.D.Gibson
1976	P.G.Lee	1992	C.A.Walsh	2008	M.van Jaarsveld
1977	M.J.Procter	1993	S.L.Watkin	2009	M.E.Trescothick
1978	J.K.Lever	1994	B.C.Lara	2010	N.M.Carter
1979	J.K.Lever	1995	D.G.Cork	2011	M.E.Trescothick
1980	R.D.Jackman	1996	P.V.Simmons	2012	N.R.D.Compton
1981	R.J.Hadlee	1997	S.P.James	2013	M.M.Ali
1982	M.D.Marshall	1998	M.B.Loye	2014	A.Lyth
1983	K.S.McEwan	1999	S.G.Law	2015	C.Rushworth
1984	R.J.Hadlee	2000	M.E.Trescothick	2016	B.M.Duckett

2016 FIRST-CLASS AVERAGES

These averages involve the 531 players who appeared in the 170 first-class matches played by 29 teams in England and Wales during the 2016 season.

'Cap' denotes the season in which the player was awarded a 1st XI cap by the county he represented in 2016. If he played for more than one county in 2016, the county(ies) who awarded him his cap is (are) underlined. Durham abolished both their capping and 'awards' system after the 2005 season. Glamorgan's capping system is based on a player's number of appearances. Gloucestershire now cap players on first-class debut. Worcestershire now award county colours when players make their Championship debut.

Team abbreviations: CU – Cambridge University/Cambridge MCCU; CfU – Cardiff MCCU; De – Derbyshire; Du – Durham; DU – Durham MCCU; E – England; Ex – Essex; Gm – Glamorgan; Gs – Gloucestershire; H – Hampshire; K – Kent; La – Lancashire; LBU – Leeds/Bradford MCCU; Le – Leicestershire; LU – Loughborough MCCU; M – Middlesex; Nh – Northamptonshire; Nt – Nottinghamshire; OU – Oxford University/Oxford MCCU; P – Pakistan(is); PA – Pakistan A; Sm – Somerset; SL – Sri Lanka(ns); SLA – Sri Lanka A; Sy – Surrey; Sx – Sussex; Wa – Warwickshire; Wo – Worcestershire; Y – Yorkshire.

† Left-handed batsman. Cap: a dash (–) denotes a non-county player. A blank denotes uncapped by his current county.

BATTING AND FIELDING

	Cap	*M*	*I*	*NO*	*HS*	*Runs*	*Avge*	*100*	*50*	*Ct/St*
J.B.Abbott (CU)	–	2	4	–	53	73	18.25	–	1	1
K.J.Abbott (Wo)	2016	2	3	–	10	18	6.00	–	–	–
Abdur Rehman Muz' (PA)	–	1	1	–	14	14	14.00	–	–	2
T.B.Abell (Sm)		13	22	1	135	538	25.61	2	1	10
M.R.Adair (Wa)		1	1	–	32	32	32.00	–	–	–
† J.H.K.Adams (H)	2006	14	25	–	99	897	35.88	–	8	13
B.M.R.Akram (LU)	–	2	2	1	160	260	260.00	2	–	–
T.D.Alexander (DU)	–	1	–	–	–	–	–	–	–	–
A.M.Ali (Le)		5	8	–	46	117	14.62	–	–	2
† M.M.Ali (E/Wo)	2007	10	15	4	155*	778	70.72	3	4	3
A.T.A.Allchin (CU)	–	2	4	1	59*	103	34.33	–	1	–
J.Allenby (Sm)		12	17	–	63	446	26.23	–	5	20
† T.P.Alsop (H)		13	21	–	117	737	35.09	1	6	12
T.R.Ambrose (Wa)	2007	15	20	4	104	653	40.81	1	7	55/4
† J.M.Anderson (E/La)	2003	10	10	4	17	55	9.16	–	–	3
† G.M.Andrew (H)		6	7	1	25	85	14.16	–	–	2
† Z.S.Ansari (Sy)	2014	10	17	1	53	439	27.43	–	2	5
J.C.Archer (Sx)		7	8	–	73	195	24.37	–	1	4
A.T.Arif (CU)	–	2	4	–	49	64	16.00	–	–	1
J.B.T.Arksey (CU)	–	1	2	2	12*	14	–	–	–	–
U.Arshad (Du)		3	3	–	84	119	39.66	–	1	1
Asad Shafiq (P)	–	6	10	2	109	436	54.50	1	3	1
† Ashar Zaidi (Ex)		3	5	–	37	120	24.00	–	–	–
M.A.Ashraf (LBU)	–	2	–	–	–	–	–	–	–	1
Azeem Rafiq (Y)	2016	7	9	2	74	249	35.57	–	2	5
Azhar Ali (P)	–	6	12	3	145	576	64.00	3	–	4
M.Azharullah (Nh)	2015	13	15	3	14*	72	6.00	–	–	1
Azizullah (PA)	–	2	3	1	15*	26	13.00	–	–	1
Babar Azam (PA)	–	3	5	1	66*	204	51.00	–	2	1
G.J.Bailey (M)		3	5	1	110*	284	71.00	1	2	2
T.E.Bailey (La)		6	9	1	53	91	11.37	–	1	–
J.M.Bairstow (E/Y)	2011	11	17	1	246	1286	80.37	4	4	38/2
A.J.Ball (K)		5	7	–	66	141	20.14	–	1	2
J.T.Ball (E/Nt)	2016	13	20	2	33	178	9.88	–	–	3
† G.S.Ballance (E/Y)	2012	17	32	2	132	975	32.50	2	5	11

	Cap	M	I	NO	HS	Runs	Avge	100	50	Ct/St
C.T.Bancroft (Gs)	2016	5	9	–	70	192	21.33	–	1	3
S.Bardiola (CU)	–	2	4	–	20	25	6.25	–	–	1
† K.H.D.Barker (Wa)	2013	17	22	3	113	608	32.00	1	4	7
E.G.Barnard (Wo)	2015	15	21	5	73	468	29.25	–	2	5
C.A.Barrett (Nh)		2	2	2	114*	118	–	1	–	3
A.W.R.Barrow (Sm)		2	4	–	21	44	11.00	–	–	6
A.P.Barton (CU)	–	2	4	–	8	14	3.50	–	–	2
G.J.Batty (Sy)	2011	17	26	5	110*	505	24.04	1	–	4
† A.P.Beard (Ex)		3	1	1	0*	0	–	–	–	1
W.A.T.Beer (Sx)		3	2	1	12*	17	17.00	–	–	2
I.R.Bell (Wa)	2001	16	23	2	174	703	33.47	1	3	7
D.J.Bell-Drummond (K)	2015	13	20	6	206*	953	68.07	2	6	1
G.K.Berg (H)	2016	10	13	3	56	288	28.80	–	1	3
† H.R.Bernard (K)		1	1	–	14	14	14.00	–	–	–
D.M.Bess (Sm)		3	5	–	41	100	20.00	–	–	5
T.L.Best (H)		6	8	1	23*	49	7.00	–	–	3
Bilawal Bhatti (PA)	–	2	3	–	5	5	1.66	–	–	1
S.W.Billings (K)	2015	7	7	–	171	329	47.00	1	1	25/1
J.M.Bird (Nt)	2016	5	8	–	23	51	6.37	–	–	1
B.Bishnoi (OU)		1	2	–	16	16	8.00	–	–	–
† A.J.Blake (K)		8	11	3	89*	285	35.62	–	2	5
† C.J.Bodenstein (OU)	–	1	2	–	34	39	19.50	–	–	–
R.S.Bopara (Ex)	2005	17	31	2	99	880	30.34	–	7	7
S.G.Borthwick (Du)		17	29	2	188*	1084	40.14	3	5	26
† J.R.Bracey (Gs)	2016	1	2	–	12	14	7.00	–	–	–
† W.D.Bragg (Gm)	2015	17	32	1	161*	1126	36.32	2	8	10
† N.Brand (CfU)	–	1	1	1	16*	16	–	–	–	–
T.T.Bresnan (Y)	2006	11	19	4	142*	722	48.13	1	5	12
D.Brierley (CU)	–	1	2	–	12	12	6.00	–	–	–
D.R.Briggs (Sx)		13	13	3	49	197	19.70	–	–	6
† S.C.J.Broad (E/Nt)	2008	11	14	–	55	250	17.85	–	1	8
H.C.Brook (Y)		1	1	–	0	0	0.00	–	–	–
J.A.Brooks (Y)	2013	14	20	11	48	250	27.77	–	–	4
N.T.Broom (De)		14	22	1	96	530	25.23	–	2	7
B.M.Broughton (OU)	–	1	1	–	0	0	0.00	–	–	–
B.C.Brown (Sx)	2014	18	24	6	159*	980	54.44	4	4	43
† K.R.Brown (La)	2015	10	17	–	61	337	19.82	–	2	6
† N.L.J.Browne (Ex)	2015	18	28	3	255	1262	50.48	3	6	14
B.J.Bryant (CU)	–	2	4	–	10	18	4.50	–	–	3
N.L.Buck (La)		3	4	2	27*	63	31.50	–	–	–
S.F.G.Bullen (LBU)	–	2	2	–	56	74	37.00	–	1	–
M.G.K.Burgess (Le/LU)		3	3	–	98	175	58.33	–	2	1
J.E.Burke (Sy)		4	6	–	31	42	7.00	–	–	1
J.T.A.Burnham (Du)		15	25	2	135	680	29.56	1	4	6
† R.J.Burns (Sy)	2014	17	32	2	122	1248	41.60	2	8	16
J.C.Buttler (La)		1	2	–	26	42	21.00	–	–	1
Craig Cachopa (Sx)		4	6	–	34	87	14.50	–	–	4
E.Callis (Y)		1	2	1	84	114	114.00	–	1	1
† M.A.Carberry (H)	2006	8	15	1	107	411	29.35	1	1	4
L.J.Carey (Gm)		3	5	1	11	12	3.00	–	–	1
K.S.Carlson (Gm)		4	8	1	119	227	32.42	1	1	1
B.A.Carse (Du)		9	8	2	47	176	29.33	–	–	2
A.Carter (De/H)		6	6	1	39	76	15.20	–	–	3
M.Carter (Nt)		3	5	1	8	20	5.00	–	–	2
† K.Carver (Y)		1	1	–	13	13	13.00	–	–	1
P.V.D.Chameera (SL)	–	2	3	–	2	4	1.33	–	–	1

	Cap	M	I	NO	HS	Runs	Avge	100	50	Ct/St
L.D.Chandimal (SL)	–	5	7	–	126	229	32.71	1	–	5/1
Z.J.Chappell (Le)		2	3	–	10	17	5.66	–	–	–
† D.Chohan (CU)	–	1	2	–	83	85	42.50	–	1	1
V.Chopra (Ex/Wa)	2012	17	26	2	107	885	36.87	1	7	23
D.T.Christian (Nt)	2016	3	5	1	31	96	24.00	–	–	2
G.Clark (Du)		3	6	–	58	170	28.33	–	2	–
J.Clark (La)		7	10	1	84*	225	25.00	–	2	1
† J.Clark (DU)	–	2	3	–	32	58	19.33	–	–	3
J.M.Clarke (Wo)	2015	16	27	1	194	1325	50.96	6	4	7
R.Clarke (Wa)	2011	16	21	4	74	408	24.00	–	4	31
T.H.Claughton (OU)	–	1	1	–	2	2	2.00	–	–	1
† M.E.Claydon (K)	2016	15	15	3	55	187	15.58	–	1	1
B.O.Coad (Y)		2	2	1	17*	18	18.00	–	–	–
J.J.Cobb (Nh)		7	9	1	49*	209	26.12	–	–	–
I.A.Cockbain (Gs)	2011	5	9	1	129*	360	45.00	1	2	2
M.T.Coles (K)	2012	11	10	–	70	333	33.30	–	3	5
P.D.Collingwood (Du)	1998	14	24	6	106*	595	33.05	1	3	12
T.G.L.Colverd (CU)	–	2	4	–	36	60	15.00	–	–	3
N.R.D.Compton (M)	2006	13	22	2	131	487	24.35	1	2	11
† A.N.Cook (E/Ex)	2005	14	24	7	142	1278	75.17	4	6	15
S.J.Cook (LU)	–	2	1	–	0	0	0.00	–	–	–
C.B.Cooke (Gm)	2016	8	14	2	63	465	38.75	–	3	6
G.T.G.Cork (De)		1	2	–	49	53	26.50	–	–	–
† M.J.Cosgrove (Le)	2015	16	27	1	146	1279	49.19	5	5	10
B.D.Cotton (De)		8	11	3	26	102	12.75	–	–	1
† J.Coughlin (Du)		1	1	–	0	0	0.00	–	–	–
P.Coughlin (Du)		7	11	1	39	202	20.20	–	–	4
F.K.Cowdrey (K)		1	2	–	15	18	9.00	–	–	–
O.B.Cox (Wo)	2009	16	24	2	75	761	34.59	–	6	38/2
M.S.Crane (H)		13	19	6	24*	126	9.69	–	–	4
R.J.Crichard (CU)	–	1	2	1	27*	48	48.00	–	–	–
M.J.J.Critchley (De)		7	12	1	70*	263	23.90	–	1	3
S.J.Croft (La)	2010	16	25	1	100	713	29.70	1	4	30
S.P.Crook (Nh)	2013	10	15	3	145	484	40.33	2	1	1
M.H.Cross (Ex)		1	–	–	–	–	–	–	–	3
T.N.Cullen (CfU)	–	1	1	–	12	12	12.00	–	–	–
† M.L.Cummins (Wo)	2016	3	4	1	25	29	9.66	–	–	–
† S.M.Curran (Sy)		10	16	2	96	499	35.64	–	5	4
T.K.Curran (Sy)	2016	16	27	1	54	435	16.73	–	3	6
A.D.Dalgleish (CU)	–	1	2	–	41	50	25.00	–	–	2
J.H.Davey (Sm)		2	3	–	10	29	9.66	–	–	1
A.L.Davies (La)		5	6	–	55	187	31.16	–	1	17/1
R.C.Davies (Sm)		15	19	1	86	380	21.11	–	3	27/6
† S.M.Davies (Sy)	2011	16	28	2	117	1147	44.11	3	5	10
C.A.L.Davis (LBU/Sx)		4	5	–	65	115	23.00	–	1	2
W.S.Davis (De)		6	8	1	15	34	4.85	–	–	–
M.J.Dawes (OU)	–	1	1	1	0*	0	–	–	–	–
L.A.Dawson (H)	2013	12	20	1	116	644	33.89	1	5	2
D.M.de Silva (SL/SLA)	–	2	3	–	88	98	32.66	–	1	1
† H.E.Dearden (Le)		2	4	–	16	36	9.00	–	–	2
J.L.Denly (K)	2008	15	21	2	206*	733	38.57	1	4	7
† C.D.J.Dent (Gs)	2010	17	31	3	180	1336	47.71	3	8	19
J.J.N.Dewes (DU)	–	2	2	2	4*	7	–	–	–	–
N.J.Dexter (Le)		16	27	1	136	958	36.84	3	4	4
C.M.Dickinson (OU)	–	2	3	–	62	98	32.66	–	1	–
S.R.Dickson (K)		15	21	3	207*	701	38.94	1	4	8

	Cap	M	I	NO	HS	Runs	Avge	100	50	Ct/St
† D.P.D.N.Dickwella (SL/SLA)	–	3	5	–	53	112	22.40	–	1	1/2
M.W.Dixon (Ex)		5	4	1	14	23	7.66	–	–	–
B.L.D'Oliveira (Wo)	2012	15	27	1	202*	888	34.15	3	2	9
A.H.T.Donald (Gm)		17	31	1	234	1088	36.26	2	5	12
† B.M.Duckett (Nh)	2016	15	25	2	282*	1338	58.17	4	5	9/1
J.E.Dunford (DU)	–	2	2	–	1	1	0.50	–	–	2/1
† M.P.Dunn (Sy)		3	4	3	6*	18	18.00	–	–	–
W.J.Durston (De)	2012	4	4	–	43	63	15.75	–	–	3
E.J.H.Eckersley (Le)	2013	12	19	2	117	645	37.94	3	1	31
F.H.Edwards (H)		2	1	–	4	4	4.00	–	–	–
† R.D.Edwards (CfU)	–	1	–	–	–	–	–	–	–	–
E.J.Ellis (OU)	–	1	1	–	1	1	1.00	–	–	1
H.R.C.Ellison (CU)	–	2	4	–	22	44	11.00	–	–	1
C.J.Emerton (CU)	–	2	4	–	6	16	4.00	–	–	–
R.M.S.Eranga (SL)		4	6	2	2*	8	2.00	–	–	–
† S.M.Ervine (H)	2005	13	23	4	158*	1090	57.36	4	5	10
D.A.Escott (OU)	–	1	2	–	125	161	80.50	1	–	1
S.S.Eskinazi (M)		9	15	1	157	609	43.50	2	2	4
L.J.Evans (Nh/Wa)		3	6	–	74	173	28.83	–	2	5
† Fakhar Zaman (PA)		2	3	–	49	53	17.66	–	–	1
T.C.Fell (Wo)	2013	8	16	1	85	530	35.33	–	4	4
A.M.Fernando (SLA)	–	2	4	2	2	3	1.50	–	–	–
A.N.P.R.Fernando (SL)		4	6	4	13*	26	13.00	–	–	1
M.V.T.Fernando (SLA)	–	3	5	–	20	42	8.40	–	–	–
A.J.Finch (Sy)		4	6	–	110	292	48.66	1	2	2
H.Z.Finch (Sx)		9	11	3	135*	413	51.62	2	2	5
S.T.Finn (E/M)	2009	14	16	4	22*	139	11.58	–	–	3
L.J.Fletcher (De/Nt)	2014	10	14	2	32	122	10.16			4
B.T.Foakes (Sy)	2016	16	26	7	141*	836	44.00	1	4	45/3
M.H.A.Footitt (Sy)		9	11	3	16	49	6.12	–	–	3
J.S.Foster (Ex)	2001	16	20	3	113	677	39.82	1	3	48/1
† J.E.C.Franklin (M)	2015	14	19	4	99	641	42.73	–	4	10
J.K.Fuller (M)		3	2	–	93	129	64.50	–	1	3
† A.W.Gale (Y)	2008	15	26	1	83	525	21.00	–	2	2
P.L.S.Gamage (SLA)	–	3	5	1	43*	70	17.50	–	–	1
R.N.Gamble (LU)	–	2	2	–	10	14	7.00	–	–	1
† G.H.S.Garton (Sx)		5	5	2	18*	36	12.00	–	–	1
R.Gibson (Y)		1	1	–	0	0	0.00		–	–
R.A.M.Gibson (DU)	–	2	3	2	64*	111	111.00	–	1	1
† W.R.S.Gidman (K)		5	7	4	99*	362	120.66	–	5	5
R.J.Gleeson (Nh)		7	6	2	31	89	22.25	–	–	1
† J.S.D.Gnodde (OU)	–	1	2	1	27	27	27.00	–	–	2
† B.A.Godleman (De)	2015	13	24	–	204	934	38.91	3	2	6
A.M.Gowers (LBU)	–	2	1	–	38	38	38.00	–	–	1/2
† S.E.Grant (LU)	–	2	2	1	52	52	52.00	–	1	–
L.Gregory (Sm)	2015	12	16	4	73*	329	27.41	–	2	3
S.W.Griffiths (CfU)	–	2	1	–	65	65	65.00	–	1	–
T.D.Groenewald (Sm)	2016	13	18	13	26*	142	28.40	–	–	1
J.O.Grundy (OU)	–	2	3	–	53	58	19.33	–	1	–
† N.R.T.Gubbins (M)	2016	16	24	1	201*	1409	61.26	4	9	6
H.F.Gurney (Nt)	2014	14	22	10	27*	83	6.91	–	–	2
† C.J.Haggett (K)		6	5	1	33*	87	21.75	–	–	1
S.R.Hain (Wa)		16	23	1	135	457	20.77	1	1	19
† T.J.Haines (Sx)		2	3	–	11	12	4.00	–	–	1
A.D.Hales (E/Nt)	2011	9	16	–	94	580	36.25	–	5	7
O.J.P.Haley (LU)	–	1	1	–	8	8	8.00	–	–	–

	Cap	M	I	NO	HS	Runs	Avge	100	50	Ct/St
H.Hameed (La)	2016	16	27	3	122	1198	49.91	4	7	6
Hamza Ali (H)		1	–	–	–		–	–	–	1
G.T.Hankins (Gs)	2016	10	17	–	116	416	24.47	1	1	6
† O.J.Hannon-Dalby (Wa)		7	9	3	30	39	6.50	–	–	–
† A.Harinath (Sy)	2016	12	22	1	137	777	37.00	1	5	5
J.A.R.Harris (M)	2015	7	9	3	78	203	33.83	–	2	2
C.S.Harwood (LBU)	–	1	–	–	–	–	–	–	–	1
Hasan Ali (PA)	–	3	4	1	50*	121	40.33	–	1	1
† Hasan Azad (LU)	–	2	2	–	18	18	9.00	–	–	–
Hassam Mushtaq (OU)	–	1	2	–	7	13	6.50	–	–	–
† L.J.Hatchett (Sx)		3	2	–	17	20	10.00	–	–	1
† T.M.Head (Y)		1	2	–	54	56	28.00	–	1	–
A.G.Hearne (CU)	–	1	2	–	19	19	9.50	–	–	–
R.P.Hemmings (De)		1	–	–	–	–	–	–	–	1
M.J.Henry (Wo)	2016	6	6	2	49*	180	45.00	–	–	1
† H.M.R.K.B.Herath (SL)	–	4	6	–	61	164	27.33	–	2	3
C.L.Herring (CfU)	–	2	2	1	14*	14	14.00	–	–	3
R.A.Heywood (OU)	–	1	2	–	21	34	17.00	–	–	1
† A.J.Hickey (Du)		4	7	3	36*	92	23.00	–	–	1
J.C.Hildreth (Sm)	2007	17	25	3	166	1107	50.31	4	2	9
L.J.Hill (Le)		3	5	–	36	76	15.20	–	–	2
A.J.Hodd (Y)	2016	12	18	3	96*	391	26.06	–	2	35/3
M.G.Hogan (Gm)	2013	16	22	6	30	191	11.93	–	–	8
G.C.Holmes (CfU)	–	2	1	–	0	0	0.00	–	–	1
P.J.Horton (Le)	2007	16	28	2	117*	908	34.92	2	6	8
A.J.Hose (Sm)		1	2	–	10	18	9.00	–	–	–
H.R.Hosein (De)		4	8	4	108	423	105.75	1	4	9
B.A.C.Howell (Gs)	2012	6	9	2	43	179	25.57	–	–	2
F.J.Hudson-Prentice (Sx)		4	6	–	20	69	11.50	–	–	–
A.L.Hughes (De)		5	9	–	140	299	33.22	1	1	7
† C.F.Hughes (De)		11	19	4	137*	806	53.73	3	4	8
M.S.T.Hughes (OU)	–	1	2	–	116	192	96.00	1	1	–
M.D.Hunn (K)		5	3	2	32*	35	35.00	–	–	2
B.A.Hutton (Nt)		13	21	3	74	411	22.83	–	2	4
Iftikhar Ahmed (P)	–	1	1	–	4	4	4.00	–	–	1
Imran Khan (P)	–	1	–	–	–	–	–	–	–	–
Imran Qayyum (K)		2	2	1	0*	0	0.00	–	–	1
Imran Tahir (Nt)	2015	7	12	4	25	127	15.87	–	–	3
Jaahid Ali (PA)	–	3	4	–	64	160	40.00	–	1	2
C.F.Jackson (K)		3	4	–	38	61	15.25	–	–	9
K.M.Jarvis (La)	2015	16	23	4	57	338	17.78	–	1	3
† M.D.U.S.Jayasundera (SLA)	–	3	6	–	53	129	21.50	–	1	–
N.G.R.P.Jayasuriya (SLA)	–	2	3	–	31	48	16.00	–	–	–
W.H.Jenkins (DU)	–	1	2	–	9	16	8.00	–	–	–
† K.K.Jennings (Du)		17	29	4	221*	1602	64.08	7	3	18
† O.J.Jones (OU)	–	1	2	–	45	53	26.50	–	–	1
R.A.Jones (Le)		6	9	2	33	127	18.14	–	–	2
R.P.Jones (La)		4	7	2	106*	212	42.40	1	–	3
C.J.Jordan (Sx)	2014	5	7	2	131	323	64.60	1	3	6
† E.C.Joyce (Sx)	2009	13	18	1	250	1059	62.29	3	6	4
† F.D.M.Karunaratne (SL)	–	5	10	2	100	253	31.62	1	1	1
R.I.Keogh (Nh)		11	17	–	154	519	30.52	1	2	4
S.C.Kerrigan (La)	2013	13	18	7	48	225	20.45	–	–	6
A.N.Kervezee (Wo)	2009	5	9	1	59	210	26.25	–	1	1
J.M.Kettleborough (Gm)		4	7	–	42	139	19.85	–	–	2
R.K.Kleinveldt (Nh)	2016	11	15	2	97	391	30.07	–	3	11

	Cap	M	I	NO	HS	Runs	Avge	100	50	Ct/St
D.Klein (Le)		2	4	1	16*	31	10.33	–	–	–
M.Klinger (Gs)	2013	7	12	4	140	589	73.62	3	2	8
T.Kohler-Cadmore (Wo)	2014	14	23	2	169	648	30.85	2	2	20
N.R.Kumar (LU)	–	2	2	–	30	30	15.00	–	–	1
† E.E.Kurtz (DU)	–	2	3	–	17	36	12.00	–	–	–
M.J.Laidman (OU)	–	2	3	–	30	55	18.33	–	–	2/1
† M.B.Lake (OU)	–	2	3	–	1	2	0.66	–	–	1
R.A.S.Lakmal (SL)	–	3	4	1	11	11	3.66	–	–	2
M.Lamb (Wa)		1	2	–	1	2	1.00	–	–	–
† T.W.M.Latham (K)		6	9	1	90	374	46.75	–	4	9
J.L.Lawlor (CfU)	–	2	3	1	81	191	95.50	–	2	2
D.W.Lawrence (Ex)		17	24	2	154	1070	48.63	3	6	13
J.Leach (Wo)	2012	16	22	5	107*	620	36.47	1	4	4
† M.J.Leach (Sm)		16	18	5	27*	128	9.84	–	–	6
† O.G.Leach (OU)	–	2	3	–	63	80	26.66	–	1	2
J.A.Leaning (Y)	2016	10	16	2	51	266	19.00	–	1	8
† A.Z.Lees (Y)	2014	17	32	2	132	1199	39.96	3	7	13
† J.S.Lehmann (Y)		5	8	1	116	384	54.85	1	2	2
† T.J.Lester (La)		2	2	1	1	1	1.00	–	–	–
† K.S.Leverock (CfU)	–	1	1	–	14	14	14.00	–	–	–
R.E.Levi (Nh)		10	14	–	104	427	30.50	1	1	11
J.D.Libby (Nh/Nt)		16	28	1	144	920	34.07	2	4	4
A.E.Lilley (LBU)	–	2	1	1	51*	51	–	–	1	1
A.M.Lilley (La)		4	7	1	45	129	21.50	–	–	1
L.S.Livingstone (La)		15	23	7	108*	815	50.93	2	6	26
D.L.Lloyd (Gm)		16	28	1	107	817	30.25	3	2	5
C.T.Lowen (LU)	–	2	2	–	66	121	60.50	–	2	2/2
† M.J.Lumb (Nt)	2012	17	31	–	108	842	27.16	1	3	6
† A.Lyth (Y)	2010	16	30	2	202	1133	40.46	4	3	25
B.J.McCarthy (Du)		7	10	2	51*	176	22.00	–	1	2
C.M.MacDonell (De/DU)		3	5	2	91	243	81.00	–	2	1
J.N.McIver (OU)	–	2	3	1	51	97	48.50	–	1	–
C.J.McKay (Le)	2015	15	20	1	65	300	15.78	–	2	–
† R.McLaren (H)		16	26	9	100	869	51.11	1	6	7
C.S.MacLeod (Du)		1	1	–	7	7	7.00	–	–	–
L.D.McManus (H)		11	14	1	132*	493	37.92	1	3	21/6
† M.W.Machan (Sx)		9	11	–	66	304	27.63	–	1	6
W.L.Madsen (De)	2011	15	26	4	163	1292	58.72	6	3	11
† S.J.Magoffin (Sx)	2013	16	16	4	23*	122	10.16	–	–	4
S.Mahmood (La)		1	1	1	0*	0	–	–	–	–
† D.J.Malan (M)	2010	15	23	1	147	951	43.22	3	5	6
J.Marsden (OU)	–	2	2	1	27*	34	34.00	–	–	1
H.J.H.Marshall (Gs)	2006	17	27	–	135	1046	38.74	4	5	15
D.D.Masters (Ex)	2008	9	10	5	47*	105	21.00	–	–	–
A.D.Mathews (SL)	–	4	6	–	80	155	25.83	–	1	4
S.C.Meaker (Sy)	2012	11	15	6	41	126	14.00	–	–	5
A.J.Mellor (De/Wa)		5	8	1	44	164	23.42	–	–	11
B.K.G.Mendis (SL)	–	5	9	1	66	303	37.87	–	3	6
C.A.J.Meschede (Gm)		14	23	5	78	491	27.27	–	4	3
J.C.Mickleburgh (Ex)	2013	10	15	–	125	650	43.33	4	1	9
C.N.Miles (Gs)	2011	14	21	5	60*	413	25.81	–	3	4
T.P.Milnes (De)		5	9	–	56	188	20.88	–	1	1
A.G.Milton (CfU)	–	1	1	–	12	12	12.00	–	–	–
† Mir Hamza (PA)	–	3	3	3	1*	2	–	–	–	–
Misbah-ul-Haq (P)	–	6	10	–	114	369	36.90	1	3	2
D.K.H.Mitchell (Wo)	2005	16	29	2	155	1069	39.59	3	5	15

	Cap	M	I	NO	HS	Runs	Avge	100	50	Ct/St
† Mohammad Amir (P)	–	5	8	2	39*	107	17.83	–	–	–
Mohammad Asghar (PA)	–	1	1	–	15	15	15.00	–	–	1
Mohammad Hafeez (P)	–	5	10	–	42	172	17.20	–	–	6
Mohammad Hasan (PA)	–	3	4	–	98	198	49.50	–	2	7
† Mohammad Nawaz (PA)	–	3	5	–	68	138	27.60	–	2	–
T.C.Moore (Ex)		2	3	1	4*	7	3.50	–	–	4
T.J.Moores (La/Nt)		6	10	–	41	201	20.10	–	–	7
A.O.Morgan (Gm)		9	17	3	103*	406	29.00	1	1	3
C.A.J.Morris (Wo)	2014	7	9	6	11	32	10.66	–	–	1
G.J.Muchall (Du)	2005	3	3	–	70	100	33.33	–	1	3
S.J.Mullaney (Nt)	2013	17	31	2	165	1148	39.58	4	3	20
D.Murphy (Nh)		12	17	4	60*	355	27.30	–	1	33/2
† T.J.Murtagh (M)	2008	14	12	4	47	168	21.00	–	–	4
† P.Mustard (Du/Gs)	2016	7	11	2	107*	485	53.88	1	3	23
J.G.Myburgh (Sm)		3	5	1	110	234	58.50	1	2	–
J.K.H.Naik (Le)	2013	3	2	2	26*	34	–	–	–	2
G.R.Napier (Ex)	2003	15	16	2	124	304	21.71	1	–	3
C.D.Nash (Sx)	2008	15	24	1	144	1256	54.60	3	9	20
R.I.Newton (Nh)		11	20	3	202*	827	48.64	3	2	5
† K.Noema-Barnett (Gs)	2015	9	13	–	84	300	23.07	–	3	7
S.A.Northeast (K)	2012	16	23	6	191	1402	82.47	5	4	5
L.C.Norwell (Gs)	2011	12	15	3	102	224	18.66	1	–	1
† C.J.Nurse (LU)	–	1	1	1	4*	4	–	–	–	–
† N.J.O'Brien (Le)	2011	9	14	3	93	432	39.27	–	2	30
† A.Ogden (LBU)	–	2	1	–	24	24	24.00	–	–	–
G.Onions (Du)		17	19	7	65	282	23.50	–	1	2
C.Overton (Sm)	2016	13	19	2	138	435	25.58	1	–	11
J.Overton (Sm)		6	9	2	51	161	23.00	–	1	1
A.P.Palladino (De)	2012	14	20	5	49	268	17.86	–	–	2
H.J.Palmer (CU)	–	2	4	–	32	94	23.50	–	–	1
† M.S.Panesar (Nh)	2006	3	4	2	17*	28	14.00	–	–	2
C.F.Parkinson (De)		4	7	2	48*	80	16.00	–	–	–
M.W.Parkinson (La)		4	5	1	9	16	4.00	–	–	1
A.R.Patel (CU)	–	2	4	–	31	57	14.25	–	–	–
J.S.Patel (Wa)	2012	16	21	5	31	298	18.62	–	–	8
R.H.Patel (M)		1	1	1	4*	4	–	–	–	–
S.R.Patel (Nt)	2008	17	30	–	124	1058	35.26	2	7	13
L.C.Paternott (OU)	–	2	3	–	20	36	12.00	–	–	1
† S.S.Pathirana (SLA)	–	3	5	1	51	146	36.50	–	1	1
S.A.Patterson (Y)	2012	15	20	1	63*	300	15.78	–	2	–
D.A.Payne (Gs)	2011	15	18	4	67*	389	27.78	–	3	9
† M.D.K.J.Perera (SL)	–	1	1	–	42	42	42.00	–	–	–
A.N.Petersen (La)	2016	15	24	1	191	1134	49.30	3	6	8
M.L.Pettini (Le)		16	26	2	142*	694	28.91	2	1	3
W.D.P.Phillips (DU)	–	2	2	–	14	18	9.00	–	–	1
M.W.Pillans (Sy)		4	6	1	34*	73	14.60	–	–	1
L.E.Plunkett (Y)	2013	8	13	3	126	449	44.90	1	3	3
H.W.Podmore (Gm/M)		5	6	2	21	47	11.75	–	–	1
† E.J.Pollock (DU)	–	2	3	–	22	46	15.33	–	–	–
J.A.Porter (Ex)	2015	15	13	7	20*	60	10.00	–	–	7
S.W.Poynter (Du)		5	8	–	42	148	18.50	–	–	14
T.Poynton (De)		9	11	2	53	167	18.55	–	1	15/1
† J.E.Poysden (Wa)		5	4	2	7*	8	4.00	–	–	–
K.T.G.D.Prasad (SL)	–	1	1	–	13	13	13.00	–	–	–
S.Prasanna (Nh)		2	4	–	31	70	17.50	–	–	2
R.D.Pringle (Du)		12	13	2	57*	243	22.09	–	1	9

	Cap	M	I	NO	HS	Runs	Avge	100	50	Ct/St
S.M.A.Priyanjan (SLA)	–	3	5	–	66	138	27.60	–	1	–
† L.A.Procter (La)		16	25	1	137	822	34.25	2	3	5
M.R.Quinn (Ex)		4	6	1	10	29	5.80		–	1
K.Rabada (K)		2	3	–	14	25	8.33	–	–	–
Rahat Ali (P)	–	4	6	3	15*	31	10.33	–	–	–
† B.A.Raine (Le)		14	19	1	64	321	17.83	–	1	2
C.A.K.Rajitha (SLA)	–	1	1	–	4	4	4.00	–	–	–
† R.Rampaul (Sy)		5	7	4	13*	33	11.00	–	–	2
† M.B.Ranasinghe (SLA)	–	3	5	1	54*	115	28.75	–	1	7
† G.S.Randhawa (Du)		1	1	–	0	0	0.00	–	–	1
† W.B.Rankin (Wa)	2013	8	6	1	16*	22	4.40	–	–	2
A.U.Rashid (Y)	2008	10	16	2	88	393	28.07	–	3	7
O.P.Rayner (M)	2015	13	13	3	26	100	10.00	–	–	18
C.M.W.Read (Nt)	1999	13	22	4	101	572	31.77	1	4	38/2
J.Read (Y)		1	1	–	14	14	14.00	–	–	4
G.H.Rhodes (Wo)	2016	6	11	2	59	274	30.44	–	2	2
† W.M.H.Rhodes (Ex/Y)		7	8	–	20	86	10.75	–	–	3
M.J.Richardson (Du)		16	25	3	115*	625	28.40	1	3	34/1
A.E.N.Riley (K)		3	2	2	32*	37	–	–	–	–
O.E.Robinson (Sx)		12	14	4	81	389	38.90	–	3	4
A.J.Robson (Le)		17	29	1	84	771	27.53	–	9	14
S.D.Robson (M)	2013	14	21	1	231	899	44.95	3	4	16
G.H.Roderick (Gs)	2013	15	26	3	102	781	33.95	1	7	29/2
† C.J.L.Rogers (Sm)		16	25	2	132	1010	43.91	3	6	8
T.S.Roland Jones (M)	2012	15	14	3	79*	319	29.00	–	2	4
J.E.Root (E/Y)	2012	9	15	1	254	839	59.92	2	3	20
† W.T.Root (LBU/Nt)		3	4	1	133	271	90.33	1	2	–
A.M.Rossington (Nh)		13	18	5	138*	606	46.61	1	4	15/3
A.P.Rouse (K)		7	7	–	65	165	23.57	–	1	30/1
T.D.Rouse (CfU/Sm)		2	2	–	41	42	21.00			2
J.J.Roy (Sy)	2014	11	19	–	120	745	39.21	2	3	9
† J.A.Rudolph (Gm)	2014	16	30	2	87	688	24.57	–	3	10
C.Rushworth (Du)		14	16	5	31*	114	10.36		–	3
† H.D.Rutherford (De)		10	17	1	78	441	27.56		3	8
J.D.Ryder (Ex)	2014	8	10	1	51	234	26.00	–	2	4
A.Sakande (OU/Sx)		2	2	1	4	4	4.00	–	–	
P.D.Salt (Sx)		4	5	1	42	98	24.50	–	–	–
A.G.Salter (Gm)		7	11	3	45*	171	21.37	–	–	5
† Sami Aslam (P)	–	2	4	1	82	167	55.66	–	2	–
B.W.Sanderson (Nh)		13	13	3	19	58	4.83	–	–	1
G.S.Sandhu (Du)		1	1	–	0	0	0.00	–	–	–
† K.C.Sangakkara (Sy)	2015	12	22	1	171	1039	49.47	1	7	10
† M.J.Santner (Wo)	2016	1	1	1	23*	23	–	–	–	–
Sarfraz Ahmed (P)	–	6	10	3	46*	231	33.00	–	–	21
† Saud Shakeel (PA)	–	1	2	1	86	137	137.00	–	2	1
R.J.Sayer (Le)		3	4	2	32*	36	18.00	–	–	–
G.F.B.Scott (LBU)	–	2	2	1	16*	21	21.00	–	–	1
B.R.M.Scriven (CfU)	–	2	3	1	67*	110	55.00	–	1	–
N.J.Selman (Gm)		10	19	2	122*	470	27.64	2	2	7
Shadab Khan (PA)	–	1	1	–	48	48	48.00	–	–	–
A.Shahzad (Sx)		9	8	1	26	109	15.57	–	–	2
† Shan Masood (P)	–	4	8	1	62	204	29.14	–	1	–
M.D.Shanaka (SL)	–	2	3	–	112	116	38.66	1	–	–
† J.D.Shantry (Wo)	2009	12	13	4	106	255	28.33	1	–	4
† Sharjeel Khan (PA)	–	3	5	–	42	95	19.00	–	–	5
J.Shaw (Gs/Y)	2016	15	19	6	29	168	12.92	–	–	5

	Cap	M	I	NO	HS	Runs	Avge	100	50	Ct/St
A.Sheikh (Le)		1	–	–	–	–	–	–	–	–
C.E.Shreck (Le)		16	20	12	20	51	6.37	–	–	6
D.P.Sibley (Sy)		7	13	2	99	377	34.27	–	3	6
† R.J.Sidebottom (Y)	2000	9	11	3	23	75	9.37	–	–	1
A.R.S.Silva (SLA)	–	3	6	1	109	314	62.80	1	1	2
J.K.Silva (SL)	–	5	10	–	79	281	28.10	–	2	1
J.A.Simpson (M)	2011	16	23	5	100*	779	43.27	1	7	45/1
† T.A.M.Siriwardana (SL)	–	3	5	–	35	48	9.60	–	–	1
† B.T.Slater (De)		9	15	1	110	393	28.07	1	1	3
G.P.Smith (Nt)		7	12	–	54	257	21.41	–	1	3
R.A.J.Smith (Gm)		1	2	–	25	25	12.50	–	–	1
† T.C.Smith (La)	2010	8	13	–	87	417	32.07	–	4	9
W.R.Smith (H)	2015	16	28	–	210	827	29.53	1	3	11
Sohail Khan (P)	–	4	4	–	36	50	12.50	–	–	–
C.T.Steel (DU)	–	2	3	–	56	93	31.00	–	1	1
D.I.Stevens (K)	2005	15	17	–	140	782	46.00	2	5	8
P.R.Stirling (M)	2016	9	7	1	85	199	33.16	–	1	3
† B.A.Stokes (Du/E)		8	11	1	51	272	27.20	–	2	2
O.P.Stone (Nh)		4	3	–	60	83	27.66	–	1	3
† M.D.Stoneman (Du)		17	29	1	141*	1317	47.03	2	6	8
† J.S.Sykes (Le)		2	1	1	12*	12	–	–	–	1
W.A.Tavaré (Gs)	2014	6	10	–	36	112	11.20	–	–	6
B.J.Taylor (H)		1	1	–	36	36	36.00	–	–	–
B.R.M.Taylor (Nt)	2015	14	26	2	114	762	31.75	2	3	11
C.J.Taylor (Ex)		1	1	–	1	1	1.00	–	–	1
J.M.R.Taylor (Gs)	2010	16	26	2	107*	860	35.83	2	4	10
J.W.A.Taylor (Nt)	2012	1	1	–	10	10	10.00	–	–	–
L.R.P.L.Taylor (Sx)		8	11	1	142*	478	47.80	1	4	6
M.D.Taylor (Gs)	2013	5	8	5	9*	42	14.00	–	–	1
† R.M.L.Taylor (Le)		4	5	1	37*	87	21.75	–	–	3
T.A.I.Taylor (De)		3	6	–	80	147	24.50	–	1	–
R.N.ten Doeschate (Ex)	2006	17	23	5	145	1226	68.11	4	6	13
S.P.Terry (Nh)		2	3	–	54	95	31.66	–	1	1
† J.W.Tetley (CU)	–	2	4	–	9	23	5.75	–	–	4
S.J.Thakor (De)		9	13	4	130	606	67.33	2	2	–
† H.D.R.L.Thirimanne (SL)	–	4	7	1	40*	133	22.16	–	–	2
H.L.Thompson (LBU)	–	2	2	–	4	8	4.00	–	–	1
A.T.Thomson (CfU)	–	2	1	–	18	18	18.00	–	–	1
C.O.Thurston (LU)	–	2	2	–	13	15	7.50	–	–	1
P.J.A.Tice (CU)	–	1	2	–	41	60	30.00	–	–	1
† J.A.Tomlinson (H)	2008	6	9	4	23*	75	15.00	–	–	2
J.C.Tongue (Wo)		1	–	–	–	–	–	–	–	–
R.J.W.Topley (H)		1	1	–	15	15	15.00	–	–	–
† J.C.Tredwell (K)	2007	12	12	2	124	291	29.10	1	–	14
P.D.Trego (Sm)	2007	17	26	2	154*	1070	44.58	2	6	5
† M.E.Trescothick (Sm)	1999	17	29	3	218	1353	52.03	5	4	34
I.J.L.Trott (Wa)	2005	17	26	3	219*	1051	45.69	2	6	4
J.R.Turpin (CfU)	–	2	1	1	0*	0	0.00	–	–	1
† M.L.Udawatte (SLA)	–	3	6	1	64	178	35.60	–	1	2
† Umar Siddiq (PA)	–	2	3	–	39	44	14.66	–	–	1
A.R.I.Umeed (Wa)		6	10	1	101	165	18.33	1	–	4
G.L.van Buuren (Gs)	2016	7	12	2	172*	459	45.90	2	–	4
T.van der Gugten (Gm)		14	20	4	36	159	9.93	–	–	3
R.E.van der Merwe (Sm)		7	10	1	102*	180	20.00	1	–	3
P.A.van Meekeren (Sm)		1	1	–	0	0	0.00	–	–	–
K.S.Velani (Ex)		2	2	–	22	41	20.50	–	–	–

	Cap	M	I	NO	HS	Runs	Avge	100	50	Ct/St
G.C.Viljoen (K)		4	4	–	63	80	20.00	–	1	1
J.M.Vince (E/H)	2013	15	25	–	119	685	27.40	1	2	8
A.C.Voges (M)	2016	6	6	1	160*	388	77.60	1	2	5
G.G.Wagg (Gm)	2013	14	23	3	106	736	36.80	1	5	5
A.C.Waghorn (CU)	–	2	4	2	6	10	5.00	–	–	–
† N.Wagner (La)		9	12	–	37	111	9.25	–	–	2
Wahab Riaz (P)	–	4	5	–	39	62	12.40	–	–	–
† D.J.Wainwright (H)		1	2	2	35*	36	–	–	–	–
A.G.Wakely (Nh)	2012	13	20	3	104	678	39.88	1	4	11
† M.A.Wallace (Gm)	2003	15	27	5	78	669	30.40	–	6	53/1
† P.I.Walter (Ex)		2	2	–	47	75	37.50	–	–	–
M.S.Warnapura (SLA)	–	2	4	–	34	77	19.25	–	–	–
L.Watkinson (LBU)	–	2	2	1	16	16	16.00	–	–	–
J.J.Weatherley (H)		2	3	–	83	96	32.00	–	1	–
† W.J.Weighell (Du)		3	4	1	22	53	17.66	–	–	1
S.D.Weller (OU)	–	2	3	–	17	27	9.00	–	–	–
† L.W.P.Wells (Sx)	2016	17	23	1	181	955	43.40	4	2	6
T.J.Wells (Le)		2	3	1	87*	105	52.50	–	1	1
M.H.Wessels (Nt)	2014	13	22	2	159*	632	31.60	2	3	22/2
S.A.Westaway (OU)	–	1	1	–	7	7	7.00	–	–	4
T.Westley (Ex)	2013	18	25	–	254	1435	57.40	5	7	19
L.P.Weston (LBU)	–	1	1	–	22	22	22.00	–	–	–
A.A.Westphal (OU)	–	2	1	1	28*	28	–	–	–	2
† I.J.Westwood (Wa)	2008	11	17	1	127	442	27.62	1	2	3
B.T.J.Wheal (H)		9	9	4	14	37	7.40	–	–	1
A.J.A.Wheater (Ex/H)	2016	15	25	4	204*	948	45.14	2	4	23/1
G.G.White (Nh)		6	5	–	33	73	14.60	–	–	3
R.G.White (LU)	–	2	2	–	30	30	15.00	–	–	2
W.A.White (Le)		4	4	2	58	103	51.50	–	1	1
R.A.Whiteley (Wo)	2013	14	24	3	71	581	27.66	–	4	13
S.G.Whittingham (Sx)		6	4	2	8*	20	10.00	–	–	1
D.Wiese (Sx)		6	9	2	70*	153	21.85	–	1	7
D.J.Willey (Y)	2016	4	5	–	22	58	11.60	–	–	–
K.S.Williamson (Y)		2	4	–	28	42	21.00	–	–	3
G.C.Wilson (Sy)	2014	3	6	–	72	164	27.33	–	2	2
M.J.Winter (OU)	–	1	2	1	27	28	28.00	–	–	–
C.R.Woakes (E/Wa)	2009	12	19	6	121	567	43.61	1	3	5
C.P.Wood (H)		3	4	–	35	96	24.00	–	–	–
[illegible] Wood ([illegible])	–	[illegible]	[illegible]	–	14	14	[illegible]	[illegible]	[illegible]	[illegible]
† L.Wood (Nt)		4	7	2	27	102	20.40	–	–	2
M.A.Wood (Du)		4	7	–	36	147	21.00	–	–	–
T.A.Wood (De)		2	4	–	13	32	8.00	–	–	1
C.J.C.Wright (Wa)	2013	10	15	2	45	207	15.92	–	–	2
L.J.Wright (Sx)	2007	7	9	–	60	242	26.88	–	2	–
Yasir Shah (P)	–	5	8	2	30	103	17.16	–	–	5
Younus Khan (P)	–	6	9	–	218	503	55.88	2	1	8
† S.A.Zaib (Nh)		3	5	1	65*	127	31.75	–	1	3
Zulfiqar Babar (P)	–	1	–	–	–	–	–	–	–	–

BOWLING

See BATTING AND FIELDING section for details of matches and caps

	Cat	O	M	R	W	Avge	Best	5wI	10wM
J.B.Abbott (CU)	(WK)	4	0	20	0				
K.J.Abbott (Wo)	RFM	75	17	249	1	249.00	1- 93	–	–
T.B.Abell (Sm)	RM	1	0	11	0				
M.R.Adair (Wa)	RFM	15	4	47	0				
B.M.R.Akram (LU)	RMF	36.2	4	156	8	19.50	3- 50	–	–
T.D.Alexander (DU)	RFM	10	0	52	0				
A.M.Ali (Le)	OB	3	1	21	0				
M.M.Ali (E/Wo)	OB	201	28	853	14	60.92	3- 88	–	–
A.T.A.Allchin (CU)	RFM	74	13	327	5	65.40	2- 41		
J.Allenby (Sm)	RM	243.2	57	598	21	28.47	4- 67	–	–
T.P.Alsop (H)	SLA	10	0	66	2	33.00	2- 59	–	–
T.R.Ambrose (Wa)	(WK)	1.5	1	0	1	0.00	1- 0	–	–
J.M.Anderson (E/La)	RFM	334.4	103	765	45	17.00	5- 16	3	1
G.M.Andrew (H)	RMF	129	25	439	7	62.71	3-104	–	–
Z.S.Ansari (Sy)	SLA	236.4	39	691	22	31.40	6- 36	1	–
J.C.Archer (Sx)	RFM	243.1	54	778	28	27.78	4- 31	–	–
A.T.Arif (CU)	RM	30	1	173	0				
J.B.T.Arksey (CU)	SLA	32	5	173	6	28.83	3- 41	–	–
U.Arshad (Du)	RMF	41	9	131	0				
Asad Shafiq (P)	LB	1	0	1	0				
Ashar Zaidi (Ex)	SLA	19.5	3	61	2	30.50	1- 0	–	–
M.A.Ashraf (LBU)	RMF	40	7	116	0				
Azeem Rafiq (Y)	OB	119.3	31	335	6	55.83	3- 60	–	–
Azhar Ali (P)	LB	24	0	114	0				
M.Azharullah (Nh)	RFM	291.2	47	1048	25	41.92	6- 68	1	–
Azizullah (PA)	RMF	62.4	20	160	8	20.00	4- 21	–	–
Babar Azam (PA)	OB	6	1	19	1	19.00	1- 17	–	–
T.E.Bailey (La)	RMF	215.4	51	592	22	26.90	5-110	2	–
A.J.Ball (K)	LFM	51	4	201	3	67.00	2- 46	–	–
J.T.Ball (E/Nt)	RFM	390	80	1257	54	23.27	6- 57	3	–
G.S.Ballance (E/Y)	LB	1	0	11	0				
K.H.D.Barker (Wa)	LMF	540.4	156	1426	62	23.00	5- 53	1	–
E.G.Barnard (Wo)	RMF	382.2	76	1423	35	40.65	4- 62	–	–
C.A.Barrett (Nh)	RM	20	0	100	2	50.00	1- 29	–	–
A.P.Barton (CU)	LMF	59	7	262	1	262.00	1- 77	–	–
G.J.Batty (Sy)	OB	444.1	93	1325	41	32.31	7- 32	2	1
A.P.Beard (Ex)	RFM	76.2	10	300	9	33.33	4- 62	–	–
W.A.T.Beer (Sx)	LB	55.3	5	200	1	200.00	1- 39	–	–
I.R.Bell (Wa)	RM	8	2	17	0				
G.K.Berg (H)	RMF	251.2	73	694	19	36.52	6- 56	1	–
H.R.Bernard (K)	RMF	22	3	105	3	35.00	2- 65	–	–
D.M.Bess (Sm)	OB	89.5	25	264	13	20.30	6- 28	2	–
T.L.Best (H)	RF	136.5	20	554	14	39.57	5- 90	1	
Bilawal Bhatti (PA)	RMF	47	12	142	2	71.00	1- 30	–	–
J.M.Bird (Nt)	RFM	157.3	27	558	15	37.20	4- 56	–	–
C.J.Bodenstein (OU)	LMF	22	2	95	1	95.00	1- 51	–	–
R.S.Bopara (Ex)	RM	355.2	69	1171	45	26.02	5- 49	2	–
S.G.Borthwick (Du)	LBG	313.3	34	1200	23	52.17	5- 79	1	–
W.D.Bragg (Gm)	RM	9	1	29	0				
N.Brand (CfU)	SLA	11.2	1	63	0				
T.T.Bresnan (Y)	RFM	297.1	71	934	31	30.12	5- 36	1	–
D.R.Briggs (Sx)	SLA	381.5	71	1176	26	45.23	5- 93	2	–
S.C.J.Broad (E/Nt)	RFM	356.3	95	979	35	27.97	4- 21	–	–

	Cat	*O*	*M*	*R*	*W*	*Avge*	*Best*	*5wI*	*10wM*
J.A.Brooks (Y)	RFM	432.2	105	1501	60	25.01	6- 65	3	–
N.T.Broom (De)	RM	17	2	64	3	21.33	1- 9	–	–
B.C.Brown (Sx)	(WK)	3	0	48	1	48.00	1- 48	–	–
N.L.J.Browne (Ex)	LB	1	0	8	0				
B.J.Bryant (CU)	OB	5	0	39	0				
N.L.Buck (La)	RMF	63	12	210	2	105.00	1- 65	–	–
J.E.Burke (Sy)	RMF	48.3	6	232	5	46.40	3- 65	–	–
R.J.Burns (Sy)	RM	3	1	7	0				
L.J.Carey (Gm)	RFM	84.4	13	330	13	25.38	4- 92	–	–
K.S.Carlson (Gm)	OB	45	7	178	6	29.66	5- 28	1	–
B.A.Carse (Du)	RF	158.2	24	607	17	35.70	3- 38	–	–
A.Carter (De/Nt)	RM	143	20	566	12	47.16	4- 52	–	–
M.Carter (Nt)	OB	76	8	316	3	105.33	1- 46	–	–
K.Carver (Y)	SLA	16	3	91	1	91.00	1- 91	–	–
P.V.D.Chameera (SL)	RF	34	3	168	3	56.00	3- 64	–	–
Z.J.Chappell (Le)	RFM	20.2	2	98	3	32.66	2- 44	–	–
V.Chopra (Ex/Wa)	LB	2	0	12	0				
D.T.Christian (Nt)	RFM	15	1	80	1	80.00	1- 22	–	–
J.Clark (La)	RMF	132	23	456	11	41.45	3- 20	–	–
J.M.Clarke (Wo)	(WK)	2	0	22	0				
R.Clarke (Wa)	RFM	430.3	103	1223	42	29.11	4- 20	–	–
T.H.Claughton (OU)	OB	10	5	27	1	27.00	1- 16	–	–
M.E.Claydon (K)	RMF	416.4	76	1600	50	32.00	5- 42	2	–
B.O.Coad (Y)	RMF	53	16	165	2	82.50	1- 57	–	–
J.J.Cobb (Nh)	LB	45	7	113	1	113.00	1- 19	–	–
I.A.Cockbain (Gs)	RM	6.5	0	43	1	43.00	1- 23	–	–
M.T.Coles (K)	RMF	309.5	57	1134	40	28.35	5-116	1	–
P.D.Collingwood (Du)	RM	39.1	6	127	1	127.00	1- 39	–	–
S.J.Cook (LU)	RFM	44.1	8	178	4	44.50	3- 64	–	–
G.T.G.Cork (De)	LMF	17	2	70	0				
M.J.Cosgrove (Le)	RM	29.4	2	112	3	37.33	2- 14	–	–
B.D.Cotton (De)	RMF	202.3	50	661	14	47.21	4- 28	–	–
J.Coughlin (Du)	RM	26	12	45	2	22.50	1- 10	–	
P.Coughlin (Du)	RM	159.5	31	460	13	35.38	3- 65		
M.S.Crane (H)	LB	399	55	1498	35	42.80	3- 19	–	–
R.J.Crishard (CU)	RMF	40.2	11	129	2	64.50	2- 60		–
M.J.J.Critchley (De)	LB	122.2	3	639	4	159.75	2-101	–	–
S.J.Croft (La)	RMF	46	7	155	2	77.50	1- 19	–	–
S.P.Crook (Nh)	RFM	[illegible]	18	570	10	57.00	[illegible]	–	
M.L.Cummins (Wo)	RF	96.2	12	377	15	25.13	7- 84	2	1
S.M.Curran (Sy)	LMF	226	50	784	27	29.03	7- 58	2	–
T.K.Curran (Sy)	RMF	469.2	93	1565	37	42.29	4- 58	–	–
A.D.Dalgleish (CU)	LM	36.4	6	112	5	22.40	3- 49	–	–
J.H.Davey (Sm)	RMF	46	11	170	5	34.00	2- 39	–	–
C.A.L.Davis (LBU/Sx)	LFM	5	0	33	0				
W.S.Davis (De)	RFM	170.2	20	733	21	34.90	7-146	1	–
M.J.Dawes (OU)	RM	31	12	51	1	51.00	1- 26	–	–
L.A.Dawson (H)	SLA	306.5	56	877	20	43.85	4-100	–	–
J.L.Denly (K)	LB	66.3	4	222	3	74.00	2- 31	–	–
C.D.J.Dent (Gs)	SLA	61.4	11	187	3	62.33	2- 21	–	–
D.M.de Silva (SL/SLA)	OB	20	1	74	2	37.00	2- 28	–	–
J.J.N.Dewes (DU)	SLA	62	3	220	4	55.00	2- 93	–	–
N.J.Dexter (M)	RM	261.5	50	824	29	28.41	5- 52	1	–
S.R.Dickson (K)	RM	1	0	4	0				
M.W.Dixon (Ex)	RF	123.1	22	498	15	33.20	5-124	1	–
B.L.D'Oliveira (Wo)	LB	271.1	33	786	19	41.36	4- 80	–	–

	Cat	O	M	R	W	Avge	Best	5wI	10wM
B.M.Duckett (Nh)	OB	0.5	0	8	0				
M.P.Dunn (Sy)	RFM	52	5	262	2	131.00	1- 74	–	–
W.J.Durston (De)	OB	101.4	14	397	9	44.11	3-149	–	–
E.J.H.Eckersley (Le)	OB	2	0	7	0				
F.H.Edwards (H)	RFM	45	6	247	3	82.33	3-102	–	–
R.D.Edwards (CfU)	RM	13	1	56	0				
H.R.C.Ellison (CU)	OB	2	0	9	0				
C.J.Emerton (CU)	RM	34.2	2	183	2	91.50	2-100	–	–
R.M.S.Eranga (SL)	RFM	105.4	17	379	6	63.16	3- 58	–	–
S.M.Ervine (H)	RM	61	10	216	2	108.00	1- 11	–	–
D.A.Escott (OU)	LB	31	9	71	6	11.83	6- 61	1	–
T.C.Fell (Wo)	OB	2.2	1	10	0				
A.M.Fernando (SLA)	RMF	48.5	7	184	8	23.00	5- 33	1	–
A.N.P.R.Fernando (SL)	RFM	114	22	378	11	34.36	4-107	–	–
M.V.T.Fernando (SLA)	LMF	74.1	11	253	12	21.08	5- 37	1	–
A.J.Finch (Sy)	LM	3	1	10	0				
H.Z.Finch (Sx)	RMF	21	1	92	2	46.00	1- 9	–	–
S.T.Finn (E/M)	RFM	423.1	64	1461	43	33.97	4- 54	–	–
L.J.Fletcher (De/Nt)	RMF	282.1	73	745	19	39.21	4- 25	–	–
M.H.A.Footitt (Sy)	LFM	269.3	50	991	38	26.07	7- 62	3	–
J.E.C.Franklin (M)	LM	205	39	646	11	58.72	3- 26	–	–
J.K.Fuller (M)	RFM	100	17	393	12	32.75	5- 70	1	–
P.L.S.Gamage (SLA)	RFM	71	11	270	7	38.57	3- 49	–	–
R.N.Gamble (LU)	RMF	45	5	201	2	100.50	1- 63	–	–
G.H.S.Garton (Sx)	LMF	106.1	10	420	11	38.18	3- 93	–	–
R.Gibson (Y)	RM	12	1	42	1	42.00	1- 42	–	–
W.R.S.Gidman (K)	RM	44	15	123	4	30.75	2- 21	–	–
R.J.Gleeson (Nh)	RM	166	32	538	13	41.38	4-105	–	–
J.S.D.Gnodde (OU)	SLA	51	20	105	1	105.00	1- 33	–	–
S.E.Grant (LU)	LMF	41.1	4	221	0				
L.Gregory (Sm)	RMF	276.5	61	894	29	30.82	4- 58	–	–
S.W.Griffiths (CfU)	RM	42	6	189	0				
T.D.Groenewald (Sm)	RFM	369	91	1071	40	26.77	5- 90	2	–
J.O.Grundy (OU)	LMF	35	7	111	5	22.20	3- 41	–	–
N.R.T.Gubbins (M)	LB	7	0	38	0				
H.F.Gurney (Nt)	LFM	426.5	79	1326	45	29.46	6- 61	2	–
C.J.Haggett (K)	RMF	158.4	30	529	15	35.26	4- 15	–	–
S.R.Hain (Wa)	OB	6	0	24	0				
T.J.Haines (Sx)	RM	4	1	8	0				
O.J.P.Haley (LU)	OB	16	1	88	1	88.00	1- 24	–	–
H.Hameed (La)	LB	2	0	3	0				
T.R.G.Hampton (Gs)	RMF	21	1	107	1	107.00	1- 73	–	–
Hamza Ali (H)	RMF	17	4	59	2	29.50	2- 47	–	–
O.J.Hannon-Dalby (Wa)	RMF	153	26	524	8	65.50	2- 39	–	–
A.Harinath (Sy)	OB	18.2	1	59	0				
J.A.R.Harris (M)	RFM	228.2	34	807	16	50.43	3- 67	–	–
C.S.Harwood (LBU)	RMF	18	0	103	1	103.00	1-103	–	–
Hasan Ali (PA)	RMF	83.4	18	290	14	20.71	4- 63	–	–
Hasan Azad (LU)	OB	1	0	2	0				
Hassam Mushtaq (OU)	LB	22	0	137	3	45.66	2- 52	–	–
L.J.Hatchett (Sx)	LMF	54	10	212	6	35.33	5- 58	1	–
T.M.Head (Y)	OB	4	1	16	0				
R.P.Hemmings (De)	RM	19	5	58	0				
M.J.Henry (Wo)	RFM	234	48	716	27	26.51	5- 36	1	–
H.M.R.K.B.Herath (SL)	SLA	130.3	23	342	9	38.00	4- 81	–	–
A.J.Hickey (Du)	OB	62.5	7	204	6	34.00	2- 19	–	–

	Cat	O	M	R	W	Avge	Best	5wI	10wM
A.J.Hodd (Y)	(WK)	1	0	14	0				
M.G.Hogan (Gm)	RFM	512.4	140	1322	49	26.97	5- 36	2	–
G.C.Holmes (CfU)	RM	3	0	15	0				
P.J.Horton (Le)	RM	13	3	42	2	21.00	2- 6	–	–
B.A.C.Howell (Gs)	RMF	50.1	13	165	2	82.50	1- 15	–	–
A.L.Hughes (De)	RM	53	10	169	1	169.00	1- 34	–	–
C.F.Hughes (De)	SLA	106.3	11	430	9	47.77	3- 87	–	–
M.S.T.Hughes (OU)		16	3	21	1	21.00	1- 21	–	–
M.D.Hunn (K)	RFM	102	8	406	9	45.11	2- 33	–	–
B.A.Hutton (Nt)	RM	276.3	50	1048	31	33.80	4- 6	–	–
Iftikhar Ahmed (P)	OB	4.2	1	13	1	13.00	1- 1	–	–
Imran Khan (P)	RMF	13	2	60	2	30.00	2- 60	–	–
Imran Qayyum (K)	SLA	78.2	14	283	6	47.16	3-158	–	–
Imran Tahir (Nt)	LB	288.4	51	930	25	37.20	7-112	1	–
K.M.Jarvis (La)	RFM	545.2	130	1673	51	32.80	6- 70	2	1
M.D.U.S.Jayasundera (SLA)	LB	1	0	9	0				
N.G.R.P.Jayasuriya (SLA)	SLA	25	6	58	3	19.33	2- 32	–	–
W.H.Jenkins (DU)	RM	30	5	158	2	79.00	2- 87	–	–
K.K.Jennings (Du)	RMF	61	14	176	7	25.14	2- 26	–	–
O.J.Jones (OU)	RM	42	14	85	2	42.50	2- 46	–	–
R.A.Jones (Le)	RMF	115	20	446	7	63.71	2- 41	–	–
C.J.Jordan (Sx)	RFM	201	38	678	17	39.88	4- 36	–	–
F.D.M.Karunaratne (SL)	RM	15.2	1	67	0				
R.I.Keogh (Nh)	OB	242.2	42	828	31	26.70	9- 52	1	1
S.C.Kerrigan (La)	SLA	498.4	106	1326	35	37.88	6- 86	2	1
A.N.Kervezee (Wo)	OB	45	13	113	3	37.66	2- 24	–	–
R.K.Kleinveldt (Nh)	RMF	302.1	60	930	26	35.76	5- 53	1	–
D.Klein (Le)	LMF	44	5	211	9	23.44	4-107	–	–
N.R.Kumar (LU)	OB	37	0	184	3	61.33	2- 63	–	–
M.B.Lake (OU)	RM	11.3	1	58	1	58.00	1- 17	–	–
R.A.S.Lakmal (SL)	RMF	91	11	324	6	54.00	3- 90	–	–
T.W.M.Latham (K)	RM	2	0	5	0				
J.L.Lawlor (CfU)	OB	8	1	38	0				
D.W.Lawrence (Ex)	LB	25	2	129	3	43.00	1- 5	–	–
J.Leach (Wo)	RMF	519.4	81	1842	67	27.49	5- 60	5	–
M.J.Leach (Sm)	SLA	561.3	123	1536	68	22.58	6- 42	5	–
J.A.Leaning (Y)	RMF	10	2	27	0				
A.Z.Lees (Y)	LB	4	0	51	2	25.50	2- 51	–	–
T.J.Lester (La)	LFM	18	3	119	0				
R.S.Levelock (CfU)	LM	9	3	33	0				
J.D.Libby (Nh/Nt)	OB	25	4	79	2	39.50	1- 13	–	–
A.E.Lilley (LBU)	LM	40	7	120	3	40.00	1- 17	–	–
A.M.Lilley (La)	OB	105.3	21	333	8	41.62	5-130	1	–
L.S.Livingstone (La)	LB	51	7	166	1	166.00	1- 19	–	–
D.L.Lloyd (Gm)	OB	161.1	20	623	11	56.63	3- 36	–	–
A.Lyth (Y)	RM	79	10	322	7	46.00	2- 9	–	–
B.J.McCarthy (Du)	RMF	177.1	25	632	20	31.60	5- 70	1	–
C.M.MacDonell (De/DU)	RFM	31	3	128	0				
J.N.McIver (OU)	OB	52	3	238	0				
C.J.McKay Le)	RFM	411.1	78	1260	56	22.50	6- 73	1	–
R.McLaren (H)	RMF	387	83	1249	32	39.03	5-104	1	–
M.W.Machan (Sx)	RM	1	0	3	0				
W.L.Madsen (De)	OB	165.1	21	527	7	75.28	2- 24	–	–
S.J.Magoffin (Sx)	RFM	523.1	144	1249	62	20.14	5- 32	5	1
S.Mahmood (La)	RFM	33	5	121	1	121.00	1-121	–	–
D.J.Malan (M)	LB	29	4	87	2	43.50	1- 5	–	–

	Cat	O	M	R	W	Avge	Best	5wI	10wM
J.Marsden (OU)	RFM	56.4	11	160	8	20.00	5- 41	1	
H.J.H.Marshall (Gs)	RM	9	0	58	0				
D.D.Masters (Ex)	RMF	325.1	92	824	40	20.60	7- 52	1	–
A.D.Mathews (SL)	RM	49	17	117	1	117.00	1- 20	–	–
S.C.Meaker (Sy)	RMF	298.5	42	1145	37	30.94	4- 40	–	–
C.A.J.Meschede (Gm)	RMF	360.5	67	1199	27	44.40	5- 84	1	–
C.N.Miles (Gs)	RMF	404.2	62	1641	57	28.78	5- 54	2	–
T.P.Milnes (De)	RMF	172	37	509	15	33.93	6- 93	1	–
Mir Hamza (PA)	LM	104.4	23	286	11	26.00	4- 53	–	–
D.K.H.Mitchell (Wo)	RM	30.5	6	92	3	30.66	2- 5	–	–
Mohammad Amir (P)	LF	188.3	41	587	16	36.68	3- 36	–	–
Mohammad Asghar (PA)	SLA	16	3	50	1	50.00	1- 50	–	–
Mohammad Nawaz (PA)	SLA	53.5	7	160	8	20.00	4- 31	–	–
T.C.Moore (Ex)	RMF	40	8	127	4	31.75	3- 48	–	–
A.O.Morgan (Gm)	SLA	232	34	740	13	56.92	2- 37	–	–
C.A.J.Morris (Wo)	RMF	144.1	26	563	11	51.18	2- 35	–	–
G.J.Muchall (Du)	RM	7	1	24	0				
S.J.Mullaney (Nt)	RM	148.5	37	454	10	45.40	3- 54	–	–
D.Murphy (Nh)	(WK)	5	0	40	1	40.00	1- 40	–	–
T.J.Murtagh (M)	RFM	457.2	116	1227	43	28.53	5- 53	1	–
J.G.Myburgh (Sm)	OB	5	1	22	0				
J.K.H.Naik (Le)	OB	53	11	147	2	73.50	2- 61	–	–
G.R.Napier (Ex)	RM	470.3	100	1539	69	22.30	5- 29	5	–
C.D.Nash (Sx)	OB	6	0	24	0				
K.Noema-Barnett (Gs)	RM	225.2	54	604	14	43.14	3- 56	–	–
S.A.Northeast (K)	LB	1.4	0	2	0				
L.C.Norwell (Gs)	RMF	413.5	94	1271	44	28.88	4- 65	–	–
C.Nurse (LU)	SLA	11	0	58	1	58.00	1- 58	–	–
A.Ogden (LBU)	LMF	37.1	1	172	4	43.00	2- 80	–	–
G.Onions (Du)	RFM	561	99	1736	55	31.56	5- 90	1	–
C.Overton (Sm)	RMF	380.5	83	1168	34	34.35	4- 54	–	–
J.Overton (Sm)	RFM	133.3	27	382	17	22.47	5- 42	1	–
A.P.Palladino (De)	RMF	453.5	110	1201	39	30.79	5- 74	2	–
M.S.Panesar (Nh)	SLA	112	16	425	5	85.00	3-122	–	–
C.F.Parkinson (De)	SLA	170.4	28	531	14	37.92	4- 90	–	–
M.W.Parkinson (La)	LB	114.1	23	363	10	36.30	5- 49	1	–
A.R.Patel (CU)	LB	80	10	348	8	43.50	5- 86	1	–
J.S.Patel (Wa)	OB	616.4	168	1658	69	24.02	5- 32	4	1
R.H.Patel (M)	SLA	37	7	94	3	31.33	2- 54	–	–
S.R.Patel (Nt)	SLA	356.5	64	1163	32	36.34	4- 71	–	–
S.S.Pathirana (SLA)	SLA	70	10	231	6	38.50	3- 27	–	–
S.A.Patterson (Y)	RMF	440.5	138	1146	39	29.38	6- 56	1	–
D.A.Payne (Gs)	LMF	461	84	1412	43	32.83	5- 36	1	–
W.D.Phillips (DU)	RM	41	8	179	5	35.80	3- 45	–	–
M.W.Pillans (Sy)	RF	93	15	332	0				
L.E.Plunkett (Y)	RFM	172.1	23	602	10	60.20	2- 46	–	–
H.W.Podmore (Gm/M)	RM	144.3	26	465	17	27.35	4- 54	–	–
J.A.Porter (Ex)	RMF	478.2	80	1683	59	28.52	5- 46	2	–
J.E.Poysden (Wa)	LB	80.4	7	323	15	21.53	5- 53	1	–
K.T.G.D.Prasad (SL)	RFM	17.3	3	78	2	39.00	2- 78	–	–
S.Prasanna (Nh)	LB	53.2	13	165	9	18.33	5- 97	1	–
R.D.Pringle (Du)	OB	242.2	32	924	21	44.00	7-107	1	–
S.M.A.Priyanjan (SLA)	OB	15.1	2	50	2	25.00	2- 25	–	–
L.A.Procter (La)	RM	152.5	28	505	10	50.50	3- 14	–	–
M.R.Quinn (Ex)	RMF	142	24	473	22	21.50	7- 76	1	1
K.Rabada (K)	RF	77	21	232	7	33.14	4-118	–	–

	Cat	O	M	R	W	Avge	Best	5wI	10wM
Rahat Ali (P)	LFM	127	20	475	12	39.58	3- 47	–	–
B.A.Raine (Le)	RMF	338	77	1108	35	31.65	5- 66	1	–
C.A.K.Rajitha (SLA)	RMF	7	0	47	0				
R.Rampaul (Sy)	RFM	128.5	13	510	21	24.28	5- 85	2	–
G.S.Randhawa (Du)	SLA	28	4	87	1	87.00	1- 60	–	–
W.B.Rankin (Wa)	RFM	181.2	23	556	20	27.80	3- 33	–	–
A.U.Rashid (Y)	LB	293.2	36	1083	32	33.84	4- 17	–	–
O.P.Rayner (M)	OB	44.5	108	1202	51	23.56	6- 79	3	–
G.H.Rhodes (Wo)	OB	64.5	5	263	3	87.66	2- 83	–	–
W.M.H.Rhodes (Ex/Y)	RMF	144	31	452	13	34.76	2- 34	–	–
A.E.N.Riley (K)	OB	26	1	146	0				
O.E.Robinson (Sx)	RM	282.3	48	951	19	50.05	4-110	–	–
A.J.Robson (Le)	LB	8	1	32	0				
C.J.L.Rogers (Sm)	LBG	1	0	4	0				
T.S.Roland-Jones (M)	RMF	482.2	95	1524	54	28.22	6- 54	2	1
J.E.Root (E/Y)	OB	31.2	6	95	3	31.66	2- 23	–	–
W.T.Root (LBU/Nt)	OB	4	0	17	0				
A.M.Rossington (Nh)	(WK)	2	0	12	0				
T.D.Rouse (CfU/Sm)	OB	8	0	62	1	62.00	1- 62	–	–
J.A.Rudolph (Gm)	LBG	26.5	4	59	2	29.50	1- 5	–	–
C.Rushworth (Du)	RMF	355.2	74	1071	34	31.50	5- 93	1	–
H.D.Rutherford (De)	SLA	2	0	8	0				
J.D.Ryder (Ex)	RM	85	15	302	3	100.66	2- 48	–	–
A.Sakande (OU/Sx)	RFM	45	5	150	1	150.00	1- 54	–	–
A.G.Salter (Gm)	OB	136	13	492	7	70.28	3- 56	–	–
B.W.Sanderson (Nh)	RMF	420.5	98	1204	55	21.89	8- 73	4	1
G.S.Sandhu (Du)	LMF	35	2	104	4	26.00	4- 70	–	–
R.J.Sayer (Le)	OB	90.2	7	361	7	51.57	2- 41	–	–
N.J.Selman (Gm)	RM	3	1	8	0				
Shadab Khan (PA)	LB	25	2	120	5	24.00	4- 89	–	–
A.Shahzad (Sx)	RFM	225.3	32	817	16	51.06	3- 34	–	–
M.D.Shanaka (SL)	RM	29	3	114	3	38.00	3- 46	–	–
J.D.Shantry (Wo)	LM	348.3	98	114	23	48.43	5 46	1	–
Shan Masood (P)	RM	3	0	19	0				
Sharjeel Khan (PA)	LB	1	1	0	0				
J.Shaw (Gs/Y)	RMF	403.3	73	1332	41	32.48	5- 79	1	–
A.Sheikh (Le)	LFM	24	4	103	1	103.00	1- 86	–	–
C.E.Shreck (Le)	RFM	442.3	85	1455	44	33.06	4- 33	–	–
D.P.Sibley (Sy)	LB	36	6	133	2	66.50	2-103	–	–
R.J.Sidebottom (Y)	LFM	245	63	657	31	21.19	5- 51	1	–
T.A.M.Siriwardana (SL)	SLA	52.2	3	247	5	49.40	2- 35	–	–
B.T.Slater (De)	OB	13	0	71	0				
R.A.J.Smith (Gm)	RM	14	3	51	1	51.00	1- 51	–	–
T.C.Smith (La)	RMF	133	31	374	15	24.93	5- 25	1	–
W.R.Smith (H)	OB	126.1	20	401	5	80.20	1- 0	–	–
Sohail Khan (P)	RFM	126.4	14	496	17	29.17	5- 68	2	–
C.T.Steel (DU)	LB	4	0	26	0				
D.I.Stevens (K)	RM	415.1	106	1172	39	30.05	4- 74	–	–
P.R.Stirling (M)	OB	53	6	138	0				
B.A.Stokes (Du/E)	RFM	210.5	39	645	21	30.71	4- 54	–	–
O.P.Stone (Nh)	RMF	106.4	11	339	10	33.90	4- 56	–	–
M.D.Stoneman (Du)	RM	5	1	28	0				
J.S.Sykes (Le)	SLA	23	7	52	1	52.00	1- 24	–	–
B.J.Taylor (H)	OB	12	3	39	2	19.50	2- 19	–	–
J.M.R.Taylor (Gs)	OB	293.5	52	998	22	45.36	4- 16	–	–
M.D.Taylor (Gs)	LMF	143	15	543	13	41.76	4- 56	–	–

	Cat	O	M	R	W	Avge	Best	5wI	10wM
R.M.L.Taylor (Le)	LM	75.3	13	271	5	54.20	2- 34	–	–
T.A.I.Taylor (De)	RMF	63	13	250	4	62.50	2-103	–	–
R.N.ten Doeschate (Ex)	RMF	132	17	473	13	36.38	4- 31	–	–
S.J.Thakor (De)	RM	188	24	687	22	31.22	5- 63	1	–
A.T.Thomson (CfU)	OB	52.1	4	221	9	24.55	6-138	1	–
J.A.Tomlinson (H)	LMF	151.3	40	483	14	34.50	4- 74	–	–
J.C.Tongue (Wo)	RM	25	7	49	4	12.25	3- 35	–	–
J.C.Tredwell (K)	OB	300	62	921	22	41.86	4- 45	–	–
P.D.Trego (Sm)	RMF	159.3	36	471	5	94.20	1- 14	–	–
I.J.L.Trott (Wa)	RM	61	7	216	4	54.00	2- 26	–	–
J.R.Turpin (CfU)	RM	34	5	152	4	38.00	2- 44	–	–
G.L.van Buuren (Gs)	SLA	84	17	219	7	31.28	3- 15	–	–
T.van der Gugten (Gm)	RFM	461	74	1485	56	26.51	5- 52	5	–
R.E.van der Merwe (Sm)	SLA	203.4	40	614	22	27.90	4- 45	–	–
P.A.van Meekeren (Sm)	RMF	37	10	127	3	42.33	3- 78	–	–
K.S.Velani (Ex)	RM	3	0	41	0				
G.C.Viljoen (K)	RF	103.5	12	385	20	19.25	5- 55	1	–
J.M.Vince (E/H)	RM	19.2	2	85	2	42.50	1- 14	–	–
A.C.Voges (M)	SLA	15	0	65	0				
G.G.Wagg (Gm)	LM	434	73	1426	37	38.54	5- 90	1	–
A.C.Waghorn (CU)	RMF	53	4	245	5	49.00	3- 79	–	–
N.Wagner (La)	LMF	286.4	52	937	32	29.28	6- 66	2	1
Wahab Riaz (P)	LF	99.5	3	422	12	35.16	3- 93	–	–
D.J.Wainwright (H)	SLA	31	4	112	2	56.00	2-112	–	–
A.G.Wakely (Nh)	RM	5	1	12	0				
P.I.Walter (Ex)	LM	50	7	214	4	53.50	3- 44	–	–
L.Watkinson (LBU)	RM	52	1	210	3	70.00	3-132	–	–
J.J.Weatherley (H)	OB	4	0	41	0				
W.J.Weighell (Du)	RMF	112.5	22	329	16	20.56	5- 33	1	–
S.D.Weller (OU)	RFM	32	2	146	4	36.50	2- 74	–	–
L.W.P.Wells (Sx)	LB	167	13	607	9	67.44	3-105	–	–
T.J.Wells (Le)	RMF	27.1	4	117	3	39.00	2- 72	–	–
T.Westley (Ex)	OB	111.5	18	355	8	44.37	2- 13	–	–
A.A.Westphal (CfU)	RMF	44	7	186	2	93.00	2- 60	–	–
I.J.Westwood (Wa)	OB	7	0	19	0				
B.T.J.Wheal (H)	RMF	229	41	749	22	34.04	6- 51	1	–
G.G.White (Nh)	SLA	122	27	317	15	21.13	6- 44	1	–
W.A.White (Le)	RMF	64.1	13	225	10	22.50	4- 24	–	–
S.G.Whittingham (Sx)	RFM	153.4	18	576	18	32.00	4- 58	–	–
D.Wiese (Sx)	RMF	152.2	34	456	19	24.00	4- 18	–	–
D.J.Willey (Y)	LFM	102	23	334	9	37.11	3- 55	–	–
K.S.Williamson (Y)	OB	18	2	59	2	29.50	1- 19	–	–
C.R.Woakes (E/Wa)	RFM	351.1	85	1052	59	17.83	9- 36	3	1
C.P.Wood (H)	LM	63	20	195	3	65.00	2- 79	–	–
J.M.Wood (DU)	RM	39	6	167	1	167.00	1- 58	–	–
L.Wood (Nt)	LM	98.5	17	350	10	35.00	5- 40	1	–
M.A.Wood (Du)	RF	78	7	275	11	25.00	3- 24	–	–
C.J.C.Wright (Wa)	RFM	280.2	54	833	30	27.76	4- 41	–	–
Yasir Shah (P)	LB	274.1	43	891	25	35.64	6- 72	2	1
S.A.Zaib (Nh)	SLA	32	2	174	5	34.80	5-148	1	–
Zulfiqar Babar (P)	SLA	17.5	3	66	1	66.00	1- 66	–	–

FIRST-CLASS CAREER RECORDS

Compiled by Philip Bailey

The following career records are for all players who appeared in first-class cricket during the 2016 season, and are complete to the end of that season. Some players who did not appear in 2016 but may do so in 2017 are included.

BATTING AND FIELDING

'1000' denotes instances of scoring 1000 runs in a season. Where these have been achieved outside the British Isles they are shown after a plus sign.

	M	*I*	*NO*	*HS*	*Runs*	*Avge*	*100*	*50*	*1000*	*Ct/St*
Abbott, J.B.	6	11	–	53	177	16.09	–	1	–	7
Abbott, K.J.	67	94	17	80	1308	16.98	–	4	–	15
Abdul Rehman Muzammil	27	48	1	174	1511	32.14	4	8	–	21
Abell, T.B.	32	56	5	135	1600	31.37	3	9	–	21
Ackermann, C.N.	61	107	11	144	3680	38.33	6	27	0+1	46
Adair, M.R.	2	3	2	32	66	66.00	–	–	–	–
Adams, J.H.K.	205	364	28	262*	12790	38.06	21	71	5	159
Akram, B.M.R.	4	5	1	160	297	74.25	2	–	–	–
Alexander, T.D.	3	2	1	2	3	3.00	–	–	–	–
Ali, A.M.	12	20	1	80	529	27.84	–	3	–	4
Ali, M.M.	155	262	26	250	9152	38.77	17	57	2	91
Allchin, A.T.A.	3	5	1	59*	103	25.75	–	1	–	–
Allenby, J.	151	238	30	138*	7756	37.28	10	56	1	160
Alsop, T.P.	15	25	–	117	787	31.48	1	6	–	14
Ambrose, T.R.	210	316	30	251*	9742	34.06	15	60	–	553/37
Anderson, J.M.	200	250	92	81	1638	10.36	–	1	–	119
Andrew, G.M.	96	143	18	180*	2994	23.95	1	18	–	32
Ansari, Z.S.	66	108	15	112	2908	31.26	3	15	1	30
Archer, J.C.	7	8	–	73	195	24.37	–	1	–	4
Arif, A.T.	6	10	–	49	136	13.60	–	–	–	1
Arksey, J.B.T.	2	2	2	12*	14	–	–	–	–	1
Arshad, U.	17	21	1	84	548	27.40	–	3	–	6
Asad Shafiq	96	163	13	223	6090	40.60	17	26	0+1	79
Ashar Zaidi	110	177	13	202	5990	36.52	12	29	0+1	82
Ashraf, M.A.	23	19	5	10	56	4.00	–	–	–	3
Azad, M.H.	4	5	1	99	167	41.75	–	1	–	1
Azeem Rafiq	32	38	5	100	812	24.60	1	4	–	14
Azhar Ali	136	235	22	226	8406	39.46	28	33	–	121
Azharullah	104	139	71	58*	895	13.16	–	1	–	22
Azizullah	26	36	6	59	414	13.80	–	1	–	7
Babar Azam	26	41	4	266	1522	41.13	2	9	–	15
Bailey, G.J.	119	211	18	160*	7532	39.02	18	38	–	111
Bailey, T.E.	22	30	7	53	370	16.08	–	1	–	2
Bairstow, J.M.	135	217	30	246	9143	48.89	21	47	3	340/13
Ball, A.J.	29	42	3	69	800	20.51	–	3	–	17
Ball, J.T.	35	53	6	49*	529	11.25	–	–	–	4
Ballance, G.S.	115	187	18	210	8174	48.36	29	38	2+1	103
Bancroft, C.T.	42	75	4	211	2727	38.40	7	9	–	51/1
Bardolia, S.	2	4	–	20	25	6.25	–	–	–	1
Barker, K.H.D.	89	113	18	125	2784	29.30	6	9	–	30
Barnard, E.G.	19	25	6	73	503	26.47	–	2	–	7
Barrett, C.A.	3	3	3	114*	138	–	1	–	–	6
Barrow, A.W.R.	40	67	5	88	1201	19.37	–	4	–	71

F-C	M	I	NO	HS	Runs	Avge	100	50	1000	Ct/St
Barton, A.P.	3	6	1	8	15	3.00	–	–	–	2
Batty, G.J.	238	355	59	133	7095	23.96	3	30	–	161
Beard, A.P.	3	1	1	0*	0	–	–	–	–	1
Beer, W.A.T.	12	14	3	39	236	21.45	–	–	–	5
Behardien, F.	91	144	12	150*	5286	40.04	8	35	–	61
Bell, I.R.	278	467	50	262*	18500	44.36	51	96	4	211
Bell-Drummond, D.J.	68	114	11	206*	3824	37.12	9	20	1	27
Berg, G.K.	98	150	18	130*	3942	29.86	2	23	–	59
Bernard, H.R.	1	1	–	14	14	14.00	–	–	–	–
Bess, D.M.	3	5	–	41	100	20.00	–	–	–	5
Best, T.L.	121	158	26	95	1593	12.06	–	2	–	42
Bilawal Bhatti	65	86	9	106	1473	19.12	2	4	–	28
Billings, S.W.	45	65	5	171	1982	33.03	3	10	–	124/9
Bird, J.M.	54	71	24	32	422	8.97	–	–	–	21
Bishnoi, B.	1	2	–	16	16	8.00	–	–	–	–
Blake, A.J.	37	58	5	105*	1278	24.11	1	6	–	22
Bodenstein, C.J.	3	6	–	34	71	11.83	–	–	–	1
Bopara, R.S.	181	296	32	229	10785	40.85	26	45	1	93
Borthwick, S.G.	127	215	22	216	7179	37.19	15	40	4	164
Bracey, J.R.	1	2	–	12	14	7.00	–	–	–	–
Bragg, W.D.	108	190	7	161*	5608	30.64	6	35	3	44/1
Brand, N.	3	4	1	46	110	36.66	–	–	–	1
Bravo, D.J.	100	180	7	197	5302	30.64	8	30	–	89
Bresnan, T.T.	170	226	38	169*	5741	30.53	6	30	–	83
Brierley, D.	1	2	–	12	12	6.00	–	–	–	–
Briggs, D.R.	80	95	21	54	1184	16.00	–	1	–	26
Broad, S.C.J.	162	220	33	169	4148	22.18	1	19	–	55
Brook, H.C.	1	1	–	0	0	0.00	–	–	–	–
Brooks, J.A.	98	112	44	53*	1128	16.58	–	3	–	26
Broom, N.T.	130	219	23	203*	7590	38.72	17	32	–	95
Broughton, B.M.	1	1	–	0	0	0.00	–	–	–	–
Brown, B.C.	102	156	25	163	4981	38.02	13	24	1	266/15
Brown, K.R.	83	136	6	132	3505	26.96	2	22	–	51
Browne, N.L.J.	48	79	9	255	3110	44.42	11	11	2	41
Bryant, B.J.	2	4	–	10	18	4.50	–	–	–	3
Buck, N.L.	65	89	26	29*	722	11.46	–	–	–	9
Bullen, S.F.G.	3	4	–	56	135	33.75	–	1	–	–
Burgess, M.G.K.	7	8	1	98	343	49.00	–	2	–	5
Burke, J.E.	12	16	1	79	274	18.26	–	2	–	6
Burnham, J.T.A.	19	33	2	135	795	25.64	1	5	–	8
Burns, R.J.	77	136	12	199	5093	41.07	10	27	3	73
Buttler, J.C.	74	114	10	144	3336	32.07	4	19	–	160/2
Cachopa, C.	43	75	2	203	2674	36.63	5	16	–	28
Callis, E.	1	2	1	84	114	114.00	–	1	–	1
Carberry, M.A.	192	337	25	300*	13244	42.44	34	64	4	90
Carey, L.J.	3	5	1	11	12	3.00	–	–	–	1
Carlson, K.S.	4	8	1	119	227	32.42	1	1	–	1
Carse, B.A.	9	8	2	47	176	29.33	–	–	–	2
Carter, A.	35	39	14	39	296	11.84	–	–	–	8
Carter, M.	4	7	1	11	31	5.16	–	–	–	3
Carver, K.	5	7	4	16	59	19.66	–	–	–	2
Chameera, P.V.D.	30	31	12	14	137	7.21	–	–	–	9
Chanderpaul, S.	350	572	104	303*	25472	54.42	71	133	1+1	186
Chandimal, L.D.	79	131	12	244	5948	49.98	17	29	0+1	130/24
Chappell, Z.J.	3	5	–	96	120	24.00	–	1	–	–
Chapple, G.	315	436	75	155	8725	24.16	6	37	–	104

F-C	*M*	*I*	*NO*	*HS*	*Runs*	*Avge*	*100*	*50*	*1000*	*Ct/St*
Chohan, D.	2	4	–	83	91	22.75	–	1	–	1
Chopra, V.	168	275	19	233*	9358	36.55	19	48	3	195
Christian, D.T.	66	113	15	131*	3033	30.94	5	12	–	70
Clark, G.	6	12	–	58	235	19.58	–	2	–	2
Clark, J. (DU)	2	3	–	32	58	19.33	–	–	–	3
Clark, J. (La)	19	27	3	84*	644	26.83	–	3	–	4
Clarke, J.M.	27	43	2	194	1855	45.24	7	8	1	10
Clarke, R.	210	319	38	214	9488	33.76	16	49	1	323
Claughton, T.H.	2	3	–	29	50	16.66	–	–	–	1
Claydon, M.E.	91	115	23	77	1445	15.70	–	4	–	10
Coad, B.O.	2	2	1	17*	18	18.00	–	–	–	–
Cobb, J.J.	102	174	17	148*	4030	25.66	3	24	–	46
Cockbain, I.A.	49	84	6	151*	2355	30.19	4	13	–	34
Coles, M.T.	95	124	16	103*	2157	19.97	1	11	–	44
Collingwood, P.D.	280	482	50	206	15507	35.89	32	80	2	317
Colverd, T.G.L.	2	4	–	36	60	15.00	–	–	–	3
Compton, N.R.D.	175	306	35	254*	11169	41.21	25	54	6	88
Cook, A.N.	245	435	35	294	19350	48.37	55	95	6+1	243
Cook, S.C.	177	325	28	390	12279	41.34	38	49	0+4	113
Cook, S.J.	2	1	–	0	0	0.00	–	–	–	–
Cooke, C.B.	50	85	10	171	2799	37.32	3	19	–	42/1
Cork, G.T.G.	1	2	–	49	53	26.50	–	–	–	–
Cosgrove, M.J.	101	321	18	233	12078	41.64	33	72	3	123
Cosker, D.A.	248	329	96	69	3444	14.78	–	2	–	150
Cotton, B.D.	18	25	6	43	264	13.89	–	–	–	3
Coughlin, J.	1	1	–	0	0	0.00	–	–	–	–
Coughlin, P.	21	33	5	85	671	23.96	–	3	–	10
Cowdrey, F.K.	12	21	1	62	372	18.60		2		5
Cox, O.B.	74	120	20	109	2877	28.77	2	18	–	185/11
Crane, M.S.	16	23	8	24*	144	9.60	–	–	–	5
Crichard, R.J.	4	5	2	27*	80	26.66	–	–	–	2
Critchley, M.J.J.	13	20	3	137*	509	29.94	1	1	–	5
Croft, S.J.	146	227	21	156	6880	33.39	11	41	–	155
Crook, S.P.	94	126	18	145	3551	32.87	5	19	–	31
Cross, M.H.	6	8	–	30	130	16.25	–	–	–	11
Cullen, T.N.	2	3	–	26	42	14.00	–	–	–	1
Cummins, M.L.	47	56	24	29*	227	7.09	–	–	–	19
Curran, S.M.	16	24	5	96	738	38.84	–	6	–	5
Curran, T.K.	30	52	6	60	748	16.26	–	4	–	11
Dalgleish, A.D.	1	2	–	41	50	25.00	–	–	–	2
Davey, J.H.	12	20	1	72	362	19.05	–	3	–	6
Davies, A.L.	33	45	2	99	1444	33.58	–	11	–	84/6
Davies, R.C.	20	25	1	86	415	17.29	–	3	–	36/6
Davies, S.M.	182	299	30	200*	10878	40.43	21	50	6	407/20
Davis, C.A.L.	6	8	–	65	188	23.50	–	2	–	2
Davis, W.S.	7	9	2	15	42	6.00	–	–	–	–
Dawes, M.J.	1	1	1	0*	0	–	–	–	–	–
Dawson, L.A.	117	191	21	169	5809	34.17	8	31	1	126
Dearden, H.E.	2	4	–	16	36	9.00	–	–	–	2
de Lange, M.	44	58	8	38	585	11.70	–	–	–	22
Delport, C.S.	55	94	6	163	2866	32.56	2	18	–	33
Denly, J.L.	159	275	19	206*	8766	34.24	18	46	3	67
Dent, C.D.J.	100	177	16	268	6013	37.34	11	35	3	124
Dernbach, J.W.	97	121	44	56*	725	9.41	–	1	–	15
de Silva, D.M.	50	90	4	156	3290	38.25	9	14	–	54
Dewes, J.J.N.	2	2	2	4*	7	–	–	–	–	–

F-C	M	I	NO	HS	Runs	Avge	100	50	1000	Ct/St
Dexter, N.J.	133	222	25	163*	6990	35.48	16	34	–	86
Dickinson, C.M.	2	3	–	62	98	32.66	–	1	–	–
Dickson, S.R.	27	42	6	207*	1293	35.91	2	7	–	12
Dickwella, D.P.D.N.	49	82	1	209	2700	33.33	8	10	–	114/29
Dixon, M.W.	10	10	3	22	56	8.00	–	–	–	1
D'Oliveira, B.L.	27	47	2	202*	1298	28.84	3	2	–	13
Donald, A.H.T.	23	43	2	234	1439	35.09	2	8	1	17
Duckett, B.M.	46	76	6	282*	3103	44.32	10	14	2	36/3
Dunford, J.E.	2	2	–	1	1	0.50	–	–	–	2/1
Dunn, M.P.	34	35	17	31*	133	7.38	–	–	–	5
Durston, W.J.	109	188	28	151	5346	33.41	6	32	1	113
Eckersley, E.J.H.	86	153	9	147	4772	33.13	13	14	1	132/3
Edwards, F.H.	97	142	52	40	639	7.10	–	–	–	19
Edwards, G.A.	4	5	1	19	56	14.00	–	–	–	1
Edwards, R.D.	1	–	–	–	–	–	–	–	–	–
Elgar, D.	129	222	21	268	8903	44.29	26	32	0+1	93
Ellis, E.J.	3	5	–	8	27	5.40	–	–	–	6/1
Ellison, H.R.C.	4	8	–	32	102	12.75	–	–	–	1
Emerton, C.J.	2	4	–	6	16	4.00	–	–	–	–
Eranga, R.M.S.	76	103	37	100*	1314	19.90	1	4	–	33
Ervine, S.M.	210	328	41	237*	10603	36.94	21	53	1	179
Escott, D.A.	1	2	–	125	161	80.50	1	–	–	1
Eskinazi, S.S.	10	17	1	157	635	39.68	2	2	–	5
Evans, L.J.	54	92	6	213*	2926	34.02	5	16	–	44
Fakhar Zaman	26	42	2	205	1565	39.12	3	10	–	26
Fell, T.C.	47	79	4	171	2697	35.96	5	12	1	42
Fernando, A.M.	2	4	2	2	3	1.50	–	–	–	–
Fernando, A.N.P.R.	80	107	48	27*	319	5.40	–	–	–	31
Fernando, M.V.T.	45	56	24	35	223	6.96	–	–	–	16
Finch, A.J.	58	94	3	288*	3147	34.58	5	20	–	55
Finch, H.Z.	12	17	3	135*	473	33.78	2	2	–	9
Finn, S.T.	133	160	53	56	966	9.02	–	1	–	41
Fletcher, L.J.	81	118	23	92	1376	14.48	–	3	–	20
Foakes, B.T.	59	89	18	141*	2799	39.42	6	13	–	92/7
Footitt, M.H.A.	83	109	34	34	633	8.44	–	–	–	22
Foster, J.S.	273	406	52	212	13176	37.22	22	68	1	775/59
Franklin, J.E.C.	195	305	45	219	9484	36.47	21	43	–	102
Freckingham, O.H.	23	33	7	34*	296	11.38	–	–	–	4
Fuller, J.K.	41	48	5	93	859	19.97	–	4	–	17
Gale, A.W.	156	245	17	272	8211	36.01	20	31	2	49
Gamage, P.L.S.	69	96	29	43*	591	8.82	–	–	–	16
Gamble, R.N.	4	4	–	10	19	4.75	–	–	–	2
Garton, G.H.S.	5	5	2	18*	36	12.00	–	–	–	1
Gayle, C.H.	180	321	26	333	13226	44.83	32	64	0+1	158
Gibson, R.	1	1	–	0	0	0.00	–	–	–	–
Gibson, R.A.M.	4	6	2	64*	158	39.50	–	1	–	1
Gidman, W.R.S.	68	104	21	143	3327	40.08	5	20	1	22
Gleeson, R.J.	9	8	2	31	97	16.16	–	–	–	3
Gnodde, J.S.D.	2	4	1	27	33	11.00	–	–	–	2
Godleman, B.A.	115	204	9	204	6210	31.84	12	31	1	80
Gordon, R.O.	6	5	2	14*	52	17.33	–	–	–	3
Gowers, A.M.	2	1	–	38	38	38.00	–	–	–	1/2
Grant, S.E.	4	4	2	52	66	33.00	–	1	–	–
Gregory, L.	51	69	9	73*	1164	19.40	–	4	–	22
Grieshaber, P.J.	1	1	–	10	10	10.00	–	–	–	–
Griffiths, D.A.	38	52	19	31*	220	6.66	–	–	–	4

F-C	*M*	*I*	*NO*	*HS*	*Runs*	*Avge*	*100*	*50*	*1000*	*Ct/St*
Griffiths, S.W.	6	6	–	65	186	31.00	–	1	–	1
Groenewald, T.D.	114	162	50	78	2038	18.19	–	6	–	39
Grundy, J.O.	4	7	2	53	94	18.80	–	1	–	–
Gubbins, N.R.T.	33	55	2	201*	2156	40.67	4	14	1	11
Guptill, M.J.	98	177	11	227	6087	36.66	11	33	–	100
Gurney, H.F.	80	102	48	27*	289	5.35	–	–	–	10
Haggett, C.J.	33	42	10	80	800	25.00	–	2	–	8
Hain, S.R.	38	58	5	208	1827	34.47	7	5	–	33
Haines, T.J.	2	3	–	11	12	4.00	–	–	–	1
Hales, A.D.	99	171	6	236	6192	37.52	12	37	3	83
Haley, O.J.P.	1	1	–	8	8	8.00	–	–	–	–
Hameed, H.	20	33	3	122	1455	48.50	4	9	1	8
Hampton, T.R.G.	4	4	3	1*	1	1.00	–	–	–	–
Hamza Ali	1	–	–	–	–	–	–	–	–	1
Handscomb, P.S.P.	58	96	5	137	3491	38.36	8	22	–	92/4
Hankins, G.T.	10	17	–	116	416	24.47	1	1	–	6
Hannon-Dalby, O.J.	48	53	20	40	218	6.60	–	–	–	5
Harinath, A.	70	122	6	154	3729	32.14	6	21	–	19
Harmer, S.R.	76	118	25	100*	2448	26.32	1	15	–	73
Harris, J.A.R.	110	152	33	87*	2551	21.43	–	12	–	31
Harrison, J.	18	30	5	65	436	17.44	–	2	–	–
Hartley, C.F.	2	3	–	2	2	0.66	–	–	–	–
Harwood, C.S.	1	–	–	–	–	–	–	–	–	1
Hasan Ali	23	33	11	50*	359	16.31	–	1	–	7
Hassam Mushtaq	1	2	–	7	13	6.50	–	–	–	–
Hastings, J.W.	68	98	6	93	2061	22.40	–	10	–	30
Hatchett, L.J.	27	34	11	25	224	9.73	–	–	–	10
Head, T.M.	45	83	2	192	2663	32.87	3	19	–	16
Hearne, A.G.	6	11	1	88	265	26.50	–	1	–	–
Helm, T.G.	8	12	3	27	90	10.00	–	–	–	2
Hemmings, R.P.	1	–	–	–	–	–	–	–	–	1
Henry, M.J.	36	45	9	75*	895	24.86	–	3	–	13
Herath, H.M.R.K.B.	245	354	80	80*	4466	16.29	–	14	–	103
Herring, C.L.	13	16	2	114*	296	21.14	1	–	–	35/1
Heywood, R.A.	1	2	–	21	34	17.00	–	–	–	1
Hickey, A.J.	4	7	3	36*	92	23.00	–	–	–	1
Hildreth, J.C.	220	357	28	303*	14588	44.34	39	66	6	181
Hill, L.J.	12	23	2	126	432	20.57	1	1	–	17
Hodd, A.J.	70	[illegible]	[illegible]	[illegible]	[illegible]	[illegible]	[illegible]	[illegible]	[illegible]	[illegible]
Hogan, M.G.	118	168	61	57	1752	16.37	–	2	–	64
Holmes, G.C.	2	1	–	0	0	0.00	–	–	–	1
Horton, P.J.	180	303	24	209	10429	37.37	23	57	3	176/1
Hose, A.J.	1	2	–	10	18	9.00	–	–	–	–
Hosein, H.R.	18	28	6	108	713	32.40	1	5	–	56/1
Howell, B.A.C.	60	93	12	102	2112	26.07	1	11	–	31
Hudson-Prentice, F.J.	5	8	–	20	84	10.50	–	–	–	–
Hughes, A.L.	31	52	7	140	1162	25.82	2	4	–	17
Hughes, C.F.	70	128	8	270*	4018	33.48	10	17	–	50
Hughes, M.S.T.	2	4	–	116	349	87.25	2	1	–	2
Hunn, M.D.	16	15	10	32*	94	18.80	–	–	–	7
Hutton, B.A.	24	38	6	74	760	23.75	–	3	–	10
Iftikhar Ahmed	32	53	4	150*	1663	33.93	3	9	–	28
Imran Khan	73	102	38	27*	476	7.43	–	–	–	8
Imran Qayyum	2	2	1	0*	0	0.00	–	–	–	1
Imran Tahir	188	238	60	77*	2529	14.20	–	4	–	78
Ingram, C.A.	97	171	15	190	5852	37.51	12	29	–	69

F-C	M	I	NO	HS	Runs	Avge	100	50	1000	Ct/St
Jackson, C.F.	4	5	–	38	87	17.40	–	–	–	10
Jahid Ali	18	31	–	155	1007	32.48	1	7	–	19
Jarvis, K.M.	63	87	30	57	871	15.28	–	1	–	17
Javid, A.	31	49	6	133	1068	24.83	2	3	–	16
Jayasundera, M.D.U.S.	68	122	4	318	5147	43.61	12	28	–	45
Jayasuriya, N.G.R.P.	23	35	8	31	293	10.85	–	–	–	9
Jenkins, W.H.	5	8	–	19	52	6.50	–	–	–	2
Jennings, K.K.	72	127	8	221*	4272	35.89	12	16	1	39
Jones, O.J.	6	11	1	83	349	34.90	–	3	–	2
Jones, R.A.	56	85	15	62	850	12.14	–	2	–	20
Jones, R.P.	4	7	2	106*	212	42.40	1	–	–	3
Jordan, C.J.	83	112	18	131	2262	24.06	1	10	–	101
Joyce, E.C.	247	406	33	250	17925	48.05	45	92	9	220
Junaid Khan	72	98	30	71	729	10.72	–	2	–	12
Karunaratne, F.D.M.	112	188	17	210*	7754	45.34	24	34	0+1	120/1
Keogh, R.I.	47	75	5	221	2296	32.80	6	6	–	10/1
Kerrigan, S.C.	98	115	40	62*	881	11.74	–	1	–	33
Kervezee, A.N.	97	164	9	155	4621	29.81	6	27	1	46
Kettleborough, J.M.	22	39	1	81	950	25.00	–	6	–	12
Klein, D.	44	62	12	66	928	18.56	–	4	–	12
Kleinveldt, R.K.	127	175	21	115*	3110	20.19	1	15	–	61
Klinger, M.	172	303	33	255	10889	40.32	30	45	1+2	164
Kohler-Cadmore, T.	33	55	4	169	1521	29.82	3	8	–	43
Kulasekara, K.M.D.N.	87	114	22	95	1684	18.30	–	5	–	35
Kumar, N.R.	13	21	1	103	469	23.45	1	2	–	5
Kurtz, E.E.	2	3	–	17	36	12.00	–	–	–	–
Laidman, M.J.	2	3	–	30	55	18.33	–	–	–	2/1
Lake, M.B.	4	7	–	66	84	12.00	–	1	–	2
Lakmal, R.A.S.	84	97	25	58*	666	9.25	–	1	–	31
Lamb, M.	1	2	–	1	2	1.00	–	–	–	–
Latham, T.W.M.	70	123	9	261	4736	41.54	9	30	–	85/1
Lawlor, J.L.	4	6	1	81	194	38.80	–	2	–	2
Lawrence, D.W.	24	36	3	161	1479	44.81	4	7	1	21
Leach, J.	56	83	10	114	2039	27.93	2	14	–	13
Leach, M.J.	33	36	11	43	296	11.84	–	–	–	9
Leach, S.G.	6	10	–	63	211	21.10	–	1	–	4
Leaning, J.A.	40	63	7	123	1751	31.26	3	8	–	33
Lees, A.Z.	69	116	9	275*	4104	38.35	10	20	2	50
Lehmann, J.S.	16	27	1	205	1164	44.76	4	4	–	11
Lester, T.J.	10	11	7	2*	6	1.50	–	–	–	2
Leverock, K.S.	2	3	–	25	48	16.00	–	–	–	–
Levi, R.E.	75	121	12	168	4092	37.54	7	26	–	54
Libby, J.D.	21	37	2	144	1158	33.08	3	5	–	5
Liddle, C.J.	25	25	13	53	143	11.91	–	1	–	7
Lilley, A.E.	6	5	2	51*	95	31.66	–	1	–	2
Lilley, A.M.	13	17	5	63	398	33.16	–	2	–	4
Livingstone, L.S.	15	23	7	108*	815	50.93	2	6	–	26
Lloyd, D.L.	36	59	8	107	1515	29.70	3	5	–	11
Lowen, C.T.	2	2	–	66	121	60.50	–	2	–	2/2
Lumb, M.J.	202	343	18	221*	11151	34.31	20	58	3	116
Lyth, A.	133	219	10	251	8397	40.17	20	46	3	166
McCarthy, B.J.	9	14	4	51*	231	23.10	–	1	–	4
McCullum, B.B.	150	261	13	302	9210	37.13	17	46	–	308/19
Macdonell, C.M.	5	8	2	91	299	49.83	–	2	–	1
McIver, J.N.	4	7	1	51	146	24.33	–	1	–	1
McKay, C.J.	74	104	12	65	1750	19.02	–	7	–	16

F-C	*M*	*I*	*NO*	*HS*	*Runs*	*Avge*	*100*	*50*	*1000*	*Ct/St*
McLaren, R.	128	191	39	140	5187	34.12	6	27	–	61
MacLeod, C.S.	25	37	6	84	735	23.70	–	4	–	17
McManus, L.D.	13	18	2	132*	613	38.31	1	4	–	25/6
Machan, M.W.	44	67	4	192	2089	33.15	5	6	–	18
Madsen, W.L.	143	255	22	231*	9364	40.18	25	46	4	123
Magoffin, S.J.	152	205	53	79	2587	17.01	–	5	–	35
Mahmood, S.	1	1	1	0*	0	–	–	–	–	–
Malan, D.J.	135	227	17	182*	7963	37.91	17	40	2	149
Marsden, J.	7	8	4	27*	47	11.75	–	–	–	5
Marshall, H.J.H.	255	419	28	170	14286	36.53	30	72	3	134
Masters, D.D.	202	246	40	119	2829	13.73	1	6	–	60
Mathews, A.D.	98	162	24	270	6997	50.70	16	36	0+1	70
Meaker, S.C.	74	97	19	94	1230	15.76	–	6	–	13
Mellor, A.J.	5	8	1	44	164	23.42	–	–	–	11
Mendis, B.K.G.	20	47	2	176	1508	33.51	2	6	–	41/8
Mendis, B.M.A.J.	130	202	27	206*	6396	36.54	16	31	–	111
Meschede, C.A.J.	59	84	12	107	1803	25.04	2	10	–	20
Mickleburgh, J.C.	101	175	3	243	4978	28.94	10	21	–	71
Miles, C.N.	44	61	8	62*	1005	18.96	–	5	–	11
Mills, T.S.	32	38	15	31*	260	11.30	–	–	–	9
Milnes, T.P.	21	28	4	56	529	22.04		2		4
Milton, A.G.	1	1	–	12	12	12.00	–	–	–	–
Mir Hamza	37	44	21	24	151	6.56	–	–	–	9
Misbah-ul-Haq	218	359	42	284	16033	50.57	43	92	0+2	193
Mitchell, D.K.H.	164	295	34	298	10284	39.40	24	44	5	221
Mohammad Amir	37	57	11	66	780	16.95	–	2	–	6
Mohammad Asghar	12	13	4	15	24	2.66	–	–	–	7
Mohammad Hafeez	188	327	14	224	11172	35.69	24	52	0+1	167
Mohammad Hasan	64	95	9	251*	2496	29.02	3	11	–	192/15
Mohammad Nawaz	29	45	2	170	1440	33.48	3	7	–	18
Moore, T.C.	9	10	5	17	50	10.00	–	–	–	6
Moores, T.J.	6	10	–	41	201	20.10	–	–	–	7
Morgan, A.O.	10	18	4	103*	434	31.00	1	1	–	3
Morgan, E.J.G.	93	153	16	209*	4791	34.97	11	22	1	71/1
Morris, C.A.J.	44	60	33	33*	274	10.14	–	–	–	12
Morris, C.H.	48	71	8	154	1957	31.06	3	10	–	43
Muchall, G.J.	163	282	17	219	7947	29.98	14	39	–	117
Mullaney, S.J.	99	168	8	165*	5292	33.07	11	27	1	91
Murphy, D.	[illegible]	97	22	135*	2124	28.32	1	12	–	195/16
Murphy, J.R.	2	3	–	22	39	13.00	–	–	–	1
Murtagh, T.J.	190	247	72	74*	3559	20.33	–	10	–	57
Mustard, P.	195	301	36	130	8098	30.55	7	49	–	648/19
Myburgh, J.G.	108	190	23	203	6841	40.96	16	39	–	61
Naik, J.K.H.	77	118	29	109*	1888	21.21	1	5	–	42
Napier, G.R.	179	239	43	196	5739	29.28	7	31	–	63
Nash, C.D.	172	293	19	184	10846	39.58	22	56	4	102
Neesham, J.D.S.	42	73	8	147	2232	34.33	5	9	–	39
Newton, R.I.	68	118	11	202*	3765	35.18	10	13	–	22
Noema-Barnett, K.	62	93	12	107	2275	28.08	2	14	–	29
Northeast, S.A.	123	210	15	191	7511	38.51	16	41	2	64
Norwell, L.C.	55	71	29	102	601	14.30	1	1	–	11
Nurse, C.J.	1	1	1	4*	4	–	–	–	–	–
O'Brien, K.J.	35	49	8	171*	1458	35.56	1	9	–	30
O'Brien, N.J.	168	269	28	182	8518	35.34	14	45	–	474/47
Ogden, A.	2	1	–	24	24	24.00	–	–	–	–
Onions, G.	162	209	81	65	1842	14.39	–	1	–	32

F-C	M	I	NO	HS	Runs	Avge	100	50	1000	Ct/St
Overton, C.	46	61	9	138	1318	25.34	1	7	–	27
Overton, J.	39	52	16	56	659	18.30	–	4	–	2
Palladino, A.P.	132	182	39	106	2303	16.10	1	7	–	36
Palmer, H.J.	2	4	–	32	94	23.50	–	–	–	1
Panesar, M.S.	219	270	87	46*	1536	8.39	–	–	–	44
Parkinson, C.F.	4	7	2	48*	80	16.00	–	–	–	–
Parkinson, M.W.	4	5	1	9	16	4.00	–	–	–	1
Parry, S.D.	9	10	1	37	138	15.33	–	–	–	2
Patel, A.R.	3	5	–	61	118	23.60	–	1	–	–
Patel, J.S.	226	290	67	120	5016	22.49	2	23	–	109
Patel, R.H.	21	28	14	26*	175	12.50	–	–	–	5
Patel, S.R.	183	298	15	256	10418	36.81	24	51	4	122
Paternott, L.C.	6	10	–	50	160	16.00	–	1	–	4
Pathirana, S.S.	72	113	5	117	2740	25.37	2	16	–	45
Patterson, S.A.	122	139	35	63*	1674	16.09	–	3	–	18
Payne, D.A.	65	79	23	67*	1099	19.62	–	5	–	25
Penrhyn Jones, D.	2	2	1	17	26	26.00	–	–	–	1
Perera, M.D.K.J.	52	82	5	336	3697	48.01	11	12	–	94/22
Petersen, A.N.	226	388	19	286	14765	40.01	42	60	2+2	175
Pettini, M.L.	171	284	41	209	8630	35.51	14	47	1	119
Philander, V.D.	128	168	30	168	3457	25.05	2	10	–	31
Phillips, W.D.B.	3	4	–	14	33	8.25	–	–	–	1
Pietersen, K.P.	217	358	26	355*	16522	49.76	50	71	3	152
Pillans, M.W.	35	49	5	49	602	13.68	–	–	–	19
Plunkett, L.E.	151	209	39	126	4269	25.11	3	22	–	86
Podmore, H.W.	5	6	2	21	47	11.75	–	–	–	1
Pollock, E.J.	3	4	–	22	61	15.25	–	–	–	–
Porter, J.A.	34	37	14	34	163	7.08	–	–	–	13
Porterfield, W.T.S.	117	193	7	186	5729	30.80	8	31	–	129
Poynter, S.W.	15	20	–	125	514	25.70	1	1	–	38/2
Poynton, T.	47	70	8	106	1155	18.62	1	6	–	107/10
Poysden, J.E.	10	8	2	47	71	11.83	–	–	–	2
Prasad, K.T.G.D.	108	132	14	103*	2174	18.42	1	8	–	29
Prasanna, S.	93	146	7	81	2956	21.26	–	16	–	66
Pringle, R.D.	23	34	4	99	796	26.53	–	5	–	12
Priyanjan, S.M.A.	88	141	15	235	4676	37.11	6	33	–	87
Procter, L.A.	62	94	6	137	2799	31.80	3	14	–	14
Quinn, M.R.	24	31	5	50	279	10.73	–	1	–	4
Rabada, K.	24	29	8	48*	292	13.90	–	–	–	6
Rahat Ali	64	79	31	35*	323	6.72	–	–	–	19
Raine, B.A.	44	71	5	72	1307	19.80	–	5	–	9
Rajitha, C.A.K.	14	20	10	52	127	12.70	–	1	–	4
Rampaul, R.	67	98	20	64*	1064	13.64	–	2	–	20
Ranasinghe, M.B.	17	27	2	342	1231	49.24	4	3	–	37/6
Randhawa, G.S.	2	2	–	5	5	2.50	–	–	–	1
Rankin, W.B.	97	111	46	56*	577	8.87	–	1	–	25
Rashid, A.U.	152	213	35	180	6174	34.68	10	35	–	75
Rayner, O.P.	115	149	25	143*	2728	22.00	2	12	–	154
Read, C.M.W.	334	507	85	240	15700	37.20	25	89	3	995/52
Read, J.	1	1	–	14	14	14.00	–	–	–	4
Reece, L.M.	29	51	5	114*	1503	32.67	1	12	–	17
Rhodes, G.H.	6	11	2	59	274	30.44	–	2	–	2
Rhodes, W.M.H.	19	28	2	95	693	26.65	–	3	–	9
Richardson, M.J.	82	140	10	148	3979	30.60	5	21	2	158/5
Riley, A.E.N.	51	65	23	34	429	10.21	–	–	–	27
Robinson, O.E.	23	31	7	110	671	27.95	1	3	–	7

F-C	M	I	NO	HS	Runs	Avge	100	50	1000	Ct/St
Robson, A.J.	53	97	2	120	2995	31.52	2	27	2	42
Robson, S.D.	115	203	16	231	7224	38.63	17	29	2	116
Roderick, G.H.	60	96	14	171	3159	38.52	5	21	–	151/3
Rogers, C.J.L.	313	554	40	319	25470	49.55	76	122	9+2	244
Roland-Jones, T.S.	81	107	22	103*	1927	22.67	1	7	–	27
Root, J.E.	96	164	20	254	7533	52.31	19	35	3	87
Root, W.T.	6	9	1	133	351	43.87	1	2	–	–
Rossington, A.M.	42	67	8	138*	2074	35.15	4	14	–	80/7
Rossouw, R.R.	78	138	6	319	5837	44.21	18	24	0+1	101
Rouse, A.P.	12	15	–	65	298	19.86	–	1	–	43/3
Rouse, T.D.	4	5	–	41	80	16.00	–	–	–	4
Roy, J.J.	73	120	10	143	4119	37.44	8	18	1	72
Rudolph, J.A.	282	487	30	228*	19191	41.99	49	92	4+1	241
Rushworth, C.	87	120	33	46	1148	13.19	–	–		17
Russell, A.D.	17	24	1	128	609	26.47	2	–	–	6
Russell, C.J.	18	22	4	22	129	7.16	–	–	–	4
Rutherford, H.D.	70	125	2	239	4220	34.30	8	21	0+1	52
Ryder, J.D.	120	196	16	236	7925	44.02	22	36	–	111
Sakande, A.	5	7	1	33	72	12.00	–	–	–	3
Salt, P.D.	4	5	1	42	98	24.50	–	–	–	–
Salter, A.G.	31	47	9	73	755	19.86	–	2	–	14
Sami Aslam	32	55	1	221	1976	36.59	6	6	–	23
Sanderson, B.W.	22	23	6	42	115	6.76	–	–	–	3
Sandhu, G.S.	6	4	2	8	21	10.50	–	–	–	–
Sangakkara, K.C.	250	414	29	319	19420	50.44	56	84	1+1	366/33
Santner, M.J.	30	44	4	118	1154	28.85	2	6	–	29
Sarfraz Ahmed	120	188	40	213*	6334	42.79	10	42	–	375/47
Saud Shakil	11	18	4	121	772	55.14	3	5	–	5
Sayer, R.J.	7	7	2	34	94	18.80	–	–	–	1
Scott, G.F.B.	4	5	2	16*	37	12.33	–	–	–	2
Scriven, B.R.M.	5	7	2	67*	172	34.40	–	1	–	–
Selman, N.J.	10	19	2	122*	470	27.64	2	2	–	7
Shadab Khan	1	1	–	48	48	48.00	–	–	–	–
Shahzad, A.	95	126	31	88	2231	23.48	–	6	–	15
Shanaka, M.D.	33	43	5	127	1415	37.23	4	6	–	25
Shan Masood	83	140	7	199	4547	34.18	7	25	0+1	55
Shantry, J.D.	86	110	28	106	1546	18.85	2	2	–	27
Sharjeel Khan	73	129	4	279	4612	36.89	11	10	0+1	39
Shaw, J.	15	19	6	29	168	12.92	–	–		3
Sheikh, A.	9	13	4	12	40	4.44	–	–	–	3
Shreck, C.E.	173	209	109	56	775	7.75	–	1	–	49
Sibley, D.P.	22	37	2	242	1039	29.68	1	5	–	18
Sidebottom, R.J.	222	273	83	61	2627	13.82	–	3	–	62
Silva, A.R.S.	87	135	26	225*	5514	50.58	17	21	–	88
Silva, J.K.	176	281	31	225	11526	46.10	35	49	0+2	356/48
Simpson, J.A.	115	181	29	143	4763	31.33	5	29	–	348/19
Siriwardana, T.A.M.	97	164	14	185*	5385	35.90	7	38	0+1	79
Slater, B.T.	47	87	2	119	2422	28.49	3	15	–	16
Smith, G.P.	101	188	8	158*	4799	26.66	8	20	–	78
Smith, R.A.J.	15	19	4	57*	285	19.00	–	1	–	3
Smith, T.C.	107	160	25	128	3972	29.42	3	26	–	112
Smith, T.M.J.	41	56	11	80	1024	22.75	–	2	–	12
Smith, W.R.	171	290	21	210	8966	33.33	17	35	1	109
Sodhi, I.S.	47	69	8	82*	1376	22.55	–	8	–	14
Sohail Khan	83	111	28	56	1132	13.63	–	1	–	19
Steel, C.T.	6	9	–	80	315	35.00	–	3	–	4

F-C	M	I	NO	HS	Runs	Avge	100	50	1000	Ct/St
Stevens, D.I.	265	416	23	208	13899	35.36	31	70	3	190
Stevenson, R.A.	3	3	–	30	34	11.33	–	–	–	–
Steyn, D.W.	127	151	34	82	1666	14.23	–	4	–	28
Stirling, P.R.	48	72	4	146	2003	29.45	4	10	–	24
Stokes, B.A.	98	160	8	258	5207	34.25	11	25	–	55
Stone, O.P.	25	32	7	60	407	16.28	–	1	–	14
Stoneman, M.D.	135	238	6	187	7659	33.01	16	37	4	70
Sykes, J.S.	12	19	4	34	186	12.40	–	–	–	6
Tavaré, W.A.	43	74	5	139	2189	31.72	4	12	1	29
Taylor, B.J.	3	4	1	36	57	19.00	–	–	–	2
Taylor, B.R.M.	117	214	12	217	8208	40.63	28	29	1+1	131/4
Taylor, C.J.	2	3	–	26	49	16.33	–	–	–	1
Taylor, J.M.R.	42	64	4	156	1801	30.01	4	6	–	22
Taylor, J.W.A.	139	231	29	291	9306	46.06	20	47	5	91
Taylor, L.R.P.L.	138	233	19	290	9381	43.83	22	48	–	179
Taylor, M.D.	23	31	15	32*	215	13.43	–	–	–	3
Taylor, R.M.L.	44	75	11	101*	1461	22.82	1	6	–	22
Taylor, T.A.I.	18	28	5	80	395	17.17	–	1	–	3
ten Doeschate, R.N.	145	213	33	259*	8864	49.24	25	40	1	89
Terry, S.P.	13	20	2	62*	535	29.72	–	6	–	10
Tetley, J.W.	4	7	–	21	63	9.00	–	–	–	7/1
Thakor, S.J.	45	69	11	134	2243	38.67	4	12	–	10
Thirimanne, H.D.R.L.	83	145	17	156	5218	40.76	14	24	0+1	68
Thomas, I.A.A.	19	30	14	13	97	6.06	–	–	–	3
Thompson, H.L.	6	9	–	40	114	12.66	–	–	–	2
Thomson, A.T.	4	3	–	25	43	14.33	–	–	–	1
Thurston, C.O.	2	2	–	13	15	7.50	–	–	–	1
Tice, P.J.A.	2	3	–	41	67	22.33	–	–	–	1/1
Tomlinson, J.A.	129	162	73	51	945	10.61	–	1	–	27
Tongue, J.C.	1	–	–	–	–	–	–	–	–	–
Topley, R.J.W.	32	38	17	15	71	3.38	–	–	–	8
Tredwell, J.C.	170	237	28	124	4543	21.73	4	16	–	189
Trego, P.D.	207	306	37	154*	9207	34.22	15	52	1	85
Trescothick, M.E.	361	620	34	284	24884	42.46	63	122	8	513
Trott, I.J.L.	251	417	43	226	16519	44.16	39	81	7	202
Turpin, J.R.	2	1	1	0*	0	–	–	–	–	1
Tye, A.J.	7	7	–	10	33	4.71	–	–	–	1
Udawatte, M.L.	125	218	16	212	6887	34.09	9	38	–	80
Umar Siddiq	36	62	9	187*	2404	45.35	8	6	–	22
Umeed, A.R.I.	7	11	1	101	172	17.20	1	–	–	4
van Buuren, G.L.	59	91	16	235	3753	50.04	10	21	–	37
van der Gugten, T.	19	27	6	57	236	11.23	–	1	–	4
van der Merwe, R.E.	57	92	14	205*	2695	34.55	4	18	–	42
van Meekeren, P.A.	5	9	–	34	95	10.55	–	–	–	1
van Zyl, S.	127	210	32	172	7653	42.99	18	35	0+1	74
Velani, K.S.	11	16	1	58	351	23.40	–	1	–	3
Vilas, D.J.	92	139	16	216*	5050	41.05	12	24	–	257/13
Viljoen, G.C.	87	116	16	72	1519	15.19	–	6	–	27
Vince, J.M.	120	198	18	240	7064	39.24	18	28	2	106
Voges, A.C.	192	320	46	269*	13205	48.19	32	67	0+1	251
Wade, M.S.	96	146	26	152	4740	39.50	9	29	–	321/12
Wagg, G.G.	144	210	21	200	5191	27.46	4	31	–	47
Waghorn, A.C.	2	4	2	6	10	5.00	–	–	–	–
Wagner, N.	119	156	31	70	1960	15.68	–	6	–	33
Wahab Riaz	117	164	28	84	2277	16.74	–	8	–	35
Wainwright, D.J.	81	114	28	109	2270	26.39	3	9	–	28

F-C	M	I	NO	HS	Runs	Avge	100	50	1000	Ct/St
Wakely, A.G.	108	169	10	123	4941	31.07	5	29	–	66
Wallace, M.A.	264	422	36	139	11159	28.90	15	55	1	707/56
Waller, M.T.C.	8	9	1	28	91	11.37	–	–	–	5
Walter, P.I.	2	2	–	47	75	37.50	–	–	–	–
Warnapura, M.S.	63	104	12	200*	3410	37.06	8	17	–	51
Watkinson, L.	4	4	1	35	71	23.66	–	–	–	1
Weatherley, J.J.	2	3	–	83	96	32.00	–	1	–	–
Weighell, W.J.	5	8	1	25	122	17.42	–	–	–	2
Weller, S.D.	6	10	2	18*	74	9.25	–	–	–	1
Wells, L.W.P.	98	161	9	208	5254	34.56	13	22	1	50
Wells, T.J.	14	23	2	87*	412	19.61	–	2	–	7
Wessels, M.H.	170	284	24	199	9259	35.61	19	48	2	274/16
Westaway, S.A.	5	8	2	63*	174	29.00	–	1	–	24
Westley, T.	128	213	15	254	7129	36.00	15	36	1	92
Weston, L.P.	3	4	–	22	30	7.50	–	–	–	5
Westphal, A.A.	6	4	2	28*	39	19.50	–	–	–	2
Westwood, I.J.	155	259	22	196	7824	33.01	15	41	–	82
Wheal, B.T.J.	13	15	5	14	54	5.40	–	–	–	2
Wheater, A.J.A.	108	161	20	204*	5321	37.73	10	29	–	165/8
White, G.G.	36	51	5	65	571	12.41	–	2	–	12
White, R.G.	4	4	–	30	34	8.50	–	–	–	3
White, W.A.	86	134	20	101*	2769	24.28	1	14	–	23
Whiteley, R.A.	66	106	11	130*	2618	27.55	3	13	–	41
Whittingham, S.G.	7	5	2	8*	20	6.66	–	–	–	1
Wiese, D.	78	126	15	208	3916	35.27	9	20	–	53
Willey, D.J.	62	87	10	104*	2110	27.40	2	14	–	14
Williamson, K.S.	114	197	16	284*	8793	48.58	24	45	–	108
Wilson, G.C.	83	125	19	160*	3822	36.05	3	23	–	148/5
Winter, M.J.	5	8	1	56	210	30.00	–	2	–	2
Woakes, C.R.	119	171	43	152*	4719	36.86	9	19	–	52
Wood, C.P.	39	55	5	105*	1265	25.30	1	6	–	12
Wood, J.M.	4	4	2	14	16	8.00	–	–	–	–
Wood, L.	16	25	5	100	539	26.95	1	2	–	4
Wood, M.A.	36	58	12	66	953	20.71	–	2	–	9
Wood, S.K.W.	3	4	1	45	77	25.66	–	–	–	–
Wood, T.A.	2	4	–	14	32	8.00	–	–	–	1
Wright, C.J.C.	122	153	37	77	2116	18.24	–	9	–	20
Wright, L.J.	122	185	22	226*	6531	40.06	16	33	1	51
Yasir Arafat	205	300	43	170	6973	27.13	5	36	–	55
Yasir Shah	97	131	17	71	1911	16.76	–	6	–	54
Younus Khan	216	360	40	313	16396	51.23	54	60	0+1	224
Zaib, S.A.	5	7	1	65*	148	24.66	–	1	–	3
Zulfiqar Babar	88	119	19	89	1681	16.81	–	6	–	35

BOWLING

'50wS' denotes instances of taking 50 or more wickets in a season. Where these have been achieved outside the British Isles they are shown after a plus sign.

	Runs	Wkts	Avge	Best	5wI	10wM	50wS
Abbott, J.B.	20	0					
Abbott, K.J.	5470	241	22.69	8-45	15	2	0+1
Abdul Rehman Muzammil	103	1	103.00	1-33	–	–	–
Abell, T.B.	33	1	33.00	1-11	–	–	–
Ackermann, C.N.	1111	31	35.83	3-85	–	–	–
Adair, M.R.	108	1	108.00	1-61	–	–	–
Adams, J.H.K.	718	13	55.23	2-16	–	–	–

F-C	Runs	Wkts	Avge	Best	5wI	10wM	50wS
Akram, B.M.R.	398	10	39.80	3-50	–	–	–
Alexander, T.D.	200	5	40.00	4-80	–	–	–
Ali, A.M.	40	0					
Ali, M.M.	9741	234	41.62	6-29	6	1	–
Allchin, A.T.A.	505	6	84.16	2-41	–	–	–
Allenby, J.	7877	298	26.43	6-54	5	1	1
Alsop, T.P.	66	2	33.00	2-59	–	–	–
Ambrose, T.R.	1	1	1.00	1- 0	–	–	–
Anderson, J.M.	20342	773	26.31	7-43	38	6	3
Andrew, G.M.	8232	238	34.58	5-40	6	–	1
Ansari, Z.S.	4204	122	34.45	6-30	6	–	–
Archer, J.C.	778	28	27.78	4-31	–	–	–
Arif, A.T.	488	7	69.71	2-29	–	–	–
Arksey, J.B.T.	205	7	29.28	3-41	–	–	–
Arshad, U.	955	36	26.52	4-78	–	–	–
Asad Shafiq	169	2	84.50	1-14	–	–	–
Ashar Zaidi	2760	91	30.32	4-50	–	–	–
Ashraf, M.A.	1384	43	32.18	5-32	1	–	–
Azad, M.H.	2	0					
Azeem Rafiq	2345	61	38.44	5-50	1	–	–
Azhar Ali	1626	39	41.69	4-34	–	–	–
Azharullah	9668	331	29.20	7-74	15	2	0+1
Azizullah	2309	105	21.99	7-52	6	1	–
Babar Azam	423	5	84.60	1-13	–	–	–
Bailey, G.J.	46	0					
Bailey, T.E.	2123	64	33.17	5-12	3	–	–
Bairstow, J.M.	1	0					
Ball, A.J.	1434	29	49.44	3-36	–	–	–
Ball, J.T.	2972	115	25.84	6-49	4	–	1
Ballance, G.S.	154	0					
Bancroft, C.T.	0	0					
Barker, K.H.D.	7446	289	25.76	6-40	12	1	3
Barnard, E.G.	1768	47	37.61	4-62	–	–	–
Barrett, C.A.	209	2	104.50	1-29	–	–	–
Barrow, A.W.R.	36	1	36.00	1- 4	–	–	–
Barton, A.P.	332	2	166.00	1-25	–	–	–
Batty, G.J.	20638	625	33.02	8-68	26	3	2
Beard, A.P.	300	9	33.33	4-62	–	–	–
Beer, W.A.T.	719	14	51.35	3-31	–	–	–
Behardien, F.	1147	32	35.84	3-48	–	–	–
Bell, I.R.	1615	47	34.36	4- 4	–	–	–
Bell-Drummond, D.J.	54	0					
Berg, G.K.	6416	202	31.76	6-56	4	–	–
Bernard, H.R.	105	3	35.00	2-68	–	–	–
Bess, D.M.	264	13	20.30	6-28	2	–	–
Best, T.L.	9693	330	29.37	7-33	13	2	–
Bilawal Bhatti	6296	272	23.14	8-56	11	2	0+2
Billings, S.W.	4	0					
Bird, J.M.	5410	220	24.59	7-45	11	3	0+1
Blake, A.J.	129	3	43.00	2- 9	–	–	–
Bodenstein, C.J.	236	6	39.33	3-53	–	–	–
Bopara, R.S.	8278	226	36.62	5-49	3	–	–
Borthwick, S.G.	7216	195	37.00	6-70	3	–	–
Bragg, W.D.	459	5	91.80	2-10	–	–	–
Brand, N.	130	0					
Bravo, D.J.	5918	177	33.43	6-11	7	–	–
Bresnan, T.T.	14927	481	31.03	5-36	8	–	–

F-C	Runs	Wkts	Avge	Best	5wI	10wM	50wS
Briggs, D.R.	7315	217	33.70	6- 45	8	–	–
Broad, S.C.J.	16336	593	27.54	8- 15	26	3	–
Brooks, J.A.	9574	360	26.59	6- 65	13	–	3
Broom, N.T.	489	8	61.12	1- 8	–	–	–
Brown, B.C.	93	1	93.00	1- 48	–	–	–
Brown, K.R.	65	2	32.50	2- 30	–	–	–
Browne, N.L.J.	171	0					
Bryant, B.J.	39	0					
Buck, N.L.	6087	158	38.52	5- 76	4	–	–
Burke, J.E.	647	23	28.13	4- 19	–	–	–
Burns, R.J.	127	2	63.50	1- 18	–	–	–
Buttler, J.C.	11	0					
Cachopa, C.	73	0					
Carberry, M.A.	1069	17	62.88	2- 85	–		–
Carey, L.J.	330	13	26.00	4- 92	–	–	–
Carlson, K.S.	178	6	29.66	5- 28	1	–	–
Carse, B.A.	607	17	35.70	3- 38	–	–	–
Carter, A.	3110	103	30.19	5- 40	2	–	–
Carter, M.	511	13	39.30	7- 56	1	1	–
Carver, K.	425	14	30.35	4-106	–	–	–
Chameera, P.V.D.	2501	78	32.06	5- 42	3	–	–
Chanderpaul, S.	2537	60	42.28	4- 48	–	–	
Chandimal, L.D.	18	1	18.00	1- 13	–	–	–
Chappell, Z.J.	204	5	40.80	2- 44	–	–	–
Chapple, G.	26314	985	26.71	7- 53	39	3	7
Chopra, V.	128	0					
Christian, D.T.	4843	136	35.61	5- 24	3	–	–
Clark, J.	1336	30	44.53	4-101		–	–
Clarke, J.M.	22	0					
Clarke, R.	12352	375	32.93	6- 63	3	–	–
Claughton, T.H.	27	1	27.00	1- 16	–	–	–
Claydon, M.E.	8166	232	32.40	6-104	7	–	2
Coad, B.O.	165	2	82.50	1- 57	–	–	–
Cobb, J.J.	1292	14	92.28	2- 11	–	–	–
Cockbain, I.A.	44	1	44.00	1- 23	–	–	–
Coles, M.T.	8457	302	28.00	6- 51	10	2	2
Collingwood, P.D.	6070	155	39.16	5- 52	2	–	–
Compton, N.R.D.	227	3	75.66	1- 1	–	–	–
Cook, A.N.	211	7	30.14	3- 13	–	–	–
Cook, S.C.	428	10	42.80	3- 42	–	–	–
Cook, S.J.	178	4	44.50	3- 64	–	–	–
Cork, G.T.G.	70	0					
Cosgrove, M.J.	2186	50	43.72	3- 3	–	–	–
Cosker, D.A.	21683	597	36.31	6- 91	12	1	1
Cotton, B.D.	1517	37	41.00	4- 20	–	–	–
Coughlin, J.	45	2	22.50	1- 10	–	–	–
Coughlin, P.	1290	42	30.71	4- 10	–	–	–
Cowdrey, F.K.	129	3	43.00	3- 59	–	–	–
Crane, M.S.	1834	45	40.75	5- 35	1	–	–
Crichard, R.J.	372	9	41.33	5- 62	1	–	–
Critchley, M.J.J.	1002	8	125.25	3- 50	–	–	–
Croft, S.J.	2845	71	40.07	6- 41	1	–	–
Crook, S.P.	7546	191	39.50	5- 48	3	–	–
Cummins, M.L.	3183	140	22.73	7- 45	8	1	–
Curran, S.M.	1359	49	27.73	7- 58	4	–	–
Curran, T.K.	3845	132	29.12	7- 20	6	1	1
Dalgleish, A.D.	112	5	22.40	3- 49	–	–	–

F-C	Runs	Wkts	Avge	Best	5wI	10wM	50wS
Davey, J.H.	589	22	26.77	4- 53	–	–	–
Davis, C.A.L.	33	0					
Davis, W.S.	814	24	33.91	7-146	1	–	–
Dawes, M.J.	51	1	51.00	1- 26	–	–	–
Dawson, L.A.	4872	130	37.47	7- 51	3	–	–
de Lange, M.	4811	174	27.64	7- 76	6	2	–
Delport, C.S.	624	11	56.72	2- 25	–	–	–
Denly, J.L.	1616	31	52.12	3- 43	–	–	–
Dent, C.D.J.	663	7	94.71	2- 21	–	–	–
Dernbach, J.W.	8734	267	32.71	6- 47	10	–	1
de Silva, D.M.	1364	59	23.11	6- 33	1	–	–
Dewes, J.J.N.	220	4	55.00	2- 93	–	–	–
Dexter, N.J.	4435	134	33.09	6- 63	4	–	–
Dickson, S.R.	44	2	22.00	1- 15	–	–	–
Dickwella, D.P.D.N.	16	0					
Dixon, M.W.	986	22	44.81	5-124	1	–	–
D'Oliveira, B.L.	1502	33	45.51	5- 48	1	–	–
Duckett, B.M.	8	0					
Dunn, M.P.	3405	96	35.46	5- 48	3	–	–
Durston, W.J.	4751	119	39.92	6-109	4	–	–
Eckersley, E.J.H.	65	2	32.50	2- 29	–	–	–
Edwards, F.H.	10161	317	32.05	7- 87	19	2	–
Edwards, G.A.	346	8	43.25	4- 44	–	–	–
Edwards, R.D.	56	0					
Elgar, D.	2447	48	50.97	4- 22	–	–	–
Ellison, H.R.C.	9	0					
Emerton, C.J.	183	2	91.50	2-100	–	–	–
Eranga, R.M.S.	6028	186	32.40	6- 21	3	–	–
Ervine, S.M.	11495	273	42.10	6- 82	5	–	–
Escott, D.A.	71	6	11.83	6- 71	1	–	–
Evans, L.J.	259	2	129.50	1- 29	–	–	–
Fakhar Zaman	49	0					
Fell, T.C.	17	0					
Fernando, A.M.	184	8	23.00	5- 33	1	–	–
Fernando, A.N.P.R.	6359	190	33.46	5- 36	4	–	–
Fernando, M.V.T.	3916	128	30.59	5- 35	6	–	–
Finch, A.J.	257	4	64.25	1- 0	–	–	–
Finch, H.Z.	107	2	53.50	1- 9	–	–	–
Finn, S.T.	13893	488	28.46	9- 37	12	1	2
Fletcher, L.J.	6908	232	29.77	5- 52	3	–	–
Foakes, B.T.	6	0					
Footitt, M.H.A.	8080	314	25.73	7- 62	19	1	2
Foster, J.S.	128	1	128.00	1-122	–	–	–
Franklin, J.E.C.	13149	467	28.15	7- 14	14	1	–
Freckingham, O.H.	2466	65	37.93	6-125	2	–	–
Fuller, J.K.	3817	113	33.77	6- 24	5	1	–
Gale, A.W.	238	1	238.00	1- 33	–	–	–
Gamage, P.L.S.	5424	185	29.31	7- 58	8	2	0+1
Gamble, R.N.	528	6	88.00	1- 41	–	–	–
Garton, G.H.S.	420	11	38.18	3- 93	–	–	–
Gayle, C.H.	5194	132	39.34	5- 34	2	–	–
Gibson, R.	42	1	42.00	1- 42	–	–	–
Gidman, W.R.S.	4774	202	23.63	6- 15	9	1	2
Gleeson, R.J.	675	17	39.70	4-105	–	–	–
Gnodde, J.S.D.	126	1	126.00	1- 33	–	–	–
Godleman, B.A.	35	0					
Gordon, R.O.	413	13	31.76	4- 53	–	–	–

F-C	*Runs*	*Wkts*	*Avge*	*Best*	*5wI*	*10wM*	*50wS*
Grant, S.E.	401	1	401.00	1- 42	–	–	–
Gregory, L.	4175	140	29.82	6- 47	7	1	–
Griffiths, D.A.	3828	113	33.87	6- 63	4	–	–
Griffiths, S.W.	529	3	176.33	2- 63	–	–	–
Groenewald, T.D.	10158	336	30.23	6- 50	14	–	–
Grundy, J.O.	247	8	30.87	3- 41	–	–	–
Gubbins, N.R.T.	48	0					
Guptill, M.J.	627	10	62.70	3- 11	–	–	–
Gurney, H.F.	7303	233	31.34	6- 61	6	–	–
Haggett, C.J.	2581	74	34.87	4- 15	–	–	–
Hain, S.R.	24	0					
Haines, T.J.	8	0					
Hales, A.D.	173	3	57.66	2- 63	–	–	–
Haley, O.J.P.	88	1	88.00	1- 24	–	–	–
Hameed, H.	12	0					
Hampton, T.R.G.	320	3	106.66	1- 15	–	–	–
Hamza Ali	59	2	29.50	2- 47	–	–	–
Handscomb, P.S.P.	21	0					
Hannon-Dalby, O.J.	3781	94	40.22	5- 68	2	–	–
Harinath, A.	190	5	38.00	2- 1	–	–	–
Harmer, S.R.	9226	283	32.60	8- 60	12	1	0+1
Harris, J.A.R.	10752	362	29.70	9- 34	12	2	2
Harrison, J.	1573	52	30.25	[illegible]- 31	2	–	–
Hartley, C.F.	190	5	38.00	2- 40	–	–	–
Harwood, C.S.	103	1	103.00	1-103	–	–	–
Hasan Ali	2600	106	24.52	8-107	6	1	–
Hassam Mushtaq	137	3	45.66	2- 52	–	–	–
Hastings, J.W.	5819	219	26.57	7- 60	7	–	–
Hatchett, L.J.	2526	72	35.08	5- 47	3	–	–
Head, T.M.	952	14	68.00	3- 42	–	–	–
Helm, T.G.	605	20	30.25	3- 46	–	–	–
Hemmings, R.P.	58	0					
Henry, M.J.	3936	139	28.31	5- 18	6		–
Herath, H.M.R.K.B.	24095	961	25.07	9-127	61	11	0+2
Hickey, A.J.	204	6	34.00	2- 19	–	–	–
Hildreth, J.C.	492	6	82.00	[illegible]- 20	–	–	–
Hill, L.J.	6	0					
Hodd, A.J.	21	0					
Hogan, M.G.	11289	451	25.03	7- 92	17	1	2
Holmes, G.C.	13	0					
Horton, P.J.	66	2	33.00	2- 6	–	–	–
Howell, B.A.C.	2756	84	32.80	5- 57	1	–	–
Hudson-Prentice, F.J.	51	0					
Hughes, A.L.	1120	22	50.90	4- 46	–	–	–
Hughes, C.F.	1261	27	46.70	3- 87	–	–	–
Hughes, M.S.T.	21	1	21.00	1- 16	–	–	–
Hunn, M.D.	1383	38	36.39	5- 99	1	–	–
Hutton, B.A.	2138	69	30.98	5- 29	2	1	–
Iftikhar Ahmed	725	28	25.89	3- 23	–	–	–
Imran Khan	6327	279	22.67	9- 69	18	3	0+3
Imran Qayyum	283	6	47.16	3-158	–	–	–
Imran Tahir	20285	766	26.48	8- 42	51	11	2+2
Ingram, C.A.	1889	48	39.35	4- 16	–	–	–
Jarvis, K.M.	6654	248	26.83	7- 35	14	2	2
Javid, A.	340	3	113.33	1- 1	–	–	–
Jayasundera, M.D.U.S.	1086	25	43.44	3- 30	–	–	–
Jayasuriya, N.G.R.P.	1841	66	27.89	7- 56	6	2	–

F-C	Runs	Wkts	Avge	Best	5wI	10wM	50wS
Jenkins, W.H.	407	5	81.40	2- 27	–	–	–
Jennings, K.K.	467	14	33.35	2- 8	–	–	–
Jones, O.J.	408	12	34.00	4- 70	–	–	–
Jones, R.A.	5048	157	32.15	7-115	5	–	–
Jordan, C.J.	7978	248	32.16	7- 43	8	–	1
Joyce, E.C.	1033	11	93.90	2- 34	–	–	–
Junaid Khan	7286	299	24.36	7- 46	20	3	0+1
Karunaratne, F.D.M.	234	1	234.00	1- 15	–	–	–
Keogh, R.I.	2132	56	38.07	9- 52	1	1	–
Kerrigan, S.C.	9168	305	30.05	9- 51	13	3	2
Kervezee, A.N.	378	8	47.25	3- 72	–	–	–
Klein, D.	4215	163	25.85	8- 72	8	1	–
Kleinveldt, R.K.	10764	374	28.78	8- 47	17	1	1
Klinger, M.	3	0					
Kulasekara, K.M.D.N.	6569	272	24.15	7- 27	9	1	0+1
Kumar, N.R.	511	10	51.10	3- 58	–	–	–
Lake, M.B.	172	5	34.40	2- 41	–	–	–
Lakmal, R.A.S.	7430	218	34.08	6- 68	4	–	–
Latham, T.W.M.	18	1	18.00	1- 7	–	–	–
Lawlor, J.L.	49	0					
Lawrence, D.W.	129	3	43.00	1- 5	–	–	–
Leach, J.	5134	177	29.00	6- 73	8	–	2
Leach, M.J.	2748	107	25.68	7-106	7	1	1
Leach, S.G.	2	0					
Leaning, J.A.	244	3	81.33	2- 30	–	–	–
Lees, A.Z.	77	2	38.50	2- 51	–	–	–
Lehmann, J.S.	20	0					
Lester, T.J.	821	9	91.22	3- 50	–	–	–
Leverock, K.S.	125	1	125.00	1- 61	–	–	–
Libby, J.D.	183	3	61.00	1- 13	–	–	–
Liddle, C.J.	1736	34	51.05	3- 42	–	–	–
Lilley, A.E.	412	15	27.46	5- 41	1	–	–
Lilley, A.M.	1296	36	36.00	5- 23	2	–	–
Livingstone, L.S.	166	1	166.00	1- 19	–	–	–
Lloyd, D.L.	1691	36	46.97	3- 36	–	–	–
Lumb, M.J.	255	6	42.50	2- 10	–	–	–
Lyth, A.	1115	26	42.88	2- 9	–	–	–
McCarthy, B.J.	786	24	32.75	5- 70	1	–	–
McCullum, B.B.	140	1	140.00	1- 1	–	–	–
Macdonell, C.M.	248	0					
McIver, J.N.	356	3	118.66	3- 64	–	–	–
McKay, C.J.	6978	259	26.94	6- 40	7	–	2
McLaren, R.	10543	380	27.74	8- 38	14	1	1+1
MacLeod, C.S.	358	15	23.86	4- 66	–	–	–
Machan, M.W.	103	1	103.00	1- 36	–	–	–
Madsen, W.L.	1108	18	61.55	3- 45	–	–	–
Magoffin, S.J.	13429	576	23.31	8- 20	26	4	5
Mahmood, S.	121	1	121.00	1-121	–	–	–
Malan, D.J.	1910	45	42.44	5- 61	1	–	–
Marsden, J.	595	21	28.33	5- 41	1	–	–
Marshall, H.J.H.	1923	42	45.78	4- 24	–	–	–
Masters, D.D.	16905	672	25.15	8- 10	31	–	4
Mathews, A.D.	2791	61	45.75	5- 47	1	–	–
Meaker, S.C.	7363	252	29.21	8- 52	11	2	1
Mendis, B.K.G.	37	0					
Mendis, B.M.A.J.	5988	226	26.49	6- 37	12	–	–
Meschede, C.A.J.	4501	119	37.82	5- 84	1	–	–

F-C	*Runs*	*Wkts*	*Avge*	*Best*	*5wI*	*10wM*	*50wS*
Mickleburgh, J.C.	50	0					
Miles, C.N.	4618	170	27.16	6- 63	10	1	2
Mills, T.S.	2008	55	36.50	4- 25	–	–	–
Milnes, T.P.	1528	42	36.38	7- 39	2	–	–
Mir Hamza	3271	164	19.94	7- 73	14	3	0+1
Misbah-ul-Haq	246	3	82.00	1- 2	–	–	–
Mitchell, D.K.H.	979	22	44.50	4- 49	–	–	–
Mohammad Amir	3403	152	22.38	7- 61	8	1	0+1
Mohammad Asghar	1168	47	24.85	5- 28	4	1	–
Mohammad Hafeez	6386	232	27.52	8- 57	6	2	–
Mohammad Nawaz	1074	44	24.40	7- 31	1	1	–
Moore, T.C.	642	18	35.66	4- 78	–	–	–
Morgan, A.O.	827	15	55.13	2- 37	–	–	–
Morgan, E.J.G.	90	2	45.00	2- 24	–	–	–
Morris, C.A.J.	4057	127	31.94	5- 54	2	–	2
Morris, C.H.	3859	152	25.38	8- 44	2	1	–
Muchall, G.J.	657	15	43.80	3- 26	–	–	–
Mullaney, S.J.	2376	59	40.27	4- 31	–	–	–
Murphy, D.	43	1	43.00	1- 40	–	–	–
Murphy, J.R.	135	2	67.50	2- 90	–	–	–
Murtagh, T.J.	17436	652	26.74	7- 82	27	4	6
Mustard, P.	9	1	9.00	1- 9		–	
Myburgh, J.G.	2160	45	48.00	4- 56	–	–	–
Naik, J.K.H.	6657	170	39.15	8-179	6	–	–
Napier, G.R.	14760	490	30.12	7- 21	17	–	3
Nash, C.D.	3139	75	41.85	4- 12	–	–	–
Needham, J.D.S.	2754	83	33.18	5- 65	2	–	–
Newton, R.I.	25	0					
Noema-Barnett, K.	3329	97	34.31	4- 20	–	–	–
Northeast, S.A.	147	1	147.00	1- 60	–	–	–
Norwell, L.C.	5601	189	29.63	6- 33	5	1	1
Nurse, C.J.	58	1	58.00	1- 58	–	–	–
O'Brien, K.J.	1011	34	29.73	5- 39	1	–	–
O'Brien, N.J.	19	2	9.50	1- 4	–	–	–
Ogden, A.	172	4	43.00	2- 80	–	–	–
Onions, G.	15702	587	26.74	9- 67	25	3	7
Overton, C.	3818	136	28.07	6- 74	2	–	–
Overton, J.	3213	86	37.36	6- 95	2		–
Palladino, A.P.	10674	364	29.32	7- 53	13		2
Panesar, M.S.	22135	709	31.22	7- 60	39	6	6
Parkinson, C.F.	531	14	37.92	4- 90	–	–	–
Parkinson, M.W.	363	10	36.30	5- 49	1	–	–
Parry, S.D.	650	18	36.11	5- 23	1	–	–
Patel, A.R.	436	13	33.53	5- 86	2	–	–
Patel, J.S.	22411	648	34.58	7- 38	24	2	5
Patel, R.H.	2036	59	34.50	5- 69	1	–	–
Patel, S.R.	10930	277	39.45	7- 68	3	1	–
Pathirana, S.S.	7207	245	29.41	7- 49	17	2	0+1
Patterson, S.A.	8957	321	27.90	6- 56	6	–	2
Payne, D.A.	5683	170	33.42	6- 26	3	–	–
Penrhyn Jones, D.	190	5	38.00	3- 55	–	–	–
Petersen, A.N.	876	17	51.52	3- 58	–	–	–
Pettini, M.L.	263	1	263.00	1- 72	–	–	–
Philander, V.D.	9774	456	21.43	7- 61	20	2	0+2
Phillips, W.D.B.	272	7	38.85	3- 45	–	–	–
Pietersen, K.P.	3760	73	51.50	4- 31	–	–	–
Pillans, M.W.	3037	114	26.64	6- 67	3	1	0+1

F-C	Runs	Wkts	Avge	Best	5wI	10wM	50wS
Plunkett, L.E.	14071	445	31.62	6- 33	11	1	3
Podmore, H.W.	465	17	27.35	4- 54	–	–	–
Porter, J.A.	3356	121	27.73	5- 46	2	–	2
Porterfield, W.T.S.	138	2	69.00	1- 29	–	–	–
Poynton, T.	96	2	48.00	2- 96	–	–	–
Poysden, J.E.	752	21	35.80	5- 53	1	–	–
Prasad, K.T.G.D.	8855	312	28.38	6- 25	5	1	–
Prasanna, S.	9949	472	21.07	8- 59	36	8	0+4
Pringle, R.D.	1598	43	37.16	7-107	2	1	–
Priyanjan, S.M.A.	1454	38	38.26	5- 71	1	–	–
Procter, L.A.	2388	68	35.11	7- 71	2	–	–
Quinn, M.R.	2648	95	27.87	7- 76	1	1	–
Rabada, K.	2285	96	23.80	9- 33	5	2	–
Rahat Ali	5596	229	24.43	6- 40	10	–	0+1
Raine, B.A.	3818	123	31.04	5- 43	3	–	1
Rajitha, C.A.K.	1369	30	45.63	7- 86	3	1	–
Rampaul, R.	5995	203	29.53	7- 51	9	1	–
Randhawa, G.S.	149	3	49.66	2- 54	–	–	–
Rankin, W.B.	8368	317	26.39	6- 55	8	–	1
Rashid, A.U.	15615	450	34.70	7-107	19	1	2
Rayner, O.P.	8316	254	32.74	8- 46	10	1	1
Read, C.M.W.	90	0					
Reece, L.M.	542	14	38.71	4- 28	–	–	–
Rhodes, G.H.	263	3	87.66	2- 83	–	–	–
Rhodes, W.M.H.	829	25	33.16	3- 42	–	–	–
Richardson, M.J.	13	0					
Riley, A.E.N.	4182	115	36.36	7-150	5	–	1
Robinson, O.E.	2088	65	32.12	6- 33	1	–	–
Robson, A.J.	127	0					
Robson, S.D.	98	2	49.00	1- 4	–	–	–
Rogers, C.J.L.	137	1	137.00	1- 16	–	–	–
Roland-Jones, T.S.	7650	302	25.33	6- 50	14	3	2
Root, J.E.	1398	27	51.77	3- 33	–	–	–
Root, W.T.	23	0					
Rossington, A.M.	18	0					
Rossouw, R.R.	70	3	23.33	1- 1	–	–	–
Rouse, T.D.	126	3	42.00	1- 3	–	–	–
Roy, J.J.	495	14	35.35	3- 9	–	–	–
Rudolph, J.A.	2696	61	44.19	5- 80	3	–	–
Rushworth, C.	7541	312	24.16	9- 52	17	2	3
Russell, A.D.	1104	54	20.44	5- 36	3	–	–
Russell, C.J.	1566	38	41.21	4- 43	–	–	–
Rutherford, H.D.	47	0					
Ryder, J.D.	4445	152	29.24	6- 47	7	2	–
Sakande, A.	429	10	42.90	3- 38	–	–	–
Salter, A.G.	2592	50	51.84	3- 5	–	–	–
Sami Aslam	24	0					
Sanderson, B.W.	1617	72	22.45	8- 73	5	1	1
Sandhu, G.S.	461	11	41.90	4- 49	–	–	–
Sangakkara, K.C.	150	1	150.00	1- 13	–	–	–
Santner, M.J.	1884	40	47.10	3- 51	–	–	–
Sarfraz Ahmed	5	0					
Saud Shakil	240	3	80.00	1- 30	–	–	–
Sayer, R.J.	713	11	64.81	2- 41	–	–	–
Scott, G.F.B.	121	2	60.50	2- 67	–	–	–
Selman, N.J.	8	0					
Shadab Khan	120	5	24.00	4- 89	–	–	–

F-C	*Runs*	*Wkts*	*Avge*	*Best*	*5wI*	*10wM*	*50wS*
Shahzad, A.	8418	243	34.64	5- 46	4	–	–
Shanaka, M.D.	815	30	27.16	6- 69	1	–	–
Shan Masood	309	4	77.25	2- 52	–	–	–
Shantry, J.D.	7473	255	29.30	7- 60	12	2	2
Sharjeel Khan	312	8	39.00	3- 19	–	–	–
Shaw, J.	1537	41	37.48	5- 79	1	–	–
Sheikh, A.	975	23	42.39	4- 97	–	–	–
Shreck, C.E.	18170	575	31.60	8- 31	23	2	4
Sibley, D.P.	197	3	65.66	2-103	–	–	–
Sidebottom, R.J.	17620	737	23.90	7- 37	30	4	4
Silva, A.R.S.	128	2	64.00	2- 22	–	–	–
Silva, J.K.	33	1	33.00	1- 11	–	–	–
Siriwardana, T.A.M.	4431	142	31.20	5- 26	6	–	–
Slater, B.T.	107	0					
Smith, G.P.	73	1	73.00	1- 64	–	–	–
Smith, R.A.J.	1146	29	39.51	3- 23	–	–	–
Smith, T.C.	6882	241	28.55	6- 46	7	–	1
Smith, T.M.J.	3378	65	51.96	4- 35	–	–	–
Smith, W.R.	1394	28	49.78	3- 34	–	–	–
Sodhi, I.S.	5300	124	42.74	7-102	5	–	–
Sohail Khan	9268	368	25.18	9-109	29	6	0+3
Steel, C.T.	118	1	118.00	1- 39	–		–
Stevens, D.I.	10127	358	[illegible]	7- 21	12	1	2
Stevenson, R.A.	215	3	71.66	1- 15	–	–	–
Steyn, D.W.	13362	575	23.23	8- 41	34	7	0+2
Stirling, P.R.	832	19	43.78	2- 27	–	–	–
Stokes, B.A.	6721	221	30.41	7- 67	4	1	–
Stone, O.P.	2210	72	30.69	5- 44	2	–	–
Stoneman, M.D.	150	0					
Sykes, J.S.	1166	21	55.52	4-176	–	–	
Tavaré, W.A.	30	0					
Taylor, B.J.	219	7	31.28	4- 64	–	–	–
Taylor, B.R.M.	225	4	56.25	2- 36	–	–	–
Taylor, C.J.	6	1	6.00	1- 6	–	–	–
Taylor, J.M.R.	2657	61	43.55	4- 16	–	–	–
Taylor, J.W.A.	176	0					
Taylor, L.R.P.L.	378	6	63.00	2- 4	–	–	–
Taylor, M.D.	2296	52	44.15	5- 75	2	–	
Taylor, R.M.L.	3691	90	41.01	5- 55	3		
Taylor, T.A.I.	1647	17	33.04	6- 61	2	–	–
ten Doeschate, R.N.	7069	208	33.98	6- 20	7	–	–
Thakor, S.J.	2150	51	42.15	5- 63	1	–	–
Thirimanne, H.D.R.L.	129	0					
Thomas, I.A.A.	1390	43	32.32	4- 48	–	–	–
Thompson, H.L.	6	0					
Thomson, A.T.	325	9	36.11	6-138	1	–	–
Tomlinson, J.A.	12196	382	31.92	8- 46	12	1	2
Tongue, J.C.	49	4	12.25	3- 35	–	–	–
Topley, R.J.W.	3223	125	25.78	6- 29	7	2	–
Tredwell, J.C.	15165	419	36.19	8- 66	12	3	1
Trego, P.D.	13562	372	36.45	7- 84	4	1	1
Trescothick, M.E.	1551	36	43.08	4- 36	–	–	–
Trott, I.J.L.	3376	69	48.92	7- 39	1	–	–
Turpin, J.R.	152	4	38.00	2- 44	–	–	–
Tye, A.J.	710	21	33.80	3- 47	–	–	–
Udawatte, M.L.	278	5	55.60	2- 31	–	–	–
Umar Siddiq	29	1	29.00	1- 19	–	–	–

F-C	Runs	Wkts	Avge	Best	5wI	10wM	50wS
van Buuren, G.L.	1863	71	26.23	4- 12	–	–	–
van der Gugten, T.	1933	73	26.47	7- 68	7	1	1
van der Merwe, R.E.	3766	100	37.66	4- 45	–	–	–
van Meekeren, P.A.	395	13	30.38	3- 44	–	–	–
van Zyl, S.	1743	48	36.31	5- 32	1	–	–
Velani, K.S.	62	0					
Vilas, D.J.	3	0					
Viljoen, G.C.	9046	345	26.22	8-105	20	4	0+1
Vince, J.M.	945	21	45.00	5- 41	1	–	–
Voges, A.C.	1896	54	35.11	4- 92	–	–	–
Wade, M.S.	32	1	32.00	1- 23	–	–	–
Wagg, G.G.	14509	422	34.38	6- 29	12	1	2
Waghorn, A.C.	245	5	49.00	3- 79	–	–	–
Wagner, N.	13319	495	26.90	7- 46	26	2	0+2
Wahab Riaz	11177	393	28.44	9- 59	15	5	0+2
Wainwright, D.J.	6991	181	38.62	6- 33	6	–	1
Wakely, A.G.	351	6	58.50	2- 62	–	–	–
Wallace, M.A.	3	0					
Waller, M.T.C.	493	10	49.30	3- 33	–	–	–
Walter, P.I.	214	4	53.50	3- 44	–	–	–
Warnapura, M.S.	217	2	108.50	1- 14	–	–	–
Watkinson, L.	347	5	69.40	3-132	–	–	–
Weatherley, J.J.	41	0					
Weighell, W.J.	508	17	29.88	5- 33	1	–	–
Weller, S.D.	393	15	26.20	3- 26	–	–	–
Wells, L.W.P.	2202	46	47.86	3- 35	–	–	–
Wells, T.J.	692	13	53.23	3- 68	–	–	–
Wessels, M.H.	115	3	38.33	1- 10	–	–	–
Westley, T.	2418	52	46.50	4- 55	–	–	–
Westphal, A.A.	437	10	43.70	3- 45	–	–	–
Westwood, I.J.	337	7	48.14	2- 39	–	–	–
Wheal, B.T.J.	1142	30	38.06	6- 51	1	–	–
Wheater, A.J.A.	86	1	86.00	1- 86	–	–	–
White, G.G.	2425	62	39.11	6- 44	1	–	–
White, W.A.	6808	202	33.70	6- 25	7	–	–
Whiteley, R.A.	1626	29	56.06	2- 6	–	–	–
Whittingham, S.G.	685	19	36.05	4- 58	–	–	–
Wiese, D.	6076	231	26.30	6- 58	6	1	–
Willey, D.J.	4735	157	30.15	5- 29	5	1	–
Williamson, K.S.	3605	85	42.41	5- 75	1	–	–
Wilson, G.C.	89	0					
Woakes, C.R.	10302	418	24.64	9- 36	18	4	3
Wood, C.P.	2894	99	29.23	5- 39	3	–	–
Wood, J.M.	235	3	78.33	2- 32	–	–	–
Wood, L.	1437	43	33.41	5- 40	1	–	–
Wood, M.A.	3145	116	27.11	5- 32	5	–	–
Wood, S.K.W.	92	3	30.66	3- 64	–	–	–
Wright, C.J.C.	11559	345	33.50	6- 22	9	–	1
Wright, L.J.	4862	120	40.51	5- 65	3	–	–
Yasir Arafat	18851	787	23.95	9- 35	44	5	0+4
Yasir Shah	10280	393	26.15	7- 76	20	2	–
Younus Khan	2120	44	48.18	4- 52	–	–	–
Zaib, S.A.	230	5	46.00	5-148	1	–	–
Zulfiqar Babar	9778	421	23.22	10-143	27	4	0+2

LIMITED-OVERS CAREER RECORDS

Compiled by Philip Bailey

The following career records, to the end of the 2016 season, include all players currently registered with first-class counties. These records are restricted to performances in limited-overs matches of 'List A' status as defined by the Association of Cricket Statisticians and Historians now incorporated by ICC into their Classification of Cricket. The following matches qualify for List A status and are included in the figures that follow: Limited-Overs Internationals; Other International matches (e.g. Commonwealth Games, 'A' team internationals); Premier domestic limited-overs tournaments in Test status countries; Official tourist matches against the main first-class teams.

The following matches do NOT qualify for inclusion: World Cup warm-up games; Tourist matches against first-class teams outside the major domestic competitions (e.g. Universities, Minor Counties etc.); Festival, pre-season friendly games and Twenty20 Cup matches.

	M	*Runs*	*Avge*	*HS*	*100*	*50*	*Wkts*	*Avge*	*Best*	*Econ*
Abbott, K.J.	86	391	17.00	45*	–	–	108	29.99	4-21	5.12
Abell, T.B.	12	343	38.11	106	1	1	–	–	–	–
Ackermann, C.N.	41	932	32.13	92	–	7	20	36.90	3-35	4.38
Adams, J.H.K.	106	3547	40.30	131	2	27	1	105.00	1-34	7.97
Ali, A.M.	9	155	19.37	84	–	1	0	–	–	5.16
Ali, M.M.	146	3890	30.15	158	9	17	97	40.91	3-28	5.36
Allenby, J.	113	2658	27.97	91*	–	16	83	34.56	5-43	4.89
Alsop, T.P.	8	327	46.71	116	1	2	–	–	–	–
Ambrose, T.R.	162	3586	32.01	135	3	20	–	–	–	156/32
Anderson, J.M.	247	366	9.15	28	–	–	343	28.15	5-23	4.83
Andrew, G.M.	122	1327	18.95	104	1	3	111	35.87	5-31	6.27
Ansari, Z.S.	42	819	34.12	66*		4	38	31.97	4-42	5.65
Archer, J.C.	3	46	23.00	35	–	–	7	19.42	5-42	4.66
Arshad, U.	14	56	10.66	23	–	–	9	52.33	3-50	6.23
Ashar Zaidi	89	2540	34.79	141	4	11	67	29.91	4-39	4.29
Ashraf, M.A.	23	3	1.50	3*	–	–	25	36.80	3-38	5.93
Azeem Rafiq	26	174	15.81	34*	–	–	25	34.68	5-30	5.59
Azharullah	57	84	6.46	9	–	–	84	28.10	5-38	5.60
Bailey, G.J.	240	7195	36.15	156	9	45	1	40.00	1-19	4.52
Bailey, T.E.	7	12	–	5*	–		10	29.00	3-31	5.28
Bairstow, J.M.	80	1973	32.34	123	2	11	–	–	–	58/7
Ball, A.J.	26	163	13.58	28	–	–	22	35.50	3-36	5.68
Ball, J.T.	53	122	11.09	27	–	–	62	30.06	4-25	5.56
Ballance, G.S.	88	3336	47.65	139	6	20	–	–	–	–
Bancroft, C.T.	28	782	31.28	176	1	4	–	–		–
Barker, K.H.D.	49	440	17.60	56		1	53	30.92	4-33	5.73
Barnard, E.G.	15	168	18.66	51	–	1	21	31.33	3-45	5.72
Batty, G.J.	247	2279	15.50	83*	–	5	232	31.68	5-35	4.60
Beer, W.A.T.	50	334	15.90	45*	–	–	44	40.45	3-27	5.15
Bell, I.R.	302	10494	40.51	158	11	76	33	34.48	5-41	5.29
Bell-Drummond, D.J.	35	1245	40.16	171*	1	10	0	–	–	7.50
Berg, G.K.	70	1114	24.75	75	–	5	51	35.96	4-24	5.49
Billings, S.W.	64	2084	45.30	175	5	13	–	–	–	54/7
Blake, A.J.	61	1037	28.80	89	–	7	3	24.66	2-13	5.28
Bopara, R.S.	298	8936	39.89	201*	14	53	220	28.08	5-63	5.28
Borthwick, S.G.	79	1024	21.78	87	–	7	63	38.49	5-38	5.98
Bragg, W.D.	41	1070	30.57	88	–	8	1	54.00	1-11	7.36
Bresnan, T.T.	255	2677	20.43	95*	–	7	290	33.53	5-48	5.19
Briggs, D.R.	74	252	13.26	25	–	–	77	35.72	4-32	5.10

L-O	M	Runs	Avge	HS	100	50	Wkts	Avge	Best	Econ
Broad, S.C.J.	140	578	11.79	45*	–	–	206	29.71	5-23	5.26
Brooks, J.A.	36	49	4.90	10	–	–	37	34.48	3-30	4.83
Brown, B.C.	54	720	23.22	62	–	4	–	–	–	52/10
Brown, K.R.	68	2016	38.03	129	2	11	0	–	–	17.00
Browne, N.L.J.	17	511	36.50	99	–	3	–	–	–	–
Buck, N.L.	42	91	8.27	21	–	–	51	35.01	4-39	6.15
Burke, J.E.	10	94	11.75	26*	–	–	17	20.58	5-28	5.88
Burnham, J.T.A.	5	69	17.25	26	–	–	–	–	–	–
Burns, R.J.	32	1062	37.92	95	–	9	–	–	–	–
Buttler, J.C.	145	4183	45.96	129	6	26	–	–	–	146/15
Callis, E.	1	10	10.00	10	–	–	–	–	–	–
Carberry, M.A.	168	4650	32.97	150*	6	34	11	27.00	3-37	5.53
Carlson, K.S.	1	17	17.00	17	–	–	–	–	–	–
Carver, K.	9	47	–	35*	–	–	7	23.28	3- 5	4.65
Chanderpaul, S.	408	13031	42.03	150	12	96	56	24.78	4-22	4.95
Chappell, Z.J.	2	32	32.00	31	–	–	1	53.00	1-28	4.89
Chapple, G.	284	2062	17.77	81*	–	9	320	28.55	6-18	4.50
Chopra, V.	91	3506	42.75	115	7	24	0	–	–	6.00
Christian, D.T.	110	2734	34.60	117	2	14	102	32.50	6-48	5.46
Clark, G.	10	170	17.00	42	–	–	–	–	–	–
Clark, J.	32	416	23.11	72	–	1	19	43.00	2-27	6.05
Clarke, J.M.	17	431	33.15	131*	1	2	–	–	–	–
Clarke, R.	213	3762	24.91	98*	–	19	129	38.13	5-26	5.38
Claydon, M.E.	92	228	7.35	19	–	–	118	30.98	4-39	5.53
Coad, B.O.	7	3	–	2*	–	–	3	94.00	1-34	6.50
Cobb, J.J.	77	2576	38.44	137	6	15	31	45.58	3-34	5.86
Cockbain, I.A.	52	1036	28.00	98*	–	7	–	–	–	–
Coles, M.T.	61	414	15.33	100	1	1	104	21.65	6-32	5.77
Collingwood, P.D.	417	10997	34.15	132	10	62	264	33.33	6-31	4.81
Compton, N.R.D.	114	3045	36.25	131	6	19	1	53.00	1- 0	5.21
Cook, A.N.	150	5204	37.71	137	9	31	0	–	–	3.33
Cook, S.C.	148	5087	38.83	127*	9	37	5	45.20	1- 2	6.02
Cooke, C.B.	64	1849	36.98	137*	2	11	–	–	–	26/2
Cork, G.T.G.	3	8	8.00	8	–	–	5	19.60	2-17	7.35
Cosgrove, M.J.	137	4043	31.58	121	4	31	18	63.38	2-21	6.41
Cosker, D.A.	252	827	10.88	50*	–	1	260	32.83	5-54	4.83
Cotton, B.D.	20	61	30.50	18*	–	–	26	30.00	4-43	5.42
Coughlin, P.	13	33	6.60	17	–	–	4	98.50	1-34	5.25
Cowdrey, F.K.	25	555	27.75	75	–	4	14	41.07	3-32	5.32
Cox, O.B.	48	460	16.42	39	–	–	–	–	–	42/6
Crane, M.S.	13	30	10.00	16*	–	–	18	35.05	4-30	6.26
Critchley, M.J.J.	14	99	14.14	43	–	–	12	52.00	4-48	6.56
Croft, S.J.	136	3449	34.49	107	1	28	59	38.93	4-24	5.40
Crook, S.P.	80	1073	20.63	100	1	5	81	33.30	5-36	5.73
Cross, M.H.	43	718	20.51	88	–	4	–	–	–	54/7
Curran, S.M.	20	295	26.81	57	–	1	22	35.18	4-32	5.32
Curran, T.K.	34	261	15.35	44	–	–	51	26.88	5-34	5.52
Davey, J.H.	64	1111	24.68	91	–	5	77	26.20	6-28	5.53
Davies, A.L.	16	380	38.00	73*	–	3	–	–	–	16/3
Davies, R.C.	6	76	25.33	46	–	–	–	–	–	8/1
Davies, S.M.	170	5459	37.64	127*	9	34	–	–	–	131/41
Davis, C.A.L.	5	60	20.00	54	–	1	1	69.00	1-25	6.57
Davis, W.S.	1	–	–	–	–	–	–	–	–	–
Dawson, L.A.	126	2720	32.38	113*	2	14	101	35.84	6-47	4.91

L-O	M	Runs	Avge	HS	100	50	Wkts	Avge	Best	Econ
de Lange, M.	49	258	11.72	29	–	–	92	23.52	5-64	5.43
Delport, C.S.	88	2223	30.04	169*	2	12	33	37.60	4-42	5.85
Denly, J.L.	128	3892	35.06	115	6	20	18	19.05	3-19	4.74
Dent, C.D.J.	49	1221	30.52	151*	3	2	12	34.33	4-43	5.64
Dernbach, J.W.	132	213	7.60	31	–	–	207	26.96	6-35	5.93
Dexter, N.J.	100	1949	30.45	135*	2	8	42	51.04	4-22	5.61
Dickson, S.R.	6	151	30.20	99	–	1	–	–	–	–
Dixon, M.W.	11	17	5.66	12	–	–	7	67.14	3-40	5.73
D'Oliveira, B.L.	36	293	16.27	42	–	–	24	45.33	3-35	5.29
Donald, A.H.T.	12	158	17.55	53	–	1	–	–	–	–
Duckett, B.M.	33	1370	54.80	220*	3	7	–	–	–	24/3
Dunn, M.P.	1	–	–	–	–	–	2	16.00	2-32	5.33
Eckersley, E.J.H.	30	680	26.15	108	1	3	–	–	–	18/1
Edwards, F.H.	78	131	10.07	21*	–	–	92	31.17	6-22	5.07
Elgar, D.	132	4189	39.51	117	4	30	49	48.81	3-43	5.40
Ervine, S.M.	236	5486	30.64	167*	7	26	204	34.29	5-50	5.61
Evans, L.J.	37	719	28.76	70*	–	2	0	–	–	8.83
Fell, T.C.	26	950	43.18	116*	1	9	–	–	–	–
Finch, A.J.	142	4965	37.61	154	11	28	7	39.28	2-44	5.32
Finch, H.Z.	11	376	47.00	92*	–	3	0	–	–	9.00
Finn, S.T.	120	264	9.42	42*	–	–	171	28.16	5-33	5.07
Fletcher, L.J.	54	221	13.81	40*	–	–	51	40.29	4-44	5.60
Foakes, B.T.	28	651	27.12	90	–	5	–	–	–	26/3
Footitt, M.H.A.	36	28	4.66	11*	–	–	47	30.51	5-28	6.23
Foster, J.S.	219	3322	28.39	83*	–	16	–	–	–	240/65
Franklin, J.E.C.	276	5413	32.60	133*	4	31	223	34.12	5-42	4.92
Fuller, J.K.	45	506	24.09	45	–	–	68	26.75	6-35	5.76
Garton, G.H.S.	8	6	3.00	4	–	–	15	26.33	4-43	6.26
Gibson, R.	5	19	6.33	9	–	–	5	31.60	1-17	5.44
Gidman, W.R.S.	51	639	24.57	76	–	2	48	30.33	4-36	4.83
Gleeson, R.J.	8	7	3.50	4*	–	–	13	22.46	5-47	5.29
Godleman, B.A.	44	1228	33.18	109*	1	6	–	–	–	–
Gregory, L.	45	557	19.89	105*	1	2	65	24.84	4-23	6.03
Grieshaber, P.J.	1	20	20.00	20	–	–	–	–	–	2/0
Griffiths, G.T.	5	7		5*	–	–	4	45.00	3-41	4.77
Groenewald, T.D.	92	670	19.70	57	–	2	102	31.54	4-22	5.19
Gubbins, N.R.T.	17	629	37.00	141	1	3	–	–	–	–
Gurney, H.F.	73	44	4.88	13*	–	–	90	32.77	5-24	5.63
Haggett, C.J.	10	57	8.14	36	–	–	8	46.87	2-54	6.69
Hain, S.R.	11	541	54.10	107	2	3	–	–	–	–
Hales, A.D.	129	4561	37.38	171	13	22	0	–	–	15.00
Handscomb, P.S.P.	44	982	31.67	72	–	5	–	–	–	35/2
Hannon-Dalby, O.J.	30	50	16.66	21*	–	–	44	29.75	5-27	5.85
Harinath, A.	7	108	21.60	52	–	1	0	–	–	5.33
Harmer, S.R.	49	640	19.39	43*	–	–	49	38.28	4-42	4.95
Harris, J.A.R.	56	295	11.34	32	–	–	75	28.98	4-38	5.67
Hartley, C.F.	4	24	8.00	15	–	–	6	28.16	2-23	4.97
Hastings, J.W.	98	1054	20.26	69*	–	1	157	26.10	6-45	4.83
Helm, T.G.	6	14	–	10*	–	–	6	26.16	3-27	4.48
Hemmings, R.P.	1	25	–	25*	–	–	0	–	–	7.00
Herring, C.L.	1	6	6.00	6	–	–	–	–	–	2/0
Higgins, R.F.	10	147	18.37	39	–	–	1	97.00	1-53	6.46
Hildreth, J.C.	186	4711	33.65	151	6	19	6	30.83	2-26	7.40
Hill, L.J.	22	395	20.78	86	–	2	–	–	–	8/1

L-O	M	Runs	Avge	HS	100	50	Wkts	Avge	Best	Econ
Hodd, A.J.	71	916	22.34	91	–	2	–	–	–	69/16
Hogan, M.G.	57	141	17.62	27	–	–	93	26.19	5-44	4.99
Horton, P.J.	107	2584	30.40	111*	2	13	1	7.00	1- 7	3.50
Hose, A.J.	12	263	23.90	77	–	1	–	–	–	–
Hosein, H.R.	3	42	42.00	40	–	–	–	–	–	1/1
Howell, B.A.C.	63	1461	35.63	122	1	8	46	35.15	3-37	4.98
Hughes, A.L.	40	408	19.42	59*	–	1	29	41.93	3-31	5.24
Hunn, M.D.	5	6	–	5*	–	–	5	38.20	2-31	5.78
Hutton, B.A.	9	66	22.00	33*	–	–	9	48.66	3-72	6.34
Imran Tahir	173	424	11.45	41*	–	–	265	23.30	7-45	4.62
Ingram, C.A.	157	6273	47.16	130	14	41	19	29.84	3-38	5.15
Jarvis, K.M.	50	131	8.18	33*	–	–	59	35.55	4-31	5.56
Javid, A.	36	540	30.00	43	–	–	22	44.18	4-42	5.71
Jennings, K.K.	29	678	37.66	71*	–	6	3	122.66	1- 9	5.93
Jones, R.A.	13	49	12.25	26	–	–	5	110.80	1-25	7.33
Jordan, C.J.	72	560	14.73	55	–	1	109	28.84	5-28	5.71
Joyce, E.C.	292	9535	38.76	160*	16	55	6	51.50	2-10	7.02
Junaid Khan	109	275	9.16	32	–	–	154	29.35	5-45	5.18
Keogh, R.I.	28	644	28.00	134	1	5	1	487.00	1-49	5.66
Kerrigan, S.C.	33	28	3.11	10	–	–	23	52.47	3-21	5.28
Kervezee, A.N.	104	2632	29.90	121*	2	13	0	–	–	8.38
Klein, D.	18	40	6.66	17	–	–	28	23.00	5-35	4.54
Kleinveldt, R.K.	141	1505	20.90	128	1	3	161	30.93	4-22	4.71
Klinger, M.	158	6509	48.93	166*	15	41	–	–	–	–
Kohler-Cadmore, T.	23	527	23.95	119	1	1	–	–	–	–
Latham, T.W.M.	88	2419	34.07	130	3	12	–	–	–	62/3
Lawrence, D.W.	8	93	13.28	35	–	–	6	42.50	3-35	5.54
Leach, J.	22	388	32.33	63	–	1	24	37.79	4-30	5.70
Leach, M.J.	15	21	7.00	18	–	–	18	35.22	3-52	4.83
Leaning, J.A.	32	786	35.72	131*	2	4	7	20.14	5-22	5.42
Leask, M.A.	33	317	13.20	50	–	1	12	67.50	2-23	6.42
Lees, A.Z.	41	1095	30.41	102	1	8	–	–	–	–
Levi, R.E.	106	3374	35.89	166	6	18	–	–	–	–
Liddle, C.J.	63	119	6.61	18	–	–	79	29.22	5-18	5.86
Lilley, A.M.	11	20	6.66	10	–	–	15	21.40	4-30	5.17
Livingstone, L.S.	13	355	39.44	98	–	3	3	44.00	3-51	6.28
Lloyd, D.L.	22	342	22.80	65	–	2	9	40.88	4-10	5.64
Lumb, M.J.	210	6312	32.87	184	7	43	0	–	–	14.00
Lyth, A.	97	2827	34.06	136	3	13	3	72.33	1- 6	6.38
McCarthy, B.J.	7	19	4.75	10*	–	–	18	20.00	4-59	6.06
McCullum, B.B.	308	7368	30.95	170	9	37	–	–	–	305/17
Macdonell, C.M.	1	19	19.00	19	–	–	–	–	–	–
McKay, C.J.	119	561	11.93	57	–	1	172	27.88	5-28	4.70
McLaren, R.	190	2879	30.30	88	–	13	243	27.39	5-38	5.10
McManus, L.D.	8	90	18.00	35	–	–	–	–	–	6/3
Machan, M.W.	58	1810	35.49	126*	2	9	12	51.75	3-31	5.82
Madsen, W.L.	80	2390	40.50	138	3	15	9	17.00	3-27	4.50
Magoffin, S.J.	53	228	20.72	24*	–	–	66	31.57	4-58	4.72
Mahmood, S.	9	6	–	6*	–	–	8	45.12	3-55	6.11
Malan, D.J.	129	4356	40.71	185*	8	21	33	30.93	4-25	5.70
Meaker, S.C.	59	87	5.43	21*	–	–	65	34.76	4-47	6.23
Mellor, A.J.	2	–	–	–	–	–	–	–	–	–
Mendis, B.M.A.J.	174	2918	23.72	99*	–	13	109	29.88	5-12	4.68
Meschede, C.A.J.	44	370	15.41	45	–	–	47	29.59	4- 5	5.48

L-O	*M*	*Runs*	*Avge*	*HS*	*100*	*50*	*Wkts*	*Avge*	*Best*	*Econ*
Miles, C.N.	30	76	7.60	16	–	–	37	34.10	4-29	6.10
Mills, T.S.	23	7	1.75	3*	–	–	22	35.77	3-23	5.97
Milnes, T.P.	4	22	11.00	16	–	–	3	80.66	2-73	8.34
Mitchell, D.K.H.	112	2787	33.98	107	2	17	62	36.11	4-19	5.56
Moores, T.J.	4	22	11.00	10	–	–	–	–	–	2/1
Morgan, A.O.	2	29	29.00	29	–	–	2	33.50	2-49	5.58
Morgan, E.J.G.	287	8370	37.03	161	15	48	0	–	–	7.00
Morris, C.A.J.	17	43	14.33	16*	–	–	18	38.55	3-46	5.79
Mullaney, S.J.	87	1207	25.68	89*	–	6	78	31.01	4-29	5.07
Murphy, D.	40	271	22.58	31*	–	–	–	–	–	26/12
Murphy, J.R.	1	6	6.00	6	–	–	0	–	–	6.40
Murtagh, T.J.	168	720	11.07	35*	–	–	216	29.93	4-14	5.15
Mustard, P.	198	5304	30.83	143	7	33	–	–	–	205/47
Myburgh, J.G.	107	2611	29.01	112	1	16	25	60.96	2-22	5.05
Nash, C.D.	108	2944	30.35	124*	2	18	43	32.53	4-40	5.50
Newton, R.I.	32	760	27.14	88*	–	3	–	–	–	–
Noema-Barnett, K.	66	1061	23.06	67	–	5	41	41.51	3-42	4.93
Northeast, S.A.	71	1951	32.51	132	2	11	–	–	–	–
Norwell, L.C.	11	28	9.33	10	–	–	18	27.05	6-52	5.79
O'Brien, K.J.	168	3987	30.66	142	3	19	132	33.70	4-13	5.38
O'Brien, N.J.	204	4895	30.78	121	3	31	–	–	–	160/36
Onions, G.	87	130	5.90	19	–	–	99	31.04	4-45	5.09
Overton, C.	34	290	13.18	49	–	–	33	39.66	3-37	5.20
Overton, J.	20	130	21.66	40*	–	–	28	28.78	4-42	6.30
Palladino, A.P.	54	267	10.68	31	–	–	54	35.42	5-49	5.33
Parry, S.D.	81	288	13.09	31	–	–	103	27.78	5-17	4.95
Patel, J.S.	188	651	9.57	50	–	1	229	30.34	5-43	4.61
Patel, R.H.	11	0	0.00	0*	–	–	11	47.63	3-71	5.75
Patel, S.R.	216	5260	33.50	129*	4	29	198	31.60	6-13	5.33
Patterson, S.A.	78	202	15.53	25*	–	–	96	28.50	6-32	4.99
Payne, D.A.	58	102	11.33	23	–	–	101	22.76	7-29	5.65
Pettini, M.L.	180	4517	29.33	144	8	29	–	–	–	–
Philander, V.D.	123	1327	23.28	79*	–	5	125	32.16	4-12	4.68
Pietersen, K.P.	253	8112	40.76	147	15	46	41	51.75	3-14	5.32
Pillans, M.W.	12	79	19.75	20*	–	–	16	21.50	3-14	4.91
Plunkett, L.E.	156	1421	21.20	72	–	3	193	31.02	4-15	5.42
Podmore, H.W.	6	1	–	1*	–	–	4	68.00	2-46	6.91
Pope, O.J.D.	1	20	20.00	20	–	–	–	–	–	–
Porter, J.A.	8	5	–	5*	–	–	5	60.20	3-39	5.42
Porterfield, W.T.S.	210	6389	31.94	112*	9	37	–	–	–	–
Poynter, S.W.	17	285	25.90	109	1	–	–	–	–	–
Poynton, T.	31	173	11.53	40	–	–	–	–	–	18/5
Poysden, J.E.	16	22	7.33	10*	–	–	17	35.82	3-33	5.66
Prasanna, S.	129	1524	15.71	95	–	7	175	24.69	6-23	4.44
Pringle, R.D.	28	379	18.95	125	1	–	9	71.66	2-39	6.05
Procter, L.A.	29	450	32.14	97	–	4	12	44.50	3-29	6.28
Quinn, M.R.	26	117	16.71	36	–	–	36	34.88	4-71	5.84
Raine, B.A.	14	164	16.40	43	–	–	13	50.46	3-62	6.30
Rampaul, R.	153	599	12.47	86*	–	1	218	25.16	5-49	4.77
Rankin, W.B.	105	122	7.17	18*	–	–	129	28.35	4-34	4.97
Rashid, A.U.	133	1280	20.64	71	–	2	162	32.06	5-33	5.33
Rayner, O.P.	56	486	24.30	61	–	1	47	37.93	4-35	5.21
Read, C.M.W.	321	5416	29.43	135	2	22	–	–	–	307/73
Reece, L.M.	22	409	25.56	59	–	2	6	69.66	4-35	6.20

L-O	M	Runs	Avge	HS	100	50	Wkts	Avge	Best	Econ
Rhodes, G.H.	5	5	5.00	5*	–	–	5	32.40	2-34	5.78
Rhodes, W.M.H.	19	242	17.28	46	–	–	10	34.40	2-22	5.44
Richardson, M.J.	9	273	45.50	64	–	3	–	–	–	–
Riley, A.E.N.	23	11	5.50	5*	–	–	19	40.57	2-32	5.58
Robinson, O.E.	8	75	25.00	30	–	–	4	64.75	2-61	6.16
Robson, A.J.	15	333	22.20	90	–	2	–	–	–	–
Robson, S.D.	15	395	30.38	88	–	2	–	–	–	–
Roderick, G.H.	37	727	29.08	104	1	5	–	–	–	37/4
Roland-Jones, T.S.	57	355	16.13	31*	–	–	90	24.83	4-40	5.25
Root, J.E.	108	3835	42.14	125	9	21	25	49.64	2-10	5.49
Rossington, A.M.	28	713	33.95	97	–	5	–	–	–	16/4
Rossouw, R.R.	125	4357	37.23	137	8	27	1	44.00	1-17	5.86
Rouse, A.P.	3	15	5.00	7	–	–	–	–	–	3/2
Roy, J.J.	110	3543	36.15	162	10	16	0	–	–	12.00
Rudolph, J.A.	254	9980	48.68	169*	17	68	13	36.38	4-40	5.74
Rushworth, C.	58	108	8.30	38*	–	–	93	23.65	5-31	5.39
Sakande, A.	1	–	–	–	–	–	1	46.00	1-46	5.87
Salt, P.D.	6	149	24.83	81	–	1	–	–	–	–
Salter, A.G.	23	201	22.33	51	–	1	11	61.09	2-41	4.99
Sanderson, B.W.	14	18	18.00	12*	–	–	9	42.11	2-17	6.76
Sandhu, G.S.	4	3	1.50	3	–	–	8	21.25	3-28	5.63
Sangakkara, K.C.	519	18908	43.07	169	37	117	–	–	–	515/123
Santner, M.J.	38	921	34.11	86	–	4	45	29.40	4-38	4.90
Sayer, R.J.	10	71	10.14	26	–	–	7	64.00	1-31	5.53
Selman, N.J.	1	6	6.00	6	–	–	–	–	–	–
Shahzad, A.	84	511	13.10	59*	–	1	118	28.63	5-51	5.41
Shantry, J.D.	67	176	10.35	31	–	–	86	29.40	4-29	5.60
Sharjeel Khan	78	2979	38.68	194	7	15	2	52.50	1- 6	6.36
Shreck, C.E.	60	47	5.22	9*	–	–	73	31.01	5-19	5.16
Sibley, D.P.	8	85	21.25	37	–	–	1	53.00	1-20	6.62
Sidebottom, R.J.	186	552	11.04	32	–	–	198	30.97	6-40	4.47
Simpson, J.A.	65	881	23.81	82	–	4	–	–	–	47/9
Slater, B.T.	14	561	51.00	148*	3	1	–	–	–	–
Smith, G.P.	48	1130	26.90	135*	2	5	–	–	–	–
Smith, R.A.J.	13	33	6.60	10	–	–	12	38.33	4-76	6.86
Smith, T.F.	1	6	6.00	6	–	–	–	–	–	–
Smith, T.M.J.	61	388	22.82	65	–	1	50	39.46	4-26	5.51
Smith, W.R.	110	2516	29.25	120*	2	20	12	35.58	2-19	5.78
Sodhi, I.S.	46	205	11.38	35	–	–	57	31.80	4-10	4.83
Sowter, N.A.	2	0	0.00	0	–	–	0	–	–	7.75
Stevens, D.I.	287	7069	30.08	133	6	45	126	31.88	5-32	4.86
Stevenson, R.A.	3	0	0.00	0	–	–	2	71.00	1-28	7.10
Stirling, P.R.	138	4161	32.76	177	10	16	55	39.89	4-11	4.90
Stokes, B.A.	109	2690	31.64	164	4	12	94	28.06	5-61	5.62
Stone, O.P.	17	90	22.50	24*	–	–	11	50.54	3-34	5.26
Stoneman, M.D.	60	2119	39.98	136*	5	12	1	8.00	1- 8	12.00
Sykes, J.S.	20	46	6.57	15	–	–	15	44.40	3-34	5.63
Tait, S.W.	101	109	6.05	22*	–	–	182	23.84	8-43	5.14
Tavaré, W.A.	8	221	27.62	77	–	2	–	–	–	–
Taylor, B.J.	2	2	–	2*	–	–	4	18.25	2-23	4.86
Taylor, B.R.M.	264	7784	33.55	145*	13	44	20	30.20	5-28	5.98
Taylor, J.M.R.	29	388	24.25	53	–	1	27	28.03	4-38	5.03
Taylor, L.R.P.L.	222	7685	43.41	132*	19	48	3	81.00	1-13	4.58
Taylor, M.D.	10	32	32.00	16	–	–	10	41.10	2-33	5.80

L-O	M	Runs	Avge	HS	100	50	Wkts	Avge	Best	Econ
Taylor, T.A.I.	4	–	–	–	–	–	5	34.80	3-48	5.93
ten Doeschate, R.N.	194	5219	45.78	180	9	28	162	30.32	5-50	5.76
Terry, S.P.	11	177	22.12	63	–	2	–	–	–	–
Thakor, S.J.	39	537	19.88	83*	–	4	38	29.18	4-49	5.98
Thomas, I.A.A.	6	1	1.00	1	–	–	6	42.33	3-31	6.35
Thomason, A.D.	1	0	–	0*	–	–	0	–	–	5.75
Topley, R.J.W.	40	41	6.83	19	–	–	69	23.72	4-26	5.45
Tredwell, J.C.	255	1807	17.37	88	–	4	267	31.91	6-27	4.70
Trego, P.D.	171	3884	31.32	147	7	19	164	32.25	5-40	5.58
Trescothick, M.E.	372	12229	37.28	184	28	63	57	28.84	4-50	4.90
Trott, I.J.L.	258	9473	48.08	137	20	64	54	29.29	4-55	5.63
Tye, A.J.	14	126	18.00	28*	–	–	29	22.72	5-46	5.59
van Buuren, G.L.	58	1248	30.43	119*	1	5	47	28.59	5-35	4.60
van der Gugten, T.	31	181	16.45	36	–	–	45	26.55	5-24	5.19
van der Merwe, R.E.	142	1902	24.38	93	–	7	192	25.75	5-26	4.75
van Meekeren, P.A.	21	52	7.42	15*	–	–	15	36.66	3-42	5.18
van Zyl, S.	103	3037	37.03	114*	5	16	18	38.33	4-24	5.22
Velani, K.S.	10	79	13.16	27	–	–	1	14.00	1-14	7.00
Vilas, D.J.	114	2812	32.69	120	5	12	–	–	–	127/21
Viljoen, G.C.	71	459	15.82	54*	–	2	103	30.23	6-19	5.88
Vince, J.M.	96	3064	36.04	131	5	15	1	84.00	1-18	6.00
Voges, A.C.	178	5582	42.93	112*	5	42	37	42.62	3-20	5.11
Wagg, G.G.	124	1643	18.88	62*	–	3	138	34.07	4-35	5.93
Wagner, N.	84	467	12.28	42	–	–	133	26.65	5-34	5.27
Wainman, J.C.	1	33	33.00	33	–	–	3	17.00	3-51	6.37
Waite, M.J.	3	61	30.50	38	–	–	3	39.00	3-48	5.85
Wakely, A.G.	67	1664	29.71	102	1	11	5	26.20	2-14	5.77
Waller, M.T.C.	50	97	16.16	25*	–	–	38	38.86	3-39	5.63
Weatherley, J.J.	2	29	14.50	27	–	–	0	–	–	5.66
Wells, L.W.P.	17	110	9.16	23	–	–	6	29.66	3-19	5.11
Wells, T.J.	16	230	23.00	32*	–	–	5	53.20	2-45	8.06
Wessels, M.H.	151	3876	30.51	146	4	20	1	48.00	1-0	5.87
Westley, T.	62	1778	33.54	111*	3	14	20	40.90	4-60	4.96
Westwood, I.J.	60	941	22.95	65	–	3	3	75.66	1-28	5.15
Wheal, B.T.J.	7	21	21.00	13	–	–	12	22.41	4-38	5.01
Wheater, A.J.A.	66	1252	27.21	135	2	5	–	–	–	74/8
White, G.G.	63	335	15.95	40	–	–	72	25.79	6-37	5.14
White, W.A.	69	783	19.09	46*	–	–	66	37.21	6-29	6.47
Whiteley, R.A.	52	844	22.21	77	–	5	8	52.87	1-17	6.66
Wiese, D.	111	2643	34.77	108	1	15	94	37.45	5-25	5.32
Willey, D.J.	91	1232	22.40	167	2	3	93	32.46	5-62	5.59
Wilson, G.C.	162	3105	23.34	113	1	20	–	–	–	123/26
Woakes, C.R.	126	1206	20.44	95*	–	1	141	35.14	6-45	5.54
Wood, C.P.	62	311	12.44	41	–	–	88	25.63	5-22	5.49
Wood, L.	2	56	56.00	52	–	1	3	25.33	2-44	5.84
Wood, M.A.	33	62	10.33	15*	–	–	43	29.34	3-23	5.25
Wood, T.A.	1	44	44.00	44	–	–	–	–	–	–
Wright, C.J.C.	97	219	10.42	42	–	–	99	35.28	4-20	5.56
Wright, L.J.	191	4243	31.19	143*	9	14	111	38.11	4-12	5.34
Zaib, S.A.	3	27	13.50	16	–	–	0	–	–	10.00

FIRST-CLASS CRICKET RECORDS

To the end of the 2016 season

TEAM RECORDS

HIGHEST INNINGS TOTALS

1107	Victoria v New South Wales	Melbourne	1926-27
1059	Victoria v Tasmania	Melbourne	1922-23
952-6d	Sri Lanka v India	Colombo	1997-98
951-7d	Sind v Baluchistan	Karachi	1973-74
944-6d	Hyderabad v Andhra	Secunderabad	1993-94
918	New South Wales v South Australia	Sydney	1900-01
912-8d	Holkar v Mysore	Indore	1945-46
910-6d	Railways v Dera Ismail Khan	Lahore	1964-65
903-7d	England v Australia	The Oval	1938
900-6d	Queensland v Victoria	Brisbane	2005-06
887	Yorkshire v Warwickshire	Birmingham	1896
863	Lancashire v Surrey	The Oval	1990
860-6d	Tamil Nadu v Goa	Panjim	1988-89
850-7d	Somerset v Middlesex	Taunton	2007

Excluding penalty runs in India, there have been 34 innings totals of 800 runs or more in first-class cricket. Tamil Nadu's total of 860-6d was boosted to 912 by 52 penalty runs.

HIGHEST SECOND INNINGS TOTAL

770	New South Wales v South Australia	Adelaide	1920-21

HIGHEST FOURTH INNINGS TOTAL

654-5	England (set 696 to win) v South Africa	Durban	1938-39

HIGHEST MATCH AGGREGATE

2376-37	Maharashtra v Bombay	Poona	1948-49

RECORD MARGIN OF VICTORY

Innings and 851 runs: Railways v Dera Ismail Khan	Lahore	1964-65

MOST RUNS IN A DAY

721	Australians v Essex	Southend	1948

MOST HUNDREDS IN AN INNINGS

6	Holkar v Mysore	Indore	1945-46

LOWEST INNINGS TOTALS

12	†Oxford University v MCC and Ground	Oxford	1877
12	Northamptonshire v Gloucestershire	Gloucester	1907
13	Auckland v Canterbury	Auckland	1877-78
13	Nottinghamshire v Yorkshire	Nottingham	1901
14	Surrey v Essex	Chelmsford	1983
15	MCC v Surrey	Lord's	1839
15	†Victoria v MCC	Melbourne	1903-04
15	†Northamptonshire v Yorkshire	Northampton	1908
15	Hampshire v Warwickshire	Birmingham	1922

† *Batted one man short*

There have been 28 instances of a team being dismissed for under 20.

LOWEST MATCH AGGREGATE BY ONE TEAM

34 (16 and 18)	Border v Natal	East London	1959-60

LOWEST COMPLETED MATCH AGGREGATE BY BOTH TEAMS

105	MCC v Australians	Lord's	1878

FEWEST RUNS IN AN UNINTERRUPTED DAY'S PLAY

95	Australia (80) v Pakistan (15-2)	Karachi	1956-57

TIED MATCHES

Before 1949 a match was considered to be tied if the scores were level after the fourth innings, even if the side batting last had wickets in hand when play ended. Law 22 was amended in 1948 and since then a match has been tied only when the scores are level after the fourth innings has been completed. There have been 56 tied first-class matches, five of which would not have qualified under the current law. The most recent are:

Warwickshire (446-7d & forfeit) v Essex (66-0d & 380)	Birmingham	2003
Worcestershire (262 & 247) v Zimbabweans (334 & 175)	Worcester	2003
Habib Bank (245 & 178) v WAPDA (233 & 190)	Lahore	2011-12
Border (210 & 210) v Boland (219 & 201)	East London	2012-13

BATTING RECORDS

35,000 RUNS IN A CAREER

	Career	*I*	*NO*	*HS*	*Runs*	*Avge*	*100*
J.B.Hobbs	1905-34	1315	106	316*	**61237**	50.65	197
F.E.Woolley	1906-38	1532	85	305*	**58969**	40.75	145
E.H.Hendren	1907-38	1300	166	301*	**57611**	50.80	170
C.P.Mead	1905-36	1340	185	280*	**55061**	47.67	153
W.G.Grace	1865-1908	1493	105	344	**54896**	39.55	126
W.R.Hammond	1920-51	1005	104	336*	**50551**	56.10	167
H.Sutcliffe	1919-45	1088	123	313	**50138**	51.95	149
G.Boycott	1962-86	1014	162	261*	**48426**	56.83	151
T.W.Graveney	1948-71/72	1223	159	258	**47793**	44.91	122
G.A.Gooch	1973-2000	990	75	333	**44846**	49.01	128
T.W.Hayward	1893-1914	1138	96	315*	**43551**	41.79	104
D.L.Amiss	1960-87	1139	126	262*	**43423**	42.86	102
M.C.Cowdrey	1950-76	1130	134	307	**42719**	42.89	107
A.Sandham	1911-37/38	1000	79	325	**41284**	44.82	107
G.A.Hick	1983/84-2008	871	84	405*	**41112**	52.23	136
L.Hutton	1934-60	814	91	364	**40140**	55.51	129
M.J.K.Smith	1951-75	1091	139	204	**39832**	41.84	69
W.Rhodes	1898-1930	1528	237	267*	**39802**	30.83	58
J.H.Edrich	1956-78	979	104	310*	**39790**	45.47	103
R.E.S.Wyatt	1923-57	1141	157	232	**39405**	40.04	85
D.C.S.Compton	1936-64	839	88	300	**38942**	51.85	123
G.E.Tyldesley	1909-36	961	106	256*	**38874**	45.46	102
J.T.Tyldesley	1895-1923	994	62	295*	**37897**	40.60	86
K.W.R.Fletcher	1962-88	1167	170	228*	**37665**	37.77	63
C.G.Greenidge	1970-92	889	75	273*	**37354**	45.88	92
J.W.Hearne	1909-36	1025	116	285*	**37252**	40.98	96
L.E.G.Ames	1926-51	951	95	295	**37248**	43.51	102
D.Kenyon	1946-67	1159	59	259	**37002**	33.63	74
W.J.Edrich	1934-58	964	92	267*	**36965**	42.39	86
J.M.Parks	1949-76	1227	172	205*	**36673**	34.76	51
M.W.Gatting	1975-98	861	123	258	**36549**	49.52	94
D.Denton	1894-1920	1163	70	221	**36479**	33.37	69
G.H.Hirst	1891-1929	1215	151	341	**36323**	34.13	60
I.V.A.Richards	1971/72-93	796	63	322	**36212**	49.40	114
A.Jones	1957-83	1168	72	204*	**36049**	32.89	56
W.G.Quaife	1894-1928	1203	185	255*	**36012**	35.37	72
R.E.Marshall	1945/46-72	1053	59	228*	**35725**	35.94	68
M.R.Ramprakash	1987-2012	764	93	301*	**35659**	53.14	114
G.Gunn	1902-32	1061	82	220	**35208**	35.96	62

HIGHEST INDIVIDUAL INNINGS

501*	B.C.Lara	Warwickshire v Durham	Birmingham	1994
499	Hanif Mohammed	Karachi v Bahawalpur	Karachi	1958-59
452*	D.G.Bradman	New South Wales v Queensland	Sydney	1929-30
443*	B.B.Nimbalkar	Maharashtra v Kathiawar	Poona	1948-49
437	W.H.Ponsford	Victoria v Queensland	Melbourne	1927-28
429	W.H.Ponsford	Victoria v Tasmania	Melbourne	1922-23
428	Aftab Baloch	Sind v Baluchistan	Karachi	1973-74
424	A.C.MacLaren	Lancashire v Somerset	Taunton	1895
405*	G.A.Hick	Worcestershire v Somerset	Taunton	1988
400*	B.C.Lara	West Indies v England	St John's	2003-04
394	Naved Latif	Sargodha v Gujranwala	Gujranwala	2000-01
390	S.C.Cook	Lions v Warriors	East London	2009-10
385	B.Sutcliffe	Otago v Canterbury	Christchurch	1952-53
383	C.W.Gregory	New South Wales v Queensland	Brisbane	1906-07
380	M.L.Hayden	Australia v Zimbabwe	Perth	2003-04
377	S.V.Manjrekar	Bombay v Hyderabad	Bombay	1990-91
375	B.C.Lara	West Indies v England	St John's	1993-94
374	D.P.M.D.Jayawardena	Sri Lanka v South Africa	Colombo	2006
369	D.G.Bradman	South Australia v Tasmania	Adelaide	1935-36
366	N.H.Fairbrother	Lancashire v Surrey	The Oval	1990
366	M.V.Sridhar	Hyderabad v Andhra	Secunderabad	1993-94
365*	C.Hill	South Australia v NSW	Adelaide	1900-01
365*	G.St A.Sobers	West Indies v Pakistan	Kingston	1957-58
364	L.Hutton	England v Australia	The Oval	1938
359*	V.M.Merchant	Bombay v Maharashtra	Bombay	1943-44
359	R.B.Simpson	New South Wales v Queensland	Brisbane	1963-64
357*	R.Abel	Surrey v Somerset	The Oval	1899
357	D.G.Bradman	South Australia v Victoria	Melbourne	1935-36
356	B.A.Richards	South Australia v W Australia	Perth	1970-71
355*	G.R.Marsh	W Australia v S Australia	Perth	1989-90
355*	K.P.Pietersen	Surrey v Leicestershire	The Oval	2015
355	B.Sutcliffe	Otago v Auckland	Dunedin	1949-50
353	V.V.S.Laxman	Hyderabad v Karnataka	Bangalore	1999-00
352	W.H.Ponsford	Victoria v New South Wales	Melbourne	1926-27
352	C.A.Pujara	Saurashtra v Karnataka	Rajkot	2012-13
351	K.D.K.Vithanage	Tamil Union v SL Air	Katunayake	2014-15
350	Rashid Israr	Habib Bank v National Bank	Lahore	1976-77

There have been 205 triple hundreds in first-class cricket, W.V.Raman (313) and Arjan Kripal Singh (302*) for Tamil Nadu v Goa at Panjim in 1988-89 providing the only instance of two batsmen scoring 300 in the same innings.

MOST HUNDREDS IN SUCCESSIVE INNINGS

6	C.B.Fry	Sussex and Rest of England	1901
6	D.G.Bradman	South Australia and D.G.Bradman's XI	1938-39
6	M.J.Procter	Rhodesia	1970-71

TWO DOUBLE HUNDREDS IN A MATCH

244	202*	A.E.Fagg	Kent v Essex	Colchester	1938

TRIPLE HUNDRED AND HUNDRED IN A MATCH

333	123	G.A.Gooch	England v India	Lord's	1990
319	105	K.C.Sangakkara	Sri Lanka v Bangladesh	Chittagong	2013-14

DOUBLE HUNDRED AND HUNDRED IN A MATCH MOST TIMES

4	Zaheer Abbas	Gloucestershire	1976-81

TWO HUNDREDS IN A MATCH MOST TIMES

8	Zaheer Abbas	Gloucestershire and PIA	1976-82
8	R.T.Ponting	Tasmania, Australia and Australians	1992-2006
7	W.R.Hammond	Gloucestershire, England and MCC	1927-45
7	M.R.Ramprakash	Middlesex, Surrey	1990-2010

MOST HUNDREDS IN A SEASON

18	D.C.S.Compton	1947	16	J.B.Hobbs	1925

100 HUNDREDS IN A CAREER

	Total		*100th Hundred*	
	Hundreds	*Inns*	*Season*	*Inns*
J.B.Hobbs	197	1315	1923	821
E.H.Hendren	170	1300	1928-29	740
W.R.Hammond	167	1005	1935	679
C.P.Mead	153	1340	1927	892
G.Boycott	151	1014	1977	645
H.Sutcliffe	149	1088	1932	700
F.E.Woolley	145	1532	1929	1031
G.A.Hick	136	871	1998	574
L.Hutton	129	814	1951	619
G.A.Gooch	128	990	1992-93	820
W.G.Grace	126	1493	1895	1113
D.C.S.Compton	123	839	1952	552
T.W.Graveney	122	1223	1964	940
D.G.Bradman	117	338	1947-48	295
I.V.A.Richards	114	796	1988-89	658
M.R.Ramprakash	114	764	2008	676
Zaheer Abbas	108	768	1982-83	658
A.Sandham	107	1000	1935	871
M.C.Cowdrey	107	1130	1973	1035
T.W.Hayward	104	1138	1913	1076
G.M.Turner	103	792	1982	779
J.H.Edrich	103	979	1977	945
L.E.G.Ames	102	951	1950	915
G.E.Tyldesley	102	961	1934	919
D.L.Amiss	102	1139	1986	1081

MOST 400s: 2 – B.C.Lara, W.H.Ponsford

MOST 300s or more: 6 – D.G.Bradman, 4 – W.R.Hammond, W.H.Ponsford

MOST 200s or more: 37 – D.G.Bradman; 36 – W.R.Hammond; 22 – E.H.Hendren

MOST RUNS IN A MONTH

1294 (avge 92.42)	L.Hutton	Yorkshire	June 1949

MOST RUNS IN A SEASON

Runs			*I*	*NO*	*HS*	*Avge*	*100*	*Season*
3816	D.C.S.Compton	Middlesex	50	8	246	90.85	18	1947
3539	W.J.Edrich	Middlesex	52	8	267*	80.43	12	1947
3518	T.W.Hayward	Surrey	61	8	219	66.37	13	1906

The feat of scoring 3000 runs in a season has been achieved 28 times, the most recent instance being by W.E.Alley (3019) in 1961. The highest aggregate in a season since 1969 is 2755 by S.J.Cook in 1991.

1000 RUNS IN A SEASON MOST TIMES

28 W.G.Grace (Gloucestershire), F.E.Woolley (Kent)

HIGHEST BATTING AVERAGE IN A SEASON

(Qualification: 12 innings)

Avge			*I*	*NO*	*HS*	*Runs*	*100*	*Season*
115.66	D.G.Bradman	Australians	26	5	278	2429	13	1938
104.66	D.R.Martyn	Australians	14	5	176*	942	5	2001
103.54	M.R.Ramprakash	Surrey	24	2	301*	2278	8	2006
102.53	G.Boycott	Yorkshire	20	5	175*	1538	6	1979
102.00	W.A.Johnston	Australians	17	16	28*	102	–	1953
101.70	G.A.Gooch	Essex	30	3	333	2746	12	1990
101.30	M.R.Ramprakash	Surrey	25	5	266*	2026	10	2007
100.12	G.Boycott	Yorkshire	30	5	233	2503	13	1971

FASTEST HUNDRED AGAINST AUTHENTIC BOWLING

35 min	P.G.H.Fender	Surrey v Northamptonshire	Northampton	1920

FASTEST DOUBLE HUNDRED

113 min	R.J.Shastri	Bombay v Baroda	Bombay	1984-85

FASTEST TRIPLE HUNDRED

181 min	D.C.S.Compton	MCC v NE Transvaal	Benoni	1948-49

MOST SIXES IN AN INNINGS

23	C.Munro	Central Districts v Auckland	Napier	2014-15

MOST SIXES IN A MATCH

23	C.Munro	Central Districts v Auckland	Napier	2014-15

MOST SIXES IN A SEASON

80	I.T.Botham	Somerset and England		1985

MOST FOURS IN AN INNINGS

72	B.C.Lara	Warwickshire v Durham	Birmingham	1994

MOST RUNS OFF ONE OVER

36	G.St A.Sobers	Nottinghamshire v Glamorgan	Swansea	1968
36	R.J.Shastri	Bombay v Baroda	Bombay	1984-85

Both batsmen hit for six all six balls of overs bowled by M.A.Nash and Tilak Raj respectively.

MOST RUNS IN A DAY

390*	B.C.Lara	Warwickshire v Durham	Birmingham	1994

There have been 19 instances of a batsman scoring 300 or more runs in a day.

LONGEST INNINGS

1015 min	R.Nayyar (271)	Himachal Pradesh v Jammu & Kashmir	Chamba	1999-00

HIGHEST PARTNERSHIPS FOR EACH WICKET

First Wicket

561	Waheed Mirza/Mansoor Akhtar	Karachi W v Quetta	Karachi	1976-77
555	P.Holmes/H.Sutcliffe	Yorkshire v Essex	Leyton	1932
554	J.T.Brown/J.Tunnicliffe	Yorkshire v Derbys	Chesterfield	1898

Second Wicket

580	Rafatullah Mohmand/Aamer Sajjad	WAPDA v SSGC	Sheikhupura	2009-10
576	S.T.Jayasuriya/R.S.Mahanama	Sri Lanka v India	Colombo	1997-98
480	D.Elgar/R.R.Rossouw	Eagles v Titans	Centurion	2009-10
475	Zahir Alam/L.S.Rajput	Assam v Tripura	Gauhati	1991-92
465*	J.A.Jameson/R.B.Kanhai	Warwickshire v Glos	Birmingham	1974

Third Wicket				
624	K.C.Sangakkara/D.P.M.D.Jayawardena	Sri Lanka v South Africa	Colombo	2006
539	S.D.Jogiyani/R.A.Jadeja	Saurashtra v Gujarat	Surat	2012-13
523	M.A.Carberry/N.D.McKenzie	Hampshire v Yorkshire	Southampton	2011
501	A.N.Petersen/A.G.Prince	Lancashire v Glamorgan	Colwyn Bay	2015
Fourth Wicket				
577	V.S.Hazare/Gul Mahomed	Baroda v Holkar	Baroda	1946-47
574*	C.L.Walcott/F.M.M.Worrell	Barbados v Trinidad	Port-of-Spain	1945-46
502*	F.M.M.Worrell/J.D.C.Goddard	Barbados v Trinidad	Bridgetown	1943-44
470	A.I.Kallicharran/G.W.Humpage	Warwickshire v Lancs	Southport	1982
Fifth Wicket				
520*	C.A.Pujara/R.A.Jadeja	Saurashtra v Orissa	Rajkot	2008-09
494	Marshall Ayub/Mehrab Hossain Jr	Central Zone v East Zone	Bogra	2012-13
479	Misbah-ul-Haq/Usman Arshad	Sui NGP v Lahore Shalimar	Lahore	2009-10
464*	M.E.Waugh/S.R.Waugh	NSW v W Australia	Perth	1990-91
423	Mosaddek Hossain/Al-Amin	Barisal v Rangpur	Savar	2014-15
420	Mohd. Ashraful/Marshall Ayub	Dhaka v Chittagong	Chittagong	2006-07
410*	A.S.Chopra/S.Badrinath	India A v South Africa A	Delhi	2007-08
405	S.G.Barnes/D.G.Bradman	Australia v England	Sydney	1946-47
401	M.B.Loye/D.Ripley	Northants v Glamorgan	Northampton	1998
Sixth Wicket				
487*	G.A.Headley/C.C.Passailaigue	Jamaica v Tennyson's	Kingston	1931-32
428	W.W.Armstrong/M.A.Noble	Australians v Sussex	Hove	1902
417	W.P.Saha/L.R.Shukla	Bengal v Assam	Kolkata	2010-11
411	R.M.Poore/E.G.Wynyard	Hampshire v Somerset	Taunton	1899
Seventh Wicket				
460	Bhupinder Singh jr/P.Dharmani	Punjab v Delhi	Delhi	1994-95
371	M.R.Marsh/S.M.Whiteman	Australia A v India A	Brisbane	2014
366*	J.M.Bairstow/T.T.Bresnan	Yorkshire v Durham	Chester-le-Street	2015
Eighth Wicket				
433	V.T.Trumper/A.Sims	Australians v C'bury	Christchurch	1913-14
392	A.Mishra/J.Yadav	Haryana v Karnataka	Hubli	2012-13
332	I.J.L.Trott/S.C.J.Broad	England v Pakistan	Lord's	2010
Ninth Wicket				
283	J.Chapman/A.Warren	Derbys v Warwicks	Blackwell	1910
268	J.B.Commins/N.Boje	SA 'A' v Mashonaland	Harare	1994-95
261	W.L.Madsen/T.Poynton	Derbys v Northants	Northampton	2012
251	J.W.H.T.Douglas/S.N.Hare	Essex v Derbyshire	Leyton	1921
Tenth Wicket				
307	A.F.Kippax/J.E.H.Hooker	NSW v Victoria	Melbourne	1928-29
249	C.T.Sarwate/S.N.Banerjee	Indians v Surrey	The Oval	1946
239	Aqil Arshad/Ali Raza	Lahore Whites v Hyderabad	Lahore	2004-05

BOWLING RECORDS – 2000 WICKETS IN A CAREER

	Career	*Runs*	*Wkts*	*Avge*	*100w*
W.Rhodes	1898-1930	69993	**4187**	16.71	23
A.P.Freeman	1914-36	69577	**3776**	18.42	17
C.W.L.Parker	1903-35	63817	**3278**	19.46	16
J.T.Hearne	1888-1923	54352	**3061**	17.75	15
T.W.J.Goddard	1922-52	59116	**2979**	19.84	16
W.G.Grace	1865-1908	51545	**2876**	17.92	10
A.S.Kennedy	1907-36	61034	**2874**	21.23	15
D.Shackleton	1948-69	53303	**2857**	18.65	20
G.A.R.Lock	1946-70/71	54709	**2844**	19.23	14
F.J.Titmus	1949-82	63313	**2830**	22.37	16
M.W.Tate	1912-37	50571	**2784**	18.16	13+1
G.H.Hirst	1891-1929	51282	**2739**	18.72	15

	Career	Runs	Wkts	Avge	100w
C.Blythe	1899-1914	42136	**2506**	16.81	14
D.L.Underwood	1963-87	49993	**2465**	20.28	10
W.E.Astill	1906-39	57783	**2431**	23.76	9
J.C.White	1909-37	43759	**2356**	18.57	14
W.E.Hollies	1932-57	48656	**2323**	20.94	14
F.S.Trueman	1949-69	42154	**2304**	18.29	12
J.B.Statham	1950-68	36999	**2260**	16.37	13
R.T.D.Perks	1930-55	53771	**2233**	24.07	16
J.Briggs	1879-1900	35431	**2221**	15.95	12
D.J.Shepherd	1950-72	47302	**2218**	21.32	12
E.G.Dennett	1903-26	42571	**2147**	19.82	12
T.Richardson	1892-1905	38794	**2104**	18.43	10
T.E.Bailey	1945-67	48170	**2082**	23.13	9
R.Illingworth	1951-83	42023	**2072**	20.28	10
F.E.Woolley	1906-38	41066	**2068**	19.85	8
N.Gifford	1960-88	48731	**2068**	23.56	4
G.Geary	1912-38	41339	**2063**	20.03	11
D.V.P.Wright	1932-57	49307	**2056**	23.98	10
J.A.Newman	1906-30	51111	**2032**	25.15	9
A.Shaw	1864-97	24580	**2026**+1	12.12	9
S.Haigh	1895-1913	32091	**2012**	15.94	11

ALL TEN WICKETS IN AN INNINGS

This feat has been achieved 81 times in first-class matches (excluding 12-a-side fixtures).
Three Times: A.P.Freeman (1929, 1930, 1931)
Twice: V.E.Walker (1859, 1865); H.Verity (1931, 1932); J.C.Laker (1956)

Instances since 1945:

W.E.Hollies	Warwickshire v Notts	Birmingham	1946
J.M.Sims	East v West	Kingston on Thames	1948
J.K.R.Graveney	Gloucestershire v Derbyshire	Chesterfield	1949
T.E.Bailey	Essex v Lancashire	Clacton	1949
R.Berry	Lancashire v Worcestershire	Blackpool	1953
S.P.Gupte	President's XI v Combined XI	Bombay	1954-55
J.C.Laker	Surrey v Australians	The Oval	1956
K.Smales	Nottinghamshire v Glos	Stroud	1956
G.A.R.Lock	Surrey v Kent	Blackheath	1956
J.C.Laker	England v Australia	Manchester	1956
P.M.Chatterjee	Bengal v Assam	Jorhat	1956-57
J.D.Bannister	Warwicks v Combined Services	Birmingham (M & B)	1959
A.J.G.Pearson	Cambridge U v Leicestershire	Loughborough	1961
N.I.Thomson	Sussex v Warwickshire	Worthing	1964
P.J.Allan	Queensland v Victoria	Melbourne	1965-66
I.J.Brayshaw	Western Australia v Victoria	Perth	1967-68
Shahid Mahmood	Karachi Whites v Khairpur	Karachi	1969-70
E.E.Hemmings	International XI v W Indians	Kingston	1982-83
P.Sunderam	Rajasthan v Vidarbha	Jodhpur	1985-86
S.T.Jefferies	Western Province v OFS	Cape Town	1987-88
Imran Adil	Bahawalpur v Faisalabad	Faisalabad	1989-90
G.P.Wickremasinghe	Sinhalese v Kalutara	Colombo	1991-92
R.L.Johnson	Middlesex v Derbyshire	Derby	1994
Naeem Akhtar	Rawalpindi B v Peshawar	Peshawar	1995-96
A.Kumble	India v Pakistan	Delhi	1998-99
D.S.Mohanty	East Zone v South Zone	Agartala	2000-01
O.D.Gibson	Durham v Hampshire	Chester-le-Street	2007
M.W.Olivier	Warriors v Eagles	Bloemfontein	2007-08
Zulfiqar Babar	Multan v Islamabad	Multan	2009-10

MOST WICKETS IN A MATCH

19	J.C.Laker	England v Australia	Manchester	1956

MOST WICKETS IN A SEASON

Wkts		*Season*	*Matches*	*Overs*	*Mdns*	*Runs*	*Avge*
304	A.P.Freeman	1928	37	1976.1	423	5489	18.05
298	A.P.Freeman	1933	33	2039	651	4549	15.26

The feat of taking 250 wickets in a season has been achieved on 12 occasions, the last instance being by A.P.Freeman in 1933. 200 or more wickets in a season have been taken on 59 occasions, the last being by G.A.R.Lock (212 wickets, average 12.02) in 1957.

The highest aggregates of wickets taken in a season since the reduction of County Championship matches in 1969 are as follows:

Wkts		*Season*	*Matches*	*Overs*	*Mdns*	*Runs*	*Avge*
134	M.D.Marshall	1982	22	822	225	2108	15.73
131	L.R.Gibbs	1971	23	1024.1	295	2475	18.89
125	F.D.Stephenson	1988	22	819.1	196	2289	18.31
121	R.D.Jackman	1980	23	746.2	220	1864	15.40

Since 1969 there have been 50 instances of bowlers taking 100 wickets in a season.

MOST HAT-TRICKS IN A CAREER

7	D.V.P.Wright
6	T.W.J.Goddard, C.W.L.Parker
5	S.Haigh, V.W.C.Jupp, A.E.G.Rhodes, F.A.Tarrant

ALL-ROUND RECORDS
THE 'DOUBLE'

3000 runs and 100 wickets: J.H.Parks (1937)
2000 runs and 200 wickets: G.H.Hirst (1906)
2000 runs and 100 wickets: F.E.Woolley (4), J.W.Hearne (3), W.G.Grace (2), G.H.Hirst (2), W.Rhodes (2), T.E.Bailey, D.E.Davies, G.L.Jessop, V.W.C.Jupp, J.Langridge, F.A.Tarrant, C.L.Townsend, L.F.Townsend
1000 runs and 200 wickets: M.W.Tate (3), A.E.Trott (2), A.S.Kennedy
Most Doubles: 16 – W.Rhodes; 14 – G.H.Hirst; 10 – V.W.C.Jupp
Double in Debut Season: D.B.Close (1949) – aged 18, the youngest to achieve this feat.

The feat of scoring 1000 runs and taking 100 wickets in a season has been achieved on 305 occasions, R.J.Hadlee (1984) and F.D.Stephenson (1988) being the only players to complete the 'double' since the reduction of County Championship matches in 1969.

WICKET-KEEPING RECORDS
1000 DISMISSALS IN A CAREER

	Career	*Dismissals*	*Ct*	*St*
R.W.Taylor	1960-88	**1649**	1473	176
J.T.Murray	1952-75	**1527**	1270	257
H.Strudwick	1902-27	**1497**	1242	255
A.P.E.Knott	1964-85	**1344**	1211	133
R.C.Russell	1981-2004	**1320**	1192	128
F.H.Huish	1895-1914	**1310**	933	377
B.Taylor	1949-73	**1294**	1083	211
S.J.Rhodes	1981-2004	**1263**	1139	124
D.Hunter	1889-1909	**1253**	906	347
H.R.Butt	1890-1912	**1228**	953	275
J.H.Board	1891-1914/15	**1207**	852	355
H.Elliott	1920-47	**1206**	904	302
J.M.Parks	1949-76	**1181**	1088	93
R.Booth	1951-70	**1126**	948	178
L.E.G.Ames	1926-51	**1121**	703	418

	Career	Dismissals	Ct	St
D.L.Bairstow	1970-90	**1099**	961	138
G.Duckworth	1923-47	**1096**	753	343
H.W.Stephenson	1948-64	**1082**	748	334
J.G.Binks	1955-75	**1071**	895	176
T.G.Evans	1939-69	**1066**	816	250
C.M.W.Read	1997-2016	**1047**	995	52
A.Long	1960-80	**1046**	922	124
G.O.Dawkes	1937-61	**1043**	895	148
R.W.Tolchard	1965-83	**1037**	912	125
W.L.Cornford	1921-47	**1017**	675	342

MOST DISMISSALS IN AN INNINGS

9	(8ct, 1st)	Tahir Rashid	Habib Bank v PACO	Gujranwala	1992-93
9	(7ct, 2st)	W.R.James	Matabeleland v Mashonaland CD	Bulawayo	1995-96
8	(8ct)	A.T.W.Grout	Queensland v W Australia	Brisbane	1959-60
8	(8ct)	D.E.East	Essex v Somerset	Taunton	1985
8	(8ct)	S.A.Marsh	Kent v Middlesex	Lord's	1991
8	(6ct, 2st)	T.J.Zoehrer	Australians v Surrey	The Oval	1993
8	(7ct, 1st)	D.S.Berry	Victoria v South Australia	Melbourne	1996-97
8	(7ct, 1st)	Y.S.S.Mendis	Bloomfield v Kurunegala Youth	Colombo	2000-01
8	(7ct, 1st)	S.Nath	Assam v Tripura (*on debut*)	Gauhati	2001-02
8	(8ct)	J.N.Batty	Surrey v Kent	The Oval	2004
8	(8ct)	Golam Mabud	Sylhet v Dhaka	Dhaka	2005-06
8	(8ct)	D.C.de Boorder	Otago v Wellington	Wellington	2009-10
8	(8ct)	R.S.Second	Free State v North West	Bloemfontein	2011-12
8	(8ct)	T.L.Tsolekile	South Africa A v Sri Lanka A	Durban	2012

MOST DISMISSALS IN A MATCH

14	(11ct, 3st)	I.Khaleel	Hyderabad v Assam	Guwahati	2011-12
13	(11ct, 2st)	W.R.James	Matabeleland v Mashonaland CD	Bulawayo	1995-96
12	(8ct, 4st)	E.Pooley	Surrey v Sussex	The Oval	1868
12	(9ct, 3st)	D.Tallon	Queensland v NSW	Sydney	1938-39
12	(9ct, 3st)	H.B.Taber	NSW v South Australia	Adelaide	1968-69
12	(12ct)	P.D.McGlashan	Northern Districts v Central Districts	Whangarei	2009-10
12	(11ct, 1st)	T.L.Tsolekile	Lions v Dolphins	Johannesburg	2010-11
12	(12ct)	Kashif Mahmood	Lahore Shalimar v Abbottabad	Abbottabad	2010-11
12	(12ct)	R.S.Second	Free State v North West	Bloemfontein	2011-12

MOST DISMISSALS IN A SEASON

128	(79ct, 49st)	L.E.G.Ames	1929

FIELDING RECORDS

750 CATCHES IN A CAREER

1018	F.E.Woolley	1906-38	784	J.G.Langridge	1928-55
887	W.G.Grace	1865-1908	764	W.Rhodes	1898-1930
830	G.A.R.Lock	1946-70/71	758	C.A.Milton	1948-74
819	W.R.Hammond	1920-51	754	E.H.Hendren	1907-38
813	D.B.Close	1949-86			

MOST CATCHES IN AN INNINGS

7	M.J.Stewart	Surrey v Northamptonshire	Northampton	1957
7	A.S.Brown	Gloucestershire v Nottinghamshire	Nottingham	1966
7	R.Clarke	Warwickshire v Lancashire	Liverpool	2011

MOST CATCHES IN A MATCH

10	W.R.Hammond	Gloucestershire v Surrey	Cheltenham	1928
9	R.Clarke	Warwickshire v Lancashire	Liverpool	2011

MOST CATCHES IN A SEASON

78	W.R.Hammond	1928	77	M.J.Stewart	1957

ENGLAND LIMITED-OVERS INTERNATIONALS 2016

SOUTH AFRICA v ENGLAND

LIMITED-OVERS INTERNATIONALS

Mangaung Oval, Bloemfontein, 3 February. Toss: England. **ENGLAND** won by 39 runs (D/L method). England 399-9 (50; J.C.Buttler 105, A.D.Hales 57, B.A.Stokes 57, J.E.Root 52, C.H.Morris 3-74). South Africa 250-5 (33.3; Q.de Kock 138*, F.du Plessis, M.M.Ali 3-43). Award: Q.de Kock.

St George's Park, Port Elizabeth, 6 February. Toss: South Africa. **ENGLAND** won by five wickets. South Africa 262-7 (50; A.B.de Villiers 73, R.J.W.Topley 4-50). England 263-5 (46.2; A.D.Hales 99, K.J.Abbott 3-58). Award: A.D.Hales.

SuperSport Park, Centurion, 9 February. Toss: England. **SOUTH AFRICA** won by seven wickets. England 318-8 (50; J.E.Root 125, A.D.Hales 65, B.A.Stokes 53). South Africa 319-3 (46.2; Q.de Kock 135, H.M.Amla 127). Award: Q.de Kock.

New Wanderers Stadium, Johannesburg, 12 February. Toss: South Africa. **SOUTH AFRICA** won by one wicket. England 262 (47.5; J.E.Root 109, A.D.Hales 50, K.Rabada 4-45, Imran Tahir 3-46). South Africa 266-9 (47.2; C.H.Morris 62). Award: C.H.Morris.

Newlands, Cape Town, 14 February. Toss: South Africa. **SOUTH AFRICA** won by five wickets. England 236 (45; A.D.Hales 112, K.Rabada 3-34, D.Wiese 3-50, Imran Tahir 3-53). South Africa 237-5 (44; A.B.de Villiers 101*, H.M.Amla 59, R.J.W.Topley 3-41). Award: A.B.de Villiers. Series award; A.D.Hales.

TWENTY20 INTERNATIONALS

Newlands, Cape Town, 19 February. Toss: South Africa. **SOUTH AFRICA** won by three wickets. England 134-8 (20; Imran Tahir 4-21). South Africa 135-7 (20; C.J.Jordan 3-23). Award: Imran Tahir.

New Wanderers Stadium, Johannesburg, 21 February. Toss: South Africa. **SOUTH AFRICA** won by nine wickets. England 171 (19.4; J.C.Buttler 54, K.J.Abbott 3-26). South Africa 172-1 (14.4; A.B.de Villiers 71, H.M.Amla 69). Award: A.B.de Villiers. Series award: Imran Tahir.

ICC WORLD T20

Wankhede Stadium, Mumbai, 16 March. Toss: West Indies. **WEST INDIES** won by six wickets. England 182-6 (20). West Indies 183-4 (18.1; C.H.Gayle 100*). Award: C.H.Gayle.

Wankhede Stadium, Mumbai, 18 March. Toss: England. **ENGLAND** won by two wickets. South Africa 229-4 (20; H.M.Amla 58, J.P.Duminy 54*, Q.de Kock 52). England 230-8 (19.4; J.E.Root 83, K.J.Abbott 3-41). Award: J.E.Root.

Feroz Shah Kotla, Delhi, 23 March. Toss: England. **ENGLAND** won by 15 runs. England 142-7 (20). Afghanistan 127-9 (20). Award: M.M.Ali (41*).

Feroz Shah Kotla, Delhi, 26 March. Toss: Sri Lanka. **ENGLAND** won by 10 runs. England 171-4 (20; J.C.Buttler 66*). Sri Lanka 161-8 (20; A.D.Mathews 73*, C.J.Jordan 4-28). Award: J.C.Buttler.

Semi-final

Feroz Shah Kotla, Delhi, 30 March. Toss: England. **ENGLAND** won by seven wickets. New Zealand 153-8 (20; B.A.Stokes 3-26). England 159-3 (17.1; J.J.Roy 78). Award: J.J.Roy.

Final

Eden Gardens, Kolkata, 3 April. Toss: West Indies. **WEST INDIES** won by four wickets. England 155-9 (20; J.E.Root 54, C.R.Brathwaite 3-23, D.J.Bravo 3-37). West Indies 161-6 (19.4; M.N.Samuels 85*, D.J.Willey 3-20). Award: M.N.Samuels.
C.R.Brathwaite hit the first four balls of the final over for six to win the match.

ENGLAND v SRI LANKA

ROYAL LONDON LIMITED-OVERS INTERNATIONAL SERIES

Trent Bridge, Nottingham, 21 June. Toss: England. **MATCH TIED**. Sri Lanka 286-9 (50; A.D.Mathews 73, S.Prasanna 59). England 286-8 (50; C.R.Woakes 95*, J..Buttler 93). Award: C.R.Woakes.
C.R.Woakes made the highest score in all LOIs by a player batting at No. 8 or lower.

Edgbaston, Birmingham, 24 June. Toss: Sri Lanka. **ENGLAND** won by ten wickets. Sri Lanka 254-7 (50; W.U.Tharanga 53*, L.D.Chandimal 52). England 256-0 (A.D.Hales 133*, J.J.Roy 112*). Award: J.J.Roy.
The highest score for a ten-wicket win in all LOIs; England's highest LOI partnership for any wicket.

County Ground, Bristol, 26 June. Toss: England. **NO RESULT**. Sri Lanka 248 (50; L.D.Chandimal 62, A.D.Mathews 56, B.K.G.Mendis 53, C.R.Woakes 3-34, L.E.Plunkett 3-46). England 16-1 (4).

The Oval, London, 29 June. Toss: England. **ENGLAND** won by six wickets. Sri Lanka 305-5 (50; B.K.G.Mendis 77, A.D.Mathews 67*, L.D.Chandimal 63, M.D.Gunathilaka 62). England 309-4 (40.1; J.J.Roy 162, J.E.Root 65). Award: J.J.Roy.

Sophia Gardens, Cardiff, 2 July. Toss: Sri Lanka. **ENGLAND** won by 122 runs. England 324-7 (50; J.E.Root 93, J.C.Buttler 70, J.M.Vince 51, M.D.Gunathilaka 3-48). Sri Lanka 202 (42.4; L.D.Chandimal 53, D.J.Willey 4-34, L.E.Plunkett 3-44). Award: J.C.Buttler. Series award: J.J.Roy.

NATWEST TWENTY20 INTERNATIONAL

The Rose Bowl, Southampton, 5 July. Toss: Sri Lanka. **ENGLAND** won by eight wickets. Sri Lanka 140 (20: L.A.Dawson 3-27, C.J.Jordan 3-29). England 144-2 (17.3; J.C.Buttler 73*). Award: J.C.Buttler. England debuts: L.A.Dawson, T.S.Mills.

ENGLAND v PAKISTAN

ROYAL LONDON LIMITED-OVERS INTERNATIONAL SERIES

The Rose Bowl, Southampton, 24 August. Toss: Pakistan. **ENGLAND** won by 44 runs (D/L method). Pakistan 260-6 (50; Azhar Ali 82, Sarfraz Ahmed 55). England 194-3 (34.3, target 151; J.J.Roy 65, J.E.Root 61). Award: J.J.Roy.

Lord's, London, 27 August. Toss: Pakistan. **ENGLAND** won by four wickets. Pakistan 251 (49.5; Sarfraz Ahmed 105, Imran Wasim 63*, C.R.Woakes 3-42, M.A.Wood 3-46). England 255-6 (47.3; J.E.Root 89, E.J.G.Morgan 68). Award: J.E.Root.

Trent Bridge, Nottingham, 30 August. Toss: England. **ENGLAND** won by 169 runs. England 444-3 (50; A.D.Hales 171, J.C.Buttler 90*, J.E.Root 85, E.J.G.Morgan 57*). Pakistan 275 (42.4; Sharjeel Khan 58, Mohammad Amir 58, C.R.Woakes 4-41). Award: A.D.Hales.

England's total was the highest in all LOIs; A.D.Hales made the highest score for England in all LOIs; J.C.Buttler took an England record 22 balls to score 50; Mohammad Amir's 58 was the first 50 in LOIs by any No. 11.

Headingley, Leeds, 1 September. Toss: Pakistan. **ENGLAND** won by four wickets. Pakistan 247-8 (50; Azhar Ali 80, Imad Wasim 57*, A.U.Rashid 3-47). England 252-6 (48; B.A.Stokes 69, J.M.Bairstow 61). Award: J.M.Bairstow.

Sophia Gardens, Cardiff, 4 September. Toss: Pakistan. **PAKISTAN** won by four wickets. England 302-9 (50; J.J.Roy 87, B.A.Stokes 75, Hasan Ali 4-60, Mohammad Amir 3-50). Pakistan 304-6 (48.2; Sarfraz Ahmed 90, Shoaib Malik 77). Award: Sarfraz Ahmed. England debut: L.A.Dawson.

NATWEST TWENTY20 INTERNATIONAL

Old Trafford, Manchester, 7 September. Toss: England. **PAKISTAN** won by nine wickets. England 135-7 (20; Wahab Riaz 3-18). Pakistan 139-1 (14.5; Khalid Latif 59*, Sharjeel Khan 59). Award: Wahab Riaz.

BANGLADESH v ENGLAND

LIMITED-OVERS INTERNATIONALS

Shere Bangla National Stadium, Mirpur, 7 October. Toss: England. **ENGLAND** won by 21 runs. England 309-8 (50; B.A.Stokes 101, J.C.Buttler 63, B.M.Duckett 60). Bangladesh 288 (47.5; Imrul Kayes 112, Shakib Al Hasan 79, J.T.Ball 5-51, A.U.Rashid 4-49). Award: J.T.Ball. England debuts: J.T.Ball, B.M.Duckett.

Shere Bangla National Stadium, Mirpur, 9 October. Toss: England. **BANGLADESH** won by 34 runs. Bangladesh 238-8 (50; Mahmudullah 75). England 204 (J.C.Buttler 57, Mashrafe Mortaza 4-29, Taskin Ahmed 3-47). Award: Mashrafe Mortaza.

Zahur Ahmed Chowdhury Stadium, Chittagong, 12 October. Toss: England. **ENGLAND** won by four wickets. Bangladesh 277-6 (50; Mushfiqur Rahim 67*, A.U.Rashid 4-43). England 278-6 (47.5; B.M.Duckett 63, S.W.Billings 62). Award: A.U.Rashid. Series award: B.A.Stokes.

ENGLAND RESULTS IN 2016

	P	*W*	*L*	*T*	*NR*
Limited Overs	18	11	5	1	1
Twenty20	10	5	5	–	–
Overall	28	16	10	1	1

600 RUNS IN LIMITED-OVERS INTERNATIONALS IN 2016

	M	*I*	*NO*	*HS*	*Runs*	*Avge*	*100*	*50*	*S/Rate*
J.E.Root	15	14	1	125	796	61.23	2	6	91.81
A.D.Hales	14	13	1	171	743	61.91	3	4	101.36
J.J.Roy	17	17	2	162	647	43.13	2	2	108.01

15 WICKETS IN LIMITED-OVERS INTERNATIONALS IN 2016

	Pl	*O*	*M*	*R*	*W*	*Avge*	*Best*	*4wI*	*Econ*
A.U.Rashid	17	158.2	–	822	29	28.34	4-43	2	5.19
C.R.Woakes	14	115.3	8	618	17	36.35	4-41	1	5.35
L.E.Plunkett	10	90	–	515	15	34.33	3-44	–	5.72

LIMITED-OVERS INTERNATIONALS CAREER RECORDS

These records, complete to 14 March 2017, include all players registered for county cricket for the 2017 season at the time of going to press, plus those who have appeared in LOI matches for ICC full member countries since 1 December 2015.

ENGLAND – BATTING AND FIELDING

	M	*I*	*NO*	*HS*	*Runs*	*Avge*	*100*	*50*	*Ct/St*
M.M.Ali	52	48	7	128	1061	25.87	2	4	18
T.R.Ambrose	5	5	1	6	10	2.50	–	–	3
J.M.Anderson	194	79	43	28	273	7.58	–	–	53
Z.S.Ansari	1	–	–	–	–	–	–	–	–
J.M.Bairstow	23	19	3	83*	514	32.12	–	3	16/2
J.T.Ball	6	1	–	28	28	28.00	–	–	1
G.S.Ballance	16	15	1	79	279	21.21	–	2	8
G.J.Batty	10	8	2	17	30	5.00	–	–	4
I.R.Bell	161	157	14	141	5416	37.87	4	35	54
S.W.Billings	9	9	–	62	239	29.87	–	2	6
R.S.Bopara	120	109	21	101*	2695	30.62	1	14	35
S.G.Borthwick	2	2	–	15	18	9.00	–	–	–
T.T.Bresnan	85	64	20	80	871	19.79	–	1	20
D.R.Briggs	1	–	–	–	–	–	–	–	–
S.C.J.Broad	121	68	25	45*	529	12.30	–	–	27
J.C.Buttler	87	75	12	129	2290	36.34	4	12	110/13
M.A.Carberry	6	6	–	63	114	19.00	–	1	2
G.Chapple	1	1	–	14	14	14.00	–	–	–
R.Clarke	20	13	–	39	144	11.07	–	–	11
P.D.Collingwood	197	181	37	120*	5092	35.36	5	26	108
A.N.Cook	92	92	4	137	3204	36.40	5	19	36
S.M.Davies	8	8	–	87	244	30.50	–	1	8
L.A.Dawson	1	1	–	10	10	10.00	–	–	–
J.L.Denly	9	9	–	67	268	29.77	–	2	5
J.W.Dernbach	24	8	1	5	19	2.71	–	–	5
B.M.Duckett	3	3	–	63	123	41.00	–	2	–
S.T.Finn	68	29	13	35	133	8.31	–	–	15
J.S.Foster	11	6	3	13	41	13.66	–	–	13/7
H.F.Gurney	10	6	4	6*	15	7.50	–	–	1
A.D.Hales	41	39	1	171	1455	38.28	5	6	12
C.J.Jordan	31	21	7	38*	169	12.07	–	–	19
E.C.Joyce †	17	17	–	107	471	27.70	1	3	6
M.J.Lumb	3	3	–	106	165	55.00	1	–	1
S.C.Meaker	2	2	–	1	2	1.00	–	–	–
E.J.G.Morgan †	153	142	22	124*	4574	38.11	9	26	59
P.Mustard	10	10	–	83	233	23.30	–	1	9/2
G.Onions	4	1	–	1	1	1.00	–	–	–
S.D.Parry	2	–	–	–	–	–	–	–	–
S.R.Patel	36	22	7	70*	482	32.13	–	1	7
K.P.Pietersen	136	125	16	130	4440	40.73	9	25	40
L.E.Plunkett	49	35	13	56	483	21.95	–	1	16
W.B.Rankin †	7	2	1	4	5	2.50	–	–	–
A.U.Rashid	41	19	6	69	336	25.84	–	1	15
C.M.W.Read	36	24	7	30*	300	17.64	–	–	41/2
J.E.Root	83	78	8	125	3344	47.77	9	20	37
J.J.Roy	38	37	2	162	1411	40.31	3	9	11
A.Shahzad	11	8	2	9	39	6.50	–	–	4
R.J.Sidebottom	25	18	8	24	133	13.30	–	–	6
B.A.Stokes	53	47	5	101	1244	29.61	1	9	25

ENGLAND – BATTING AND FIELDING (continued)

	M	*I*	*NO*	*HS*	*Runs*	*Avge*	*100*	*50*	*Ct/St*
R.J.W.Topley	10	5	4	6	7	7.00	–	–	2
J.C.Tredwell	45	25	11	30	163	11.64	–	–	14
M.E.Trescothick	123	122	6	137	4335	37.37	12	21	49
I.J.L.Trott	68	65	10	137	2819	51.25	4	22	14
J.M.Vince	5	4	–	51	104	26.00	–	1	4
D.J.Willey	25	14	7	13*	99	14.14	–	–	14
C.R.Woakes	61	47	15	95*	794	24.81	–	2	28
M.A.Wood	11	4	3	13	34	34.00	–	–	3
L.J.Wright	50	39	4	52	707	20.20	–	2	18

ENGLAND – BOWLING

	O	*M*	*R*	*W*	*Avge*	*Best*	*4wI*	*R/Over*
M.M.Ali	424.5	5	2137	44	48.56	3-32	–	5.03
J.M.Anderson	1597.2	125	7861	269	29.22	5-23	13	4.92
J.T.Ball	55.5	0	342	12	28.50	5-51	1	6.12
G.J.Batty	73.2	1	366	5	73.20	2-40	–	4.99
I.R.Bell	14.4	0	88	6	14.66	3- 9	–	6.00
R.S.Bopara	310	11	1523	40	38.07	4-38	1	4.91
S.G.Borthwick	9	0	72	0	–	–	–	8.00
T.T.Bresnan	703.3	35	3813	109	34.98	5-48	4	5.42
D.R.Briggs	10	0	39	2	19.50	2-39	–	3.90
S.C.J.Broad	1018.1	56	5364	178	30.13	5-23	10	5.26
M.A.Carberry	1	0	12	0	–	–	–	12.00
G.Chapple	4	0	14	0	–	–	–	3.50
R.Clarke	78.1	3	415	11	37.72	2-28	–	5.30
P.D.Collingwood	864.2	14	4294	111	38.68	6-31	4	4.96
L.A.Dawson	8	0	70	2	35.00	2-70	–	8.75
J.W.Dernbach	205.4	6	1308	31	42.19	4-45	1	6.35
S.T.Finn	584.4	37	2961	102	29.02	5-33	6	5.06
H.F.Gurney	75.5	4	432	11	39.27	4-55	1	5.69
C.J.Jordan	255.2	5	1521	43	35.37	5-29	1	5.95
S.C.Meaker	19	1	110	2	55.00	1-45	–	5.78
G.Onions	34	1	185	4	46.25	2-58	–	5.44
S.D.Parry	19	2	92	4	23.00	3-32	–	4.84
S.R.Patel	197.5	4	1091	24	45.45	5-41	1	5.51
K.P.Pietersen	66.4	0	370	7	52.85	2-22	–	5.55
L.E.Plunkett	401.2	12	2348	73	32.16	4-40	1	5.85
W.B.Rankin	53.1	3	241	10	24.10	4-46	1	4.53
A.U.Rashid	344.4	3	1945	55	35.36	4-43	4	5.64
J.E.Root	156	2	908	13	69.84	2-15	–	5.82
A.Shahzad	98	5	490	17	28.82	3-41	–	5.00
R.J.Sidebottom	212.5	12	1039	29	35.82	3-19	–	4.88
B.A.Stokes	286.2	5	1744	46	37.91	5-61	2	6.09
R.J.W.Topley	77.1	6	410	16	25.62	4-50	1	5.31
J.C.Tredwell	350.4	18	1666	60	27.76	4-41	3	4.75
M.E.Trescothick	38.4	0	219	4	54.75	2- 7	–	5.66
I.J.L.Trott	30.3	0	166	2	83.00	2-31	–	5.44
D.J.Willey	186.4	13	1048	32	32.75	4-34	1	5.61
C.R.Woakes	494	25	2771	85	32.60	6-45	9	5.60
M.A.Wood	99	2	578	12	48.16	3-46	–	5.83
L.J.Wright	173	2	884	15	58.93	2-34	–	5.10

† *E.C.Joyce has also made 46 appearances for Ireland; E.J.G.Morgan has also made 23 appearances for Ireland; and W.B.Rankin has also made 39 appearances for Ireland (see below).*

AUSTRALIA – BATTING AND FIELDING

	M	I	NO	HS	Runs	Avge	100	50	Ct/St
G.J.Bailey	90	85	10	156	3044	40.58	3	22	48
S.M.Boland	14	4	1	4	9	3.00	–	–	3
D.T.Christian	19	18	5	39	273	21.00	–	–	10
M.J.Cosgrove	3	3	–	74	112	37.33	–	1	–
N.M.Coulter-Nile	16	11	5	16	76	12.66	–	–	4
P.J.Cummins	28	13	6	36	113	16.14	–	–	6
J.P.Faulkner	67	50	21	116	988	34.06	1	4	20
A.J.Finch	79	75	1	148	2580	34.86	7	15	36
P.S.P.Handscomb	5	4	–	82	90	22.50	–	1	5
J.W.Hastings	28	21	11	51	271	27.10	–	1	5
J.R.Hazlewood	35	8	6	11*	20	10.00	–	–	9
T.M.Head	22	21	1	128	744	37.20	1	5	10
S.D.Heazlett	1	1	–	4	4	4.00	–	–	–
M.C.Henriques	8	8	1	12	46	6.57	–	–	2
U.T.Khawaja	18	17	2	98	469	31.26	–	4	3
C.A.Lynn	1	1	–	16	16	16.00	–	–	–
N.M.Lyon	13	6	4	30	46	23.00	–	–	2
C.J.McKay	59	31	10	30	190	9.04	–	–	7
M.R.Marsh	48	44	9	102*	1242	35.48	1	9	23
S.E.Marsh	53	52	2	151	1896	37.92	3	12	13
G.J.Maxwell	74	67	8	102	1957	33.16	1	15	42
J.M.Mennie	2	2	–	1	1	1.00	–	–	–
J.S.Paris	2	–	–	–	–	–	–	–	1
K.W.Richardson	12	4	2	19	30	15.00	–	–	1
S.P.D.Smith	95	81	10	164	3101	43.67	8	16	57
B.Stanlake	2	1	1	1*	1	–	–	–	–
M.A.Starc	65	31	15	52*	259	16.18	–	1	18
M.P.Stoinis	3	3	1	146*	192	96.00	1	–	1
C.P.Tremain	4	3	2	23*	23	23.00	–	–	1
A.C.Voges	31	28	9	112*	870	45.78	1	4	7
M.S.Wade	87	75	10	100*	1741	26.78	1	10	102/9
D.A.Warner	93	91	3	179	3946	44.84	13	16	42
D.J.Worrall	3	1	1	6*	6	–	–	–	1
A.Zampa	22	11	3	12	51	6.37	–	–	6

AUSTRALIA – BOWLING

	O	M	R	W	Avge	Best	4wI	R/Over
S.M.Boland	119.2	3	725	16	45.31	3-67	–	6.07
D.T.Christian	121.1	4	595	20	29.75	5-31	1	4.91
M.J.Cosgrove	5	0	13	1	13.00	1- 1	–	2.60
N.M.Coulter-Nile	136.2	5	734	27	27.18	4-48	1	5.38
P.J.Cummins	236	7	1303	51	25.54	4-41	3	5.52
J.P.Faulkner	519.2	11	2858	95	30.08	4-32	4	5.50
A.J.Finch	19.1	0	95	2	47.50	1- 2	–	4.95
J.W.Hastings	228.4	7	1187	40	29.67	6-45	2	4.97
J.R.Hazlewood	297.2	22	1385	55	25.18	5-31	3	4.65
T.M.Head	89.4	0	516	11	46.90	2-22	–	5.75
M.C.Henriques	48	1	245	6	40.83	3-32	–	5.10
N.M.Lyon	120	9	592	17	34.82	4-44	1	4.93
C.J.McKay	494.1	38	2364	97	24.37	5-28	6	4.78
M.R.Marsh	265.2	5	1483	41	36.17	5-33	2	5.58
G.J.Maxwell	310.4	7	1717	45	38.15	4-46	2	5.52
J.M.Mennie	20	2	131	3	43.66	3-49	–	6.55
J.S.Paris	16	0	93	1	93.00	1-40	–	5.81
K.W.Richardson	101	9	540	14	38.57	5-68	1	5.34
S.P.D.Smith	174.2	1	931	27	34.48	3-16	–	5.34

AUSTRALIA – BOWLING (continued)

	O	M	R	W	Avge	Best	4wI	R/Over
B.Stanlake	13	1	68	1	68.00	1-55	–	5.23
M.A.Starc	532.2	30	2566	129	19.89	6-28	12	4.82
M.P.Stoinis	18	0	88	3	29.33	3-49	–	4.88
C.P.Tremain	40	0	255	7	36.42	3-64	–	6.37
A.C.Voges	50.1	1	276	6	46.00	1- 3	–	5.50
D.A.Warner	1	0	8	0	–	–	–	8.00
D.J.Worrall	26.2	0	171	1	171.00	1-43	–	6.49
A.Zampa	101.2	2	991	34	29.14	3-16	–	5.46

SOUTH AFRICA – BATTING AND FIELDING

	M	I	NO	HS	Runs	Avge	100	50	Ct/St
K.J.Abbott	28	13	4	23	76	8.44	–	–	7
H.M.Amla	150	147	10	159	6880	50.21	24	31	75
T.Bavuma	1	1	–	113	113	113.00	1	–	1
F.Behardien	55	45	12	70	1016	30.78	–	6	26
Q.de Kock	79	79	4	178	3273	43.64	12	12	104/5
M.de Lange	4	–	–	–	–	–	–	–	–
A.B.de Villiers	211	202	38	162*	9025	55.03	24	51	166/5
F.du Plessis	107	103	13	185	3943	43.81	8	26	55
J.P.Duminy	172	155	34	150*	4529	37.42	4	24	72
D.Elgar	6	5	1	42	98	24.50	–	–	3
Imran Tahir	74	23	11	29	117	9.75	–	–	14
C.A.Ingram	31	29	3	124	843	32.42	3	3	12
R.K.Kleinveldt	10	7	–	43	105	15.00	–	–	4
R.McLaren	54	41	15	71*	485	18.65	–	1	13
D.A.Miller	93	83	25	138*	2220	38.27	4	8	44
M.Morkel	103	39	15	32*	217	9.04	–	–	28
C.H.Morris	23	14	2	62	232	19.33	–	1	5
W.D.Parnell	61	35	13	56	482	21.90	–	1	10
A.M.Phangiso	21	13	2	20	81	7.36	–	–	4
A.L.Phehlukwayo	14	6	5	42*	125	125.00	–	–	3
V.D.Philander	30	19	7	30*	151	12.58	–	–	6
D.Pretorius	9	4	–	50	86	21.50	–	1	3
K.Rabada	34	12	7	19*	87	17.40	–	–	9
R.R.Rossouw	36	35	3	132	1239	38.71	3	7	22
J.A.Rudolph	45	39	6	81	1174	35.57	–	7	11
T.Shamsi	5	1	1	0*	0	–	–	–	1
D.W.Steyn	114	45	11	35	294	8.64	–	–	26
R.E.van der Merwe	13	7	3	12	39	9.75	–	–	3
D.Wiese	6	6	1	41*	102	20.40	–	–	–

SOUTH AFRICA – BOWLING

	O	M	R	W	Avge	Best	4wI	R/Over
K.J.Abbott	217.1	13	1051	34	30.91	4-21	1	4.83
F.Behardien	124.4	2	719	14	51.35	3-19	–	5.76
M.de Lange	34.5	1	198	10	19.80	4-46	1	5.68
A.B.de Villiers	30	0	180	7	25.71	2-15	–	6.00
F.du Plessis	32	0	189	2	94.50	1- 8	–	5.90
J.P.Duminy	507.3	8	2700	63	42.85	4-16	1	5.32
D.Elgar	16	1	67	2	33.50	1-11	–	4.18
Imran Tahir	648.4	29	3004	127	23.65	7-45	7	4.63
C.A.Ingram	1	0	17	0	–	–	–	17.00
R.K.Kleinveldt	85.3	6	448	12	37.33	4-22	1	5.23
R.McLaren	400.3	13	2102	77	27.29	4-19	5	5.24
M.Morkel	868	41	4287	173	24.78	5-21	9	4.93
C.H.Morris	173	3	956	29	32.96	4-31	2	5.52

SOUTH AFRICA – BOWLING (continued)

	O	M	R	W	Avge	Best	4wI	R/Over
W.D.Parnell	456.1	20	2569	90	28.54	5-48	5	5.63
A.M.Phangiso	160.5	6	829	26	31.88	3-40	–	4.58
A.L.Phehlukwayo	91.4	5	521	15	34.73	4-44	1	5.68
V.D.Philander	213.1	20	986	41	24.04	4-12	2	4.62
D.Pretorius	64.2	4	304	12	25.33	3- 5	–	4.72
K.Rabada	282.1	15	1442	57	25.29	6-16	3	5.11
R.R.Rossouw	7.3	0	44	1	44.00	1-17	–	5.86
J.A.Rudolph	4	0	26	0	–	–	–	6.50
T.Shamsi	44	3	212	7	30.28	3-36	–	4.81
D.W.Steyn	960	66	4751	178	26.69	6-39	7	4.94
R.E.van der Merwe	117.3	2	561	17	33.00	3-27	–	4.77
D.Wiese	49	0	316	9	35.11	3-50	–	6.44

WEST INDIES – BATTING AND FIELDING

	M	I	NO	HS	Runs	Avge	100	50	Ct/St
S.J.Benn	47	30	7	31	182	7.91	–	–	9
D.Bishoo	17	10	4	12*	32	5.33	–	–	3
C.R.Brathwaite	23	22	2	33*	270	13.50	–	–	8
K.C.Brathwaite	10	10	–	78	278	27.80	–	1	3
D.M.Bravo	94	91	10	124	2595	32.03	3	17	30
J.L.Carter	20	19	2	54	453	26.64	–	3	6
S.Chanderpaul	268	251	40	150	8778	41.60	11	59	73
J.Charles	48	48	–	130	1283	26.72	2	4	21/1
M.L.Cummins	2	–	–	–	–	–	–	–	–
F.H.Edwards	50	22	14	13	73	9.12	–	–	4
A.D.S.Fletcher	25	25	–	54	354	14.16	–	2	5/3
S.T.Gabriel	10	8	3	2	7	1.40	–	–	1
J.O.Holder	52	40	12	57	627	22.39	–	2	17
S.D.Hope	7	7	–	101	250	35.71	1	–	7
A.S.Joseph	3	2	1	22*	24	24.00	–	–	2
E.Lewis	8	8	–	148	253	31.62	1	–	2
J.N.Mohammed	5	5	–	72	138	27.60	–	2	–
S.P.Narine	65	45	12	36	363	11.00	–	–	14
A.R.Nurse	7	6	1	21	47	9.40	–	–	4
K.A.Pollard	101	95	6	119	2289	25.71	3	9	53
K.O.A.Powell	31	31	–	83	788	25.41	–	7	9
R.Powell	4	4	–	44	77	19.25	–	–	4
D.Ramdin	139	110	22	169	2200	25.00	2	8	181/7
R.Rampaul	92	40	11	86*	362	12.48	–	1	14
M.N.Samuels	187	177	26	133*	5180	34.30	10	28	50
J.E.Taylor	85	40	9	43*	276	8.90	–	–	20

WEST INDIES – BOWLING

	O	M	R	W	Avge	Best	4wI	R/Over
S.J.Benn	397.5	15	1913	39	49.05	4-18	3	4.80
D.Bishoo	142	4	642	26	24.69	3-30	–	4.52
C.R.Brathwaite	174	6	997	21	47.47	4-48	1	5.72
K.C.Brathwaite	25.2	0	140	1	140.00	1-56	–	5.52
J.L.Carter	17.1	0	111	3	37.00	2-14	–	6.46
S.Chanderpaul	123.2	0	636	14	45.42	3-18	–	5.15
J.Charles	0.5	0	12	0	–	–	–	14.40
M.L.Cummins	16	2	82	1	82.00	1-42	–	5.12
F.H.Edwards	356.2	23	1812	60	30.20	6-22	2	5.08
A.D.S.Fletcher	4.4	0	26	0	–	–	–	5.57
S.T.Gabriel	70.1	2	388	16	24.25	3-17	–	5.52
J.O.Holder	414.2	27	2259	71	31.81	4-13	3	5.45

WEST INDIES – BOWLING (continued)

	O	M	R	W	Avge	Best	4wI	R/Over
A.S.Joseph	28	0	200	8	25.00	4-76	1	7.14
J.N.Mohammed	15	0	65	0	–	–	–	4.33
S.P.Narine	590	35	2435	92	26.46	6-27	6	4.12
A.R.Nurse	66	1	334	14	23.85	3-27	–	5.06
K.A.Pollard	340.4	4	1956	50	39.12	3-27	–	5.74
R.Rampaul	672.1	33	3434	117	29.35	5-49	10	5.10
M.N.Samuels	816.5	22	3932	85	46.25	3-25	–	4.81
J.E.Taylor	690.3	34	3549	126	28.16	5-48	4	5.13

NEW ZEALAND – BATTING AND FIELDING

	M	I	NO	HS	Runs	Avge	100	50	Ct/St
C.J.Anderson	44	40	5	131*	1047	29.91	1	4	9
T.A.Boult	48	23	15	21*	102	12.75	–	–	10
D.A.J.Bracewell	14	8	1	30	74	10.57	–	–	2
N.T.Broom	30	30	4	109*	646	24.84	1	3	8
D.G.Brownlie	16	15	1	63	361	25.78	–	1	6
C.de Grandhomme	9	7	2	36	165	33.00	–	–	2
A.P.Devcich	12	11	–	58	195	17.72	–	1	3
G.D.Elliott	83	69	11	115	1976	34.06	2	11	17
L.H.Ferguson	7	6	2	4*	15	3.75	–	–	–
J.E.C.Franklin	110	80	27	98*	1270	23.96	–	4	26
M.J.Guptill	143	140	16	237*	5414	43.66	12	32	68
M.J.Henry	30	13	5	48*	165	20.62	–	–	9
T.W.M.Latham	54	53	7	137	1367	29.71	2	6	31/4
M.J.McClenaghan	48	14	10	34*	108	27.00	–	–	4
B.B.McCullum	260	228	28	166	6083	30.41	5	32	262/15
A.F.Milne	33	12	6	36	130	21.66	–	–	16
C.Munro	20	16	–	87	419	26.18	–	3	4
J.D.S.Neesham	35	31	7	74	676	28.16	–	3	16
H.M.Nicholls	11	10	2	82	211	27.75	–	2	8
J.S.Patel	42	14	7	34	88	12.57	–	–	13
L.Ronchi †	78	61	9	170*	1215	23.36	1	3	99/10
M.J.Santner	32	26	9	48	452	26.58	–	–	15
I.S.Sodhi	15	5	–	5	6	1.20	–	–	2
T.G.Southee	116	68	22	55	522	11.34	–	1	27
L.R.P.L.Taylor	183	169	28	131*	6144	43.57	17	33	115
B.J.Watling	27	25	2	96*	573	24.91	–	5	20
K.S.Williamson	111	105	10	145*	4362	45.91	8	29	45

NEW ZEALAND – BOWLING

	O	M	R	W	Avge	Best	4wI	R/Over
C.J.Anderson	226.3	10	1376	55	25.01	5-63	3	6.07
T.A.Boult	434	31	2162	87	24.85	6-33	6	4.98
D.A.J.Bracewell	119.2	15	593	18	32.94	3-31	–	4.96
C.de Grandhomme	50	1	263	7	37.57	2-40	–	5.26
A.P.Devcich	54	1	291	4	72.25	2-33	–	5.38
G.D.Elliott	217	8	1179	39	30.23	4-31	1	5.43
L.H.Ferguson	63	1	407	8	50.87	3-54	–	6.46
J.E.C.Franklin	641.2	34	3354	81	41.40	5-42	1	5.22
M.J.Guptill	18.1	0	98	4	24.50	2- 6	–	5.39
M.J.Henry	255.5	12	1456	58	25.10	5-30	6	5.69
M.J.McClenaghan	389.2	11	2313	82	28.20	5-58	7	5.94
A.F.Milne	243.5	5	1259	31	40.61	3-49	–	5.16
C.Munro	16	0	94	1	94.00	1-20	–	5.87
J.D.S.Neesham	172.2	2	1113	32	34.78	4-42	2	6.45
J.S.Patel	325.4	9	1636	47	34.80	3-11	–	5.02

NEW ZEALAND – BOWLING (continued)

	O	M	R	W	Avge	Best	4wI	R/Over
M.J.Santner	242.2	3	1219	35	34.82	3-31	–	5.03
I.S.Sodhi	119.1	3	668	15	44.53	3-38	–	5.60
T.G.Southee	968.5	60	5212	155	33.62	7-33	6	5.37
L.R.P.L.Taylor	7	0	35	0	–	–	–	5.00
K.S.Williamson	209.3	2	1156	33	35.03	4-22	1	5.51

† *L.Ronchi played 4 times for Australia early in his career, and 74 times for New Zealand.*

INDIA – BATTING AND FIELDING

	M	I	NO	HS	Runs	Avge	100	50	Ct/St
R.Ashwin	105	60	19	65	674	16.43	–	1	30
J.J.Bumrah	11	2	1	0*	0	0.00	–	–	4
Y.S.Chahal	3	–	–	–	–	–	–	–	1
R.Dhawan	3	2	1	9	12	12.00	–	–	–
S.Dhawan	76	75	3	137	3090	42.91	9	17	35
M.S.Dhoni	283	246	66	183*	9101	50.56	9	61	266/91
F.Y.Fazal	1	1	1	55*	55	–	–	1	–
Gurkeerat Singh	3	3	1	8	13	6.50	–	–	1
R.A.Jadeja	129	90	31	87	1888	32.00	–	10	45
K.M.Jadhav	15	11	3	120	468	58.50	2	1	7
V.Kohli	179	171	25	183	7755	53.11	27	39	86
D.S.Kulkarni	12	2	2	25*	27	–	–	–	2
B.Kumar	59	31	9	31	207	9.40	–	–	17
A.Mishra	36	11	3	14	43	5.37	–	–	5
K.K.Nair	2	2	–	39	46	23.00	–	–	–
M.K.Pandey	12	9	3	104*	261	43.50	1	1	2
H.H.Pandya	7	5	2	56	160	53.33	–	1	3
A.R.Patel	30	18	6	38	170	14.16	–	–	13
A.M.Rahane	73	71	2	111	2237	32.42	2	16	42
K.L.Rahul	6	6	2	100*	220	55.00	1	1	4
A.T.Rayudu	34	30	9	124*	1055	50.23	2	6	11
I.Sharma	80	28	13	13	72	4.80	–	–	19
R.G.Sharma	153	147	23	264	5131	41.37	10	29	54
B.B.Sran	6	–	–	–	–	–	–	–	1
J.Yadav	1	1	1	1*	1	–	–	–	1
U.T.Yadav	63	21	13	18*	77	9.62	–	–	18
Yuvraj Singh	293	268	38	150	8447	36.72	14	51	92

INDIA – BOWLING

	O	M	R	W	Avge	Best	4wI	R/Over
R.Ashwin	955.3	34	4695	145	32.37	4-25	1	4.91
J.J.Bumrah	97.3	5	477	22	21.68	4-22	2	4.89
Y.S.Chahal	24	3	77	6	12.83	3-25	–	3.20
R.Dhawan	25	0	160	1	160.00	1-74	–	6.40
M.S.Dhoni	6	0	31	1	31.00	1-14	–	5.16
Gurkeerat Singh	10	0	68	0	–	–	–	6.80
R.A.Jadeja	1072.2	44	5237	151	34.68	5-36	6	4.88
K.M.Jadhav	27	0	141	6	23.50	3-29	–	5.22
V.Kohli	101.5	1	636	4	159.00	1-15	–	6.24
D.S.Kulkarni	99.4	5	508	19	26.73	4-34	1	5.09
B.Kumar	487.5	45	2417	61	39.62	4- 8	2	4.95
A.Mishra	319.3	19	1511	64	23.60	6-48	4	4.72
A.R.Patel	241	11	1057	35	30.20	3-39	–	4.38
H.H.Pandya	51	1	296	9	32.88	3-31	–	5.80
A.T.Rayudu	18	1	111	3	37.00	1- 5	–	6.16
I.Sharma	622.1	29	3563	115	30.98	4-34	6	5.72

INDIA – BOWLING (continued)

	O	M	R	W	Avge	Best	4wI	R/Over
R.G.Sharma	98.5	2	515	8	64.37	2-27	–	5.21
B.B.Sran	50.2	2	269	7	38.42	3-56	–	5.34
J.Yadav	4	0	8	1	8.00	1- 8	–	2.00
U.T.Yadav	492.5	20	2965	88	33.69	4-31	3	6.01
Yuvraj Singh	826.2	18	4202	110	38.20	5-31	3	5.08

PAKISTAN – BATTING AND FIELDING

	M	I	NO	HS	Runs	Avge	100	50	Ct/St
Ahmed Shehzad	75	75	1	124	2510	33.91	6	13	26
Anwar Ali	22	16	5	43*	321	29.18		–	4
Asad Shafiq	60	58	4	84	1336	24.74	–	9	14
Azhar Ali	45	45	3	102	1605	38.21	3	9	6
Babar Azam	23	23	1	123	1168	53.09	4	6	9
Hasan Ali	13	7	3	13	37	9.25	–	–	2
Imad Wasim	18	14	5	63*	332	36.88	–	3	7
Junaid Khan	56	25	12	25	60	4.61	–	–	5
Mohammad Amir	29	21	6	73*	269	17.93	–	2	6
Mohammad Hafeez	182	182	10	140*	5527	32.13	11	29	68
Mohammad Irfan	60	33	21	12	48	4.00	–	–	11
Mohammad Nawaz [b3]	9	8	2	53	143	23.83	–	–	2
Mohammad Rizwan	25	22	6	75*	460	28.75	–	3	24
Rahat Ali	14	7	4	6*	8	2.66	–	–	1
Sami Aslam	4	4	–	45	78	19.50	–	–	–
Sarfraz Ahmed	67	52	9	105	1498	34.83	2	6	60/20
Sharjeel Khan	25	25	–	152	812	32.48	1	6	6
Shoaib Malik	244	221	34	143	6548	35.01	8	38	88
Sohaib Maqsood	26	25	2	89*	735	31.95	–	5	9
Sohail Khan	13	6	1	7	25	5.00	–	–	3
Umar Akmal	116	105	17	102*	3044	34.59	2	20	77/13
Umar Gul	130	65	18	39	457	9.72	–	–	17
Wahab Riaz	77	56	13	54*	589	13.69	–	2	21
Yasir Shah	17	9	3	32*	102	17.00	–	–	4

PAKISTAN – BOWLING

	O	M	R	W	Avge	Best	4wI	R/Over
Ahmed Shehzad	19.1	0	140	2	70.00	1-22	–	7.30
Anwar Ali	154.3	1	944	18	52.44	3-66	–	6.11
Asad Shafiq	2	0	18	0	–	–	–	9.00
Azhar Ali	43	0	260	4	65.00	2-26	–	6.04
Hasan Ali	109.4	2	651	23	28.30	5-52	2	5.93
Imad Wasim	143.5	1	690	23	30.00	5-14	1	4.79
Junaid Khan	444.2	24	2388	83	28.77	4-12	3	5.37
Mohammad Amir	252	13	1221	45	27.13	4-28	1	4.84
Mohammad Hafeez	1135.2	44	4694	129	36.38	4-41	1	4.13
Mohammad Irfan	518.1	31	2549	83	30.71	4-30	2	4.91
Mohammad Nawaz [b3]	67.3	0	362	11	32.90	4-42	1	5.36
Rahat Ali	113.1	1	658	18	36.55	3-40	–	5.81
Shoaib Malik	1254.5	38	5852	153	38.24	4-19	1	4.66
Sohaib Maqsood	9	0	42	1	42.00	1-16	–	4.66
Sohail Khan	111	4	597	19	31.42	5-55	1	5.37
Umar Gul	1010.4	68	5253	179	29.34	6-42	6	5.19
Wahab Riaz	598.1	19	3347	101	33.13	5-46	5	5.59
Yasir Shah	141.3	1	766	18	42.55	6-26	2	5.41

SRI LANKA – BATTING AND FIELDING

	M	*I*	*NO*	*HS*	*Runs*	*Avge*	*100*	*50*	*Ct/St*
M.A.Aponso	5	5	4	2*	6	6.00	–	–	–
K.M.C.Bandara	1	1	1	1*	1	–	–	–	–
P.V.D.Chameera	9	5	3	13*	36	18.00	–	–	2
L.D.Chandimal	122	111	20	111	3095	34.01	4	20	53/6
D.M.de Silva	16	15	2	78*	334	25.69	–	3	7
P.C.de Silva	7	7	1	44	94	15.66	–	–	4
D.P.D.N.Dickwella	11	10	–	94	380	38.00	–	3	6/1
T.M.Dilshan	330	303	41	161*	10290	39.27	22	47	123/1
R.M.S.Eranga	19	11	8	12*	34	11.33	–	–	5
A.N.P.R.Fernando	16	7	6	7	12	12.00	–	–	2
W.I.A.Fernando	1	1	–	0	0	0.00	–	–	–
D.A.S.Gunaratne	10	8	2	114*	222	37.00	1	–	4
M.D.Gunathilaka	16	15	–	65	377	25.13	–	3	7
G.S.N.F.G.Jayasuriya	6	4	1	31	51	17.00	–	–	1
C.K.Kapugedera	97	79	7	95	1551	21.54	–	8	30
K.M.D.N.Kulasekara	181	120	35	73	1319	15.51	–	4	44
C.B.R.L.S.Kumara	3	2	1	5	6	6.00	–	–	1
R.A.S.Lakmal	58	27	14	20*	74	5.69	–	–	13
L.D.Madushanka	3	3	–	7	13	4.33	–	–	–
A.D.Mathews	180	151	39	139*	4492	40.10	1	32	43
B.A.W.Mendis	87	42	19	21*	188	8.17	–	–	15
B.K.G.Mendis	22	21	1	94	685	34.25	–	8	11
B.M.A.J.Mendis	54	40	10	72	604	20.13	–	1	13
S.S.Pathirana	14	11	1	56	292	29.20	–	1	4
A.K.Perera	4	2	–	7	8	4.00	–	–	1
M.D.K.Perera	10	9	–	30	99	11.00	–	–	2
M.D.K.J.Perera	68	65	3	135	1635	26.37	3	8	26/2
N.L.T.C.Perera	114	85	13	80*	1233	17.12	–	5	49
S.Prasanna	34	31	3	95	370	13.21	–	2	4
P.A.D.L.R.Sandakan	5	4	2	2*	3	1.50	–	–	1
K.C.Sangakkara	397	373	40	169	13975	41.96	25	90	396/96
S.M.S.M.Senanayake	49	33	11	42	290	13.18	–	–	19
M.D.Shanaka	9	7	1	42	119	19.83	–	–	2
T.A.M.Siriwardana	14	11	1	66	281	28.10	–	2	4
W.U.Tharanga	198	187	12	174*	5810	33.20	14	30	35
H.D.R.L.Thirimanne	107	87	12	139*	2586	34.48	4	16	34
J.D.F.Vandersay	7	3	1	8	22	11.00	–	–	1
D.S.Weerakkody	3	3	–	58	73	24.33	–	1	2

SRI LANKA – BOWLING

	O	*M*	*R*	*W*	*Avge*	*Best*	*4wI*	*R/Over*
M.A.Aponso	43.2	1	181	7	25.85	4-18	1	4.17
K.M.C.Bandara	10	0	83	1	83.00	1-83	–	8.30
P.V.D.Chameera	50.1	0	349	10	34.90	3-51	–	6.95
D.M.de Silva	39	0	209	4	52.25	2-35	–	5.35
P.C.de Silva	52.4	2	256	5	51.20	2-29	–	4.86
T.M.Dilshan	980	22	4778	106	45.07	4- 4	3	4.87
R.M.S.Eranga	119.2	4	686	21	32.66	3-46	–	5.74
A.N.P.R.Fernando	123.2	4	755	18	41.94	2-21	–	6.12
D.A.S.Gunaratne	49	2	236	9	26.22	3-10	–	4.81
M.D.Gunathilaka	25	0	142	5	28.40	3-48	–	5.68
G.S.N.F.G.Jayasuriya	16	0	89	1	89.00	1-15	–	5.56
C.K.Kapugedera	44	0	225	2	112.50	1-24	–	5.11
K.M.D.N.Kulasekara	1366.4	106	6689	195	34.30	5-22	4	4.89
C.B.R.L.S.Kumara	22	0	182	3	60.66	2-73	–	8.27
R.A.S.Lakmal	435.2	24	2397	80	29.96	4-30	2	5.50
L.D.Madushanka	22	0	154	4	38.50	2-70	–	7.00

SRI LANKA – BOWLING (continued)

	O	*M*	*R*	*W*	*Avge*	*Best*	*4wI*	*R/Over*
A.D.Mathews	816.1	49	3779	111	34.04	6-20	2	4.63
B.A.W.Mendis	692.2	34	3324	152	21.86	6-13	10	4.80
B.K.G.Mendis	3.2	0	28	0	–	–	–	8.40
B.M.A.J.Mendis	222.5	2	1134	28	40.50	3-15	–	5.08
S.S.Pathirana	105.3	1	581	13	44.69	3-37	–	5.50
A.K.Perera	4	0	22	0	–	–	–	5.50
M.D.K.Perera	63	1	337	11	30.63	3-48		5.34
N.L.T.C.Perera	692.3	23	3989	127	31.40	6-44	6	5.75
S.Prasanna	275.1	8	1503	28	53.67	3-32	–	5.46
P.A.D.L.R.Sandakan	37	0	214	4	53.50	2-33	–	5.78
S.M.S.M.Senanayake	393	11	1874	53	35.35	4-13	1	4.76
M.D.Shanaka	25	0	144	6	24.00	5-43	1	5.76
T.A.M.Siriwardana	50.1	1	278	8	34.75	2-27		5.54
H.D.R.L.Thirimanne	17.2	0	94	3	31.33	2-36	–	5.42
J.D.F.Vandersay	40	1	266	6	44.33	3-50	–	6.65

A.N.P.R.Fernando is also known as N.Pradeep.

ZIMBABWE – BATTING AND FIELDING

	M	*I*	*NO*	*HS*	*Runs*	*Avge*	*100*	*50*	*Ct/St*
R.P.Burl	5	4	–	28	69	17.25	–	–	3
B.B.Chari	8	8	–	39	128	16.00	–	–	2/1
T.L.Chatara	34	23	10	23	109	8.38	–	–	4
C.J.Chibhabha	100	100	2	99	2346	23.93	–	16	32
E.Chigumbura	202	187	24	117	4178	25.63	2	19	69
T.S.Chisoro	12	9	5	42*	84	21.00	–	–	6
A.G.Cremer	74	53	16	58	611	16.51	–	1	25
C.R.Ervine	58	55	8	130*	1645	35.00	2	9	27
S.M.Ervine	42	34	7	100	698	25.85	1	2	5
K.M.Jarvis	24	15	5	13	52	5.20	–	–	6
L.M.Jongwe	22	19	3	46	236	14.75	–	–	10
N.Madziva	12	12	3	25	67	7.44	–	–	3
T.Maruma	17	16	–	32	157	9.81	–	–	8
H.Masakadza	171	170	4	178*	4715	28.40	4	30	66
W.P.Masakadza	10	5	–	10	14	2.80	–	–	4
S.F.Mire	15	15	–	54	306	20.40	–	3	5
P.J.Moor	19	18	1	52	335	19.70	–	2	13
C.B.Mpofu	76	39	19	6	46	2.30	–	–	11
C.T.Mumba	1	1	–	1	1	1.00	–	–	1
T.Mupariwa	40	32	10	33	185	8.40	–	–	9
T.K.Musakanda	6	6	1	60	114	22.80	–	1	6
R.Mutumbami	31	29	2	74	552	20.44	–	3	21/5
T.Muzarabani	8	7	3	5	12	3.00	–	–	–
R.Ngarava	5	3	–	10	10	3.33	–	–	1
T.Panyangara	65	49	13	33	239	6.63	–	–	9
V.Sibanda	127	126	4	116	2994	24.54	2	21	42
Sikandar Raza	63	60	7	141	1645	31.03	3	6	26
B.R.M.Taylor	167	166	15	145*	5258	34.82	8	32	98/20
D.T.Tiripano	13	10	3	19	84	12.00	–	–	–
B.V.Vitori	20	11	3	20*	63	7.87	–	–	2
M.N.Waller	63	57	4	99*	964	18.18	–	4	17
S.C.Williams	104	100	14	102	2742	31.88	1	24	36

ZIMBABWE – BOWLING

	O	M	R	W	Avge	Best	4wI	R/Over
T.L.Chatara	303.2	26	1515	48	31.56	3-30	–	4.99
C.J.Chibhabha	274.5	12	1593	35	45.51	4-25	1	5.79
E.Chigumbura	723.1	23	4274	101	42.31	4-28	1	5.91
T.S.Chisoro	85	6	343	13	26.38	3-16	–	4.03
A.G.Cremer	577.5	22	2690	84	32.02	6-46	4	4.65
S.M.Ervine	274.5	10	1561	41	38.07	3-29	–	5.67
K.M.Jarvis	202.5	9	1221	27	45.22	3-36	–	6.01
L.M.Jongwe	143.5	11	759	25	30.36	5- 6	1	5.27
N.Madziva	86.4	2	519	20	25.95	4-49	1	5.98
T.Maruma	37.3	1	230	4	57.50	2-50	–	6.13
H.Masakadza	300.2	5	1590	38	41.84	3-39	–	5.29
W.P.Masakadza	88.1	7	376	15	25.06	4-21	1	4.26
S.F.Mire	55.3	0	327	6	54.50	3-49	–	5.89
C.B.Mpofu	597.5	40	3209	85	37.75	6-52	3	5.36
C.T.Mumba	4	0	31	0	–	–	–	7.75
T.Mupariwa	336.3	23	1690	57	29.64	4-39	3	5.02
T.Muzarabani	53.5	3	262	7	37.42	2-32	–	4.86
R.Ngarava	36	2	178	7	25.42	2-37	–	4.94
T.Panyangara	540.2	41	3024	65	46.52	3-28	–	5.59
V.Sibanda	44.3	1	265	3	88.33	1-12	–	5.95
Sikandar Raza	208.2	7	1048	24	43.66	3-40	–	5.03
B.R.M.Taylor	66	0	406	9	45.11	3-54	–	6.15
D.T.Tiripano	72.5	6	396	14	28.28	5-63	1	5.43
B.V.Vitori	170.2	4	998	29	34.41	5-20	2	5.85
M.N.Waller	78	0	418	6	69.66	1- 9	–	5.35
S.C.Williams	475.4	18	2310	45	51.33	3-15	–	4.85

BANGLADESH – BATTING AND FIELDING

	M	I	NO	HS	Runs	Avge	100	50	Ct/St
Imrul Kayes	65	65	1	112	1873	29.26	2	13	20
Mahmudullah	134	117	30	128*	2858	32.85	2	16	40
Mashrafe Mortaza	167	126	21	51*	1526	14.53	–	1	52
Mosaddek Hossain	8	8	3	50*	180	36.00	–	1	3
Mosharraf Hossain	5	5	1	8	26	6.50	–	–	1
Mushfiqur Rahim	165	152	23	117	4118	31.92	4	23	134/39
Mustafizur Rahman	11	7	4	9	15	5.00	–	–	2
Nasir Hossain	58	47	8	100	1262	32.35	1	6	34
Nurul Hasan	2	2	–	44	68	34.00	–	–	2/1
Rubel Hossain	69	36	19	17	100	5.88	–	–	11
Sabbir Rahman	32	28	4	65	696	29.00	–	3	20
Shafiul Islam	56	31	11	24*	126	6.30	–	–	8
Shakib Al Hasan	166	158	24	134*	4650	34.70	6	32	41
Soumya Sarkar	20	20	2	127*	724	40.22	1	4	13
Subashis Roy	1	1	1	1*	1	–	–	–	–
Taijul Islam	4	2	–	11	21	10.50	–	–	1
Tamim Iqbal	162	161	3	154	5120	32.40	7	34	37
Tanbir Hayder	2	2	–	3	5	2.50	–	–	1
Taskin Ahmed	23	12	4	4*	12	1.50	–	–	5

BANGLADESH – BOWLING

	O	M	R	W	Avge	Best	4wI	R/Over
Mahmudullah	604	14	3083	70	44.04	3- 4	–	5.10
Mashrafe Mortaza	1392	108	6535	218	29.97	6-26	7	4.69
Mosaddek Hossain	38	1	190	6	31.66	2-30	–	5.00
Mosharraf Hossain	33	1	147	4	36.75	3-24	–	4.45
Mustafizur Rahman	94.4	6	415	30	13.83	6-43	3	4.38

BANGLADESH – BOWLING (continued)

	O	*M*	*R*	*W*	*Avge*	*Best*	*4wI*	*R/Over*
Nasir Hossain	175.2	4	809	21	38.52	3-26	–	4.61
Rubel Hossain	520.2	20	2932	88	33.31	6-26	6	5.63
Sabbir Rahman	31.1	0	201	2	100.50	1-12	–	6.44
Shafiul Islam	390.2	24	2294	63	36.41	4-21	1	5.87
Shakib Al Hasan	1416.1	75	6176	220	28.07	5-47	8	4.36
Soumya Sarkar	11	0	57	0	–	–	–	5.18
Subashis Roy	10	1	45	1	45.00	1-45	–	4.50
Taijul Islam	37	2	151	5	30.20	4-11	1	4.08
Tamim Iqbal	1	0	13	0	–	–	–	13.00
Tanbir Hayder	10	0	67	0	–	–	–	6.70
Taskin Ahmed	170.4	5	973	35	27.80	5-28	2	5.70

ASSOCIATES – BATTING AND FIELDING

	M	*I*	*NO*	*HS*	*Runs*	*Avge*	*100*	*50*	*Ct/St*
J.H.Davey (Scotland)	28	25	5	64	463	23.15	–	2	9
E.C.Joyce (Ireland)	46	45	6	160*	1639	42.02	4	9	16
A.N.Kervezee (Neth)	39	36	3	92	924	28.00	–	4	18
M.A.Leask (Scotland)	16	13	1	50	215	17.91	–	1	6
B.J.McCarthy (Ireland)	8	6	1	13	32	6.40	–	–	2
M.W.Machan (Scotland)	23	22	–	114	734	33.36	1	3	4
E.J.G.Morgan (Ireland)	23	23	2	115	744	35.42	1	5	9
D.Murphy (Scotland)	8	7	2	20*	58	11.60	–	–	8/3
T.J.Murtagh (Ireland)	23	15	5	23*	117	11.70	–	–	6
W.T.S Porterfield (Ireland)	95	94	3	112*	2804	30.81	8	13	46
S.W.Poynter (Ireland)	12	11	1	36	124	12.40	–	–	15
W.B.Rankin (Ireland)	39	18	13	18*	53	10.60	–	–	6
R.A.J.Smith (Scotland)	2	1	–	10	10	10.00	–	–	–
P.R.Stirling (Ireland)	73	72	2	177	2285	32.64	5	9	32
R.N.ten Doeschate (Neth)	33	32	9	119	1541	67.00	5	9	13
T.van der Gugten (Neth)	4	2	–	2	4	2.00	–	–	–
P.A.van Meekeren (Neth)	2	1	1	15*	15	–	–	–	–
B.T.J.Wheal (Scotland)	5	4	3	2*	2	2.00	–	–	–
G.C.Wilson (Ireland)	73	69	7	113	1575	25.40	1	11	53/10

ASSOCIATES – BOWLING

	O	*M*	*R*	*W*	*Avge*	*Best*	*4wI*	*R/Over*
J.H.Davey	191.3	16	998	46	21.69	6-28	3	5.20
A.N.Kervezee	4	0	34	0		–	–	8.50
M.A.Leask	61.2	0	387	3	129.00	1-26	–	6.30
B.J.McCarthy	66.2	3	417	18	23.16	4-59	2	6.28
M.W.Machan	67	2	384	9	42.66	3-31	–	5.73
T.J.Murtagh	192	13	885	26	34.03	4-32	1	4.60
W.B.Rankin	303.2	19	1522	46	33.08	3-32	–	5.01
R.A.J.Smith	15	0	97	1	97.00	1-34	–	6.46
P.R.Stirling	324.4	7	1512	32	47.25	4-11	1	4.65
R.N.ten Doeschate	263.2	18	1327	55	24.12	4-31	3	5.03
T.van der Gugten	21	3	85	8	10.62	5-24	1	4.04
P.A.van Meekeren	11	0	79	1	79.00	1-54	–	7.18
B.T.J.Wheal	43.1	2	218	7	31.14	2-31	–	5.05

LIMITED-OVERS INTERNATIONALS RESULTS

1970-71 to 14 March 2017

This chart excludes all matches involving multinational teams.

	Opponents	*Matches*						*Won*						*Tied*	*NR*
			E	*A*	*SA*	*WI*	*NZ*	*I*	*P*	*SL*	*Z*	*B*	*Ass*		
England	Australia	**136**	51	80	–	–	–	–	–	–	–	–	–	2	3
	South Africa	**56**	24	–	28	–	–	–	–	–	–	–	–	1	3
	West Indies	**91**	45	–	–	42	–	–	–	–	–	–	–	–	4
	New Zealand	**83**	36	–	–	–	41	–	–	–	–	–	–	2	4
	India	**96**	39	–	–	–	–	52	–	–	–	–	–	2	3
	Pakistan	**81**	49	–	–	–	–	–	30	–	–	–	–	–	2
	Sri Lanka	**69**	33	–	–	–	–	–	–	34	–	–	–	1	1
	Zimbabwe	**30**	21	–	–	–	–	–	–	–	8	–	–	–	1
	Bangladesh	**19**	15	–	–	–	–	–	–	–	–	4	–	–	–
	Associates	**22**	19	–	–	–	–	–	–	–	–	–	1	–	2
Australia	South Africa	**96**	–	47	45	–	–	–	–	–	–	–	–	3	1
	West Indies	**139**	–	73	–	60	–	–	–	–	–	–	–	3	3
	New Zealand	**135**	–	90	–	–	39	–	–	–	–	–	–	–	6
	India	**123**	–	72	–	–	–	41	–	–	–	–	–	–	10
	Pakistan	**98**	–	62	–	–	–	–	32	–	–	–	–	1	3
	Sri Lanka	**96**	–	60	–	–	–	–	–	32	–	–	–	–	4
	Zimbabwe	**30**	–	27	–	–	–	–	–	–	2	–	–	–	1
	Bangladesh	**19**	–	18	–	–	–	–	–	–	–	1	–	–	–
	Associates	**23**	–	22	–	–	–	–	–	–	–	–	0	–	1
S Africa	West Indies	**61**	–	–	44	15	–	–	–	–	–	–	–	1	1
	New Zealand	**70**	–	–	41	–	24	–	–	–	–	–	–	–	5
	India	**76**	–	–	45	–	–	28	–	–	–	–	–	–	3
	Pakistan	**72**	–	–	47	–	–	–	24	–	–	–	–	–	1
	Sri Lanka	**65**	–	–	34	–	–	–	–	29	–	–	–	1	1
	Zimbabwe	**38**	–	–	35	–	–	–	–	–	2	–	–	–	1
	Bangladesh	**17**	–	–	14	–	–	–	–	–	–	3	–	–	–
	Associates	**23**	–	–	23	–	–	–	–	–	–	–	0	–	–
W Indies	New Zealand	**61**	–	–	–	30	24	–	–	–	–	–	–	–	7
	India	**116**	–	–	–	60	–	53	–	–	–	–	–	1	2
	Pakistan	**130**	–	–	–	69	–	–	58	–	–	–	–	3	–
	Sri Lanka	**56**	–	–	–	28	–	–	–	25	–	–	–	–	3
	Zimbabwe	**47**	–	–	–	35	–	–	–	–	10	–	–	1	1
	Bangladesh	**28**	–	–	–	19	–	–	–	–	–	7	–	–	2
	Associates	**22**	–	–	–	19	–	–	–	–	–	–	2	–	1
N Zealand	India	**98**	–	–	–	–	43	49	–	–	–	–	–	1	5
	Pakistan	**98**	–	–	–	–	42	–	53	–	–	–	–	1	2
	Sri Lanka	**95**	–	–	–	–	45	–	–	41	–	–	–	1	8
	Zimbabwe	**38**	–	–	–	–	27	–	–	–	9	–	–	1	1
	Bangladesh	**28**	–	–	–	–	20	–	–	–	–	8	–	–	–
	Associates	**15**	–	–	–	–	15	–	–	–	–	–	0	–	–
India	Pakistan	**127**	–	–	–	–	–	51	72	–	–	–	–	–	4
	Sri Lanka	**149**	–	–	–	–	–	83	–	54	–	–	–	1	11
	Zimbabwe	**63**	–	–	–	–	–	51	–	–	10	–	–	2	–
	Bangladesh	**32**	–	–	–	–	–	26	–	–	–	5	–	–	1
	Associates	**27**	–	–	–	–	–	25	–	–	–	–	2	–	–
Pakistan	Sri Lanka	**147**	–	–	–	–	–	–	84	58	–	–	–	1	4
	Zimbabwe	**54**	–	–	–	–	–	–	47	–	4	–	–	1	2
	Bangladesh	**35**	–	–	–	–	–	–	31	–	–	4	–	–	–
	Associates	**29**	–	–	–	–	–	–	27	–	–	–	1	–	1
Sri Lanka	Zimbabwe	**50**	–	–	–	–	–	–	–	41	7	–	–	–	2
	Bangladesh	**38**	–	–	–	–	–	–	–	33	–	4	–	–	1
	Associates	**22**	–	–	–	–	–	–	–	21	–	–	1	–	–
Zimbabwe	Bangladesh	**67**	–	–	–	–	–	–	–	–	28	39	–	–	–
	Associates	**67**	–	–	–	–	–	–	–	–	45	–	19	1	2
Bangladesh	Associates	**38**	–	–	–	–	–	–	–	–	–	26	12	–	–
Associates	Associates	**198**	–	–	–	–	–	–	–	–	–	–	187	1	10
		3839	332	551	356	377	320	459	458	368	125	101	226	34	132

MERIT TABLE OF ALL L-O INTERNATIONALS

	Matches	*Won*	*Lost*	*Tied*	*No Result*	*% Won (exc NR)*
South Africa	574	356	196	6	16	64.15
Australia	895	551	303	9	32	63.84
Pakistan	871	458	387	8	18	53.69
India	907	459	402	7	39	52.88
West Indies	751	377	341	9	24	51.85
England	683	332	320	8	23	50.30
Sri Lanka	787	368	379	5	35	48.83
New Zealand	721	320	357	6	38	46.85
Bangladesh	321	101	216	–	4	31.86
Zimbabwe	484	125	342	6	11	26.42
Associate Members (v Full*)	288	39	241	1	7	13.87

* Results of games between two Associate Members and those involving multi national sides are excluded from this list; Associate Members have participated in 486 LOIs, 198 LOIs being between Associate Members.

TEAM RECORDS

HIGHEST TOTALS

† Batting Second

444-3	(50 overs)	England v Pakistan	Nottingham	2016
443-9	(50 overs)	Sri Lanka v Netherlands	Amstelveen	2006
439-2	(50 overs)	South Africa v West Indies	Johannesburg	2014-15
438-9†	(49.5 overs)	South Africa v Australia	Johannesburg	2005-06
438-4	(50 overs)	South Africa v India	Mumbai	2015-16
434-4	(50 overs)	Australia v South Africa	Johannesburg	2005-06
418-5	(50 overs)	South Africa v Zimbabwe	Potchefstroom	2006-07
418-5	(50 overs)	India v West Indies	Indore	2011-12
417-6	(50 overs)	Australia v Afghanistan	Perth	2014-15
414-7	(50 overs)	India v Sri Lanka	Rajkot	2009-10
413-5	(50 overs)	India v Bermuda	Port of Spain	2006-07
411-8†	(50 overs)	Sri Lanka v India	Rajkot	2009-10
411-4	(50 overs)	South Africa v Ireland	Canberra	2014-15
408-5	(50 overs)	South Africa v West Indies	Sydney	2014-15
408-9	(50 overs)	England v New Zealand	Birmingham	2015
404-5	(50 overs)	India v Sri Lanka	Kolkata	2014-15
402-2	(50 overs)	New Zealand v Ireland	Aberdeen	2008
401-3	(50 overs)	India v South Africa	Gwalior	2009-10
399-6	(50 overs)	South Africa v Zimbabwe	Benoni	2010-11
399-9	(50 overs)	England v South Africa	Bloemfontein	2015-16
398-5	(50 overs)	Sri Lanka v Kenya	Kandy	1995-96
398-5	(50 overs)	New Zealand v England	The Oval	2015
397-5	(44 overs)	New Zealand v Zimbabwe	Bulawayo	2005
393-6	(50 overs)	New Zealand v West Indies	Wellington	2014-15
392-6	(50 overs)	South Africa v Pakistan	Pretoria	2006-07
392-4	(50 overs)	India v New Zealand	Christchurch	2008-09
391-4	(50 overs)	England v Bangladesh	Nottingham	2005
387-5	(50 overs)	India v England	Rajkot	2008-09
385-7	(50 overs)	Pakistan v Bangladesh	Dambulla	2010
384-6	(50 overs)	South Africa v Sri Lanka	Centurion	2016-17
383-6	(50 overs)	India v Australia	Bangalore	2013-14
381-6	(50 overs)	India v England	Cuttack	2016-17
378-5	(50 overs)	Australia v New Zealand	Canberra	2016-17
377-6	(50 overs)	Australia v South Africa	Basseterre	2006-07
377-8	(50 overs)	Sri Lanka v Ireland	Dublin	2016
376-2	(50 overs)	India v New Zealand	Hyderabad, India	1999-00
376-9	(50 overs)	Australia v Sri Lanka	Sydney	2014-15
375-3	(50 overs)	Pakistan v Zimbabwe	Lahore	2015
374-4	(50 overs)	India v Hong Kong	Karachi	2008

373-6	(50 overs)	India v Sri Lanka	Taunton	1999
373-8	(50 overs)	New Zealand v Zimbabwe	Napier	2011-12
372-6	(50 overs)	New Zealand v Zimbabwe	Whangarei	2011-12
372-2	(50 overs)	West Indies v Zimbabwe	Canberra	2014-15
372-6†	(49.2 overs)	South Africa v Australia	Durban	2016-17
371-9	(50 overs)	Pakistan v Sri Lanka	Nairobi	1996-97
371-6	(50 overs)	Australia v South Africa	Durban	2016-17
370-4	(50 overs)	India v Bangladesh	Dhaka	2010-11
369-5	(50 overs)	New Zealand v Pakistan	Napier	2014-15
368-5	(50 overs)	Australia v Sri Lanka	Sydney	2005-06
368-4	(50 overs)	Sri Lanka v Pakistan	Hambantota	2015
367-5	(50 overs)	South Africa v Sri Lanka	Cape Town	2016-17
366-8†	(50 overs)	England v India	Cuttack	2016-17
365-2	(50 overs)	South Africa v India	Ahmedabad	2009-10
365-9†	(46 overs)	England v New Zealand	The Oval	2015

The highest score for Zimbabwe is 351-7 (v Kenya, Mombasa, 2008-09), and for Bangladesh 329-6 (v Pakistan, Dhaka, 2014-15).

HIGHEST TOTALS BATTING SECOND

WINNING:	438-9	(49.5 overs)	South Africa v Australia	Johannesburg	2005-06
LOSING:	411-8	(50.0 overs)	Sri Lanka v India	Rajkot	2009-10

HIGHEST MATCH AGGREGATES

872-13	(99.5 overs)	South Africa v Australia	Johannesburg	2005-06
825-15	(100 overs)	India v Sri Lanka	Rajkot	2009-10

LARGEST RUNS MARGINS OF VICTORY

290 runs	New Zealand beat Ireland	Aberdeen	2008
275 runs	Australia beat Afghanistan	Perth	2014-15
272 runs	South Africa beat Zimbabwe	Benoni	2010-11
258 runs	South Africa beat Sri Lanka	Paarl	2011-12
257 runs	India beat Bermuda	Port of Spain	2006-07
257 runs	South Africa beat West Indies	Sydney	2014-15
256 runs	Australia beat Namibia	Potschefstroom	2002-03
256 runs	India beat Hong Kong	Karachi	2008
255 runs	Pakistan beat Ireland	Dublin	2016
245 runs	Sri Lanka beat India	Sharjah	2000-01
243 runs	Sri Lanka beat Bermuda	Port of Spain	2006-07
234 runs	Sri Lanka beat Pakistan	Lahore	2008-09
233 runs	Pakistan beat Bangladesh	Dhaka	1999-00
232 runs	Australia beat Sri Lanka	Adelaide	1984-85
231 runs	South Africa beat Netherlands	Mohali	2010-11
229 runs	Australia beat Netherlands	Basseterre	2006-07
224 runs	Australia beat Pakistan	Nairobi	2002
221 runs	South Africa beat Netherlands	Basseterre	2006-07
217 runs	Pakistan beat Sri Lanka	Sharjah	2001-02
215 runs	Australia beat New Zealand	St George's	2006-07
215 runs	West Indies beat Netherlands	Delhi	2010-11
214 runs	South Africa Beat India	Mumbai	2015-16
212 runs	South Africa beat Zimbabwe	Centurion	2009-10
210 runs	New Zealand beat USA	The Oval	2004
210 runs	Sri Lanka beat Canada	Hambantota	2010-11
210 runs	England beat New Zealand	Birmingham	2015
209 runs	South Africa beat West Indies	Cape Town	2003-04
208 runs	South Africa beat Kenya	Cape Town	2001-02
208 runs	Australia beat India	Sydney	2003-04
208 runs	West Indies beat Canada	Kingston	2009-10
206 runs	New Zealand beat Australia	Adelaide	1985-86
206 runs	Sri Lanka beat Netherlands	Colombo (RPS)	2002-03
206 runs	South Africa beat Bangladesh	Dhaka	2010-11
206 runs	South Africa beat Ireland	Benoni	2016-17

205 runs	Pakistan beat Kenya	Hambantota	2010-11
203 runs	Australia beat Scotland	Basseterre	2006-07
203 runs	West Indies beat New Zealand	Hamilton	2013-14
202 runs	England beat India	Lord's	1975
202 runs	South Africa beat Kenya	Nairobi	1996-97
202 runs	Zimbabwe beat Kenya	Dhaka	1998-99
202 runs	New Zealand beat Zimbabwe	Napier	2011-12
201 runs	South Africa beat Ireland	Canberra	2014-15
200 runs	India beat Bangladesh	Dhaka	2002-03
200 runs	New Zealand beat India	Dambulla	2010
200 runs	Australia beat Scotland	Edinburgh	2013

LOWEST TOTALS (Excluding reduced innings)

35	(18.0 overs)	Zimbabwe v Sri Lanka	Harare	2003-04
36	(18.4 overs)	Canada v Sri Lanka	Paarl	2002-03
38	(15.4 overs)	Zimbabwe v Sri Lanka	Colombo (SSC)	2001-02
43	(19.5 overs)	Pakistan v West Indies	Cape Town	1992-93
43	(20.1 overs)	Sri Lanka v South Africa	Paarl	2011-12
44	(24.5 overs)	Zimbabwe v Bangladesh	Chittagong	2009-10
45	(40.3 overs)	Canada v England	Manchester	1979
45	(14.0 overs)	Namibia v Australia	Potchefstroom	2002-03
54	(26.3 overs)	India v Sri Lanka	Sharjah	2000-01
54	(23.2 overs)	West Indies v South Africa	Cape Town	2003-04
55	(28.3 overs)	Sri Lanka v West Indies	Sharjah	1986-87
58	(18.5 overs)	Bangladesh v West Indies	Dhaka	2010-11
58	(17.4 overs)	Bangladesh v India	Dhaka	2014
58	(16.1 overs)	Afghanistan v Zimbabwe	Sharjah	2015-16
61	(22.0 overs)	West Indies v Bangladesh	Chittagong	2011-12
63	(25.5 overs)	India v Australia	Sydney	1980-81
63	(18.3 overs)	Afghanistan v Scotland	Abu Dhabi	2014-15
64	(35.5 overs)	New Zealand v Pakistan	Sharjah	1985-86
65	(24.0 overs)	USA v Australia	Southampton	2004
65	(24.3 overs)	Zimbabwe v India	Harare	2005
67	(31.0 overs)	Zimbabwe v Sri Lanka	Harare	2008-09
67	(24.4 overs)	Canada v Netherlands	King City	2013
67	(24.0 overs)	Sri Lanka v England	Manchester	2014
68	(31.3 overs)	Scotland v West Indies	Leicester	1999
69	(28.0 overs)	South Africa v Australia	Sydney	1993-94
69	(22.5 overs)	Zimbabwe v Kenya	Harare	2005-06
69	(23.5 overs)	Kenya v New Zealand	Chennai	2010-11
70	(25.2 overs)	Australia v England	Birmingham	1977
70	(26.3 overs)	Australia v New Zealand	Adelaide	1985-86
70	(20.5 overs)	West Indies v Australia	Perth	2012-13
70	(24.4 overs)	Bangladesh v West Indies	St George's	2014

The lowest for England is 86 (v A, Manchester, 2001).

LOWEST MATCH AGGREGATES

73-11	(23.2 overs)	Canada (36) v Sri Lanka (37-1)	Paarl	2002-03
75-11	(27.2 overs)	Zimbabwe (35) v Sri Lanka (40-1)	Harare	2003-04
78-11	(20.0 overs)	Zimbabwe (38) v Sri Lanka (40-1)	Colombo (SSC)	2001-02

BATTING RECORDS
5000 RUNS IN A CAREER

		LOI	*I*	*NO*	*HS*	***Runs***	*Avge*	*100*	*50*
S.R.Tendulkar	I	463	452	41	200*	**18426**	44.83	49	96
K.C.Sangakkara	SL/Asia/ICC	404	380	41	169	**14234**	41.98	25	93
R.T.Ponting	A/ICC	375	365	39	164	**13704**	42.03	30	82
S.T.Jayasuriya	SL/Asia	445	433	18	189	**13430**	32.36	28	68
D.P.M.D.Jayawardena	SL/Asia	448	418	39	144	**12650**	33.37	19	77
Inzamam-ul-Haq	P/Asia	378	350	53	137*	**11739**	39.52	10	83
J.H.Kallis	SA/Afr/ICC	328	314	53	139	**11579**	44.36	17	86

		LOI	*I*	*NO*	*HS*	***Runs***	*Avge*	*100*	*50*
S.C.Ganguly	I/Asia	311	300	23	183	**11363**	41.02	22	72
R.S.Dravid	I/Asia/ICC	344	318	40	153	**10889**	39.16	12	83
B.C.Lara	WI/ICC	299	289	32	169	**10405**	40.48	19	63
T.M.Dilshan	SL	330	303	41	161*	**10290**	39.27	22	47
Mohammad Yousuf	P/Asia	288	272	40	141*	**9720**	41.71	15	64
A.C.Gilchrist	A/ICC	287	279	11	172	**9619**	35.89	16	55
M.Azharuddin	I	334	308	54	153*	**9378**	36.92	7	58
P.A.de Silva	SL	308	296	30	145	**9284**	34.90	11	64
M.S.Dhoni	I/Asia	286	249	67	183*	**9275**	50.96	10	61
C.H.Gayle	WI/ICC	269	264	17	215	**9221**	37.33	22	47
A.B.de Villiers	SA/Afr	216	207	38	162*	**9175**	54.28	24	52
Saeed Anwar	P	247	244	19	194	**8824**	39.21	20	43
S.Chanderpaul	WI	268	251	40	150	**8778**	41.60	11	59
D.L.Haynes	WI	238	237	28	152*	**8648**	41.37	17	57
Yuvraj Singh	I/Asia	296	271	39	150	**8539**	36.80	14	51
M.S.Atapattu	SL	268	259	32	132*	**8529**	37.57	11	59
M.E.Waugh	A	244	236	20	173	**8500**	39.35	18	50
V.Sehwag	I/Asia/ICC	251	245	9	219	**8273**	35.05	15	38
H.H.Gibbs	SA	248	240	16	175	**8094**	36.13	21	37
Shahid Afridi	P/Asia/ICC	398	369	27	124	**8064**	23.57	6	39
S.P.Fleming	NZ/ICC	280	269	21	134*	**8037**	32.40	8	49
M.J.Clarke	A	245	223	44	130	**7981**	44.58	8	58
V.Kohli	I	179	171	25	183	**7755**	53.11	27	39
S.R.Waugh	A	325	288	58	120*	**7569**	32.90	3	45
A.Ranatunga	SL	269	255	47	131*	**7456**	35.84	4	49
Javed Miandad	P	233	218	41	119*	**7381**	41.70	8	50
Younus Khan	P	265	255	23	144	**7249**	31.24	7	48
Salim Malik	P	283	256	38	102	**7170**	32.88	5	47
N.J.Astle	NZ	223	217	14	145*	**7090**	34.92	16	41
G.C.Smith	SA/Afr	197	194	10	141	**6989**	37.98	10	47
M.G.Bevan	A	232	196	67	108*	**6912**	53.58	6	46
H.M.Amla	SA	150	147	10	159	**6880**	50.21	24	31
G.Kirsten	SA	185	185	19	188*	**6798**	40.95	13	45
A.Flower	Z	213	208	16	145	**6786**	35.34	4	55
I.V.A.Richards	WI	187	167	24	189*	**6721**	47.00	11	45
G.W.Flower	Z	221	214	18	142*	**6571**	33.52	6	40
Ijaz Ahmed	P	250	232	29	139*	**6564**	32.33	10	37
Shoaib Malik	P	244	221	34	143	**6548**	35.01	8	38
A.R.Border	A	273	252	39	127*	**6524**	30.62	3	39
R.B.Richardson	WI	224	217	30	122	**6248**	33.41	5	44
L.R.P.L.Taylor	NZ	183	169	28	131*	**6144**	43.57	17	33
M.L.Hayden	A/ICC	161	155	15	181*	**6133**	43.80	10	36
B.B.McCullum	NZ	260	228	28	166	**6083**	30.41	5	32
D.M.Jones	A	164	161	25	145	**6068**	44.61	7	46
D.C.Boon	A	181	177	16	122	**5964**	37.04	5	37
J.N.Rhodes	SA	245	220	51	121	**5935**	35.11	2	33
Ramiz Raja	P	198	197	15	119*	**5841**	32.09	9	31
W.U.Tharanga	SL/Asia	198	187	12	174*	**5810**	33.20	14	30
R.R.Sarwan	WI	181	169	33	120*	**5804**	42.67	5	38
C.L.Hooper	WI	227	206	43	113*	**5761**	35.34	7	29
S.R.Watson	A	190	169	27	185*	**5757**	40.54	9	33
S.K.Raina	I	223	192	35	116*	**5568**	35.46	5	36
W.J.Cronje	SA	188	175	31	112	**5565**	38.64	2	39
Mohammad Hafeez	P	182	182	10	140*	**5527**	32.13	11	29
M.E.K.Hussey	A	185	157	44	109*	**5442**	48.15	3	39
I.R.Bell	E	161	157	14	141	**5416**	37.87	4	35
M.J.Guptill	NZ	143	140	16	237*	**5414**	43.66	12	32
A.Jadeja	I	196	179	36	119	**5359**	37.47	6	30
D.R.Martyn	A	208	182	51	144*	**5346**	40.80	5	37
E.J.G.Morgan	E	176	165	24	124*	**5318**	37.71	10	31
B.R.M.Taylor	Z	167	166	15	145*	**5258**	34.82	8	32

		LOI	I	NO	HS	Runs	Avge	100	50
G.Gambhir	I	147	143	11	150*	**5238**	39.68	11	34
A.D.R.Campbell	Z	188	184	14	131*	**5185**	30.50	7	30
M.N.Samuels	WI	187	177	26	133*	**5180**	34.30	10	28
R.S.Mahanama	SL	213	198	23	119*	**5162**	29.49	4	35
C.G.Greenidge	WI	128	127	13	133*	**5134**	45.03	11	31
R.G.Sharma	I	153	147	23	264	**5131**	41.37	10	29
Misbah-ul-Haq	P	162	149	31	96*	**5122**	43.40	–	42
Tamim Iqbal	B	162	161	3	154	**5120**	32.40	7	34
P.D.Collingwood	E	197	181	37	120*	**5092**	35.36	5	26
A.Symonds	A	198	161	33	156	**5088**	39.75	6	30
Abdul Razzaq	P/Asia	265	228	57	112	**5080**	29.70	3	23

HIGHEST INDIVIDUAL INNINGS

264	R.G.Sharma	India v Sri Lanka	Kolkata	2014-15
237*	M.J.Guptill	New Zealand v West Indies	Wellington	2014-15
219	V.Sehwag	India v West Indies	Indore	2011-12
215	C.H.Gayle	West Indies v Zimbabwe	Canberra	2014-15
209	R.G.Sharma	India v Australia	Bangalore	2013-14
200*	S.R.Tendulkar	India v South Africa	Gwalior	2009-10
194*	C.K.Coventry	Zimbabwe v Bangladesh	Bulawayo	2009
194	Saeed Anwar	Pakistan v India	Madras	1996-97
189*	I.V.A.Richards	West Indies v England	Manchester	1984
189*	M.J.Guptill	New Zealand v England	Southampton	2013
189	S.T.Jayasuriya	Sri Lanka v India	Sharjah	2000-01
188*	G.Kirsten	South Africa v UAE	Rawalpindi	1995-96
186*	S.R.Tendulkar	India v New Zealand	Hyderabad	1999-00
185*	S.R.Watson	Australia v Bangladesh	Dhaka	2010-11
185	F.du Plessis	South Africa v Sri Lanka	Cape Town	2016-17
183*	M.S.Dhoni	India v Sri Lanka	Jaipur	2005-06
183	S.C.Ganguly	India v Sri Lanka	Taunton	1999
183	V.Kohli	India v Pakistan	Dhaka	2011-12
181*	M.L.Hayden	Australia v New Zealand	Hamilton	2006-07
181	I.V.A.Richards	West Indies v Sri Lanka	Karachi	1987-88
180*	M.J.Guptill	New Zealand v South Africa	Hamilton	2016-17
179	D.A.Warner	Australia v Pakistan	Adelaide	2016-17
178*	H.Masakadza	Zimbabwe v Kenya	Harare	2009-10
178	D.A.Warner	Australia v Afghanistan	Perth	2014-15
178	Q.de Kock	South Africa v Australia	Centurion	2016-17
177	P.R.Stirling	Ireland v Canada	Toronto	2010
175*	Kapil Dev	India v Zimbabwe	Tunbridge Wells	1983
175	H.H.Gibbs	South Africa v Australia	Johannesburg	2005-06
175	S.R.Tendulkar	India v Australia	Hyderabad, India	2009-10
175	V.Sehwag	India v Bangladesh	Dhaka	2010-11
175	C.S.MacLeod	Scotland v Canada	Christchurch	2013-14
174*	W.U.Tharanga	Sri Lanka v India	Kingston	2013
173	M.E.Waugh	Australia v West Indies	Melbourne	2000-01
173	D.A.Warner	Australia v South Africa	Cape Town	2016-17
172*	C.B.Wishart	Zimbabwe v Namibia	Harare	2002-03
172	A.C.Gilchrist	Australia v Zimbabwe	Hobart	2003-04
172	L.Vincent	New Zealand v Zimbabwe	Bulawayo	2005
171*	G.M.Turner	New Zealand v East Africa	Birmingham	1975
171*	R.G.Sharma	India v Australia	Perth	2015-16
171	A.D.Hales	England v Pakistan	Nottingham	2016
170*	L.Ronchi	New Zealand v Sri Lanka	Dunedin	2014-15
169*	D.J.Callaghan	South Africa v New Zealand	Pretoria	1994-95
169	B.C.Lara	West Indies v Sri Lanka	Sharjah	1995-96
169	K.C.Sangakkara	Sri Lanka v South Africa	Colombo (RPS)	2013
169	D.Ramdin	West Indies v Bangladesh	Basseterre	2014
167*	R.A.Smith	England v Australia	Birmingham	1993
166	B.B.McCullum	New Zealand v Ireland	Aberdeen	2008

The highest for Bangladesh is 154 by Tamim Iqbal (v Zimbabwe, Bulawayo, 2009).

HUNDRED ON DEBUT

D.L.Amiss	103	England v Australia	Manchester	1972
D.L.Haynes	148	West Indies v Australia	St John's	1977-78
A.Flower	115*	Zimbabwe v Sri Lanka	New Plymouth	1991-92
Salim Elahi	102*	Pakistan v Sri Lanka	Gujranwala	1995-96
M.J.Guptill	122*	New Zealand v West Indies	Auckland	2008-09
C.A.Ingram	124	South Africa v Zimbabwe	Bloemfontein	2010-11
R.J.Nicol	108*	New Zealand v Zimbabwe	Harare	2011-12
P.J.Hughes	112	Australia v Sri Lanka	Melbourne	2012-13
M.J.Lumb	106	England v West Indies	North Sound	2013-14
M.S.Chapman	124*	Hong Kong v UAE	Dubai	2015-16
K.L.Rahul	100*	India v Zimbabwe	Harare	2016
T.Bavuma	113	South Africa v Ireland	Benoni	2016-17

Shahid Afridi scored 102 for P v SL, Nairobi, 1996-97, in his second match having not batted in his first.

Fastest 100	31 balls	A.B.de Villiers (149)	SA v WI	Johannesburg	2014-15
Fastest 50	16 balls	A.B.de Villiers (149)	SA v WI	Johannesburg	2014-15

15 HUNDREDS

		Inns	***100***	*E*	*A*	*SA*	*WI*	*NZ*	*I*	*P*	*SL*	*Z*	*B*	*Ass*
S.R.Tendulkar	I	452	**49**	2	9	5	4	5	–	5	8	5	1	5
R.T.Ponting	A	365	**30***	5	–	2	2	6	6	1	4	1	1	1
S.T.Jayasuriya	SL	433	**28**	4	2	–	1	5	7	3	–	1	4	1
V.Kohli	I	171	**27**	3	5	1	3	3	–	2	6	1	3	–
K.C.Sangakkara	SL	380	**25**	4	2	2	–	2	6	2	–	–	5	2
H.M.Amla	SA	147	**24**	2	1	–	5	2	2	2	4	3	1	2
A.B.de Villiers	SA	207	**24**	2	1	–	5	1	6	3	2	3	–	1
C.H.Gayle	WI	264	**22**	2	–	3	–	2	4	3	1	3	1	3
S.C.Ganguly	I	300	**22**	1	1	3	–	3	–	2	4	3	1	4
T.M.Dilshan	SL	303	**22**	2	1	2	–	3	4	2	–	2	4	2
H.H.Gibbs	SA	240	**21**	2	3	–	5	2	2	2	1	2	1	1
Saeed Anwar	P	244	**20**	–	1	–	2	4	4	–	7	2	–	–
B.C.Lara	WI	289	**19**	1	3	3	–	2	–	5	2	1	1	1
D.P.M.D.Jayawardena	SL	418	**19***	5	–	–	1	3	4	2	–	–	1	2
M.E.Waugh	A	236	**18**	1	–	2	3	3	3	1	1	3	–	1
L.R.P.L.Taylor	NZ	169	**17**	3	2	1	1	–	2	3	1	2	2	–
D.L.Haynes	WI	237	**17**	2	6	–	–	2	2	4	1	–	–	–
J.H.Kallis	SA	314	**17**	1	1	–	4	3	2	1	3	1	–	1
N.J.Astle	NZ	217	**16**	2	1	1	1	–	5	2	–	3	–	1
A.C.Gilchrist	A	279	**16***	2	–	2	–	2	1	1	6	1	–	–
V.Sehwag	I	245	**15**	1	–	–	2	6	–	2	2	–	1	1
Mohammad Yousuf	P	273	**15**	–	1	2	2	1	1	–	2	3	3	–

* = Includes hundred scored against multi-national side. The most for England is 12 by M.E.Trescothick (in 122 innings), for Zimbabwe 8 by B.R.M.Taylor (167), and for Bangladesh 7 by Tamim Iqbal (161).

HIGHEST PARTNERSHIP FOR EACH WICKET

1st	286	W.U.Tharanga/S.T.Jayasuriya	Sri Lanka v England	Leeds	2006
2nd	372	C.H.Gayle/M.N.Samuels	West Indies v Zimbabwe	Canberra	2014-15
3rd	258	D.M.Bravo/D.Ramdin	West Indies v Bangladesh	Basseterre	2014
4th	275*	M.Azharuddin/A.Jadeja	India v Zimbabwe	Cuttack	1997-98
5th	256*	D.A.Miller/J.P.Duminy	South Africa v Zimbabwe	Hamilton	2014-15
6th	267*	G.D.Elliott/L.Ronchi	New Zealand v Sri Lanka	Dunedin	2014-15
7th	177	J.C.Buttler/A.U.Rashid	England v New Zealand	Birmingham	2015
8th	138*	J.M.Kemp/A.J.Hall	South Africa v India	Cape Town	2006-07
9th	132	A.D.Mathews/S.L.Malinga	Sri Lanka v Australia	Melbourne	2010-11
10th	106*	I.V.A.Richards/M.A.Holding	West Indies v England	Manchester	1984

BOWLING RECORDS

200 WICKETS IN A CAREER

		LOI	Balls	R	W	Avge	Best	5w	R/Over
M.Muralitharan	SL/Asia/ICC	350	18811	12326	**534**	23.08	7-30	10	3.93
Wasim Akram	P	356	18186	11812	**502**	23.52	5-15	6	3.89
Waqar Younis	P	262	12698	9919	**416**	23.84	7-36	13	4.68
W.P.J.U.C.Vaas	SL/Asia	322	15775	11014	**400**	27.53	8-19	4	4.18
Shahid Afridi	P/Asia/ICC	398	17620	13632	**395**	34.51	7-12	9	4.62
S.M.Pollock	SA/Afr/ICC	303	15712	9631	**393**	24.50	6-35	5	3.67
G.D.McGrath	A/ICC	250	12970	8391	**381**	22.02	7-15	7	3.88
B.Lee	A	221	11185	8877	**380**	23.36	5-22	9	4.76
A.Kumble	I/Asia	271	14496	10412	**337**	30.89	6-12	2	4.30
S.T.Jayasuriya	SL	445	14874	11871	**323**	36.75	6-29	4	4.78
J.Srinath	I	229	11935	8847	**315**	28.08	5-23	3	4.44
D.L.Vettori	NZ/ICC	295	14060	9674	**305**	31.71	5-7	2	4.12
S.K.Warne	A/ICC	194	10642	7541	**293**	25.73	5-33	1	4.25
S.L.Malinga	SL	191	9207	8082	**291**	27.77	6-38	7	5.26
Saqlain Mushtaq	P	169	8770	6275	**288**	21.78	5-20	6	4.29
A.B.Agarkar	I	191	9484	8021	**288**	27.85	6-42	2	5.07
Z.Khan	I/Asia	200	10097	8301	**282**	29.43	5-42	1	4.93
J.H.Kallis	SA/Afr/ICC	328	10750	8680	**273**	31.79	5-30	2	4.84
A.A.Donald	SA	164	8561	5926	**272**	21.78	6-23	2	4.15
J.M.Anderson	E	194	9584	7861	**269**	29.22	5-23	2	4.92
Abdul Razzaq	P/Asia	265	10941	8564	**269**	31.83	6-35	3	4.69
Harbhajan Singh	I/Asia	236	12479	8973	**269**	33.35	5-31	3	4.31
M.Ntini	SA/ICC	173	8687	6559	**266**	24.65	6-22	4	4.53
Kapil Dev	I	225	11202	6945	**253**	27.45	5-43	1	3.72
Shoaib Akhtar	P/Asia/ICC	163	7764	6169	**247**	24.97	6-16	4	4.76
K.D.Mills	NZ	170	8230	6485	**240**	27.02	5-25	1	4.72
M.G.Johnson	A	153	7489	6038	**239**	25.26	6-31	3	4.83
H.H.Streak	Z/Afr	189	9468	7129	**239**	29.82	5-32	1	4.51
D.Gough	E/ICC	159	8470	6209	**235**	26.42	5-44	2	4.39
C.A.Walsh	WI	205	10822	6918	**227**	30.47	5- 1	1	3.83
C.E.L.Ambrose	WI	176	9353	5429	**225**	24.12	5-17	4	3.48
Shakib Al Hasan	B	166	8497	6176	**220**	28.07	5-47	1	4.36
Mashrafe Mortaza	B/Asia	169	8447	6643	**219**	30.33	6-26	1	4.71
Abdur Razzak	B	153	7965	6065	**207**	29.29	5-29	4	4.56
C.J.McDermott	A	138	7460	5018	**203**	24.71	5-44	1	4.03
C.Z.Harris	NZ	250	10667	7613	**203**	37.50	5-42	1	4.28
C.L.Cairns	NZ/ICC	215	8168	6594	**201**	32.80	5-42	1	4.84

SIX WICKETS IN AN INNINGS

8-19	W.P.J.U.C.Vaas	Sri Lanka v Zimbabwe	Colombo (SSC)	2001-02
7-12	Shahid Afridi	Pakistan v West Indies	Providence	2013
7-15	G.D.McGrath	Australia v Namibia	Potchefstroom	2002-03
7-20	A.J.Bichel	Australia v England	Port Elizabeth	2002-03
7-30	M.Muralitharan	Sri Lanka v India	Sharjah	2000-01
7-33	T.G.Southee	New Zealand v England	Wellington	2014-15
7-36	Waqar Younis	Pakistan v England	Leeds	2001
7-37	Aqib Javed	Pakistan v India	Sharjah	1991-92
7-51	W.W.Davis	West Indies v Australia	Leeds	1983
6- 4	S.T.R.Binny	India v Bangladesh	Dhaka	2014
6-12	A.Kumble	India v West Indies	Calcutta	1993-94
6-13	B.A.W.Mendis	Sri Lanka v India	Karachi	2008
6-14	G.J.Gilmour	Australia v England	Leeds	1975
6-14	Imran Khan	Pakistan v India	Sharjah	1984-85
6-14	M.F.Maharoof	Sri Lanka v West Indies	Mumbai	2006-07
6-15	C.E.H.Croft	West Indies v England	Kingstown	1980-81
6-16	Shoaib Akhtar	Pakistan v New Zealand	Karachi	2001-02
6-16	K.Rabada	South Africa v Bangladesh	Dhaka	2015
6-18	Azhar Mahmood	Pakistan v West Indies	Sharjah	1999-00
6-19	H.K.Olonga	Zimbabwe v England	Cape Town	1999-00
6-19	S.E.Bond	New Zealand v Zimbabwe	Harare	2005

6-20	B.C.Strang	Zimbabwe v Bangladesh	Nairobi	1997-98
6-20	A.D.Mathews	Sri Lanka v India	Colombo (RPS)	2009-10
6-22	F.H.Edwards	West Indies v Zimbabwe	Harare	2003-04
6-22	M.Ntini	South Africa v Australia	Cape Town	2005-06
6-23	A.A.Donald	South Africa v Kenya	Nairobi	1996-97
6-23	A.Nehra	India v England	Durban	2002-03
6-23	S.E.Bond	New Zealand v Australia	Port Elizabeth	2002-03
6-25	S.B.Styris	New Zealand v West Indies	Port of Spain	2002
6-25	W.P.J.U.C.Vaas	Sri Lanka v Bangladesh	Pietermaritzburg	2002-03
6-26	Waqar Younis	Pakistan v Sri Lanka	Sharjah	1989-90
6-26	Mashrafe Mortaza	Bangladesh v Kenya	Nairobi	2006
6-26	Rubel Hossain	Bangladesh v New Zealand	Dhaka	2013-14
6-26	Yasir Shah	Pakistan v Zimbabwe	Harare	2015-16
6-27	Naved-ul-Hasan	Pakistan v India	Jamshedpur	2004-05
6-27	C.R.D.Fernando	Sri Lanka v England	Colombo (RPS)	2007-08
6-27	M.Kartik	India v Australia	Mumbai	2007-08
6-27	K.A.J.Roach	West Indies v Netherlands	Delhi	2010-11
6-27	S.P.Narine	West Indies v South Africa	Providence	2016
6-28	H.K.Olonga	Zimbabwe v Kenya	Bulawayo	2002-03
6-28	J.H.Davey	Scotland v Afghanistan	Abu Dhabi	2014-15
6-28	M.A.Starc	Australia v New Zealand	Auckland	2014-15
6-29	B.P.Patterson	West Indies v India	Nagpur	1987-88
6-29	S.T.Jayasuriya	Sri Lanka v England	Moratuwa	1992-93
6-29	B.A.W.Mendis	Sri Lanka v Zimbabwe	Harare	2008-09
6-30	Waqar Younis	Pakistan v New Zealand	Auckland	1993-94
6-31	P.D.Collingwood	England v Bangladesh	Nottingham	2005
6-31	M.G.Johnson	Australia v Sri Lanka	Pallekele	2011
6-33	T.A.Boult	New Zealand v Australia	Hamilton	2016-17
6-34	Zahoor Khan	UAE v Ireland	Dubai (ICCA)	2016-17
6-35	S.M.Pollock	South Africa v West Indies	East London	1998-99
6-35	Abdul Razzaq	Pakistan v Bangladesh	Dhaka	2001-02
6-38	Shahid Afridi	Pakistan v Australia	Dubai	2009
6-38	S.L.Malinga	Sri Lanka v Kenya	Colombo (RPS)	2010-11
6-39	K.H.MacLeay	Australia v India	Nottingham	1983
6-39	D.W.Steyn	South Africa v Pakistan	Port Elizabeth	2013-14
6-41	I.V.A.Richards	West Indies v India	Delhi	1989-90
6-41	C.A.Soper	Papua New Guinea v Hong Kong	Mong Kok	2016-17
6-42	A.B.Agarkar	India v Australia	Melbourne	2003-04
6-42	Umar Gul	Pakistan v England	The Oval	2010
6-43	D.J.Bravo	West Indies v Zimbabwe	St George's	2012-13
6-43	M.A.Starc	Australia v India	Melbourne	2014-15
6-43	Mustafizur Rahman	Bangladesh v India	Dhaka	2015
6-44	Waqar Younis	Pakistan v New Zealand	Sharjah	1996-97
6-44	N.L.T.C.Perera	Sri Lanka v Pakistan	Pallekele	2012
6-45	C.R.Woakes	England v Australia	Brisbane	2010-11
6-45	J.W.Hastings	Australia v Sri Lanka	Dambulla	2016
6-46	A.G.Cremer	Zimbabwe v Kenya	Harare	2009-10
6-47	C.R.Woakes	England v Sri Lanka	Pallekele	2014-15
6-48	A.Mishra	India v Zimbabwe	Bulawayo	2013
6-49	L.Klusener	South Africa v Sri Lanka	Lahore	1997-98
6-50	A.H.Gray	West Indies v Australia	Port of Spain	1990-91
6-52	C.B.Mpofu	Zimbabwe v Kenya	Nairobi (Gym)	2008-09
6-55	S.Sreesanth	India v England	Indore	2005-06
6-59	Waqar Younis	Pakistan v Australia	Nottingham	2001
6-59	A.Nehra	India v Sri Lanka	Colombo (RPS)	2005

HAT-TRICKS

Jalaluddin	Pakistan v Australia	Hyderabad	1982-83
B.A.Reid	Australia v New Zealand	Sydney	1985-86
C.Sharma	India v New Zealand	Nagpur	1987-88
Wasim Akram	Pakistan v West Indies	Sharjah	1989-90
Wasim Akram	Pakistan v Australia	Sharjah	1989-90
Kapil Dev	India v Sri Lanka	Calcutta	1990-91
Aqib Javed	Pakistan v India	Sharjah	1991-92

D.K.Morrison	New Zealand v India	Napier	1993-94
Waqar Younis	Pakistan v New Zealand	East London	1994-95
Saqlain Mushtaq	Pakistan v Zimbabwe	Peshawar	1996-97
E.A.Brandes	Zimbabwe v England	Harare	1996-97
A.M.Stuart	Australia v Pakistan	Melbourne	1996-97
Saqlain Mushtaq	Pakistan v Zimbabwe	The Oval	1999
W.P.J.U.C.Vaas	Sri Lanka v Zimbabwe	Colombo (SSC)	2001-02
Mohammad Sami	Pakistan v West Indies	Sharjah	2001-02
W.P.J.U.C.Vaas[1]	Sri Lanka v Bangladesh	Pietermaritzburg	2002-03
B.Lee	Australia v Kenya	Durban	2002-03
J.M.Anderson	England v Pakistan	The Oval	2003
S.J.Harmison	England v India	Nottingham	2004
C.K.Langeveldt	South Africa v West Indies	Bridgetown	2004-05
Shahadat Hossain	Bangladesh v Zimbabwe	Harare	2006
J.E.Taylor	West Indies v Australia	Mumbai	2006-07
S.E.Bond	New Zealand v Australia	Hobart	2006-07
S.L.Malinga[2]	Sri Lanka v South Africa	Providence	2006-07
A.Flintoff	England v West Indies	St Lucia	2008-09
M.F.Maharoof	Sri Lanka v India	Dambulla	2010
Abdur Razzak	Bangladesh v Zimbabwe	Dhaka	2010-11
K.A.J.Roach	West Indies v Netherlands	Delhi	2010-11
S.L.Malinga	Sri Lanka v Kenya	Colombo (RPS)	2010-11
S.L.Malinga	Sri Lanka v Australia	Colombo (RPS)	2011
D.T.Christian	Australia v Sri Lanka	Melbourne	2011-12
N.L.T.C.Perera	Sri Lanka v Pakistan	Colombo (RPS)	2012
C.J.McKay	Australia v England	Cardiff	2013
Rubel Hossain	Bangladesh v New Zealand	Dhaka	2013-14
P.Utseya	Zimbabwe v South Africa	Harare	2014
Taijul Islam	Bangladesh v Zimbabwe	Dhaka	2014-15
S.T.Finn	England v Australia	Melbourne	2014-15
J.P.Duminy	South Africa v Sri Lanka	Sydney	2014-15
K.Rabada	South Africa v Bangladesh	Mirpur	2015
J.P.Faulkner	Australia v Sri Lanka	Colombo (RPS)	2016

[1] The first three balls of the match. Took four wickets in opening over (W W W 4 wide W 0).
[2] Four wickets in four balls.

WICKET-KEEPING RECORDS

100 DISMISSALS IN A CAREER

Total			*LOI*	*Ct*	*St*
482†‡	K.C.Sangakkara	Sri Lanka/Asia/ICC	360	384	98
472†	A.C.Gilchrist	Australia/ICC	287	417	55
424	M.V.Boucher	South Africa/Africa	295	402	22
363	M.S.Dhoni	India/Asia	286	269	94
287‡	Moin Khan	Pakistan	219	214	73
242†‡	B.B.McCullum	New Zealand	185	227	15
233	I.A.Healy	Australia	168	194	39
220‡	Rashid Latif	Pakistan	166	182	38
206‡	R.S.Kaluwitharana	Sri Lanka	187	131	75
204‡	P.J.L.Dujon	West Indies	169	183	21
189	R.D.Jacobs	West Indies	147	160	29
188	D.Ramdin	West Indies	139	181	7
187	Kamran Akmal	Pakistan	154	156	31
181	B.J.Haddin	Australia	126	170	11
171	Mushfiqur Rahim	Bangladesh	165	132	39
165	D.J.Richardson	South Africa	122	148	17
165†‡	A.Flower	Zimbabwe	213	133	32
163†‡	A.J.Stewart	England	170	148	15
154‡	N.R.Mongia	India	140	110	44
145	T.Taibu	Zimbabwe/Africa	150	112	33
136†‡	A.C.Parore	New Zealand	179	111	25
126	Khaled Masud	Bangladesh	126	91	35

Total			LOI	Ct	St
124	R.W.Marsh	Australia	92	120	4
123	J.C.Buttler	England	87	110	13
111	M.S.Wade	Australia	87	102	9
109	Q.de Kock	South Africa	79	104	5
109	L. Ronchi	New Zealand	78	99	10
103	Salim Yousuf	Pakistan	86	81	22

† *Excluding catches taken in the field.* ‡ *Excluding matches when not wicket-keeper.*

SIX DISMISSALS IN AN INNINGS

6	(6ct)	A.C.Gilchrist	Australia v South Africa	Cape Town	1999-00
6	(6ct)	A.J.Stewart	England v Zimbabwe	Manchester	2000
6	(5ct/1st)	R.D.Jacobs	West Indies v Sri Lanka	Colombo (RPS)	2001-02
6	(5ct/1st)	A.C.Gilchrist	Australia v England	Sydney	2002-03
6	(6ct)	A.C.Gilchrist	Australia v Namibia	Potchefstroom	2002-03
6	(6ct)	A.C.Gilchrist	Australia v Sri Lanka	Colombo (RPS)	2003-04
6	(6ct)	M.V.Boucher	South Africa v Pakistan	Cape Town	2006-07
6	(5ct/1st)	M.S.Dhoni	India v England	Leeds	2007
6	(6ct)	A.C.Gilchrist	Australia v India	Baroda	2007-08
6	(5ct/1st)	A.C.Gilchrist	Australia v India	Sydney	2007-08
6	(6ct)	M.J.Prior	England v South Africa	Nottingham	2008
6	(6ct)	J.C.Buttler	England v South Africa	The Oval	2013
6	(6ct)	M.H.Cross	Scotland v Canada	Christchurch	2013-14
6	(5ct/1st)	Q.de Kock	South Africa v New Zealand	Mt Maunganui	2014-15
6	(6ct)	Sarfraz Ahmed	Pakistan v South Africa	Auckland	2014-15

FIELDING RECORDS

100 CATCHES IN A CAREER

Total			LOI
218	D.P.M.D.Jayawardena	Sri Lanka/Asia	448
160	R.T.Ponting	Australia/ICC	375
156	M.Azharuddin	India	334
140	S.R.Tendulkar	India	463
133	S.P.Fleming	New Zealand/ICC	280
131	J.H.Kallis	South Africa/Africa/ICC	328
130	Younus Khan	Pakistan	265
130	M.Muralitharan	Sri Lanka/Asia/ICC	350
127	A.R.Border	Australia	273
127	Shahid Afridi	Pakistan/Asia/ICC	398
124	R.S.Dravid	India/Asia/ICC	344
123	S.T.Jayasuriya	Sri Lanka/Asia	445
120	C.L.Hooper	West Indies	227
120	B.C.Lara	West Indies/ICC	299
118	T.M.Dilshan	Sri Lanka	330
115	L.R.P.L.Taylor	New Zealand	183
114	C.H.Gayle	West Indies/ICC	269
113	Inzamam-ul-Haq	Pakistan/Asia	378
111	S.R.Waugh	Australia	325
109	R.S.Mahanama	Sri Lanka	213
108	P.D.Collingwood	England	197
108	M.E.Waugh	Australia	244
108	H.H.Gibbs	South Africa	248
108	S.M.Pollock	SA/Africa/ICC	303
106	M.J.Clarke	Australia	245
105	M.E.K.Hussey	Australia	185
105	G.C.Smith	South Africa/Africa	197
105	J.N.Rhodes	South Africa	245
100	I.V.A.Richards	West Indies	187
100	S.K.Raina	India	223
100	S.C.Ganguly	India/Asia	311

The most for Zimbabwe is 86 by G.W.Flower (221), and for Bangladesh 52 by Mashrafe Mortaza (167).

FIVE CATCHES IN AN INNINGS

5	J.N.Rhodes	South Africa v West Indies	Bombay (BS)	1993-94

APPEARANCE RECORDS

250 MATCHES

463	S.R.Tendulkar	India
448	D.P.M.D.Jayawardena	Sri Lanka/Asia
445	S.T.Jayasuriya	Sri Lanka/Asia
404	K.C.Sangakkara	Sri Lanka/Asia/ICC
398	Shahid Afridi	Pakistan/Asia/ICC
378	Inzamam-ul-Haq	Pakistan/Asia
375	R.T.Ponting	Australia/ICC
356	Wasim Akram	Pakistan
350	M.Muralitharan	Sri Lanka/Asia/ICC
344	R.S.Dravid	India/Asia/ICC

334	M.Azharuddin	India	280	S.P.Fleming	New Zealand/ICC
330	T.M.Dilshan	Sri Lanka	273	A.R.Border	Australia
328	J.H.Kallis	South Africa/Africa/ICC	271	A.Kumble	India/Asia
325	S.R.Waugh	Australia	269	C.H.Gayle	West Indies/ICC
322	W.P.J.U.C.Vaas	Sri Lanka/Asia	269	A.Ranatunga	Sri Lanka
311	S.C.Ganguly	India/Asia	268	M.S.Atapattu	Sri Lanka
308	P.A.de Silva	Sri Lanka	268	S.Chanderpaul	West Indies
303	S.M.Pollock	South Africa/Africa/ICC	265	Abdul Razzaq	Pakistan/Asia
299	B.C.Lara	West Indies/ICC	265	Younus Khan	Pakistan
296	Yuvraj Singh	India/Asia	262	Waqar Younis	Pakistan
295	M.V.Boucher	South Africa/Africa	260	B.B.McCullum	New Zealand
295	D.L.Vettori	New Zealand/ICC	251	V.Sehwag	India/Asia/ICC
288	Mohammad Yousuf	Pakistan/Asia	250	C.Z.Harris	New Zealand
287	A.C.Gilchrist	Australia/ICC	250	Ijaz Ahmed	Pakistan
286	M.S.Dhoni	India/Asia	250	G.D.McGrath	Australia/ICC
283	Salim Malik	Pakistan			

The most for England is 197 by P.D.Collingwood, for Zimbabwe 221 by G.W.Flower, and for Bangladesh 175 by Mohammad Ashraful.

The most consecutive appearances is 185 by S.R.Tendulkar for India (Apr 1990-Apr 1998).

100 MATCHES AS CAPTAIN

LOI			*W*	*L*	*T*	*NR*	*% Won (exc NR)*
230	R.T.Ponting	Australia/ICC	165	51	2	12	73.08
210	S.P.Fleming	New Zealand	98	106	1	13	47.80
199	M.S.Dhoni	India	110	74	4	11	58.51
193	A.Ranatunga	Sri Lanka	89	95	1	8	48.10
178	A.R.Border	Australia	107	67	1	3	61.14
174	M.Azharuddin	India	90	76	2	6	53.57
150	G.C.Smith	South Africa/Africa	92	51	1	6	63.88
147	S.C.Ganguly	India/Asia	76	66	–	5	53.52
139	Imran Khan	Pakistan	75	59	1	4	55.55
138	W.J.Cronje	South Africa	99	35	1	3	73.33
129	D.P.M.D.Jayawardena	Sri Lanka	71	49	1	8	58.67
125	B.C.Lara	West Indies	59	59	–	7	50.42
118	S.T.Jayasuriya	Sri Lanka	66	47	2	3	57.39
109	Wasim Akram	Pakistan	66	41	2	–	60.55
106	S.R.Waugh	Australia	67	35	3	1	63.80
105	I.V.A.Richards	West Indies	67	36	–	2	65.04

The most for England is 69 by A.N.Cook, for Zimbabwe 86 by A.D.R.Campbell, and for Bangladesh 69 by Habibul Bashar.

100 LOI UMPIRING APPEARANCES

209	R.E.Koertzen	South Africa	09.12.1992	to	09.06.2010
200	B.F.Bowden	New Zealand	23.03.1995	to	06.02.2016
182	Alim Dar	Pakistan	16.02.2000	to	09.10.2016
181	S.A.Bucknor	West Indies	18.03.1989	to	29.03.2009
174	D.J.Harper	Australia	14.01.1994	to	19.03.2011
174	S.J.A.Taufel	Australia	13.01.1999	to	02.09.2012
172	D.R.Shepherd	England	09.06.1983	to	12.07.2005
152	R.B.Tiffin	Zimbabwe	25.10.1992	to	19.02.2017
139	D.B.Hair	Australia	14.12.1991	to	24.08.2008
137	S.J.Davis	Australia	12.12.1992	to	17.06.2015
122	E.A.R.de Silva	Sri Lanka	22.08.1999	to	13.06.2012
114	I.J.Gould	England	20.06.2006	to	15.06.2016
112	B.R.Doctrove	West Indies	04.04.1998	to	20.01.2012
107	N.J.Llong	England	17.06.2006	to	09.12.2016
107	D.L.Orchard	South Africa	02.12.1994	to	07.12.2003
100	R.S.Dunne	New Zealand	06.02.1989	to	26.02.2002

INTERNATIONAL TWENTY20 RECORDS

MATCH RESULTS

2004-05 to 7 March 2017

	Opponents	*Matches*	*Won*											*Tied*	*NR*
			E	*A*	*SA*	*WI*	*NZ*	*I*	*P*	*SL*	*Z*	*B*	*Ass*		
England	Australia	**13**	5	7	–	–	–	–	–	–	–	–	–	–	1
	South Africa	**12**	4	–	7	–	–	–	–	–	–	–	–	–	1
	West Indies	**14**	4	–	–	10	–	–	–	–	–	–	–	–	–
	New Zealand	**14**	9	–	–	–	4	–	–	–	–	–	–	–	1
	India	**11**	6	–	–	–	–	5	–	–	–	–	–	–	–
	Pakistan	**14**	9	–	–	–	–	–	4	–	–	–	–	1	–
	Sri Lanka	**8**	4	–	–	–	–	–	–	4	–	–	–	–	–
	Zimbabwe	**1**	1	–	–	–	–	–	–	–	0	–	–	–	–
	Bangladesh	**0**	0	–	–	–	–	–	–	–	–	0	–	–	–
	Associates	**5**	2	–	–	–	–	–	–	–	–	–	2	–	1
Australia	South Africa	**17**	–	11	6	–	–	–	–	–	–	–	–	–	–
	West Indies	**11**	–	5	–	6	–	–	–	–	–	–	–	–	–
	New Zealand	**6**	–	4	–	–	1	–	–	–	–	–	–	1	–
	India	**13**	–	4	–	–	–	9	–	–	–	–	–	–	–
	Pakistan	**14**	–	6	–	–	–	–	7	–	–	–	–	1	–
	Sri Lanka	**13**	–	5	–	–	–	–	–	8	–	–	–	–	–
	Zimbabwe	**1**	–	0	–	–	–	–	–	–	1	–	–	–	–
	Bangladesh	**4**	–	4	–	–	–	–	–	–	–	0	–	–	–
	Associates	**1**	–	1	–	–	–	–	–	–	–	–	0	–	–
S Africa	West Indies	**10**	–	–	6	4	–	–	–	–	–	–	–	–	–
	New Zealand	**15**	–	–	11	–	4	–	–	–	–	–	–	–	–
	India	**10**	–	–	4	–	–	6	–	–	–	–	–	–	–
	Pakistan	**11**	–	–	6	–	–	–	5	–	–	–	–	–	–
	Sri Lanka	**9**	–	–	5	–	–	–	–	4	–	–	–	–	–
	Zimbabwe	**3**	–	–	3	–	–	–	–	–	0	–	–	–	–
	Bangladesh	**4**	–	–	4	–	–	–	–	–	–	0	–	–	–
	Associates	**4**	–	–	4	–	–	–	–	–	–	–	0	–	–
W Indies	New Zealand	**10**	–	–	–	3	4	–	–	–	–	–	–	3	–
	India	**7**	–	–	–	4	–	2	–	–	–	–	–	–	1
	Pakistan	**7**	–	–	–	2	–	–	5	–	–	–	–	–	–
	Sri Lanka	**9**	–	–	–	3	–	–	–	6	–	–	–	–	–
	Zimbabwe	**3**	–	–	–	2	–	–	–	–	1	–	–	–	–
	Bangladesh	**6**	–	–	–	3	–	–	–	–	–	2	–	–	1
	Associates	**5**	–	–	–	2	–	–	–	–	–	–	2	–	1
N Zealand	India	**5**	–	–	–	–	5	0	–	–	–	–	–	–	–
	Pakistan	**15**	–	–	–	–	7	–	8	–	–	–	–	–	–
	Sri Lanka	**15**	–	–	–	–	7	–	–	6	–	–	–	1	1
	Zimbabwe	**6**	–	–	–	–	6	–	–	–	0	–	–	–	–
	Bangladesh	**7**	–	–	–	–	7	–	–	–	–	0	–	–	–
	Associates	**4**	–	–	–	–	4	–	–	–	–	–	0	–	–
India	Pakistan	**8**	–	–	–	–	–	6	1	–	–	–	–	1	–
	Sri Lanka	**10**	–	–	–	–	–	6	–	4	–	–	–	–	–
	Zimbabwe	**7**	–	–	–	–	–	5	–	–	2	–	–	–	–
	Bangladesh	**5**	–	–	–	–	–	5	–	–	–	0	–	–	–
	Associates	**5**	–	–	–	–	–	4	–	–	–	–	0	–	1
Pakistan	Sri Lanka	**15**	–	–	–	–	–	–	10	5	–	–	–	–	–
	Zimbabwe	**9**	–	–	–	–	–	–	9	–	0	–	–	–	–
	Bangladesh	**10**	–	–	–	–	–	–	8	–	–	2	–	–	–
	Associates	**7**	–	–	–	–	–	–	7	–	–	–	0	–	–
Sri Lanka	Zimbabwe	**3**	–	–	–	–	–	–	–	3	0	–	–	–	–
	Bangladesh	**5**	–	–	–	–	–	–	–	4	–	1	–	–	–
	Associates	**6**	–	–	–	–	–	–	–	6	–	–	0	–	–
Zimbabwe	Bangladesh	**9**	–	–	–	–	–	–	–	–	4	5	–	–	–
	Associates	**12**	–	–	–	–	–	–	–	–	5	–	6	1	–
Bangladesh	Associates	**15**	–	–	–	–	–	–	–	–	–	10	4	–	1
Associates	Associates	**135**	–	–	–	–	–	–	–	–	–	–	131	–	4
		598	44	47	56	39	49	48	64	50	13	20	145	9	14

MATCH RESULTS SUMMARY

	Matches	*Won*	*Lost*	*Tied*	*NR*	*Win %*
Afghanistan	55	36	19	0	0	65.45
India	81	48	30	1	2	60.75
South Africa	95	56	38	0	1	59.57
Pakistan	110	64	43	3	0	58.18
Netherlands	45	24	19	0	2	55.81
Sri Lanka	93	50	41	1	1	54.34
New Zealand	97	49	41	5	2	51.57
Australia	93	47	43	2	1	51.08
England	92	44	33	1	4	50.00
Ireland	58	26	26	0	6	50.00
Papua New Guinea	6	3	3	0	0	50.00
West Indies	82	39	37	3	3	49.36
Scotland	44	18	23	0	3	43.90
Hong Kong	24	10	14	0	0	41.66
Kenya	29	10	19	0	0	34.48
Bangladesh	65	20	43	0	2	31.74
Oman	17	5	11	0	1	31.25
United Arab Emirates	23	6	17	0	0	26.08
Nepal	11	3	8	0	0	27.27
Zimbabwe	54	13	40	1	0	24.07
Canada	19	4	14	1	0	21.05
Bermuda	3	0	3	0	0	0.00

INTERNATIONAL TWENTY20 RECORDS

(To 7 March 2017)

TEAM RECORDS

HIGHEST INNINGS TOTALS

† Batting Second

263-3	Australia v Sri Lanka	Pallekele	2016
260-6	Sri Lanka v Kenya	Johannesburg	2007-08
248-6	Australia v England	Southampton	2013
245-6	West Indies v India	Lauderhill	2016
244-4†	India v West Indies	Lauderhill	2016
241-6	South Africa v England	Centurion	2009-10
236-6†	West Indies v South Africa	Johannesburg	2014-15
231-7	South Africa v West Indies	Johannesburg	2014-15
230-8†	England v South Africa	Mumbai	2015-16
229-4	South Africa v England	Mumbai	2015-16
225-7	Ireland v Afghanistan	Abu Dhabi	2013-14
221-5	Australia v England	Sydney	2006-07
219-4	South Africa v India	Johannesburg	2011-12
218-4	India v England	Durban	2007-08
215-5	Sri Lanka v India	Nagpur	2009-10
215-3	Sri Lanka v West Indies	Pallekele	2015-16
215-6	Afghanistan v Zimbabwe	Sharjah	2015-16
214-5	Australia v New Zealand	Auckland	2004-05
214-6	New Zealand v Australia	Christchurch	2009-10
214-4†	Australia v New Zealand	Christchurch	2009-10
214-7	England v New Zealand	Auckland	2012-13
213-4	Australia v England	Hobart	2013-14
211-5	South Africa v Scotland	The Oval	2009
211-4†	India v Sri Lanka	Mohali	2009-10
211-3	Sri Lanka v Pakistan	Dubai	2013-14
211-6	Ireland v Scotland	Dubai	2016-17
210-5	Afghanistan v Scotland	Edinburgh	2015

The highest total for Pakistan is 203-5 (v Bangladesh, Karachi, 2008), for Zimbabwe 200-2 (v New Zealand, Hamilton, 2011-12) and for Bangladesh is 190-5 (v Ireland, Belfast, 2012).

LOWEST COMPLETED INNINGS TOTALS † Batting Second

39 (10.3)	Netherlands v Sri Lanka	Chittagong	2013-14
53 (14.3)	Nepal v Ireland	Belfast	2015
56† (18.4)	Kenya v Afghanistan	Sharjah	2013-14
60† (15.3)	New Zealand v Sri Lanka	Chittagong	2013-14
67 (17.2)	Kenya v Ireland	Belfast	2008
68† (16.4)	Ireland v West Indies	Providence	2009-10
69† (17.0)	Hong Kong v Nepal	Chittagong	2013-14
69† (17.4)	Nepal v Netherlands	Amstelveen	2015
70	Bermuda v Canada	Belfast	2008
70† (15.4)	Bangladesh v New Zealand	Kolkata	2015-16
71 (19.0)	Kenya v Ireland	Dubai	2011-12
71 (13.2)	Ireland v Afghanistan	Dubai	2016-17
72 (17.1)	Afghanistan v Bangladesh	Dhaka	2013-14
72	Nepal v Hong Kong	Colombo (PSS)	2014-15
73 (16.5)	Kenya v New Zealand	Durban	2007-08
73† (16.4)	UAE v Netherlands	Dubai	2015-16
74 (17.3)	India v Australia	Melbourne	2007-08
74† (19.1)	Pakistan v Australia	Dubai	2012
75† (19.2)	Canada v Zimbabwe	King City (NW)	2008-09
78 (17.3)	Bangladesh v New Zealand	Hamilton	2009-10
78† (18.5)	Kenya v Scotland	Aberdeen	2013
79† (14.3)	Australia v England	Southampton	2005
79-7†	West Indies v Zimbabwe	Port of Spain	2009-10
79† (18.1)	India v New Zealand	Nagpur	2015-16
80† (16.0)	Afghanistan v South Africa	Bridgetown	2009-10
80† (15.5)	New Zealand v Pakistan	Christchurch	2010-11
80† (17.2)	Afghanistan v England	Colombo (RPS)	2012-13
80† (14.4)	England v India	Colombo (RPS)	2012-13

The lowest total for South Africa is 100 (v Pakistan, Centurion, 2012-13), for Sri Lanka 82 (v India, Visakhapatnam, 2015-16), and for Zimbabwe 84 (v New Zealand, Providence, 2009-10).

BATTING RECORDS – 1200 RUNS IN A CAREER

Runs			*M*	*I*	*NO*	*HS*	*Avge*	*50*	*R/100B*
2140	B.B.McCullum	NZ	71	70	10	123	35.66	15	136.2
1889	T.M.Dilshan	SL	80	79	12	104*	28.19	14	120.5
1806	M.J.Guptill	NZ	61	59	7	101*	34.73	11	131.4
1709	V.Kohli	I	48	44	12	90*	53.40	16	134.7
1690	Umar Akmal	P	82	77	14	94	26.82	8	122.9
1686	D.A.Warner	A	63	63	3	90*	28.10	12	139.5
1683	J.P.Duminy	SA	71	65	21	96*	38.25	9	124.2
1656	Mohammad Shahzad	Af	55	55	3	118*	31.84	12	136.6
1614	Mohammad Hafeez	P	77	75	4	86	22.73	9	115.0
1568	E.J.G.Morgan	E	67	66	13	85*	29.58	8	130.9
1548	Shoaib Malik	P	82	76	20	75	27.64	5	113.9
1519	C.H.Gayle	WI	50	47	4	117	35.32	15	145.4
1493	D.P.M.D.Jayawardena	SL	55	55	8	100	31.76	10	133.1
1462	S.R.Watson	A	58	56	6	124*	29.24	11	145.3
1457	A.B.de Villiers	SA	73	70	10	79*	24.28	9	132.6
1413	H.Masakadza	Z	50	50	2	93*	29.43	10	119.7
1405	Shahid Afridi	P	98	90	12	54*	18.01	4	150.7
1382	K.C.Sangakkara	SL	56	53	9	78	31.40	8	119.5
1364	R.G.Sharma	I	62	55	12	106	31.72	12	129.4
1307	S.K.Raina	I	65	55	11	101	29.70	5	132.9
1257	A.D.Hales	E	45	45	5	116*	31.42	8	133.8
1256	L.R.P.L.Taylor	NZ	73	65	13	63	24.15	5	120.0
1209	M.S.Dhoni	I	76	66	33	56	36.63	1	123.4
1202	Tamim Iqbal	B	55	55	5	103*	24.04	5	115.3

HIGHEST INDIVIDUAL INNINGS

Score	*Balls*				
156	63	A.J.Finch	A v E	Southampton	2013
145*	65	G.J.Maxwell	A v SL	Pallekele	2016
124*	71	S.R.Watson	A v I	Sydney	2015-16
123	58	B.B.McCullum	NZ v B	Pallekele	2012-13
122	60	Babar Hayat	HK v Oman	Fatullah	2015-16
119	56	F.du Plessis	SA v WI	Johannesburg	2014-15
118*	67	Mohammad Shahzad	Af v Z	Sharjah	2015-16
117*	51	R.E.Levi	SA v NZ	Hamilton	2011-12
117	57	C.H.Gayle	WI v SA	Johannesburg	2007-08
116*	56	B.B.McCullum	NZ v A	Christchurch	2009-10
116*	64	A.D.Hales	E v SL	Chittagong	2013-14
114*	70	M.van Wyk	SA v WI	Durban	2014-15
111*	62	Ahmed Shehzad	P v B	Dhaka	2013-14
110	51	K.L.Rahul	I v WI	Lauderhill	2016
106	66	R.G.Sharma	I v SA	Dharamsala	2015-16
104*	57	T.M.Dilshan	SL v A	Pallekele	2011
103*	63	Tamim Iqbal	B v Oman	Dharmasala	2015-16
101*	69	M.J.Guptill	NZ v SA	East London	2012-13
101	60	S.K.Raina	I v SA	Gros Islet	2009-10
101	54	C.Munro	NZ v B	Mt Maunganui	2016-17
100*	48	C.H.Gayle	WI v E	Mumbai	2015-16
100	64	D.P.M.D.Jayawardena	SL v Z	Providence	2009-10
100	58	R.D.Berrington	Sc v B	The Hague	2012
100	49	E.Lewis	WI v I	Lauderhill	2016

The highest score for Zimbabwe is 93* by H.Masakadza (v B, Khulna, 2015-16).

HIGHEST PARTNERSHIP FOR EACH WICKET

1st	171*	M.J.Guptill/K.S.Williamson	NZ v P	Hamilton	2015-16
2nd	166	D.P.M.D.Jayawardena/K.C.Sangakkara	SL v WI	Bridgetown	2009-10
3rd	152	A.D.Hales/E.J.G.Morgan	E v SL	Chittagong	2013-14
4th	161	D.A.Warner/G.J.Maxwell	A v SA	Johannesburg	2015-16
5th	119*	Shoaib Malik/Misbah-ul-Haq	P v A	Johannesburg	2007-08
6th	101*	C.L.White/M.E.K.Hussey	A v SL	Bridgetown	2009-10
7th	91	P.D.Collingwood/M.H.Yardy	E v WI	The Oval	2007
8th	80	P.L.Mommsen/S.M.Sharif	Sc v Ne	Edinburgh	2015
9th	66	D.J.Bravo/J.E.Taylor	WI v P	Dubai	2016-17
10th	31*	Wahab Riaz/Shoaib Akhtar	P v NZ	Auckland	2010-11

BOWLING RECORDS – 50 WICKETS IN A CAREER

Wkts			*Matches*	*Overs*	*Mdns*	*Runs*	*Avge*	*Best*	*R/Over*
97	Shahid Afridi	P	98	357.2	4	2362	24.35	4-11	6.61
85	Umar Gul	P	60	200.3	2	1443	16.97	5- 6	7.19
85	Saeed Ajmal	P	64	238.2	2	1516	17.83	4-19	6.36
84	S.L.Malinga	SL	65	229.5	–	1677	19.96	5-31	7.29
67	Shakib Al Hasan	B	57	207.5	1	1406	20.98	4-15	6.76
66	B.A.W.Mendis	SL	39	147.3	5	952	14.42	6- 8	6.45
65	K.M.D.N.Kulasekara	SL	56	197.1	6	1456	22.40	4-31	7.38
65	S.C.J.Broad	E	56	195.3	2	1491	22.93	4-24	7.62
58	D.W.Steyn	SA	42	150.1	2	1009	17.39	4- 9	6.71
58	N.L.McCullum	NZ	63	187.1	–	1278	22.03	4-16	6.82
56	Mohammad Nabi	Af	52	187.2	5	1305	23.30	4-10	6.96
54	Imran Tahir	SA	31	115.5	–	740	13.70	5-24	6.38
52	G.H.Dockrell	Ire	43	130.4	1	821	15.78	4-20	6.28
52	R.Ashwin	I	45	167.0	2	1154	22.19	4- 8	6.91

Wkts			Matches	Overs	Mdns	Runs	Avge	Best	R/Over
52	Sohail Tanvir	P	54	191.2	3	1364	26.23	3-12	7.12
52	D.J.Bravo	WI	66	173.4	–	1470	28.26	4-28	8.46
51	G.P.Swann	E	39	135.0	4	859	16.84	3-13	6.36

The most wickets for Australia is 48 by S.R.Watson, and for Zimbabwe 33 by A.G.Cremer.

BEST FIGURES IN AN INNINGS

6- 8	B.A.W.Mendis	SL v Z	Hambantota	2012-13
6-16	B.A.W.Mendis	SL v A	Pallekele	2011
6-25	Y.S.Chahal	I v E	Bangalore	2016-17
5- 3	H.M.R.K.B.Herath	SL v NZ	Chittagong	2013-14
5- 6	Umar Gul	P v NZ	The Oval	2009
5- 6	Umar Gul	P v SA	Centurion	2012-13
5-13	Elias Sunny	B v Ire	Belfast	2012
5-13	Samiullah Shenwari	Af v K	Sharjah	2013-14
5-14	Imad Wasim	P v WI	Dubai	2016-17
5-18	T.G.Southee	NZ v P	Auckland	2010-11
5-19	R.McLaren	SA v WI	North Sound	2009-10
5-19	Ahsan Malik	Neth v SA	Chittagong	2013-14
5-20	N.Odhiambo	K v Sc	Nairobi (Gym)	2009-10
5-22	Mustafizur Rahman	B v NZ	Kolkata	2015-16
5-23	D.Wiese	SA v WI	Durban	2014-15
5-24	A.C.Evans	Sc v Neth	Edinburgh	2015
5-24	Imran Tahir	SA v NZ	Auckland	2016-17
5-26	D.J.G.Sammy	WI v Z	Port of Spain	2009-10
5-27	M.R.J.Watt	Sc v Neth	Dubai	2015-16
5-27	J.P.Faulkner	A v P	Mohali	2015-16
5-31	S.L.Malinga	SL v E	Pallekele	2012-13
4- 2	S.O.Tikolo	K v Sc	Dubai	2013-14

The best figures for England are 4-10 by R.S.Bopara (v WI, The Oval, 2011), and for Zimbabwe 4-28 by W.P.Masakadza (v Sc, Nagpur, 2015-16).

HAT-TRICKS

B.Lee	Australia v Bangladesh	Melbourne	2007-08
J.D.P.Oram	New Zealand v Sri Lanka	Colombo (RPS)	2009
T.G.Southee	New Zealand v Pakistan	Auckland	2010-11
N.L.T.C.Perera	Sri Lanka v India	Ranchi	2015-16

WICKET-KEEPING RECORDS
25 DISMISSALS IN A CAREER

Dis			Matches	Ct	St
65	M.S.Dhoni	India	76	42	23
60	Kamran Akmal	Pakistan	54	28	32
51	D.Ramdin	West Indies	58	32	19
49	Mohammad Shahzad	Afghanistan	55	25	24
45	K.C.Sangakkara	Sri Lanka	56	25	20
45	Mushfiqur Rahim	Bangladesh	57	22	23
39	Q.de Kock	South Africa	30	30	9
32†	B.B.McCullum	New Zealand	71	24	8
29	L.Ronchi	New Zealand	32	24	5
28†	A.B.de Villiers	South Africa	73	21	7
27	W.Barresi	Netherlands	34	26	1
25	N.J.O'Brien	Ireland	30	15	10

† *Excluding catches taken in the field*. The most for England is 20 (17 ct, 3 st) by C.Kieswetter.

MOST DISMISSALS IN AN INNINGS

5 (3 ct, 2 st)	Mohammad Shahzad	Afghanistan v Oman	Abu Dhabi	2015-16

FIELDING RECORDS

25 CATCHES IN A CAREER

Total			*Matches*	*Total*			*Matches*
42	L.R.P.L.Taylor	New Zealand	73	30	D.J.G.Sammy	West Indies	66
40	A.B.de Villiers	South Africa	73	30	E.J.G.Morgan	England	67
38	Umar Akmal	Pakistan	82	30	Shahid Afridi	Pakistan	98
35	M.J.Guptill	New Zealand	61	29	D.A.Miller	South Africa	49
35	D.J.Bravo	West Indies	66	28	P.W.Borren	Netherlands	43
34	J.P.Duminy	South Africa	71	27	Mohammad Nabi	Afghanistan	52
34	Shoaib Malik	Pakistan	82	26	N.L.McCullum	New Zealand	63
33	D.A.Warner	Australia	63	26	T.M.Dilshan	Sri Lanka	80
32	S.K.Raina	India	65				

MOST CATCHES IN AN INNINGS

4	D.J.G.Sammy	West Indies v Ireland	Providence	2009-10
4	P.W.Borren	Netherlands v Bangladesh	The Hague	2012
4	C.J.Anderson	New Zealand v South Africa	Port Elizabeth	2012-13
4	L.D.Chandimal	Sri Lanka v Bangladesh	Chittagong	2013-14
4	A.M.Rahane	India v England	Birmingham	2014
4	Babar Hayat	Hong Kong v Afghanistan	Dhaka	2015-16

APPEARANCE RECORDS

60 APPEARANCES

98	Shahid Afridi	Pakistan	67	E.J.G.Morgan	England
82	Shoaib Malik	Pakistan	66	D.J.Bravo	West Indies
82	Umar Akmal	Pakistan	66	D.J.G.Sammy	West Indies
80	T.M.Dilshan	Sri Lanka	65	S.L.Malinga	Sri Lanka
77	Mohammad Hafeez	Pakistan	65	S.K.Raina	India
76	M.S.Dhoni	India	64	Saeed Ajmal	Pakistan
73	A.B.de Villiers	South Africa	63	N.L.McCullum	New Zealand
73	L.R.P.L.Taylor	New Zealand	63	D.A.Warner	Australia
71	J.P.Duminy	South Africa	62	R.G.Sharma	India
71	B.B.McCullum	New Zealand	61	M.J.Guptill	New Zealand
68	A.D.Mathews	Sri Lanka	60	Umar Gul	Pakistan

25 MATCHES AS CAPTAIN

			W	*L*	*T*	*NR*	*%age wins*
72	M.S.Dhoni	India	41	28	1	2	58.57
53	W.T.S.Porterfield	Ireland	26	23		4	53.06
47	D.J.G.Sammy	West Indies	27	17	1	2	60.00
43	Shahid Afridi	Pakistan	19	23	1	–	44.18
37	P.W.Borren	Netherlands	21	15	–	1	58.33
32	F.du Plessis	South Africa	19	13	–	–	59.37
30	Asghar Stanikzai	Afghanistan	24	6	–	–	80.00
30	P.D.Collingwood	England	17	11	–	2	60.71
29	Mohammad Hafeez	Pakistan	17	11	1	–	58.62
28	G.J.Bailey	Australia	14	13	1	–	50.00
28	B.B.McCullum	New Zealand	13	14	–	1	48.14
28	D.L.Vettori	New Zealand	13	13	2	–	46.42
27	G.C.Smith	South Africa	18	9	–	–	66.66
27	S.C.J.Broad	England	11	15	–	1	42.30
26	Mashrafe Mortaza	Bangladesh	9	16	–	1	36.00

INDIAN PREMIER LEAGUE 2016

The ninth IPL tournament was held in India between 9 April and 29 May.

	Team	*P*	*W*	*L*	*T*	*NR*	*Pts*	*Net RR*
1	Gujarat Lions (-)	14	9	5	–	–	18	–0.37
2	Royal Challengers Bangalore (3)	14	8	6	–	–	16	+0.93
3	Sunrisers Hyderabad (6)	14	8	6	–	–	16	+0.24
4	Kolkata Knight Riders (5)	14	8	6	–	–	16	+0.10
5	Mumbai Indians (2)	14	7	7	–	–	14	–0.14
6	Delhi Daredevils (7)	14	7	7	–	–	14	–0.15
7	Rising Pune Supergiants (-)	14	5	9	–	–	10	+0.01
8	Kings XI Punjab (8)	14	4	10	–	–	8	–0.64

1st Qualifying Match: At M.Chinnaswamy Stadium, Bangalore, 24 May (floodlit). Toss: Royal Challengers Bangalore. **ROYAL CHALLENGERS BANGALORE** won by four wickets. Gujarat Lions 158 (20; D.R.Smith 73, S.R.Watson 4-29). Royal Challengers Bangalore 159-6 (18.2; A.B.de Villiers 79*, D.S.Kulkarni 4-14). Award: A.B.de Villiers.

Elimination Final: At Feroz Shah Kotla, Delhi, 25 May (floodlit). Toss: Kolkata Knight Riders. **SUNRISERS HYDERABAD** won by 22 runs. Sunrisers Hyderabad 162-8 (20; Kuldeep Yadav 3-35). Kolkata Knight Riders 140-8 (20; B.Kumar 3-19). Award: M.C.Henriques (Sunrisers Hyderabad 31 & 2-17).

2nd Qualifying Match: At Feroz Shah Kotla, Delhi, 27 May (floodlit). Toss: Sunrisers Hyderabad. **SUNRISERS HYDERABAD** won by four wickets. Gujarat Lions 162-7 (20; A.J.Finch 50). Sunrisers Hyderabad 163-6 (19.2; D.A.Warner 93*). Award: D.A.Warner.

FINAL: At M.Chinnaswamy Stadium, Bangalore, 29 May (floodlit). Toss: Sunrisers Hyderabad. **SUNRISERS HYDERABAD** won by 8 runs. Sunrisers Hyderabad 208-7 (20; D.A.Warner 69, C.J.Jordan 3-45). Royal Challengers Bangalore 200-7 (20; C.H.Gayle 76, V.Kohli 54). Award: B.C.J.Cutting (Sunrisers Hyderabad 39* in 15b & 2-35). Series award: V.Kohli (Royal Challengers Bangalore).

IPL winners:	2008	Rajasthan Royals	2009	Deccan Chargers
	2010	Chennai Super Kings	2011	Chennai Super Kings
	2012	Kolkata Knight Riders	2013	Mumbai Indians
	2014	Kolkata Knight Riders	2015	Mumbai Indians

TEAM RECORDS

HIGHEST TOTALS

263-5 (20)	Bangalore v Pune	Bangalore	2013
248-3 (20)	Bangalore v Gujarat	Bangalore	2016

LOWEST TOTALS

58 (15.1)	Rajasthan v Bangalore	Cape Town	2009
67 (15.2)	Kolkata v Mumbai	Mumbai	2008

LARGEST MARGINS OF VICTORY

144 runs	Bangalore (248-3) v Gujarat (104)	Bangalore	2016
10 wickets	Mumbai (154-7) v Deccan (155-0)	Mumbai	2008
10 wickets	Rajasthan (92) v Bangalore (93-0)	Bangalore	2010
10 wickets	Mumbai (133-5) v Rajasthan (134-0)	Mumbai	2011
10 wickets	Rajasthan (162-6) v Mumbai (163-0)	Jaipur	2012
10 wickets	Punjab (138) v Chennai (139-0)	Mohali	2013
10 wickets	Delhi (95) v Bangalore (99-0)	Delhi	2015
10 wickets	Gujarat (135-8) v Hyderabad (137-0)	Rajkot	2016

Delhi beat Punjab by ten wickets in a reduced game in 2009.

BATTING RECORDS

800 RUNS IN A SEASON

Runs			*Year*	*M*	*I*	*NO*	*HS*	*Ave*	*100*	*50*	*6s*	*4s*	*R/100B*
973	V.Kohli	Bangalore	2016	16	16	4	113	81.08	4	7	38	83	152.0
848	D.A.Warner	Hyderabad	2016	17	17	3	93*	60.57	–	9	31	88	151.4

HIGHEST SCORES

Score	*Balls*				
175*	66	C.H.Gayle	Bangalore v Pune	Bangalore	2013
158*	73	B.B.McCullum	Kolkata v Bangalore	Bangalore	2008
133*	59	A.B.de Villiers	Bangalore v Mumbai	Mumbai	2015
129*	52	A.B.de Villiers	Bangalore v Mumbai	Bangalore	2016
128*	62	C.H.Gayle	Bangalore v Delhi	Delhi	2012
127	56	M.Vijay	Chennai v Rajasthan	Chennai	2010

FASTEST HUNDRED

30 balls	C.H.Gayle (175*)	Bangalore v Pune	Bangalore	2013

MOST SIXES IN AN INNINGS

17	C.H.Gayle	Bangalore v Pune	Bangalore	2013

HIGHEST STRIKE RATE IN A SEASON (Qualification: 100 runs or more)

R/100B	*Score*	*Balls*			
204.34	188	92	B.B.McCullum	Kolkata	2008

HIGHEST STRIKE RATE IN AN INNINGS (Qualification: 25 runs, 350+ strike rate)

R/100B	*Score*	*Balls*				
400.0	28	7	J.A.Morkel	Chennai v Bangalore	Chennai	2012
387.5	31	8	A.B.de Villiers	Bangalore v Pune	Bangalore	2013
385.7	27*	7	B.Akhil	Bangalore v Deccan	Hyderabad	2008
372.7	41	11	A.B.de Villiers	Bangalore v Mumbai	Bangalore	2015
350.0	35	10	C.H.Gayle	Bangalore v Hyderabad	Hyderabad	2015
350.0	35*	10	S.N.Khan	Bangalore v Hyderabad	Bangalore	2016

BOWLING RECORDS
25 WICKETS IN A SEASON

Wkts			*Year*	*P*	*O*	*M*	*Runs*	*Avge*	*Best*	*4w*	*R/Over*
32	D.J.Bravo	Chennai	2013	18	62.3	–	497	15.53	4-42	1	7.95
28	S.L.Malinga	Mumbai	2011	16	63.0	2	375	13.39	5-13	1	5.95
28	J.P.Faulkner	Rajasthan	2013	16	63.1	2	427	15.25	5-16	2	6.75
26	D.J.Braveo	Chennai	2015	17	52.2	–	426	16.38	3-22	–	8.14

BEST BOWLING FIGURES IN AN INNINGS

6-14	Sohail Tanvir	Rajasthan v Chennai	Jaipur	2008
6-19	A.Zampa	Pune v Hyderabad	Visakhapatnam	2016
5-5	A.Kumble	Bangalore v Rajasthan	Cape Town	2009
5-12	I.Sharma	Deccan v Kochi	Kochi	2011
5-13	S.L.Malinga	Mumbai v Delhi	Delhi	2011

MOST ECONOMICAL BOWLING ANALYSIS

O	*M*	*R*	*W*				
4	1	6	0	F.H.Edwards	Deccan v Kolkata	Cape Town	2009
4	1	6	1	A.Nehra	Delhi v Punjab	Bloemfontein	2009

MOST EXPENSIVE BOWLING ANALYSIS

O	*M*	*R*	*W*				
4	0	66	0	I.Sharma	Hyderabad v Chennai	Hyderabad	2013
4	0	65	0	U.T.Yadav	Delhi v Bangalore	Delhi	2013
4	0	65	1	Sandeep Sharma	Punjab v Hyderabad	Hyderabad	2014
4	0	63	2	V.R.Aaron	Delhi v Chennai	Chennai	2012
4	0	63	0	A.B.Dinda	Pune v Mumbai	Mumbai	2013
4	0	62	0	M.G.Neser	Punjab v Bangalore	Mohali	2013
4	0	61	2	S.R.Watson	Bangalore v Hyderabad	Bangalore	2016

ENGLAND WOMEN INTERNATIONALS

The following players have played for England since 1 September 2015. Details correct to 6 April 2017.

BEAUMONT, Tamsin ('**Tammy**') Tilley, b Dover, Kent 11 Mar 1991. RHB, WK. Kent 2007 to date. Diamonds 2007-12. Sapphires 2008. Emeralds 2011-13. Surrey Stars 2016. **Tests**: 2 (2013 to 2014); HS 12 v I (Wormsley) 2014. **LOI**: 35 (2009-10 to 2016-17); HS 168* v P (Taunton) 2016. **IT20**: 44 (2009-10 to 2016); HS 82 v P (Bristol) 2016.

BRUNT, Katherine Helen, b Barnsley, Yorks 2 Jul 1985. RHB, RMF. Yorkshire 2004 to date. Sapphires 2006-08. Diamonds 2011-12. Yorkshire Diamonds 2016. **Tests**: 10 (2004 to 2015); HS 52 v A (Worcester) 2005; BB 6-69 v A (Worcester) 2009. **LOI**: 94 (2004-05 to 2016-17); HS 31 v A (Worcester) 2015; BB 5-18 v A (Wormsley) 2011. **IT20**: 57 (2005 to 2016); HS 35 v WI (Arundel) 2012; BB 3-6 v NZ (Lord's) 2009.

CROSS, Kathryn ('**Kate**') Laura, b Manchester, Lancs 3 Oct 1991. RHB, RMF. Lancashire 2005 to date. Sapphires 2007-08. Emeralds 2012. Lancashire Thunder 2016. **Tests**: 3 (2013-14 to 2015); HS 4* v A (Canterbury) 2015; BB 3-29 v I (Wormsley) 2014. **LOI**: 14 (2013-14 to 2016); HS 4* v I (Scarborough) 2014; BB 5-24 v NZ (Lincoln) 2014-15. **IT20**: 4 (2013-14 to 2014-15); HS – ; BB 2-27 v NZ (Whangarei) 2014-15.

ECCLESTONE, Sophie (Helsby HS), b Chester 6 May 1999. RHB, SLA. Cheshire 2013-14. Lancashire 2015 to date. Lancashire Thunder 2016. **LOI**: 2 (2016-17); HS 3 and BB 2-28 v WI (Florence Hall) 2016-17. **IT20**: 2 (2016); HS –; BB 2-26 v P (Southampton) 2016.

EDWARDS, Charlotte Marie, b Huntingdon, Cambs 17 Dec 1979. RHB, LB. East Anglia 1994-99. Kent 2000 to date. N Districts 2000-01 to 2002-03. Diamonds 2006-12. Sapphires 2013. W Australia 2014-15. Southern Vipers 2016. S Australia 2016-17. MBE 2009. CBE 2014. *Wisden* 2013. **Tests**: 23 (1996 to 2015, 10 as captain); HS 117 v NZ (Scarborough) 2004; BB 2-28 v A (Harrogate) 1998. **LOI**: 191 (1997 to 2015-16, 117 as captain); HS 173* v Ire (Pune) 1997-98; BB 4-30 v SL (Colombo, PSS) 2010-11. **IT20**: 95 (2004 to 2015-16, 93 as captain); HS 92* v A (Hobart) 2013-14; BB 3-21 v SL (Colombo, NCC) 2010-11.

ELWISS, Georgia Amanda, b Wolverhampton, Staffs 31 May 1991. RHB, RMF. Staffordshire 2004-10. Sapphires 2006-12. Diamonds 2008. Australia CT 2009-10 to 2010-11. Emeralds 2011. Sussex 2011 to date. Rubies 2013. Loughborough Lightning 2016. **Tests**: 1 (2015); HS 46 and BB – v A (Canterbury) 2015. **LOI**: 25 (2011-12 to 2016-17); HS 77 v P (Taunton) 2016; BB 3-17 v I (Wormsley) 2012. **IT20**: 13 (2011-12 to 2016); HS 18 v SA (Paarl) 2015-16; BB 2-9 v P (Chennai) 2015-16.

FARRANT, Natasha ('**Tash**') Eleni (Sevenoaks S), b Athens, Greece 29 May 1996. LHB, LM. Kent 2012 to date. Sapphires 2013. Southern Vipers 2016. **LOI**: 1 (2013-14); HS 1* and BB 1-14 v WI (Port of Spain) 2013-14. **IT20**: 9 (2013 to 2016); HS 1* and BB 2-15 v P (Loughborough) 2013.

GREENWAY, Lydia Sophie, b Farnborough, Kent 6 Aug 1985. LHB, OB. Kent 2000 to date. Rubies 2006-13. Diamonds 2008. Southern Vipers 2016. **Tests**: 14 (2002-03 to 2015); HS 70 v SA (Shenley) 2003. **LOI**: 126 (2003 to 2015-16); 125* v SA (Potchefstroom) 2011-12. **IT20**: 85 (2004 to 2015-16); HS 80* v A (Southampton) 2013.

GRUNDY, Rebecca Louise, b Solihull, Warwicks 12 Jul 1990. LHB, SLA. Warwickshire 2007 to date. Rubies 2013. Loughborough Lightning 2016. **LOI**: 7 (2014-15 to 2015-16); HS 1* v NZ (Mt Maunganui) 2014-15 – twice; BB 3-36 v NZ (Lincoln) 2014-15 – twice. **IT20**: 12 (2013-14 to 2015-16); HS 2* v A (Hove) 2015; BB 2-13 v SL (Sylhet) 2013-14.

GUNN, Jennifer ('**Jenny**') Louise, b Nottingham 9 May 1986. RHB, RMF. Nottinghamshire 2001-15. Emeralds 2006-08. S Australia 2006-07 to 2007-08. Diamonds 2007. W Australia 2008-09. Yorkshire 2011. Rubies 2012-13. Warwickshire 2016. Yorkshire Diamonds 2016. MBE 2014. **Tests**: 11 (2004 to 2014); HS 62* and BB 5-19 v I (Wormsley) 2014. **LOI**: 132 (2003-04 to 2016-17); HS 73 v NZ (Taunton) 2007; BB 5-22 v P (Louth) 2013. **IT20**: 95 (2004 to 2016, 3 as captain); HS 69 v SL (Colombo, NCC) 2010-11; BB 5-18 v NZ (Bridgetown) 2013-14.

HARTLEY, Alexandra, b Blackburn, Lancs 26 Sep 1993. RHB, SLA. Lancashire 2008-12. Emeralds 2011-13. Rubies 2012. Middlesex 2013 to date. Surrey Stars 2016. **LOI**: 9 (2016 to 2016-17); HS 2* v WI (Florence Hall) 2016-17; BB 4-24 v WI (Kingston) 2016-17. **IT20**: 1 (2016); BB 2-19 v P (Chelmsford) 2016.

HAZELL, Danielle ('**Danni**'), b Durham 13 May 1988. RHB, OB. Durham 2002-04. Sapphires 2006-13. Emeralds 2007. Yorkshire 2008 to date. Diamonds 2011-12. Yorkshire Diamonds 2016. **Tests**: 3 (2010-11 to 2013-14); HS 15 v A (Perth) 2013-14; BB 2-32 v A (Sydney) 2010-11. **LOI**: 45 (2009-10 to 2016-17); HS 45 and BB 3-21 v SL (Colombo, RPS) 2016-17. **IT20**: 70 (2009-10 to 2016); HS 18* v WI (Arundel) 2012; BB 4-12 v WI (Hove) 2012.

JONES, Amy Ellen, b Solihull, Warwicks 13 Jun 1993. RHB, WK. Warwickshire 2008 to date. Diamonds 2011. Emeralds 2012. Rubies 2013. Loughborough Lightning 2016. **LOI**: 20 (2012-13 to 2016-17); HS 41 v SL (Mumbai, BS) 2012-13. **IT20**: 15 (2013 to 2016); HS 14 v A (Melbourne) 2013-14 and 14 v SA (Johannesburg) 2015-16.

KNIGHT, Heather Clare, b Rochdale, Lancs 26 Dec 1990. RHB, OB. Devon 2008-09. Emeralds 2008-13. Berkshire 2010 to date. Sapphires 2011-12. Tasmania 2014-15 to 2015-16. Western Storm 2016. **Tests**. 5 (2010-11 to 2015); HS 157 v A (Wormsley) 2013; BB 1-7 v I (Wormsley) 2014. **LOI**: 66 (2009-10 to 2016-17, 11 as captain); HS 79 v NZ (Mt Maunganui) 2014-15, BB 5-26 v P (Leicester) 2016. **IT20**. 36 (2010-11 to 2016, 3 as captain); HS 30 v NZ (Whangarei) 2014-15; BB 3-10 v NZ (Whangarei) 2014-15 – separate matches.

LANGSTON, Bethany Alice, b Harold Wood, Essex 6 Sep 1992. RHB, RM. Essex 2009-15. Diamonds 2011-12. Emeralds 2013. Yorkshire 2016. Otago 2016-17. Loughborough Lightning 2016. **LOI**: 4 (2016-17); HS 21 v SL (Colombo, RPS) 2016-17; BB 1-23 v SL (Colombo, SSC) 2016-17. **IT20**: 2 (2013-14); HS –; BB 1-16 v WI (Bridgetown) 2013-14.

MARSH, Laura Alexandra, b Pembury, Kent 5 Dec 1986. RHB, RMF/OB. Sussex 2003-10. Rubies 2006-07. Emeralds 2008. Sapphires 2011. Kent 2011 to date. New South Wales 2015-16. Otago 2015-16. Surrey Stars 2016. **Tests**: 7 (2006 to 2015); HS 55 v A (Wormsley) 2013; BB 3-44 v I (Leicester) 2006. **LOI**: 83 (2006 to 2016-17); HS 67 v Ire (Kibworth) 2010; BB 5-15 v P (Sydney) 2008-09. **IT20**: 60 (2007 to 2015-16); HS 54 v P (Galle) 2012-13; BB 3-12 v P (Chennai) 2015-16.

SCIVER, Natalie Ruth, b Tokyo, Japan 20 Aug 1992. RHB, RM. Surrey 2010 to date. Rubies 2011. Emeralds 2012-13. Surrey Stars 2016. **Tests**: 3 (2013-14 to 2015); HS 49 and BB 1-30 v A (Perth) 2013-14. **LOI**: 32 (2013 to 2016-17); HS 80 v P (Worcester) 2016; BB 3-19 v WI (Port of Spain) 2013-14. **IT20**: 37 (2013 to 2016-17); HS 47 and BB 4-15 v A (Cardiff) 2015.

SHRUBSOLE, Anya, b Bath, Somerset 7 Dec 1991. RHB, RMF. Somerset 2004 to date. Rubies 2006-12. Emeralds 2006-13. Western Storm 2016. **Tests**: 4 (2013 to 2015); HS 14 v I (Wormsley) 2014; BB 4-51 v A (Perth) 2013-14. **LOI**: 37 (2008 to 2016); HS 29 v NZ (Mt Maunganui) 2014-15; BB 5-17 v SA (Cuttack) 2012-13. **IT20**: 47 (2008 to 2015-16); HS 10* v SA (Paarl) 2015-16; BB 5-11 v NZ (Wellington) 2011-12.

TAYLOR, Sarah Jane, b Whitechapel, London 20 May 1989. RHB, WK. Sussex 2004 to date. Rubies 2006-12. Emeralds 2008-13. Wellington 2010-11 to 2011-12. S Australia 2014-15 to date. **Tests**: 8 (2006 to 2015); HS 40 v I (Wormsley) 2014. **LOI**: 101 (2006 to 2015-16); HS 129 v SA (Lord's) 2008. **IT20**: 81 (2006 to 2015-16); HS 77 v A (Chelmsford) 2013.

WILSON, Frances Claire, b Aldershot, Hants 7 Nov 1991. RHB, OB. Somerset 2006-14. Diamonds 2011. Emeralds 2012. Rubies 2013. Middlesex 2015 to date. Wellington 2016-17. Western Storm 2016. **LOI**: 6 (2010-11 to 2016-17); HS 30 v SL (Colombo, RPS) 2016-17. **IT20**: 7 (2010-11 to 2016); HS 43* v P (Southampton) 2016.

WINFIELD, Lauren, b York 16 Aug 1990. RHB, WK. Yorkshire 2007 to date. Diamonds 2011. Sapphires 2012. Rubies 2013. Yorkshire Diamonds 2016. **Tests**: 2 (2014 to 2015); HS 35 v I (Wormsley) 2014. **LOI**: 25 (2013 to 2016-17); HS 123 v P (Worcester) 2016. **IT20**: 18 (2013 to 2016); HS 74 v SA (Birmingham) 2014 and 74 v P (Bristol) 2016.

WYATT, Danielle ('**Danni**') Nicole, b Stoke-on-Trent, Staffs 22 Apr 1991. RHB, OB. Staffordshire 2005-12. Emeralds 2006-08. Sapphires 2011-13. Victoria 2011-12 to 2015-16. Nottinghamshire 2013-15. Sussex 2016. Lancashire Thunder 2016. **LOI**: 48 (2009-10 to 2016-17); HS 44 v WI (Florence Hall) 2016-17; BB 3-7 v SA (Cuttack) 2012-13. **IT20**: 70 (2009-10 to 2016); HS 41 v P (Loughborough) 2012; BB 4-11 v SA (Basseterre) 2010.

WOMEN'S LIMITED-OVERS RECORDS

1973 to 12 March 2017

RESULTS SUMMARY

	Matches	*Won*	*Lost*	*Tied*	*NR*	*% Won (exc NR)*
Australia	300	232	60	2	6	78.91
England	312	181	119	2	10	59.93
India	234	126	103	1	4	54.78
New Zealand	311	157	146	2	6	51.47
South Africa	158	75	74	2	7	49.66
West Indies	149	72	72	1	4	49.65
Sri Lanka	142	54	83	–	5	39.41
Trinidad & Tobago	6	2	4	–		33.33
Pakistan	137	40	95	–	2	29.62
Ireland	141	39	96	–	6	28.88
Bangladesh	30	7	21	–	2	25.00
Jamaica	5	1	4	–	–	20.00
Netherlands	101	19	81	–	1	19.00
Denmark	33	6	27	–	–	18.18
International XI	18	3	14	–	1	17.64
Young England	6	1	5	–	–	16.66
Scotland	8	1	7	–	–	12.50
Japan	5	–	5	–	–	0.00

TEAM RECORDS

HIGHEST INNINGS TOTALS

455-5 (50 overs)	New Zealand v Pakistan	Christchurch	1996-97
412-3 (50 overs)	Australia v Denmark	Mumbai	1997-98
397-4 (50 overs)	Australia v Pakistan	Melbourne	1996-97
378-5 (50 overs)	England v Pakistan	Worcester	2016
376-2 (50 overs)	England v Pakistan	Vijayawada	1997-98

LARGEST RUNS MARGIN OF VICTORY

408 runs	New Zealand beat Pakistan	Christchurch	1996-97
374 runs	Australia beat Pakistan	Melbourne	1996-97

LOWEST INNINGS TOTALS

22 (23.4 overs)	Netherlands v West Indies	Deventer	2008
23 (24.1 overs)	Pakistan v Australia	Melbourne	1996-97
[illegible]	Scotland v England	Reading	2001

BATTING RECORDS

2000 RUNS IN A CAREER

Runs		*Career*	*M*	*I*	*NO*	*HS*	*Avge*	*100*	*50*
5992	C.M.Edwards (E)	1997-2016	191	180	23	173*	38.16	9	46
5614	M.Raj (I)	1999-2017	172	155	45	114*	51.03	5	43
4844	B.J.Clark (A)	1991-2005	118	114	12	229*	47.49	5	30
4814	K.L.Rolton (A)	1995-2009	141	132	32	154*	48.14	8	33
4101	S.C.Taylor (E)	1998-2011	126	120	18	156*	40.20	8	23
4064	D.A.Hockley (NZ)	1982-2000	118	115	18	117	41.89	4	34
3732	S.R.Taylor (WI)	2008-2016	98	97	13	171	44.42	5	26
3492	S.W.Bates (NZ)	2006-2017	98	94	9	168	41.08	7	22
3261	S.J.Taylor (E)	2006-2016	101	94	12	129	39.76	5	16
3177	A.J.Blackwell (A)	2003-2017	133	116	25	114	34.91	3	23
2970	A.E.Satterthwaite (NZ)	2007-2017	95	90	11	137*	37.59	6	15
2919	H.M.Tiffen (NZ)	1999-2009	117	111	16	100	30.72	1	18
2856	A.Chopra (I)	1995-2012	127	112	21	100	31.38	1	18
2844	E.C.Drumm (NZ)	1992-2006	101	94	13	116	35.11	2	19
2728	L.C.Sthalekar (A)	2001-2013	125	111	22	104*	30.65	2	16

Runs		Career	M	I	NO	HS	Avge	100	50
2671	M.M.Lanning (A)	2011-2017	57	57	6	135*	52.37	10	10
2630	L.M.Keightley (A)	1995-2005	82	78	12	156*	39.84	4	21
2554	L.S.Greenway (E)	2003-2016	126	111	26	125*	30.04	1	12
2438	S.J.McGlashan (NZ)	2002-2016	134	125	16	97*	22.36	–	14
2422	M.du Preez (SA)	2007-2017	94	89	14	116*	32.29	2	11
2337	D.J.S.Dottin (WI)	2008-2016	98	93	9	95	27.82	–	17
2201	R.J.Rolls (NZ)	1997-2007	104	91	3	114	25.01	2	12
2121	J.A.Brittin (E)	1979-1998	63	59	9	138*	42.42	5	8
2091	J.Sharma (I)	2002-2008	77	75	7	138*	30.75	2	14
2089	T.Chetty (SA)	2007-2017	86	78	12	95	31.65	–	14
2072	Bismah Maroof (P)	2006-2017	90	88	10	99	26.56	–	11
2047	S.Nitschke (A)	2004-2011	80	69	9	113*	34.11	1	14
2002	N.J.Browne (NZ)	2002-2014	125	102	28	63	27.05	–	10

HIGHEST INDIVIDUAL INNINGS

229*	B.J.Clark	Australia v Denmark	Mumbai	1997-98
173*	C.M.Edwards	England v Ireland	Pune	1997-98
171	S.R.Taylor	West Indies v Sri Lanka	Mumbai	2012-13
168*	T.T.Beaumont	England v Pakistan	Taunton	2016
168	S.W.Bates	New Zealand v Pakistan	Sydney	2008-09
157	R.H.Priest	New Zealand v Sri Lanka	Lincoln	2015-16
156*	L.M.Keightley	Australia v Pakistan	Melbourne	1996-97
156*	S.C.Taylor	England v India	Lord's	2006
154*	K.L.Rolton	Australia v Sri Lanka	Christchurch	2000-01
153*	J.Logtenberg	South Africa v Netherlands	Deventer	2007
151	K.L.Rolton	Australia v Ireland	Dublin	2005

HIGHEST PARTNERSHIP FOR EACH WICKET

1st	268	S.J.Taylor/C.M.G.Atkins	England v South Africa	Lord's	2008
2nd	262	H.M.Tiffen/S.W.Bates	New Zealand v Pakistan	Sydney	2008-09
3rd	244	K.L.Rolton/L.C.Sthalekar	Australia v Ireland	Dublin	2005
4th	224*	J.Logtenberg//M.du Preez	South Africa v Netherlands	Deventer	2007
5th	188*	S.C.Taylor/J.Cassar	England v Sri Lanka	Lincoln	2000-01
6th	142	S.Luus/C.L.Tryon	South Africa v Ireland	Dublin	2016
7th	104*	S.J.Tsukigawa/N.J.Browne	New Zealand v England	Chennai	2006-07
8th	85*	S.L.Clarke/N.J.Shaw	England v Scotland	Reading	2001
9th	73	L.R.F.Askew/I.T.Guha	England v New Zealand	Chennai	2006-07
10th	58	A.Sharma/G.Sultana	India v England	Taunton	2012

BOWLING RECORDS
100 WICKETS IN A CAREER

		LOI	Balls	R	W	Avge	Best	4w	R/Over
C.L.Fitzpatrick (A)	1993-2007	109	6017	3023	**180**	16.79	5-14	11	3.01
J.Goswami (I)	2002-2016	151	7339	3910	**177**	22.09	6-31	6	3.19
L.C.Sthalekar (A)	2001-2013	125	5964	3646	**146**	24.97	5-35	2	3.66
N.David (I)	1995-2008	97	4892	2305	**141**	16.34	5-20	6	2.82
A.Mohammed (WI)	2003-2016	101	4580	2524	**136**	18.55	7-14	11	3.30
J.L.Gunn (E)	2004-2016	132	5396	3397	**123**	27.61	5-22	5	3.77
K.H.Brunt (E)	2005-2016	94	4685	2624	**120**	21.86	5-18	6	3.36
S.R.Taylor (WI)	2008-2016	98	4134	2140	**114**	18.77	4-17	5	3.10
E.A.Perry (A)	2007-2017	83	3808	2752	**113**	24.35	5-19	3	4.33
H.A.S.D.Siriwardene (SL)	2003-2016	93	4218	2639	**106**	24.89	4-11	6	3.75
D.van Niekerk (SA)	2009-2017	78	3352	1970	**105**	18.76	5-17	5	3.52
Sana Mir (P)	2005-2017	95	4591	2768	**104**	26.61	5-32	4	3.61
L.A.Marsh (E)	2006-2016	83	4282	2706	**103**	26.27	5-15	3	3.79
C.E.Taylor (E)	1988-2005	105	5140	2443	**102**	23.95	4-13	2	2.85
I.T.Guha (E)	2001-2011	83	3767	2345	**101**	23.21	5-14	4	3.73
N.Al Khadeer (I)	2002-2012	78	4036	2402	**100**	24.02	5-14	5	3.57

SIX OR MORE WICKETS IN AN INNINGS

7- 4	Sajjida Shah	Pakistan v Japan	Amsterdam	2003
7- 8	J.M.Chamberlain	England v Denmark	Haarlem	1991
7-14	A.Mohammed	West Indies v Pakistan	Dhaka	2011-12
7-24	S.Nitschke	Australia v England	Kidderminster	2005
6-10	J.Lord	New Zealand v India	Auckland	1981-82
6-10	M.Maben	India v Sri Lanka	Kandy	2003-04
6-10	S.Ismail	South Africa v Netherlands	Savar	2011-12
6-20	G.L.Page	New Zealand v Trinidad & T	St Albans	1973
6-20	D.B.Sharma	India v Sri Lanka	Ranchi	2015-16
6-31	J.Goswami	India v New Zealand	Southgate	2011
6-32	B.H.McNeill	New Zealand v England	Lincoln	2007-08
6-36	S.Luus	South Africa v Ireland	Dublin	2016

WICKET-KEEPING AND FIELDING RECORDS

100 DISMISSALS IN A CAREER

Total			*LOI*	*Ct*	*St*
133	R.J.Rolls	New Zealand	104	89	44
126	T.Chetty	South Africa	86	87	39
114	J.Smit	England	109	69	45
113	S.J.Taylor	England	101	73	40

SIX DISMISSALS IN AN INNINGS

6 (4ct, 2st)	S.L.Illingworth	New Zealand v Australia	Beckenham	1993
6 (1ct, 5st)	V.Kalpana	India v Denmark	Slough	1993
6 (2ct, 4st)	Batool Fatima	Pakistan v West Indies	Karachi	2003-04
6 (4ct, 2st)	Batool Fatima	Pakistan v Sri Lanka	Colombo (PSS)	2011

50 CATCHES IN THE FIELD IN A CAREER

Total			*LOI*	*Career*
52	L.S.Greenway	England	126	2003-2016
52	J.Goswani	India	151	2002-2016
52	C.M.Edwards	England	191	1997-2016
51	S.W.Bates	New Zealand	98	2006-2017
51	A.J.Blackwell	Australia	133	2003-2017

FOUR CATCHES IN THE FIELD IN AN INNINGS

4	Z.J.Goss	Australia v New Zealand	Adelaide	1995-96
4	J.L.Gunn	England v New Zealand	Lincoln	2014-15

APPEARANCE RECORDS

125 APPEARANCES

191	C.M.Edwards	England	1997-2016
172	M.Raj	India	1999-2017
151	J.Goswami	India	2002-2016
141	K.L.Rolton	Australia	1995-2009
134	S.J.McGlashan	New Zealand	2002-2016
133	A.J.Blackwell	Australia	2003-2017
132	J.L.Gunn	England	2004-2016
127	A.Chopra	India	1995-2012
126	L.S.Greenway	England	2003-2016
126	S.C.Taylor	England	1998-2011
125	N.J.Browne	New Zealand	2002-2014
125	L.C.Sthalekar	Australia	2001-2013

100 CONSECUTIVE APPEARANCES

109	M.Raj	India	17.04.2004 to 07.02.2013

100 MATCHES AS CAPTAIN

			Won	*Lost*	*No Result*	
117	C.M.Edwards	England	72	38	7	2005-2016
101	B.J.Clark	Australia	83	17	1	1994-2005

WOMEN'S INTERNATIONAL TWENTY20 RECORDS

2004 to 6 April 2017

MATCH RESULTS SUMMARY

	Matches	*Won*	*Lost*	*Tied*	*NR*	*Win %*
England	102	73	26	2	1	72.27
Australia	98	59	37	2	–	60.20
West Indies	96	56	34	4	2	59.57
New Zealand	92	53	36	2	1	58.24
India	73	37	36	–	–	50.68
South Africa	71	29	41	–	1	41.42
Pakistan	77	31	43	2	1	40.78
Sri Lanka	68	19	46	–	3	29.23
Ireland	44	10	34	–	–	22.72
Bangladesh	34	5	29	–	–	14.70
Netherlands	11	–	10	–	1	0.00

WOMEN'S INTERNATIONAL TWENTY20 RECORDS

(To 6 April 2017)

TEAM RECORDS – HIGHEST INNINGS TOTALS

205-1	South Africa v Netherlands	Potchefstroom	2010-11
191-4	West Indies v Netherlands	Potchefstroom	2010-11
191-4	Australia v Ireland	Sylhet	2013-14
188-3	New Zealand v Sri Lanka	Christchurch	2015-16
187-5	England v Pakistan	Bristol	2016
186-7	New Zealand v South Africa	Taunton	2007
186-1	Australia v Ireland	Dublin	2015
185-2	Australia v Pakistan	Sylhet	2013-14
184-4	West Indies v Ireland	Dublin	2008
180-5	England v South Africa	Taunton	2007
180-5	New Zealand v West Indies	Gros Islet	2010

HIGHEST INNINGS TOTAL BATTING SECOND

165-2	England (set 164) v Australia	The Oval	2009

LOWEST COMPLETED INNINGS TOTALS † Batting Second

44 (15.3)	Bangladesh v Pakistan	Bangkok	2016-17
54† (18.2)	Bangladesh v India	Bangkok	2016-17
57† (19.4)	Sri Lanka v Bangladesh	Guangzhou	2012-13
58-9†	Bangladesh v England	Sylhet	2013-14
59-8	Sri Lanka v Australia	Colombo (SSC)	2016-17
60† (16.5)	Pakistan v England	Taunton	2009
60 (19.4)	New Zealand v England	Whangarei	2014-15

BATTING RECORDS – 1200 RUNS IN A CAREER

Runs			*M*	*I*	*NO*	*HS*	*Avge*	*50*	*R/100B*
2605	C.M.Edwards	E	95	93	14	92*	32.97	12	106.9
2389	S.R.Taylor	WI	77	76	13	90	37.92	19	102.0†
2214	S.W.Bates	NZ	87	85	3	94*	27.00	13	106.0
2045	S.J.Taylor	E	81	79	11	77	30.20	15	109.6
1930	M.M.Lanning	A	70	69	8	126	31.63	11	115.8
1805	D.J.S.Dottin	WI	91	90	18	112*	25.06	10	123.3†
1708	M.Raj	I	63	61	16	73*	37.95	10	93.7†
1351	Bismah Maroof	P	74	68	16	65*	25.98	4	84.6
1314	A.J.Blackwell	A	95	81	19	61	21.19	1	92.9
1223	H.Kaur	I	68	60	11	77	24.95	4	93.7†

† *No information on balls faced for games at Roseau on 22 and 23 February 2012.*

HIGHEST INDIVIDUAL INNINGS

Score	*Balls*				
126	65	M.M.Lanning	A v Ire	Sylhet	2013-14
116*	71	S.A.Fritz	SA v Neth	Potchefstroom	2010-11
112*	45	D.J.S.Dottin	WI v SA	Basseterre	2010
96*	53	K.L.Rolton	A v E	Taunton	2005
94*	61	S.W.Bates	NZ v P	Sylhet	2013-14
92*	59	C.M.Edwards	E v A	Hobart	2013-14

HIGHEST PARTNERSHIP FOR EACH WICKET

1st	170	S.A.Fritz/T.Chetty	SA v Neth	Potchefstroom	2010-11
2nd	118*	S.W.Bates/A.L.Watkins	NZ v A	Taunton	2009
3rd	124	T.D.Smartt/S.A.C.A.King	WI v Neth	Potchefstroom	2010-11
4th	147*	K.L.Rolton/K.A.Blackwell	A v E	Taunton	2005
5th	118	S.F.Daley/D.J.S.Dottin	WI v SA	Basseterre	2010
6th	68	K.L.Rolton/A.J.Blackwell	A v SA	Taunton	2009
7th	51	S.R.Taylor/M.R.Aguilleira	WI v SL	Cayon	2010
8th	39	L.E.Kaushalya/K.A.D.A.Kanchana	SL v I	Ranchi	2015-16
9th	33*	D.Hazell/H.L.Colvin	E v WI	Bridgetown	2013-14
10th	23*	L.N.McCarthy/E.J.Tice	Ire v SL	Dublin	2013

BOWLING RECORDS
60 WICKETS IN A CAREER

Wkts			*Matches*	*Overs*	*Mdns*	*Runs*	*Avge*	*Best*	*R/Over*
104	A.Mohammed	WI	89	302.3	6	1611	15.49	5-10	5.32
77	E.A.Perry	A	82	265.5	4	1513	19.64	4-12	5.69
73	D.Hazell	E	70	266.0	6	1384	18.95	4-12	5.20
72	S.F.Daley	WI	68	227.1	8	1113	15.45	5-15	4.89
68	A.Shrubsole	E	47	159.3	5	870	12.79	5-11	5.45
67	S.R.Taylor	WI	77	199.1	4	1079	16.10	3-10	5.41
66	J.L.Gunn	E	95	202.5	1	1240	18.78	5-18	6.11
66	Sana Mir	P	75	264.2	7	1364	20.66	4-13	5.16
63	H.L.Colvin	E	50	186.5	4	971	15.41	4- 9	5.19
60	Nida Dar	P	70	209.4	6	1074	17.90	3-12	5.12
60	L.C.Sthalekar	A	54	199.2	1	1161	19.35	4-18	5.82
60	L.A.Marsh	E	60	224.3	4	1169	19.48	3-12	5.20

BEST FIGURES IN AN INNINGS

6-17	A.E.Satterthwaite	NZ v E	Taunton	2007
5- 8	S.Luus	SA v Ire	Chennai	2015-16
5-10	A.Mohammed	WI v SA	Cape Town	2009-10
5-10	M.Strano	A v NZ	Geelong	2016-17
5-11	A.Shrubsole	E v NZ	Wellington	2011-12
5-11	J.Goswami	I v A	Visakhapatnam	2011-12
5-12	A.Mohammed	WI v NZ	Bridgetown	2013-14
5-15	S.F.Daley	WI v SL	Colombo (RPS)	2012-13
5-16	P.Roy	I v P	Taunton	2009
5-16	S.L.Quintyne	WI v E	Bridgetown	2013-14
5-18	J.L.Gunn	E v NZ	Bridgetown	2013-14
5-22	J.L.Hunter	A v WI	Colombo (RPS)	2012-13

HAT-TRICKS

Asmavia Iqbal	Pakistan v England	Loughborough	2012
Ekta Bisht	Sri Lanka v India	Colombo (NCC)	2012-13

M.Kapp	South Africa v Bangladesh	Potchefstroom	2013-14
N.R.Sciver	England v New Zealand	Bridgetown	2013-14
Sana Mir	Pakistan v Sri Lanka	Sharjah	2014-15
A.M.Peterson	New Zealand v Australia	Geelong	2016-17

WICKET-KEEPING RECORDS

30 DISMISSALS IN A CAREER

Dis			*Matches*	*Ct*	*St*
68	R.H.Priest	New Zealand	68	38	30
68	S.J.Taylor	England	81	22	46
57	T.Chetty	South Africa	68	34	23
51	M.R.Aguilleira	West Indies	81	26	25
50	Batool Fatima	Pakistan	45	11	39
43	A.J.Healy	Australia	72	15	28
40	J.M.Fields	Australia	37	25	15
31	S.Naik	India	31	10	21

FIVE DISMISSALS IN AN INNINGS

5 (1ct, 4st)	Kycia A.Knight	West Indies v Sri Lanka	Colombo (RPS)	2012-13
5 (1ct, 4st)	Batool Fatima	Pakistan v Ireland	Dublin	2013
5 (1ct, 4st)	Batool Fatima	Pakistan v Ireland	Dublin	2013

FIELDING RECORDS

30 CATCHES IN A CAREER

Total			*Matches*	*Total*			*Matches*
55	J.L.Gunn	England	95	33	J.E.Cameron	Australia	64
54	L.S.Greenway	England	85	33	A.J.Blackwell	Australia	95
39	S.W.Bates	New Zealand	87	32	S.A.C.A.King	West Indies	76

FOUR CATCHES IN AN INNINGS

4	L.S.Greenway	England v New Zealand	Chelmsford	2010

APPEARANCE RECORDS

75 APPEARANCES

95	A.J.Blackwell	Australia	81	M.R.Aguilleira	West Indies
95	C.M.Edwards	England	81	S.J.Taylor	England
95	J.L.Gunn	England	79	S.A.Campbelle	West Indies
91	D.J.S.Dottin	West Indies	77	S.R.Taylor	West Indies
89	A.Mohammed	West Indies	76	S.A.C.A.King	West Indies
87	S.W.Bates	New Zealand	76	S.J.McGlashan	New Zealand
85	L.S.Greenway	England	75	Sana Mir	Pakistan
82	E.A.Perry	Australia	75	A.E.Satterthwaite	New Zealand

30 MATCHES AS CAPTAIN

			W	*L*	*T*	*NR*	*%age wins*
93	C.M.Edwards	England	68	23	1	1	73.91
70	M.R.Aguilleira	West Indies	38	28	2	2	55.88
65	Sana Mir	Pakistan	26	36	2	1	40.62
50	S.W.Bates	New Zealand	28	21	1	–	56.00
50	M.du Preez	South Africa	24	25	–	1	48.97

MCCA FIXTURES 2017

Sun 23 April	**KNOCK-OUT TROPHY**
North Devon	Devon v Dorset (1)
Banbury	Oxfordshire v Cornwall (1)
Shrewsbury	Shropshire v Staffordshire (2)
Newport	Wales MC v Herefordshire (2)
Saffron Walden	Cambridgeshire v Northumberland (3)
North Mymms	Hertfordshire v Suffolk (4)
Warminster	Wiltshire v Buckinghamshire (4)
Sun 30 April	**KNOCK-OUT TROPHY**
Henley	Berkshire v Devon (1)
Bashley	Dorset v Oxfordshire (1)
Oxton	Cheshire v Shropshire (2)
Himley	Staffordshire v Wales MC (2)
Grantham	Lincolnshire v Cambridgeshire (3)
S Northumberland	Northumberland v Cumberland (3)
Ampthill	Bedfordshire v Hertfordshire (4)
Ipswich School	Suffolk v Wiltshire (4)
Mon 1 May	**KNOCK-OUT TROPHY**
Manor Park	Norfolk v Cambridgeshire (3)
Sun 7 May	**KNOCK-OUT TROPHY**
Truro, Grampound Rd	Cornwall v Dorset (1)
Bicester & N Ox	Oxfordshire v Berkshire (1)
Eastnor	Herefordshire v Staffordshire (2)
Newport	Wales MC v Cheshire (2)
Penrith	Cumberland v Lincolnshire (3)
Manor Park	Norfolk v Northumberland (3)
Tring	Buckinghamshire v Suffolk (4)
Warminster	Wiltshire v Bedfordshire (4)
Sun 14 May	**KNOCK-OUT TROPHY**
Wokingham	Berkshire v Cornwall (1)
Sidmouth	Devon v Oxfordshire (1)
Alderley Edge	Cheshire v Herefordshire (2)
Oswestry	Shropshire v Wales MC (2)
Leys School	Cambridgeshire v Cumberland (3)
Bracebridge Heath	Lincolnshire v Norfolk (3)
Dunstable	Bedfordshire v Buckinghamshire (4)
Hertford	Hertfordshire v Wiltshire (4)
Sun 21 May	**KNOCK-OUT TROPHY**
Werrington	Cornwall v Devon (1)
North Perrott	Dorset v Berkshire (1)
Brockhampton	Herefordshire v Shropshire (2)
Knypersley	Staffordshire v Cheshire (2)
Netherfield	Cumberland v Norfolk (3)
Jesmond	Northumberland v Lincolnshire (3)
Gerrards Cross	Buckinghamshire v Hertfordshire (4)
Woolpit	Suffolk v Bedfordshire (4)
Sun 4 – Tue 6 June	**MCCA CHAMPIONSHIP**
Wargrave	Berkshire v Cornwall
Saffron Walden	Cambridgeshire v Lincolnshire
Netherfield	Cumberland v Bedfordshire
Sherborne School	Dorset v Devon
Brockhampton	Herefordshire v Cheshire

Hertford	Hertfordshire v Norfolk
Gt & Little Tew	Oxfordshire v Wiltshire
Longton	Staffordshire v Northumberland
Bury St Edmunds	Suffolk v Buckinghamshire
Pontarddulais	Wales MC v Shropshire
Sun 11 June	**KNOCK-OUT TROPHY – Quarter-finals**
Match 1	Winner Gp 3 v Runner-up Gp 1
Match 2	Winner Gp 4 v Runner-up Gp 2
Match 3	Winner Gp 1 v Runner-up Gp 4
Match 4	Winner Gp 2 v Runner-up Gp 3
Sun 18 – Tue 20 June	**MCCA CHAMPIONSHIP**
Luton	Bedfordshire v Cambridgeshire
Burnham	Buckinghamshire v Norfolk
Nantwich	Cheshire v Cornwall
Bishop's Stortford	Hertfordshire v Cumberland
Sleaford	Lincolnshire v Staffordshire
S Northumberland	Northumberland v Suffolk
Banbury	Oxfordshire v Devon
Whitchurch	Shropshire v Herefordshire
Abergavenny	Wales MC v Berkshire
Corsham	Wiltshire v Dorset
Sun 25 June	**EAST ANGLIA T20**
Bury St Edmunds	
Sun 2 – Tue 4 July	**MCCA CHAMPIONSHIP**
Falkland	Berkshire v Wiltshire
March	Cambridgeshire v Northumberland
Truro	Cornwall v Wales MC
Sidmouth	Devon v Cheshire
Colwall	Herefordshire v Dorset
Grantham	Lincolnshire v Buckinghamshire
Shifnal	Shropshire v Oxfordshire
West Brom Dartmth	Staffordshire v Bedfordshire
Copdock	Suffolk v Hertfordshire
Sun 9 July	**KNOCK-OUT TROPHY – Semi-finals**
tbc	Winner Match 2 v Winner Match 1
tbc	Winner Match 4 v Winner Match 3
Sun 16 – Tue 18 July	**MCCA CHAMPIONSHIP**
Bedford School	Bedfordshire v Lincolnshire
Finchampstead	Berkshire v Herefordshire
High Wycombe	Buckinghamshire v Staffordshire
Alderley Edge	Cheshire v Wales MC
St Austell	Cornwall v Shropshire
Furness	Cumberland v Northumberland
Bournemouth	Dorset v Oxfordshire
Long Marston	Hertfordshire v Cambridgeshire
Manor Park	Norfolk v Suffolk
South Wilts	Wiltshire v Devon
Wed 19 – Thu 20 July	
Loughborough	England Under-19 v Unicorns
Sun 23 – Tue 25 July	**MCCA CHAMPIONSHIP**
Manor Park	Norfolk v Cumberland

Sun 30 July – Tue 1 August	**MCCA CHAMPIONSHIP**
Chesham	Buckinghamshire v Cambridgeshire
Penzance	Cornwall v Herefordshire
Sandford	Devon v Shropshire
Manor Park	Norfolk v Bedfordshire
Jesmond	Northumberland v Lincolnshire
Challow & Childrey	Oxfordshire v Berkshire
Checkley	Staffordshire v Hertfordshire
Ipswich School	Suffolk v Cumberland
Usk	Wales MC v Dorset
Devizes	Wiltshire v Cheshire
Sun 10 August	
Torquay	MCCA v MCC
Sun 13 – Tue 15 August	**MCCA CHAMPIONSHIP**
Flitwick	Bedfordshire v Suffolk
Wisbech	Cambridgeshire v Staffordshire
Boughton H, Chester	Cheshire v Oxfordshire
Sedbergh School	Cumberland v Buckinghamshire
Exeter	Devon v Berkshire
North Perrott	Dorset v Cornwall
Eastnor	Herefordshire v Wales MC
Cleethorpes	Lincolnshire v Hertfordshire
Jesmond	Northumberland v Norfolk
Bridgnorth	Shropshire v Wiltshire
Wed 23 August	**KNOCK-OUT TROPHY**
tbc	FINAL (Reserve day Thu 24)
Sun 27 – Wed 30 August	**MCCA CHAMPIONSHIP**
Banbury	FINAL

MCCA KNOCK OUT TROPHY GROUPS

Group 1	*Group 2*	*Group 3*	*Group 4*
Berkshire	Cheshire	Cambridgeshire	Bedfordshire
Cornwall	Herefordshire	Cumberland	Buckinghamshire
Devon	Shropshire	Lincolnshire	Hertfordshire
Dorset	Staffordshire	Norfolk	Suffolk
Oxfordshire	Wales MC	Northumberland	Wiltshire

SECOND XI CHAMPIONSHIP FIXTURES 2017

THREE-DAY MATCHES

APRIL		
Mon 10	H Wycombe	MCC YC v Warwicks
	Notts SC	Notts v Leics
Tue 18	Hem Heath	Derbyshire v Lancashire
	Southampton	Hampshire v Surrey
	Radlett	Middlesex v Kent
	RGS Worcester	Worcs v Warwicks
Wed 26	Newport	Glamorgan v Glos
MAY		
Tue 2	Milton Keynes	Northants v Durham
Wed 3	H Wycombe	MCC YC v Yorkshire
	EFSG, Birm	Warwicks v Leics
Mon 8	Southampton	Hampshire v Essex
Tue 9	Chester-le-St	Durham v Notts
	Polo Farm Cant	Kent v Sussex
	Liverpool	Lancashire v Northants
	Purley	Surrey v Glos
	Harrogate	Yorkshire v Warwicks
Wed 10	Barnt Green	Worcs v MCC YC
Mon 15	Billericay	Essex v Surrey
	Basingstoke	Hampshire v Glamorgan
	Notts SC	Notts v Warwicks

Date	Venue	Match
Tue 16	Bristol U	Glos v Middlesex
	Taunton Vale	Somerset v Kent
Mon 22	Polo Farm Cant	Kent v Hampshire
	EFSG, Birm	Warwicks v Derbyshire
Tue 23	Chester-le-St	Durham v Leics
	Northern CC	Lancashire v Worcs
	Milton Keynes	Northants v Notts
	Preston Nom	Sussex v Glamorgan
Tue 30	Neath	Glamorgan v Kent
	Kibworth	Leics v Yorkshire

JUNE

Date	Venue	Match
Mon 5	Belper Mead	Derbyshire v Northants
	Beckenham	Kent v Surrey
	Radlett	Middlesex v Somerset
	Notts SC	Notts v Lancashire
Tue 6	Billericay	Essex v Glos
Mon 12	H Wycombe	MCC YC v Notts
Tue 13	Taunton S	Somerset v Glamorgan
	Stourbridge	Worcs v Derbyshire
	Scarborough	Yorkshire v Lancashire
Mon 19	Neath	Glamorgan v Surrey
	Desborough	Leics v Lancashire
	Richmond	Middlesex v Sussex
Tue 20	Holcot	Northants v Worcs
	York	Yorkshire v Derbyshire
Mon 26	Glossop	Derbyshire v MCC YC
Tue 27	Burnopfield	Durham v Worcs
	Horsham	MCC Univs v Hampshire
	LSE, N Malden	Surrey v Somerset
	Blackstone	Sussex v Glos
	Stamford Brg	Yorkshire v Notts

JULY

Date	Venue	Match
Tue 4	Pontarddulais	Glamorgan v Essex
	RGS Worcester	Worcs v Leics
Wed 5	Hastings	MCC Univs v Sussex
Mon 10	Newclose IoW	Hampshire v Sussex
	EFSG, Birm	Warwicks v Lancashire
Tue 11	Belper Mead	Derbyshire v Durham
	Northwood	Middlesex v Glamorgan
	York	Yorkshire v Northants
Wed 12	Taunton Vale	Somerset v MCC Univs
Mon 17	Bristol U	Glos v Hampshire
	Polo Farm Cant	Kent v Essex
	Radlett	MCC Univs v Middlesex
Tue 18	S N'berland	Durham v Warwicks
	Urmston	Lancashire v MCC YC
Wed 19	Kibworth	Leics v Derbyshire
	Horsham	Sussex v Somerset
Mon 24	Southampton	Hampshire v Middlesex
	Hove	Sussex v Surrey
Tue 25	Billericay	Essex v MCC Univs
	Bristol CC	Glos v Kent
	EFSG, Birm	Warwicks v Northants
	RGS Worcester	Worcs v Yorkshire
Mon 31	Notts SC	Notts v Worcs

AUGUST

Date	Venue	Match
Tue 1	Coggeshall	Essex v Middlesex
	Bristol CC	Glos v Somerset
	Mumbles	MCC Univs v Glamorgan
	H Wycombe	MCC YC v Durham
Mon 7	Beckenham	MCC Univs v Kent
	Milton Keynes	Northants v MCC YC
	Taunton Vale	Somerset v Hampshire
Mon 14	Swarkestone	Derbyshire v Notts
	LSE, N Malden	Surrey v Middlesex
Tue 15	Chester-le-St	Durham v Yorkshire
	Bath	Glos v MCC Univs
	H Wycombe	MCC YC v Leics
Wed 16	Halstead	Essex v Sussex
Mon 21	Todmorden	Lancashire v Durham
	Taunton Vale	Somerset v Essex
Tue 22	Desborough	Leics v Northants
Wed 23	LSE, N Malden	Surrey v MCC Univs

SEPTEMBER

Date	Venue	Match
Tue 5	tbc	FINAL (Four days)

SECOND XI TROPHY FIXTURES 2017

ONE-DAY MATCHES

APRIL

Date	Venue	Match
Thu 13	Northwood	MCC YC v Warwicks
	Notts SC	Notts v Leics
Mon 17	Hem Heath	Derbyshire v Lancashire
	Radlett	Middlesex v Kent
Tue 18	Dunstable	Northants v MCC YC
Wed 19	Northampton	Northants v Leics
Mon 24	Denby	Derbyshire v Notts
	Billericay	Essex v Sussex
	Purley	Surrey v Somerset
Tue 25	Denby	Derbyshire v Northants
	Newport	Glamorgan v Glos
	Purley	Surrey v Middlesex
	Southampton	Unicorns v Hampshire
	Moseley	Warwicks v Worcs
	Leeds	Yorkshire v Lancashire
Wed 26	Hinckley Town	Leics v Lancashire
	Radlett	Middlesex v Essex
	Taunton Vale	Somerset v Unicorns
Thu 27	Preston Nom	Sussex v Hampshire
Fri 28	Moseley	Warwicks v Notts

MAY

Date	Venue	Match
Mon 1	Milton Keynes	Northants v Durham
	Oakham S	Notts v Worcs

	Taunton Vale	Somerset v Essex
	Croydon	Surrey v Hampshire
Tue 2	Northwood	MCC YC v Yorkshire
	Southgate	Middlesex v Sussex
Wed 3	Billericay	Essex v Surrey
	Newport	Glamorgan v Somerset
	Beckenham	Kent v Glos
Thu 4	Horsham	Sussex v Surrey
	Kidderminster	Worcs v Derbyshire
Fri 5	Bristol U	Glos v Somerset
Mon 8	Chester-le-St	Durham v Notts
	Canterbury	Kent v Sussex
	Northop Hall	Lancs v Northants
	Purley	Surrey v Glos
	York	Yorkshire v Warwicks
Tue 9	Falkland CC	Unicorns v Middlesex
	Kidderminster	Worcs v MCC YC
Wed 10	Falkland CC	Unicorns v Glamorgan
Thu 11	Southampton	Hampshire v Essex
Mon 15	Bedminster	Glos v Middlesex
	Lutterworth	Leics v Yorkshire
	Taunton Vale	Somerset v Kent
	Worcester	Worcs v Durham
Tue 16	Bowdon	Lancashire v Durham
Thu 18	Southampton	Hampshire v Glamorgan
	Northwood	MCC YC v Leics
Fri 19	Brandon	Durham v Yorkshire
	Newport	Glamorgan v Kent
	tbc	Leics v Warwicks
Mon 22	Chester-le-St	Durham v MCC YC
	Bristol U	Glos v Unicorns
	Neston	Lancashire v Worcs
	Bedford S	Northants v Notts
	Blackstone	Sussex v Glamorgan
Tue 23	Billericay	Essex v Unicorns
Thu 25	Polo Farm Cant	Kent v Hampshire
	Cov/N Wrwk	Warwicks v Derbyshire
JUNE		
Fri 2	tbc	Semi-finals
Thu 8	tbc	FINAL

SECOND XI TWENTY20 CUP FIXTURES 2017

APRIL		
Thu 20	Kibworth	Leics v MCC YC
JUNE		
Wed 7	Northwood	MCC YC v Worcs
Fri 9	East Grinstead	Sussex v Kent
Tue 13	Gt/Little Tew	Unicorns v Essex
Wed 14	tbc	Hampshire v Unicorns
	Sunbury	Middlesex v Surrey
Thu 15	Northwood	MCC YC v Notts
Sun 18	Neath	Glamorgan v Surrey
Mon 19	Northampton	Northants v Worcs
	Worksop Col	Notts v Warwicks
Thu 22	Trent Coll	Notts v Lancashire
Mon 26	Burnopfield	Durham v Worcs
	Preston Nom	Sussex v Glos
	Moseley	Warwicks v Leics
	Barnsley	Yorkshire v Notts
Thu 29	Glossop	Derbyshire v MCC YC
Fri 30	Uxbridge	Middlesex v Somerset
JULY		
Mon 3	St Fagans	Glamorgan v Essex
	Polo Farm Cant	Kent v Middlesex
	Northampton	Northants v Lancashire
	Taunton Vale	Somerset v Glos
	Worcester	Worcs v Leics
Tue 4	LSE N Malden	Surrey v Sussex
Wed 5	tbc	Kent v Surrey
	Westhoughton	Lancashire v Derbyshire
	Grantham	Notts v Northants
	Taunton Vale	Somerset v Hampshire
Thu 6	Marske	Yorkshire v Durham
Mon 10	Belper Mead	Derbyshire v Durham
	Richmond	Middlesex v Glamorgan
	Saff Walden	Unicorns v Kent
	Pudsey Congs	Yorkshire v Northants
Tue 11	LSE N Malden	Surrey v Unicorns
Thu 13	Newclose IoW	Hampshire v Sussex
	Cov/N Wrwk	Warwicks v Lancashire
Fri 14	Bristol U	Glos v Glamorgan
Mon 17	S N'berland	Durham v Warwicks
	Manchester	Lancashire v MCC YC
	Worksop Coll	Notts v Derbyshire
Tue 18	tbc	Leics v Northants
	Horsham	Sussex v Somerset
Thu 20	Clifton Coll	Glos v Hampshire
	Polo Farm Cant	Kent v Essex
Mon 24	Chelmsford	Essex v Somerset
	Bristol CC	Glos v Kent
	Leicester GS	Leics v Derbyshire
	Moseley	Warwicks v Northants
	RGS Worcester	Worcs v Yorkshire
Thu 27	Chester-le-St	Durham v Leics
	Southampton	Hampshire v Middlesex
	Taunton Vale	Somerset v Glamorgan
Mon 31	Alvaston & B	Derbyshire v Yorkshire
	Northwood	MCC YC v Durham
AUGUST		
Wed 2	Southampton	Hampshire v Surrey
	Blackpool	Lancashire v Yorkshire
Thu 3	Long Marston	Unicorns v Sussex
	RGS Worcester	Worcs v Warwicks
Fri 4	Coggeshall	Essex v Middlesex
	Port Talbot	Glamorgan v Unicorns
Thu 10	Arundel	FINALS DAY

WOMEN'S FIXTURES 2017

SL	ECB Women's Cricket Super League
WC	ICC Women's World Cup 2017

Sat 24 June

WC	Bristol	New Zealand v Sri Lanka
WC	Derby	England v India

Sun 25 June

WC	Leicester	Pakistan v South Africa

Mon 26 June

WC	Taunton	Australia v West Indies

Tue 27 June

WC	Leicester	England v Pakistan

Wed 28 June

WC	Derby	South Africa v New Zealand

Thu 29 June

WC	Taunton	West Indies v India
WC	Bristol	Sri Lanka v Australia

Sun 2 July

WC	Taunton	England v Sri Lanka
WC	Bristol	Australia v New Zealand
WC	Derby	India v Pakistan
WC	Leicester	South Africa v West Indies

Wed 5 July

WC	Bristol	England v South Africa
WC	Derby	Sri Lanka v India
WC	Leicester	Pakistan v Australia

Thu 6 July

WC	Taunton	New Zealand v West Indies

Sat 8 July

WC	Taunton	New Zealand v Pakistan
WC	Leicester	South Africa v India

Sun 9 July

WC	Bristol	England v Australia
WC	Derby	West Indies v Sri Lanka

Tue 11 July

WC	Leicester	West Indies v Pakistan

Wed 12 July

WC	Taunton	Sri Lanka v South Africa
WC	Bristol	Australia v India
WC	Derby	England v New Zealand

Sat 15 July

WC	Taunton	South Africa v Australia
WC	Bristol	England v West Indies
WC	Derby	India v New Zealand
WC	Leicester	Pakistan v Sri Lanka

Tue 18 July

WC	Bristol	Semi-final 1

Wed 19 July

WC	Derby	Semi-final 2

Sun 23 July

WC	Lord's	FINAL

Thu 10 August

SL	Southampton	Vipers v Storm

Fri 11 August

SL	Leeds	Diamonds v Thunder

Sat 12 August

SL	Taunton	Storm v Lightning

Sun 13 August

SL	The Oval	Stars v Diamonds

Tue 15 August

SL	Derby	Lightning v Vipers

Wed 16 August

SL	Manchester	Thunder v Stars

Fri 18 August

SL	Loughborough	Lightning v Diamonds

Sun 20 August

SL	Blackpool	Thunder v Lightning
SL	York	Diamonds v Storm
SL	Southampton	Vipers v Stars

Wed 23 August

SL	Guildford	Stars v Storm
SL	Liverpool	Thunder v Vipers

Sat 26 August

SL	Guildford	Stars v Lightning
SL	Bristol	Storm v Thunder
SL	Arundel	Vipers v Diamonds

Fri 1 September

SL	Hove	FINAL

TEST MATCH CHAMPIONSHIP SCHEDULE

Months indicate the start of a series. Number of Tests in brackets. All series, especially those involving Pakistan and Zimbabwe, are subject to confirmation.

2017	Apr	West Indies hosts Pakistan (3)
	Jun	Sri Lanka hosts Zimbabwe (2)
	Jul	**England hosts South Africa (4)**
	Jul	Bangladesh hosts Pakistan (2)
	Jul	Sri Lanka hosts India (3)
	Aug	**England hosts West Indies (3)**
	Aug	Australia hosts Bangladesh (2)
	Sep	South Africa hosts Bangladesh (2)
	Oct	Pakistan hosts Sri Lanka (3)
	Oct	Zimbabwe hosts West Indies (2)
	Nov	**Australia hosts England (5)**
	Nov	India hosts Pakistan (3)
	Nov	New Zealand hosts West Indies (3)
	Nov	South Africa hosts Sri Lanka (3)
2018	Jan	Bangladesh hosts Sri Lanka (2)
	Jan	South Africa hosts India (4)
	Mar	South Africa hosts Australia (4)
	Mar	West Indies hosts Bangladesh (2)
	Mar	India hosts Sri Lanka (3)
	Mar	**New Zealand hosts England (2)**
	May	**England hosts Pakistan (2)**
	Jun	Zimbabwe hosts Australia (2)
	Jun	**England hosts India (5)**
	Aug	Sri Lanka hosts South Africa (3)
	Aug	Zimbabwe hosts Pakistan (2)

ICC CHAMPIONS TROPHY FIXTURES 2017

Thu 1 June	10.30	The Oval	England v Bangladesh
Fri 2 June	10.30	Birmingham	Australia v New Zealand
Sat 3 June	10.30	The Oval	Sri Lanka v South Africa
Sun 4 June	10.30	Birmingham	India v Pakistan
Mon 5 June	13.30	The Oval	Australia v Bangladesh
Tue 6 June	10.30	Cardiff	England v New Zealand
Wed 7 June	13.30	Birmingham	Pakistan v South Africa
Thu 8 June	10.30	The Oval	India v Sri Lanka
Fri 9 June	10.30	Cardiff	New Zealand v Bangladesh
Sat 10 June	10.30	Birmingham	England v Australia
Sun 11 June	10.30	The Oval	India v South Africa
Mon 12 June	10.30	Cardiff	Sri Lanka v Pakistan
Wed 14 June	10.30	Cardiff	First Semi Final
Thu 15 June	10.30	Birmingham	Second Semi-Final
Sun 18 June	10.30	The Oval	FINAL

PRINCIPAL FIXTURES 2017

CC1	Specsavers County Championship Division 1
CC2	Specsavers County Championship Division 2
FCF	First-Class Friendly
LOI	Royal London Limited-Overs International
50L	Royal London One-Day Cup
T20	NatWest T20 Blast
IT20	NatWest Twenty20 International
TM	Investec Test Match
MCCU	MCC University
Uni	University match
F	Floodlit

Sun 26 – Wed 29 March
FCF[F]	Abu Dhabi	MCC v Middlesex

Tue 28 – Thu 30 March
Uni	Cambridge	Cambridge MCCU v Notts
Uni	Cardiff	Glamorgan v Cardiff MCCU
Uni	Bristol	Glos v Durham MCCU
Uni	Canterbury	Kent v Leeds/Brad MCCU
Uni	Leicester	Leics v Loughboro MCCU
Uni	Oxford	Oxford MCCU v Surrey

Sun 2 – Tue 4 April
Uni	Cambridge	Cambridge MCCU v Lancashire
Uni	Chelmsford	Essex v Durham MCCU
Uni	Southampton	Hampshire v Cardiff MCCU
Uni	Northampton	Northants v Loughboro MCCU
Uni	Oxford	Oxford MCCU v Warwicks
Uni	Leeds	Yorkshire v Leeds/Brad MCCU

Fri 7 – Mon 10 April
CC1	Chelmsford	Essex v Lancashire
CC1	The Oval	Surrey v Warwicks
CC1	Leeds	Yorkshire v Hampshire
CC2	Canterbury	Kent v Glos
CC2	Leicester	Leics v Notts
CC2	Northampton	Northants v Glamorgan

Fri 7 – Sun 9 April
Uni	Cambridge	Cambridge MCCU v Middlesex
Uni	Chester-le-St	Durham v Durham MCCU
Uni	Leeds, Wwd	Leeds/Brad MCCU v Worcs
Uni	Loughborough	Loughboro MCCU v Derbyshire
Uni	Taunton	Somerset v Oxford MCCU
Uni	Hove	Sussex v Cardiff MCCU

Fri 14 – Mon 17 April
CC1	Southampton	Hampshire v Middlesex
CC1	Taunton	Somerset v Essex
CC1	The Oval	Surrey v Lancashire
CC1	Birmingham	Warwicks v Yorkshire
CC2	Derby	Derbyshire v Northants
CC2	Chester-le-St	Durham v Notts
CC2	Cardiff	Glamorgan v Worcs
CC2	Bristol	Glos v Leics
CC2	Hove	Sussex v Kent

Fri 21 – Mon 24 April
CC1	Southampton	Hampshire v Yorkshire
CC1	Manchester	Lancashire v Somerset
CC1	Lord's	Middlesex v Essex
CC1	Birmingham	Warwicks v Surrey
CC2	Bristol	Glos v Durham
CC2	Canterbury	Kent v Derbyshire
CC2	Leicester	Leics v Glamorgan
CC2	Nottingham	Notts v Sussex
CC2	Worcester	Worcs v Northants

Thu 27 April
50L	Chester-le-St	Durham v Derbyshire
50L	Bristol	Glos v Glamorgan
50L	Canterbury	Kent v Hampshire
50L	Lord's	Middlesex v Sussex
50L[F]	Northampton	Northants v Warwicks
50L	Worcester	Worcs v Notts

Fri 28 April
50L[F]	Manchester	Lancashire v Leics
50L	Taunton	Somerset v Surrey

Sat 29 April
50L	Nottingham	Notts v Yorkshire

Sun 30 April
50L	Derby	Derbyshire v Northants
50L	Chelmsford	Essex v Hampshire
50L	Cardiff	Glamorgan v Surrey
50L	Leicester	Leics v Worcs
50L	Lord's	Middlesex v Glos
50L	Hove	Sussex v Somerset

Mon 1 May
50L	Birmingham	Warwicks v Durham
50L	Leeds	Yorkshire v Lancashire

Tue 2 May
50L	Derby	Derbyshire v Notts
50L[F]	Leicester	Leics v Warwicks
50L	Taunton	Somerset v Kent
50L	The Oval	Surrey v Esssex
50L	Hove	Sussex v Glamorgan

Wed 3 May

50L[F]	Southampton	Hampshire v Middlesex
50L[F]	Northampton	Northants v Worcs
50L	Leeds	Yorkshire v Durham

Thu 4 May

50L	Chelmsford	Essex v Glos

Fri 5 May

LOI	**Bristol**	**England v Ireland**
50L	S N'berland	Durham v Leics
50L	Cardiff	Glamorgan v Somerset
50L	Canterbury	Kent v Sussex
50L	Liverpool	Lancashire v Northants
50L	The Oval	Surrey v Middlesex
50L	Birmingham	Warwicks v Notts
50L	Worcester	Worcs v Yorkshire

Sun 7 May

LOI	**Lord's**	**England v Ireland**
50L	Chester-le-St	Durham v Northants
50L	Cardiff	Glamorgan v Essex
50L	Southampton	Hampshire v Glos
50L	Canterbury	Kent v Middlesex
50L	Welbeck	Notts v Leics
50L	Hove	Sussex v Surrey
50L	Birmingham	Warwicks v Lancashire
50L	Leeds	Yorkshire v Derbyshire

Wed 10 May

50L	Derby	Derbyshire v Warwicks
50L[F]	Chelmsford	Essex v Sussex
50L	Bristol	Glos v Kent
50L	Manchester	Lancashire v Worcs
50L	Radlett	Middlesex v Glamorgan
50L[F]	Northampton	Northants v Yorkshire
50L	Taunton	Somerset v Hampshire

Thu 11 May

50L[F]	Nottingham	Notts v Durham

Fri 12 May

50L[F]	Chelmsford	Essex v Middlesex
50L	Bristol	Glos v Somerset
50L	Southampton	Hampshire v Glamorgan
50L	Blackpool	Lancashire v Derbyshire
50L[F]	Leicester	Leics v Northants
50L	The Oval	Surrey v Kent
50L	Worcester	Worcs v Warwicks

Sun 14 May

50L	Swansea	Glamorgan v Kent
50L	Leicester	Leics v Derbyshire
50L	Nottingham	Notts v Lancashire
50L	Taunton	Somerset v Essex
50L	The Oval	Surrey v Hampshire
50L	Eastbourne	Sussex v Glos
50L	Birmingham	Warwicks v Yorkshire
50L	Worcester	Worcs v Durham

Tue 16 May

50L[F]	Derby	Derbyshire v Worcs
50L[F]	Chester-le-St	Durham v Lancashire
50L[F]	Northampton	Northants v Notts
50L[F]	Leeds	Yorkshire v Leics

Wed 17 May

50L[F]	Bristol	Glos v Surrey
50L[F]	Southampton	Hampshire v Sussex
50L[F]	Canterbury	Kent v Essex
50L[F]	Lord's	Middlesex v Somerset

Fri 19 – Mon 22 May

CC1	Chelmsford	Essex v Hampshire
CC1	Manchester	Lancashire v Yorkshire
CC1	Lord's	Middlesex v Surrey
CC1	Taunton	Somerset v Warwicks
CC2	Derby	Derbyshire v Worcs
CC2	Cardiff	Glamorgan v Notts
CC2	Leicester	Leics v Kent

Fri 19 May

[F]	Hove	Sussex v South Africans

Sun 21 – Wed 24 May

CC2	Hove	Sussex v Durham

Sun 21 May

	Northampton	Northants v South Africans

Wed 24 May

LOI[F]	**Leeds**	**England v South Africa**

Thu 25 – Sun 28 May

CC2	Derby	Derbyshire v Leics

Fri 26 – Mon 29 May

CC1	Chelmsford	Essex v Surrey
CC1	Taunton	Somerset v Hampshire
CC2	Swansea	Glamorgan v Durham
CC2	Tunbridge W	Kent v Sussex
CC2	Northampton	Northants v Worcs
CC2	Nottingham	Notts v Glos

Sat 27 May

LOI	**Southampton**	**England v South Africa**
	Leeds	Yorkshire v S Africa A

Mon 29 May

LOI	**Lord's**	**England v South Africa**
	Derby	Derbyshire v S Africa A

Thu 1 June

	Nottingham	England Lions v S Africa A

Fri 2 – Mon 5 June

CC1	Southampton	Hampshire v Warwicks
CC1	Lord's	Middlesex v Somerset

CC1 Leeds Yorkshire v Lancashire
CC2 Chester-le-St Durham v Northants
CC2 Nottingham Notts v Derbyshire
CC2 Hove Sussex v Worcs

Sat 3 June
Northampton England Lions v S Africa A

Mon 5 June
[F] Northampton England Lions v S Africa A

Thu 8 – Sun 11 June
CC2 Canterbury Kent v Durham
FCF[F] Southampton Hampshire v S Africa A

Fri 9 – Mon 12 June
CC1 Southport Lancashire v Middlesex
CC1 Taunton Somerset v Yorkshire
CC1 Guildford Surrey v Essex
CC2 Bristol Glos v Notts
CC2 Leicester Leics v Sussex
CC2 Northampton Northants v Derbyshire
CC2 Worcester Worcs v Glamorgan

Tue 13 June
50L[F] tbc Quarter-final 1 & 2
Second-placed side in each group has a home tie against third-placed side in opposite group.

Wed 14 – Sat 17 June
FCF Arundel Sussex v S Africa A
If Sussex in 50L semis, v Duke of Norfolk's XI

Fri 16 June
50L[F] tbc Semi-final 1

Sat 17 June
50L tbc Semi-final 2
Winner of each group has home tie against winner of the quarter-final.

Sun 18 June
Leicester Leics v South Africans
Match cancelled if SA in Champ Trophy final

Mon 19 – Thu 22 June
CC1 Chelmsford Essex v Warwicks
CC1 Manchester Lancashire v Hampshire
CC1 Lord's Middlesex v Yorkshire
CC2 Chester-le-St Durham v Glamorgan
CC2 Nottingham Notts v Leics
CC2 Worcester Worcs v Kent

Wed 21 – Sat 24 June
FCF Canterbury England Lions v S Africa A

Wed 21 June
IT20[F] Southampton England v South Africa

Fri 23 June
IT20 Taunton England v South Africa
Lord's Cambridge U v Oxford U

Sun 25 June
IT20 Cardiff England v South Africa

Mon 26 –Thu 29 June
CC1[F] Chelmsford Essex v Middlesex
CC1[F] Southampton Hampshire v Somerset
CC1[F] Birmingham Warwicks v Lancashire
CC1[F] Leeds Yorkshire v Surrey
CC2[F] Chester-le-St Durham v Worcs
CC2[F] Cardiff Glamorgan v Derbyshire
CC2[F] Northampton Northants v Leics
CC2[F] Nottingham Notts v Kent
CC2[F] Hove Sussex v Glos

Thu 29 June – Sat 1 July
FCF Worcester England Lions v South Africans

Sat 1 July
50L Lord's FINAL

Mon 3 – Thu 6 July
CC1 The Oval Surrey v Hampshire
CC1 Birmingham Warwicks v Middlesex
CC1 Scarborough Yorkshire v Somerset
CC2 Chesterfield Derbyshire v Durham
CC2 Cheltenham Glos v Glamorgan
CC2 Beckenham Kent v Northants

Tue 4 – Fri 7 July
FCF Cambridge Cambridge U v Oxford U

Wed 5 – Sat 8 July
CC2 Arundel Sussex v Leics

Thu 6 – Mon 10 July
TM1 Lord's ENGLAND v SOUTH AFRICA

Fri 7 July
T20[F] Chester-le-St Durham v Lancashire
T20[F] Chelmsford Essex v Surrey
T20[F] Cardiff Glamorgan v Hampshire
T20 Cheltenham Glos v Middlesex
T20[F] Northampton Northants v Derbyshire
T20 Worcester Worcs v Warwicks
T20[F] Leeds Yorkshire v Notts

Sat 8 July
T20 Chesterfield Derbyshire v Yorkshire
T20[F] Birmingham Warwicks v Notts

Sun 9 – Wed 12 July
CC2 Cheltenham Glos v Worcs

Sun 9 July
T20 Chester-le-St Durham v Northants
T20 Beckenham Kent v Essex

T20	Manchester	Lancashire v Leics
T20	The Oval	Surrey v Somerset
T20	Arundel	Sussex v Glamorgan
Tue 11 July		
T20[F]	Northampton	Northants v Yorkshire
Wed 12 July		
T20[F]	Hove	Sussex v Hampshire
Thu 13 July		
T20[F]	Chelmsford	Essex v Somerset
T20	Cheltenham	Glos v Kent
T20[F]	Lord's	Middlesex v Surrey
Fri 14 – Tue 18 July		
TM2	**Nottingham**	**ENGLAND v SOUTH AFRICA**
Fri 14 July		
T20[F]	Southampton	Hampshire v Middlesex
T20[F]	Manchester	Lancashire v Yorkshire
T20[F]	The Oval	Surrey v Kent
T20[F]	Birmingham	Warwicks v Northants
T20	Worcester	Worcs v Leics
Sat 15 July		
T20[F]	Cardiff	Glamorgan v Somerset
Sun 16 July		
T20	Chelmsford	Essex v Glamorgan
T20	Cheltenham	Glos v Sussex
T20	Manchester	Lancashire v Derbyshire
T20	Uxbridge	Middlesex v Somerset
T20	Birmingham	Warwicks v Leics
Tue 18 July		
T20[F]	Canterbury	Kent v Glos
Wed 19 July		
T20[F]	The Oval	Surrey v Essex
T20	Worcester	Worcs v Derbyshire
Thu 20 July		
T20[F]	Chester-le-St	Durham v Leics
T20[F]	Southampton	Hampshire v Sussex
T20	Richmond	Middlesex v Kent
Fri 21 July		
T20[F]	Chelmsford	Essex v Hampshire
T20[F]	Cardiff	Glamorgan v Sussex
T20[F]	Leicester	Leics v Northants
T20[F]	Nottingham	Notts v Derbyshire
T20	Taunton	Somerset v Glos
T20[F]	The Oval	Surrey v Middlesex
T20	Worcester	Worcs v Lancashire
T20[F]	Leeds	Yorkshire v Warwicks
Sat 22 July		
T20	Nottingham	Notts v Northants
Sun 23 July		
T20	Cardiff	Glamorgan v Essex
T20	Southampton	Hampshire v Surrey
T20	Manchester	Lancashire v Durham
T20	Taunton	Somerset v Middlesex
T20	Hove	Sussex v Kent
T20	Birmingham	Warwicks v Derbyshire
T20	Leeds	Yorkshire v Worcs
Tue 25 July		
T20[F]	Derby	Derbyshire v Lancashire
T20[F]	Chester-le-St	Durham v Notts
T20[F]	Bristol	Glos v Glamorgan
T20[F]	Leicester	Leics v Warwicks
Wed 26 July		
T20[F]	Nottingham	Notts v Worcs
T20	Taunton	Somerset v Hampshire
T20[F]	Leeds	Yorkshire v Durham
Thu 27 – Mon 31 July		
TM3	**The Oval**	**ENGLAND v SOUTH AFRICA**
Thu 27 July		
T20[F]	Canterbury	Kent v Somerset
T20[F]	Lord's	Middlesex v Essex
T20[F]	Northampton	Northants v Worcs
Fri 28 July		
T20[F]	Derby	Derbyshire v Notts
T20[F]	Cardiff	Glamorgan v Surrey
T20[F]	Bristol	Glos v Hampshire
T20[F]	Manchester	Lancashire v Notts
T20[F]	Leicester	Leics v Durham
T20[F]	Hove	Sussex v Middlesex
T20[F]	Birmingham	Warwicks v Yorkshire
Sat 29 July		
T20[F]	Chelmsford	Essex v Glos
Sun 30 July		
T20	Derby	Derbyshire v Leics
T20	Canterbury	Kent v Glamorgan
T20	Nottingham	Notts v Yorkshire
T20	Taunton	Somerset v Sussex
T20	Birmingham	Warwicks v Lancashire
T20	Worcester	Worcs v Durham
Tue 1 – Thu 3 August		
FCF	Chelmsford	Essex v West Indians
Tue 1 August		
T20[F]	Southampton	Hampshire v Kent
T20[F]	Northampton	Northants v Warwicks
Wed 2 August		
T20[F]	Leicester	Leics v Notts

Thu 3 August

T20F	Cardiff	Glamorgan v Glos
T20F	Lord's	Middlesex v Hampshire
T20F	Northampton	Northants v Lancashire
T20F	Hove	Sussex v Surrey
T20F	Leeds	Yorkshire v Derbyshire

Fri 4 – Tue 8 August

TM4	**Manchester**	**ENGLAND v SOUTH AFRICA**

Fri 4 August

T20F	Derby	Derbyshire v Notts
T20F	Chester-le-St	Durham v Yorkshire
T20F	Bristol	Glos v Somerset
T20F	Southampton	Hampshire v Essex
T20F	Canterbury	Kent v Sussex
T20F	Leicester	Leics v Lancashire
T20F	The Oval	Surrey v Glamorgan
T20F	Birmingham	Warwicks v Worcs

Sat 5 August

T20	Nottingham	Notts v Durham
T20	Worcester	Worcs v Northants

Sun 6 – Wed 9 August

CC1	Southampton	Hampshire v Lancashire
CC1	Lord's	Middlesex v Warwicks
CC1	Scarborough	Yorkshire v Essex
CC2	Derby	Derbyshire v Notts
CC2	Leicester	Leics v Durham
CC2	Northampton	Northants v Glos
CC2	Worcester	Worcs v Sussex

Sun 6 – Tue 8 August

FCF	Canterbury	Kent v West Indians

Sun 6 August

T20	Taunton	Somerset v Surrey

Mon 7 – Thu 10 August

CC1	Taunton	Somerset v Surrey

Thu 10 August

T20F	Southampton	Hampshire v Glamorgan
T20F	Lord's	Middlesex v Sussex

Fri 11 – Sun 13 August

FCFF	Derby	Derbyshire v West Indians

Fri 11 August

T20F	Chester-le-St	Durham v Worcs
T20F	Chelmsford	Essex v Middlesex
T20F	Canterbury	Kent v Hampshire
T20F	Northampton	Northants v Leics
T20F	Nottingham	Notts v Warwicks
T20F	Hove	Sussex v Glos
T20F	Leeds	Yorkshire v Lancashire

Sat 12 August

T20	Leicester	Leics v Yorkshire
T20	Taunton	Somerset v Kent

Sun 13 August

T20	Chester-le-St	Durham v Warwicks
T20	Bristol	Glos v Essex
T20	Taunton	Somerset v Glamorgan
T20	The Oval	Surrey v Sussex
T20	Worcester	Worcs v Notts

Tue 15 August

T20F	Derby	Derbyshire v Durham
T20	Uxbridge	Middlesex v Glos

Wed 16 August

T20F	Manchester	Lancashire v Worcs

Thu 17 – Mon 21 August

TM1F	**Birmingham**	**ENGLAND v WEST INDIES**

Thu 17 August

T20F	Chelmsford	Essex v Kent
T20F	Leicester	Leics v Derbyshire
T20F	The Oval	Surrey v Glos
T20F	Leeds	Yorkshire v Northants

Fri 18 August

T20F	Derby	Derbyshire v Worcs
T20F	Cardiff	Glamorgan v Middlesex
T20F	Southampton	Hampshire v Somerset
T20F	Canterbury	Kent v Surrey
T20F	Manchester	Lancashire v Warwicks
T20F	Northampton	Northants v Durham
T20F	Nottingham	Notts v Leics
T20F	Hove	Sussex v Essex

Tue 22 August

T20F	tbc	Quarter-final 1

Wed 23 August

T20F	tbc	Quarter-final 2

Thu 24 August

T20F	tbc	Quarter-final 3

Fri 25 – Tue 29 August

TM2	**Leeds**	**ENGLAND v WEST INDIES**

Fri 25 August

T20F	tbc	Quarter-final 4

Mon 28 – Thu 31 August

CC1	Chelmsford	Essex v Somerset
CC1	Manchester	Lancashire v Warwicks
CC1	The Oval	Surrey v Middlesex
CC2	Chester-le-St	Durham v Derbyshire
CC2	Colwyn Bay	Glamorgan v Sussex
CC2	Canterbury	Kent v Leics
CC2	Nottingham	Notts v Northants

CC2 Worcester Worcs v Glos

Sat 2 – Sun 3 September

Leicester Leics v West Indians

An ECB XI will play if Leicestershire in T20 finals day

Sat 2 September

T20[F] Birmingham Semi-finals and FINAL

Tue 5 – Fri 8 September

CC1 Southampton Hampshire v Surrey
CC1 Manchester Lancashire v Essex
CC1 Birmingham Warwicks v Somerset
CC1 Leeds Yorkshire v Middlesex
CC2 Derby Derbyshire v Glamorgan
CC2 Chester-le-St Durham v Kent
CC2 Leicester Leics v Glos
CC2 Northampton Northants v Sussex
CC2 Nottingham Notts v Worcs

Thu 7 – Mon 11 September

TM3 Lord's ENGLAND v WEST INDIES

Tue 12 – Fri 15 September

CC1 Uxbridge Middlesex v Hampshire
CC1 Taunton Somerset v Lancashire
CC1 The Oval Surrey v Yorkshire
CC1 Birmingham Warwicks v Essex
CC2 Cardiff Glamorgan v Northants
CC2 Bristol Glos v Kent
CC2 Hove Sussex v Derbyshire
CC2 Worcester Worcs v Leics

Wed 13 September

LOI tbc Ireland v West Indies

Sat 16 September

IT20[F] Chester-le-St England v West Indies

Tue 19 – Fri 22 September

CC1 Southampton Hampshire v Essex
CC1 Lord's Middlesex v Lancashire
CC1 The Oval Surrey v Somerset
CC1 Leeds Yorkshire v Warwicks
CC2 Derby Derbyshire v Kent
CC2 Chester-le-St Durham v Sussex
CC2 Cardiff Glamorgan v Glos
CC2 Northampton Northants v Notts

Tue 19 September

LOI[F] Manchester England v West Indies

Thu 21 September

LOI[F] Nottingham England v West Indies

Sun 24 September

LOI Bristol England v West Indies

Mon 25 – Thu 28 September

CC1 Chelmsford Essex v Yorkshire
CC1 Manchester Lancashire v Surrey
CC1 Taunton Somerset v Middlesex
CC1 Birmingham Warwicks v Hampshire
CC2 Bristol Glos v Derbyshire
CC2 Canterbury Kent v Glamorgan
CC2 Leicester Leics v Northants
CC2 Hove Sussex v Notts
CC2 Worcester Worcs v Durham

Wed 27 September

LOI[F] The Oval England v West Indies

Fri 29 September

LOI[F] Southampton England v West Indies

First published in 2017

by HEADLINE PUBLISHING GROUP

1

Cataloguing in Publication Data is available from the British Library

ISBN 978 1 4722 3256 4

Cover photograph Jonny Bairstow (Yorkshire and England) © Action Images via Reuters/Paul Childs Livepic

Back cover photograph © Glyn Kirk/AFP/Getty Images

Typeset in Times by
Letterpart Limited, Caterham on the Hill, Surrey

Printed and bound in Great Britain by
Clays Ltd St Ives plc

Headline's policy is to use papers that are natural, renewable and recyclable products and made from wood grown in sustainable forests. The logging and manufacturing processes are expected to conform to the environmental regulations of the country of origin.

HEADLINE PUBLISHING GROUP

An Hachette UK Company
Carmelite House
50 Victoria Embankment
London EC4Y 0DZ

www.headline.co.uk
www.hachette.co.uk